1994 Children's Writer's & Illustrator's Market

1994

Children's Writer's & Illustrator's Market

Edited by
Christine Martin

WRITER'S DIGEST BOOKS

CINCINNATI, OHIO

Distributed in Canada by McGraw-Hill Ryerson,
300 Water St., Whitby, Ontario L1N 9B6.
Also distributed in Australia by
Kirby Books, Private Bag No. 19, P.O. Alex-
andria NSW/2015.

Managing Editor, Market Books Department:
Constance J. Achabal;
Supervising Editor: Michael Willins;
Production Editor: Alice P. Buening.

Children's Writer's & Illustrator's Market.

International Standard Serial Number
0897-9790
International Standard Book Number
0-89879-614-8

Cover illustration by Tom Post
Portraits by Leslie Sowers Slaughter

Contents

The Markets

The book publishers listed here are focusing their lists and specializing. Now more than ever, writers and illustrators must learn from those already in the field: Anne Diebel, art director at Clarion Books, on page 56; Rosemary Wells, author and illustrator of the Max series, on page 66; Margery Cuyler, author and editor-in-chief at Holiday House, on page 84; illustrator Michael Paraskevas on page 96; and writer Candy Dawson Boyd on page 124.

© 1993 Charles Jordan

© Handprint Signature Inc.®

Resources

© 1993 Elizabeth Sayles

From the Editor

If you're new to the field of children's writing and illustrating, you're probably wondering where to begin. After all, it's a little daunting when you're just starting out. If you're a published writer or illustrator, you may be wondering how to keep abreast of changes in the industry—as cliché as it may sound, editors and publishers do come and go. In either case, you've found your answer: *Children's Writer's & Illustrator's Market*.

This directory (now 32 pages larger than the previous edition) provides more than 600 *up-to-date* listings of book publishers, magazines, audiovisual and audiotape markets, scriptwriter's markets, special markets (such as paper product companies), markets where young writers and illustrators may send work, and contests and awards—all of which seek material for children. And approximately 150 of these listings are *new* outlets. Like the answer to many complex questions, however, there's even more.

Discover the latest trends

In addition to containing detailed market listings, each section begins with an introduction that discusses trends, concerns and changes in that area. You'll discover, for example, that children's magazines are booming. In fact, this year the Magazines section contains more new listings than any other. You'll also learn that magazines for kids are much more specialized than in the past.

Other trends you'll read about affect the entire industry, such as the ever-increasing demand for multicultural materials for youngsters and the predicted growth of the educational market. To help children's writers and illustrators on all levels, this edition features two articles which discuss the concerns related to these movements.

In Writing and Illustrating from Another Culture's Tradition, Susan Strauss, a European-American who tells Native American stories, shares how writers and illustrators may gain confidence working outside their traditions. And in Getting Started in the Educational Market, Barbara Gregorich, author of educational resources ranging from textbooks to filmstrips and flash cards, explains the various opportunities for writers and illustrators in this area.

Besides articles addressing trends, you'll also find specific information on the business aspects of the field. Everything from proper formats for your manuscripts and the question of simultaneous submissions to negotiating contracts, royalties and rights is detailed in The Business of Children's Writing & Illustrating, beginning on page 19. This annually-updated article is a must read for beginners and a quick refresher course for established artists.

Gain insider information

One of our standard features continues to be interviews with industry professionals, including editors and art directors, established writers and illustrators. Formerly called Close-ups, these interviews are now called Insider Reports, to reflect our belief that those on the inside provide the best advice for those trying to break into the field.

In the Book Publishers section, you'll hear from Rosemary Wells, writer and illustrator of the humorous Max books; Candy Dawson Boyd, an author filling the gaps in children's literature; and Margery Cuyler, author and Holiday House editor-in-chief who aims to pass good culture on to kids. You'll also discover what it takes to illustrate for Clarion Books, and other publishers, from Art Director Anne Diebel. And Michael Paraskevas discusses his success with editorial renderings in charcoal, acrylic and gouache—not your typical children's illustration.

In the Magazines section, you'll learn what catches the eyes of Suzanne Harper, managing editor of *Disney Adventures*, and Gerald Bishop, editor of *Ranger Rick*. And, in Young Writer's & Illustrator's Markets, Editor Arun Toké shares the philosophy behind *Skipping Stones*, his multicultural children's publication.

In addition, for the first time ever, we've included an interview in our Special Markets section. There you'll hear from Paula Carlson, president of Handprint Signature, a greeting card company that creates cards for kids to sign and send. Like all of our interview subjects, Carlson provides advice and insight into a particular aspect of the children's field.

Yet we know sometimes advice just isn't enough. So last year we initiated First Books, a feature that also provides inspiration. In this year's First Books, you'll hear how authors Mary Bahr and Deborah Hopkinson and illustrator Elaine Sandeen each published their first children's books. Their accounts relay not only the struggles faced when just beginning but how hard work and perseverance lead to success.

Utilize the resources

To help you discover the right market for your first book—or your first children's article or illustration—we've compiled a Subject Index which lists book and magazine publishers according to the fiction and nonfiction subjects they are seeking. Using this Subject Index in conjunction with our Age-Level Index will help you further hone the list of potential markets.

Other resources here include sections on Clubs & Organizations, which offer a multitude of educational, business and legal support services, and Workshops, where successful writing and illustrating techniques are shared. In addition, you'll find a list of other recommended books and publications.

Of course, while we try to include all the resources you need within these pages, we're always ready to answer any questions or concerns. In fact, I invite you to let me know who you would like to hear from next year and/or what topics you would like to see covered. After all, sometimes it takes more than one person to refine even the best answer. And, as the new editor of *Children's Writer's & Illustrator's Market*, I want you to know we're in this together.

Christine Martin

How to Use Children's Writer's & Illustrator's Market

As a children's writer, illustrator or photographer you may be asking yourself questions about the 1994 *Children's Writer's & Illustrator's Market*. "How do I use this book to find editors who will buy my work?" "Do I actually need to read every listing in this directory to sell my material?"

It's easy to open this book, quickly find the names of numerous contacts who purchase freelance material, and then mail submissions with the hope that editors will want to use them. More than likely, if this is your modus operandi, you will end up angering most of the editors you contact. Editors hate to receive inappropriate submissions. Sorting through stacks of mail that contain everything but the type of material they're seeking wastes time and energy.

To avoid irritating editors—and to increase your chances of acceptance—you must target your work appropriately. And the information in this book *can* help you. Besides providing listings of markets, this directory includes a number of tools to help you determine which markets are the best ones for your work.

Start with the indexes

This directory has over 600 potential buyers of freelance material and about 150 listings (all marked with an asterisk [*]) are new in this edition. The easiest way to narrow down the listings, to learn which ones publish the type of material you are interested in submitting, is to start with the indexes.

In many listings you will find four categories of children's writing/illustrating; they are defined as: "picture books," written/illustrated for preschoolers to 8 year-olds; "young readers" for 5- to 8-year-olds; "middle readers" for 9- to 11-year-olds; and "young adults," for those ages 12 and up. These age breakdowns may vary slightly from publisher to publisher, but they can help you identify buyers who may be interested in your work.

If you have a manuscript about teenage sports heroes, identify and contact those book publishers who publish titles for young adults. If you have an exciting tale about dragons, princes and princesses that would interest 6-year-olds, search for picture book or young reader markets. The Age-Level Index in the back of this book can help you quickly accomplish this task.

Using the Age-Level Index in combination with the new Subject Index will further hone your list of potential markets. The Subject Index lists book and magazine publishers by the fiction and nonfiction subjects they are seeking.

If you're a writer trying to place a health article written for middle readers, make a list of those markets under Health in the Magazines: Nonfiction section of the Subject Index. Then go to the Age-Level Index and compare your list with the list of magazines under Middle Readers. Circle those that are the same, and read the circled listings to discover submission procedures.

If you're an illustrator, use the Subject Index to determine which publishers are seeking your preferred subject matter. If you enjoy painting animals, for instance, consider sending samples to book and magazine publishers listed under Animals and, perhaps, Nature/Environment. Children's photographers can use the Subject Index in this fashion as well.

Of course, read the listings for the potential markets to discover the type of artwork the art directors prefer and what type of samples they will keep on file.

Study the listings

Many listings use the "Tips" section to describe the freelancing credentials an editor wants to see. Some editors in this directory are interested in the work of newer, lesser-known writers and illustrators. Others may only be interested in established writers or artists with plenty of credits.

Besides providing subject information, markets also state whether they're seeking fiction and/or nonfiction. To guarantee you are sending an editor exactly what he wants, see if specific submission guidelines are available (this is usually stated, "Ms guidelines available for SASE.")—and send for them.

Throughout this book, the abbreviations "ms" or "mss" refer to "manuscript" or "manuscripts," respectively. The letters "SASE" stand for self-addressed, stamped envelope, while SAE (self-addressed envelope) is often used in conjunction with IRC (International Reply Coupon). Many markets require SASEs and you must include one if you want your work returned. IRCs are required when sending mail to countries other than your own.

In the Book Publishers section a solid block [■] appears before markets that subsidy publish manuscripts. In Contests & Awards a double dagger [‡] indicates contests for students.

If you're a parent or teacher you may be interested in our Young Writer's & Illustrator's Markets beginning on page 273. These markets encourage submissions from children and your students or kids may have material that could get published. Some markets, however, require a written statement from a teacher or parent, noting the work is original. Also watch for age limits.

Along with information for writers, markets provide plenty of information for photographers and illustrators. If you're a photographer, check to see what format a buyer prefers. For example, some want 35mm color transparencies, others want b&w prints. Most important, note the type of photos a buyer wants to purchase and the procedures for submitting. It's not uncommon for a market to want a résumé and promotional literature, as well as tearsheets from previous work. Listings also note whether model releases and/or captions are required.

Illustrators will find numerous markets in which samples are kept on file for possible future assignments. If you are both a writer and illustrator, look for those markets that accept manuscript/illustration packages.

In researching listings you will also find payment information. Some markets pay on acceptance, others on publication. Some pay a flat rate for manuscripts and artwork, others pay advances and royalties. Know how a market operates. This will keep you from being shocked when you discover your paycheck won't arrive until your manuscript is published—18 months after it was accepted. For details about contracts and other business tips, see The Business of Children's Writing & Illustrating beginning on page 19.

First Books

by Christine Martin

Children's writers and illustrators share many common concerns, yet their paths to publication are unique. The three individuals featured here recount the steps toward publication of their first children's books and discuss, not only the writing and illustrating process, but how they market material.

Mary Bahr
The Memory Box (Albert Whitman & Company)

"Like Dorothy Gale, for me it all began in Kansas when a 'tornado' in my life pushed me to write," says Mary Bahr Fritts. That tornado was a car accident that injured her 3-year-old son and caused the pain of watching a child suffer, and the joy of friends who cared, to spill out on paper.

At the time, Fritts, a librarian, was volunteering in a large parish library and writing book reviews for the parish newsletter. When she offered the personal piece to the editor in lieu of her column, the editor not only printed it, but suggested she send it out for publication.

"When *Parish Family Digest* bought it, I knew I'd discovered 'what I wanted to do when I grew up,'" Fritts says. "I *had* to publish again, but knowing nothing about the writing profession, I read every 'how-to-write' book in the library, plus subscribed to *Writer's Digest* and *The Writer*, devouring every word."

An ad in one of those magazines led Fritts to sign up for writing courses from The Institute of Children's Literature. "It was time to make a commitment of time and money. These, plus assignments and deadlines, would force me to finish and market a piece," she says. "I chose the ICL because, by then, as volunteer in two school libraries, I knew what children were reading, plus we had four sons, one for each area of the juvenile market."

Fritts did publish again, starting with adult humor, how-to and inspirational articles in 1987, then adding children's stories in 1989. She's now sold juvenile material to about a dozen magazines, including *Guide*, *Hopscotch*, *Junior Trails* and *On the Line*.

"I write more for children than any other market," she says, "because I admire their honesty, passion and sense of adventure. But mostly because I *remember* the bully who washed my face in the snow, the best friend who wasn't, that awful first kiss, the teacher who humiliated me in front of the class, the ecstasy of first love. Of these, I write with a passion. That's an important word. If your story or article doesn't have passion, it won't sell."

In addition to recalling her own childhood experiences, Fritts synthesizes ideas she gleans while reading books, studying newspapers, attending church, glimpsing characters on the street, driving carpool, observing what people choose to read, and gathering with other writers.

This synthesis is particularly true of her first book, *The Memory Box*, the story of a young boy who, during a summer visit with his grandparents, learns his grandfather has Alzheimer's and helps create a "memory box" in which Gramps can save memories of the times they've spent together.

"Books for children are like puzzles: The answer to the whole, does not come all at once," Fritts explains. "The first piece of *The Memory Box* came as a need to write about family because I had the best of childhoods. And the setting came without question as I grew up in the land of 10,000 lakes.

"Another piece came during church when a man in a handsome tan suit and sneakers shuffled down the aisle, lost and disoriented. I knew he had Alzheimer's, and I wondered, 'What if I were his grandson and I knew he'd forget me someday?' "

The final piece came to her at the *Highlights* Foundation Writers Workshop at Chautauqua. Children's book writer and editor James Cross Giblin spoke of the responsibility of writing for children, noting how stories become part of their "boxful of memories." Those words struck a chord. "When I flip-flopped them, I knew I had the title for the book that was marinating," she says. "The puzzle pieces took one and a half years to fall into place, but the story took less than two weeks to write."

Then, of course, came the marketing. The book went to four editors and through two requested rewrites before Giblin suggested Fritts try Kathy Tucker at Albert Whitman & Company, a publisher known for carrying concept books in picture book format. Fritts sent her story and "waited for what seemed the longest months of my life, until they offered a contract." When her acceptance letter arrived, it read, "You've written touchingly not only of the sadness of Alzheimer's but also of the strength of family love."

Fritts actually wrote the story, however, before she researched Alzheimer's. "Although my grandfather didn't have Alzheimer's, I'd hear him conversing with my grandmother many times after she died. As a child, it made me feel sad when he'd leave me there, in the present, and go back to visit her in the past," she says. "I read about the disease after I wrote the book and it still seemed truthful to me. However, the publisher requested I have two Alzheimer's experts read the manuscript to verify its authenticity."

The book, illustrated in gouache by David Cunningham, was published in 1992 under her maiden name, Mary Bahr. "I use my maiden name on anything I publish for children. A wonderful childhood was my parents' and grandparents' gift to me. My stories about those memories are my gift to them," she says. Likewise, Fritts uses her married name when publishing in the adult market — as a tribute to the nurture and support she's received from her husband and sons.

Regarding the book-publishing process, Fritts says one thing that surprised her was the barrage of blue slips attached to the manuscript "with what seemed like trillions of edits. I remember a day at the mailbox saying so loud that the mailman came back, 'If you didn't like what I wrote, why did you buy it?' When I saw the finished product, I knew the answer." *The Memory Box* not only received a starred review in *Booklist*, but is now in its second printing.

While Fritts believes each writer must glean what works for her from all the advice that's given to beginning writers, she says the advice she took to heart was to begin (*now*), to never stop perfecting your craft and to revise, market and persist. Overall, she says, "A manuscript in the drawer does not sell, but neither does a manuscript in the mail too soon. If you work hard and never give up, you will succeed."

Elaine Sandeen
Jenna's Big Jump (Atheneum)

"My mom used to tell everybody that I started drawing as soon as I was old enough to hold a pencil," says Elaine Sandeen. Though she doesn't quite remember her age at that time, Sandeen does recall her family predicting she would be an artist. Becoming a children's book illustrator, however, wasn't what first came to mind.

"When I was in junior high school, about 12 years old, I used to draw on my homework and my desk and all kinds of stuff," Sandeen says, "and the teacher asked me if I would do a portrait of his baby son." When she agreed, he gave her a photograph and she did the portrait. "After that, all the kids in school started wanting me to do portraits because I only charged like a dollar or 50 cents. I had to eventually quit doing them, though, because I had so many portraits to do, I didn't have time to do my schoolwork," she says.

Yet the experience stayed with Sandeen and she began envisioning herself as a gallery artist. "I always wanted to be more of a fine artist doing oil paintings," Sandeen explains. "In fact, I have done quite a few portraits and murals for people . . . but I don't like art shows at all.

"Then when my daughter got to be about two or three years old, just as soon as she was old enough to hold a book without tearing the pages out, I started reading her books from the library and discovered just how wonderful they are. The more I read them, the more I fell in love with children's books. That's when I got the idea to start looking into what it would take to become a children's book illustrator."

The self-taught artist soon discovered, however, that finding information was far from easy. "What little information I do know about illustrating and things like how to get a job is mainly from books. *Getting Started as a Freelance Illustrator or Designer* (by Michael Fleishman), in fact, is basically the one that got me started," she says.

Sandeen also took a class at an adult school called the Learning Tree University. It was an eight-week class on children's book illustration and design. There the instructor suggested eliciting the interest of publishing companies by sending out postcards with sample artwork on the front.

Having read *Children's Writer's & Illustrator's Market*, Sandeen decided to start as recommended—with magazines. "I mailed about 50 postcards to magazine publishing companies," she says, "but they would send me their illustrator's guidelines which would be talking about color separations and stuff I didn't know anything about." Sandeen then took an illustration class at the Antelope Valley College. In that class, she learned how to do mechanicals, paste-up work and color separations.

By 1992, Sandeen, who works as a seamstress for a uniform company, was ready to try again. This time, however, she decided to target book publishing companies. "I went through all the book publishing companies in *Children's Writer's & Illustrator's Market* and made a mailing list of 100 publishers that I thought would want black & white or full-color artwork in pencil, colored pencil or oils (her preferred media)."

She then sent out postcards in the beginning of June and almost immediately got calls from three or four publishing companies requesting to see her portfolio. After sending her portfolio, she gave them all follow-up calls. And, in the beginning of July, she got her very first illustration job. "I was just totally thrilled to death," she says.

The assignment came from Atheneum. "The art director, Patrice Fodero, called and said they had a manuscript she wanted to send," recalls Sandeen. "They needed one color illustration for the jacket and 10 black & white illustrations for the book. I was to pick any parts I wanted to illustrate but space them evenly throughout the book. And I was to do up some very detailed, almost-finished sketches first."

The manuscript Sandeen received was *Jenna's Big Jump*, a chapter book about a new fourth-grader named Jenna who not only tries to stand up to the class bully, but also plans to prove herself to her mother by learning to swing from a rope in her friend's hayloft. The story was written by Faythe Dyrud Thureen and happens to be Thureen's first children's book as well.

Knowing the importance of consistent characters, Sandeen began by using her friend's daughter as a model for Jenna. She got a Polaroid camera, placed the youngster in the positions she wanted Jenna to be in, and used the resulting snapshots as a guide for Jenna's facial features and body proportions.

Sandeen then sketched the jacket illustration and sent it to Atheneum for review while she worked on the inside illustrations. When she received her sketch back, however, she was asked to totally redo the illustration. Realizing one of her interior illustrations was stronger, she simply switched the original jacket illustration with the illustration inside. Once approved, she completed the cover in oils, and finished the rest of the artwork in pencil.

Regarding the experience, she says, "I think the thing that surprised me the most was that everybody was just such normal, nice people. I kind of expected these really mean, critical art directors, but even when they would criticize or want a change, they were just so nice about it."

Although Sandeen admits she got more encouragement than discouragement, her advice to aspiring children's book illustrators is not to be discouraged by what other people say. "When I first started this," she says, "my husband said I probably had as much chance of becoming a children's book illustrator as his youngest son has of becoming a rock star. But I thought, well, you don't become really rich and famous as a children's book illustrator, so why should it be as hard?"

Deborah Hopkinson
Sweet Clara and the Freedom Quilt (Alfred A. Knopf, Inc.)

"Anyone reading this publication is more knowledgeable than I was when I began!'', says Deborah Hopkinson. "My research efforts were quite laughable in retrospect. I spent half my time trying to figure out what an imprint was and where to send manuscripts, and the other half getting rejections."

Hopkinson, who works as development director for Hawaii's East West Center (a federally funded research and educational institution devoted to the Asia-Pacific region), wanted to write ever since she was a child, but didn't begin writing fiction until 1987. "As a New Year's resolution," she says, "I set a goal of submitting one story a month. I chose children's stories because, with a fulltime career and a three-year-old, children's books were the only kind of books I was reading!"

Despite disappointments, Hopkinson stuck to her resolution. In the fall of 1988, after almost two years of rejections, she attended her first children's writing workshop. "I learned for the first time about the Society of Children's Book Writers and Illustrators and was encouraged to break into the market through magazines," she says.

Her first magazine submission was accepted by *Cricket* that November. "I later sold the first children's story I had ever written—which had been rejected countless times by book publishers—to *Ladybug Magazine*, where it was illustrated by David McPhail. Since then I have sold about two dozen stories—a number of which are historical fiction—to children's magazines and anthologies," Hopkinson adds.

In the spring of 1989, she also received what she calls "a gift"—the idea for what would become her first children's book. "As I was getting ready for work, I heard a story on National Public Radio about an African-American quilt exhibition at Williams College. The story made reference to 'escape routes being sewn into quilts.' And the enormity of that story hit me," she says.

Hopkinson then began reading primary and secondary sources about slavery and the Underground Railroad. She says she carried the characters around in her head for awhile and late that summer finished *Sweet Clara and the Freedom*

Quilt, the story of a young slave girl who stitches a map of the land into a quilt, creating an escape route to the North—and her freedom.

If the idea for the story had somehow been "given" to Hopkinson, the publication of the story would require more effort. In August 1989, Hopkinson submitted her story to a publisher who had expressed interest in her work. That publisher, however, held it until May 1990 before rejecting it. "I tried three or four more publishers during the summer of 1990, sometimes getting a letter in return, often just a form rejection," she says.

Determined not to be discouraged, Hopkinson did something she had never done before (or since): She simultaneously submitted her manuscript. "I felt the story was publishable, but at the rate things were going it might take years!", she says. "So, in October 1990, I decided to submit *Sweet Clara* simultaneously to publishers that indicated they would accept such submissions."

About three weeks later, Hopkinson picked up the phone at work and heard Anne Schwartz, executive editor at Alfred A. Knopf Books for Young Readers, say she liked the story. "My letter was in the slush pile," Hopkinson explains. "Anne said that, because she noticed it said simultaneous submission on it, she decided to give it a quick glance—just in case. Ironically, months after I sent letters to the other publishers—withdrawing my manuscript—I received a couple of rejection letters."

Once accepted, *Sweet Clara* went through three or four revisions, and author Patricia McKissack was kind enough to review the dialect, Hopkinson says. When the picture book finally arrived in the mail in late 1992, it was two years after it was first accepted by Knopf. And it was beautifully illustrated by the paintings of James Ransome, a descendant of slaves who lived on the Verona Plantation, a model for the plantation pictured in *Sweet Clara*.

"I'm very much aware of the recent debate about multiculturalism and the issue of writing outside your ethnic or cultural group," says Hopkinson. "Although I have written other stories with Asian- or African-American characters, I do so with hesitation and believe this issue should be approached with sensitivity. I have been touched and humbled by the warm acceptance of African-Americans to my writing this book."

Now in its third printing, *Sweet Clara and the Freedom Quilt* has received more than just warm acceptance. In addition to being a Reading Rainbow and Children's Book-of-the-Month Club selection, it has been adapted as a play to tour in elementary schools by the St. Louis Black Repertory Company.

Hopkinson says during the whole publishing process she received two bits of good advice. "The practical advice is to systematically do your best to break into the market through magazines and build up your publishing credits. The best artistic advice I've been given is simply to find and write the story you want to tell without worrying about format, formulas or market needs. I guess in the end you do a little of both."

Her own advice to beginning writers is to read widely and keep putting as much time and energy as you can toward your dream. "I don't listen to anyone who says write at the same time every day; sometimes it's just not possible with a fulltime job and kids. I just do what I can and try not to be discouraged by how little that sometimes is. The most important thing is to take one step at a time down the path you want to go. And use rejection the same way you use encouragement—as a spur."

Writing and Illustrating from Another Culture's Tradition

by Susan Strauss

Maybe, just maybe it is my karma that I, a first generation European-American with three-quarters Jewish heritage and an appearance "as goyish (Yiddish for Wasp) as the girls on Wall Street," would write books on Native American myths. "Must a writer be a member of a particular ethnic group to write about it?" is a question that has followed my entire career, first as a storyteller and now as a writer.

Today, I write and perform stories from a wide variety of cultures. During the years when I was only working with Native American Coyote Tales, I once asked a Native friend if she thought I should stop telling Coyote Stories. "Why?" she asked. "Because I'm not Native," I said. "Yeah," she said, "but you're not a Coyote either."

Every time I decided I had no business working with the Native tradition, I was mysteriously pulled back into it by circumstance. Finally, I realized that I am a Coyote, in the mythic sense. After 14 years of working with myth, I believe every culture has a special medicine carried in the style with which it expresses truth.

If people are deeply called to work with particular cultural traditions, they should embark on the journey. By answering this calling, they will find their psyche balanced by the work. Every artist who is truly doing work is spiritually and psychologically enriched by the progress. A cultural tradition, be it music, dance or storytelling, does not choose us by color, but by soul.

One thing is certain: My oral and written renditions of Native myths will never be as authentic as a traditional teller raised in the culture. But this does not mean they will not be as good or as close to the soul of the story. I have received confirmation of this several times from traditional Natives.

Still, one should deeply examine one's own attraction to another culture's artistic traditions to make sure this attraction is not false or part of some fad. A colleague of mine once told me "I just don't like Coyote Stories. . . . " I commend her, because even though Native American stories are popular with schools (which is her market), she is true to herself.

Susan Strauss is an internationally known storyteller and author of Coyote Stories for Children, Wolf Stories: Myths and True Life Tales from Around the World *and several audiocassettes. Her work has brought her engagements with the Oregon Symphony, the Smithsonian, Columbia University and numerous national parks and forests. Her third book,* The Passionate Fact: Storytelling in Natural History Interpretation, *will be available from North American Press this spring. She lives in Bend, Oregon.*

Discover your purpose

The act of taking stories from an oral tradition and putting them into print does diminish their authenticity and power. Therefore, writers must discover their purpose for regenerating the stories in print.

From my own experience, this purpose or vision for the Coyote Stories became clear about four o'clock in the morning in a motel room in western Idaho. All night a colleague attempted to convince me that I should stop telling Native American stories. After she had fallen asleep, I lay awake for hours. Finally, I decided to accept her reasoning. At that moment, I felt a deep despair. I felt like someone had just told me that several of my closest friends had died. I wept quietly as I imagined saying goodbye to the characters of Coyote, Fox and Bear, and the landscapes of North America as I had generated them through myself.

Within this experience, I realized why I told Native stories. These stories were a way for me to express my love for the continent and creatures we call America . . . and home. My vision became larger than personal growth or the translation of a cultural tradition. It became a way to give Americans of all ethnicities an experience of their true homeland and a reverence for the life forms that sustain it.

Can there be pitfalls even with a good vision? One vision that inspired my second book, *Wolf Stories: Myths and True Life Tales from Around the World*, was to show a universal reverence for the wolf which is expressed by many world cultures. Universality is a noble vision for any book. All cultures are yearning to express the same wisdom, only each culture has its particular style for approaching that wisdom. A writer should not sacrifice the specific details of that style in an effort to show universality.

With the best interests at heart, writers and publishers can perpetrate "cultural colonialism" under the guise of universality. The details of a folk-story style are like tastes. Each culture has its own version of the pancake. How wonderful are the variations of tastes, textures and uses of each! Would we want to lose those differences? Not in pancakes; not in folklore or mythology.

From an illustrator's point of view, this is equally a concern. Imagine illustrating a story from India in which a female beauty is drawn with a slender, tall, New York model figure rather than with full hips and bust. Or Coyote carrying salmon in a backpack that looks like it was bought in a sports shop rather than the type that was traditionally carried, with the strap across the forehead, by the fishing Natives of Oregon.

Only in recent illustrations have distinctions been made between the traditional clothing and dwellings of Plains Indians and those of all other tribes. Not so far in the past, all Native people were illustrated with tepees and buckskin clothing.

Research, research, research

How can we avoid losing these details and bring forth the most authentic work? The most important answer for writers and illustrators is research. This essential homework can be delineated into two types: head and heart research.

Head research should be obvious. A writer should make great efforts to read every version of a story to decipher the story's truest form and meaning. Greek myths, for instance, have gone through dramatic changes depending on whether they were recorded during matriarchal or patriarchal historic periods. Following this head research, an author must do some soul searching (heart research) to decide what is the true story and what is the truth of the story. This heart research usually requires that an author live with the story as a flaming interest for some period of time.

This beginning process will be aided by research in the culture itself. Cultural research will provide the writer and illustrator with ideas for creating a cultural context for the story and an authentic style as well as dissolve false assumptions. Especially in regard to Native American stories, writers, publishers, readers and Native Americans not familiar with their own mythology overromanticize the culture and wash out bawdy or violent aspects of a story which are vital to its healing and instructive worth.

The bawdy or violent images in Native American stories are used to show the consequences of disrespectful behavior or the severity of sacrifice and initiation. They served the moral development of Native children for thousands of years. For this reason, they are considered sacred, not crass.

Some of the earliest anthropological recordings of Native myths censored these parts of the stories or transcribed them in Latin so only a select readership could understand. Also, some Native informants censored themselves because they knew the dominant culture could not accept certain parts of their myths. This kind of pre-publishing censorship is evident in several Native American books published within the past two years and was a concern during the production of my first book, *Coyote Stories for Children: Tales from Native America*.

Visit the natives

Writers and illustrators can begin to prepare themselves for this struggle to preserve the truest story by gaining personal experience with the culture or subject. One cannot expect to gather all knowledge from books, but must "visit the natives" . . . whether the natives be traditional people of a particular culture or in the case of *Wolf Stories*, live wolves.

I spent some time in cages with captive wolves, watching their movement and character, and some time interviewing biologists who have observed wolves in the wild. This was the most important aspect of my research. It helped me understand the similarity between the biological wolf and the positive representations of the wolf in world mythology . . . and how negative wolf myths might have developed. In short, I learned who the wolf really was.

With animals or humans, it is hard for me to understand how an illustrator could create without this kind of research, also. An illustrator might find examples of a particular ethnic dress in a book, but will this source also show the way in which people wear their clothes? For instance, is a hat worn straight or tilted in one direction? Is a man's wrap worn around his waist or does it hang from his hips with his belly relaxed and exposed?

And what about body shapes? Style is more than type of clothing. With serious research, illustrations will avoid looking like a *Woman's Day* magazine Sunday picnic photospread in which models are dressed in ethnic clothing. As writer or illustrator, your head research will help you examine the inconsistencies between what you read and what you experience.

At last, writers and illustrators must sift all this through their own ability of self-reflection. This kind of heart research is a fearless exploration of your own and others' delights and dislikes of authentic story elements. This exploration will help you translate the story and cultural context without censorship or "cultural colonialism."

If all of this does not help convince your publisher to print your material without dominant culture whitewashing, find a worthy co-author, cultural consultant or editor who is from the culture and will support the authenticity of your efforts.

In my first book, *Coyote Stories for Children*, I was determined to keep the violent and bawdy elements of stories that I knew, from years of storytelling experience, were magical, provocative and healing for modern children. I was determined not to produce another collection of Native American stories for children that was softened and sweetened. I was coerced by my publisher to eliminate some of these parts, until we brought on a Native American editor. He had the clout to convince my publisher to include the story "Coyote and the Grass People." In this story, Coyote develops a tremendous farting problem because of his arrogance and lack of respect.

Today, every time someone approaches me at a book signing with their child and says, "Do you know which story is our favorite?", I already know the answer.

66 A cultural tradition, be it music, dance or storytelling, does not choose us by color, but by soul. **99**

—Susan Strauss

Getting Started in the Educational Market

by Barbara Gregorich

For writers and illustrators, the educational market is not like a quiet library floor of study carrels, each sequestering a student laboring over tomes. It's more like a feature film that enthralls with great acting, color, sound, movement and special effects. Make that a *large* feature film, an epic with a cast of thousands.

In the U.S. there are approximately two million teachers and 40 million students. Last year book sales of elementary and secondary textbooks totaled more than $2 billion dollars. Sales of audiovisual and other media for schools totaled more than $164 million. And this doesn't include the various nontextbook juvenile hardbacks and paperbacks used in the classroom. The publishers who produce these educational materials are always in need of writers and illustrators, and this interesting field is fairly easy to enter.

Breaking in

Although the educational market, like others, is tightening in a tough economy, publishers still need reliable writers to create the endless round of new and revised textbooks and supplementary materials. They also need illustrators to provide the art. For writers, the market is especially kind to beginners because it's skill-oriented. Publishers are looking for writers who can explain the how and why of various rules (grammar, math, cooking) in clear and simple language.

Imagine yourself a writer who hasn't been published. You may be circulating a trade book manuscript to various editors. But in the meantime, you could be seeking freelance work as a writer of educational materials. You could write end-of-chapter summaries of an eighth-grade history textbook or a fifth-grade social studies book. An educational editor looking for somebody to write ancillary textbook materials hires several writers for each textbook project. Those writers who prove reliable at entry-level writing can move up to a higher level. If you're a published writer, you could break into the educational market by proposing a particular activity book, video or audiotape.

Not all writing is creative writing. Much of it is expository, or explanatory writing. And while there is creative writing in the educational market, it's easier to break in by writing the "straight stuff." Take that fifth-grade social studies textbook. Most likely two or three teachers of long-standing reputation have been hired to write the text (as outlined and designed by the publisher). Each

Barbara Gregorich's *educational materials include textbooks, workbooks, storybooks, filmstrips, audiocassettes, flash cards and computer software. Author of* Writing for the Educational Market *(J. Weston Walch, Publisher), she gives seminars at writers' and teachers' conferences. Her adult trade books include* Women at Play: The Story of Women in Baseball *(Harcourt Brace & Co., 1993). She lives in Chicago, Illinois.*

chapter will, according to the publisher's plans, contain items such as chapter summaries, discussion questions, activity suggestions and test questions.

If you can read somebody else's material and write a 75-word summary of its main points, or write 5-10 student test questions based on the material, you're a good candidate for writing ancillary text materials. Pay for such writing is in the range of $50 for 10 test questions. If you do well in this area, your requests to be considered to write other materials (possibly activity pages, which pay $20-60 per page) will be heard and possibly met. You will be an insider, somebody who has worked for the company already.

Unlike beginning writers, beginning illustrators can't break into the market with end-of-chapter materials—there are no end-of-chapter illustrations in textbooks. For illustrators, the place to begin is with supplementary materials, particularly worksheets and activity books. The pay for illustrations runs from roughly $10-100 per page for black & white, and $75-350 per page for color. In illustrating, as in writing, fees are negotiable.

Teacher materials

Educational products for the kindergarten through twelfth grade market can be classified into two categories: those used by teachers (or parents) and those used by the students themselves.

Teacher materials are never seen by the student. Such materials comprise questions and *answers* written in a separate teacher edition of textbooks; teacher manuals that accompany posters, audiovisual programs, videos, multimedia kits; even software programs designed to allow teachers to type in their own questions and change the format from multiple choice to true/false or fill-in-the-blank. In most cases, educational publishers seek teachers or former teachers to write these materials, mainly because classroom experience helps when writing for those who must function in the classroom.

As for illustrators, even when it comes to teacher materials, publishers do not require that illustrators have a teaching background. Generally one must be a published illustrator to land a large educational assignment. Few publishers want to take risks with an unknown in the final stages of production, when printing and shipping deadlines loom large. Smaller independent publishers of supplemental materials are more likely to hire a beginning illustrator. Large educational houses such as Macmillan Publishing Company are interested in professional portfolios.

Student materials

Unlike publishers of teacher materials, publishers of student materials are more open to hiring writers who have never been or even thought of being teachers. This bodes well for writers because student materials are the most fun of any educational writing assignments. They are also the most creative. Working on student materials designed and solicited by a publisher can soon lead a writer to create her own proposals for student materials—when you reach this point in educational writing, you will be writing query letters to educational editors just as you would to trade book or magazine editors.

There are many kinds of student materials. Textbooks are aimed at students, of course, but so are activity books, worksheets, audiotapes, videos, storybooks, posters, puzzles, board games, flash cards and software. The real challenge in writing these materials is to convey specific information in a clear but interest-holding way. In creating activity books, you must visualize the way an activity will look and work on a page, be it a crossword puzzle, a true/false quiz or an unscramble-the-words test. In writing audiotapes, you must be lively and inventive to convey the information but not put the audience to sleep.

Writing audiotapes is a good way to break into the educational market. If you have a special knack with young children (talking to them, singing to them, playing games with them), you might try to write an audiotape of stories, games or sing-alongs. If your skill is in explaining how things work, or if you're particularly good at understanding the conflicting emotions young adults feel, audiotapes for grades 7-12 might be more along your line. Educational publishers produce audios on diverse subjects such as art, business, computers, foreign languages, health and fitness, math, music and social studies.

The range of topics isn't the only thing that's wide in educational publishing: The range of media is wider than in any other field. Educational writers can work in several media without much difficulty—print, film, audio, software and manipulatives such as flash cards and board games. This means that if you develop a product for one field, say an audiotape on substance abuse, you might later develop a workbook on the same topic—or a video, or a computer program.

Be aware of market needs

In business publishing the buzzwords seem to change every few years, and in trade publishing hot topics come and go. But in educational publishing, the topics remain the same: Reading will always be taught, as will math, history and physical education.

Nevertheless, the *way* in which subjects are taught is not static. Every decade or so there seems to be a change in how educators approach addition and subtraction—terms such as "borrowing" are replaced with "regrouping." And while reading will always be taught, today's educators are debating which approach to reading is best: the phonics approach, the whole language approach, or a combination of the two.

If you want to write reading materials for children in the primary grades, you should be aware of the current debate over whole language versus phonics: Should children learn the meaning of words in context, and thus learn to comprehend what they read, or should they be taught phonics skills so they can pronounce any word they encounter? More important, you should be aware of which approach the publisher you are working with takes and what the publisher's needs are. If the publisher wants a whole language approach to reading, then the editor will most likely reject a story built around the use of 10 words which contain a short "a" sound.

Anybody wishing to illustrate for the educational market should be aware of the issues teachers (and thus educational publishers) are concerned with—issues such as nonviolence, separation of church and state, nonstereotyping and multiculturalism. If you want to know what types of art various educational publishers are looking for, be sure to study *current* books, not the old Dick and Jane materials.

In both writing and illustrating, educational publishers are looking for people who can make the page fun, integrate art with text, and make the child want to learn.

Introductory letters and query letters

In trade book and magazine publishing, writers send query letters to editors, pitching an idea for a particular book or article. In educational publishing, the beginning writer can start with an introductory letter. The writer with a proposal in mind will send a query letter just as in trade publishing.

The introductory letter should be written if you are seeking work as a freelance writer of ancillary materials. In this letter, state your strengths and qualifications for the assignment. For example, if you have a degree in biology and are good at writing how-to materials, state so in your letter. Include a short résumé and no more than three samples of published work (if any). Always ask that your letter and résumé be kept on file for appropriate assignments. Address such letters to editors in charge of a particular department: for example, the secondary-level biology editor or the primary-level math editor.

When writing query letters to educational publishers, act as if you were writing to magazine or trade book editors: Be interesting and concise, and enclose a self-addressed, stamped envelope.

Illustrators should write a cover letter to go with their portfolio. If appropriate, mention your educational background — college degree, art training, and any speciality areas such as cartography, which would qualify you for geography texts and activity pages.

Finding educational publishers

Although educational publishing is a billion-dollar business, its publications aren't immediately visible to the freelance writer who is used to walking into a bookstore and purchasing books or magazines. For one thing, most educational products are confined to the school system. For another, educational publishers aren't listed in their own separate directory.

This book, *Children's Writer's & Illustrator's Market*, is an easy place to find accessible educational publishers. In addition, *Literary Market Place* lists publishers by subject matter, classifying more than 300 of them as educational.

An excellent way to find educational publishers is to visit a teacher's supply house. These stores, which sell poster paper, grade books and other such items, are a wonderful place to browse a variety of supplementary educational materials. Writers and illustrators can get the names and addresses of publishers from their products, then write to them.

Another good way to find educational publishers is to attend trade shows aimed at the educational marketplace. The International Reading Association, for example, packs educational publishers back-to-back in exhibition booths at its yearly conferences. You can pay to attend one of these conferences. Wander the aisles, pick up materials that interest you, study the catalogs, talk to editors if they aren't too busy with teachers (who buy their books). When you get home, write to the publishing houses that interest you.

After you've worked with one educational publisher, you can continue to develop materials for that publisher, or you can move on to others — there are hundreds of them, and they're always looking for materials.

The Business of Children's Writing & Illustrating

When a writer or illustrator decides to market her freelancing talents she will encounter many unexpected problems, and develop numerous questions about the field of children's writing and illustrating. "What is the proper way to submit my work?" "Do I need an agent?" "How much should I ask for my material?" This section is designed to answer your questions and expose you to the business techniques needed to successfully market your work.

Researching markets

There are two basic elements to submitting your work successfully: good research and persistence. Read through the listings in this book and familiarize yourself with the publications that interest you. Then study the specific needs and the required submission procedures of each publisher or publication. Editors hate to receive inappropriate submissions because handling them wastes precious time. By randomly sending out manuscripts without knowledge of the markets' needs, you risk irritating the editors. As editors may remember your name and associate it with inappropriate submissions, this practice actually hurts you more than it helps.

If you're interested in submitting to a particular magazine, write to request a sample copy. For a book publisher, obtain a book catalog or a couple of books produced by that publisher. By doing this, you can better acquaint yourself with that market's writing and illustration styles and formats.

Most of the book publishers and magazines listed offer some sort of writer's/artist's guidelines. Read these guidelines *before* submitting work.

Formats for submission

Throughout these listings you will read editors' requests for a query letter, cover letter, book proposal, complete manuscript or résumé as all or part of the initial contact procedure. Any submission should be directed to a specific person. Turnover at publishing companies and magazines is rampant. Therefore, it is a good idea to call the publisher to confirm a contact name before sending anything. You do not need to disturb the contact person by asking to speak with him; merely ask the receptionist or secretary if the person still works there and if he still handles the same manuscripts/artwork.

Query letters. A query letter should be no more than a one-page, well-written piece to arouse an editor's interest in your manuscript. Queries are usually required from writers submitting nonfiction material to a publisher. In the query letter you want to convince the editor that your idea is perfect for his readership and you're the writer qualified to do the job. Include any previous writing experience in your letter and published samples to prove your credentials, especially any samples related to the subject matter about which you're querying.

Many query letters start with a lead similar to the lead of the actual manuscript. Next, you want to briefly outline the work and include facts, anecdotes, interviews or other pertinent information that give the editor a feel for the manuscript's premise. Your goal is to entice him to want to know more. End your letter with a straightforward request to write (or submit) the work, and include information on its approximate length, date it could be completed, and the availability of accompanying photos or artwork.

More and more, queries are being used for fiction manuscripts because slush piles at some publishing houses have become virtually uncontrollable. As the number of submissions continues to skyrocket, several publishers have stopped accepting unsolicited submissions. However, they are still open to queries. For a fiction query, explain the story's plot, main characters, conflict and resolution. Just as in nonfiction queries, make the editor eager to see more. For more information on writing good queries, consult *How to Write Irresistible Query Letters*, by Lisa Collier Cool (Writer's Digest Books).

Cover letters. Many editors prefer to review a complete manuscript, especially for fiction. In such a case, the cover letter serves as your introduction, establishes your credentials as a writer, and gives the editor an overview of the manuscript.

If an editor asked you for a manuscript because of a query, note this in your cover letter. Also, if a rejection letter includes an invitation to submit other work, mention that as well. Editors should understand the work was solicited.

For an illustrator, the cover letter serves as your introduction to the art director and establishes your credentials as a professional artist. Be sure to explain what services you can provide as well as what type of follow-up contact you plan to make, if any. When sending samples of your work, indicate whether they should be returned or filed. Never send original artwork! If you wish to have the samples returned, include a self-addressed, stamped envelope (SASE). Cover letters, like queries, should be no longer than one page.

Résumés. Often writers and illustrators are asked to submit résumés with their cover letters and writing/art samples. Résumés can be created in a variety of formats ranging from a single page listing information to color brochures featuring your art. Keep the résumé brief, and focus on your artistic achievements. Include your clients and the work you've done for them as well as your educational background and any awards you've received. Do not use the same résumé that you use for a typical job application.

Book proposals. Throughout the listings in the Book Publishers section you will find references to submission of a synopsis, outline and sample chapters. Depending on an editor's preference, some or all of these components, as well as inclusion of a cover letter, comprise a book proposal.

A synopsis summarizes the book. Such a summary includes the basic plot of the book (including the ending), is easy to read and flows well.

An outline can also be used to set up fiction, but is more effective as a tool for nonfiction. The outline covers your book chapter by chapter and provides highlights of each. If you are developing an outline for fiction include major characters, plots and subplots, and length of the book. An outline can run to 30 pages depending on the complexity of your manuscript.

Sample chapters give a more comprehensive idea of your writing skill. Some editors may request the first two or three chapters to see how your material is set up; others may request a beginning, middle and ending chapter to get a better feel for the entire plot. Be sure to determine what the editor needs to see before investing time in writing sample chapters.

Many picture book editors require an outline or synopsis, sample chapters and a variation of roughs or finished illustrations from the author/illustrator. Listings specifying an interest in picture books will detail what type of artwork should accompany manuscripts. If you want to know more about putting together a book proposal, read *How to Write and Sell Children's Picture Books*, by Jean Karl (Writer's Digest Books).

Manuscript formats. If an editor specifies that you should submit a complete manuscript, here is some format information to guide you. In the upper left corner of your title page, type your legal name (not pseudonym), address, phone number and Social Security number (publishers must have this to file payment records with the government). In the upper right corner, type the approximate word length. All material in the upper corners should be typed single-spaced. Then type the title (centered) almost halfway down the page with the word "by" two spaces under that and your name or pseudonym two spaces under "by."

The first page should also include the title (centered) one-third of the way down. Two spaces under that type "by" and your name or pseudonym. To begin the body of your manuscript, drop down two double spaces and indent five spaces for each new paragraph. There should be 1¼ inch margins around all sides of a full typewritten page. (Manuscripts with wider margins are more readable and easier to edit.) Set your typewriter on double-space for the manuscript body. From page 2 to the end of your manuscript include your last name followed by a comma and the title (or key words of the title) in the upper left corner. The page number should go in the top right corner. Drop down two double spaces to begin the body of each page. If you're submitting a novel, type each chapter title one-third of the way down the page.

When typing the text of a picture book, it is not necessary to include page breaks or supply art. Editors prefer to find the illustrators for picture books. Most of the time, a writer and an illustrator who work on the same book never meet. In this kind of arrangement, the editor acts as a go-between in case either the writer or illustrator has any problems with text or artwork.

If you are an illustrator who has written your own book, create a dummy or storyboard containing both art and text. Then submit it along with sample pieces of final art (color photocopies—no originals). For a step-by-step guide on creating a good dummy, refer to Frieda Gates's book, *How to Write, Illustrate, and Design Children's Books* (Lloyd-Simone Publishing Company).

For more information on manuscript formats read *Manuscript Submission*, by Scott Edelstein (Writer's Digest Books).

Mailing and recording submissions

Your primary concern in packaging material is to ensure that it arrives undamaged. If your manuscript is fewer than six pages it is safe to simply fold it in thirds and send it out in a #10 (business-size) envelope. For a self-addressed, stamped envelope (SASE) you can then fold another #10 envelope in thirds or insert a #9 (reply) envelope which fits in a #10 neatly without any folding. Some editors appreciate receiving a manuscript folded in half in a 6×9 envelope. For larger manuscripts use a 9 × 12 envelope both for mailing the submission out and as a SASE for its return. The SASE can be folded in half. Book manuscripts require a sturdy box such as a typing paper or envelope box for mailing. Include a self-addressed mailing label and return postage so it can double as your SASE.

Artwork requires a bit more packaging care to guarantee that it arrives in presentable form. Sandwich illustrations between heavy cardboard that is slightly larger than the work, and tape it closed. Write your name and address on each piece in case the inside material becomes separated from the outer envelope. For the outer wrapping use either a manila envelope, foam-padded envelope, a mailer with plastic air bubbles as a liner or brown paper. Bind non-joined edges with reinforced mailing tape and clearly write your address.

Mail material first class to ensure quick delivery. Also, first-class mail is forwarded for one year if the addressee has moved, and can be returned if undeliverable. If you are concerned about your material safely reaching its destination, consider other mailing options, such as UPS or certified mail. If material needs to reach your editor or art director quickly, you can elect to use overnight delivery services.

Occasionally throughout this book you will see the term International Reply Coupon (IRC). Keep in mind markets outside your own country cannot use your country's postage when returning a manuscript to you, which therefore renders moot any SASE you may have sent. When mailing a submission to another country, include a self-addressed envelope and IRCs. Your post office can help you determine, based on the package's weight, the correct number of IRCs to include to ensure its return.

If it is not necessary for an editor to return your work, such as with photocopies of manuscripts or art, don't include return postage. Instead, track the status of your submission by enclosing a postage-paid reply postcard (which requires less postage) with options for the editor to check, such as "Yes, I am interested" or "No, the material is not appropriate for my needs at this time."

Some writers or illustrators simply include a deadline date. If nothing is heard from the editor or art director by this date, the manuscript or artwork is automatically withdrawn from consideration. Because many publishing houses are overstocked with manuscripts, a minimum deadline should be no less than three months.

One thing you should never do is use a publisher's fax number to send queries, manuscripts or illustration samples. Only use a fax number after acquiring proper authorization. Don't disrupt the publisher's pace of doing internal business by sending a long manuscript via fax.

Many times writers and illustrators devote their attention to submitting material to editors or art directors, then fail to follow up on overdue responses because they feel the situation is out of their hands. By tracking those submissions still under consideration and then following up, you may refresh the memory of a buyer who temporarily forgot about your submission, or revise a troublesome point to make your work more enticing to him. At the very least you will receive a definite "no," thereby freeing you to send your material to another market.

When recording your submissions be sure to include the date they were sent, the business and contact name, and any enclosures such as samples of writing, artwork or photography. Keep copies of the article or manuscript as well as related correspondence for easier follow up. When you sell rights to a manuscript or artwork you can "close" your file by noting the date the material was accepted, what rights were purchased, the publication date and payment.

Simultaneous submissions

If you opt for simultaneous submissions—sending the same material to several editors at the same time—be sure to inform each editor your work is being considered elsewhere. Doing so is a professional courtesy that is encouraged throughout the field. Most editors are reluctant to receive simultaneous submissions, but understand the frustration experienced by hopeful authors who must wait many months for a response. In some cases, an editor may actually be more inclined to read your manuscript sooner because he knows it's being considered elsewhere.

The Society of Children's Book Writers and Illustrators, however, warns against simultaneous submissions, believing they will eventually cause publishers to quit accepting unsolicited material altogether. Also, since manuscripts that are simultaneously submitted are not specifically tailored to any one publisher, SCBWI feels the act will result in less than serious consideration of work received. The official recommendation of the SCBWI is to submit to one publisher at a time, but wait only three months (note you will do so in your cover letter). If no response is received, then send a note withdrawing your manuscript from consideration. SCBWI considers simultaneous submissions acceptable only if you have a manuscript dealing with a timely issue.

It is especially important to keep track of submissions when you are submitting simultaneously. This way if you get an offer on that manuscript, you can notify the other publishers to withdraw your work from consideration.

Agents

Many children's writers and illustrators, especially those who are just beginning, are confused about whether to utilize the services of an agent. The decision is strictly one that each writer or illustrator must decide for herself. There are some who are confident enough with their own negotiation skills and feel acquiring an agent is not in their best interest. Still, others scare easily at the slightest mention of business and are not willing to sacrifice valuable writing or illustrating time for the time it takes to market their work. Before you consider contacting an agent, read on to become familiar with what an agent can—and cannot—do.

Enough demand for children's material exists that breaking into children's publishing without an agent is easier than breaking into the adult market without one. In fact, many agents avoid working with children's books because traditionally low advances and trickling royalty payments over long periods of time make children's books less lucrative. Acquiring an agent to market short stories is next to impossible—there just isn't enough financial incentive for an agent to be interested.

One benefit of having an agent, though, is it may expedite the process of getting your work reviewed, especially with publishers who don't accept unagented submissions. If an agent has a good reputation and submits your manuscript to an editor, that manuscript may actually bypass the first-read stage (which is done by editorial assistants and junior editors) and end up on that editor's desk sooner. And illustrators who live elsewhere often seek representatives based in New York City when they want their work shown to New York City publishers.

When agreeing to have a reputable agent represent you, remember that she should be familiar with the needs of the current market and evaluate your manuscript/artwork accordingly. She should also determine the quality of your piece and whether it is saleable. Upon selling your manuscript, your agent should negotiate a favorable contract and clear up any questions you have about monetary payments. One advantage to having an agent be the "go-between" is her acting as the "bad guy" during negotiations. This allows you, as an individual, to preserve your good faith with the publisher.

Keep in mind, though, however reputable the agent is, she has limitations. An agent's representation does not guarantee sale of your work. It just means she sees potential in your writing or art. Though an agent may offer criticism or advice on how to improve your book, she cannot make you a better writer or give you fame.

Agents typically charge a 15 percent commission from the sale of writing or art. Such fees are taken from advances and royalty earnings. If your agent sells foreign rights to your work, she will deduct 20 percent because she will most likely be dealing with an overseas agent with whom she must split the fee.

Some agents offer reading services. If you are a new writer, you will probably be charged a fee of less than $75. Many times, if an agent agrees to represent you, the fee will be reimbursed (though not always). If you with to use an agency's critique service, expect to pay $25-200 depending on the length of the manuscript. The purpose of a critique service is not to polish the manuscript, but to offer advice based on the agent's knowledge of what sells in juvenile publishing.

Prior to engaging in a reading or critique service, find out up front what results to expect. Watch out for agencies that derive most of their income from reading and critique services. Unfortunately, there are "quacks" in this business who are more interested in earning their money from services than from selling books.

Other standard fees incurred from an agent include miscellaneous expenses such as photocopying, phone bills, postage or messenger services. Before signing a contract with an agent, know exactly what the terms are, such as what rate of commission is charged and what expenses you will be expected to pay.

Be advised that not every agent is open to representing a writer or artist who lacks an established track record. Your manuscript or artwork, and query or cover letter, must be attractive and professional looking. Your first impression must be that of an organized, articulate person.

Feel free to investigate an agent before contacting her. Determine how familiar and successful she is with selling to children's publishers. For a detailed directory of literary agents and art/photo reps refer to *Guide to Literary Agents and Art/Photo Reps* (Writer's Digest Books). The 1994 edition has a new index which lists art reps who specialize in children's books.

Negotiating contracts and royalties

Negotiation is a two-way street on which, hopefully, both the author/artist and editor/art director will feel mutual satisfaction prior to signing a contract.

Book publishers pay authors and artists in royalties, or rather, a percentage of either the wholesale or retail price of each book sold. With large publishing houses, the author usually receives an advance issued against future royalties before the book is published. Half of the advance amount is issued upon signing the book contract. The other half is issued when the book is finished. For illustrations, one-third of the advance should be collected upon signing the contract; one-third upon delivery of sketches; and one-third upon delivery of finished art.

After your book has sold enough copies to earn back your advance, you will start to get royalty checks. Some publishers hold a reserve against returns. In other words, a percentage of royalties is held back in case books are returned. If you have such a reserve clause in your contract, make sure to be informed of the exact percentage of total sales that will be withheld and the time period the publisher will hold this money. You should be reimbursed this amount after a reasonable time period, such as a year. Royalty percentages vary with each publisher, but there are standard ranges.

For picture books, the writer and illustrator (if two people) should each be able to get $2,000-5,000 advances. Royalties range from 6-10% and are usually split equally between the writer and illustrator. A writer who also does the illustrations usually gets a higher advance ($4,000-7,000) and the full royalty.

Writers of chapter books or middle grade novels should expect royalties of 5-10% and an advance of $3,000-6,000. Illustrators who do 10-15 black & white illustrations and a color cover for these books should get a $3,000-5,000 advance and 2-5% royalties.

Authors of young adult novels can expect a $3,500-6,000 advance with royalty rates of 2-5%. Usually, an artist is paid one flat fee to do one color illustration for the cover.

For all types of books, royalty rates for hardcover books should be higher than percentage rates for paperbacks.

Writers will find that price structures for magazines are based on a per-word rate or range for a specific length of article. Artists, however, have a few more variables to contend with prior to contracting their services.

Payment for illustrations can be set by such factors as whether the piece will be rendered in black & white or four-color, how many illustrations are to be purchased, and the artist's prior experience. Determine an hourly rate by using the annual salary of a staff artist doing similar work in an economically similar geographic area (try to find an artist willing to share this information), then dividing that salary by 52 (the number of weeks in a year) and again by 40 (the number of hours in a work week). Add overhead expenses such as rent, utilities, art supplies, etc. to this answer by multiplying your hourly rate by 2.5. Research again to be sure your rate is competitive within the marketplace.

Once you make a sale you will probably sign a contract. A contract is an agreement between two or more parties that specifies the fee to be paid, services to be rendered, deadlines, rights purchased and, for artists, return (or not) of original artwork. Most publishers have a standard contract they offer to writers and illustrators. The specifics (such as royalty rates, advances, delivery dates, etc.) are typed in after negotiations.

Though it is okay to conduct negotiations over the telephone, be sure to secure a tangible written contract once both parties have agreed on terms. Do not depend on oral stipulations; written contracts protect both parties from misunderstandings and faulty memories. Watch for clauses that may not be in your best interest, such as "work-for-hire." When you do work for hire, you give up all rights to your creations. There are several reputable children's magazines that buy all rights, and many writers and illustrators believe it is worth the concession in order to break into the field. However, once you've entered the field of book publishing, it's in your best interest to keep the rights to your work.

Be sure you know whether your contract contains an option clause. This clause requires the author to give the publisher a first look at her next work before marketing it to other publishers. Though it is editorial etiquette to give the publisher the first chance at publishing your next work, be wary of statements in the contract which could trap you. Don't allow the publisher to consider the next project for more than 30 days and be specific about what type of work should actually be considered "next work" (i.e., if the book under contract is a young adult novel, specify that the publisher will only receive an exclusive look at the next young adult novel).

If there are clauses that appear vague or confusing, get legal advice. The time and money invested in counseling up front could protect you from more serious problems later. If you have an agent, she will review any contract.

One final note. When a book goes out of print, a publisher will sell any existing copies to a wholesaler who, in turn, sells the copies to stores at a discount. When the books are "remaindered" to a wholesaler, they are usually sold at a price just above the cost of printing. When negotiating a contract with a publisher you may want to discuss the possibility of purchasing the remaindered copies before they are sold to a wholesaler. Then you can market the copies you purchased and still make a healthy profit.

Copyright protection

A copyright is a form of protection provided to creators of original works, published or unpublished. The Copyright Act of 1976 (which went into effect January 1, 1978) states that work is protected as soon as it's created.

So the United States may have copyright relations with 80 other countries, in March 1989, Congress amended our copyright law and ratified the Berne Convention, the major international copyright convention. Because of this, most works created after March 1989 that are protected by United States copyright are also protected under the laws of most other countries.

The international recognition of copyright protection provided in the Berne Convention prevents foreign piracy of works copyrighted in the U.S. and allows prosecution of foreign copyright infringers in foreign courts. (A few principal countries, such as China, have yet to adopt the convention.)

Although works are protected once they are created, to proceed with an infringement lawsuit, the work must be registered. A person who infringes upon a registered copyright is subject to greater liabilities, even when no damages or profits are made as a result of the infringement. Some feel a copyright notice should be included on all work, registered or not. Others feel it is not necessary and a copyright notice will only confuse publishers about whether the material is registered (acquiring rights to previously registered material is a more complicated process).

Most publishers are reputable and will not steal your work; therefore, including a copyright notice on unregistered work is not necessary. However, if you don't feel your work is safe without a copyright notice, it is your right to include one. Including a copyright notice — © (year of work, your name) — should help ensure your work against plagiarism.

Registration is a legal formality intended to make copyright public record. As stated above, registration of work is necessary to file any infringement suits. Also, registration can help you win more money in a court case. By registering work within three months of publication or before an infringement occurs, you are eligible to collect statutory damages and attorney's fees. If you register later than three months after publication, you will qualify only for actual damages and profits.

Keep in mind that ideas and concepts are not copyrightable, but expressions of those ideas and concepts are. A character type or basic plot outline is not subject to a copyright infringement lawsuit. Also, titles, names, short phrases or slogans, and lists of contents are not subject to copyright protection, though titles and names may be protected through the Trademark Office.

In general, copyright protection ensures you, the writer or illustrator, the power to decide how the work is used and allows you to receive payment for each use. Essentially a copyright also encourages you to create new works by guaranteeing the power to sell rights to their use in the marketplace. As the copyright holder you can print, reprint or copy your work; sell or distribute copies of your work; or prepare derivative works such as plays, collages or recordings. The Copyright Law is designed to protect a writer's or illustrator's work (copyrighted on or after January 1, 1978) for her lifetime plus 50 years.

If you collaborate with someone else on a written or artistic project, the copyright will last for the lifetime of the last survivor plus 50 years. A writer's heirs may hold a copyright for an additional 50 years. After that, the work becomes public domain. In addition, works created anonymously or under a pseudonym are protected for 100 years, or 75 years after publication, whichever is shorter. Incidentally, this latter rule is also true of work-for-hire agreements. Under work-for-hire you relinquish your copyright to your "employer." Try to avoid agreeing to such terms.

For work published before January 1, 1978, the copyright protection is valid for 28 years with an option to renew the last year of the first term. For most copyrights, the law has extended renewal terms from 28 to 47 years, so these works can now be protected for up to 75 years.

For members of the Society of Children's Book Writers and Illustrators, in-depth information about copyrights and the law is available. Send a self-addressed, stamped envelope to the Society of Children's Book Writers and Illustrators, Suite 106, 22736 Vanowen St., West Hills CA 91307 and request their brochure, "Copyright Facts for Writers."

For more information about the proper procedure to register works, contact the Register of Copyrights, Copyright Office, Library of Congress, Washington

DC 20559. The forms available are **TX** for writing (books, articles, etc.); **VA** for pictures (photographs, illustrations); and **PA** for plays and music. To learn more about how to go about using the copyright forms, request a copy of Circular I on Copyright Basics. All of these forms are free. Send the completed registration form along with the stated fee and a copy of the work to the Copyright Office. You can register a group of articles or illustrations if:

- the group is assembled in order, such as in a notebook;
- the works bear a single title, such as "Works by (your name)";
- they are the work of one writer or artist;
- the material is the subject of a single claim to copyright.

It is the publisher's responsibility to register your book for copyright. If you have previously registered the same material, you must inform your editor and supply the previous copyright information. Otherwise, the publisher cannot register the book in its published form.

Rights for the writer and illustrator

The copyright law specifies that writers generally sell one-time rights to their work unless they and the buyer agree otherwise in writing. Be forewarned that many editors aren't aware of this. Many publications will want more exclusive rights from you than just one-time usage of your work; some will even require you to sell all rights. Be sure that you are monetarily compensated for the additional rights you relinquish. It is always to your benefit to retain as much control as possible over your work.

Writers who only give up limited rights to their work can then sell reprint rights to other publications, foreign rights to international publications, or even movie rights, should the opportunity arise. Likewise, artists can sell their illustrations to other book and magazine markets as well as to paper-product companies who may use an image on a calendar or greeting card. In some cases, illustrators are now selling original artwork after it has been published. And there are now galleries throughout the U.S. that display the works of children's illustrators.

You can see that exercising more control over ownership of your work gives you a greater marketing edge for resale. If you must give up all rights to a work, scrutinize the price you are being offered to determine whether it will compensate you for the loss of other sales.

Rights acquired through sale of a book manuscript are explained in each publisher's contract. Take time to read through relevant clauses to be sure you understand what each contract is specifying prior to signing. Make sure your contract contains a clause allowing all rights to revert back to you in the event the publisher goes out of business. The rights you will most often be selling to publishers and periodicals in the marketplace are:

- *One-time rights*—The buyer has no guarantee that he is the first to use a piece. One-time permission to run a written or illustrated work is acquired, then the rights revert back to the creator.
- *First rights*—The creator offers rights to use the work for the first time in any medium. All other rights remain with the creator. When material is excerpted from a soon-to-be-published book for use in a newspaper or periodical, first serial rights are also purchased.

- *First North American serial rights*—This is similar to first rights, except that publishers who distribute both in the U.S. and Canada will stipulate these rights to ensure that a publication in the other country won't come out with simultaneous usage of the same work.
- *Second serial (reprint) rights*—In this case newspapers and magazines are granted the right to reproduce a work that already has appeared in another publication. These rights also are purchased by a newspaper or magazine editor who wants to publish part of a book after the book has been published (such as an excerpt from a just-published biography). The proceeds from reprint rights are often split 50/50 between the author and his publishing company.
- *Simultaneous rights*—Use of such rights occurs among magazines with circulations that don't overlap, such as many religious publications. Many spiritual stories or illustrations are appropriate for a variety of denominational periodicals. Be sure you submit to a publication that allows simultaneous submissions, and be sure to state in your cover letter to the editor that the submission is being considered elsewhere (to a non-competing market).
- *All rights*—Rights such as these are purchased by publishers who pay premium usage fees, have an exclusive format, or have other book or magazine interests from which the purchased work can generate more "mileage." (Some magazines that purchase all rights to artwork use the same work again several years later.) When the writer or illustrator sells all rights to a market she no longer has any say in who acquires rights to use her piece.

Synonymous with purchase of all rights is the term "work-for-hire." Under such an agreement the creator of a work gives away all rights—and her copyright—to the company buying her work. Avoid such agreements; they're not in your best interest. If a market is insistent upon acquiring all rights to your work, see if you can negotiate for the rights to revert back to you after a reasonable period of time. It can't hurt to ask. If they're agreeable to such a proposal, be sure you get it in writing.

- *Foreign serial rights*—Be sure before you market to foreign publications that you have only sold North American—not worldwide—serial rights to previous markets. If so, you are free to market to publications you think may be interested in material that has appeared in a North American-based periodical.
- *Syndication rights*—This is a division of serial rights. For example, if a syndicate prints portions of a book in installments in its newspapers, it would be syndicating second serial rights. The syndicate would receive a commission and leave the remainder to be split between the author and publisher.
- *Subsidiary rights*—These include serial rights, dramatic rights, book club rights or translation rights. The contract should specify what percentage of profits from sales of these rights go to the author and publisher.
- *Dramatic, television and motion picture rights*—During the specified time the interested party tries to sell the story to a producer or director. Many times options are renewed because the selling process can be lengthy.
- *Display rights*—Watch out for these. They're also known as "Electronic Publishing Rights" or "Data, Storage and Retrieval." Usually listed under subsidiary rights, they're not clear. They refer to many means of publication not yet invented. If a display rights clause is listed in your contract, try to negotiate its elimination. Otherwise, demand the clause be restricted to things designed to

be read only. By doing this, you maintain your rights to use your work for things such as games and interactive software.

Business records

It is imperative to keep accurate business records to determine if you are making a profit as a writer or illustrator. Keep a bank account and ledger apart from your personal finances. Also, if writing or illustrating is secondary to another freelance career, maintain separate business records from that as well.

If you're just starting your career, you will likely accumulate some business expenses prior to showing any profit. To substantiate your income and expenses to the IRS keep all invoices, cash receipts, sales slips, bank statements, cancelled checks and receipts related to travel expenses and entertaining clients. For entertainment expenditures record the date, place and purpose of the business meeting as well as gas mileage.

Be sure to file all receipts in chronological order; if you maintain a separate file for each month of the year it will provide for easier retrieval of records at year's end. Keeping receipts is important for all purchases, big and small. Don't take the small purchases for granted. Enough of them can result in a rather substantial monetary figure.

When setting up a single-entry bookkeeping system, record income and expenses separately. It may prove easier to use some of the subheads that appear on Schedule C (the form used for recording income from a business) of the 1040 tax form. This way you can transfer information more easily onto the tax form when filing your return. In your ledger include a description of each transaction—date, source of income (or debts from business purchases), description of what was purchased or sold, the amount of the transaction, and whether payment was by cash, check or credit card.

You don't have to wait until January 1 to start keeping records, either. The moment you first make a business-related purchase or sell an article, book manuscript or illustrations begin tracking your profits and losses. If you keep records from January 1 to December 31 you are using a calendar-year accounting method. Any other accounting period is known as a fiscal year.

You also can choose between two types of accounting methods—the cash method and the accrual method. The cash method is used more often: You record income when it is received and expenses when they are disbursed. Under the accrual method you report income at the time you earn it rather than when it is actually received. Similarly, expenses are recorded at the time they are incurred rather than when you actually pay them. If you choose this method keep separate records for "accounts receivable" and "accounts payable."

Taxes

To successfully (and legally) compete in the business of writing or illustrating, you must know what income you should report and deductions you can claim. Yet before you can do this, you must prove to the IRS that you are in business to make a profit, that your writing or illustrations are not merely a hobby. Under the Tax Reform Act of 1986 it was determined you should show a profit for three years out of a five-year period to attain professional status. What does the IRS look for as proof of your professionalism? Keeping accurate financial records (see previous section on business records), maintaining a business bank account separate from your personal account, the time you devote to your profession and whether it is your main or secondary source of income, and your history of profits and losses. The amount of training you have invested in your field — as well as your expertise — is also a contributing factor.

If your business is unincorporated, you will fill out tax information on Schedule C of Form 1040. If you're unsure of what deductions you can take, request the appropriate IRS publication containing this information. Under the Tax Reform Act, only 50 percent (formerly it was 80 percent) of business meals, entertainment and related tips and parking charges are deductible. Other deductibles allowed on Schedule C include: car expenses for business-related trips, professional courses and seminars, depreciation of office equipment (such as a computer), dues and publications, and miscellaneous expenses, such as postage used for business needs, etc.

If you're working out of a home office, a portion of your mortgage (or rent), related utilities, property taxes, repair costs and depreciation may be deducted as business expenses — under special circumstances. To learn more about the possibility of home office deductions, consult IRS Publication 587 (Business Use of Your Home).

The method of paying taxes on income not subject to withholding is your "estimated tax." If you expect to owe more than $500 at year's end and if the total amount of income tax that will be withheld during the year will be less than 90% of the tax shown on the current year's return, you will generally make estimated tax payments. Estimated tax payments are made in four equal installments due on April 15, June 15, September 15 and January 15 (assuming you're a calendar-year taxpayer). For more information, request Publication 505, Self-Employment Tax.

Depending on your net income you may be liable for a Social Security tax. This is a tax designed for those who don't have Social Security withheld from their paychecks. You're liable if your net income is $400 or more per year. Net income is the difference between your income and allowable business deductions. Request Schedule SE, Computation of Social Security Self-Employment Tax, if you qualify.

If completing your income tax return proves to be a complex affair, call the IRS for assistance. In addition to walk-in centers, the IRS has numerous publications to instruct you in various facets of preparing a tax return.

Insurance

As a self-employed professional be aware of what health and business insurance coverage is available to you. Unless you're a Canadian who is covered by national health insurance or a fulltime freelancer covered by your spouse's policy, health insurance will no doubt be one of your biggest expenses. Under the terms of the Consolidated Omnibus Budget Reconciliation Act (COBRA) of 1985, if you leave a job with health benefits, you are entitled to continue that coverage for at least 18 months at the insurer's cost plus a small administration charge. Eventually, though, you must search for your own health plan. Be mindful of the fact that you may also need disability and life insurance.

Disability insurance is offered through many private insurance companies and state governments, and pays a monthly fee that covers living and business expenses during periods of long-term recuperation from a health problem. The amount of money paid is based on the writer's or artist's annual earnings.

Before contacting any insurance representative, talk to other writers or illustrators to find out about insurance companies they could recommend. If you belong to a writer's or artist's organization, be sure to contact them to determine if any insurance coverage for professionals is offered to members. Such group coverage may prove less expensive and yield more comprehensive coverage than an individual policy.

Key to Symbols

* *Symbol indicating listing is new in this edition*
■ *Symbol indicating a market subsidy publishes manuscripts*
‡ *Symbol indicating a contest is for students*
● *Symbol indicating comment from editor of* Children's Writer's & Illustrator's Market

Important Market Listing Information

● *Listings are based on questionnaires, phone calls and updated copy. They are not advertisements nor are markets reported here necessarily endorsed by the editor of this book.*
● *Information in the listings comes directly from the company and is as accurate as possible, but situations change and needs fluctuate between the publication of this directory and the time you use it.*
● Children's Writer's & Illustrator's Market *reserves the right to exclude any listing that does not meet its requirements.*

The Markets

Book Publishers

Indications are the children's book business is slowing down. The number of children's-only bookstores—which more than doubled from 1985 to 1992—is stabilizing, as is the amount of space all booksellers are devoting to children's books. And, now that the baby boomers' baby boom is behind us, market consultants Veronis, Suhler & Associates forecast children's book sales growing at only half the rate during 1992 to 1997 as they did from 1987 to 1992.

Limits on sales space and ever-increasing competition between stores—in addition to the predicted drop in the growth rate of consumer spending—are forcing retailers to be more selective, purchasing only what they truly believe can sell.

Just like booksellers deciding which titles to stock, publishers are more selective when determining which manuscripts to pursue. While such news may initially be disheartening for newcomers to the children's field, the end result is sure to be a curb in "over publishing" and the production of stronger titles—ones that will attract the attention of both bookstore owners and prospective book buyers.

Though some publishers are no longer producing children's books (see Book Publishers/'93-'94 Changes at the end of this section) and a few of those listed in last year's edition have called a halt to the endless march of unsolicited manuscripts, not all publishers are closing their doors to submissions. The good news, in fact, is that some view the children's book market as merely cyclical and are joining the bandwagon now instead of trying to catch it the next time around. Consequently, new children's book publishing ventures are continuing to form.

Many publishers believe the key is to focus their lists, to specialize, to find and fill the niches unaddressed by the book boom of the '80s. This means children's writers and illustrators must study the market even more carefully than in the past, submit highly polished work and persevere.

Multiculturalism

While the interest in children's books with multicultural themes remains strong, not all groups are finding equal representation. As Karen Ellis, children's backlist buyer at the Tattered Cover bookstore in Denver, said in the January 11, 1993 issue of *Publishers Weekly*, "There are beginning to be more African-American stories, but Hispanic literature is still sadly lacking and that's a good segment of our population."

Not only has the expansion of multicultural titles been uneven regarding representation, but category growth has also been lopsided. While more and more multicultural picture books are being found on store shelves, multicultural books aimed at older children are still scarce. In fact, booksellers say readers would like to see more chapter books and young adult novels with ethnic characters. Writers and illustrators stand to benefit from these gaps in children's literature.

Just as the demand for multicultural books continues, however, so does the debate over whether writers and illustrators must be members of the ethnic groups about which they are creating materials. Though some publishers believe writers and illustrators can transcend cultural differences, others prefer working with members of specific ethnic groups for specific ethnic stories — to avoid possible stereotyping. While it helps to have an inside perspective, research is also crucial, and the key for *all* writers and illustrators in this area is proving authenticity.

If you're considering writing or illustrating material about an ethnic group other than your own, read Writing and Illustrating from Another Culture's Tradition, on page 11, for more information.

Expanding categories

As always, some types of children's books appear to be more popular than others. Picture books, for instance, was the booming category for many years. Now, however, their status is changing as the offspring of the baby boomer generation grow up. In fact, a report in the January 11, 1993 *Publishers Weekly* noted that picture books was the major area in which retailers were noticing a slowdown in growth — and increased price resistance.

Yet, while picture books may be a concern in the retail sector, nonfiction picture books are expanding their audience and, perhaps, their slice of the educational market. No longer are picture books with nonfiction subjects just for preschoolers and elementary school children. In fact, artwork and photographs are being integrated into nonfiction books aimed at even older readers. According to the April 1993 *Children's Writer*, "A trickle of nonfiction picture books has turned into a deluge of mainstream selections from concept books for toddlers to photo essays for teens."

While picture books is an area to watch, other categories are also expanding. One area that's undoubtedly booming is the easy-to-read market, comprising the first books children read on their own. Another area in which interest is increasing, though much more slowly, is that of historical fiction for middle readers. The growth in this area, as well as the growth in nonfiction picture books, is due in large part to teachers who are incorporating more trade books into their classrooms.

Though Veronis, Suhler & Associates forecast a decrease in the growth rate of consumer spending on books, they also predict an increase in the growth rate of educational and professional spending, particularly on the elementary through high school level. This not only means the above categories could expand even further, but it also translates into increased opportunities for writers and illustrators. Those particularly interested in the educational market can find information about breaking into the field in Getting Started in the Educational Market on page 15.

Finally, when it comes to young adults, the interest in science fiction and fantasy books appears to be growing, but it's the interest in horror that has many publishers creating new series. According to the June 1993 *Children's Writer*, editors expect teen horror to be the most popular genre of the decade. "Horror novels are replacing the teen romances that appeared on young adult bestseller lists only two or three years ago," the newsletter reports.

Why are today's teens reading the latest novel by R.L. Stine or Christopher Pike (the "superstars" of the genre) instead of Sweet Valley High? Part of the reason is that young adult horror novels appeal to both boys and girls, though the protagonists are primarily female. In addition, the books are very teen-centered; adults are merely peripheral characters. And these stories of graphic violence and multiple murders have room for a bit of romance. Watch for this category to continue to expand with books for 8- to 12-year-olds in which editors are looking for "creepy suspense rather than serial killers," reports *Children's Writer*.

Be wary of trends

Although areas of need exist and a number of trends have emerged, the best advice remains the same: "Write about what you know or what interests you." In other words, if you aren't familiar with the horror movies of the '70s and '80s—which are believed to have spawned today's teenage interest in the horror series—then don't try writing a young adult horror novel. If you're not truly excited about a subject, obviously your readers won't be either.

The same advice holds true for illustrators. As Anne Diebel, art director at Clarion Books, says in the interview on page 56, "If you really love to draw cars and ships, send us pictures of cars and ships. Don't send us what you think we want to see. Do what you do best and we'll both be happy."

The key to marketing both children's writing and illustration is to match your interests with that of the publisher. To help you locate markets seeking the work you're creating, we've added a Subject Index at the back of this book. This index lists book and magazine publishers according to their fiction and nonfiction needs and/or interests. Use the Age-Level Index in conjunction with the Subject Index and you'll narrow the list of possible markets even further.

For instance, if you write fictitious sports stories for young readers and you're trying to place a book manuscript, go first to the Subject Index. Locate the Fiction categories under Book Publishers and find Sports. Make a list of the book publishers listed there. Now go to the Age-Level Index and see if any of the publishers on your list are included under the heading Young Readers. Circle them. Look up the listings for those publishers and see if your work matches their needs.

Subsidy publishing

Some writers who are really determined to get their work into print, but who receive rejections from royalty publishers, may look to subsidy publishers as an option. Subsidy publishers ask writers to pay all or part of the costs of producing a book. Some of the listings in this section give percentages of subsidy-published material and are marked with a solid block (■).

Aspiring writers should strongly consider working solely with publishers who pay. Such publishers will be active in marketing your work because they profit only through these efforts. Subsidy publishers, on the other hand, make their money from writers who pay to have their books published. In fact, some operations are more interested in the contents of your wallet than the contents of your book. And you must do your own marketing and promotion. Though there are reputable subsidy publishers, those considering such services should take a "buyer beware" attitude. Any contracts offered by these houses should be carefully inspected by a lawyer or someone qualified to analyze these types of documents.

If you're interested in publishing your book just to share it with friends and relatives, self publishing is a viable option. In self publishing, you oversee all of the book production details. A local printer may be able to help you, or you may want to arrange some type of desktop computer publishing.

Whatever course you choose, don't treat writing for children as a starter course into the world of "real writing." Creating a children's book is *not* a quick and easy project. Actually, aspects of the craft make writing for this audience more difficult. Writing for children *is* real writing, and what follows in this section are listings of *real* markets—one of which might make your dreams of being published a reality.

ADDISON-WESLEY PUBLISHING CO., General Books Dept., One Jacob Way, Reading MA 01867-3999. (617)944-3700. Book publisher. Estab. 1942. Associate Editor: John Bell. Publishes 10 middle reader titles/year. 33% of books by first-time authors.
Nonfiction: Middle readers: science, hobbies, nature/environment. Young readers, young adults: science. "All of our children's books are science activity books." No fiction or picture books. "We don't publish them."
How to Contact/Writers: Nonfiction: Query. Reports on queries in 6 weeks; on mss in 2 months. Publishes a book 2 years after acceptance. Will consider simultaneous submissions.
Illustration: Works with 15 illustrators/year. Will review ms/illustration packages. Will review artwork for future assignments. Prefers "4-color representational art for covers and b&w for interior."
How to Contact/Illustrators: Ms/illustration packages: "Query first." Illustrations only: "Send promo sheet." Original artwork returned at job's completion.
Terms: Pays authors in royalties based on retail price. Pays illustrators by the project. Sends galleys to authors; dummies to illustrators. Book catalog for 7×10 SASE.
Tips: The writer and/or illustrator have the best chance of selling "science activity books *only*. Increasing competition in our field (science projects) means finding more focused and more imaginative books. Many more book-toy packages have appeared lately. Adults buy them (they're too expensive for most kids that age), so they're being shaped by what adults think kids should like."

ADVOCACY PRESS, P.O. Box 236, Santa Barbara CA 93102. (805)962-2728. Fax: (805)963-3580. Division of The Girls Incorporated of Greater Santa Barbara. Book publisher. Editorial Contact: Bill Sheehan. Publishes 2-4 children's books/year.
Fiction: Picture books, young readers, middle readers: animal, concepts in self-esteem, fantasy, gender equity, nature/environment. "Illustrated children's stories incorporate self-esteem, gender equity, self-awareness concepts." Recently published *Nature's Wonderful World in Rhyme* (birth-age 12, collection of poems); *Kylie's Song* (32-page picture book). "Most publications are 32-48 page picture stories for readers 4-11 years. Most feature adventures of animals in interesting/educational locales."
How to Contact/Writers: "Because of the required focus of our publications, most have been written in-house." Reports on mss in 1-2 months. Include SASE.

Illustration: "Require intimate integration of art with story. Therefore, almost always use local illustrators." Average about thirty illustrations per story. Will review ms/illustration packages.

How to Contact/Illustrators: Ms/illustration packages: Query first.

Terms: Authors and illustrators paid by royalty.

■**AEGINA PRESS/UNIVERSITY EDITIONS, INC.**, 59 Oak Lane, Spring Valley, Huntington WV 25704. (304)429-7204. Book publisher. Estab. 1983. Managing Editor: Ira Herman. Art Coordinator: Claire Nudd. Publishes 3 picture books/year; 4 young readers/year; 4 middle readers/year; 6 young adults/year. 40% of books by first-time authors; 5% of books from agented writers; "more than 50% of books are subsidy published."

Fiction: All ages: adventure, animal, fantasy, humor, poetry, religion, romance, science fiction, sports, suspense/mystery. "Will consider most categories." Average word length: picture books—1,000; young readers—2,000; middle readers—10,000; young adults—20,000. Recently published *Prairie Pups*, by Ruth Scouler Johnson, illustrated by Ellisa Mitchell (ages 5-8, animal story); *Me and Daffodil*, text and illustrations by Barbara Garber (ages 5-8, animal story); *Two*, by Shelby Coy-Tobias Laney, art by Joan C. Waites (ages 8-11, adventure); *Anna, The Little Peasant Girl*, by Virginia Hughes, art by Matthew Richardson (ages 6-8, fantasy).

Nonfiction: All ages: animal, history, nature/environment, sports, textbooks. "Will consider all types of manuscripts, especially those usable in classrooms." Recently published *C.I.T.E.S. Endangered Species Coloring Book*, by George Furness, illustrated by Linda Silk (ages 4-10, coloring book).

How to Contact/Writers: Fiction/nonfiction: Submit complete ms. Reports on queries in 1 week; mss in 1 month. Publishes a book 5-6 months after acceptance. Will consider simultaneous submissions.

Illustration: Works with 20 illustrators/year. Will review ms/illustration packages. Will review artwork for future assignments. Primarily uses b&w artwork only.

How to Contact/Illustrators: Ms/illustration packages: Query first. Illustrations only: Query with nonreturnable samples. "We generally use our own artists. We will consider outside art. Artists should send photocopies or non-returnable samples." Reports on art samples in 1 month.

Terms: Pays authors in royalties of 10-15% based on retail price. Pays freelance artists per project ($60 minimum). Payment "negotiated individually for each book." Sends galleys to authors. Book catalog available for $2 and SAE and 4 first-class stamps; ms guidelines for #10 envelope and 1 first-class stamp.

Tips: "Focus your subject and plotline. For younger readers, stress visual imagery and fantasy characterizations. A cover letter should accompany the manuscript, which states the approximate length (not necessary for poetry). A brief synopsis of the manuscript and a listing of the author's publishing credits (if any) should also be included. Queries, sample chapters, synopses and completed manuscripts are welcome." For the future, "we plan to stress stories for middle readers and older children. Will consider all types, however."

AFRICA WORLD PRESS, P.O. Box 1892, Trenton NJ 08607. (609)771-1666. Book publisher. Editor: Kassahun Checole. Publishes 20-30 picture books/year; 10 young reader and young adult titles/year; 15 middle readers/year. Books concentrate on African-American life.

 The solid block before a listing indicates the market subsidy publishes manuscripts.

Fiction: Picture books, young readers: adventure, concept, contemporary, folktales, history, multicultural. Middle readers, young adults: adventure, contemporary, folktales, history, multicultural. Publishes very little fiction.
Nonfiction: Picture books, young readers, middle readers, young adults: concept, history, multicultural. Does not want to see self-help, gender or health books.
How to Contact/Writers: Submit outline/synopsis and 2 sample chapters. Reports on queries in 30-45 days; mss in 3 months. Will consider previously published work.
Illustration: Works with 10-20 illustrators/year. Will review ms/illustration packages. Contact: Kassahun Checole, editor. Will review artwork for future assignments.
How to Contact/Illustrators: Ms/illustration packages: Query. Illustrations only: Query with samples. Reports in 3 months.
Terms: Pays authors royalty based on retail price. Pays illustrators by the project or royalty based on retail price. Book catalog available for SAE; ms and art guidelines available for SASE.

AFRICAN AMERICAN IMAGES, 1909 W. 95th St., Chicago IL 60643. (312)445-0322. Fax: (312)445-9844. Book publisher. Editor: Jawanza Kunjufu. Publishes 2 picture books/year; 1 young reader title/year; 1 middle reader title/year; 1 young adult title/year. 90% of books by first-time authors.
Fiction/Nonfiction: All levels: black culture.
How to Contact/Writers: Fiction/nonfiction: Submit complete ms. Reports on queries in 1 week; mss in 3 weeks. Publishes a book 9 months after acceptance. Will consider simultaneous submissions.
Illustration: Editorial will review ms/illustration packages.
How to Contact/Illustrators: Ms/illustration packages: Send 3 chapters of ms with 1 piece of final art. Illustrations only: Send tearsheets. Reports on art samples in 2 weeks. Original artwork returned at job's completion.
Terms: Buys ms outright. Illustrator paid by the project. Book catalog, ms/artist's guidelines free on request.

ALADDIN BOOKS/COLLIER BOOKS FOR YOUNG READERS, 24th Floor, 866 Third Avenue, New York NY 10022. Paperback imprints of Macmillan Children's Book Group.
  • In November 1993 all imprints of the Macmillan Children's Book Group and all other divisions of Macmillan were sold to Paramount Communications.

ALYSON PUBLICATIONS, INC., 40 Plympton St., Boston MA 02118. (617)542-5679. Book publisher. Editorial Contact: Sasha Alyson. Publishes 4 (projected) picture books/year; 1 (projected) young adult title/year. "Alyson Wonderland is the line of children's books. We are looking for diverse depictions of family life for children of gay and lesbian parents."
Fiction: All levels: Books aimed at the children of lesbian and gay parents. "Our YA books should deal with issues faced by kids growing up gay or lesbian." Recently published *Uncle What-Is-It Is Coming to Visit!*, by Michael Willhoite; *Two Moms, The Zark, and Me*, by Johnny Valentine.
How to Contact/Writers: Submit outline/synopsis and sample chapters (young adults); submit complete manuscript (picture books/young readers). Reports on queries in 3 weeks; on mss in 4-5 weeks. Include SASE.
Illustration: Works with 4 illustrators/year. Will review mss/illustration packages. Will review artwork for future assignments. Send "representative art that can be *kept on file*. Good quality photocopies are OK."
Terms: Pays authors and illustrators royalties. Prefers to discuss terms with the authors and artists. "We *do* offer advances." Book catalog and/or ms guidelines free on request.
Tips: "We only publish kids' books aimed at the children of gay or lesbian parents."

AMERICAN BIBLE SOCIETY, 1865 Broadway, New York NY 10023. (212)408-1235. Fax: (212)408-1435. Book publisher. Estab. 1816. Product Development Manager: Charles Houser. Publishes 2 picture books/year; 4 young readers/year; 4 young adults/year. Publishes books with spiritual/religious themes based on the Bible.

Nonfiction: Picture books, young readers, middle readers, young adults: multicultural, religion, self help. Multicultural needs include African-American, Hispanic/Latino, Native American, Asian; mixed groups (such as choirs, classrooms, church events). "Fiction and nonfiction. We do not accept unsolicited mss, but people are sending them in anyway. We prefer published writing samples with résumés so that we can contact copywriters when an appropriate project comes up." Recently published *Bible for Today's Family New Testament* (for children ages 7-11, full color wrap cover illustration; 200 b&w interior illustrations).

How to Contact/Writers: All manuscripts developed in-house. Query with résumé and writing samples. Contact Barbara Bernstengel. Unsolicited mss rejected. No credit lines given.

Illustration: Works with 2-5 illustrators/year. Editorial will review artwork for possible future assignments. "Would be more interested in artwork for children and teens which is influenced by the visual 'vocabulary' of videos."

How to Contact/Illustrators: Ms/illustration packages: "Query first." Illustrations only: Query with samples; arrange a personal interview to show portfolio; send "résumés, tearsheets and promotional literature to keep; slides will be returned promptly." Reports on queries in 6 weeks; mss in 1 week. Factors used to determine payment for ms/illustration package include "nature and scope of project; complexity of illustration and continuity of work; number of illustrations." Pays illustrators $200-30,000; based on fair market value. Sends two complimentary copies of published work to illustrators. Original artwork returned at job's completion. Book catalog free on request.

Photography: Contact Charles Houser. Buys stock and assigns work. Looking for "nature, scenic, interracial, intergenerational people shots." Model/property releases required. Uses any size b&w prints; 35mm, 2¼×2¼ and 4×5 transparencies. Photographers should query with samples; arrange a personal interview to show portfolio; provide résumé, promotional literature or tearsheets.

Terms: Photographers paid by the project (range: $800-5,000); per photo (range $150-1,500). Pays $100-1,500 for copy writing, depending on nature and size of project. Credit line given on most projects. Most photos purchased on one-time use basis. ABS owns all publication rights to illustrations and mss.

*AMERICAN EDUCATION PUBLISHING, Suite 145, 150 E. Wilson Bridge Rd., Columbus OH 43085-2328. (614)848-8866. Book publisher. Director, Retail Product Development: Diane Mangan. Publishes 10-12 picture books/year; 12-15 middle readers/year. 50% of books by first-time authors; 15% of books from agented authors; 35% of books developed in house.

Fiction: Picture books: adventure, animal, concept, contemporary, nature/environment. Young readers: adventure, animal, concept, contemporary, fantasy, folktales, humor, nature/environment. Middle readers: adventure, animal, contemporary, fantasy, science fiction. Young adults: adventure, animal, contemporary, fantasy, science fiction. Recently published *The Wind*, *The Alphabet* and *The Colors*, all by Monique Felix (8×8 softcover for toddlers).

Nonfiction: Picture books: activity books, animal, concept, nature/environment, reference, science, self help, social issues. Young readers: activity books, animal, concept, hobbies, nature/environment, reference, science, self help, social issues. Middle readers and young adults: animal, biography, hobbies, how-to, nature/environment, reference, science, self help, social needs. Recently published *Gnat* and *Fire* both by Kitty Benedict (8×8 softcover for beginners).

Lynn Adams rendered this full-page illustration in black & white ink with wash as part of a major project for the American Bible Society entitled Bible for Today's Family. *Adams was commissioned to create a cover and more than 200 drawings for this illustrated New Testament for children. Charles Houser of the ABS says Adams's work was chosen "because of the warmth and naturalness of her figures and her sensitivity to the religious content of the illustrations." The artist was required to do some historical research for the assignment and depict lively, interesting scenes in a realistic style. It was important that characters were consistently rendered so children can easily follow the continuity of the story.*

How to Contact/Writers: Fiction: Submit outline/synopsis and 3 sample chapters. Nonfiction: Query. Reports on queries in 6 weeks; mss in 2-3 months. Publishes a book 6-8 months after acceptance. Will consider simultaneous submissions and previously published work.

Illustration: Works with 6 illustrators/year. Will review ms/illustration packages. Will review artwork for future assignments. Contact Diane Mangan, director, retail product development.

How to Contact/Illustrators: Ms/illustration packages: Submit ms with 4 pieces of final art. Illustrations only: Query with samples, résumé, tearsheets. Reports in 2 months. Samples returned with SASE; samples kept on file. Original artwork returned at job's completion.

Terms: Pays authors royalty of 5-10% based on wholesale price or work purchased outright. Pays illustrators by the project or royalty of 5-10% based on wholesale price. Sends galleys to authors.

APPALACHIAN MOUNTAIN CLUB BOOKS, 5 Joy St., Boston MA 02108. (617)523-0636. Fax: (617)523-0722. Book publisher. Editor: Gordon Hardy. 50% of books by first-time authors; 5% of books from agented authors. Publishes environmental, conservation and oudoor recreation books.

Nonfiction: Young readers: activity books, history, how-to, nature/environment, travel, outdoor recreation. Middle readers, young adults: activity books, history, nature/environment, travel, outdoor recreation. Recently published *Seashells in My Pocket*, by Judith Hansen, illustrations by Donna Sabaka (ages 6 and up, child's nature guide to exploring); *The Conservation Works Book*, by Lisa Capone, illustrated by Cady Goldfield (ecology book with humorous sketches for the entire family).

How to Contact/Writers: Fiction/nonfiction: Query; submit outline/synopsis. Reports on queries in 1 month; mss in 4 months. Publishes a book 6 months after receipt of acceptable ms. Will consider simultaneous submissions and electronic submissions.

 The asterisk before a listing indicates the listing is new in this edition.

Illustration: Works with 2 illustrators/year. Will review ms/illustration packages. Contact: Gordon Hardy, editor. Will review artwork for future assignments. Uses primarily b&w artwork only.

How to Contact/Illustrators: Ms/illustration packages: Query; submit ms with dummy. Illustrations only: Query with samples. Reports in 1 month. Samples returned with SASE.

Photography: Purchases photos from freelancers. Uses cover photos. Model/property releases required; captions required. Uses 5×8 glossy b&w prints and 35 mm transparencies. Photographers should submit cover letter, stock photo list and color promo piece.

Terms: Pays authors royalty of 6-9% based on retail price or work purchased outright. Offers advances (amount varies with assignment). Pays illustrators by the project (range: $25-50). Photographers paid $25/photo. Sends galleys to authors. Book catalog available for $8\frac{1}{2} \times 11$ SAE and 4 first-class stamps; ms guidelines for SASE, art guidelines not available.

Tips: "Make sure writer has an illustrator to propose!" Publishes books that are "outdoor/conservation oriented (New England focus is best)."

AQUILA COMMUNICATIONS LTD., 8354 Labarre St., Montreal, Quebec H4P 2E7 Canada. (514)738-7071. Book publisher. Manager: Mike Kelada. 100% of books by first-time authors. "We specialize in teaching French as a second language."

How to Contact/Writers: Fiction: Submit outline/synopsis and 5 sample chapters. Nonfiction: Submit outline/synopsis and 10 sample chapters. Reports on queries and mss in 1 week to 2 months. Will consider previously published work.

Illustration: Will review ms/illustration packages. Will review artwork for future assignments. Uses b&w and color artwork.

How to Contact/Illustrators: Ms/illustration packages: Submit ms with copies of artwork. Illustrations only: Submit photocopies of sample artwork. Reports in 3 weeks. Cannot return samples; samples filed.

Photography: Purchases photos from freelancers. Buys stock and assigns work.

ARCHWAY/MINSTREL BOOKS, 1230 Avenue of the Americas, New York NY 10020. (212)698-7000. Fax: (212)698-7337. Imprint of Pocket Books. Book publisher. Editorial Director: Patricia MacDonald. Publishes originals and reprints. Minstrel Books (ages 7-11) and Archway Paperbacks (ages 12-16).

Fiction: Middle readers: animal stories, adventures, fantasy, funny school stories, thrillers. Young adults: adventure, contemporary stories, horror, suspense. Recently published (Archway) *Bury Me Deep, Christopher Pike* and *Fear Street Super Chill*, by R.L. Stine; *Help Wanted*, by Richie Tenkersley Cusick. Recently published (Minstrel) *Aliens Ate My Homework*, by Bruce Coville; *My Babysitter is a Vampire*, by Ann Hodjman; *My Crazy Cousin Courtney*, by Judi Miller.

Nonfiction: Middle readers: animal, environment, sports. Young adults: sports.

How to Contact/Writers: Fiction/nonfiction: Query, submit outline/synopsis and sample chapters. SASE mandatory.

Terms: Pays authors in royalties.

ATHENEUM PUBLISHERS, 866 Third Ave., New York NY 10022. (212)702-2000. Macmillan Children's Book Group. Book publisher. Vice President/Editorial Director: Jonathan Lanman. Editorial Contacts: Marcia Marshall, Senior Editor; Ana Cerro, Associate Editor. Publishes 15-20 picture books/year; 4-5 young reader titles/year; 20-25 middle reader titles/year; 10-15 young adult titles/year. 20% of books by first-time authors; 50% of books from agented writers.

 • At press time, Macmillan Children's Book Group, as well as other parts of the company, were be sold to Paramount Communications. This could affect the publisher's policies, so watch *Publishers Weekly* and other trade journals for details.

Fiction: Picture books and middle readers: animal, contemporary, fantasy. Young readers and young adults: contemporary, fantasy.

Nonfiction: All levels: animal, biography, education, history.

How to Contact/Writers: Fiction/nonfiction: Query; will consider complete picture book ms; submit outline/synopsis and sample chapters for longer works. Reports on queries in 6-8 weeks; mss in 3 months. Publishes a book 18-24 months after acceptance. Will consider simultaneous submissions from previously unpublished authors; "we request that the author let us know it is a simultaneous submission."

Illustration: Editorial will review ms/illustration packages.

How to Contact/Illustrators: Ms/illustration packages: Query first, 3 chapters of ms with 1 piece of final art. Illustrations only: Résumé, tearsheets. Reports on art samples only if interested. Original artwork returned at job's completion.

Terms: Pays authors in royalties of 8-12½% based on retail price. Illustrators paid royalty or flat fee depending on the project. Sends galleys to authors; proofs to illustrators. Book catalog available for 9×12 SAE and 5 first-class stamps; ms guidelines for #10 SAE and 1 first-class stamp.

AVON BOOKS/BOOKS FOR YOUNG READERS (AVON FLARE, AVON CAMELOT AND YOUNG CAMELOT), 1350 Avenue of the Americas, New York NY 10019. (212)261-6817. Division of The Hearst Corporation. Book publisher. Editorial Director: Ellen Krieger. Senior Editor: Gwen Montgomery. Assistant Editor: Margaret Draesel. Publishes 25-30 middle reader titles/year; 20-25 young adult titles/year. 10% of books by first-time authors; 20% of books from agented writers.

Fiction: Middle readers: comedy, contemporary, problem novels, sports, spy/mystery/adventure. Young adults: contemporary, problem novels, romance. Average length: middle readers—100-150 pages; young adults—150-250 pages. Avon does not publish preschool picture books.

Nonfiction: Middle readers: hobbies, music/dance, sports. Young adults: music/dance, "growing up." Average length: middle readers—100-150 pages; young adults—150-250 pages.

How to Contact/Writers: Fiction: Submit complete ms. Nonfiction: Submit outline/synopsis and sample chapters. Reports on queries in 1 month; mss in 1-2 months. Publishes a book 18-24 months after acceptance. Will consider simultaneous submissions.

Illustration: Very rarely will review ms/illustration packages.

How to Contact/Illustrators: "Send samples we can keep. Need line art and cover art."

Terms: Pays authors in royalties of 6% based on retail price. Average advance payment is "very open." Sends galleys to authors; sometimes sends dummies to illustrators. Book catalog available for 9×12 SAE and 4 first-class stamps; ms guidelines for #10 SASE.

Tips: "We have three young readers imprints, Young Camelot books for beginner readers, Avon Camelot books for the middle grades and Avon Flare for young adults. Our list includes both individual titles and series, with the emphasis in our paperback originals on high quality recreational reading—a fresh and original writing style; identifiable, three dimensional characters; a strong, well-paced story that pulls readers in and keeps them interested." Writers: "Make sure that you really know what a company's list looks like before you submit work. Is your work in line with what they usually do? Is your

A bullet has been placed within some listings to introduce special comments by the editor of Children's Writer's & Illustrator's Market.

work appropriate for the age group that this company publishes for? Keep aware of what's in your bookstore (but not what's in there for too long!)" Illustrators: "Submit work to art directors and people who are in charge of illustration at publishers. This is usually not handled entirely by the editorial department."

BANDANNA BOOKS, 319-B Anacapa St., Santa Barbara CA 93101. (805)962-9915. Fax: (805)564-3278. Imprint: Little Humanist Classics. Book Publisher. Editor: Sasha Newborn. Fiction Editor: Joan Blake. Publishes 1 young adult title/year. "Most books have been translations in the humanist tradition. Looking for themes of intellectual awakening."
Fiction: Young adults (16 and older): history, multicultural, problem novels, romance. Multicultural needs include "cultural encounters." No religious, fantasy. Average word length: 60,000. Recently published *The First Detective*, by Edgar Allan Poe (ages 14 and up); and *Benigna Mechiavelli*, by Charlotte Perkins Gillman (ages 15 and up).
Nonfiction: Young adults (16 and older): biography, history, multicultural, social issues, textbooks. No religious, fantasy. Average word length: 50,000. Recently published *Sappho*, by N. Browne, illustrated by Jeanne Morgan (ages 16-24, translation of Sappho's poems); *Dante and His Circle*, by D.G. Rossetti (ages 18 and up, poems on love).
How to Contact/Writers: Nonfiction: Submit outline/synopsis and 1 sample chapter. Reports on queries in 1 month; mss in 3 months. Publishes a book up to a year after acceptance. Will consider simultaneous submissions.
Illustration: Works with 2 illustrators/year. Will review ms/illustration packages. Will review artwork for future assignments. Contact: Sasha Newborn, publisher. Uses primarily b&w artwork only. Prefers woodblock, scratchboard artwork.
How to Contact/Illustrators: Ms/illustration packages: Submit ms with dummy. Illustrations only: Query with samples, portfolio and tearsheets. Reports back only if interested. Cannot return samples.
Terms: Pays authors royalty of 5-10% based on retail price; also advances (average amount: $200). Pays illustrators by the project (range: $25-200). Sends galleys to authors. Book catalog available; ms and art guidelines not available.

BANTAM DOUBLEDAY DELL, 1540 Broadway, New York NY 10036. (212)354-6500. Book publisher. Publisher: Craig Virden. Publishes 25 picture books/year; 12 young reader titles/year; 60 middle reader books/year; 60 young adult titles/year. 10% of books by first-time authors; 70% of books from agented writers.
Fiction: Picture books: adventure, animal, contemporary, easy-to-read, fantasy, humor. Young readers: animal, contemporary, humor, easy-to-read, fantasy, sports, suspense/ mystery. Middle Readers: adventure, animal, contemporary, humor, easy-to-read, fantasy, sports, suspense/mystery. Young adults: adventure, contemporary issues, humor, coming-of-age, suspense/mystery. Recently published *Baby*, by Patricia MacLachlan; *Nate the Great and the Pillowcase*, by Marjorie Weinman Sharmat and Rosalind Weinman; *Between Madison and Palmetto*, by Jacqueline Woodson; *Who is Eddie Leonard*, by Harry Mazer.
Nonfiction: "Bantam Doubleday Dell Books for Young Readers publishes a very limited number of nonfiction titles."
How to Contact/Writers: Submit through agent only. "All unsolicited manuscripts returned unopened with the following exceptions: unsolicited manuscripts accepted for the Delacorte Press Prize for a First Young Adult Novel contest and the Marguerite de Angeli Prize for a First Middle Grade Novel contest (see contest section)." Reports on queries in 6-8 weeks; mss in 3 months.
Illustration: Number of illustrations used per fiction title varies considerably.
How to Contact/Illustrators: Query first. Do not send originals. Cannot return samples; samples filed. "If you submit a dummy, please submit the text separately." Illustrations only: tearsheets, résumé, samples that do not need to be returned. Reports on ms/

art samples only if interested. Original artwork returned at job's completion.

Terms: Pays authors royalty based on retail price. Pays illustrators royalty based on retail price or work purchased outright.

BARRONS EDUCATIONAL SERIES, 250 Wireless Blvd., Hauppauge NY 11788. (516)434-3311. Fax: (516)434-3723. Book publisher. Estab. 1945. Managing/Acquisitions Editor: Grace Freedson. Publishes 20 picture books/year; 20 young reader titles/year; 20 middle reader titles/year; 10 young adult titles/year. 25% of books by first-time authors; 25% of books from agented writers.

Fiction: Picture books, young readers: animal, concept, health-related, multicultural, nature/environment. Middle readers, young adults: health, nature/environment. Published *Get Ready, Get Set, Read* (beginning reader series).

Nonfiction: Picture books, young readers: activity books, animal, careers, concept, reference, science. Middle readers: animal, history, nature/environment, reference, science, social issues. Young adults: animal, careers, cooking, history, how-to, nature/environment, reference, science, social issues.

How to Contact/Writers: Fiction: Query. Nonfiction: Submit outline/synopsis and sample chapters. Reports on queries in 1 month; mss in 6-8 months. Publishes a book 1 year after acceptance. Will consider simultaneous submissions.

Illustration: Works with 10 illustrators/year. Editorial will review ms/illustration packages. Will review artwork for future assignments.

How to Contact/Illustrators: Ms/illustration packages: Query first; 3 chapters of ms with 1 piece of final art, remainder roughs. Illustrations only: Tearsheets or slides plus résumé. Reports in 3-8 weeks.

Terms: Pays authors in royalties of 6% based on retail price or buys ms outright for $2,000 minimum. Illustrators paid by the project based on retail price. Sends galleys to authors; dummies to illustrators. Book catalog, ms/artist's guidelines free on request. Please send 9×12 SAE.

Tips: Writers: "We are predominately on the lookout for preschool storybooks and concept books. No YA fiction/romance or novels." Illustrators: "We are happy to receive a sample illustration to keep on file for future consideration. Periodic notes reminding us of your work is acceptable." Children's book themes "are becoming much more contemporary and relevant to a child's day-to-day activities."

BEHRMAN HOUSE INC., 235 Watchung Ave., West Orange NJ 07052. (201)669-0447. Fax: (201)669-9769. Book publisher. Project Editor: Adam Siegel. Publishes 3 young reader titles/year; 3 middle reader titles/year; 3 young adult titles/year. 12% of books by first-time authors; 2% of books from agented writers. Publishes books on all aspects of Judaism: history, cultural, textbooks, holidays.

Nonfiction: All levels: history, religion, Jewish educational textbooks. Average word length: young reader—1,200; middle reader—2,000; young adult—4,000.

How to Contact/Writers: Fiction/nonfiction: Submit outline/synopsis and sample chapters. Reports on mss/queries in 2 months. Publishes a book 2½ years after acceptance. Will consider simultaneous submissions.

Illustration: Will review ms/illustration packages. Will review artwork for future assignments.

How to Contact/Illustrators: Ms/illustration packages: "Query first." Illustrations only: Query with samples; send unsolicited art samples by mail. Reports in 2 months.

Photography: Purchases photos from freelancers. Contact Adam Siegel. Uses photos of families involved in Jewish activities. Uses color and b&w prints. Photographers should query with samples. Send unsolicited photos by mail. Submit portfolio for review.

Terms: Pays authors in royalties of 3-8% based on retail price or buys ms outright for $1,000-5,000. Offers advance (average amount: $500). Pays illustrators by the project (range: $500-5,000). Sends galleys to authors; dummies to illustrators. Book catalog free on request.

Tips: Looking for "religious school texts" with Judaic themes.

*BERKLEY PUBLISHING GROUP, Imprints: Berkley, Joye, Diamond, Ace, Pacer. 200 Madison Ave., New York NY 10016. Book publisher. Editor: Melinda Metz. Senior Editor: Gary Goldstein. "We are mainly pubilshing young adult horror, thrillers and romance."

Fiction: Young adults: problem novels, romance, suspense/horror. Length: young adults—55,000.

How to Contact/Writers: Fiction: Submit outline/synopsis and 3 sample chapters. Reports on queries in 2 weeks; mss in 2-3 months. Publishes a book in 12-18 months after acceptance.

Terms: Pays authors royalty based on retail price. Offers advance. Sends galleys to authors.

*BESS PRESS, P.O. Box 22388, Honolulu HI 96823. (808)734-7159. Editor: Revé Shapard. Publishes 1-2 picture books/year; 1-2 young readers/year; 0-1 middle readers/year. 60% of books by first-time authors. "Books must be about Hawaii, Asia or the Pacific."

Fiction: Picture books, young readers: adventure, animal, anthology, concept, contemporary, folktales, hi-lo, history, humor, multicultural, nature/environment, sports, suspense/mystery. Middle readers: adventure, animal, anthology, contemporary, folktales, hi-lo, history, humor, multicultural, nature/environment, problem novels, sports, suspense/mystery. Young adults: adventure, anthology, contemporary, hi-lo, history, humor, multicultural, problem novels, sports, suspense/mystery. Recently published *Angel of Rainbow Gulch*, by Helen Swanson (ages 9-11, novel); *Too Many Curls*, by Marilyn Kahalewai (ages 3-8, picture book); *Let's Call Him Lau-wili-wili-humuhumu-nukunuku-nukunuku-apuaa-oioi*, by Tim Myers, illustrated by Daryl Arakaki (ages 3-8, picture book).

Nonfiction: Picture books: activity books, biography, concept, geography, hi-lo, history, multicultural, reference, sports, textbooks. Young readers: activity books, biography, geography, hi-lo, history, multicultural, reference, sports, textbooks. Middle readers, young adults: biography, geography, hi-lo, history, multicultural, reference, sports, textbooks. Recently published *Filipino Word Book*, by Teresita V. Ramos and Josie Clausen, illustrated by Jerri Asuncion and Boboy Betco (ages 5-11, introductory language book); *Flowers of Hawaii Coloring Book*, by Wren (ages 3-8, coloring book); Keiki's First Books, by Maile and Wren (for toddlers, concept books).

How to Contact/Writers: Fiction/nonfiction: Submit complete ms. Reports on queries in 2 weeks; on mss in 3-4 weeks. Publishes a book 6-12 months after acceptance. Will consider simultaneous submissions and previously published work.

Illustration: Works with 5 illustrators/year. Will review ms/illustration packages. Will review artwork for future assignments.

How to Contact/Illustrators: Ms/illustration packages: Submit ms with dummy. Illustrations only: Query with samples. Reports in 3 weeks. Samples returned with SASE; samples filed. Original artwork returned at job's completion.

Terms: Pays authors royalty of 5-10% based on wholesale price or work purchased outright. Pays illustrators by the project, royalty of 2½-5% based on wholesale price. Sends galleys to authors; dummies to illustrators. Book catalog available for SASE; ms and art guidelines available for SASE.

Tips: This publisher wants books that have the potential for high sales in primary markets—Hawaii, Micronesia, the Western United States and libraries.

*BETHANY HOUSE PUBLISHERS, 11300 Hampshire Ave. S., Minneapolis MN 55438. (612)829-2500. Book publisher. Children's Book Editor: Barbara Lilland. Managing Editor: Lance Wubbles. Publishes 16 young readers/year; 16 young adult titles/year. Publishes books with spiritual and religious themes.
Fiction: Middle readers, young adults: adventure, contemporary, problem novels, romance, suspense/mystery. Does not want to see poetry or science fiction. Average word length: young readers—20,000; young adults—35,000. Recently published *Too Many Secrets*, by Patricia H. Rushford (young adult/teens, mystery-adventure series); *Becky's Brainstorm*, by Elaine L. Schulte (young readers, adventure series with a strong Christian values theme); *Mandie and the Fiery Rescue*, by Lois Leppard (young readers, adventure series).
Nonfiction: Middle readers, young adults: religion, self-help, social issues. Recently published *Can I Be a Christian Without Being Weird?*, by Kevin Johnson (early teens, devotional book); *Dear Judy, Did You Ever Like a Boy (who didn't like you?)*, by Judy Baer (young adult/teen, advice book on social issues).
How to Contact/Writers: Fiction: Query. Nonfiction: Query. Reports on queries in 1 month; on mss in 2 months. Publishes a book 9-12 months after acceptance. Will consider simultaneous submissions and previously published work.
Illustration: Works with 4 illustrators/year. Will review/ms/illustration packages. Will review artwork for future assignments.
How to Contact/Illustrators: Ms/illustration packages: Query. Illustrations only: Query with samples. Reports in 6 weeks. Samples returned with SASE.
Terms: Pays authors royalty based on retail price. Pays illustrators by the project. Sends galleys to authors. Book catalog available for 11 × 14 SAE and 5 first-class stamps.
Tips: "Research the market, know what is already out there. Study our catalog before submitting material. We look for an evangelical message woven delicately into a strong plot and topics that seek to broaden the reader's experience and perspective."

BETHEL PUBLISHING, 1819 S. Main, Elkhart IN 46516. (219)293-8585. Book publisher. Contact: Senior Editor. Publishes 1-2 young readers/year; 1-2 middle readers/year.
Fiction: Young readers: animal, religion. Middle readers and young adults: adventure, religion. Does not want to see "New-Age—Dungeon & Dragons type." Recently published *The Great Forest*, by Jean Springer (ages 9-14, religion); *Pordy's Prickly Problem*, by Janette Oke (ages 7-12, religion); *Peace Porridge*, by Marjie Douglas (ages 8-13, religion). Does not want to see workbooks, cookbooks, coloring books, books on theological studies, poetry or preschool/elementary age stories. Average word length: 30,000-50,000.
Nonfiction: Young readers, middle readers and young adults: religion.
How to Contact/Writers: Fiction/nonfiction: Query. Submit complete ms. Reports on queries in 3 weeks; mss in 3 months. Publishes a book 1 year after acceptance. Will consider simultaneous submissions and previously published work.
Illustration: Works with 2 illustrators/year. Will review ms/illustration packages. Will review artwork for future assignments.
How to Contact/Illustrators: Ms/illustration packages: Query. Reports in 1 month. Samples returned with SASE. Originals not returned.
Photography: Purchases photos from freelancers. Contact Senior Editor. Buys stock. Model/property releases required. Uses color and b&w glossy prints; 35mm and 2¼ × 2¼ transparencies. Photographers should send cover letter.
Terms: Pays authors royalty of 5-10% on wholesale price. Pays illustrators by the project. Photographers paid by the project. Sends galleys to authors. Book catalog available for 9 × 12 SAE and 3 first-class stamps. Ms guidelines available for SASE. Artist's guidelines not available.

BLACK MOSS PRESS, 2450 Byng Rd., Windsor, Ontario N8W 3E8 Canada. (519)252-2551. Editor: Kristina Russelo. Publishes 2-4 picture books/year. 75% of books by first-time authors.
Fiction: Picture books: adventure, contemporary, humor. Does not want to see fantasy or food material. Average word length: Picture books—1,000. Published *Moving Gives Me A Stomach Ache*, by Heather McKend, illustrated by Heather Collins (ages 3-8, picture book).
How to Contact/Writers: Fiction: Submit complete ms. Reports on queries in 4-6 weeks; mss in 2 months. Publishes a book 2 years after acceptance.
Illustration: Works with 3-4 illustrators/year, however, "we aren't really looking for illustrators right now."
Terms: Pays authors royalty of 4-5% based on retail price. Pays illustrators by the project (range: $1,000-1,500). Sends galleys to authors; dummies to illustrators. Book catalog available for 6×8 SAE and 84¢ in Canadian first-class postage. Ms guidelines available for SASE; art guidelines not available.
Tips: "Read the books out loud. So many books sound stiff and unnatural. We want books with a realistic story with an interesting set of characters and strong setting. We will only publish Canadian citizens or landed immigrants."

BLUE HERON PUBLISHING, INC., 24450 NW Hansen Rd., Hillsboro OR 97124. (503)621-3911. Book publisher. Publisher: Dennis Stovall. Publishes 1-2 young adult titles/year. Wants "reprints of YA classics and/or well published authors. Only interested in the previously described from Northwest authors."
Fiction: Middle readers: adventure, animal, contemporary, history, nature/environment. Young adults: adventure, anthology, animal, contemporary, history, nature/environment. Average word length: young adult—60,000. Published *Death Walk*, by Walt Morey (YA, adventure novel); *Morning Glory Afternoon*, by Irene Bennett Brown (YA, historical adventure/romance); and *Angry Waters*, by Walt Morey (YA, adventure).
Nonfiction: Middle readers, young adults: history, nature/environment, writing/publishing.
How to Contact/Writers: Nonfiction: Query. Reports on queries in 4-6 weeks; mss in 6 weeks. Publishes a book 18 months after acceptance. Will consider simultaneous submissions, electronic submissions via disk or modem and previously published work.
Illustration: Will review artwork for future assignments (only Northwest artists). Contact Linny Stovall, publisher.
How to Contact/Illustrators: Illustrations only: Query with samples.
Terms: Pays author royalty of 5-8% on retail price. Pays illustrators by the project (range: $100-600). Sends galleys to authors; dummies to illustrators. Book catalog available for 6×9 SAE and 52¢ postage. Ms guidelines available.

BOYDS MILLS PRESS, 815 Church St., Honesdale PA 18431. (717)253-1164. Imprint: Wordsong (poetry). Book publisher. Manuscript Coordinator: Beth Troop. Art Director: Tim Gillner. 5% of books from agented writers.
Fiction: All levels: adventure, animal, contemporary, folktales, history, humor, multicultural, poetry, sports. Middle readers, young adults: suspense/mystery. Multicultural themes vary. "Please query us on the appropriateness of suggested topics for middle grade and young adult. For all other submissions send entire manuscript." Recently published *Naomi Knows It's Springtime*, by Virginia Kroll (ages 5-8, picture book); *Annie's Choice*, by Clara Gillow Clark (ages 10 and up, historical); *Poems That Sing to You*, by Michael Strickland (ages 10 and up, poetry).
Nonfiction: Picture books, young readers, middle readers: activity books, animal, arts/crafts, history, how-to, multicultural, nature/environment. Picture books, young readers: concept. Young readers, middle readers, young adult: geography. Recently published

Chi-Hoon, by Patricia McMahon (ages 8 and up, multicultural); *Sea Snakes*, by Sneed Collard (ages 8-12, animal).

How to Contact/Writers: Fiction/nonfiction: Submit complete manuscript or submit through agent. Query on middle reader, young adult and nonfiction. Reports on queries/mss in 1 month.

Illustration: Works with 70-100 illustrators/year. Will review ms/illustration packages. Will review artwork for future assignments. Contact: Tim Gillner, art director.

How to Contact/Illustrators: Ms/illustration packages: Submit complete ms. Illustrations only: Query with samples; send résumé and slides.

Terms: Authors paid royalty or outright purchase. Offers advances. Illustrators paid by the project, royalty. Catalog available for 9 × 12 SASE. Ms and art guidelines available for free.

Tips: "Picture books are our strongest need at this time."

© 1993 Charles Jordan

Charles Jordan captured the little pig's excitement and enthusiasm in colored pencil in this illustration for the book A Pile of Pigs, *by Judith Ross Enderle and Stephanie Gordon Tessler, from Boyds Mills Press. "Along with the opportunity of vast exposure of my work," Jordan says of the assignment, "I was able to break into the picture book field, in which I hope to grow."*

BRADBURY PRESS, 866 Third Ave., New York NY 10022. (212)702-9809. Imprint of Macmillan Publishing Company. Book publisher. Vice President and Editorial Director: Barbara Lalicki. Art Director: Julie Quan. Publishes 20-25 picture books/year; 5 young reader titles/year; 5 middle reader titles/year. 15% of books by first-time authors; 85% of books from previously published or agented writers.

● At press time, Macmillan Children's Book Group, as well as other parts of the company, were sold to Paramount Communications. This could affect the publisher's policies, so watch *Publishers Weekly* and other trade journals for details.

Fiction: Picture books: animal, contemporary, history. Young readers: animal, contemporary, easy-to-read, history. Middle readers: contemporary, fantasy, history, science fiction, spy/mystery/adventure. Average length: picture books—32 pages; young readers—48 pages; middle readers—90 pages.

Nonfiction: Picture books: animal, history, music/dance, nature/environment. Young readers, middle readers: animal, biography, education, history, hobbies, music/dance, nature/environment, sports. Average length: picture books—2-3 ms pages; young and middle readers—48-96 ms pages.

How to Contact/Writers: Fiction: Query. Nonfiction: Submit outline/synopsis and sample chapters. "We have extremely limited nonfiction interest because of commitments to authors." Reports on queries in 2-3 weeks; on mss in 6-8 weeks. Publishes a book 18 months after acceptance.

Illustration: Will review illustrator's work for future assignments.

How to Contact/Illustrators: Ms/illustration packages: Submit ms with color photocopies of art. Illustrations only: Portfolio drop off last Thursday of every month. Reports on art samples only if interested. Original artwork returned at job's completion.

Terms: Pays author in royalties based on retail price. Average advance: varies. Book catalog available for 8×10 SAE and 4 first-class stamps; manuscript and/or artist's guidelines for business-size SAE and 1 first-class stamp.

Tips: Looks for "a strong story, nothing gimmicky, no pop-ups." Trends include "nonfiction for pre-schoolers."

BRIGHT RING PUBLISHING, 1900 N. Shore Dr., Box 5768, Bellingham WA 98227-5768. (206)734-1601. Fax: (206)676-1271. Estab. 1985. Editor: MaryAnn Kohl. Publishes 1 young reader title/year. 50% of books by first-time authors. Uses only recipe format— "but no cookbooks unless woven into another subject like art, music, science."

Nonfiction: Young readers and middle readers: activity books involving art ideas, hobbies, how-to, music/dance, nature/environment, science. "No picture books, no poetry, no stories of any kind and no crafts." Average length: "about 125 ideas/book." Published *Good Earth Art* by MaryAnn Kohl, illustrated by Cindy Gaines (picture book, young reader, middle reader—art ideas). "We are moving into only recipe-style resource books in any variety of subject areas—useful with children 2-12. 'Whole language' is the buzz word in early education—so books to meet the new demands of that subject will be needed."

How to Contact/Writers: Nonfiction: submit complete ms. Reports on queries in 2 weeks; mss in 1 month. Publishes a book 1 year after acceptance. Will consider simultaneous submissions.

Illustration: Works with 2 illustrators/year. Will review ms/illustration packages. Prefers to review "black line (drawings) for text." Will review artwork for future assignments.

How to Contact/Illustrators: Ms/illustration packages: "Query first." Illustrations only: Query with samples; send tearsheets and "sample of ideas I request after query." Reports in 6-8 weeks. Original artwork returned at job's completion.

Terms: Pays authors in royalties of 3-10% based on wholesale price. Work purchased outright (range: $500-2,000). Pays illustrators $500-2,000. Also offers "free books and discounts for future books." Book catalog, ms/artist's guidelines for business-size SAE and 29¢ postage.

Tips: Illustrators: "Build your portfolio by taking a few jobs at lower pay—then grow. Bright Ring Publishing is not looking for picture books, juvenile fiction, or poetry at this time. We are, however, highly interested in creative activity and resource books for children to use independently or for teachers and parents to use with children. Must work for pre-school through age twelve."

"Picture books" are geared toward the preschool to 8-year-old group; *"Young readers"* are for 5- to 8-year-olds; *"Middle readers"* are for 9- to 11-year-olds; and *"Young adults"* are for those 12 and up.

CAPSTONE PRESS INC., P.O. Box 669, N. Mankato MN 56001. (612)551-0513. Book publisher. Publisher: John Coughlan. Publishes "nonfiction only, ages 8-15." 15% of books by first-time authors; 1% from agented authors.
Nonfiction: Animals, sports, vehicles. Published *Hot Air Ballooning*, by Christie Constanzo (grade 5, sports); *BMX Bikes*, by Karol Carstensen (grade 5, sports); *18 Wheelers*, by Linda Maifair (grade 5, sports).
How to Contact/Writers: Nonfiction: Query. Reports in 2 weeks. Publishes a book in "6 months to 1 year depending upon publishing program."
How to Contact/Illustrators: Query first. Submit résumé and photocopies of work. Reports in 2 weeks. Does not return original artwork.
Terms: Outright purchase. Offers advance of one third of purchase price. Illustrators are paid by the project. Does not send galleys to authors; dummies to illustrators.

CAROLINA WREN PRESS/LOLLIPOP POWER BOOKS, 120 Morris St., Durham NC 27701. (919)560-2738. Book publisher. Carolina Wren estab. 1976; Lollipop Power Estab. 1971. Both are nonprofit, small presses. Children's Editor: Ruth A. Smullin. Designer: Martha Scotford. Publishes 1 picture book/year.
Fiction: Picture books: bilingual (English/Spanish), multicultural, multiracial, nonsexist. Average length: 30 pages. Published *The Boy Toy*, by Phyllis Johnson, illustrated by Lena Schiffman; *Maria Teresa*, by Mary Atkinson, illustrated by Christine Engla Eber; *In Christina's Toolbox*, by Dianne Homan, illustrated by Mary Heine.
How to Contact/Writers: "Query and request guidelines; enclose SASE with request. All manuscripts must be typed, double-spaced and accompanied by an SASE of appropriate size with sufficient postage. If you do not wish your manuscript returned, you may simply enclose a SASE for our response. Do not send illustrations." Reports on queries/ms in 3 months. Publishes a book 2-3 years after acceptance.
Illustration: Will review ms/illustration packages. Will review artwork for future assignments. Contact: Martha Scotford, designer.
How to Contact/Illustrators: Query with tearsheets. Reports on art samples only if SASE enclosed. Original artwork returned at job's completion.
Terms: Pays authors in royalties of 5% of print-run based on retail price, or cash, if available. Pays illustrators in royalties of 5% of print-run based on retail price, or cash, if available. Sends galleys to authors; dummies to illustrators.
Tips: "Lollipop Power Books offer alternative points of view to prevailing stereotypes. Our books show children: girls and women who are self-sufficient, with responsibilities beyond those of home and family; boys and men who are emotional and nurturing and involved in domestic responsibilities; families that use day care or alternative child care; families that consist of one parent only, working parents, or extended families; realistic portrayals of children of all races and ethnic groups, who have in common certain universal feelings and experiences. We believe that children must be taken seriously. Our books present their problems honestly and without condescension. Lollipop Power Books must be well-written stories that will appeal to children. We are not interested in preachy tales where message overpowers plot and character. We are looking for good stories told from a child's point of view. Our current publishing priorities are: a) African-American, Hispanic or Native American characters; b) bilingual books (English/Spanish); c) books that show gay men or lesbian women as ordinary people who can raise children. To request a catalog, send a 9×12 envelope with postage sufficient for 2 ounces."

CAROLRHODA BOOKS, INC., 241 First Ave. N., Minneapolis MN 55401. (612)332-3344. Book publisher. Estab. 1969. Submissions Editor: Rebecca Poole. Publishes 5 picture books/year; 25 young reader titles/year; 30 middle reader titles/year. 20% of books by first-time authors; 10% of books from agented writers.

Fiction: Picture books: folktales, multicultural, nature/environment, special needs. Young readers, middle readers: historical. Average word length: picture books—1,000-1,500; young readers—2,000. Recently published *Agassu: Legend of the Leopard King*, by Rick Dupré.

Nonfiction: Picture books: animal, hobbies, nature/environment. Young readers, middle readers: animal, biography, history, hobbies, multicultural, nature/environment, science, social issues, special needs. Multicultural needs include biographies. Average word length: young readers— 2,000; middle readers—6,000. Recently published *Mummies & Their Mysteries*, by Charlotte Wilcox (photo essay); *Mammolina: A Story About Maria Montessori*, by Barbara O'Connor.

How to Contact/Writers: Fiction/nonfiction: Submit complete ms. Reports on queries in 3-4 weeks; mss in 3 months. Publishes a book 18 months after acceptance. Will consider simultaneous submissions. Must enclose SASE.

Illustration: Will review ms/illustration packages. Will review artwork for future assignments. "Do not send originals."

How to Contact/Illustrators: Ms/illustration packages: At least one sample illustration (in form of photocopy, slide, duplicate photo) with full ms. Illustrations only: Query with samples; send résumé/slides. "We like illustrators to send samples we can keep on file." Reports on art samples only if interested.

Photography: Purchases photos from freelancers. Buys stock and assigns work.

Terms: Buys ms outright for variable amount. Factors used to determine final payment: color vs. b&w, number of illustrations, quality of work. Sends galleys to authors; dummies to illustrators. Book catalog available for 9×12 SAE and 3 first-class stamps; manuscript guidelines for #10 SAE and 1 first-class stamp.

Tips: Writers: "Research the publishing company to be sure it is in the market for the type of book you're interested in writing. Familiarize yourself with the company's list. We specialize in beginning readers, photo essays and books published in series. We do very few single-title picture books and no novels. For more detailed information about our publishing program, consult our catalog. We do not publish any of the following: textbooks, workbooks, songbooks, puzzles, plays and religious material. In general, we suggest that you steer clear of alphabet books; preachy stories with a moral to convey; stories featuring anthropomorphic protagonists ('Amanda the Amoeba,' 'Frankie the Fire Engine,' 'Tonie the Tornado'); and stories that revolve around trite, unoriginal plots. Be sure to avoid racial and sexual stereotypes in your writing, as well as sexist language." (See also Lerner Publications.)

CHARIOT BOOKS, 20 Lincoln Ave., Elgin IL 60120. (708)741-9558. An imprint of Chariot Family Products and a division of David C. Cook Publishing Co. Book publisher. Design Coordinator: Helen Lannis. Managing Editor: Julie Smith. Publishes 20-30 picture books/year; 6-8 young readers/year; 10-15 middle readers/year; 4-6 young adult titles/year. Less than 5% of books by first-time authors; 15% of books from agented authors. "All books have overt Christian values, but there is no primary theme."

  ● This publisher is no longer soliciting manuscripts because they have been inundated with work.

Illustration: Works with 25 illustrators/year. Will review artwork for future assignments. Contact Helen Lannis, design coordinator.

How to Contact/Illustrators: Illustrations only: Query with samples; send résumé, promo sheet, portoflio, tearsheets. Reports only if interested. Original artwork returned at job's completion.

Terms: Pays illustrators by the project, royalty or work purchased outright. Sends dummies to illustrators. Ms guidelines available for SASE.

CHARLESBRIDGE, 85 Main St., Watertown MA 02172. (617)926-0329. Book publisher. Publishes 12 nonfiction picture books/year. Trade Acquisitions Editor: Katherine Keller. Publishes nature/science and multicultural books.
Nonfiction: Picture books: geography, nature/environment, science. "No anthropomorphism, pure fiction—look at what we publish before you send us your manuscript." Average word length: picture books—1,500. Published: *Icky Bug Counting Book*, by Jerry Pallotta (picture book); *Woodhoopoe Willie*, by Virginia Kroll (multicultural book).
How to Contact/Writers: Nonfiction: Submit complete ms. Reports on mss in 2 months. Publishes a book 1-2 years after acceptance.
Illustration: Works with 10-12 illustrators/year. Will review ms/illustration packages. Welcomes samples.
How to Contact/Illustrators: Illustrations only: Query with samples; provide résumé, tearsheets and slides to be kept on file. Reports back only if interested.
Terms: Pays authors in royalties or work purchased outright. Pays illustrators by the project.
Tips: "We have a reputation for the accuracy of the information we present in text and illustrations. We only work with illustrators and writers who meet these standards."

CHICAGO REVIEW PRESS, 814 N. Franklin St., Chicago IL 60610. (312)337-0747. Book publisher. Editorial Director: Amy Teschner. Art Director: Fran Lee. Publishes 1 middle reader/year; "about 4" young adult titles/year. 50% of books by first-time authors; 10% of books from agented authors. "We publish art activity books for young children and project books in the arts and sciences for ages 10 and up (our Ziggurat Series). We do not publish fiction."
Nonfiction: Young readers, middle readers and young adults: activity books, arts/crafts, geography, hobbies, how-to, science. "We're interested in hands-on, educational books; anything else probably will be rejected." Average word length: young readers and young adult—175 pages. Recently published *A Handbook to the Universe: Explorations of Matter, Energy, Space, and Time for Beginning Scientific Thinkers*, by Richard Paul (ages 12 and up); *Seeing for Yourself: Techniques and Projects for Beginning Photographers*, by Roger Gleason (ages 11 and up); *Exploring The Sky: Projects for Beginning Astronomers, Revised Edition*, by Richard Moeschl (ages 11 and up); *Real Toads in Imaginary Gardens: Suggestions and Starting Points for Young Creative Writers*, by Stephen Phillip Policoff and Jeffrey Skinner (ages 12 and up). Reports on queries/mss in 2 months. Publishes a book 1-2 years after acceptance. Will consider simultaneous submissions and previously published work.
Illustration: Works with 2 illustrators/year. Will review ms/illustration packages. Will review artwork for future assignments.
How to Contact/Illustrators: Ms/illustration packages: Submit 1-2 chapters of ms with corresponding pieces of final art. Illustrations only: Send samples. Reports back only if interested. Original artwork "usually" returned at job's completion.
Photography: Purchases photos from freelancers ("but not often"). Contact Fran Lee, art director. Buys stock and assigns work. Wants "instructive photos. We consult our files when we know what we're looking for on a book-by-book basis." Uses b&w prints.
Terms: Pays authors royalty of 7½-12½% based on retail price. Offers advances ("but not always") of $500-1,500. Pays illustrators by the project (range varies considerably). Photographers paid by the project (range varies considerably). Sends galleys to authors. Book catalog available for SASE; ms guidelines available for SASE.
Tips: "We're looking for original activity books for small children and the adults caring for them—new themes and enticing projects to occupy kids' imaginations and promote their sense of personal creativity. We like activity books that are as much fun as they are constructive. For older kids, age 10 and up, we publish Ziggurat Books—activity books geared to teach a discipline in the arts or sciences. As for the future, we expect parents to become increasingly engaged in their children's educations. Our Ziggurat

books are intended to encourage children to pursue interests and talents inspired but not thoroughly covered by their schoolwork or other influences. We think parents are buying our books so their kids can pick up where a particularly exciting lesson or museum visit left off. When a kid becomes curious about say, photography or astronomy, we want to provide the challenging hands-on book that will cultivate enthusiasm while teaching him or her all about that intriguing subject."

*CHILDREN'S BOOK PRESS, Suite 4, 6400 Hollis St., Emeryville CA 94608. (510)655-3395. Contact: Publisher. Publishes 3 picture books/year. 50% of books by first-time authors. "Children's Book Press is a nonprofit publisher of bilingual and multicultural children's literature. We publish folktales and contemporary stories reflecting the traditions and culture of the emerging majority in the United States and from countries around the world. Our goal is to help broaden the base of children's literature in this country to include more stories from the African-American, Asian-American, Hispanic and Native American communities as well as the diverse Spanish-speaking communities throughout the Americas."

Fiction: Picture books: contemporary, multicultural. Average word length: picture books—800-1,600.

How to Contact/Writers: Fiction: Submit complete ms. Reports on mss in 1-12 months. Publishes a book 1 year after acceptance. Will consider simultaneous submissions.

Illustration: Works with 3 illustrators/year. Will review ms/illustration packages. Will review artwork for future assignments. Uses color artwork only.

How to Contact/Illustrators: Ms/illustration packages: Send ms with 3 or 4 color photocopies. Illustrations only: Send slides. Reports in 1-12 months. Samples returned with SASE. Original artwork returned at job's completion.

Terms: Pays authors royalty. Pays illustrators by the project. Book catalog available for SAE; ms guidelines available for SASE.

Tips: "Vocabularly level should be approximately third grade (eight years old) or below. Keep in mind, however, that many of the young people who read our books may be nine, ten, or eleven years old or older. Their life experience is often more advanced than their reading level, so try to write a story that will appeal to a fairly wide age range. We are especially interested in humorous stories."

CHILDRENS PRESS, 5440 N. Cumberland, Chicago IL 60656. (312)693-0800. Book publisher. Vice President of Editorial: M.F. Dyra. Creative Director: M. Fiddle. Publishes 20 picture books and 30 middle readers/year. 5% of books by first-time authors. Publishes informational (nonfiction) for K-6; picture books for young readers K-3.

Fiction: Picture books, young readers: adventure, animal, concept, contemporary, folktales, multicultural. Middle readers: contemporary, hi-lo, humor, multicultural. Young adults: hi-lo. Does not want to see young adult fiction, romance or science fiction. Average word length: picture book—300; middle readers—4,000.

Nonfiction: Picture books: arts/crafts, biography, concept, geography, hi-lo, history, hobbies, how-to, multicultural, nature/environment, science, special needs. Young readers: animal, arts/crafts, biography, careers, concept, geography, health, hi-lo, history, hobbies, multicultural, nature/environment, science, social issues, sports. Middle read-

---

Market conditions are constantly changing! If you're still using this book and it is 1995 or later, buy the newest edition of Children's Writer's & Illustrator's Market *at your favorite bookstore or order directly from Writer's Digest Books.*

ers: hi-lo, history, multicultural, reference, science. Average word length: picture books—400; young readers—2,000; middle readers—8,000; young adult—12,000.

How to Contact/Writers: Fiction: Query; submit outline/synopsis or submit outline/synopsis and 1 sample chapter. Nonfiction: Query; submit outline/synopsis. Reports in 2-3 months. Publishes a book 18 months after acceptance. Will consider simultaneous submissions.

Illustration: Works with 14 illustrators/year. Will review ms/illustration packages. Contact: M. Fiddle, creative director. Will review artwork for future assignments. Uses color artwork only.

How to Contact/Illustrators: Illustrations only: Query with samples or arrange personal portfolio review. Reports back only if interested. Samples returned with SASE. Samples filed. Originals not returned.

Photography: Purchases photos from freelancers. Contact: Jan Izzo, photo editor. Buys stock and assigns work. Model/property releases and captions required. Uses color and b&w prints; 2¼ × 2¼, 35 mm transparencies. Photographers should send cover letter and stock photo list.

Terms: Pays authors royalty of 5% based on net or work purchased outright (range: $500-1,000). Offers average advances of $1,000. Pays illustrators by the project (range: $1,800-3,500). Photographers paid per photo (range: $50-100). Sends galleys to authors; dummies to illustrators. Book catalog available for SAE; ms guidelines for SASE.

Tips: "Never write down to reader; keep language lively."

CHILDREN'S WRITER'S & ILLUSTRATOR'S MARKET, 1507 Dana Ave., Cincinnati OH 45207. Publication of Writer's Digest Books. Contact: Editor. Publishes annual directory of freelance markets for children's writers and illustrators. Send b&w samples—photographs, photostats or good quality photocopies of artwork. "Since *Children's Writer's & Illustrator's Market* is published only once a year, submissions are kept on file for the next upcoming edition until selections are made. Material is then returned by SASE." Buys one-time rights. Buys 10-20 illustrations/year. "I need examples of art that have been sold to one of the listings in *CWIM*. Thumb through the book to see the type of art I'm seeking. The art must have been freelanced; it cannot have been done as staff work. Include the name of the listing that purchased the work, what the art was used for and the payment you received." Pays $50 to holder of reproduction rights and free copy of *CWIM* when published.

■CHINA BOOKS, 2929 24th St., San Francisco CA 94110. (415)282-2994. Fax: (415)282-0994. Book publisher. Independent book producer/packager. Estab. 1960. Art Director: Wendy Lee. 10% of books by first-time authors; 10% of books from agented writers. 10% subsidy published.

Fiction: Picture books: animal, anthology, folktales, health, history, multicultural, nature/environment, poetry. Young readers: animal, contemporary, folktales, health, history, multicultural, nature/environment, religion. Middle readers: animal, contemporary, fantasy, folktales, nature/environment, poetry. Subjects must relate to China or Chinese-Americans." Recently published: *The Moon Maiden & Other Asian Folktales*, adapted and illustrated by the Hua Long (ages 10-12); *The Banker*, by Chang Naishan (adult fiction); *The Beijinger in New York*, by Glen Cao (adult fiction).

Nonfiction: Picture books, young readers, middle readers: activity books, arts/crafts, biography, cooking, geography, history, hobbies, multicultural, music/dance, nature/environment, religion, sports. Average word length: young readers—2,000; middle readers—4,000. Subjects must relate to China or Chinese-Americans.

How to Contact/Writers: Fiction/nonfiction: Query; submit outline/synopsis and sample chapters. Reports on queries in 2 weeks; mss in 1 month. Publishes a book 9 months after acceptance. Will consider simultaneous and electronic submissions via disk or modem.

Illustration: Works with 10 illustrators/year. Editorial will review ms/illustration packages. Will review artwork for future assignments.
How to Contact/Illustrators: Illustrations only: Query with samples, tearsheets.
Photography: Buys stock and assigns work. Looking for Chinese or Chinese-American subjects. Uses color and b&w prints; 35mm and 2¼ × 2¼ transparencies. Photographers should query with samples.
Terms: Pays authors in royalties of 8-10% based on retail price; buys ms outright for $100-500. Offers average advance payment of "1/3 of total royalty." Pays illustrators by the project (range: $100-500); royalties of 8% based on retail price. Pays photographers by the project (range: $50-500); per photo (range: $25-100); royalty of 4-8% based on retail price. Sends galleys to authors; dummies to illustrators. Book catalog free on request; manuscript/artist's guidelines for SASE.
Tips: Looks for "something related to China or to Chinese-Americans."

CHRONICLE BOOKS, 275 Fifth St., San Francisco CA 94103. (415)777-7240. Fax: (415)777-2289. Book publisher. Director: Victoria Rock. Editorial Assistant: Molly Ker. Publishes 18-20 (both fiction and nonfiction) picture books/year; 2-4 middlegrade nonfiction titles/year; 2-4 beginning readers or middlegrade fiction/year. 10-50% of books by first-time authors; 10-50% of books from agented writers.
Fiction: Picture books, young readers, middle readers: animal, fantasy, folktales, history, multicultural, nature/environment. Published *Ten Little Rabbits*, by Virginia Crossman and Sylvia Long (picture book); *Mama, Do You Love Me?*, by Barbara Joosse and Barbara Lavallee (picture book).
Nonfiction: Picture books: activity books, history, science. Young readers: animal, cooking, history, nature/environment, science. Middle readers: animal, arts/crafts, cooking, nature/environment, science, social issues. Recently published *Cities in the Sand: The Ancient Civilizations of the Southwest* (ages 8-12); *Beneath the Waves: Exploring the Hidden World of the Kelp Forest* (ages 8-12); *N.C. Wyeth's Pilgrims* (ages 6-12); *Among le Orangutans* (ages 8-12).
How to Contact/Writers: Fiction and nonfiction: Submit complete manuscript (picture books); submit outline/synopsis and sample chapters (for older readers). Reports on queries in 1-2 months; mss in 2-3 months. Publishes a book 1-3 years after acceptance. Will consider simultaneous submissions, as long as they are marked "multiple submission." Will not consider submissions by fax.
Illustration: Works with 15-20 illustrators/year. Editorial will review ms/illustration packages. "Indicate if project *must* be considered jointly, or if editor may consider text and art separately." Will review artwork for future assignments. Wants "unusual art. Something that will stand out on the shelves. Either bright and modern or very traditional. Fine art, not mass market."
How to Contact/Illustrators: Send samples of artist's work (not necessarily from book, but in the envisioned style). Slides, tearsheets and color photocopies OK. (No original art.) Dummies helpful. Résumé helpful. "If samples sent for files, generally no response — unless samples are not suited to list, in which case samples are returned. Queries and project proposals responded to in same time frame as author query/proposals."
Photography: Purchases photos from freelancers. Works on assignment only. Wants nature/natural history photos.
Terms: Generally pays authors in royalties based on retail price "though we do occasionally work on a flat fee basis." Advance varies. Illustrators paid royalty based on retail price or flat fee. Sends galleys to authors; proofs to illustrators. Book catalog for 9 × 12 SAE and 8 first-class stamps; manuscript guidelines for #10 SASE.
Tips: "Chronicle Books publishes an eclectic mixture of traditional and innovative children's books. We are interested in taking on projects that have a unique bent to them — be it in subject matter, writing style, or illustrative technique. As a small list, we are looking for books that will lend our list a distinctive flavor. Primarily we are interested

---

Clues to Illustrating for Clarion Books

When Anne Diebel was a freelance illustrator, sending off her samples to unfamiliar art directors, she would often read *Children's Writer's & Illustrator's Market*, searching each article for the magic formula to get her work noticed.

These days, Diebel sits at the other side of the desk. As art director for Clarion Books, Diebel reviews the work of new illustrators and knows firsthand how decisions are made. "It's tricky," says Diebel, "and there are no magic formulas." But she's quick to point out some clues.

The most important advice Diebel offers is to send publishers the work you truly enjoy doing. "If you really love to draw cars and ships, send us pictures of cars and ships. Don't send us what you think we want to see. Do what you do best and we'll both be happy," she says.

Anne Diebel

Diebel strongly suggests sending for each publisher's guidelines for artists *before* submitting work. Clarion's one-page sheet contains lots of helpful information like what kinds of artwork Clarion is looking for, how to submit, and when portfolios may be dropped off for review. The guidelines tell you to submit art samples to the art director, but a book with illustrations should be sent to the editorial department. Often, having the guidelines can save hours of wasted time.

Diebel also advises artists who want to work for Clarion to do a little research. Review the company's recent titles by requesting a catalog, or, for a closer look, visit a children's bookstore or library to see what type of books Clarion publishes and find out if your work suits their style. Clarion usually does not use pop-ups, die-cuts or gimmicks. More in line with Clarion's needs would be figure studies of children, pre-teens, and animals in various activities and settings.

She encourages artists to keep sending samples to publishers, even if they get no response. "It must seem for most artists that all they do is send their samples out into a great void from which they never receive a response, let alone encouragement," says Diebel. At Clarion, samples typically arrive daily, in stacks of 20, along with tons of other correspondence which must be handled as quickly and efficiently as possible.

Occasionally Diebel points illustrators toward more appropriate publishers if she believes the material has potential but is not suited for her company. If the artist's work seems right for Clarion, Diebel either contacts the artist or keeps the work on file. "I keep files broken down into subjects such as 'Jackets — Realistic' or 'Picture Books — Whimsical,' " she says.

If Diebel is so impressed by a mailed-in sample that she calls a new artist about a possible project, they will often meet for a portfolio review before a contract is signed. "The sending of samples is only an introduction, not a proposal," says Diebel. Publishing a children's book is a complicated, multifaceted project, with many important deadlines that must be met. "I do not hire artists who require prodding, or I should say, I do not rehire them."

Though most of the books Clarion publishes are illustrated by seasoned artists, Diebel has enjoyed giving several illustrators their first book assignments and is always on the lookout for new illustrators with fresh styles. In fact, reveals Diebel, "Publishers actually compete to find the best new illustrators." By being the first to sign an illustrator, the publishing company develops a relationship with the artist which can last for many years.

—Mary Cox

This illustration by Elizabeth Sayles appears in Dribbles, a picture book written by Connie Heckert and published by Clarion Books. Says Art Director Anne Diebel, "Sayles comes in with sketches that are beautifully composed and thought out. And her execution is nearly flawless."

in fiction and nonfiction picture books for children ages infant-8 years, and nonfiction books for children ages 8-12 years. At this time we are not publishing any fiction for young adult readers, but we will occasionally look at projects for this age group that are particularly relevant to our publishing program."

CLARION BOOKS, 215 Park Ave. S., New York NY 10003. (212)420-5800. Houghton Mifflin Company. Book publisher. Editor and Publisher: Dorothy Briley. Art Director: Anne Diebel. Publishes 20 picture books/year; 7 young reader titles/year; 14 middle reader titles/year; 4 young adult titles/year. 10% of books by first-time authors; 15% of books from agented writers.
Fiction: All levels: adventure, animal, contemporary, fantasy, folktales, history, humor, multicultural, nature/environment, science fiction, sports, family stories. Average word length: picture books—50-1,000; young readers—1,000-2,500; middle readers—10,000-30,000; young adults—20,000-30,000.
Nonfiction: All levels: animal, biography, concept, geography, history, multicultural, nature/environment, science, social issues. Average word length: picture books—750-1,000; young readers—1,000-2,500; middle readers—10,000-30,000.
How to Contact/Writers: Fiction: Send complete ms. Nonfiction: Query. Reports on queries in 1 month; mss in 2-3 months. Publishes a book 18 months after acceptance. Will consider simultaneous submissions.
Illustration: Works with 30 illustrators/year. Will review ms/illustration packages. Will review artwork for future assignments.
How to Contact/Illustrators: Ms/illustration packages: "Query first." Illustrations only: query with samples. Reports on art samples only if interested. Original artwork returned at job's completion.
Terms: Pays in royalties of 10% based on retail price, shared 50/50 by author and illustrator. Offers advance (average amount: $2,500-5,000). Sends galleys to authors; dummies to illustrators. Book catalog, ms/artist's guidelines free on request with 8×10 SASE.

CLOVERDALE PRESS, 109 W. 17th St., New York NY 10011. (212)727-3370. Fax: (212)727-3381. Independent book producer/packager. Editorial Contact: Marian Vaarn. 50% of books by first-time authors; 10% of books from agented writers.
Fiction: Average word length: young adult/teens—30,000. Produces Sweet Dreams young adult romances for Bantam Books.
Nonfiction: Middle readers, young adult: biography, cookbooks, education, financial, how-to, sports, true crimes. Produced Great Lives series (middle readers, biography); *Designed for Living* (cookbook); *Free and Almost Free Things for Teachers* (education); *Market Movers* (financial).
How to Contact/Writers: Fiction/nonfiction: "Needs change constantly." Query first or request ms guidelines with #10 SAE and 1 first-class stamp. Reports on queries in 2-4 weeks. Publishing time for a book "varies according to publisher—usually about 1 year."
Terms: Usually purchases outright; payment varies. Illustrators are paid by the project.

COBBLEHILL BOOKS, 375 Hudson St., New York NY 10014. (212)366-2000. Affiliate of Dutton Children's Books, a division of Penguin Books USA Inc. Book publisher. Editorial Director: Joe Ann Daly. Executive Editor: Rosanne Lauer. Publishes 6 picture books/year; 14 young reader titles/year; 9 middle reader titles/year; 5 young adult titles/year.
Fiction: Picture books, young readers: adventure, animal, contemporary, easy-to-read, sports, suspense/mystery. Middle readers: adventure, contemporary, problem novels, sports, suspense/mystery. Young adults: adventure, suspense/mystery.

Nonfiction: Picture books, young readers: animal, nature/environment, sports. Middle readers: nature/environment.

How to Contact/Writers: Fiction/nonfiction: Query. Will consider simultaneous submissions "if we are informed about them."

How to Contact/Illustrators: Illustrations only: Send samples to keep on file, no original artwork. Original artwork returned at job's completion.

Terms: Pays authors in royalties. Illustrators paid royalties or a flat fee. Book catalog for 8½×11 SAE and 2 first-class stamps; ms guidelines for #10 SASE.

CONCORDIA PUBLISHING HOUSE, 3558 S. Jefferson Ave., St. Louis MO 63118. (314)268-1000. Book publisher. Family and Children's Resources Editor: Ruth Geisler. Art Director: Ed Luhmann. "Concordia Publishing House publishes a number of quality children's books each year. Most are fiction, with some nonfiction, based on a religious subject."

Fiction/Nonfiction: "Reader interest ranges from picture books to young adults. All books must contain explicit Christian content." Recently published *Little Visits on the Go*, by Mary Manz Simon (family devotional book and audio tape); *The Biggest Bully in Brookdale*, by Carol Gormon (first title in The Tree House Kids series, grades 2-3, first chapter books); *God Loves Me — So What*, by Guy Doud (preteen and teen, Christian living).

How to Contact/Writers: Fiction: Query. Submit complete manuscript (picture books); submit outline/synopsis and sample chapters (novel-length). Reports on queries in 1 month; mss in 2 months. Publishes a book 1 year after acceptance. Will consider simultaneous submissions.

Illustration: Will review artwork for future assignments. Contact Ed Luhmann, art director.

How to Contact/Illustrators: Illustrations only: Query with samples.

Terms: Pays authors in royalties based on retail price or outright purchase (minimum $500). Sends galleys to author. Manuscript guidelines for 1 first-class stamp and a #10 envelope.

Tips: "Do not send finished artwork with the manuscript. If sketches will help in the presentation of the manuscript, they may be sent. If stories are taken from the Bible, they should follow the Biblical account closely. Liberties should not be taken in fantasizing Biblical stories."

COTEAU BOOKS LTD., 401-2206 Dewdney Ave., Regina Sasketchewan, S4R 1H3 Canada. (306)777-0170. Thunder Creek Publishing Co-op Ltd. Book publisher. Managing Editor: Shelley Sopher. Publishes 1 picture book/year, 9-11 books/year. 30% of books by first-time authors.

Fiction: Picture books, young readers: contemporary, folktales, multicultural. "No didactic, message pieces, nothing religious, no fantasy (especially historical fantasy)." Average word length: picture books — 500. Published *The Potter*, by Jacolyn Caton/Stephen McCallum (ages 3-8, picture book).

How to Contact/Writers: Fiction: Submit complete ms. Reports on queries in 1 month; mss in 4 months. Publishes a book 1-2 years after acceptance. Coteau Books publishes Canadian writers only; mss from the US are returned unopened. In 1993-94 only children's writers from the Canadian Prairies will be considered.

Always include a self-addressed stamped envelope (SASE) or a self-addressed envelope (SAE) and International Reply Coupons (IRCs) with submissions.

Illustration: Works with 1 illustrator/year. Will review ms/illustration packages. Will review artwork for possible future assignments.

How to Contact/Illustrators: Ms/illustration packages: Send "roughs." Illustrations only: Send nonreturnable samples. Reports only if interested. Original artwork returned at job's completion. Only Canadian illustrators are used.

Terms: Pays authors in royalties of 5-10% based on retail price. Other method of payment: "signing bonus." Pays illustrators by the project (range: $500-2,000) or royalty of 5% maximum based on retail price. Sends galleys to authors; dummies to illustrators. Book catalog free on request with 9×12 SASE (IRC).

COUNCIL FOR INDIAN EDUCATION, Box 31215, Billings MT 59107. (406)252-7451. Book publisher. Estab. 1968. Editor: Hap Gilliland. Publishes 1 picture book/year; 1 young reader title/year; 3 middle reader titles/year; 1 young adult title/year. 75% of books by first-time authors.

Fiction: Picture books, young readers, middle readers: adventure, anthology, animal, contemporary, folktales, history, nature/environment, poetry, sports, suspense/mystery. Young adults: adventure, anthology, animal, contemporary, folktales, health-related, nature/environment, poetry, romance, sports. All must relate to Native American life and culture, past and present. Does not want to see "sex, vulgarity or anything not related to American Indian life and culture."

Nonfiction: Picture books, young readers: animal, biography, history, hobbies, nature/environment, sports. Middle readers, young adults: animal, biography, careers, health, history, hobbies, music/dance, nature/environment, sports. All of above must be related to American Indian life and culture, past and present.

How to Contact/Writers: Fiction/nonfiction: Submit outline/synopsis and sample chapters, or submit complete ms. Reports on queries in 2 months; mss in 6 months. "We accept 5% of the manuscripts received. Those with potential must be evaluated by all the members of our Indian Editorial Board, who make the final selection. This board makes sure the material is true to the Indian way of life and is the kind of material they want their children to read." Publishes a book 1 year after acceptance. Will consider simultaneous submissions. "We do not read manuscripts between June 1 and October 1 each year."

Illustration: "It is doubtful we will need new artists in the next year." Editorial will review ms/illustration packages. "Black & white artwork only."

How to Contact/Illustrators: Ms/illustration packages: Send samples with ms. Illustrations only: Query with samples. Reports on art samples in 3 months "when we report back to author on ms." Original artwork returned at job's completion "if requested."

Terms: Pays authors in royalties of 10% based on wholesale price or buys ms outright for "1½¢ per word." Additional payment for ms/illustration packages "sometimes." Factors used to determine payment for ms/illustration package include "number of illustrations used." Sends galleys to authors. Book catalog/manuscript guidelines available for SASE.

Tips: "For our publications, write about one specific tribe or group and be sure actions portrayed are culturally correct for the group and time period portrayed. What kind of material can we use? These are our preferences, in the order listed: Contemporary Indian Life—exciting stories that could happen to Indian children now. (Be sure the children act like present-day Indians, not like some other culture.) Indians of the old days—authentically portrayed. Be specific about who, where and when. How-to—Indian arts, crafts, and activities. Biography—Indians past and present. History and culture—factual material of high interest only. If you are Indian, express your ideas and ideals. Folk stories and legends—high interest expressing Indian ideas. Name the specific tribe. Poetry—possibly—if it expresses real Indian ideals. Instructional material and information for teachers of Indian children."

CRESTWOOD HOUSE, 866 Third Ave,. New York NY 10022. (212)702-2168. Macmillan Children's Book Group. Book publisher. Associate Editor: Barbie Heit Schwaeber. Publishes 70 middle readers/year. 10% of books by first-time authors; 2% of books from agented authors. Publishes "hi-lo nonfiction for reluctant readers."
Nonfiction: Middle readers: biography, careers, hi-lo, history, multicultural, nature/environment, sports. "We publish only in series. Not interested in single titles." Average word length: middle readers—5,500. Recently published *Sports Immortals: Billie Jean King*; *Cool Classics: Lamborghini*; *The Armed Forces: The Navy and You*; *Cool Classics: Porsche*; *Africa Today: Africa's Struggle to Survive*.
How to Contact/Writers: Nonfiction: Query. Submit outline/synopsis. Reports on queries in 1 month. Publishes a book 1-1½ years after acceptance. Will consider simultaneous submissions.
Illustration: Works with 2 illustrators/year.
Terms: Work purchased outright (range: $1,000-1,500). Sends galleys to authors. Book catalog available for 9×12 SASE. Ms guidelines not available.

*CROCODILE BOOKS, USA, 99 Seventh Ave., Brooklyn NY 11215. (718)797-4292. Imprint of Interlink Publishing Group, Inc. Book publisher. Vice President: Ruth Moushabeck. Publishes 16 picture books/year. 25% of books by first-time authors. *No unsolicited manuscripts accepted*.
Fiction: Picture books: animal, contemporary, history, spy/mystery/adventure.
Nonfiction: Picture book: history, nature/environment.
Terms: Pays authors in royalties. Sends galleys to author; dummies to illustrator.

CROSSWAY BOOKS, Good News Publishers, 1300 Crescent, Wheaton IL 60187. (708)682-4300. Fax: (708)682-4785. Book Publisher. Editorial Director: Leonard Goss. Publishes 1-2 picture books/year; 6-10 young readers/year; 6 middle readers/year; 5-10 young adult titles/year. "Crossway Books is committed to publishing books that bring Biblical reality to readers and that examine crucial issues through a Christian world view."
Fiction: Picture books: religion. Young readers: adventure, animal, contemporary, fantasy, history, humor, religion. Middle readers: adventure, animal, contemporary, fantasy, history, humor, religion, science fiction, suspense/mystery, supernatural, Christian realism. Young adults: contemporary, fantasy, history, humor, religion, science fiction, suspense/mystery, supernatural, Christian realism. Does not want to see horror novels, romance or prophecy novels. Recently published *Tell Me the Secrets*, by Max Lucado, illustrated by Ron DiCiann.
Nonfiction: Middle readers, young adults: history, reference, religion, social issues. Does not want to see celebrity books, popular trend books, popular experience books or books attempting cultural synthesis.
How to Contact/Writers: Fiction/nonfiction: Submit outline/synopsis. Reports on queries/mss in 3-6 weeks. Publishes a book 6-10 months after acceptance. Will consider simultaneous submissions or electronic submissions via disk or modem.
Illustration: Works with 5 illustrators/year. Will review ms/illustration packages. Will review artwork for future assignments.
How to Contact/Illustrators: Ms/illustration packages: Query. Illustrations only: Query with samples; provide résumé, promo sheet and client list.

The asterisk before a listing indicates the listing is new in this edition.

Terms: Pays authors royalty of 14% based on net sales. Pays illustrators by the project. Sends galleys to authors; dummies to illustrators. Book catalog available; ms and art guidelines available for SASE.

CROWN PUBLISHERS (CROWN BOOKS FOR CHILDREN), 201 E. 50th St., New York NY 10022. (212)940-7742. Imprint of Random House, Inc. Book publisher. Editor-in-Chief: Simon Boughton. Publishes 20 picture books/year; 10 nonfiction titles/year. 2% of books by first-time authors; 70% of books from agented writers.
Fiction: Picture books: animal, humor, nature/environment. Young readers: history, nature/environment. Does not want to see fantasy, science fiction, poetry. Average word length: picture books—750. Published: *The Giraffe That Walked to Paris*, by Nancy Milton; *Ruby Mae Has Something to Say*, by David Small (4-8 years, picture books).
Nonfiction: Picture books, young readers and middle readers: activity books, animal, biography, careers, health, history, hobbies, music/dance, nature/environment, religion, science, sports. Average word length: picture books—750-1,000; young readers—20,000; middle readers—50,000. Does not want to see ABCs. Published: *Chameleons*, by James Martin and Art Wolfe (4-8 years, picture book); *Children of the Dust Bowl*, by Jerry Stanley (9-14 years, middle reader).
How to Contact/Writers: Fiction/nonfiction: Submit complete manuscript. Reports on queries/mss in 3-4 months. Publishes book 2 years after acceptance. Will consider simultaneous submissions.
Illustration: Works with 20 illustrators/year. Will review ms/illustration packages. Will review work for future assignments. Contact: Isabel Warren-Lynch, Art Director. "Double-spaced, continuous manuscripts; do not supply page-by-page breaks. One or two photocopies of art are fine. *Do not send original art.* Dummies are acceptable."
How to Contact/Illustrators: Submit photocopies, portfolio or slides with SASE; provide business card and tearsheets. Reports on ms/art samples in 2 months. Artwork returned at job's completion.
Terms: Pays authors royalty based on retail price. Advance "varies greatly." Pays illustrators by the project or royalty. Sends galleys to authors; proofs to illustrators. Book catalog for 9×12 SAE and 4 first-class stamps. Ms guidelines for 4½×9½ SASE; art guidelines not available.

CRYSTAL RIVER PRESS, P.O. Box 1382, Healdsburg CA 95448. Book publisher. Editor-in-Chief: Thomas Watson. Managing Editor: Ed Popp. Publishes 8-15 picture books/year; approximately 8 young readers/year; 6-10 middle readers/year; 5-9 young adult titles/year. 85% of books by first-time authors and illustrators; 30% of books from agented authors.
Fiction: Picture books, young readers, middle readers, young adults: adventure, animal, anthology, contemporary, fantasy, folktales, health, hi-lo, history, humor, multicultural, nature/environment, problem novels, science fiction, special needs, sports, suspense/mystery. Does not want conceptual material. Average word length: picture books—500-1,200; young readers—800-2,000; middle readers—800-4,000; young adults 40,000-80,000. Recently published: *Why Is Franky Sooooooo Cranky?*, written and illustrated by Joni Dowling (grades 3-5, soft cover); *Scruffy's Walk*, by Rebecca Chappell, illustrated by Phyllis Rapp (grades 1-3, hard and soft cover).
Nonfiction: Picture books, young readers, middle readers, young adults: activity books, animal, arts/crafts, biography, careers, cooking, geography, health, hi-lo, history, hobbies, how-to, multicultural, music/dance, nature/environment, reference, science, social issues, special needs, sports. Wants themes to be well researched. "Try to remember, we are dealing with young minds." Average word length: picture books: 300-500; young readers: 700-2,000; middle readers: 2,000-5,000. Recently published: *Jenny's Locket*, by Christine Simpson, illustrated by Heather Daylight, (grades 5-9, softcover); *How A Picture Is Created*, written and illustrated by Steve Swentson, (grades 4-9, how-to soft cover).

How to Contact/Writers: Fiction: Query; submit complete ms if short; submit outline/synopsis and 3 sample chapters. Nonfiction: Query; submit complete ms; submit outline/synopsis. Reports on queries in 3 weeks; mss in 6-8 weeks. Will consider simultaneous submissions, electronic submissions via disk (Mac) and previously published work.
Illustration: Works with 35 illustrators/year. Will review ms/illustration package. Will review artwork for future assignment.
How to Contact/Illustrators: Ms/illustration packages: Query; submit ms with dummy. Illustrations only: Query with samples; provide resume; slides. Samples returned with SASE; samples filed. Original artwork returned at job's completion.
Photography: Purchases photos from freelancers. Buys stock and assigns work. Uses photos of people, the environment. Model/property releases required; captions required. Uses matte/glossy color and b&w prints, 2¼ × 2¼ and 8 × 10 transparencies. Photographers should submit cover letter, resume, color/b&w promo piece.
Terms: Pays authors royalty of 5-15% based on retail price of first printing. Pays illustrators royalty of 7-9% based on retail price. Photographers paid royalty of 5-15% based on retail price. Sends galleys to authors; dummies to illustrators. Writers and illustrators guidelines available for SASE. Book catalog available for SASE.
Tips: Sees popularity of audio books growing.

CSS PUBLISHING, 628 S. Main St., Lima OH 45804. (419)227-1818. Book publisher. Editor: Fred Steiner. Publishes books with religious themes.
Fiction: Picture books, young readers, middle readers, young adults: religion. Needs children's sermons (object lesson) for Sunday morning worship services; dramas for Advent, Christmas or Epiphany involving children for church services; activity and craft ideas for Sunday school or mid-week services for children (particularly pre-school and first and second grade). Does not want to see secular picture books. Recently published *That Seeing, They May Believe*, by Kenneth Mortonson (lessons for adults to present during worship services to pre-schoolers-third graders); *What Shall We Do With This Baby?*, by Jan Spence (Christmas eve worship service involving youngsters from newborn babies-high school youth); *Miracle in the Bethlehem Inn*, by Mary Lou Warstler (Advent or Christmas drama involving pre-schoolers-high school youth and adults).
Nonfiction: Picture books, young readers, middle readers, young adults: religion. Needs children's sermons (object lesson) for Sunday morning workship services; dramas for Advent, Christmas or Epiphany involving children for church services; activity and craft ideas for Sunday school or mid-week services for children (particularly pre-school and first and second grade). Does not want to see secular picture books. Recently published *Mustard Seeds*, by Ellen Humbert (activity/bulletins for pre-schoolers-first graders to use during church); *This Is The King*, by Cynthia Cowen.
How to Contact/Writers: Reports on queries in 1 week; mss in 1-6 months. Publishes a book 9 months after acceptance. Will consider simultaneous submissions.
Tips: "We are seeking material for use by clergy, Christian education directors and Sunday school teachers for mainline Protestant churches. Our market is mainline Protestant clergy."

MAY DAVENPORT, PUBLISHERS, 26313 Purissima Rd., Los Altos Hills CA 94022. (415)948-6499. Book publisher. Independent book producer/packager. Estab. 1976. Editor: May Davenport. Publishes 1-2 picture books/year; 2-3 young adult titles/year. 99% of books by first-time authors. Seeks books with literary merit. "We are overstocked with picture book/elementary reading material."
Fiction: Young adults: contemporary, history, humor, suspense/mystery. Does not want to see picture books unless the stories can be made into coloring books and are not boring for adults to read. Average word length: 40,000-60,000. Recently published *The Candy Heart*, by Carol deWolf (grades 1-2, paper); *Tug of War*, by Barbara A. Scott (grades 8-12, paper); *A Fine Line*, by Constance D. Casserly (grades 8-12, paper).

Nonfiction: Activity books to read alone or aloud, or to color.
How to Contact/Writers: Fiction: Query. Reports on queries in 1-2 weeks; mss in 2-4 weeks. "We do not answer queries or manuscripts which do not have SASE attached." Publishes a book 6-12 months after acceptance.
Illustration: Works with 2-3 illustrators/year. Will review ms/illustration packages. Will review artwork for future assignments.
How to Contact/Illustrators: Illustrations only: "Send samples for our files for future reference."
Terms: Pays authors in royalties of 15% based on retail price. Pays "by mutual agreement, no advances." Pays illustrators by the project. Book listing, ms guidelines free on request with SASE.
Tips: Writers: "Make readers laugh with your imaginative words. However, if you do not have a humorous literary talent, forget it. If you have a literary talent, avoid using alliterations so prevalent in comic books. Just describe action, without grunts."

DAVIS PUBLICATIONS, INC., 50 Portland St., Worcester MA 01608. (508)754-7201. Fax: (508)753-3834. Book publisher. Acquisitions Editor: Claire M. Golding. Publishes 10 titles total/year. 30% of books by first-time authors. "We publish books for the art education market (elementary through high school), both technique-oriented and art appreciation resource books and textbooks."
Nonfiction: Middle readers, young adults: Activity books about art and art-related textbooks; multicultural books detailing the arts of other cultures (Hispanic, Native American, African-American, Asian); textbooks. Recently published *Children and Painting*, by Cathy Weisman Topal; *Basic Printmaking Techniques*, by Bernard Toale; *Exceptional Children, Exceptional Art*, by David Henley; *Design and Drawing*, by Richard L. Shadrin; and *Native American Arts & Cultures*, by Anne D'Alleva.
How to Contact/Writers: Submit outline/synopsis and 1 sample chapter. Reports on queries in 1 month; mss in 2 months. Publishes a book 1 year after acceptance. Will consider simultaneous submissions and electronic submissions via disk.
Illustration: Works with 2 illustrators/year. "We use a combination of photos and line drawings" (200-300/nonfiction title). Will review ms/illustration packages. Will review artwork for future assignments.
How to Contact/Illustrators: Query with samples. Reports in 1 month.
Photography: "Rarely" purchases photos from freelancers. Contact: Holly Hanson. "Usually need photos of particular artists, artworks or art forms." Model/property releases required; captions required. Publishes photo concept books. Uses 5 × 7 and 8 × 10 glossy, b&w prints and 4 × 5 and 8 × 10 transparencies.
Terms: Pays authors royalties of 10-12½% based on wholesale price. Pays illustrators by the project (range $50-300). Sends galleys to authors. Book catalog available for SASE; ms guidelines available for SASE.
Tips: Seeking "nonfiction titles on art techniques, media and history/appreciation. We do not publish children's story/picture books; rather, we publish educational books for use by art teachers, art students and amateur artists."

DAWN PUBLICATIONS, 14618 Tyler Foote, Nevada City CA 95959. (916)292-3482. Fax: (916)292-4258. Book publisher. Publisher: Bob Rinzler. Publishes works with holistic themes dealing with nature, parenting and health issues.
Fiction: All levels: Animal, folktales, health, nature/environment.
Nonfiction: All levels: animal, health, nature/environment, self-help, social issues, parenting, values and morals. Recently published *A Walk in the Rainforest*, by Kristin Pratt; *I Celebrate Nature*, by Diane Iversen.
How to Contact/Writers: Fiction/nonfiction: Query; submit complete ms; submit outline/synopsis and sample chapters. Reports on queries/mss in 3 weeks. Publishes a book

1 year after acceptance. Will consider simultaneous submissions and previously published work.
Illustration: Works with 3 illustrators/year. Will review ms/illustration packages. Will review artwork for future assignments.
How to Contact/Illustrators: Ms/illustration packages: Query; submit complete package; submit chapters of ms. Illustrations only: Query with samples, résumé.
Terms: Pays authors royalty based on wholesale price. Offers advance. Pays illustrators by the project or royalties based on wholesale price. Sends galleys to authors; dummies to illustrators. Book catalog available for 6×9 SASE.

T.S. DENISON CO. INC., 9601 Newton Ave. S., Minneapolis MN 55431. Fax: (612)888-9641. Editor: Baxter Brings. 25% of books by first-time authors. Publishes teacher resource/activity books. "We mostly publish nonfiction."
Fiction: Young readers, middle readers: history, multicultural, nature/environment, poetry. "Anything that accompanies student activities." Doesn't want "fiction stories without activities for the classroom."
Nonfiction: Young readers, middle readers: activity books, animal, arts/crafts, careers, history, multicultural, music/dance, nature/environment, reference, science, social issues, textbooks. Average word length: picture books—96 pages; middle readers—150 pages. Published *Let's Meet Famous Composers*, by Harriet Kinghorn, illustrated by Margo De Paulis (grades 3-6, teacher resource); *Toddler Calendar*, by Elaine Commius, art by Anita Nelson (Pre-K, teacher resource); *FairyTale Mask*, by Gwen Rives Jones, art by Darcy Myers (grades 1-3, teacher resource).
How to Contact/Writers: Fiction/nonfiction: Query; submit complete ms; submit outline/synopsis and 2 sample chapters. Reports on queries/mss in 2 months. Publishes a book 9 months after acceptance. Will consider simultaneous submissions and electronic submissions via disk or modem.
Illustration: Works with 15 illustrators/year. Will review artwork for future assignments.
How to Contact/Illustrators: Illustrations only: Query with samples; arrange a personal interview to show portfolio. Reports in 1 month. Original artwork not returned at job's completion.
Terms: Pays authors royalty of 4-8% based on retail price (direct mail). Work purchased outright (range: $300-1,000). Pays illustrators by the project (range: $300-500 for covers; $25 for b&w; $15-30/hour for inside illustration). Book catalog available for 9×12 SAE and 3 first-class stamps; ms guidelines available for SASE.

*DIAL BOOKS FOR YOUNG READERS, Penguin Books USA Inc., 375 Hudson St., New York NY 10014. (212)366-2800. Editor-in-Chief: Phyllis J. Fogelman. Publishes 9 picture books/year; 10 young reader titles/year; 5 middle reader titles/year; 10 young adult titles/year.
Fiction: Picture books: adventure, animal, contemporary, fantasy, folktales, history, nature/environment, poetry, religion, science fiction, sports, suspense/mystery. Young readers: animal, contemporary, easy-to-read, fantasy, folktales, history, nature/environment, poetry, science fiction, sports, mystery/adventure. Middle readers, young adults: animal, contemporary, fantasy, folktales, history, health-related, nature/environment, poetry, problem novels, religion, science fiction, sports, spy/mystery/adventure. Recently published *Brother Eagle, Sister Sky*, illustrated by Susan Jeffers (all ages, picture book); *Amazing Grace*, by Mary Hoffman (ages 4-8, picture book); and *Saul Looks Back in Wonder*, by Tom Feelings, Maya Angelou, et al (ages 7 and up, poetry picture book.)
Nonfiction: Uses very little nonfiction but will consider submissions of outstanding artistic and literary merit. Picture books: animal, biography, history, nature/environment, sports. Young readers: activity books, animal, biography, history, nature/environment, religion, sports. Middle readers: animal, biography, careers, health, history, na-

INSIDER REPORT

Viewing Children's Writing as an Art Form

Rosemary Wells

To create quality humorous stories and illustrations for children, you must take the work very seriously, says Rosemary Wells. As author, and often illustrator, of 50 children's books (at last count), Wells considers children's writing an art form, much like poetry.

"A good children's book has to stand up to 500 readings aloud," she says. "The only writers who can do it well are the ones with a 'voice.' You also need a sure knowledge of what children are about. You don't necessarily have to have kids, but you have to be very close to your own childhood. There are a lot of people who try it, who love children and children's books, but it falls apart because they don't have these qualities."

Wells urges writers to avoid turning stories into vehicles for causes or moral lessons. "One mistake a writer can make is to try to teach a lesson or write a story for a cause or an idea," she says. "Write about characters and the rest will follow. Otherwise, you run the risk of having the cause *become* your character. If my books have certain points to them, that's because they come along with the story, but what I try to do most of all is to give humor and character."

Indeed, humor and character thrive in Wells's best-known series of books about bunny siblings Max and Ruby. In her most recent Max and Ruby title, *Max and Ruby's First Greek Myth*, published by Dial Books for Young Readers, the ever-instructive Ruby tries to teach Max a lesson about snooping by sharing the story (her own version, of course) of Pandora's box.

Wells has more than a dozen books featuring these characters, who were inspired by her own children. "When I wrote the first set of board books, my oldest daughter was five and my little one was nine months," she explains. "This was just what was going on. It really is based on their relationship: the older sibling trying to control everything, trying to be a kind of sub-parent. I like to write things the way they are, because the way they are is very, very funny."

She combines this realistic writing voice with a lighthearted illustration style. Good illustrators, Wells says, "need to know what appeals to children. You need to be able to draw children and draw animals, and you have to draw them in a way that is extremely appealing and warm and real." Some of the illustrations from her three Voyage to the Bunny Planet books, about a utopia headed by a bunny queen, are included in *The Very Best of Children's Book Illustration*, compiled by the Society of Illustrators.

For Wells, the writing and illustrating process differs from book to book; some start primarily as pictures and others as text. She dismisses the notion of a writer "making up" stories. "I don't make them up; they come to me," she says. "I have very little awareness of my own participation. It may sound very mysterious, but that's the way it is for me. I'm a writer. It's my job to have ideas."

Once she has an idea, she nurtures it carefully before committing it to paper. "I lie there in the darkness from five to six in the morning and think about the book. For nights after that I will think about how to solve problems and will rewrite in my head. Then I go to my computer and type out the story."

In addition to preschool board books, Wells has created books for elementary school-age students and young adults. It's a wide range for a writer to cover, but Wells says she subscribes to the idea that "a change is as good as a rest. When you do a series of board books, for example, it's nice to change. Working on three different kinds of books at once allows me to use different muscles."

Wells also enjoys just writing. "I love collaborating," she says. "My illustration is funny, but when I do a book that's not funny, I need someone else to illustrate it. I have added to my range by writing for other artists. I have three books at Dial right now being illustrated by other people."

While juggling a schedule that includes a picture book, another Max and Ruby book, and a novel about the Civil War, Wells also participates in book readings and signings. "Writers perform without an audience on a daily basis," she says. "Reading gives me an audience. For commercial purposes it's necessary for authors to get out. But it's also a wonderful way to see America. I love meeting people. I think I meet the best Americans because I meet the ones who care enough about their kids to bring them out to buy books and meet authors."

—Glenda Tennant Neff

Meet Max, the younger bunny in Rosemary Wells's popular series of books about bunny siblings named Max and Ruby. Wells began writing the series after listening to the relationship between her own children. The older sibling was trying to be a "sub-parent" to the younger one, she says. The situation provided not only humor but inspiration. In this illustration, also created by Wells, Max eyes a new shirt.

© 1991 Rosemary Wells, from *Max's Dragon Shirt*, published by Dial Books

ture/environment, religion, sports. Young adults: animal, biography, careers, health, history, hobbies, music/dance, nature/environment, religion, sports. Published *A Flower Grows*, by Ken Robbins (ages 4-8, picture book); *Extraordinay Eyes*, by Sandra Sinclair (middle readers).

How to Contact/Writers: Fiction: Query, submit outline/synopsis and sample chapters for longer work, submit complete ms for short material.

Illustration: Editorial will review ms/illustration packages. Prefers to use own artists for mss submitted by authors. Will review work for possible future assignments.

How to Contact/Illustrators: Ms/illustration packages: Query first or submit 1 piece of final color art and sketches. Illustrations only: Query with samples; submit portfolio for review; arrange a personal interview to show portfolio; provide tearsheets to be kept on file.

Photography: Contact: Toby Sherry. Model/property releases required with submissions. Publishes photo essays. Uses b&w, glossy prints and 35mm, 2¼×2¼, 4×5 transparencies. Photographers should submit portfolio for review; arrange a personal interview to show portfolio; provide tearsheets to be kept on file.

Terms: Pays authors and illustrators in royalties based on retail price. Average advance payment "varies." Ms guidelines for SASE.

DILLON PRESS, INC., 866 Third Ave., New York NY 10022. (212)702-7839. Imprint of Macmillan Children's Book Group. Book publisher. Editor: Joyce Stanton. Publishes 40 middle readers/year. 10% of books by first-time authors; 2% of books from agented authors.

Nonfiction: Animal, biography, geography, history, multicultural, nature/environment, science, social issues. Average word length: 5,000. Published *Places in American History: The Alamo*; *People in Focus: Malcolm X*; *Ecology Watch: Polar Lands*.

How to Contact/Writers: Nonfiction: Query. Submit outline/synopsis and 2 sample chapters. Reports on queries in 2 months. Publishes a book 1 year after acceptance.

Terms: Pays authors royalty of up to 5% based on retail price; or work purchased outright (range: $1,000-1,500). Offers advances (average amount: $1,000). Sends galleys to authors. Book catalog available for 9×12 SASE; ms guidelines not available.

*■DIMI PRESS, 3820 Oak Hollow Lane, SE, Salem OR 97302-4774. (503)364-7698. Fax: (503)364-9727. Book publisher. "For children's books, we only do subsidy publishing. We have not published any children's books, but will."

Fiction: Will consider any children's fiction category.

Nonfiction: Will consider any children's nonfiction category.

How to Contact/Writers: Fiction/nonfiction: Submit outline/synopsis and 1 sample chapter. Reports on queries in 1 month; mss in 2 months. Publishes a book 3-9 months after acceptance.

Illustration: Will review ms/illustration packages. Contact: Dick Lutz, president. Will review artwork for future assignments.

How to Contact/Illustrators: Ms/illustration packages: Submit ms with 3 pieces of final art. Illustrations only: Query with samples, résumé. Reports only if interested. Cannot return samples. Original artwork returned at job's completion.

Terms: Pays illustrators/photographers by the project. Sends galleys to authors; dummies to illustrators. Book catalog available for #10 SAE and 1 first-class stamp.

Refer to the Business of Children's Writing & Illustrating for up-to-date marketing, tax and legal information.

■**DISCOVERY ENTERPRISES, LTD.**, 134 Middle St., Lowell MA 01852. (508)459-1720. Fax: (508)937-5779. Book publisher and independent book producer/packager. Executive Director: JoAnne Weisman. Publishes 6 middle readers books/year. 40% of books by first-time authors; subsidy publishes 10%. Publishes all nonfiction—serious histories and biographies, 15,000-20,000 words for ages 12-adult. Needs pen & ink drawings for history series.

Nonfiction: Middle readers: biography, history, nature/environment, Third World countries. Young adults: biography, history. "No sports figures, religious leaders, pop stars or current entertainers for biographies." Average word length: middle readers 15,000-20,000; young adults 15,000-20,000. Recently published *J. Robert Oppenheimer and the Birth of the Atomic Age*, by Kenneth M. Deitch and Joseph Yeamans (ages 12-adult, biography); *Marjory Stoneman Douglas: Guardian of the Everglades*, by Kem Knapp Sawyer, illustrated by Leslie Carow (ages 10-adult, biography); *Pride and Promise: The Harlem Renaissance*, by Kathryn Cryan-Hicks (ages 12-adult, historical); *Homer in the Classroom: A New Approach to Critical Thinking*, by Prof. Fred Stopsky (guide to teaching methods for teachers of grades 2-12); *Edna Hibel: Her Life and Her Art*, by Olga Cossi (ages 10-adult, biography).

How to Contact/Writers: Nonfiction: Query. Submit outline/synopsis and 3 sample chapters. Reports on queries in 1-2 weeks; reports on mss in 3 months. Publishes a book 6 months after acceptance. Will consider simultaneous submissions.

Illustration: Works with 6-8 illustrators/year. Will review ms/illustration packages after query only. Will review artwork for future assignments. Contact: JoAnne Weisman, executive director. "No preference in medium or style, but artist must be able to do portraits, as these are biographies."

How to Contact/Illustrators: Ms/illustration packages: Submit 2-3 chapters of ms with copies of 4-6 pieces of final art. Send samples of artwork—color copies OK with text. Illustrations only: Query with samples; provide résumé, promotional literature and tearsheets to be kept on file. Reports in 4-6 weeks. Original artwork returned at job's completion "but not for 2 years."

Photography: Photographers should contact JoAnne Weisman, executive director. Uses all types of photos. Model/property releases required; captions required. Interested in stock photos. Uses 35mm, 2¼×2¼ and 4×5 transparencies. Photographers should query with samples; provide resume, business card, promotional literature and tearsheets to be kept on file.

Terms: Pays authors royalty of 5-10% based on wholesale price. Offers $1,000 advance on book assignments only. Pays illustrators by the project (range: $600-1,500) or royalty of 5-10% based on wholesale price. Photographers paid per photo (range: $25-400). Sends galleys to authors; dummies to illustrators. Book catalog available for #10 SASE.

Tips: Wants "neat, clean artwork, presented professionally." For writers, good cover letter, outline and sample chapters necessary. "Watch for grammatical errors. I prefer separate submissions from artists and authors. Carefully research and accurately illustrate art for histories and biographies in any medium. We are looking for biographies of women in sciences/computers; curriculum guides regarding Turn of the Century for grades 5-8; biography of journalist or newspaper publisher (15,000-20,000 words); historical plays." Sees trend toward more nonfiction for use in classrooms to supplement or replace textbooks, as well as more emphasis on multi-racial books, women's history, peace, etc.

The solid block before a listing indicates the market subsidy publishes manuscripts.

DISTINCTIVE PUBLISHING CORP., P.O. Box 17868, Plantation FL 33318-7868. (305)975-2413. Fax: (305)972-3949. Book publisher. Independent book producer/packager. Editor: F. Knauf. Publishes 1-2 books/year. 95% of books by first-time authors.
Fiction: Picture books; adventure, animal, history, nature/environment. Young readers: adventure, animal, history, humor, multicultural, nature/environment, suspense/mystery. "We will consider all submissions." Published *Ships of Children*, by Richard Taylor (middle-young adult, adventure).
Nonfiction: Picture book, young readers: animal, biography, careers, geography, history, social issues. "As with fiction we will consider all submissions."
How to Contact/Writers: Nonfiction: Submit complete ms. Reports on queries in 2-4 weeks; mss in 1-3 months. Publishes book 6-12 months after acceptance. Will consider simultaneous submissions and previously published work.
Illustration: Will review ms/illustration packages.
How to Contact/Illustrators: Ms/illustration packages: Submit complete package. Reports in 1 month. Original artwork is returned at job's completion.
Photography: Contact: Alan Erdlee, publisher. Type of photos used depends on project. Model/property release required; captions required. Interested in stock photos. Publishes photo concept books. Uses 4×6 glossy color prints, 2¼×2¼ transparencies. Photographer should query with samples; query with resume of credits; provide résumé, business card, tearsheets to be kept on file.
Terms: Pays authors royalty based on wholesale and retail price or work purchased outright. "Each project is different." Offers advances. Pays illustrators by the project or royalty. Photographers are paid by the project or per photo. Sends galleys to author; dummies to illustrators. Book catalog available for 9×12 SASE.
Tips: Best chance of selling to this market is with adventure and educational mss.

DORLING KINDERSLEY, INC., 232 Madison Ave., New York NY 10016. (212)684-0404. Book publisher. Senior Editor, Children's Books: B. Alison Weir. Publishes 10 picture books/year. 50% of books by first-time authors; 50% of books from agented authors (fiction list only).
Fiction: Picture books: adventure, contemporary, folktales, history, multicultural, nature/environment. Multicultural needs include relationship stories/family stories. Does not want to see fiction with licensed characters. Average word length: picture books— 48 pages.
Nonfiction: Young readers: animal, biography (international only), hobbies, how-to, multicultural, music/dance, nature/environment, science. "We produce almost all nonfiction in-house." Does not want to see "manuscripts imitating books we've already published." Average length: young readers—32 pages. Recently published Look Closer series, Eyewitness Books and Eyewitness Explorers Guides.
How to Contact/Writers: Fiction/nonfiction: Submit agented ms. Reports on queries/ mss in 2 months. Publishes a book about 1½ years after acceptance. Will consider simultaneous submissions.
Illustration: Works with about 15 illustrators/year. Will review ms/illustration packages. Will review artwork for future assignments.
How to Contact/Illustrators: Submit ms with dummy. Illustrations only: Query with samples; provide promo sheet and tearsheets. Reports only if immediately interested. Otherwise samples go in file. Samples returned with SASE (if requested).
Photography: Purchases photos from freelancers. Contact: Dirk Kaufman, designer. Works on assignment only. Photographers should submit cover letter and résumé.
Terms: Pays author royalty based on retail price. Pays illustrators by the project or royalty. Pays photographers by the project. Sends galleys to authors; dummies to illustrators. Book catalog available for 9×12 SAE and 3 first-class stamps; ms guidelines available for SASE; artist's guidelines not available.

Tips: A writer has the best chance of selling well-written picture book stories that work internationally. Also, innovative manuscripts that combine fiction and nonfiction. "See our recently published book, *Yankee Doodle*, by Gary Chalk."

DUTTON CHILDREN'S BOOKS, 375 Hudson St., New York NY 10014. (212)366-2600. Penguin USA. Book publisher. Editor-in-Chief: Lucia Monfried. Art Associate: Carolyn Boschi. Publishes approximately 60 picture books/year; 4 young reader titles/year; 10 middle reader titles/year; 8 young adult titles/year. 10% of books by first-time authors.
Fiction: Picture books: adventure, animal, folktales, history, multicultural, nature/environment, poetry. Young readers: adventure, animal, contemporary, easy-to-read, fantasy, suspense/mystery. Middle readers: adventure, animal, contemporary, fantasy, history, multicultural, nature/environment, suspense/mystery. Young adults: adventure, animal, anthology, contemporary, fantasy, history, multicultural, nature/environment, poetry, science fiction, suspense/mystery. Recently published *The Fortune Teller*, by Lloyd Alexander (picture book); *Dark Heart*, by Betsy James (ages 10 and up, novel); *It Happened at Pickle Lake*, by Chrisel Kleitsch (ages 7-10, Speedster series for reluctant readers).
Nonfiction: Picture books: animal, history, multicultural, nature/environment. Young readers: animal, history, multicultural, nature/environment. Middle readers: animal, biography, history, multicultural, nature/environment. Young adults: animal, biography, history, multicultural, nature/environment, social issues. Recently published *Jack in the Pulpit*, by Jerome Wexler (ages 8 and up, photo essay); *Talking Peace*, by Jimmy Carter (young adult).
How to Contact/Writers: Query. Reports on queries in 1 month; mss in 3 months. Publishes a book 12-18 months after acceptance. Will consider simultaneous submissions.
Illustration: Works with 40-60 illustrators/year. Will review ms/illustration packages. Will review artwork for future assignments.
How to Contact/Illustrators: Ms/illustration packages: Query first. Illustrations only: Query with samples; send résumé, portfolio, slides—no original art please. Reports on art samples in 2 months. Original artwork returned at job's completion.
Photography: Purchases photos from freelancers. Assigns work. Wants "nature photography."
Terms: Pays authors royalties of 4-10% based on retail price. Book catalog, ms guidelines for SAE. Pays illustrators royalties of 2-10% based on retail price unless jacket illustration—then pays by flat fee. Photographers paid royalty per photo.
Tips: Writers: "We publish high-quality trade books and are interested in well-written manuscripts with fresh ideas and child appeal. Avoid topics that appear frequently. We have a complete publishing program. Though we publish mostly picture books, we are very interested in acquiring more novels for young, middle and young adult readers. In nonfiction, we are looking for history, general biography, science and photo essays for all age groups." Illustrators: "We would like to see samples and portfolios from potential illustrators of picture books (full color), young novels (b&w) and jacket artists (full color)." Foresee "even more multicultural publishing, plus more books published in both Spanish and English."

*EAKIN PRESS, P.O. Box 90159, Austin TX 78709-0159. (512)288-1771. Book publisher. Publishes 4 picture books/year; 2 young readers/year; 6 middle readers/year; 2 young adult titles/year. "We publish children's books about Texas-picture books for preschool, grades 1, 2 and 3; middle reader books 25-35,000 words, nonfiction for grades 4-7; young adult books for grades 7-12."
How to Contact/Writers: Fiction: Query. Reports on queries in 2 weeks; mss in 6 weeks. Will consider simultaneous submissions.

Melanie Hope Greenberg wrote and illustrated **My Father's Luncheonette** *as a nostalgic look back on her own childhood, as conveyed in this gouache and pen and ink illustration. The book, published by Dutton Children's Books, won an American Institute of Graphic Artists award for book illustration.*

Illustration: Works with 4 illustrators/year.
How to Contact/Illustrators: Ms/Illustration packages: Query. Samples returned with SASE. Originals not returned.

WM. B. EERDMANS PUBLISHING COMPANY, 255 Jefferson Ave. SE, Grand Rapids MI 49503. (616)459-4591. Book publisher. Children's Book Editor: Amy Eerdmans. Publishes 6 picture books/year; 4 young reader titles/year; 4 middle reader titles/year.
Fiction: All levels: fantasy, parables, problem novels, religion, retold Bible stories from a Christian perspective.
Nonfiction: All levels: biography, history, nature/environment, religion.
How to Contact/Writers: Fiction/nonfiction: Query; submit complete ms. Reports on queries in 1-2 weeks; mss in 4-6 weeks.
Illustration: Reviews ms/illustration packages. Will review illustrator's work for possible future assignments. Contact: Willem Mineur, art director.

How to Contact/Illustrators: Illustrations only: Submit résumé, slides or color photocopies. Reports on ms/art samples in 1 month. Original artwork returned at job's completion.
Terms: Pays authors in royalties of 5-10%. Pays in royalty for the author. The illustrator receives royalty or permission fee. Sends galleys to authors; dummies to illustrators. Book catalog free on request; ms and/or artist's guidelines free on request.
Tips: "We're looking for fiction and nonfiction that project a positive spiritual message and imply Christian values. We are also looking for material that will help children explore their faith. Accept all genres."

*ENSLOW PUBLISHERS INC., Box 777, Bloy St. & Ramsey Ave., Hillside NJ 07205. (201)964-4116. Vice President: Brian D. Enslow. Estab. 1978. Publishes 30 middle reader titles/year; 30 young adult titles/year. 30% of books by first-time authors.
Nonfiction: Young readers, middle readers, young adults: activity books, animal, biography, careers, health, history, hobbies, nature/environment, sports. Average word length: middle readers-5,000; young adult-15,000. Published *Louis Armstrong*, by Patricia and Fredrick McKissack (grades 2-3, biography); *Lotteries: Who Wins, Who Loses?*, by Ann E. Weiss (grades 6-12, issues book).
How to Contact/Writers: Nonfiction: Query. Reports on queries/mss in 2 weeks. Publishes a book 18 months after acceptance. Will not consider simultaneous submissions.
Illustration: Number of illustrations used for nonfiction: middle readers—20; young adults—20.
How to Contact/Illustrators: Provide résumé, business card or tearsheets to be kept on file.
Terms: Pays authors royalties or work purchased outright. Sends galleys to authors. Book catalog/ms guidelines available for $2.

*FACTS ON FILE, 460 Park Ave. S., New York NY 10016. (212)683-2244. Book publisher. Editorial Contact: James Warren. Publishes 35 young adult titles/year. 5% of books by first-time authors; 25% of books from agented writers; additional titles through book packagers, co-publishers and unagented writers.
Nonfiction: Young adults: animal, biography, science, history, music/dance, nature/environment, religion, sports. Published *Martin Luther King, Jr. and the Freedom Movement*, by Lillie Patterson; *The Encyclopedia of the Animal World*; *Charles Darwin: The Evolution of a Naturalist*, by Richard Milner.
How to Contact/Writers: Nonfiction: Submit outline/synopsis and sample chapters. Reports on queries in 6-8 weeks. Publishes a book 10 months after acceptance. Will consider simultaneous submissions. Sends galleys to authors. Book catalog free on request.
Tips: "Most projects have high reference value and fit into a series format."

*FALCON PRESS PUBLISHING CO., SkyHouse, P.O. Box 1718, Helena MT 59624. (406)442-6597. Book publisher, independent book producer/packager (SkyHouse). Publishes 2 picture books/year; 6 middle readers/year; 2 young adult titles/year. Focuses on nature/environment and outdoor recreation.
Nonfiction: Picture books: animal, geography, nature/environment. Young readers, young adults: animal, nature/environment. Middle readers: animal, biography, history, nature/environment. Does not want to see anthropomorphized animal stories. Average word length: picture books—650; middle readers—6,500; young adults—20,000-40,000. Recently published *The Battle of the Little Bighorn*, by Mark Henckel (ages 8-12, history); *Montana Wildlife*, by Gayle C. Shirley (ages 8 and up, animal field guide); *Where Dinosaurs Still Rule*, by Debbie Tewell (ages 8 and up, nature); *Four-Legged Legends of Montana*, by Gayle C. Shirley (young adult, animal).

How to Contact/Writers: Nonfiction: Query, submit outline/synopsis. Reports on queries/mss in 2-3 months. Publishes a book 18 months after acceptance. Will consider simultaneous submissions, electronic submissions via disk or modem.

Illustration: Works with 4 illustrators/year.

How to Contact/Illustrators: Illustrations only: Query with samples, résumé, slides, tearsheets. Reports in 2-3 months. Samples returned with SASE; samples filed. Originals returned at job's completion.

Terms: Pays authors 5-15% royalty based on wholesale price, or work purchased outright ($750 minimum). Pays illustrators by the project, royalty based on wholesale price. Sends galleys to authors. Book catalog available for 9 × 12 SAE and 2 first-class stamps; ms guidelines available for SASE; artist guidelines not available.

Tips: "Research each publishing house before you submit to make sure your manuscript is appropriate for it." Looking for "books that fit into our existing history and natural history series."

FARRAR, STRAUS & GIROUX, 19 Union Square W., New York NY 10003. (212)741-6934. Book publisher. Children's books Editor-in-Chief: Margaret Ferguson. Estab. 1946. Publishes 21 picture books/year; 6 middle reader titles/year; 5 young adult titles/year. 5% of books by first-time authors; 5% of books from agented writers.

Fiction: "Original and well-written material for all ages." Recently published *Tell Me Everything*, by Carolyn Coman (ages 12 up).

How to Contact/Writers: Fiction/nonfiction: Query; submit outline/synopsis and sample chapters. Reports on queries in 6 weeks; mss in 12 weeks. Publishes a book 18 months after acceptance. Will consider simultaneous submissions.

Illustration: Will review ms/illustration packages.

How to Contact/Illustrators: Ms/illustration packages: Ms with 1 example of final art, remainder roughs. Illustrations only: Tearsheets. Reports on art samples only if interested. Original artwork returned at job's completion.

Terms: "We offer an advance against royalties for both authors and illustrators." Sends galleys to authors; dummies to illustrators. Book catalog available for 6½ × 9½ SAE and 56¢ postage; ms guidelines for 1 first-class stamp.

Tips: "Study our catalog before submitting. We will see illustrator's portfolios by appointment."

FAWCETT JUNIPER, 201 E. 50 St., New York NY 10022. (212)751-2600. Imprint of Ballantine/DelRey/Fawcett Books. Book publisher. Editor-in-Chief/Vice President: Leona Nevler. Publishes 36 young adult titles/year.

Fiction: Middle readers: contemporary, romance, science fiction. Young adults: contemporary, fantasy, romance.

How to Contact/Writers: Fiction: Query.

Terms: Pays authors in royalties.

*THE FEMINIST PRESS AT THE CITY UNIVERSITY OF NEW YORK, 311 E. 94 St., New York NY 10128. (212)360-5790. Book publisher. Senior Editor: Susannah Driver. Publishes 1-2 middle reader, young reader and young adult books/year.

How to Contact/Writers: Fiction/nonfiction: Query. Reports on queries/mss in 2-3 weeks. Publishes a book 1-2 years after acceptance.

Illustration: Works with 1 illustrator/year. Will review ms/illustration packages. Uses primarily b&w artwork only.

Terms: Pays authors royalty. Offers advances (Average amount: $100). Pays illustrators by the project or royalty; "depends on project." Sends galleys to authors. Book catalog available; ms guidelines available.

*FIESTA CITY PUBLISHERS, Box 5861, Santa Barbara CA 93150-5861. (805)733-1984. Book publisher. Editorial contact: Ann Cooke. Publishes 1 middle reader title/year; 1 young adult title/year. 25% of books by first-time authors. Publishes books about cooking and music or the 2 combined.

Nonfiction: Young adult: cooking, music/dance, self-help. Average word length: 30,000. Does not want to see "cookbooks about healthy diets or books on rap music." Recently published *Kids Can Write Songs, Too!* (revised second printing), by Eddie Franck; *Bent-Twig*, by Frank E. Cooke, with some musical arrangements by Johnny Harris (a three-act musical for young adolescents).

How to Contact/Writers: Fiction/nonfiction: Query. Reports on queries in 2 weeks; on mss in 1 month. Publishes a book 1 year after acceptance. Will consider simultaneous submissions.

Illustration: Works with 1 illustrator/year. Will review ms/illustrations packages (query first). Contact: Frank E. Cooke, president.

How to Contact/Illustrators: Send résumé.

Terms: Pays authors royalty based on wholesale price.

Tips: "Write clearly and simply. Do not write 'down' to young adults (or children). Looking for self-help books on current subjects, original and unusual cookbooks, and books about music, or a combination of cooking and music."

FOUR WINDS PRESS, 866 Third Ave., New York NY 10022. (212)702-2000. Imprint of Macmillan Publishing Co. Book publisher. Editor-in-Chief: Virginia Duncan.

 • In November, 1993, all imprints of the Macmillan Children's Book Group and all other divisions of Macmillan were sold to Paramount Communications. This could affect future editorial policies, so watch *Publishers Weekly* and other trade journals for details.

Fiction: Picture books: animal, contemporary, humor. Middle readers: history, family, contemporary. Average word length: picture books—750-1,500; middle readers—10,000-30,000. "Young adult books are no longer being considered."

Nonfiction: Picture books: animal, biography, concepts, history, nature/environment. Middle readers: animal, biography, history, hobbies, music/dance, nature/environment, sports. Average word length: picture books—750-1,500; middle readers—10,000-30,000.

How to Contact/Writers: Fiction: Submit outline/synopsis and complete ms. Nonfiction: Query. Reports on queries/mss in 3 months. "Due to volume of submissions received, we cannot guarantee a quick response time or answer queries about manuscript status." Publishes a book 18-24 months after acceptance.

Illustration: Editorial will review ms/illustration packages.

How to Contact/Illustrators: Picture books: Submit full ms or dummy with art samples (not originals!). Illustrations only: "Illustration portfolios are reviewed every Thursday on a drop-off basis. If you cannot drop off your portfolio, mail tearsheets. Your portfolio should contain samples of work that best reflect your technical and creative ability to illustrate a text for children. These samples should include two or three different scenes of animals and/or children rendered in a setting. These should show your ability to handle composition, create interesting characters and maintain consistency between scenes. Use whatever medium is best suited to your technique." Reports on ms/art samples in 6-8 weeks; art samples only if interested. Original artwork returned at job's completion.

Terms: Pays authors in royalties of 5-10% based on retail price (depends on whether artist is sharing royalties). Pays illustrators by the project; royalties range from 2-5%; "fees and royalties vary widely according to budget for book. Ms and/or artist's guidelines for 1 first-class stamp and a business-size envelope. "No calls, please."

Tips: "The length of your story depends on the age of the child for whom it is intended. There are no fixed lengths. A good story is almost always the right length." (See also

Aladdin Books/Collier Books for Young Adults, Atheneum Publishers, Bradbury Press, Margaret K. McElderry Books.)

*FRANKLIN WATTS, INC., 11th Floor, 95 Madison Ave., New York NY 10016. (212)951-2650. Subsidiary of Grolier Inc. Book publisher. Editorial contact: John Selfridge. 5% of books by first-time authors; 10% of books from agented writers.
Nonfiction: Young readers: activity books. Middle readers: activity books, animal, arts/crafts, biography, cooking, geography, health, history, multicultural, music/dance, nature/environment, reference, religion, science, social issues, special needs, sports. Young adults: arts/crafts, biography, geography, health, history, multicultural, music/dance, nature/environment, reference, religion, science, social issues, special needs, sports. Average word length: middle readers—5,000; young adult/teens—16,000-35,000.
How to Contact/Writers: Query. No mss. SASE.
Illustration: Works with 10-20 illustrators/year. Will review ms/illustration packages. Will review artwork for future assignments. Contact: Vicki Fishman, art director.
How to Contact/Illustrators: Query with samples, résumé; promo sheet; client list. Original artwork returned at job's completion.
Photography: Purchases photos from freelancers. Contact photo editor. Buys stock and assigns work.
Terms: Pays authors royalties and buys photos outright. Illustrators paid by the project. Book catalog for 10×13 SASE.
Tips: Looks for children's nonfiction grades 5-8 or 9-12.

FREE SPIRIT PUBLISHING, Suite 616, 400 First Ave. N., Minneapolis MN 55401-1730. (612)338-2068. Fax: (612)337-5050. Book publisher. Publisher/President: Judy Galbraith. Publishes 3-4 middle reader titles/year; 3-4 young adult titles/year. 80% of books by first-time authors. "Our books pertain to the education and psychological well being of young people."
  ● This publisher received several awards in 1993 for children's publishing. Children's Books of Distinction awards from the *Hungry Mind Review* were given to *It's All in Your Head*, by Susan Barrett and *The First Honest Book About Lies*, by Jonni Kincher. Free Spirit also received honors from the American Library Association, The New York Public Library and the Midwest Independent Publishers Association.
Fiction: Picture books, young readers, middle readers, young adults: contemporary, mental health, multicultural, special needs. Recently published *Sofia and the Heartmender*, by Marie Olofsdotter (ages 5 and up, self-esteem/assertiveness); *If I Ran the Family*, by Lee and Sue Kaiser Johnson (ages 4-9, healthy family issue).
Nonfiction: Picture books, young readers, middle readers, young adults: health, hobbies, multicultural, nature/environment, self-esteem, social issues, special needs, psychology, education. Recently published *School Power: Strategies for Succeeding in School*, by Jeanne Shay Schumm and Marguerite Radencich (ages 11 and up, education); *Bringing Up Parents: The Teenager's Handbook*, by Alex J. Packer, Ph.D. (ages 13 and up, family relationships/communication/self-help); *The Survival Guide for Teenagers with Learning Differences*, by Rhoda Cummings, Ed.D. and Gary Fisher, Ph.D. (ages 13 and up, self-help/education/learning disabilities). Does not want poetry, stories with religious themes, non-human characters.
How to Contact/Writers: Nonfiction: Submit résumé, outline/synopsis and sample chapters. Reports on queries/mss in 3 months. Publishes a book 12-18 months after acceptance.
Illustration: Works with 5 illustrators/year. Will review ms/illustration packages. Will review work for future assignments. "We don't keep files of artist's samples in-house."
Contact: Nancy Tuminelly, graphic designer, Maclean & Tuminelly, Suite 626, 400 First

Ave. N., Minneapolis MN 55401. "MacLean & Tuminelly is a firm that designs and produces our books."

How to Contact/Illustrators: Ms/illustrations packages: Query with samples.

Terms: Pays authors in royalties of 7-12% based on wholesale price. Offers advance payment of $500-$1,000. Pays illustrators by the project. Sends galleys to authors. Book catalog free on request.

Tips: Does not accept unsolicited artists' or photographers' samples. Wants to see "a book that helps kids help themselves, or that helps adults help kids help themselves."

LAURA GERINGER BOOKS, 10 E. 53rd St., New York NY 10022. (212)207-7554. Fax: (212)207-7192. HarperCollins Publishers. Editorial Director: Laura Geringer. Publishes 10-12 picture books/year; 2 middle readers/year; 2-4 young adult titles/year. 20% of books by first-time authors; 50% of books from agented authors.

Fiction: Picture books: adventure, animal, contemporary, fantasy, folktales, history, nature/environment, poetry. Young readers: adventure, anthology, animal, contemporary, fantasy, folktales, health-related, history, nature/environment, poetry, sports, suspense/mystery. Middle readers, young adults: adventure, anthology, animal, contemporary, fantasy, folktales, health-related, history, nature/environment, poetry, problem novels, sports, suspense/mystery. Average word length: picture books—250-1,200. Recently published *Santa Calls*, by William Joyce (all ages, picture book); *The Borning Room*, by Paul Fleischman (ages 10 and up, middle grade); *The Tub People*, by Pam Conrad (preschool-3 years, picture book); *What Hearts*, by Bruce Brooks (age 10-young adult).

How to Contact/Writers: Fiction: Submit complete ms. Reports on queries in 2-4 weeks; mss in 2-4 months. Publishes a book 1½-3 years after acceptance. Will consider simultaneous submissions.

Illustration: Works with 20-25 illustrators/year. Average number of illustrations used for fiction: picture books—12-18; middle readers—10-15. Will review ms/illustration packages. Will review artwork for future assignments. Contact: Laura Geringer or Harriett Barton (art director).

How to Contact/Illustrators: Submit complete package. Illustrations only: Query with samples; submit portfolio for review; provide résumé, business card, promotional literature or tearsheets to be kept on file. Reports in 2-4 weeks. Original artwork returned at job's completion.

Terms: Pays authors royalties of 5-6¼% (picture book) or 10-12% (novel) based on retail price. Offers advances. Pays illustrators royalties of 5-6%. Sends galleys to authors; dummies to illustrators. Book catalog available for 9×11 SASE; ms guidelines available for SASE.

Tips: "Write about what you *know*. Don't try to guess our needs. And don't forget that children are more clever than we give them credit for!" Wants "artwork that isn't overly 'cutesy' with a strong sense of style and expression."

GLOBE FEARON EDUCATIONAL PUBLISHER, (formerly Fearon/Janus/Quercus), 240 Frisch Court, Paramus NJ 07652. Imprint of Paramount Publishing. Book publisher. Production Director: Penny Gibson. Publishes 100 special education, young adult titles/year.

Fiction: Young adults: hi-lo, multicultural, special needs. Average word length: 10,000-15,000.

A bullet has been placed within some listings to introduce special comments by the editor of Children's Writer's & Illustrator's Market.

Nonfiction: Young adults: biography, careers, health, hi-lo, history, multicultural, nature/environment, science, special needs, textbooks.
How to Contact/Writers: Fiction/nonfiction: Query "but, we don't respond to all queries." Reports on queries in 6 months; mss in 12-18 months.
Illustration: Works with 20 illustrators/year. Will review samples/portfolio. Contact: Penny Gibson, production director. Will review artwork for future assignments. Uses b&w and color artwork.
How to Contact/Illustrators: Illustrations only: Query with samples, résumé, promo sheet, portfolio, slides, client list, tearsheets; arrange personal portfolio review. Reports in 2 months. Samples returned with SASE. "We prefer to keep on file."
Photography: Purchases photos from freelancers. Buys stock images and assigns work. "We don't accept general submissions. We commission as needed." Model/property releases required. Uses wide range of color and b&w prints. Photographers should submit cover letter, résumé, published samples, slides, client list, stock photo list, portfolio, promo piece.
Terms: Work purchased outright ($2,500 minimum). Pays illustrators by the project. Photographers paid by the project. Sometimes sends galleys to authors.
Tips: "Be very sure the house you approach publishes the type of work you do. Make sure your work has solid, carefully crafted development with no dangling details."

DAVID R. GODINE, PUBLISHER, 300 Massachusetts, Boston MA 02115. (617)536-0761. Book publisher. Estab. 1970. Contact: Editorial Department. Publishes 3-4 picture books/year; 2 young reader titles/year; 3-4 middle reader titles/year. 10% of books by first-time authors; 20% of books from agented writers.
Fiction: Picture books: animal. Young readers: animal, easy-to-read, fantasy, folk or fairy tales, mystery/adventure. Middle readers: animal, fantasy, folk or fairy tales. Recently published *Cuckoo Clock*, by Mary Stolz (ages 9-11, middle readers); *The Turnip*, illustrated by Kevin Hawkes (ages 8-10, early readers); *Burton and Stanley*, by Frank O'Rourke (ages 8-10, early readers).
How to Contact/Writers: Reports on queries in 2 weeks; mss in 3 weeks. Publishes a book 2 years after acceptance.
Illustration: Editorial will review all varieties of ms/illustration packages.
How to Contact/Illustrators: Ms/illustration packages: "Roughs and 1 piece of finished art plus either sample chapters for very long works or whole ms for short works." Illustrations only: "Slides, with one full-size blow-up of art." Reports on art samples in 3 weeks. Original artwork returned at job's completion.
Terms: Pays authors in royalties based on retail price. Number of illustrations used determines final payment. Pay for separate authors and illustrators "differs with each collaboration." Illustrators paid by the project. Sends galleys to authors; dummies to illustrators. Book catalog/ms guidelines free on request.

GOLDEN BOOKS, 850 Third Ave., New York NY 10022. (212)753-8500. Western Publishing Co. Editorial Director: Marilyn Salomon. Book publisher. 100% of books from agented authors.
Fiction: Picture books: "accepts a variety of age appropriate subject matter." Young readers: easy-to-read. Middle readers: series lines. Young adult titles: contemporary, sports and series lines.
Nonfiction: Picture books: education, history, nature/environment, sports. Young and middle readers: animal, education, history, nature/environment, sports.
How to Contact/Writers: "Material accepted only through agent."
Illustration: Will sometimes review ms/illustration packages. Will review an illustrator's work for possible future assignments. Contact Remo Cosentino and Georg Brewer, art directors.

How to Contact/Illustrators: Ms/illustration packages: Query first.
Terms: Pays authors in royalties based on retail price.

GREENHAVEN PRESS, 10907 Technology Place, San Diego CA 92127. (619)485-7424. Book publisher. Estab. 1970. Senior Editors: Terry O'Neill and Bonnie Szumski. Publishes 40-50 young adult titles/year. 35% of books by first-time authors.
Nonfiction: Middle readers: biography, controversial topics, history, issues. Young adults: biography, history, nature/environment. Other titles "to fit our specific series." Average word length: young adults—15,000-18,000.
How to Contact/Writers: Query only. "We accept no unsolicited manuscripts. All writing is work-for-hire."
Terms/Writers: Buys ms outright for $1,500-2,500. Offers advances. Sends galleys to authors. Book catalog available for 9×12 SAE and 65¢ postage.
Tips: "Get our guidelines first before submitting anything."

GREENWILLOW BOOKS, 1350 Avenue of the Americas, New York NY 10019. (212)261-6500. Imprint of William Morrow & Co. Book publisher. Editor-in-chief: Susan Hirschman. Art Director: Ava Weiss. Publishes 50 picture books/year; 10 middle readers books/year; 10 young adult books/year.
Fiction: Will consider all levels of fiction; various categories.
How to Contact/Writers: Fiction: Submit complete ms to editorial department "not specific editor." Do not call. Reports on mss in 10-12 weeks. Publishes a book 18-24 months after acceptance. Will consider simultaneous submissions.
Illustration: Will review ms/illustration packages.
How to Contact/Illustators: Illustrations only: Query with samples, résumé.
Terms: Pays authors royalty. Offers advances. Pays illustrators royalty or by the project. Sends galleys to authors. Book catalog available for 9×12 SAE with $2 postage; ms guidelines available for SASE.

GROSSET & DUNLAP, INC., 200 Madison Ave., New York NY 10016. (212)951-8700. Imprint of The Putnam & Grosset Group. Book publisher. Editor-in-chief: Craig Walker. Art Director: Ronnie Ann Herman. Publishes 5 picture books/year; 8 young readers/year; 12 middle readers/year; 5 young adult titles/year; 25 board books/year; 25 novelty books/year. 5% of books by first-time authors; 50% of books from agented authors. Publishes fiction and nonfiction for mass market; novelty and board books.
Fiction: Picture books: animal, concept. Young readers: adventure, animal, concept, history, nature/environment, sports. Most categories will be considered. "We publish series fiction, but not original novels in the young adult category." Sees too many trade picture books. Recently published *Yo! It's Captain Yo-Yo*, by Jon Buller and Susan Schade (grades 2-3, All Aboard Reading); *Snakes*, by Pat Demuth, illustrations by Judith Moffatt (grades 1-3, All Aboard Reading); *Nina, Nina Ballerina*, by Jane O'Connor, illustrations by DyAnne DiSalvo-Ryan (preschool-grade 1, All Aboard Reading).
Nonfiction: Picture books: animal, concept, nature/environment. Young readers: activity books, animal, arts/crafts, biography, concept, history, sports. Published *Your Insides*, by Joanna Cole (ages 4-6, human body); *Dinosaur Bones!*, by C.E. Thompson, illustra-

Market conditions are constantly changing! If you're still using this book and it is 1995 or later, buy the newest edition of Children's Writer's & Illustrator's Market at your favorite bookstore or order directly from Writer's Digest Books.

tions by Paige Billin-Frye (ages 4-8, book & mobile); *Zoom!*, written and illustrated by Margaret A Hartelius (ages 4-8, paper airplane kit).

How to Contact/Writers: Fiction/nonfiction: Query. Reports in 2-4 weeks on queries; 1-2 months on mss. Publishes book 1-2 years after acceptance. Will consider simultaneous submissions.

Illustrations: Works with 50 illustrators/year. Will review ms/illustration packages. Will review artwork for future assignments. Contact: Ronnie Ann Herman, art director.

How to Contact/Illustrators: Ms/illustration packages: Query. Illustrations only: Query with samples; provide résumé, promo sheet, portfolio, slides, tearsheets. "Portfolio drop-off on Wednesdays." Reports only if interested. Original artwork returned at job's completion.

Photography: Photographers should contact Ronnie Ann Herman, art director. Buys stock images. Uses photos of babies and toddlers, interactive children, animals—full color. Interested in stock photos. Publishes photo concept books. Uses color prints; 35mm, 2¼ × 2¼, 4 × 5 and 8 × 10 transparencies. To contact, photographers should query with samples, send unsolicited photos by mail, submit portfolio, provide promotional literature or tearsheets to be kept on file.

Terms: Pays authors royalty or by outright purchase. Offers advances. Pays illustrators by the project or by royalty. Photographers paid by the project or per photo. Book catalog available for 9 × 12 SASE. Ms guidelines available for SASE.

HARCOURT BRACE & CO., (formerly Harcourt Brace Jovanovich), Suite 1900, 525 B St., San Diego CA 92101-4495. (619)699-6810. Children's Books Division which includes: Harcourt Brace Children's Books, Gulliver Books, Voyager Paperbacks, Odyssey Paperbacks, Jane Yolen Books. Book publisher. Attention: Manuscript Submissions, Children's Books Division. Publishes 40-45 picture books/year; 15-20 middle reader titles/year; 8-12 young adult titles/year. 20% of books by first-time authors; 50% of books from agented writers.

Fiction: Picture books, young readers: animal, contemporary, fantasy, history. Middle readers, young adults: animal, contemporary, fantasy, history, problem novels, romance, science fiction, sports, spy/mystery/adventure. Average word length: picture books—"varies greatly"; middle readers—20,000-50,000; young adults—35,000-65,000.

Nonfiction: Picture books, young readers: animal, biography, history, hobbies, music/dance, nature/environment, religion, sports. Middle readers, young adults: animal, biography, education, history, hobbies, music/dance, nature/environment, religion, sports. Average word length: picture books—"varies greatly"; middle readers—20,000-50,000; young adults—35,000-65,000.

How to Contact/Writers: Fiction/nonfiction: Query; submit outline/synopsis and sample chapters; submit complete ms for picture books only. "Only Harcourt Brace Children's Books accepts unsolicited manuscripts." Reports on queries/mss in 6-8 weeks.

Illustration: Editorial will review ms/illustration packages. Art Director of Children's Books, Michael Farmer, will review an illustrator's work for possible future assignments.

How to Contact/Illustrators: Ms/illustration packages: picture books ms—complete ms acceptable. Longer books—outline and 2-4 sample chapters. Send several samples of art; no original art. Illustrations only: Résumé, tearsheets, color photocopies, color stats all accepted. "Please DO NOT send original artwork or transparencies. Include SASE for return, please." Reports on art samples in 6-10 weeks. Original artwork returned at job's completion.

Terms: Pays authors in royalties based on retail price. Pays illustrators by the project. Sends galleys to authors; dummies to illustrators. Book catalog available for 9 × 12 SASE; ms/artist's guidelines for business-size SASE.

Tips: "Become acquainted with Harcourt Brace's books in particular if you are interested in submitting proposals to us."

HARPERCOLLINS CHILDREN'S BOOKS, 10 E. 53rd St., New York NY 10022. (212)207-7044. Contact: Submissions Editor. Creative Director: Harriet Barton. Book publisher.
Fiction: All levels: adventure, animal, anthology, concept, contemporary, fantasy, folktales, hi-lo, history, multicultural, nature/environment, poetry, problem novels, romance, science fiction, special needs, sports, suspense/mystery. Published *The Magic Wood*, by Henry Treece (ages 6 and up, picture book); *The Noisy Giants' Tea Party*, by Kate and Jim McMullan (ages 3-8, picture book).
Nonfiction: All levels: activity books, animal, arts/crafts, biography, concept, geography, hi-lo, history, hobbies, multicultural, music/dance, nature/environment, reference, science, social issues, sports. Recently published *Marie Curie & Radium*, by Steve Parker (ages 8-12); *The Pigman & Me*, by Paul Zindel (ages 12 up, young adult); *The Moon of the Deer*, by Jean Craighead George (ages 8-12, middle reader).
How to Contact/Writers: Fiction/nonfiction: Query, submit outline/synopsis and sample chapters. Reports on mss in 2-3 months.
Illustration: Works with 50 illustrators/year. Will review ms/illustration packages (preferable to see picture books without art). Will review work for possible future assignments. (No original art, please).
How to Contact/Illustrators: Ms/illustrations packages: Query first. Query with samples, portfolio, slides, arrange personal portfolio review.
Terms: Pays authors in royalties based on retail price. Illustrators paid by the project; royalty based on retail price.

HARVEST HOUSE PUBLISHERS, 1075 Arrowsmith, Eugene OR 97402. (503)343-0123. Book publisher. Manuscript Coordinator: LaRae Weikert. Publishes 5-6 picture books/year; 3 young reader titles/year; 3 young adult titles/year. 25% of books by first-time authors. Books follow a Christian theme.
Fiction: Picture books: easy-to-read. Young readers: contemporary, easy-to-read. Middle readers: contemporary, fantasy. Young adults: fantasy, problem novels, romance. Recently published *Lullabies to Dreamland*, illustrated with text by Deniece Williams.
Nonfiction: All levels: religion.
How to Contact/Writers: Fiction/nonfiction: Query; submit outline/synopsis and sample chapters; submit complete ms. Reports on queries in 2-4 weeks; mss in 6-8 weeks. Publishes a book 1 year after acceptance. Will consider simultaneous submissions.
Illustration: Editorial will review ms/illustration package. Will review artwork for future assignments.
How to Contact/Illustrators: Ms/illustration packages: "3 chapters of ms with 1 piece of final art and any approximate rough sketches." Illustrations only: send résumé, tearsheets. Submit to Fred Renich, production manager. Reports on art samples in 2 months. Original artwork returned at job's completion.
Terms: Pays authors in royalties of 10-15%. Average advance payment: "negotiable." Pays illustrator: "Sometimes by project." Sends galleys to authors; sometimes sends dummies to illustrators. Book catalog, ms/artist's guidelines free on request.

HENDRICK-LONG PUBLISHING COMPANY, P.O. Box 25123, Dallas TX 75225. Book publisher. Contact: Joann Long, Vice President. Publishes 1 picture book/year; 4 young reader titles/year; 4 middle reader titles/year. 20% of books by first-time authors.
Fiction: All levels: history books on Texas and the Southwest. No fantasy or poetry. Published *Boomer's Kids*, by Ruby Tolliver, illustrations by Lyle Miller (ages 12 and above); *The Adventures of Jason Jackrabbit*, by M.M. Dee, illustrations by Donna Newsom (ages 6-9); *Swept Back to a Texas Future: An Original Historical Musical*, by Peggy Purser Freeman, illustrations by Holly Haas (grades 4 and 7).
Nonfiction: All levels: history books on Texas and the Southwest. Published *Trails of Tears: American Indians Driven from Lands*, by Jeanne Williams, illustrations and map by Michael Taylor (ages 12 and above); *Miss Ima and the Hogg Family*, by Gwen Cone

Neeley, photographs from archives and museums (ages 12 and above).
How to Contact/Writers: Fiction and nonfiction: Query with outline/synopsis and sample chapter. Reports on queries in 1 month; mss in 2 months. Publishes a book 18 months after acceptance. No simultaneous submissions. Include SASE.
Illustration: Number of illustrations used for fiction and nonfiction: picture books—22; middle readers—11; young readers—11. Uses primarily b&w artwork only. Editorial will review ms/illustration packages. Will review artwork for future assignments.
How to Contact/Illustrators: Query first. Submit résumé, promotional literature, photocopies or tearsheets—no original work sent unsolicited. Material kept on file. No reply sent.
Terms: Pays authors in royalty based on selling price. Advances vary. Sends galleys to authors; dummies to illustrators. Book catalog for $1, 52¢ postage and large SAE; ms/artist's guidelines for 1 first-class stamp and #10 SAE.

HERALD PRESS, 616 Walnut Ave., Scottdale PA 15683. (412)887-8500. Fax: (412)887-3111. Division of Mennonite Publishing House. Estab. 1908. Publishes 1 picture storybook/year; 1 young reader title/year; 2-3 middle reader titles/year; 1-2 young adult titles/year. Editorial Contact: S. David Garber. Art Director: Jim Butti. 20% of books by first-time authors; 3% of books from agented writers.
Fiction: Young readers, middle readers, young adults: contemporary, history, problem novels, religious, self-help, social concerns. Does not want stories on fantasy, science fiction, war, drugs, cops and robbers.
Nonfiction: Young readers, middle readers, young adults: how-to, religious, self-help, social concerns.
How to Contact/Writers: Fiction/nonfiction: "Send to Book Editor, the following: (1) a one-page summary of your book, (2) a one- or two-sentence summary of each chapter, (3) the first chapter and one other, (4) your statement of the significance of the book, (5) a description of your target audience, (6) a brief biographical sketch of yourself, and (7) SASE for return of the material. You may expect a reply in about a month. If your proposal appears to have potential for Herald Press, a finished manuscript will be requested. Herald Press depends on capable and dedicated authors to continue publishing high-quality Christian literature." Publishes a book 12 months after acceptance. Will consider simultaneous submissions but prefers not to.
Illustration: Works with 3 illustrators/year. Will review ms/illustration packages. Will review artwork for future assignments. Contact: Jim Butti, art director.
How to Contact/Illustrators: Illustrations only: Query with samples. Send résumé, tearsheets and slides.
Photography: Purchases photos from freelancers. Contact: Debbie Cameron. Buys stock and assigns work.
Terms: Pays authors in royalties of 10-12% based on retail price. Pay for illustrators: by the project; $220-600. Sends galleys to authors. Book catalog for 3 first-class stamps; ms guidelines free on request.
Tips: "We invite book proposals from Christian authors in the area of juvenile fiction. Our purpose is to publish books which are consistent with Scripture as interpreted in the Anabaptist/Mennonite tradition. Books that are honest in presentation, clear in thought, stimulating in content, appropriate in appearance, superior in printing and binding, and conducive to the spiritual growth and welfare of the reader."

HOLIDAY HOUSE INC., 425 Madison Ave., New York NY 10017. (212)688-0085. Fax: (212)421-6134. Book publisher. Vice President/Editor-in-Chief: Margery Cuyler. Assistant Editor: Ashley Mason. Publishes 30 picture books/year; 7 young reader titles/year; 7 middle reader titles/year; 3 young adult titles/year. 20% of books by first-time authors; 10% from agented writers.

Fiction: Picture book: animal, folktales, sports. Young reader: contemporary, easy-to-read, history, sports, spy/mystery/adventure. Middle reader: contemporary, fantasy, history, sports, spy/mystery/adventure. Recently published *The Battle for the Castle*, by Elizabeth Winthrop (middle reader, fantasy novel); *Peeping Beauty*, by Mary Jane Auch (humorous picture book).

Nonfiction: Picture books: biography, history, nature. Young reader: biography, history, nature/environment, sports. Middle reader: biography, history, nature/environment, sports. Recently published *African Elephants*, by Dorothy Hinshaw Patent (young reader, nature/environment); *The Wright Brothers*, by Russell Freedman (middle reader, historical); *The Sioux*, by Virginia Driving Hawk Sneve, illustrated by Ronald Himler (picture book).

How to Contact/Writers: Fiction/nonfiction: Submit complete ms. Reports on queries in 2 weeks; on mss in 6 weeks. Publishes a book 10 months after acceptance. Will consider simultaneous submissions.

Illustration: Works with 25 illustrators/year. Editorial will review ms/illustration packages. Will review artwork for future assignments. Ashley Mason will also view artists' portfolios inhouse.

How to Contact/Illustrators: Ms/illustration packages: Query first. Illustrations only: Send résumé and tearsheets. Reports within 6 weeks with SASE or if interested (if no SASE). Original art work returned at job's completion.

Terms: Pays authors royalties. Pays illustrators royalties. Ms/artist's guidelines for #10 SASE.

HENRY HOLT & CO., INC., 115 W. 18th St., New York NY 10011. (212)886-9200. Book publisher. Editor-in-Chief/Vice President/Associate Publisher: Brenda Bowen. Publishes 20-30 picture books/year; 40-60 young reader titles/year; 6 middle reader titles/year; 6 young adult titles/year. 5% of books by first-time authors; 40% of books from agented writers.

How to Contact/Writers: Fiction/nonfiction: Submit complete ms. Reports on queries/mss in 2 months. Publishes a book 12-18 months after acceptance. Will consider simultaneous submissions.

Illustration: Will review ms/illustration packages.

How to Contact/Illustrators: Ms/illustration packages: Random samples OK. Illustrations only: Tearsheets, slides. Do *not* send originals. Reports on art samples only if interested. If accepted, original artwork returned at job's completion.

Terms: Pays authors/illustrators royalty based on retail price. Sends galleys to authors; dummies to illustrators.

HOMESTEAD PUBLISHING, Box 193, Moose WY 83012. Book publisher. Editor: Carl Schreier. Publishes 8 picture books/year; 2 young reader titles/year; 2 middle reader titles/year; 2 young adult titles/year. 30% of books by first-time authors; 1% of books from agented writers.

Fiction: Average word length: young readers—1,000; middle readers—5,000; young adults—5,000-150,000.

Nonfiction: Picture books, middle readers: animal (wildlife), biography, history, nature/environment. Young readers: animal (wildlife), nature/environment. Young adults: animal (wildlife), history, nature/environment. Average word length: young readers—1,000; middle readers—5,000; young adults—5,000-250,000.

How to Contact/Writers: Fiction/nonfiction: Query; submit outline/synopsis and sample chapters. Reports on queries/mss in 1 month. Publishes a book 1 year after acceptance. Will consider simultaneous submissions.

Illustration: Will review ms/illustration packages. Prefers to see "watercolor, opaque, oil" illustrations.

Passing Good Culture on to Children

"I feel that as a children's book publisher, we have a responsibility to pass 'good' culture on to children," says Margery Cuyler. "The texts of our children's books should be literate, the characterization strong, and the plots and themes adeptly engineered."

Cuyler is vice president and editor-in-chief of Holiday House, a small, independent children's book publisher in New York City. "Holiday House, which was founded in 1935, has always prided itself on publishing books of high quality — both in terms of content and design — that also have child appeal," she says.

Assisted by Ashley Mason, Cuyler acquires 50 titles a year and guides them through the various stages of production. Their list evolves from back-

Margery Cuyler

list authors and illustrators who continue to submit projects, authors and illustrators dissatisfied with their regular publishers or too prolific to stay with one house, commissioned work, a small number of imports, and, of course, unsolicited submissions.

"It's *always* a joy to find a new author in the slush pile, which is why we continue to read every manuscript that arrives in the mail," Cuyler says. In total, they receive about 4,500 manuscripts a year, out of which they usually accept four to six — depending upon their luck.

Manuscripts are first read and screened by Mason, who looks for good writing and, after that, originality of subject matter. She wants writers who can effectively communicate a theme and, at the same time, tell an entertaining story, Cuyler explains.

Once the pile is narrowed down, Cuyler evaluates the remaining submissions. "I look for 'voice' first, since it's voice which immediately distinguishes one writer from another," she says. "I also look for warmth, charm, and a sense of fun. I like fiction that has a strong story line. And I especially favor *humorous* middle grade novels."

Like all editors and publishers, Cuyler and company have likes *and* dislikes. "We're seeing too many sentimental picture books, folktales and cutesy fantasies," she says. "Since many of our backlist illustrators write their own picture book texts, we're primarily on the lookout for middle grade fiction." They also want to see holiday books (for any age), Judaica, photo essays with a multicultural focus, contemporary stories about children from different cultural backgrounds and historical nonfiction.

Cuyler encourages writers and illustrators to request publishers' catalogs to discover the differing characteristics of their lists. While some publishers are series oriented, others specialize in picture books. Still others are noted for strong young adult fiction.

She also suggests visiting local bookstores to see what's being published and talking to teachers, librarians and children about what's needed. "Sometimes, it's easier to get published if your work addresses an area in publishing that hasn't been well covered," she says. And Cuyler should know. In addition to serving 20 years as Holiday House's editor-in-chief, she is a children's author.

Cuyler's first book for children, *Jewish Holidays*, was published by Henry Holt & Company in 1978. "I wrote that book because, at the time, I realized there was a sparsity of good material on Jewish holidays for children. Most of what I found in the library was sentimental or patronizing, with mediocre artwork. I was inspired to fill the gap because I was interested in learning more about the subject myself," she says.

She then wrote a few other nonfiction books and two novels before concentrating on picture books. All told she has about a dozen picture books to her credit. In fact, her most recent one, *Buddy Bear and the Bad Guys*, was published by Clarion Books last fall. And though Cuyler keeps her roles as editor and author separate, editing children's books has helped her spot marketing trends, which sometimes affect the subjects she writes about.

Regarding trends in the industry, however, Cuyler notes some concerns: "My main worry about picture books today is that they're getting farther and farther away from the child. I've seen absolutely beautifully produced picture books with mediocre texts. Picture books, with some exceptions, generally don't seem to be funny anymore. And what has happened to the good, old-fashioned animal story? Or family story? Where are the guts in fairy tales?" Cuyler sees so many that look pretty but don't capture a tale's original appearance of truthfulness.

On the other hand, she says, "There is a recent positive trend toward nonfiction or books in which information is introduced visually, through images, in tandem with a story line. And multicultural materials are in demand, particularly Mideastern and Asian stories. Also, stories with strong heroines." Expecting the school market to expand dramatically by the end of the century, she believes the multicultural and nonfiction trends will continue to develop.

Yet, Cuyler cautions writers and illustrators about following trends too closely. "Having said all of the above, my advice would be *not* to write and illustrate to please others — those editors and reviewers who will ultimately be judging your work — or you'll become paralyzed and your originality will be compromised. Rather, write and illustrate to please yourself and see what comes out of it."

As a children's writer, she says, "The best advice I ever received was to treat writing like alchemy; it's a process of turning the baser metal of 'real experience' into the gold of something imaginary."

— Christine Martin

How to Contact/Illustrators: Ms/illustration packages: "Query first with sample writing and art style." Illustrations only: "Résumés, style samples." Reports on art samples in 1-2 months. Original artwork returned at job's completion with SASE.

Terms: Pays authors in royalties of 5-10% based on wholesale price. Work purchased outright "depending on project." Pays illustrators by the project (range: $50-10,000) or royalty of 3-10% based on wholesale price. Sends galleys to authors; dummies to illustrators.

HOUGHTON MIFFLIN CO., Children's Trade Books, 222 Berkeley St., Boston MA 02108. (617)351-5000. Book publisher. Vice President/Director: Walter Lorraine. Senior Editor: Matilda Welter; Editor: Audrey Bryant. Coordinating Editor: Laura Hornick. Art Director: Amy Bernstein. Averages 50-55 titles/year. Publishes hardcover originals and trade paperback reprints (some simultaneous hard/soft).

Fiction: All levels: all categories except religion. "We do not rule out any theme. Though we do not publish specifically religious material." Published *The Widow's Broom*, by Chris Van Allsburg (picture book).

How to Contact/Writers: Fiction: Submit complete ms. Nonfiction: Submit outline/synopsis and sample chapters. Reports on queries in 2 weeks; on mss in 1-8 weeks.

Illustration: Works with 60 illustrators/year. Will review ms/illustration packages. Will review artwork for future assignments.

How to Contact/Illustrators: Query with samples (colored photocopies, fine); provide slides and tearsheets.

Terms: Pays standard royalty; offers advance. Book catalog free on request.

Tips: "The growing independent-retail book market will no doubt affect the number and kinds of books we publish in the near future. Booksellers are more informed about children's books today than ever before."

HUMANICS LIMITED PUBLISHING GROUP, 1482 Mecaslin St. NW, Atlanta GA 30309. (404)874-2176. Fax: (404)874-1976. Book publisher. Acquisitions Editor: Karen S. Parmett. Publishes 4 picture books/year. 50% of books by first-time authors.

Fiction: Picture books: adventure, animal, contemporary, easy-to-read, folktales, multicultural, nature/environment, poetry, self-image, self esteem. Average word length: picture books—250-350. Published *The Planet of the Dinosaurs*, by Barbara Carr, Ph.D.; *The Adventure Of Paz In The Land Of Numbers*, by Miriam Bowden.

Nonfiction: Picture books: multicultural. Young readers: activity books, arts/crafts, geography, multicultural, music/dance, nature/environment, science, special needs. Multicultural stories must be accurate.

How to Contact/Writers: Fiction/Nonfiction: Submit outline/synopsis and sample chapters or submit complete ms. Reports on queries/mss in 3 months.

Illustration: Works with 2-4 illustrators/year. Will review ms/illustration packages. Will review artwork for future assignments.

How to Contact/Illustrators: Illustrations only: Send résumé, tearsheets, slides, photographs, color photocopies. Do not send original artwork for preliminary contact. When an illustrator has been hired, he/she will receive artwork back once the project has been completed.

"Picture books" are geared toward the preschool to 8-year-old group; "Young readers" are for 5- to 8-year-olds; "Middle readers" are for 9- to 11-year-olds; and "Young adults" are for those 12 and up.

Terms: Pays authors and illustrators royalties. Book catalog free upon request, but a 9×12 SAE is required and 98¢ postage; ms/artist's guidelines for #10 SAE and 29¢ postage.
Tips: Enclose proper postage and 9×12 SAE if you would like to have your manuscript returned."

■**HUNTER HOUSE PUBLISHERS,** P.O.Box 2914, Alameda CA 94501-0914. Book publisher. Independent book producer/packager. Editor: Lisa Lee. Publishes 1-2 young adult titles/year. 80% of books by first-time authors; 5% of books from agented writers. **Nonfiction:** Young readers, middle readers: social issues. Young adults: self-help, social issues. "We emphasize that all our books try to take multicultural experiences and concerns into account. We would be interested in a social issues or self-help book on multicultural issues." Books are therapy/personal growth-oriented. Does not want to see "fiction; illustrated, picture books." Recently published *Turning Yourself Around: Self-Help Strategies for Troubled Teens*, by Kendall Johnson, Ph.D.; *Safe Dieting For Teens*, by Linda Ojeda, Ph.D.
How to Contact/Writers: Nonfiction: Query; submit overview and chapter-by-chapter synopsis, sample chapters and statistics on your subject area, support organizations or networks and marketing ideas. "Testimonials from professionals or well-known authors are important." Reports on queries in 1 month; mss in 3 months. Publishes a book 18 months after acceptance. Will consider simultaneous submissions.
Illustration: Works with 1 illustrator/year. Will review ms/illustration packages. Will review artwork for future assignments. Contact: Paul Frindt or Lisa Lee. Uses primarily b&w artwork only.
How to Contact/Illustrators: Query with samples. Provide résumé and client list. Contact: Lisa Lee.
Photography: Purchases photos from freelancers. Contact: Paul Frindt. Buys stock images.
Terms: Pays authors in royalties based on wholesale price or outright purchase. Pays illustrators by the project. Sends galleys to authors. Book catalog available for 9×12 SAE and 65¢ postage; manuscript guidelines for standard SAE and 1 first-class stamp.
Tips: Wants therapy/personal growth workbooks.

HUNTINGTON HOUSE PUBLISHERS, P.O. Box 53788, Lafayette LA 70505. (318)237-7049. Book publisher. Editor-in-Chief: Mark Anthony. Publishes 2 young readers/year. 100% of books by first-time authors. "All books have spiritual/religious themes."
Fiction: Picture books: folktales, religion. Young readers: folktales, history, religion. Middle readers, young adults: contemporary, folktales, history, religion. Does not want to see romance, nature/environment,multicultural. Average word length: picture books — 12-50; young readers — 100-300; middle readers — 4,000-15,000; young adults/teens — 10,000-40,000. Recently published *Greatest Star of All*, by Greg Gulley and David Watts (ages 9-11, adventure/religion).
Nonfiction: Picture books: animal, religion. Young readers, middle readers, young adults/teens: biography, history, religion. No nature/environment, multicultural. Average word length: picture books — 12-50 ; young readers — 100-300; middle readers — 4,000-15,000; young adult/teens — 10,000-40,000. Recently published *To Grow By Storybook Readers*, by Marie Le Doux and Janet Friend (preschool to age 8, textbook).
How to Contact/Writers: Fiction/nonfiction: Query. Submit outline/synopsis, table of contents and proposal letter. One or two sample chapters are optional. Send SASE. Reports on queries in 1 month; mss in 2 months. Publishes a book 8 months after acceptance. Will consider simultaneous submissions.
Illustration: Works with 2 illustrators/year. Will review ms/illustration packages. Will review artwork for future assignments.

How to Contact/Illustrators: Ms/illustration packages: Query; submit ms with dummy. Illustrations only: Query with samples; send résumé and client list. Ms/illustration packages: Reports in 1 month. Illustrations only: Reports only if interested. Samples returned with SASE; samples filed. Original artwork returned at job's completion.
Photography: Purchases photos from freelancers. Contact: Managing Editor. Buys stock images. Model/property releases required. Photographers should submit cover letter and résumé to be kept on file.
Terms: Pays authors royalty of 10% based on wholesale price. Pays illustrators by the project (range: $50-250) or royalty of 10% based on wholesale price. Sends galleys to authors; dummies to illustrators. Book catalog available for #10 SAE and 2 first-class stamps; ms guidelines for SASE; artist's guidelines not available.

HYPERION BOOKS FOR CHILDREN, 114 Fifth Ave., New York NY 10011. (212)633-4400. Fax: (212)633-4833. An operating unit of Walt Disney Publishing Group, Inc. Book publisher. Editorial Director: Andrea Cascardi. 30% of books by first-time authors; 40% of books from agented authors. Publishes various categories.
Fiction: Picture books, young readers, middle readers, young adults: adventure, animal, anthology (short stories), contemporary, fantasy, folktales, history, humor, multicultural, poetry, science fiction, sports, suspense/mystery. Middle readers, young adults: problem novels, romance. Published *Rescue Josh McGuire*, by Ben Mikaelsen (ages 10-14, adventure).
Nonfiction: All trade subjects for all levels.
How to Contact/Writers: Fiction: Submit complete ms. Nonfiction: Query. Submit outline/synopsis and 2 sample chapters. Reports on queries in 3 months; mss in 4 months.
Illustration: Works with 100 illustrators/year. "Picture books are fully illustrated throughout. All others depend on individual project." Will review ms/illustration packages. Will review artwork for future assignments. Contact: Ellen Friedman, art director.
How to Contact/Illustrators: Ms/illustration packages: Submit complete package. Illustrations only: provide résumé, business card, promotional literature or tearsheets to be kept on file. Reports back only if interested. Original artwork returned at job's completion.
Photography: Contact: Ellen Friedman, art director. Works on assignment only. Publishes photo essays and photo concept books. Provide résumé, business card, promotional literature or tearsheets to be kept on file.
Terms: Pays authors royalty based on retail price. Offers advances. Pays illustrators and photographers royalty based on retail price or a flat fee. Sends galleys to authors; dummies to illustrators. Book catalog available for 9×12 SAE and 3 first-class stamps; ms guidelines available for SASE.

*IDEALS CHILDREN'S BOOKS, (formerly Ideals Publishing Corporation), Box 140300, Nashville TN 37214. (615)885-8270. Book publisher. Children's Book Editor: Peggy Schaefer. Publishes 40-50 picture books/year; 5-8 young reader titles/year. 5-10% of books by first-time authors; 5-10% of books from agented writers.
Fiction: Picture books: adventure, animal, concept, contemporary, easy-to-read, fantasy, folktales, history, multicultural, nature/environment. sports. Average word length: picture books—200-1,200; young readers—1,200-2,400. Recently published *Nobiah's Well*, by Donna Guthrie (ages 4-8); *Alpha Zoo Christmas*, by Susan Harrison (ages 4-8).
Nonfiction: Picture books, young readers: activity books, animal, biography, history, hobbies, music/dance, nature/environment, sports. Does not want "ABC" and counting books of a general nature. "Only interested in them if they relate to specific themes." Average word length: picture books—200-1,200; young readers—1,000-2,400. Recently published: *The Blue Whale*, by Melissa Kim (ages 6-10); *How's the Weather*, by Melvin and Gilda Berger (ages 5-9, early reader).

How to Contact/Writers: Fiction/nonfiction: Submit complete ms. Reports on queries/mss in 3-6 months. Publishes a book 18-24 months after acceptance. Must include SASE for response.

Illustration: Works with 20 illustrators/year. Number of illustrations used for fiction and nonfiction: picture books—12-18; young readers—12-18. Editorial will review ms/illustration packages. Will review artwork for future assignments. Preference: No cartoon—tight or loose, but realistic watercolors, acrylics.

How to Contact/Illustrators: Ms/illustration packages: Ms with 1 color photocopy of final art and remainder roughs. Illustrations only: Résumé and tearsheets showing variety of styles. Reports on art samples only if interested. "No original artwork, please."

Terms: "All terms vary according to individual projects and authors/artists."

Tips: "Trend is placing more value on nonfiction and packaging. (i.e., We are not interested in young adult romances.)" Illustrators: "Be flexible in contract terms—and be able to show as much final artwork as possible." Work must have strong storyline with realistic characters. Shows little interest in anthropomorphism.

INCENTIVE PUBLICATIONS, INC., 3835 Cleghorn Ave., Nashville TN 37215. (615)385-2934. Editor: Jan Keeling. Approximately 20% of books by first-time authors.

Nonfiction: Young reader, middle reader, young adult: education. Recently published *Cooperative Learning Teacher Timesavers*, by Imogene Forte (grades 1-6, plans, aids and ideas); *Teacher's Gold Mine II*, by Michener and Muschlitz (grades 1-6, ideas and activities).

How to Contact/Writers: Nonfiction: Submit outline/synopsis and sample chapters. Usually reports on queries/mss in approximately 1 month. Typically publishes a book 18 months after acceptance. Will consider simultaneous submissions.

Terms: Pays in royalties or work purchased outright. Book catalog for SAE and 90¢ postage.

Tips: "We buy only teacher resource material. Please do not submit fiction!"

JALMAR PRESS, #204, 2675 Skypark Dr., Torrance CA 90505. (310)784-0016. Fax: (310)784-1379. Subsidiary of B.L. Winch and Associates. Book publisher. Estab. 1971. President: B.L. Winch. Publishing Assistant: Jeanne Iler. Publishes 3 picture books and young reader titles/year. 10% of books by first-time authors. Publishes self-esteem (curriculum content related), drug and alcohol abuse prevention, peaceful conflict resolution, stress management, whole brain learning materials and gender equity.

Fiction: All levels: concept, self-esteem. Does not want to see "fiction children's books that have to do with cognitive learning (as opposed to affective learning)." Published *Scooter's Tail of Terror: A Fable of Addiction and Hope*, by Larry Shles (ages 5-105). "All submissions must teach (by metaphor) in the areas listed above."

Nonfiction: All levels: activity books, concept, how-to, textbooks within areas specified above.

How to Contact/Writers: Fiction/nonfiction: Submit complete ms. Reports on queries in 1 month; mss in 1-6 months. Publishes a book 6-12 months after acceptance. Will consider simultaneous submissions.

Illustration: Works with 1-4 illustrators/year. Editorial will review ms/illustration packages.

How to Contact/Illustrators: Ms/illustration packages: Submit complete package. Illustrations only: Send unsolicited art samples by mail. Reports in 2 weeks. Originals returned upon job's completion.

Terms: Pays authors 7-12% royalty based on net receipts. Average advance "varies." Pays illustrators a share in royalties with author or work purchased outright. Book catalog free on request.

Tips: Wants "thoroughly researched, tested, practical, activity-oriented, curriculum content and grade/level correlated books on self-esteem, peaceful conflict resolution, stress management, drug and alcohol abuse prevention and whole brain learning. Books bridging self-esteem to various 'trouble' areas, such as 'at risk,' 'dropout prevention,' etc."

JEWISH LIGHTS PUBLISHING, P.O. Box 237, Woodstock VT 05091. (802)457-4000. A division of LongHill Partners, Inc. Book publisher. President: Stuart M. Matlins. Publishes 1 picture book/year; 1 young readers/year; 1 middle readers/year; 1 young adult title/year. 50% of books by first-time authors; 50% of books from agented authors. All books have spiritual/religious themes.
Fiction: Picture books: multicultural, religion. Young readers, middle readers, young adults: religion. "We are not interested in anything other than religion/spiritual."
Nonfiction: All levels: religion. Published *God's Paintbrush*, by Rabbi Sandy Eisenberg Sasso and Annette Carroll Compton (K-4, spiritual).
How to Contact/Writers: Fiction/nonfiction: Query. Submit outline/synopsis. Reports on queries in 1 month; mss in 3 months. Publishes a book 6 months after acceptance. Will consider simultaneous submissions and previously published work.
Illustration: Works with 3 illustrators/year. Will review ms/illustration packages. Will review artwork for future assignments.
How to Contact/Illustrators: Query. Illustrations only: Query with samples; provide résumé. Reports in 1 month. Samples returned with SASE; samples filed. Original artwork not returned at job's completion.
Terms: Pays authors royalty of 10% of revenue received. Offers advances. Pays illustrators by the project or royalty. Pays photographers by the project, per photo or royalty. Sends galleys to authors; dummies to illustrators. Book catalog available for 9 × 12 SAE and 59¢ postage; ms and artist's guidelines not available.

JEWISH PUBLICATION SOCIETY, 1930 Chestnut St., Philadelphia PA 19103. (215)564-5925. Editor-in-Chief: Dr. Ellen Frankel. Editor: Bruce Black. Book publisher. All work must have Jewish content.
Fiction: Picture books, young readers, middle readers and young adults: adventure, contemporary, folktales, history, mystery, problem novels, religion, romance, sports. Recently published: *God Must Like Cookies, Too*, by Carol Snyder, illustrated by Beth Glick (ages 3-8, picture book); *K'tonton's Sukkot Adventure*, by Sadie Rose Weilerstein, illustrated by Joe Boddy (ages 3-8, picture book).
Nonfiction: Picture books: biography, history, religion. Young readers, middle readers, young adults: biography, history, religion, sports. Recently published: *Raoul Wallenbert: The Man Who Stopped Death*, by Sharon Linner (ages 10 and up, biography); *Leonard Bernstein: A Passion for Music*, by Johanna Hurwitz, illustrated by Sonia D. Lisher (ages 10 and up, biography).
How to Contact/Writers: Fiction/nonfiction: Query, submit outline/synopsis and sample chapters. Will consider simultaneous submissions (please advise).
Illustration: Will review ms/illustration packages.
How to Contact/Illustrators: Ms/illustration packages: Query first or send three chapters of ms with one piece of final art, remainder roughs. Illustrations only: Query with photocopies; arrange a personal interview to show portfolio.
Terms: Pays authors in royalties based on retail price.
Tips: Writer/illustrator currently has best chance of selling picture books to this market.

BOB JONES UNIVERSITY PRESS/LIGHT LINE BOOKS, 1500 Wade Hampton Blvd. Greenville SC 29614. (803)242-5100, ext. 4315. Book publisher. Contact: Mrs. Gloria Repp, Editor. Publishes 4 young reader titles/year; 4 middle reader titles/year; 4 young adult titles/year. 50% of books by first-time authors.
Fiction: Young readers: animal, contemporary, easy-to-read, history, sports, spy/mystery/adventure. Middle readers: animal, contemporary, history, problem novels, sports, spy/mystery/adventure. Young adults/teens: contemporary, history, problem novels,

sports, spy/mystery/adventure. Average word length: young readers—20,000; middle readers—30,000; young adult/teens—50,000. Published *The Treasure of Pelican Cove*, by Milly Howard (grades 2-4, adventure story); *Right Hand Man*, by Connie Williams (grades 5-8, contemporary)

Nonfiction: Young readers: animal, biography, nature/environment. Middle readers: animal, biography, history, nature/environment. Young adults/teens: biography, history, nature/environment. Average word length: young readers—20,000; middle readers—30,000; young adult/teens—50,000. Published *With Daring Faith*, by Becky Davis (grades 5-8, biography); *Morning Star of the Reformation*, by Andy Thomson (grades 9-12, biography).

How to Contact/Writers: Fiction: "Send the complete manuscript for these genres: Christian biography, modern realism, historical realism, regional realism and mystery/adventure. Query with a synopsis and five sample chapters for these genres: Fantasy and science fiction (no extra-terrestrials). We do not publish these genres: Romance, poetry and drama." Nonfiction: Query, submit complete manuscript or submit outline/synopsis and sample chapters. Reports on queries in 3 weeks; mss in 2 months. Publishes book "approximately one year" after acceptance. Will consider simultaneous and electronic submissions via IBM-compatible disk or modem.

Terms: Buys ms outright for $1,000-1,500. Book catalog and ms guidelines free on request.

Tips: "Write something fresh and unique to carry a theme of lasting value. We publish only books with high moral tone, preferably with evangelical Christian content. Stories should reflect the highest Christian standards of thought, feeling and action. The text should make no reference to drinking, smoking, profanity or minced oaths. Other unacceptable story elements include unrelieved suspense, sensationalism and themes advocating secular attitudes of cynicism, rebellion or materialism."

■**JORDAN ENTERPRISES PUBLISHING CO.**, 6457 Wilcox Station, Box 38002, Los Angeles CA 90038. Book publisher. Estab. 1989. Managing Editor: Patrique Quintahlen. Publishes 2 picture books/year; 1 young reader title/year; 1 middle reader title/year; 1 young adult title/year. 90% of books by first-time authors; 95% of books from agented writers; 1% subsidy published (poetry only).

Fiction: All levels: adventure, animal, fantasy, folktales, health, hi-lo, history, humor, multicultural, nature/environment, poetry, problem novels, romance, science fiction, special needs, sports, suspense/mystery. "No horror, feminist or sexist." Average word length: picture books—2,000; young readers—3,000; middle readers—2,500; young adults—20,000. Recently published *The Strawberry Fox*; *The Christmas Toy Welcome*; *The Boy and the Boss' Breakfast*; *Rueben*.

Nonfiction: All levels: activity books, animal, arts/crafts, biography, careers, concept, cooking, health, hi-lo, history, hobbies, how-to, multicultural, music/dance, nature/environment, reference, religion, science, self-help. Recently published *Roomates, College Sublets and Living in the Dorm*.

How to Contact/Writers: Fiction/nonfiction: Query; submit outline/synopsis and sample chapters. Reports on queries in 4 months; on mss in 6-12 months. Publishes a book 1 year after acceptance. Will consider simultaneous and electronic submissions via disk or modem.

Illustration: Works with 3-5 illustrators/year. Editorial will review ms/illustration packages. Will review artwork for future assignments.

How to Contact/Illustrators: Ms/illustration packages: Query first. Illustrations only: Query with samples; provide résumé and tearsheets. Reports on art samples in 4 months. Original artwork returned at job's completion.

Photography: Purchases photos from freelancers. Contact: Patrique Quintahlen. Needs photos showing nature, art, school, dances, Christmas settings; "various culturally diverse photos with complimentary scenery." Model/property releases required; photo

captions required. Publishes photo essays and photo concept books. Uses 8×11 color, b&w prints; 35mm, 2¼×2¼, 4×5 transparencies. To contact, photographers should query with samples; provide résumé, promo sheet or tearsheets to be kept on file.
Terms: Pays authors in royalties of 4-10% based on retail price. Work purchased outright (range: $400-600). Offers advance (Average amount: $500). Pays illustrators by the project (range: $60-600) or 2-5% royalties based on retail price for juvenile novels. Photographers paid by the project (range: $60-600); per photo (range: $10-200); by royalty of 1-2% based on retail price. Sends galleys to authors; dummies to illustrators.
Tips: Wants "inspiring fantasy picture books and fantasy juvenile novels. Devote 95% of your time to finding an agent once you've completed a manuscript. Do not limit your search for an agent—look nationwide. We are searching for writers who are experienced in using the four stages of writing, and who have written inspiring fantasy stories for children. The gift of imagination combined with professional skills and techniques are a splendid mind set for creating modern classics. There is a growing need for books and articles that more clearly define the times for children."

JUST US BOOKS, INC., 301 Main St., Orange NJ 07050. (201)676-4345. Fax: (201)677-0234. Imprint of Afro-Bets Series. Book publisher; "for selected titles" book packager. Estab. 1988. Vice President/Publisher: Cheryl Willis Hudson. Publishes 4-6 picture books/year; "projected 6" young reader/middle reader titles/year. 33% books by first-time authors. Looking for "books that reflect a genuinely authentic African or African-American experience. We try to work with authors and illustrators who are from the culture itself." Also publishes *Harambee*, a newspaper for young readers, 6 times during the school year. (Target age for *Harambee* is 10-13.)
Fiction: Picture books, young readers, middle readers: adventure, contemporary, easy-to-read, history, multicultural (African-American themes), sports. Average word length: "varies" per picture book; young reader—500-2,000; middle reader—5,000. Wants African-American themes. Gets too many traditional African folktales. Recently published *Land of the Four Winds*, by Veronica Freeman Ellis, illustrated by Sylvia Walker (ages 6-9, picture book).
Nonfiction: Picture books, young readers, middle readers: activity books, biography, concept, history, multicultural (African-American themes). Published *Book of Black Heroes Vol. 2: Great Women in the Struggle*, by Toyomi Igus.
How to Contact/Writers: Fiction/nonfiction: Query or submit outline/synopsis for proposed title. Reports on queries in 6-8 weeks; ms in 8 weeks "or as soon as possible." Publishes a book 12-18 months after acceptance. Will consider simultaneous submissions (with prior notice).
Illustration: Works with 4-6 illustrators/year. Editorial will review ms/illustration packages ("but prefer to review them separately"). Will review artwork for future assignments.
How to Contact/Illustrators: Ms/illustration packages: "Query first." Illustrations only: Query with samples; send résumé, promo sheet, slides, client list, tearsheets; arrange personal portfolio review. Reports in 2-3 weeks. Original artwork returned at job's completion "depending on project."
Photography: Purchases photos from freelancers. Buys stock and assigns work. Wants "African-American themes—kids age 10-13 in school, home and social situations for *Harambee* (newspaper)."
Terms: Pays authors royalty based on retail price or work purchased outright. Royalties based on retail price. Pays illustrators by the project or royalty based on retail price. Sends galleys to authors; dummies to illustrators. Book catalog for business-size SAE and 65¢ postage; ms/artist's guidelines for business-size SAE and 65¢ postage.
Tips: "Multicultural books are tops as far as trends go. There is a great need for diversity and authenticity here. They will continue to be in the forefront of children's book publishing until there is more balanced treatment on these themes industry wide."

Writers: "Keep the subject matter fresh and lively. Avoid 'preachy' stories with stereo-typed characters. Rely more on authentic stories with sensitive three-dimensional char-acters." Illustrators: "Submit 5-10 good, neat samples. Be willing to work with an art director for the type of illustration desired by a specific house and grow into larger projects."

*KABEL PUBLISHERS, 11225 Huntover Dr., Rockville MD 20852. (301)468-6463. Fax: (301)468-6463. Manager: John Aker. Publishes 1-3 picture books/year; 1-3 young read-ers/year; 1-3 middle readers/year; 1-3 young adult titles/year. 20% of books by first-time authors.
Fiction: Will consider any children's fiction category.
Nonfiction: Will consider any children's nonfiction category.
How to Contact/Writers: Fiction/nonfiction: Submit complete ms, outline/synopsis. Reports on queries in 2-4 weeks. Publishes a book 3-6 months after acceptance.
Illustration: Will review ms/illustration packages. Uses primarily b&w artwork only.
How to Contact/Illustrators: Ms/illustration packages: Submit ms with final art. Re-ports in 2-4 weeks. Cannot return samples; samples filed. Originals not returned.
Terms: Pays authors 12 author's copies free as royalty; 20-30% gross after sale of 250 copies. Pays illustrators by the project. Sends galleys to authors (2 proofs). Ms/artist's guidelines are not available.

KAR-BEN COPIES, INC., 6800 Tildenwood Lane, Rockville MD 20852. (301)984-8733. Fax: (301)881-9195. Book publisher. Estab. 1975. Editor: Madeline Wikler. Publishes 10 picture books/year; 10 young reader titles/year. 20% of books by first-time authors.
Fiction: Picture books, young readers, middle readers: Jewish Holiday, Jewish story-book. Does not want to see "anthropomorphic Hanukkah candles or comparisons be-tween Christmas and Hanukkah." Average word length: picture books—2,000. Recently published *Kingdom of Singing Birds*, by Miriam Aroner; *Hillel Builds A House*, by Shos-hana Lepon; *Sammy Spider's First Hanukkah*, by Sylvia Rouss.
Nonfiction: Picture books, young readers, middle readers: religion—Jewish interest. Average word length: picture books—2,000. Recently published *Jewish Holiday Crafts for Little Hands*, by Ruth Brinn; *Tell Me A Mitzvah*, by Danny Siegel; *My First Jewish Word Book*, by Roz Schanzer.
How to Contact/Writers: Fiction/nonfiction: Submit complete ms. Reports on queries/ ms in 6 weeks. Publishes a book 1 year after acceptance. Will consider simultaneous submissions. "We don't like them, but we'll look at them—as long as we *know* it's a simultaneous submission."
Illustration: Works with 12 illustrators/year. Will review ms/illustration packages. Will review artwork for future assignments. Prefers "4-color art to any medium that is scan-nable."
How to Contact/Illustrators: Ms illustration packages: Send whole ms and sample of art (no originals). Illustrations only: Tearsheets, photocopies, promo sheet or anything representative that does *not* need to be returned. Enclose SASE for response. Reports on art samples in 4 weeks.
Terms: Pays authors in royalties of 6-8% based on net sales or work purchased outright (range: $500-2,000). Offers advance (Average amount: $1,000). Pays illustrators royalty of 6-8% based on net sales or by the project (range: $500-3,000). Sends galleys to authors. Book catalog free on request. Ms guidelines for #10 SAE and 1 first-class stamp.

Refer to the Business of Children's Writing & Illustrating for up-to-date marketing, tax and legal information.

Tips: Looks for "books for young children with Jewish interest and content, modern, non-sexist, not didactic. Fiction or nonfiction with a *Jewish* theme—can be serious or humorous, life cycle, Bible story, or holiday-related."

KNOPF BOOKS FOR YOUNG READERS, 29th Floor, 201 E. 20th St., New York NY 10022. (212)254-1600. Random House, Inc. Book publisher. Estab. 1915. Publisher: J. Schulman; Associate Publisher: S. Spinner. 90% of books published through agents.
Fiction: Upmarket picture books: adventure, animal, contemporary, fantasy, retellings of folktales, original stories. Young readers: adventure, animal, contemporary, nature/environment, science fiction, sports, suspense/mystery. Middle readers: adventure, animal, fantasy, nature/environment, science fiction, sports, suspense/mystery. Young adult: adventure, contemporary, fantasy, science fiction—very selective; few being published currently.
Nonfiction: Picture books, young readers, middle readers: animal, biography, nature/environment, sports.
How to Contact/Writers: Fiction/nonfiction: Submit through agent only. Publishes a book 12-18 months after acceptance. Will consider simultaneous submissions.
Illustration: Will review ms/illustration packages (through agent only). Will review an illustrator's work for possible future assignments. Contact: art director.
Terms: Pays authors in royalties. Book catalog free on request.

*LAREDO PUBLISHING CO. INC., 22930 Lockness Ave., Torrance CA 90501. (310)517-1890. Book publisher. Vice President: Clara Kohen. Publishes 5 picture books/year; 15 young readers/year. 10% of books by first-time authors. Spanish language books only.
Fiction: Picture books: multicultural (Spanish). Young readers: adventure, animal, fantasy, folktales, health, multicultural (Spanish), poetry. Middle readers: adventure, animal, contemporary, fantasy, folktales, health, multicultural (Spanish), nature/environment, poetry. Recently published *Pregones*, by Alma Flor Ada (middle readers, personal experience in Spanish); *Pajaritos*, by Clarita Kohen (young readers, counting book in Spanish); *El Conejo y el Coyote*, by Clarita Kohen (young readers, folktale in Spanish).
Nonfiction: Recently published *Los Aztecas*, by Robert Nicholson (middle readers, history, culture and traditions of the Aztecs in Spanish); *Los Sioux*, by Robert Nicholson (middle readers, history, culture and traditions of the Sioux in Spanish); *La Antigua Chine*, by Robert Nicholson (middle readers, history, culture and traditions of the Chinese in Spanish).
How to Contact/Writers: Fiction: Submit complete ms. Reports on mss in 3 months. Publishes a book 1 year after acceptance. Will consider simultaneous submissions.
Illustration: Works with 20 illustrators/year. Will review ms/illustration packages. Uses color artwork only.
How to Contact/Illustrators: Illustrations only: Query with samples, promo sheet. Reports in 2 months. Samples returned with SASE. Originals not returned.
Terms: Pays authors royalty of 5-7% based on wholesale price. Offers advances (varies). Pays illustrators by the project (range: $250-500). Sends galleys to authors; dummies to illustrators.
Tips: "We will only accept manuscripts in Spanish."

LEE & LOW BOOKS, INC., 14th Floor, 228 E. 45th St., New York NY 10017. (212)867-6155. Fax: (212)338-9059. Book publisher. Publisher: Philip Lee. Editor-in-Chief: Elizabeth Szabla. Publishes 6-8 picture books/year. "Multicultural subjects only."

 The asterisk before a listing indicates the listing is new in this edition.

Fiction: Picture books: adventure, contemporary, history, multicultural, nature/environment, sports, suspense/mystery. Young readers: adventure, anthology, contemporary, history, multicultural, nature/environment, sports, suspense/mystery. Middle readers: adventure, anthology, contemporary, history, multicultural, nature/environment, problem novels, sports, suspense/mystery. Does not want to see folktales or stories using animals as main characters. Average word length: picture books—1,000. Recently published *Amelia's Road*, by Linda Jacobs Altman, illustrations by Enrique O. Sanchez (ages 3-10, picture book); *A Crack in the Wall*, by Mary Elizabeth Haggerty, illustrations by Ruben De Anda (ages 4-10, picture book); *Abuela's Weave*, by Omar S. Castaneda, illustrations by Enrique O. Sanchez (ages 3-9, picture book); *Baseball Saved Us*, by Ken Mochizuki, illustrations by Dom Lee (ages 4 and up, picture book); *Joshua's Masai Mask*, by Dakari Hru, illustrations by Anna Rich (ages 3-10, picture book).
Nonfiction: Picture books, young readers, middle readers: biography, history, multicultural. Average word length: picture books—1,000.
How to Contact/Writers: Nonfiction: Query; submit complete ms; submit outline/synopsis and sample chapters. Reports in 1 month on queries; 2 months on mss. Publishes a book "18 months after illustration is accepted." Will consider simultaneous submissions.
Illustration: Works with 4-6 illustrators/year. Will review ms/illustration packages. Will review artwork for future assignments.
How to Contact/Illustrators: Ms/illustration packages: Query; submit complete package. Query with samples, résumé, portfolio, tearsheets. Reports in 1 month. Send SASE for return of originals.
Photography: Photographers should contact Elizabeth Szabla. Publishes photo essays and photo concept books. To contact, photographers should query with samples; query with résumé of credits.
Terms: Pays authors royalty based on retail price. Offers advances. Pays illustrators royalty based on retail price. Photographers paid by the project. Sends galleys to author.
Tips: "Do your homework. Visit a bookstore or a library and find out what kind of children's books are being published. Should it be a picture book or story book? Is the story visual? Is the idea original? Are the characters well developed and believable? We specialize in multicultural stories. We would like to see more contemporary stories that are set in the U.S."

LERNER PUBLICATIONS CO., 241 First Ave. N., Minneapolis MN 55401. (612)332-3344. Fax: (612)332-7615. Book publisher. Editor: Jennifer Martin. Publishes 9 young reader titles/year; 62 middle reader titles/year; 5 young adult titles/year. 20% of books by first-time authors; 5% of books from agented writers. "Most books are nonfiction for children, grades 3-9."
Fiction: Middle readers: adventure, contemporary, folktales, hi-lo, history, multicultural, nature/environment, sports, suspense/mystery. Young adults: contemporary, hi-lo, history, multicultural, nature/environment, poetry, problem novels, sports, suspense/mystery. "Especially interested in books with ethnic characters." Recently published *Ransom for a River Dolphin*, by Sarita Kendall (grades 5 and up, mystery).
Nonfiction: Middle readers, young adults: activity books, animal, arts/crafts, biography, careers, concept, cooking, geography, health, hi-lo, history, hobbies, how-to, multicultural, music/dance, nature/environment, sports, science/math, social issues, self-help, special needs. Multicultural material must contain authentic details. Does not want to see textbooks, workbooks, song books, audiotapes, puzzles, plays, religious material, books for teachers or parents, picture or alphabet books. Average word length: young readers—3,000; middle readers—7,000; young adults—12,000. Recently published *Marie Curie and Her Daughter Irene*, by Rosalynd Pflaum (grades 5 and up, Lerner Biographies series); *Hakeem Olajuwon: Tower of Power*, by George R. Rekela (grades 4-9,

Expanding the Limits of Kids' Book Illustration

Prior to 1990, Michael Paraskevas didn't have any of the credentials one would expect in a children's book illustrator. Having spent most of his time painting for such haute publications as *New York* magazine, *Town & Country* and *Esquire*, his style was editorial, linear, sophisticated. He'd never worked with a book publisher, much less a children's book publisher. He didn't even have kids.

But in what seemed like an overnight success, Paraskevas illustrated and published five children's books (all written by his mother, Betty) and garnered an award from the Society of Illustrators. Critics compared his work to the prolific and ever-popular Shel Silverstein. His list of credentials grew like a beanstalk into the clouds.

Michael Paraskevas

The secret to his success? Any logical competitor might assume Paraskevas metamorphosed his work to fit the mold of the kids' book universe. But in fact the opposite is true. "I didn't change my style at all," he says matter-of-factly. The trick was to convince publishers that editorial renderings in charcoal, acrylic and gouache would work for kids. "One art director even laughed at my portfolio," he recalls. "I had stuff in it from *Sports Illustrated* and *Time*, and she said, 'Well, this is very editorial, but it doesn't look like children's book work.' I said, 'I know, but I want to paint like this for kids' books.' "

Other publishers, however, didn't laugh at all. They respected Paraskevas's adamance about his style, and rather liked his quirky rejection of puffy paint and watercolor in favor of more sophisticated images. Dial Books quickly snatched up the first two mother-son collaborations: *On the Edge of the Sea* and *The Strawberry Dog*. More recently, Harcourt Brace offered a contract for an entire series — three kids' books and an adult paperback — centered around a mischievous character named Junior Kroll.

A character with universal appeal, Junior Kroll first came into existence more than three years ago. "I was doing a weekly page of jokes for the local paper and asked my mother to come up with some ideas that I could illustrate," explains Paraskevas. "She came up with the idea for this malicious little kid named Junior Kroll who did things like paint monsters on the wall with the tail of a cat. Visually, I've always based Junior on me as a kid. I had lots of old photos I used at first for reference, but now I've got him down and can draw him from memory."

Perhaps what is most unique about Junior Kroll, aside from his stark visage, is the fact that "he relates a lot to older people," adds Paraskevas. "One reviewer raved about this because a lot of kids don't have that today. Especially on children's programming. It's always little kids relating to other little kids—which is fine, but there's something missing." Kids shouldn't have to be completely segregated from the adult world, he stresses.

In fact, "kids are more sophisticated than people think," Paraskevas defends. "Some of our books contain all sorts of little innuendoes about older people—and that's OK." Books can be read at different levels and appreciated for different reasons, he says. "You can read to a little kid who will just enjoy the pictures and the basic story or you can read it when you're older [and get more out of it]." He cites as an example one bookstore in Miami which "had trouble selling *Junior Kroll* in the kids' section, so they moved it to an adult section—and sold out all the copies!"

As the kids' book market booms and shelves are jammed with new titles competing for attention, Paraskevas knows how difficult it is to be noticed. It's tempting to follow successful trends. Nevertheless, he warns authors and illustrators to think twice before tackling unfamiliar subjects. "I don't think you can write or paint truthfully about things unrelated to you," he says. "You can always spot a fake a mile away. My mother would never write about a Russian immigrant living in Poland because she doesn't know anything about that."

Finally, keeping current on kids' interests is paramount, says Paraskevas, who frequents toy stores, video parlors and children's bookstores. But studying kids, he adds, is not an exact science. Much of the creative process has to remain intuitive. "Don't draw what you *think* kids would like," he advises. "Draw what you *know* you would have liked as a kid." Remember and trust your gut.

—*Jenny Pfalzgraf*

After convincing publishers that editorial renderings in charcoal, acrylic and gouache would work for kids, Michael Paraskevas began illustrating and publishing children's books written by his mother, Betty. Junior Kroll (Harcourt Brace & Co., 1993) is the first in their popular series of books about a malicious youngster.

Sports Achievers series); *Abortion: Understanding the Controversy* by JoAnn Bren Guernsey (grades 6 and up, Pro/Con series).
How to Contact/Writers: Fiction: Submit outline/synopsis and sample chapters. Nonfiction: Query; submit outline/synopsis and sample chapters. Reports on queries in 2-3 weeks; mss in 2 months. Publishes a book 12-18 months after acceptance. Will consider simultaneous submissions.
Illustration: Works with 1-2 illustrators/year. Will review ms/illustration packages. Will review artwork for future assignments. "We tend to work only with local talent." Contact: Art Director.
How to Contact/Illustrators: Query with samples and résumé.
Photography: Contact: Photo Research Department. Buys stock and assigns work. Model/property releases required. Publishes photo essays. Photographers should query with samples.
Terms: Pays authors royalty or work purchased outright. Pays illustrators by the project. Sends galleys to authors. Book catalog available for 9×12 SAE and $1.90 postage; ms guidelines for 4×9 SAE and 1 first-class stamp.
Tips: Wants "straightforward, well-written nonfiction for children in grades 3-9 backed by solid current research or scholarship. Before you send your manuscript to us, you might first take a look at the kinds of books that our company publishes. We specialize in publishing high-quality educational books for children from second grade through high school. Avoid sex stereotypes (e.g., strong, aggressive, unemotional males/weak, submissive, emotional females) in your writing, as well as sexist language." (See also Carolrhoda Books, Inc.)

LION BOOKS, PUBLISHER, Suite B, 210 Nelson, Scarsdale NY 10583. (914)725-2280. Imprint of Sayre Ross Co. Book publisher. Editorial contact: Harriet Ross. Publishes 5 middle reader titles/year; 10 young adult titles/year. 50-70% of books by first-time authors. Publishes books "with ethnic and minority accents for young adults, including a variety of craft titles dealing with African and Asian concepts."
Nonfiction: Activity, art/crafts, biography, history, hobbies, how-to, multicultural. Average word length: young adult—30,000-50,000.
How to Contact/Writers: Nonfiction: Query, submit complete ms. Reports on queries in 3 weeks; ms in 2 months.
How to Contact/Illustrators: Reports in 2 weeks.
Terms: Work purchased outright (range: $500-5,000). Average advance: $750-2,000. Illustrators paid $500-1,500. Sends galleys to author. Book catalog free on request.

LITTLE, BROWN AND COMPANY, 34 Beacon St., Boston MA 02108. (617)227-0730. Book publisher. Editor-in-Chief: Maria Modugno. Art Director: Sue Sherman. Estab. 1837. Publishes 30% picture books/year; 10% young reader titles/year; 30% middle reader titles/year; 10% young adult titles/year.
  ● At press time, Little, Brown announced it was cutting back its number of children's titles by 30% (from 120 titles in 1993 to 85-90 by 1995) and "regrettably," is no longer accepting unsolicited mss.
Fiction: Picture books: adventure, animal, contemporary, fantasy, folktales, history, humor, multicultural, nature/environment. Young readers: adventure, animal, contemporary, fantasy, history, humor, multicultural, nature/environment, science fiction, suspense/mystery. Middle readers: adventure, contemporary, fantasy, history, humor, multicultural, nature/environment, science fiction, suspense/mystery. Young adults: contemporary, health, humor, multicultural, nature/environment, suspense/mystery. Multicultural needs include "any material by, for and about minorities." No "rhyming texts, anthropomorphic animals that learn a lesson, alphabet and counting books, and stories based on an event rather than a character." Average word length: picture books—1,000; young readers—6,000; middle readers—15,000-25,000; young adults—

20,000-40,000. Recently published *Honkers*, by Jane Yolen (ages 4-8, picture book); *Babysitting for Benjamin*, by Valiska Gregory (ages 4-8, picture book); *Howling for Home*, by Joan Carris (ages 7-9, first chapter book); *Dear Mom, Get Me Out of Here!*, by Ellen Conford (ages 8-12, middle reader).

Nonfiction: Picture books: animal, biography, concept, history, multicultural, nature/environment. Young readers: activity books, biography, multicultural. Middle readers: activity books, arts/crafts, biography, cooking, geography, history, multicultural. Young adults: multicultural, self-help, social issues. Average word length: picture books—2,000; young readers—4,000-6,000; middle readers—15,000-25,000; young adults—20,000-40,000. Recently published *In the Shogun's Shadow*, by John Langone (ages 10 and up, young adult); *Faith Ringgold*, by Robin Turner (ages 6-10, picture book).

How to Contact/Writers: Fiction/nonfiction: Submit through agent only.

Illustration: Works with 40 illustrators/year. Will review artwork for future assignments.

How to Contact/Illustrators: Illustrations only: Query with samples/slides; provide résumé, promo sheet or tearsheets to be kept on file. Reports on art samples in 6-8 weeks. Original artwork returned at job's completion.

Photography: Contact: Sue Sherman, art director. Works on assignment only. Model/property releases required; captions required. Publishes photo essays and photo concept books. Uses 35mm transparencies. Photographers should provide résumé, promo sheets or tearsheets to be kept on file.

Terms: Pays authors royalties of 3-10% based on retail price. Offers advance (Average amount: $2,000-10,000). Pays illustrators by the project (range: $1,500-5,000) or royalty of 3-10% based on retail price. Photographers paid by the project, by royalty based on retail price. Sends galleys to authors; dummies to illustrators. Book catalog, manuscript/artist's guidelines free on request.

Tips: "Publishers are cutting back their lists in response to a shrinking market and relying more on big names and known commodities. In order to break into the field these days, authors and illustrators must research their competition and try to come up with something outstandingly different."

LODESTAR BOOKS, 375 Hudson St., New York NY 10014. (212)366-2627. Fax: (212)366-2011. Affiliate of Dutton Children's Books, a division of Penguin Books, USA, Inc. Estab. 1980. Editorial Director: Virginia Buckley. Senior Editor: Rosemary Brosnan. Publishes 10 picture books/year; 8-10 middle reader titles/year; 5 young adult titles/year (25 books/year). 5-10% of books by first-time authors; 50% through agents.

● This publisher has received numerous awards in recent years including the Coretta Scott King Honor Book Award and other awards from the American Library Association and the Boston Globe-Horn Book.

Fiction: Picture books: adventure, animal, contemporary, folktales, humor, multicultural, nature/environment. Young readers: adventure, animal, contemporary, humor, multicultural, nature/environment. Middle reader: adventure, animal, contemporary, folktales, humor, multicultural, nature/environment, suspense/mystery. Young adult: adventure, contemporary, history, humor, multicultural, nature/environment. Multicultural needs include "well-written books with good characterization. Prefer books by authors of same ethnic background as subject, but not absolutely necessary." No commercial picture books, science fiction or genre novels. Recently published *Little Eight John*, by Jan Wahl with illustrations by Wil Clay (ages 5-8, picture book); *Jericho's Journey*, by G. Clifton Wisler (ages 10-14, historical novel); *Celebrating the Hero*, by Lyll Becerra de Jenkins (ages 12 and up, a novel set in Columbia).

Nonfiction: Picture books: activity books, animal, concept, geography, history, multicultural, nature/environment, science, social issues. Young reader: animal, concept, geography, history, multicultural, nature/environment, science, social issues, sports.

Middle reader: animal, biography, careers, geography, history, multicultural, music/dance, nature/environment, science, social issues, sports. Young adult: history, multicultural, music/dance, nature/environment, social issues, sports. Multicultural needs include authentic, well-written books about African-American, Native American, Hispanic and Asian-American experiences. Also, books on Jewish themes. Recently published *The Giant Book of Animal Worlds*, by Anita Ganeri, illustrations by John Butler (ages 7-10, giant board book on animal habitats); *Twins on Toes: A Ballet Debut*, by Joan Anderson, photographs by George Ancona (ages 8-12); *Witnesses to Freedom: Young People Who Fought for Civil Rights*, by Belinda Rochelle (ages 8-12).

How to Contact/Writers: Fiction: submit synopsis and sample chapters or submit complete ms. Nonfiction: Query or submit synopsis and sample chapters. Reports on queries in 1 month; mss in 3 months. Publishes a book 12-18 months after acceptance. Will consider simultaneous submissions.

Illustration: Works with approximately 12 illustrators/year. Will review ms/illustration packages. Will review artwork for possible future assignments.

How to Contact/Illustrators: Ms/illustration packages: Send "manuscript and copies of art (no original art please)." Illustrations only: Query with samples; send portfolio or slides. Drop off portfolio for review. Reports back only if interested. Original art work returned at job's completion.

Photography: Purchases photos from freelancers (infrequently).

Terms: Pays authors and illustrators royalties of 5% each for picture books; 8% to author, 2% to illustrator for illustrated novel; and 10% for novel based on retail price. Sends galleys to author. Book catalog for SASE; manuscript guidelines for #10 SAE and 1 first-class stamp.

Tips: Wants "well-written books that show awareness of children's and young people's lives, feelings and problems; arouse imagination and are sensitive to children's needs. More books by African-American, Hispanic, Asian-American and Native American writers. More novelty and interactional books."

LOOK AND SEE PUBLICATIONS, P.O. Box 64216, Tucson AZ 85728-4216. (602)529-2857. Book publisher. "We self-publish the children's activity books we write." Publishes 2 young readers/year. Publishes "history and cultures of the Southwest national parks."

Nonfiction: Middle readers, young adults: activity books.

How to Contact/Writers: Nonfiction: Query. "We are not interested in having manuscripts submitted." Reports on queries in 1 month.

Illustration: Works with 1-2 illustrators/year. Will review artwork for future assignments. Uses primarily b&w artwork only. Most of the art we use is done in charcoal or pen & ink.

How to Contact/Illustrators: Ms/illustration packages: Query. Illustrations only: Query with samples. Reports back only if interested. Cannot return samples; samples filed. Originals not returned.

Terms: Pays illustrators by the project. Sends dummies to illustrators. Book catalog available for 4¼ × 9½ SAE and 1 first-class stamp. Ms/artist's guidelines not available.

LOTHROP, LEE & SHEPARD BOOKS, 1350 Avenue of the Americas, New York NY 10019. (212)261-6500. Division and imprint of William Morrow Co. Inc., Children's Fiction and Nonfiction. Editor-in-Chief: Susan Pearson. Publishes 60 total titles/year.

Fiction: All levels: various categories. Recently published *By the Light of the Halloween Moon*, by Caroline Stutson, illustrated by Kevin Hawkes; *Down Buttermilk Lane*, by Barbara Mitchell, illustrated by John Sandford.

Nonfiction: Recently published *Pablo Remembers: The Fiesta of the Day of the Dead*, by George Ancona; *Kangaroos: On Location* by Kathy Darling, photographs by Tara Darling.

How to Contact/Writers: Fiction and nonfiction: Query; "no unsolicited mss." Reports on queries in 1-6 weeks; mss in 1-6 months (longer for novels).
Illustration: Works with 30 or more illustrators/year. Editorial will review ms/illustration packages. Will review artwork for future assignments.
How to Contact/Illustrators: Ms/illustration packages: Write for guidelines first. Illustrations only: Query with samples; submit portfolio for review.
Photography: Purchases photos from freelancers. Buys stock and assigns work.
Terms: Method of payment: "varies." Royalties/advances negotiated. Ms/artist's guidelines free for SASE.
Tips: Currently seeking picture books and young nonfiction. "Multicultural books of all types" are popular right now. Does not want books written to fill a special need instead of from the writer's experience and personal conviction. Also does not want film scripts, cartoon merchandising ideas or pedantic books. Work should come from the heart.

LUCAS/EVANS BOOKS INC., 1123 Broadway, New York NY 10010. (212)929-2583. Executive Director: Barbara Lucas. Editor and Production Manager: Cassandra Conyers. Estab. 1984. Book packager specializing in children's books, preschool through high school age. Books prepared from inception to camera-ready mechanicals for all major publishers.
Fiction/Nonfiction: Particularly interested in series ideas, especially for middle grades and beginning readers. All subject categories except problem novels and textbooks considered. Recently published fiction titles: *Ghost Dog*, by Ellen Leroe (Hyperion); *Song for the Ancient Forest*, by Nancy Luenn (Atheneum); *Second-Grade Friends*, by Miriam Cohen (Scholastic). Recently published nonfiction titles: *They Had a Dream*, Epoch Biography by Jules Archer (Viking); *The Kids' Cookbook*, by West Village Nursery School (Outlet); *Science Source Books* (Facts on File series).
How to Contact/Writers: Query. Reports on queries in 2 months.
Illustration: Works with 15-20 illustrators/year. Query first. Color photocopies of art welcome for our file.
How to Contact/Illustrators: Query with samples; provide résumé, promo sheet, slides, client list, tearsheets, arrange personal portfolio review.
Terms: Offers authors and illustrators royalty-based contracts with advance based on retail price or work purchased outright.
Tips: Prefers experienced authors and artists but will consider unpublished work. "There seems to be an enormous demand for early chapter books, although we will continue our efforts to sell to publishers in all age groups and formats. We are interested in series since publishers look to packagers for producing time-consuming projects."

LUCENT BOOKS, P.O. Box 289011, San Diego CA 92128-9009. (619)485-7424. Sister Company to Greenhaven Press. Book publisher. Editor: Bonnie Szumski. 50% of books by first-time authors; 10% of books from agented writers.
Nonfiction: Middle readers, young adults: education, heatlh, topical history, nature/environment, sports, "any overviews of specific topics—i.e., political, social, cultural, economic, criminal, moral issues." No fiction. Average word length: 15,000-20,000. Published *The Persian Gulf War*, by Don Nardo (grades 6-12, history); *Photography*, by Brad Steffens (grades 5-8, history); *Rainforests*, by Lois Warburton (grades 5-8, overview).
How to Contact/Writers: Nonfiction: "Writers should query first; we do writing by assignment only. If you want to write for us, send SASE for guidelines." Reports on queries in 2 months. Publishes a book 6 months after acceptance.
Illustration: "We use photos, mostly." Uses primarily b&w artwork only. Will review ms/illustration packages. Will review artwork for future assignments. "Prefers 7 × 9 format—4-color cover."

How to Contact/Illustrators: Ms/illustration packages: Query first. Illustrations only: Query with samples; provide résumé, business card, promotional literature or tearsheets to be kept on file.

Terms: "Fee negotiated upon review of manuscript." Sends galleys to authors. Ms guidelines free on request.

Tips: "Books must be written at a 7-8 grade reading level. There's a growing market for quality nonfiction. Tentative subjects: free speech, tobacco, alcohol, discrimination, immigration, poverty, the homeless in America, space weapons, drug abuse, terrorism, animal experimentation, endangered species, AIDS, pollution, gun control, etc. The above list is presented to give writers an example of the kinds of titles we are seeking. If you are interested in writing about a specific topic, please query us by mail before you begin writing to be sure we have not assigned a particular topic to another author. The author should strive for objectivity. There obviously will be many issues on which a position should be taken—e.g. discrimination, tobacco, alcoholism, etc. However, moralizing, self-righteous condemnations, maligning, lamenting, mocking, etc. should be avoided. Moreover, where a pro/con position is taken, contrasting viewpoints should be presented. Certain moral issues such as abortion and euthanasia, if dealt with at all, should be presented with strict objectivity."

*LUCKY BOOKS, P.O. Box 1415, Winchester VA 22604. (703)662-3424. Book publisher. Co-Publishers: Mac S. Rutherford and Donna Rutherford. Publishes 1-2 picture books/ year; 1-2 young readers/year. 90% of books by first-time authors.

Fiction: Picture books, young readers: adventure, animal, fantasy, nature/environment, poetry. No religion. Average word length: picture books—500-1,500; young readers—3,000-6,000. Recently published *Prince*, by Margery Van Susteren (8 and up, pet story); *Zonkey The Donkey*, by Virginia Athey, illustrated by Donna Rutherford (pre-school, poetic); *When The Zebras Came For Lunch*, by Barbara Van Curen (pre-school, fantasy).

Nonfiction: Picture books, young readers: animal. Not interested in how-to. Average word length: picture books—500-1,500.

How to Contact/Writers: Fiction: Submit complete ms. Nonfiction: Query. Reports on queries in 1-2 months; mss in 3-4 months. Publishes a book 1-1½ years after acceptance (varies greatly).

Illustration: Works with 1 illustrator/year. Will review ms/illustration packages. Will review artwork for future assignments. Contact: Donna Rutherford.

How to Contact/Illustrators: Ms/illustration packages: Submit ms with 2-3 pieces of final art. Illustrations only: Query with samples, résumé, slides. Reports back only if interested. Samples returned with SASE; samples filed.

Terms: Pays authors royalty of 3-6% based on wholesale or retail price. Pays illustrators royalty of 1-3% based on wholesale or retail price.

MARGARET K. McELDERRY BOOKS, 866 Third Ave., New York NY 10022. (212)702-7855. Fax: (212)605-3045. Imprint of Macmillan Publishing Co. Book publisher. Publisher: Margaret K. McElderry. Art Director: Nancy Williams. Publishes 10-12 picture books/year; 2-4 young reader titles/year; 8-10 middle reader titles/year; 5-7 young adult titles/year. 25% of books by first-time authors; 33% of books from agented writers.

● In November, 1993, all imprints of the Macmillan Children's Book Group and all other divisions of Macmillan were sold to Paramount Communications. This could affect future editorial policies, so watch *Publishers Weekly* and other trade journals for details.

Fiction: Picture books: folktales, humor, multicultural. Young readers: contemporary, fantasy, humor, multicultural, poetry. Middle readers: adventure, contemporary, fantasy, poetry, suspense/mystery. Young adult: poetry. "Always interested in publishing picture books and beginning reader books which feature minority characters. We see too many rhymed picture book manuscripts which are not terribly original or special."

Average word length: picture books—500; young readers—2,000; middle readers—10,000-20,000; young adults—45,000-50,000. Recently published *The Boggart*, by Susan Cooper; *The Christmas Knight*, by Jane Louise Curry; *Winter Camp*, by Kirkpatrick Hill.
Nonfiction: Young readers, middle readers: biography, history. Average word length: picture books—500-1,000; young readers—1,500-3,000; middle readers—10,000-20,000; young adults—30,000-45,000. Published *Climbing Jacob's Ladder: Heroes of the Bible in African-America Spirituals*, selected by John Langstaff, illustrated by Ashley Bryan (all ages); *Natural History from A to Z*, by Tim Arnold (ages 10-14, basic concepts of biology); *Hiawatha: Messenger of Peace*, by Dennis Fradin (ages 7-11).
How to Contact/Writers: Fiction/nonfiction: Submit complete ms. Reports on queries in 2 weeks; mss in 3 months. Publishes a book 12-18 months after acceptance. Will consider simultaneous submissions (only if indicated as such).
Illustration: Works with 20-30 illustrators/year. Design department will review an artwork for future assignments (2 or 3 samples only).
How to Contact/Illustrators: Ms/illustration packages: Ms (complete) and 2 or 3 copies of finished art. Illustrations only: Query with samples; provide, promo sheet or tearsheets; arrange personal portfolio review. Reports on art samples in 6-8 weeks. Original artwork returned at job's completion.
Terms: Pays authors royalty based on retail price. Pays illustrators by the project or royalty based on retail price. Photographers paid by the project. Sends galleys to authors; dummies to illustrators. Book catalog, ms/artist's guidelines free on request.
Tips: Sees "more sales of beginning chapter books; more sales of poetry books; constant interest in books for the youngest baby market." (See also Aladdin Books/Collier Books for Young Readers, Atheneum Publishers, Bradbury Press, Four Winds Press.)

MACMILLAN CHILDREN'S BOOKS, 866 Third Ave., New York NY 10022. Imprint of Macmillan Publishing Company. Contact: Submissions Editor. Publishes 45 picture books/year; 10 young readers books/year; 10 middle readers books/year; 5 young adult books/year. 5% or less of books by first-time authors; 33% from agented authors. "No primary theme—of a higher literary standard than mass market."
  • In November 1993, all imprints of the Macmillan Children's Book Group and all other divisions of Macmillan were sold to Paramount Communications. This could affect future editorial policies, so watch *Publishers Weekly* and other trade journals for details.
Fiction: All levels: adventure, anthology, animal, contemporary, fantasy, folktales, history, humor, multicultural, nature/environment, poetry, problem novels, science fiction, suspense/mystery. Does not want to see "topic" books, stories about bunnies or kittens, "New Age" themes. Published *Our Yard Is Full of Birds*, by Anne Rockwell, illustrated by Lizzy Rockwell (ages 2-7, picture book); *Meet Posy Bates*, by Helen Cresswell (grades 1-4, storybook); *Hats Off to John Stetson*, by Mary Blount Christian, illustrated by Ib Ohlsson, (grades 2-6, historical fiction).
Nonfiction: Picture books, young readers, middle readers and young adults: animal, biography, history, music/dance, nature/environment, science. No fixed lengths! Recently published *The Macmillan Book of Baseball Stories*, by Terry Egan, Stan Friedmann and Mike Levine (grades 3 and up); *Frank Thompson: Her Civil War Story*, by Bryna Stevens (grades 5-9, biography); *Man and Mustang*, by George Ancona (grades 3-7, photo essay).
How to Contact/Writers: Fiction/nonfiction: Query. Submit complete ms ("only shorter works"). Submit outline/synopsis and 2 sample chapters. "For longer works, query with sample chapter and outline. All submissions must include SASE!" Reports on queries in 1-2 weeks; mss in 2-6 weeks. Publishes a book 1-2 years after acceptance.
Illustration: Works with 45 illustrators/year. Will review ms/illustration packages. Will review artwork for future assignments. Contact: Art Director.

How to Contact/Illustrators: Ms/illustrations packages: Send complete ms with sample illustrations. Illustrations only: Query with samples and résumé; submit portfolio for review; drop off portfolio on specified days. "Should request guidelines for our portfolio review procedure—on a drop-off basis, or can mail it in." Reports back only if interested. Original artwork returned at job's completion. Publishes photo essays and photo concept books. Uses color and b&w prints.

Photography: Purchases photos from freelancers. "We do not work with stock agencies much. Most of the photos we receive come with a manuscript, written by the photographer, or an author they're collaborating with."

Terms: Advance and royalties based on retail price negotiated at time of contract. Pays illustrators by the project or royalty bsed on retail price. Pays photographers by the project, per photo, royalty. Sends galleys to authors. Book catalog available for 9 × 12 SAE and $1.20 postage; ms guidelines available for SASE.

Tips: Wants "an original story that is not based on an overworked theme. With novels, good character development is essential."

MAGE PUBLISHERS INC., 1032-29th St. NW, Washington DC 20007. (202)342-1642. Book publisher. Editorial Contact: A. Sepehri. Publishes 2-3 picture books/year.

Fiction: Contemporary/myth, Persian heritage. Average word length: 5,000.

Nonfiction: Persian heritage. Average word length: 5,000.

How to Contact/Writers: Fiction/nonfiction: Query. Reports on queries/ms in 3 months. Will consider simultaneous submissions.

Illustration: Editorial will review ms/illustration packages submitted by authors/artists; ms/illustration packages. Will review artwork for possible future assignments.

How to Contact/Illustrators: Illustrations only: Send résumé and slides. Reports in 3 months. Original artwork returned at job's completion.

Terms: Pays authors in royalties. Sends galleys to authors. Book catalog free on request.

MAGINATION PRESS, 19 Union Square West, New York NY 10003. (212)924-3344. Brunner/Mazel, Inc. Book publisher. Editor-in-Chief: Susan Kent Cakars. Publishes 4-8 picture books and young reader titles/year. Publishes "books dealing with the psycho/therapeutic treatment or resolution of children's serious problems—written by mental health professionals."

Fiction: Picture books, young readers: concept, mental health, multicultural, problem novels, special needs. Recently published *Gentle Willow: A Story for Children About Dying*, by Joyce C. Mills, Ph.D. (ages 4-8); *Sammy's Mommy Has Cancer*, by Sherry Kohlenberg (ages 4-8); *What About Me? When Brothers & Sisters Get Sick*, by Allan Peterkin, M.D. (ages 4-8).

Nonfiction: Picture books and young readers: concept, mental health, how-to, multicultural, psychotherapy, special needs. Published *Putting on the Brakes: Young People's Guide to Understanding Attention Deficit Hyperactivity Disorder (ADHD)*, by Patricia O. Quinn, M.D. and Judith M. Stern, M.A. (ages 8-13).

How to Contact/Writers: Fiction/nonfiction: Submit complete ms. Reports on queries/mss: "up to 3 months (may be only days)." Publishes a book 1 year after acceptance.

Illustration: Works with 4-8 illustrators/year. Reviews illustration packages. Will review artwork for future assignments. Prefers b&w for text, full-color for cover.

How to Contact/Illustrators: Illustrations only: Query with samples. Original artwork returned at job's completion.

A bullet has been placed within some listings to introduce special comments by the editor of Children's Writer's & Illustrator's Market.

Terms: Pays authors in royalties. Offers varied but low advance. Pays illustrators by the project, $2,000 max. Pays royalty, 2% max. Sends galleys to authors. Book catalog and ms guidelines on request with SASE.

MARCH MEDIA, INC., #256, 7003 Chadwick, Brentwood TN 37027. (615)370-3148. Independent book producer/agency. President: Etta G. Wilson. 25% of books by first-time authors.
Fiction: Picture books, young readers, middle readers: humor, multicultural, religion. Multicultural needs include Hispanic characters. Recently produced *Tennesee Trailblazers*, by Pat Kissack (9-12); *Holt and the Cowboys*, by Jim McCafferty (7-10).
Nonfiction: Picture books, young readers: religion. Middle readers: history, nature/environment, religion.
How to Contact/Writers: Fiction: Submit outline/synopsis and sample chapters. Nonfiction: submit complete ms. Reports on queries in 2 weeks, on ms in 3 months. Will consider simultaneous submissions.
Illustration: Works with 7 illustrators/year. Editorial will review ms/illustration packages. Will review artwork for future assignments.
How to Contact/Illustrators: Ms/illustration packages: "Query first." Illustrations only: Send tearsheets to be kept on file. Reports back only if interested. Original art work returned at job's completion.
Terms: Pays authors royalty or work purchased outright. Pays illustrators by the project.
Tips: Illustrators: "Be certain you can draw children. Study book design." Looking for manuscripts that present "a unique, imaginative exploration of a situation." Recent trend reflects "more nonfiction and better art."

MEADOWBROOK PRESS, 18318 Minnetonka Blvd., Deephaven MN 55391. (612)473-5400. Fax: (612)473-0736. Book publisher. Senior Editor: Elizabeth Weiss. Submissions Editor: Craig Hansen. Publishes 10-12 titles/year. 20% of books by first-time authors; 10% of books from agented writers. Publishes nonfiction—"Parenting, pregnancy and childcare; humor particularly relating to gift giving occasions, children's activity books, and gift books."
Nonfiction: Young readers and middle readers: activity books, childcare, parenting. *No fiction picture books.* Average word length: varies. Recently published: *The Joy of Parenthood*, by Jan Blaustone; *Kids' Party Games and Activities*, by Penny Warner.
Poetry: "We have several ongoing poetry projects, for young readers and adults." Poets should contact and request a list of current projects.
How to Contact/Writers: Nonfiction: Query, submit outline/synopsis and sample chapters or submit complete ms. Reports on queries/mss in 1-3 months. Publishes a book 9-12 months after acceptance. Send a business-sized SAE and 2 first-class stamps for writer's guidelines and book catalog before submitting ideas. Will consider simultaneous submissions.
Illustration: Will review illustration portfolios. Kate Laing, Production Manager, will review artwork for future assignments.
How to Contact/Illustrators: Illustration portfolios: Send photos or color copies of final art. Do not send original artwork unless requested. Reports back in 2-3 weeks.
Terms: Pays authors in royalties of 5-7½% based on retail price. Offers average advance payment of $1,000-5,000. Pay for illustrators: $100-10,000; ¼-¾% of total royalties. Sends galleys for review to authors "sometimes."
Tips: Illustrators: "Develop a commercial style—compare your style to that of published illustrators, and submit your work when it is judged 'in the ball park.' " Writers: "Don't send in just anything. Our catalog and guidelines are free for a SASE. Send for them. See what works for us, what we publish. 98% of rejected material comes from writers who never bothered to do their homework on us and find out what we do publish, first. As a result, their ideas are a total miss for our market from the word 'go.' " Poets: "Send

in only your best work. If you're writing a structured poem, stick rigidly to meter and beat. Our philosophy favors clear ideas clearly communicated. Poems that leave their message a mystery don't work well in our market."

MERIWETHER PUBLISHING LTD., 885 Elkton Dr., Colorado Springs CO 80907. Book publisher. Estab. 1969. Executive Editor: Arthur L. Zapel. Art Director: Tom Myers. "We do most of our artwork in-house; we do not usually publish for the children's elementary market." 75% of books by first-time authors; 5% of books from agented writers. Publishes primarily how-to activity books for teens. Most books are related to theater arts or activities for church youth.
Fiction: Middle readers, young adults: anthology, contemporary, humor, religion. "We are currently looking for a religious children's book at the primary level." Does not want storybooks for teens.
Nonfiction: Middle readers: activity books, religion. Young adults: activity books, how-to church activities, religion, drama/theater arts. Average length: 250 pages. Recently published *The Theatre and You*, by Marsh Cassady; *Readers Theatre Anthology*, by Mel White; *Play It Again*, by Norman and Deb Bert.
How to Contact/Writers: Nonfiction: Query or submit outline/synopsis and sample chapters. Reports on queries in 3 weeks; mss in 6 weeks. Publishes a book 6-12 months after acceptance. Will consider simultaneous submissions.
Illustration: Works with 3 illustrators/year. Will review ms/illustration packages. Will review artwork for future assignments.
How to Contact/Illustrators: Ms/illustration packages: Query first. Illustrations only: Query with samples; send résumé, promo sheet or tearsheets. Reports on art samples in 4 weeks.
Terms: Pays authors in royalties of 10% based on retail or wholesale price. Pays illustrators by the project (range: $150-3,000); royalties based on retail or wholesale price. Sends galleys to authors. Book catalog for SAE and $2 postage; ms guidelines for SAE and 1 first-class stamp.
Tips: "As indicated, we are currently looking for a unique concept for a children's book series relating to religion. It must be for the elementary level—applies to writers or illustrators, together or separately. We are new in publishing children's books. The two titles we have published were for the religous market—read aloud books for parents."

MERRILL PUBLISHING, 445 Hutchinson Ave., Columbus OH 43235. (614)841-3700. Fax: (614)841-3701. Imprint of Macmillan Publishing Co./College Division. Editor for Education: Linda Scharp. Publishes "educational books used by college students to teach them how to deal with children, children's special needs and foundations of education. Publishes some children's literature books and other disciplines in other divisions."
Illustration: Uses 30-40 illustrations/year for college level textbooks. Will review illustration packages. Contact: Cathleen Norz, cover designer, at (614)841-3699.
How to Contact/Illustrators: Query with samples; submit portfolio for review; provide tearsheets. Reports in 1 week.
Photography: Photo Editor: Ann Vega. Uses photos of children, children with teachers at school, handicapped, children at play. Model/property release required with submissions. Uses color and b&w glossy prints and 35mm transparencies. Provide transparencies; submit portfolio for review.
Terms: Pays $300-1,000 by the project.
Tips: Wants "illustrations or photos depicting real life and some illustrations based on children's responses to literature."

JULIAN MESSNER, 15 Columbus Circle, New York NY 10023. (212)373-8000. Imprint of Simon & Schuster's Children's Trade Division. Book publisher. President and Publisher: Willa Perlman. Publishes 4 young reader titles/year; 15 middle reader titles/year;

10 young adult titles/year. 25% of books by first-time authors; 50% of books from agented writers.

Nonfiction: Middle readers: animal, biography, general science, history, hobbies, nature/environment. Young adults: biography, general science, history, nature/environment, teen issues. Average word length: middle readers—30,000; young adults—40,000-45,000. Published *The Starry Sky*, Rose Wyler (5-7 years, science); *The Homeless*, by Elaine Landau (11-13 years, teenage nonfiction); *George Bush*, by George Sullivan (12-14 years, biography).

How to Contact/Writers: Nonfiction: Query. Reports on queries in 2 months; on mss in 3 months. Publishes a book 8 months after acceptance. Will consider simultaneous submissions.

Illustration: Editorial will review ms/illustration packages submitted by authors with illustrations done by separate artists.

How to Contact/Illustrators: Ms/illustration packages: Query first. Illustrations only: "Résumé and photocopies." Reports on art samples only if interested. Original artwork returned at job's completion.

Terms: Pays authors in royalties. Additional payment for ms/illustration packages. Sends galleys to authors.

■**METAMORPHOUS PRESS**, P.O. Box 10616, Portland OR 97210. (503) 228-4972. Book publisher. Acquisitions Editor: Lori Stephens. Estab. 1982. 10% of books from agented writers. Subsidy publishes 10%.

Nonfiction: Picture books: education. Young readers: education, music/dance. Middle readers: education, music/dance, self-help/esteem. Young adults: education, music/dance, self-help/esteem.

How to Contact/Writers: Fiction: Query. Nonfiction: Query; submit outline/synopsis and sample chapters. Reports on queries in 6-12 months. Publishes a book 1-2 years after acceptance. Will consider simultaneous and electronic submissions via disk or modem.

Illustration: Will review ms/illustration packages.

How to Contact/Illustrators: Ms/illustration packages: Query. Illustrations only: "vitae with samples of range and style." Reports on art samples only if interested.

Terms: Pays authors royalty of 10% based on wholesale price. Illustrators paid by author. Sends galleys to authors; dummies to illustrators. Book catalog available for large SAE and 52¢ postage.

Tips: Looks for "books that relate and illustrate the notion that we create our own realities, self-reliance and positive outlooks work best for us—creative metaphors and personal development guides given preference."

*****MILKWEED EDITIONS**, Suite 400, 430 First Ave. N., Minneapolis MN 55401-1743. (612)332-3192. Book Publisher. Writers Contact: Children's reader. Illustrators Contact: Art Director. Publishes 4 middle readers/year; 0-1 young adult titles/year. 25% of books by first-time authors. "Works must embody humane values and contribute to cultural understanding. There is no primary theme."

Fiction: Middle readers and young adults: adventure, animal, contemporary, fantasy, history, humor, multicultural, nature/environment, problem novels, science fiction, suspense/mystery. Does not want to see anthologies, folktales, health, hi-lo, poetry, religion, romance, sports. Average length: middle readers—110-350 pages; young adults—110-350 pages. Recently published *Gildaen*, by Emilie Buchwald (middle reader, fantasy); *I Am Lavina Cumming*, by Susan Lowell (middle reader, contemporary).

Nonfiction: Middle readers, young adults: biographies. Average length: middle readers—110-350 pages; young adults—110-350 pages. "We have not published any nonfiction as of yet."

How to Contact/Writers: Fiction/nonfiction: Query, submit complete manuscript. Reports on queries in 2-3 weeks; mss in 1-6 months. Publishes a book 10-12 months after acceptance. Will consider simultaneous submissions or previously published work.
Illustration: Works with 3 illustrators/year. Will review ms/illustration packages. Will review artwork for future assignments.
How to Contact/Illustrators: Ms/illustration packages: Query. Submit manuscript with dummy. Illustrations only: Query with samples; provide résumé, promo sheet, slides, tearsheets and client list. Reports in 4-6 weeks. Samples returned with SASE; samples filed. Originals returned at job's completion.
Terms: Pays authors royalty of 7½% based on retail price. Offers advance against royalties. Sends galleys to authors. Book catalog available for 8½ × 11 SAE with 2 first-class stamps; ms guidelines available for SASE.

THE MILLBROOK PRESS, 2 Old New Milford Rd., Brookfield CT 06804. (203)740-2220. Book publisher. Manuscript Coordinator: Tricia Bauer. Art Director: Judie Mills. Publishes 4 picture books/year; 40 young readers/year; 50 middle readers/year; 10 young adult titles/year. 10% of books by first-time authors; 10% of books from agented authors. Publishes curriculum-related nonfiction, primarily for the school library market.
Nonfiction: All levels: activity books, animal, arts/crafts, biography, careers, concept, geography, health, history, hobbies, multicultural, music/dance, nature/environment, reference, social issues, sports, science. No fiction or poetry. Average word length: picture books—minimal; young readers—5,000; middle readers—10,000; young adult/teens—20,000. Recently published *Maps and Mazes: A First Guide to Mapmaking*, by Gillian Chapman and Pam Robson (grades 2-4, picture book); *The Transcontinental Railroad: Triumph of a Dream*, by Dan Elish (grades 4-6, history); *Animal Rights: A Handbook for Young Adults*, by Daniel Cohen (grades 7-up, contemporary issues).
How to Contact/Writers: Nonfiction: Query. Submit outline/synopsis and 1 sample chapter. Reports on queries/mss in 1 month.
Illustration: Will review ms/illustration packages. Will review artwork for future assignments. Contact: Judie Mills, art director.
How to Contact/Illustrators: Ms/illustration packages: Query; submit 1 chapter of ms with 1 piece of final art. Illustrations only: Query with samples; provide résumé, business card, promotional literature or tearsheets to be kept on file. Reports back only if interested.
Terms: Pays author royalty 7% average based on wholesale price. Offers advances. Payment for illustrators varies. Sends galleys to authors. Book catalog for SAE; ms guidelines for SASE.

MISTY HILL PRESS, 5024 Turner Rd., Sebastopol CA 95472. (707)823-7437. Book publisher. Editor-in-Chief: Sally Karste. 100% of books by first-time authors.
Fiction: Middle readers, young adults: history.
Nonfiction: Middle readers, young adults: history. Recently published *Trails to Poosey*, by Olive Cooke (young adults, historical fiction).
How to Contact/Writers: Fiction/nonfiction: Submit outline/synopsis and sample chapters. Reports on queries in 1 week; mss in 1 month. Publishes a book 8 months after acceptance. Will consider simultaneous submissions.
Terms: Illustrators paid by the project. Sends galleys to authors.
Tips: "Historical fiction: substantial research, good adventure or action against the historical setting. Historical fiction only."

■MOREHOUSE PUBLISHING CO., 871 Ethan Allen Hwy., Ridgefield CT 06877. (203)431-3927. Fax: (203)431-3964. Book publisher. Estab. 1884. Editor: Deborah Grahame-Smith. Publishes 4 picture books/year. 75% of books by first-time authors. Subsidy publishes 25%.

Fiction: All levels: religion.

Nonfiction: All levels: religion, moral message, family values. Picture books and young readers: religion.

How to Contact/Writers: Fiction/nonfiction: Submit outline/synopsis and sample chapters to Deborah Grahame-Smith. Reports on queries in 4-6 weeks. Publishes a book 1 year after acceptance.

Illustration: Editorial will review ms/illustration packages.

How to Contact/Illustrators: Ms/illustration packages: submit 3 chapters of ms with 1 piece of final art. Illustrations only: submit résumé, tearsheets. Reports on art samples in 4-6 weeks. Original artwork returned at job's completion. Contact: Deborah Grahame-Smith, editor.

Terms: Pays authors "both royalties and outright." Offers average advance payment of $500. Sends galleys to authors. Book catalog free on request.

Tips: Writers: "Prefer authors who can do their own illustrations. Be fresh, be fun, not pedantic, but let your work have a message." Illustrators: "Work hard to develop an original style." Looks for ms/illustration packages "with a religious or moral value while remaining fun and entertaining."

© 1992 Nancy Ward Balderose

This colored pencil illustration by Nancy Ward Balderose appeared in her book Once Upon a Pony: A Mountain Christmas *from Morehouse Publishing. The book opened doors for Balderose. It "has a national and even international following," she says. "I now receive royalties, do book signings and speaking engagements."*

■**JOSHUA MORRIS PUBLISHING,** 221 Danbury Rd., Wilton CT 06897. (203)761-9999. Fax: (203)761-5655. Subsidiary of Reader's Digest, Inc. Senior Editor: Sarah Feldman. Art Director: Julia Sabbagh. "We publish mostly early concept books and books for beginning readers. Most are in series of 4 titles and contain some kind of novelty element (i.e., lift the flap, die cut holes, book and soft toy, etc.) We publish 300-400 books per year." 5% of books by first-time authors; 5% of books from agented authors; 90% of books published on commission.

Fiction: Picture books and young readers: activity books, adventure, animal, concept, nature/environment, reference, religion. Middle readers: animal, nature/environment, religion. Does not want to see poetry, short stories, science fiction. Average word length: picture books—300-400. Published *Whooo's There?*, by Lily Jones (ages 3-7, sound and light); *Ghostly Games*, by John Speirs, with additional text by Gill Speirs (ages 8-12, puzzle).

Nonfiction: Picture books, young readers and middle readers: activity books, animal, nature/environment, religion. Average word length: varies. Published *Alan Snow Complete Books (Dictionary, Atlas* and *Encyclopedia)*, by Alan Snow (ages 3-7, first reference); *Rain Forest Nature Search*, by Paul Sterry (ages 7-12, puzzle/activity).

How to Contact/Writers: Fiction: Query. Nonfiction: Query. Reports on queries/mss in 3-4 months. Publishes a book 12-18 months after acceptance. Will consider simultaneous submissions and previously published work.

Illustration: Will review ms/illustration packages. Will review artwork for future assignments. Contact Julie Sabbagh, art director.

How to Contact/Illustrators: Ms/illustration packages: Query. Illustrations only: Query with samples (non-returnable). Provide résumé, promo sheet or tearsheets to be kept on file. Reports back only if interested. Original artwork returned (only if requested).

Photography: Contact Patricia Jennings, art director. Buys stock and assigns work. Uses photos of animals and children. Model/property releases required. Publishes photo concept books. Uses 4×6 glossy, color prints and 4×5 transparencies. Photographers should provide résumé, promo sheet or tearsheets to be kept on file.

Terms: Pays authors royalty or work purchased outright. Offers advances. Pays illustrators by the project or royalty. Photographers paid per photo.

Tips: Best bets with this market are "innovative concept and beginning readers, and books that have a novelty element."

MORROW JUNIOR BOOKS, 1350 Avenue of the Americas, New York NY 10019. Does not accept unsolicited manuscripts.

JOHN MUIR PUBLICATIONS, INC., P.O. Box 613, Santa Fe NM 87504-0613. (505)982-4078. Book publisher. Editorial Contact: Ken Luboff. Art Director: Ken Wilson. Publishes 25 middle reader nonfiction picture books/year.

Nonfiction: Middle readers: activity books, animal, arts/crafts, biography, concept, hobbies, multicultural, nature/environment, science, social issues. Average word length: middle readers—12,000-15,000. Recently published *Kids Explore Series* (4 titles), by different authors (middle readers); *Kids Explore America's Hispanic Heritage, Kids Explore America's African-American Heritage*, etc.

How to Contact/Writers: Query. Reports on queries/mss in 4-6 weeks. Publishes a book 8-12 months after acceptance. Will consider simultaneous submissions.

Illustration: Reviews illustration packages. Art Director, Ken Wilson, will review artwork for future assignments.

How to Contact/Illustrators: Ms/illustration packages: Query, outline and 1 chapter for illustration; 4 original finished pieces and roughs of ideas. Illustrations only: submit

The solid block before a listing indicates the market subsidy publishes manuscripts.

résumé and samples of art that have been reproduced or samples of original art for style.

Photography: Purchases photos from freelancers. Buys stock images. Buys "travel, animal" photos.

Terms: Pays authors on work for hire basis. Occasionally royalties. Some books are paid by flat fee for illustration. Pays illustrators by the project. Book catalog free on request.

Tips: "We want nonfiction books for 8- to 12-year-old readers that can sell in bookstores as well as gift stores, libraries and classrooms."

NAR PUBLICATIONS, P.O. Box 233, Barryville NY 12719. (914)557-8713. Book publisher. 50% of books by first-time authors; 100% of books from agented writers.

Fiction: "No young adult novels or books. Short picture books with limited text preferred."

How to Contact/Writers: Fiction/nonfiction: Query. Reports on queries in 3 weeks; mss in 1 month. Publishes a book 9 months after acceptance. Will consider simultaneous and electronic submissions via disk.

Terms: Buys ms outright. Book catalog for 1 first-class stamp and #10 SAE.

Tips: "We have only published two books for children. Preschool to age 8 has best chance of acceptance. We no longer accept unagented manuscripts."

NATUREGRAPH PUBLISHER, INC., P.O. Box 1075, Happy Camp CA 96039. (916)493-5353. Contact: Barbara Brown. Publishes 2 adult titles/year, usable by young adults. ("We are not geared to young adult as such.") 100% of books by first-time authors.

Nonfiction: Animal, nature/environment, Native American. Average word length: young adults — 70,000.

How to Contact/Writers: Nonfiction: Query. Reports on queries/mss in 2 weeks. Publishes a book 18 months after acceptance.

Terms: Pays authors in royalties of 10% based on wholesale price. Sends galleys to authors. Book catalog is free on request.

NEW DISCOVERY BOOKS, 866 Third Ave., New York NY 10022. (212)702-9631. Imprint of Macmillan Children's Book Group. Book publisher. Editor: Michael Ford. Publishes 40 middle readers/year. 20% of books by first-time authors; 10% of books from agented authors. Publishes "series and select single titles for the school and library market."

Nonfiction: Middle readers: biography, history, multicultural, science, social issues. Average word length: middle readers — 20,000. Recently published *The Monster Factory*; *Getting Your Message Across*; *The New Deal*.

How to Contact/Writers: Query. Submit outline/synopsis and 2 sample chapters. Reports on queries in 1 month; mss in 2 months. Publishes book 1-1½ years after acceptance. Will consider simultaneous submissions.

Terms: Pays authors royalty of 5% maximum based on retail price. Offers advances (average amount: $2,000). Sends galleys to authors. Book catalog available for 9×12 SASE. Ms guidelines not available.

NORTHLAND PUBLISHING, P.O. Box 1389, Flagstaff AZ 86002. (602)774-5251. Book publisher. Editor: Erin Murphy. Art Director: Trina Stahl. Publishes 6 picture books/year; 2 young readers/year. 75% of books by first-time authors. Primary theme is West and Southwest regional, Native American folktales.

Fiction: Picture books and young readers: animal, contemporary, folktales, history, multicultural/bilingual, nature/environment. "Our Native American folktales are enjoyed by readers of all ages, child through adult." No religion, science fiction, anthology. Average word length: picture books — 800; young readers — 1,500. Recently published *Monster Birds*, retold by Vee Brown, illustrated by Baje Whitethorne (ages 7 and up);

Carlos the Squash Plant, by Jan Romero Stevens, illustrated by Jeanne Arnold (bilingual Spanish/English book for ages 5 and up); *Building a Bridge,* by Lisa Shook Begaya, illustrated by Libba Tracy (ages 5 and up).

Nonfiction: Picture books and young readers: animal, multicultural, nature/environment. Average word length: picture books—1,500; young readers—1,500.

How to Contact/Writers: Fiction/nonfiction: Query; submit complete ms with cover letter. Reports on queries in 1 month; mss in 8 weeks. "Acknowledgment sent immediately upon receipt." If manuscript and art are complete at time of acceptance, publication usually takes 1 year. Will consider simultaneous submissions.

Illustration: Works with 6-8 illustrators/year. Will review ms/illustration packages. Will review artwork for future assignments. Uses color artwork only.

How to Contact/Illustrators: Ms/illustration packages: Submit ms with samples; slides or color photocopies. Illustrations only: Query with samples, promo sheet, slides, tearsheets. Reports in 1 month. Samples returned with SASE. Original artwork returned at job's completion.

Terms: Pays authors/illustrators royalty of 4-7% based on wholesale price. Offers advances. "This depends so much on quality of work and quantity needed." Sends galleys to authors; dummies to illustrators. Ms guidelines available for SASE; artist's guidelines not available.

Tips: Receptive to "Native American folktales (must be retold by a Native American author)."

NORTHWORD PRESS, INC., P.O. Box 1360, Minocqua WI 54548. (715)356-9800. Imprints: Willow Creek Press, Heartland Press. Editor-in-Chief: Greg Linder. Production Coordinator: Russ Kuepper. Publishes 3 picture books/year. 50% of books by first-time authors; 10% of books from agented authors. Publishes books pertaining to nature, wildlife and the environment. Also Native American topics.

Fiction: Picture books, young readers: animal, nature/environment. Does not want to see "anything without a strong nature/animal focus; no moralizing animal/nature stories (didactic)."

Nonfiction: Picture books, young readers: activity books, animal, nature/environment. Average word length: picture books—500-3,000; young readers—2,500-3,000. Recently published *Moose for Kids,* by Jeff Fair (ages 4-10, photo picture book); *Who Lives Here?,* by Dawn Baumann Brunke (ages 4-10, animal and habitat coloring guide series).

How to Contact/Writers: Fiction: Query. Nonfiction: Query; submit outline/synopsis and 1 sample chapter. Reports on queries in 2 months; mss in 3 months. Publishes a book 9-12 months after acceptance. Will consider simultaneous submissions.

Illustration: Works with 1-3 illustrators/year. Will review ms/illustration packages. Will review artwork for future assignments. Contact Russ Kuepper, production coordinator.

How to Contact/Illustrators: Ms/illustration packages: Query. Submit 1 chapter of ms with 3 pieces of final art. Illustrations only: Query with samples. Reports back only if interested. Original artwork returned at job's completion.

Photography: Contact: Larry Mishkar photo editor. Uses nature and wildlife photos, full-color. Buys stock and assigns work. Model releases required. Publishes photo concept books. Uses color prints and 35mm transparencies. Query with samples. "Not responsible for damage to, or loss of, unsolicited materials."

Terms: Pays authors royalty based on wholesale price or work purchased outright. Offers negotiable advances. Pays illustrators by the project. Pays photographer by the project, per photo or royalty. Sends galleys to authors. Book catalog available for 9 × 12 SAE and 2 first-class stamps; ms guidelines available for SASE.

Tips: "The two key words are 'nature' and 'wildlife.' Beyond that, we're looking for fun, unusual and well-written manuscripts. We are expanding our children's line."

ORCA BOOK PUBLISHERS, P.O. Box 3626 Station B, Victoria, British Columbia V8R 6S4 Canada. (604)380-1229. Book publisher. Children's Books Editor: Ann Featherstone. Publishes 6 picture books/year; 1 or 2 middle readers/year; 1 or 2 young adult titles/year. 25% of books by first time authors. "We only consider authors and illustrators who are Canadian or who live in Canada."

Fiction: Picture books: contemporary, fairy tales, folktales, humor, nature/environment. Middle readers: adventure, contemporary, history, multicultural, nature/environment, problem novels, special needs, suspense/mystery. Young adults: contemporary, history, multicultural, nature/environment, problem novels, special needs. "Please, no cute little woodland creatures looking for their mother, name or home. Spare us also from *Alice in Wonderland* clones, where children meet talking animals that take them on 'exciting' adventures." Average word length: picture books—500-2,000; middle readers—25,000-35,000; young adult—35,000-60,000. Published *Thistle Broth*, by Richard Thompson, illustrated by Henry Fernandes; *Waiting for the Whales*, by Sheryl McFarlane, illustrated by Ron Lightburn.

Nonfiction: Picture books, young readers, middle readers: animal, nature/environment. "We have enough whale stories to hold us for a while." Average word length: picture books—300-500; middle readers—2,000-3,000. Recently published *Siwiti—A Whale's Story*, by Alexandra Morton, photographs by Robin and Alexandra Morton (ages 6-12, animal).

How to Contact/Writers: Fiction: Submit complete ms if picture book; submit outline/synopsis and 3 sample chapters. Nonfiction: Query with SASE. "All queries or unsolicited submissions should be accompanied by a SASE." Reports on queries in 3-6 weeks; mss in 1-3 months. Publishes book 12-18 months after acceptance.

Illustration: Works with 6 illustrators/year. Will review ms/illustration packages. Will review artwork for future assignments.

How to Contact/Illustrators: Ms/illustration packages: Submit ms with 3-4 pieces of final art. "Reproductions only, no original art please." Illustrations only: Query with samples; provide resume, slides. Reports in 6-8 weeks. Samples returned with SASE; samples filed. Original artwork returned at job's completion if picture books.

Terms: Pays authors royalty of 5-10% if picture book based on retail price. Offers advances (average amount: $500). Pays illustrators royalty of 5% minimum based on retail price or advance on royalty of $500. Sends galleys to authors. Book catalog available for legal or 8½ × 11 manila SAE and 2 first-class stamps. Ms guidelines available for SASE. Art guidelines not available.

Tips: "American authors and illustrators should remember that the US stamps on their reply envelopes cannot be posted in any country outside of the US."

ORCHARD BOOKS, 95 Madison Ave., New York NY 10016. (212)686-7070. Division and imprint of Grolier, Inc. Book publisher. President and Publisher: Neal Porter. "We publish between 50 and 60 books yearly including fiction, poetry, picture books, and photo essays." 10-25% of books by first-time authors.

● This publisher has received numerous awards in the last few years for children's literature. The book *Missing May*, by Cynthia Rylant, received the 1993 Newberry Medal and Orchard earned honors from *The Horn Book, School Library Journal* and Booklist.

Fiction: All levels: adventure, animal, anthology, concept, contemporary, fantasy, folktales, health, history, humor, multicultural, nature/environment, poetry, religion, romance, science fiction, sports, suspense/mystery. Does not want to see anthropomorphized animals.

Nonfiction: All levels: animal, biography, concept, geography, health, history, hobbies, multicultural, music/dance, nature/environment, religion, science, self-help, social issues, sports. "We publish nonfiction on a very selective basis."

© 1992 Sheena Lott

Rendered in watercolor, this illustration by Sheena Lott graces the cover of Jessie's Island, by Sheryl McFarlane, from Orca Book Publishers, Ltd. R.J. Tyrrell, Orca's publisher, wanted art that would convey the serenity and natural beauty of the scenes. The book received the Canadian Children's Book Centre Choice Award.

How to Contact/Writers: Fiction: Submit entire ms. Nonfiction: Submit outline/synopsis and sample chapters. Reports on queries in 2 weeks; mss in 1 month. Average length of time between acceptance of a book-length ms and publication of work "depends on the editorial work necessary. If none, about 8 months or longer if schedule of books dictates." Will consider simultaneous submissions "only in rare instances."
Illustration: Works with 40 illustrators/year. Editorial will review ms/illustration packages. "It is better to submit ms and illustration separately unless they are by the same person, or a pairing that is part of the project such as husband and wife." Will review artwork for future assignments.
How to Contact/Illustrators: Ms/illustration packages: 3 chapters of ms with 1 piece of final art, remainder roughs. Illustrations only: Send "tearsheets or photocopies or photostats of the work." Reports on art samples in 1 month. Original artwork returned at job's completion if SASE is enclosed.
Terms: Pays authors in royalties "industry standard" based on retail price. Sends galleys to authors; dummies to illustrators. Book catalog free on request with 8½×11 SASE.

OUR CHILD PRESS, 800 Maple Glen Ln., Wayne PA 19087-4797. (215)964-0606. Book publisher. President: Carol Hallenbeck. 90% of books by first-time authors.
Fiction/Nonfiction: All levels: adoption, multicultural, special needs. Average word length: Open. Recently published *Don't Call Me Marda*, by Sheila Kelly Welch; *Is That*

Your Sister? by Catherine and Sherry Burin; *Oliver: A Story About Adoption*, by Lois Wichstrom.

How to Contact/Writers: Fiction/Nonfiction: Query or submit complete ms. Reports on queries/mss in 3 months. Publishes a book 6-12 months after acceptance.

Illustration: Works with 2 illustrators/year. Reviews ms/illustration packages. Will review artwork for future assignments.

How to Contact/Illustrators: Query first. Submit résumé, tearsheets and photocopies. Reports on art samples in 2 months. Original artwork returned at job's completion.

Terms: Pays authors in royalties of 5-10% based on wholesale price. Pays illustrators royalties of 5-10% based on wholesale price. Book catalog for SAE (business envelope) and 52¢ postage.

Tips: Won't consider anything not related to adoption.

RICHARD C. OWEN PUBLISHERS, INC., Dept. CWIM-94, 135 Katonah Ave., Katonah NY 10536. (914)232-3903. Book publisher. Editor: Janice Boland. Publishes 5 storybooks a year. 95% of books by first-time authors. Publishes "child focused, meaningful books about characters and situations with which five, six, and seven-year-old children can identify. We include multicultural stories that present minorities in a positive and natural way. Our stories show the diversity in America."

Fiction: Picture books that children will read ("these are not lap books—they are books for 5-7-year-olds to read by themselves; they have brief text and pictures on every page."): adventure, animal, contemporary (multicultural and minorities), Native American folktales, nature/environment (American animals), poetry, suspense/mystery. Does not want to see holiday, religious themes, moral teaching stories. No talking animals with personified human characteristics, jingles and rhymes, holiday stories, alphabet books, lists without plots, stories with nostalgic views of childhood, soft or sugar-coated tales. No stereotyping. Average word length: picture books—up to 100 words.

Nonfiction: Picture books: animal, careers, multicultural, nature/environment. No "encyclopedic" type of information stories. Average word length: up to 100 words.

How to Contact/Writers: Fiction/nonfiction: Submit complete ms. "*Must* request guidelines first with #10 SASE." Reports on queries in 2 weeks ("we only send author's guidelines"); mss in 2-6 weeks. Publishes a book 2-3 years after acceptance. Will consider simultaneous submissions.

Illustration: Works with 2-3 illustrators/year. Will review artwork for future assignments.

How to Contact/Illustrators: Send color copies/reproductions or photos of art or provide tearsheets. Must request guidelines first. Reports in 1 month.

Photography: Contact: Janice Boland. Wants photos that are child oriented; not interested in portraits. "Natural, bright, crisp and colorful—of children and of subjects and compositions attractive to children." Sometimes interested in stock photos for special projects. Uses color transparencies.

Terms: Pays authors royalties of 8% based on "monies we receive." Offers no advances. Pays illustrators by the project (range: $500-1,000). Photographers paid by the project. Ms/artist guidelines available for SASE.

Tips: Seeking "stories that have charm, magic, impact and appeal; that children living in today's society will want to read and reread; books with strong storylines, child-appealing language, action and interesting, vivid characters." Multicultural needs include "ethnic true-to-life tales, folktales, Indian legends and stories about specific culture environments. We want our books to reflect the rich cultural heritage and diversity of this country without stereotyping." Trend is toward "quality books that portray various cultures in rich and interesting ways; well-constructed and developed books that make these cultures accessible to all."

PACIFIC PRESS, P.O. Box 7000, Boise ID 83707. (208)465-2500. Fax: (208)465-2531. Book publisher. Acquisitions Editor: Marvin Moore. Publishes 2-4 picture books, 2-4 young readers, 2-4 middle readers, 4-6 young adult titles/year. 5% of books by first-time authors. Seventh-day Adventist Christian publishing house which publishes books pertaining to religion, spiritual values (strong spiritual slant).
Fiction: All levels: religion. Does not want to see fantasy or totally non-factual stories. "We prefer true stories that are written in fiction style." Average word length: picture books—500-1,000; young readers—6,000-7,000; middle readers—25,000-33,000; young adult/teens—33,000-75,000. Published *Focus on the Edge*, by Heidi Borriuk (teens); *Mystery on Colton's Island*, by Mary Duplex (ages 8-12); *Rocky and Me*, by Paul Ricchiati (ages 4-6, picture/text for pre-school).
Nonfiction: All levels: activity books, animal, health, nature/environment, religion. "We publish very little nonfiction for children. All manuscripts must have a religious/spiritual/health theme." Average word length: picture books—500-1,000; young readers—6,000-7,000; middle readers—25,000-33,000; young adult/teens—33,000-80,000. Published *Before I Was a Kid*, by Rita Stewart (age 4-6, picture/text for preschool).
How to Contact/Writers: Fiction: Submit complete ms; submit outline/synopsis and 2 sample chapters. Nonfiction: Query; submit complete ms; submit outline/synopsis and 2 sample chapters. Reports on queries in 2 weeks; mss in 2 months. Publishes a book 6-12 months after acceptance. Will consider simultaneous submissions and electronic submissions via disk or modem.
Illustration: Will review artwork for future assignments. Contact: Randy Maxwell, director of advertising.
How to Contact/Illustrators: Ms/illustration packages: Submit complete package. Illustrations only: submit portfolio for review. Reports in 2 weeks. Original artwork returned at job's completion.
Terms: Pays authors royalty of 12-16% based on wholesale price. Offers advances ($300-500). Pays illustrators by the project (range: $500-750); 6% royalty based on wholesale price. Sends galleys to authors. Book catalog available for 9×12 SASE. Ms guidelines available for SASE.
Tips: "Character building stories with a strong spiritual emphasis" have the best chance of being published by our press. Also, "adventure, and mystery stories that incorporate spirituality and character building are especially welcome."

PANDO PUBLICATIONS, 5396 Laurie Lane, Memphis, TN 38120. (901)682-8779. Book publisher. Estab. 1988. Owner: Andrew Bernstein. Publishes 2-6 middle reader titles/year; 2-6 young adult titles/year. 20% of books by first-time authors.
Fiction: Animal, concept, folktales, history, nature/environment. No poetry, science fiction, religion.
Nonfiction: Middle readers, young adults: activity books, animal, arts/crafts, biography, concept, cooking, geography, history, hobbies, how-to, multicultural, nature/environment, reference, science, social issues, special needs, sports. Average length: middle readers—175 pages; young adults—200 pages.
How to Contact/Writers: Fiction/nonfiction: Prefers full ms. Reports on queries in 4 months; on mss in 7 months. Publishes a book 1 year after acceptance. Will consider simultaneous submissions. "Prefers" electronic submissions via disk or modem.

"Picture books" are geared toward the preschool to 8-year-old group; *"Young readers"* are for 5- to 8-year-olds; *"Middle readers"* are for 9- to 11-year-olds; and *"Young adults"* are for those 12 and up.

Illustration: Works with 2 illustrators/year. Editorial will review all illustration packages.

How to Contact/Illustrators: Ms/illustrations: Query first. Illustrations only: Query with samples. Reports on art samples in 3 months. Original artwork returned at job's completion.

Terms: Pays authors royalty of 7-10% based on retail price. Offers average advance payment of "¹/₃ royalty due on first run." Sends galleys to authors; dummies to illustrators. "Book descriptions available on request."

Tips: Writers: "Find an untapped market then write to fill the need." Illustrators: "Find an author with a good idea and writing ability. Develop the book with the author. Join a professional group to meet people—ABA, publishers' groups, as well as writers' groups and publishing auxiliary groups. Talk to printers." Looks for "how-to books, but will consider anything."

PARENTING PRESS, INC., P.O. Box 75267, Seattle WA 98125. (206)364-2900. Book publisher. Estab. 1979. Editorial Director: Alice Cummiskey. Publishes 2-3 picture books/year; 1-2 young reader titles/year; 1-2 middle reader titles/year. 40% of books by first-time authors.

Fiction: Picture books, young readers, middle readers: social skills books for children. "We rarely publish straight fiction." Published *First Day Blues*, by Peggy King Anderson, illustrations by Rebekah J. Strecker (ages 7-11); *On The Wings Of A Butterfly*, by Marilyn Maple, Ph.D., illustrations by Sandy Haight (ages 6-11); *I'm Mad*, by Elizabeth Crary, illustrations by Jean Whitney (ages 3-9).

Nonfiction: Picture books: education, health, history, multicultural, social skills building. Young readers: education, health, history, nature/environment, social skills building books. Middle readers: health, social skills building. No books on "new baby, coping with a new sibling, cookbooks, manners." Average word length: picture books—500-800; young readers—1,000-2,000; middle readers—up to 10,000. Published *Kids To The Rescue*, by Maribeth and Darwin Boelts (ages 4-12).

How to Contact/Writers: Fiction: "We publish educational books for children in story format. *No straight fiction*." Nonfiction: Query. Reports on queries in 4-6 weeks; mss in 1-2 months, "after requested." Publishes a book 10-11 months after acceptance. Will consider simultaneous submissions.

Illustrations: Works with 6 illustrators/year. Will review ms/illustration packages. "We do reserve the right to find our own illustrator, however." Will review artwork for future assignments.

How to Contact/Illustrators: Ms/illustration packages: Query. Illustrations only: Send "résumé, samples of art/drawings (no original art); photocopies or color photocopies okay." Original artwork returned at job's completion for illustrators under contract.

Terms: Pays authors in royalties of 4% based on net. Outright purchase of ms, "negotiated on a case-by-case basis. Not common for us." Offers average advance of $150. Pays illustrators by the project; 4% royalty based on net. Sends galleys to authors; dummies to illustrators. Book catalog/ms guidelines for #10 SAE and 1 first-class stamp.

Tips: Writers: "Query publishers who already market to the same audience. We often get manuscripts (good ones) totally unsuitable to our market." Illustrators: "We pay attention to artists who are willing to submit an illustration on speculation." Looking for "social skills building books for children, books that empower children, books that encourage decision making, books that are balanced ethnically and in gender."

PAULIST PRESS, 997 Macarthur Blvd., Mahwah NJ 07430. (201)825-7300. Fax: (201)825-8345. Book publisher. Estab. 1865. Editor: Kevin Lynch. Publishes 9-11 picture books/year; 6-7 young reader titles/year; 3-4 middle reader titles/year. 70% of books by first-time authors; 30% of books from agented writers.

Fiction: Picture books, young readers, middle readers: religious/moral. Average length: picture books—24 pages; young readers—24-32 pages; middle readers—64 pages. Published *A Bug From Aunt Tillie*, by Susan O'Keefe (ages 6-8, picture story book); *What Do You Do With the Rest of the Day, Mary Ann?*, by Eileen Lomasney (ages 5-7, picture book).

Nonfiction: Young readers, middle readers: religion. Published *Christopher Columbus: The Man who Unlocked the Secrets of the World*, by Teri Martini (ages 9-12, biography).

How to Contact/Writers: Fiction/nonfiction: Submit complete ms. Reports on queries in 1 month; mss in 2 months. Publishes a book 12-16 months after acceptance.

Illustration: Editorial will review all varieties of ms/illustration packages.

How to Contact/Illustrators: Ms/illustration packages: Complete ms with 1 piece of final art, remainder roughs. Illustrations only: Résumé, tearsheets. Reports on art samples in 6 weeks. Original artwork returned at job's completion, "if requested by illustrator."

Terms: Work purchased outright (range: $65-100/illustration). Offers advance (average payment $450-$650). Factors used to determine final payment: Color art, b&w, number of illustrations, complexity of work. Pay for separate authors and illustrators: Author paid by royalty rate; illustrator paid by flat fee, sometimes by royalty. Sends galleys to authors; dummies to illustrators.

Tips: Not interested in reviewing novels. Looking for "concept books for young readers, ages 7-9."

■**PEARTREE**, P.O. Box 14533, Clearwater FL 34629-4533. (813)531-4973. Book publisher. President: Barbara Birenbaum. Office Manager: H. Lapidus or Barbara Birenbaum. Publishes 1-5 young readers/year; 1-5 middle readers/year. 50% of books by first-time authors; 50% subsidy publishes. "Publishes shows on events (i.e. Liberty Centennial, Ground Hog Day, Thanksgiving) or general stories with 'lessons,' no Christian themes."

Fiction: Young readers: adventure, animal, contemporary, hi-lo, nature, holidays. Middle readers: adventure, animal, hi-lo, multicultural, nature, holidays. Does not want to see material on religion, science fiction, suspense, sports (per se), anthology or folktales.

How to Contact/Writers: Query with SASE. Reports on queries in 2 weeks; mss in 3-6 months. Publishes a book 9 months after acceptance. Will consider simultaneous submissions and previously published work.

Illustration: Works with 2 illustrators/year. Will review ms/illustration packages. Will review artwork for future assignments. Uses primarily b&w artwork with text.

How to Contact/Illustrators: Ms/illustration packages: Query; then submit ms with dummy. Illustrations only: Query with samples and SASE. Samples returned with SASE; samples filed ("if we anticipate an interest").

Terms: Work purchased outright from author. Other methods of payment include profits from sales of books. Pays illustrators by the project (range—$10/illustration-$200/book). Sends galleys to authors.

Tips: "We will consider publishing and marketing books as subsidy press when major houses reject titles. Be willing to get illustrations in books at minimum cost. Understand that small presses offer budding artists/writers chance to get in print and 'launch' careers on shoestring budgets."

PELICAN PUBLISHING CO. INC., 1101 Monroe St., Gretna LA 70053. (504)368-1175. Book publisher. Estab. 1926. Editor: Nina Kooij. Production Manager: Dana Bilbray. Publishes 6 picture books/year; 5 middle reader titles/year; 20% of books by first-time authors; 20% of books from agented writers.

Fiction: Picture books, young readers: folktales, health, history, multicultural, nature/environment, religion. Middle readers: folktales, health-related, history, multicultural, nature/environment, problem novels, religion, sports, suspense/mystery. Multicultural needs include stories about Native Americans and African-Americans. Does not want animal or general Christmas stories. Average word length: picture books—32 pages; middle readers—112 pages. Recently published *Bluebonnet at Johnson Space Center*, by Mary Brooke Casad (ages 5-8, descibes the new Texas space center); *When the Great Canoes Came*, by Mary Louise Clifford, illustrated by Joyce Haynes (ages 8-12, novel about Jamestown from the Indian's perspective).

Nonfiction: Young readers: biography, health, history, multicultural, music/dance, nature/environment, religion. Middle readers: biography, cooking, health, history, multicultural, music/dance, nature/environment, religion, sports. Published *Floridians All*, by George S. Fichter, illustrated by George Cardin (ages 8-12, collection of biographies on famous Florida figures).

How to Contact/Writers: Fiction/Nonfiction: Query. Reports on queries in 1 month; mss in 3 months. Publishes a book 12-18 months after acceptance.

Illustration: Works with 7 illustrators/year. Will review ms/illustration packages. Will file artwork for future assignments.

How to Contact/Illustrators: Ms/illustration packages: Query first. Illustrations only: query with samples (no originals). Reports on ms/art samples only if interested.

Terms: Pays authors in royalties; buys ms outright "rarely." Sends galleys to authors.

Tips: No anthropomorphic stories, pets stories (fiction or nonfiction), fantasy, poetry, science fiction, or romance. Writers: "Be as original as possible. Develop characters that lend themselves to series and always be thinking of new and interesting situations for those series. Give your story a strong hook—something that will appeal to a well-defined audience. There is a lot of competition out there for general themes." Looks for: "writers whose stories have specific 'hooks' and audiences, and who actively promote their work." Foresees more books on divorced families in the future.

PERSPECTIVES PRESS, P.O. Box 90318, Indianapolis IN 46290-0318. (317)872-3055. Book publisher. Estab. 1982. Publisher: Pat Johnston. Publishes 1-3 picture books/year; 1-3 young reader titles/year; 1-3 middle reader titles/year. 95% of books by first-time authors.

Fiction/Nonfiction: Picture books, young readers, middle readers: adoption, foster care, donor insemination or surrogacy. Does not want young adult material. Published *Lucy's Feet*, by Stephanie Stein, illustrated by Kathryn A. Imler.

How to Contact/Writers: Fiction/nonfiction: Query or submit outline/synopsis and sample chapters. "No query necessary on picture books." Reports on queries in 2 weeks; mss in 6 weeks. Publishes a book 6-10 months after acceptance. Will consider simultaneous submissions.

Illustration: Works with 1-2 illustrators/year. Will review artwork for future assignments.

How to Contact/Illustrators: Illustrators only: Submit promo sheet and client list. Reports on art samples only if interested.

Terms: Pays authors royalties of 5-15% based on net sales or work purchased outright. Pays illustrators royalty or by the project. Sends galleys to authors; dummies to illustrators. Book catalog, ms guidelines available for #10 SAE and 2 first-class stamps.

Tips: "Do your homework! I'm amazed at the number of authors who don't bother to check that we have a very limited interest area and subsequently submit unsolicited material that is completely inappropriate for us. For children, we focus exclusively on issues of adoption and interim (foster) care plus families built by donor insemination or surrogacy; for adults we also include infertility issues."

PHILOMEL BOOKS, 200 Madison Ave., New York NY 10016. (212)951-8700. Imprint of The Putnam & Grosset Group. Book publisher. Editor-in-Chief: Paula Wiseman. Editorial Director: Patricia Gauch. Editorial Contact: Laura Walsh. Art Director: Nanette Stevenson. Publishes 30 picture books/year; 5-10 young reader titles/year. 20% of books by first-time authors; 80% of books from agented writers.

Fiction: All levels: adventure, animal, fantasy, folktales, history, nature/environment, special needs, poetry, multicultural. Middle readers, young adults: problem novels. No concept picture books, mass-market "character" books, or series.

Nonfiction: All levels: arts/crafts, biography, history, multicultural, music/dance. "Creative nonfiction on any subject." Average length: "not to exceed 150 pages."

How to Contact/Writers: Fiction/nonfiction: Query; submit outline/synopsis and sample chapters; all other unsolicited mss responded to within 8-10 weeks. Reports on queries in 4-6 weeks. Publishes a book 2 years after acceptance.

Illustration: Works with 20-25 illustrators/year. Will review ms/illustration packages. Will review artwork for future assignments.

How to Contact/Illustrators: Ms/illustration packages: Query first. Illustrations only: Query with samples. Send résumé, promo sheet, portfolio, slides, client list, tearsheets or arrange personal portfolio review. Reports on art samples in 2 months. Original artwork returned at job's completion.

Terms: Pays authors in advance royalties. Average advance payment "varies." Illustrators paid by advance and in royalties. Sends galleys to authors; dummies to illustrators. Book catalog, ms/artist's guidelines free on request with SASE (9×12 envelope for catalog).

Tips: Wants "unique fiction or nonfiction with a strong voice and lasting quality. Discover your own voice and own story—and persevere." Looks for "something unusual, original, well-written. Fine art. The genre (fantasy, contemporary, or historical fiction) is not so important as the story itself, and the spirited life the story allows its main character. We are also interested in receiving adolescent novels, particularly novels that contain regional spirit, such as a story about a young boy or girl written from a Southern, Southwestern or Northwestern perspective."

PIPPIN PRESS, 229 E. 85th St., Box 1347, Gracie Station, New York NY 10028. (212)288-4920. Fax: (212)563-5703. Children's book publisher. Estab. 1987. Publisher/President: Barbara Francis. Publishes 6-8 books/year. "Not interested in young adult books." *Query letter must precede all submissions.*

Fiction: Picture books, young readers, middle readers: animal, fantasy, folktales, humorous, multicultural, nature/environment, suspense/mystery. Multicultural needs include "original material rather than retellings or adaptations and written by a person of the particular ethnic group." Average word length: picture books—750-1,500; young readers—2,000-3,000; middle readers—3,000. Recently published *The Sounds of Summer*, by David Updike, illustrated by Robert Andrew Parker (ages 7-10); *Windmill Hill*, by Hope Slaughter, illustrated by Edward Frascino (ages 7-10); *The Planet of the Grapes: Show Biz Jokes and Riddles*, compiled by Charles Keller, illustrated by Mischa Richter (ages 8-11).

Nonfiction: Picture books, young readers, middle readers: biography, history, multicultural, music/dance, nature/environment. Recently published *James Madison and Dolley Madison and Their Times*, written and illustrated by Robert Quackenbush (ages 7-11); *Take Me to Your Liter*, by Charles Keller, illustrated by Gregory Filling (ages 7-11, science and math jokes). No young adult books.

How to Contact/Writers: Fiction/nonfiction: Query with SASE. No unsolicited mss. Reports on queries in 2-3 weeks; solicited mss in 2-3 months. Publishes a book 1-2 years after acceptance. Will consider simultaneous submissions.

Illustration: Works with 6-8 illustrators/year. Send query with SASE before sending any artwork.

How to Contact/Illustrators: Illustrations only: Query. "I see illustrators by appointment." Reports on art samples only if interested. Original artwork returned at job's completion.

Terms: Pays authors in royalties. Pays illustrators royalties or by the project. Sends galleys to authors; dummies to illustrators. "The illustrator prepares the dummy on picture books; dummies for longer books prepared by the designer are submitted to the illustrator." Book catalog available for 6×9 SASE; ms/artist's guidelines for #10 SASE.
Tips: "We receive too many unsolicited mss even though our guidelines specify *query only*. We will be publishing more transitional books, i.e. picture storybooks for ages 7-10 and more imaginative nonfiction for ages 6-10. We are looking for chapter books, especially humorous ones, and will continue to publish writers and illustrators with track records."

PLAYERS PRESS, INC., P.O. Box 1132, Studio City CA 91614. (818)789-4980. Book publisher. Estab. 1965. Vice President/Editorial: R. W. Gordon. Publishes 2-10 young readers dramatic plays and musicals/year; 2-10 middle readers dramatic plays and musicals/year; 4-20 young adults dramatic plays and musicals/year. 35% of books by first-time authors; 1% of books from agented writers. "No novels or storybooks."
Fiction: "We use all categories (young readers, middle readers, young adults) but only for dramatic plays and/or musicals."
Nonfiction: "Any children's nonfiction pertaining to the entertainment industry, performing arts and how-to for the theatrical arts only."
How to Contact/Writers: Fiction/nonfiction: Submit plays or outline/synopsis and sample chapters of entertainment books. Reports on queries in 2-4 weeks; mss in 3-4 months. Publishes a book 10 months after acceptance. No simultaneous submissions.
Illustration: Associate Editor will review artwork for future assignments.
How to Contact/Illustrators: Ms/illustration packages: Query first. Illustrations only: Send résumé, tearsheets. Reports on art samples only if interested.
Terms: Pays authors in royalties of 2-20% based on retail price. Pays illustrators by the project; royalties range from 2-5%. Sends galleys to authors; dummies to illustrators. Book catalog available for $1.
Tips: Looks for "plays/musicals and books pertaining to the performing arts only."

■**POCAHONTAS PRESS, INC.,** 832 Hutcheson Dr., Blacksburg VA 24060-3259. (703)951-0467. Book Publisher. Editorial contact: Mary C. Holliman. Publishes 1-2 middle readers/year. Subsidy publishes 50%.
Nonfiction: All levels: biography, history, hobbies, nature/environment, science, sports. No pre-school or fiction. Published *Quarter-Acre of Heartache*, by C.C. Smith (young adult, Indian battle to save reservation).
How to Contact/Writers: Query; submit outline/synopsis and sample chapters. Reports on queries in 3-4 weeks; mss in 1-2 months. Publishes a book "probably as much as a year" after acceptance.
Illustrations: Will review all varieties of ms illustration packages. Prefers "black ink, though will sometimes accept pencil drawings. No color."
Terms: Pays authors in royalties of 10% based on actual receipts. Pays illustrators either by the project $20/hour or in royalties of 5-10% based on actual receipts. Sends galleys to authors; dummies to illustrators. Book catalog free on request. Ms guidelines not available.

Tips: "Have respect for your child reader, and remember that the actual reader is often an adult. Don't talk down and make jokes or references that are beyond the child's experience. Please, avoid the caricature and the scary." Looks for "a story, well told, about a real person, not necessarily well known, who has done something interesting or unusual or achieved something from a poor start." Pocahontas Press is "currently overloaded with manuscripts ready to publish, and won't be able to consider any for some time."

■**THE PRESERVATION PRESS**, 1785 Massachusetts Ave. NW, Washington DC 20036. (202)673-4057. Fax: (202)673-4172. Subsidiary of the National Trust for Historic Preservation. Book publisher. Director: Buckley Jeppson. Publishes 3 picture books/year; 4 young readers/year; 1 middle reader/year. 20% of books by first-time authors; 25% of books from agented authors; 40% subsidy published. Publishes books about architecture; "preservation of cultural sites and objects."
Nonfiction: Picture books, young readers, middle readers and young adults: activity books, history, architecture, American culture. Recently published *I Know That Building!*, by Jane D'Alelio (middle reader, activities); *What It Feels Like to Be a Building*, by Forrest Wilson (young reader, architecture); *Daily Life in a Victorian House*, by Forrest Wilson (middle reader).
How to Contact/Writers: Nonfiction: Submit outline/synopsis and 1 sample chapter. Reports on queries in 3 weeks; mss in 2 months. Publishes a book 12-18 months after acceptance. Will consider simultaneous submissions and previously published work.
Illustration: Will review ms/illustration packages.
How to Contact/Illustrators: Ms/illustration packages: Submit 1-2 chapters of ms with 3-4 pieces of final art. Reports in 3-4 weeks. Original artwork returned at job's completion.
Photography: Contact Janet Walker, managing editor. Uses architectural photos— interior and exterior. Model/property releases required. Captions required. Interested in stock photos. Publishes photo essays. Uses 5×7 or 8×10 glossy, b&w prints and 35mm, 2¼×2¼, 4×5 and 8×10 transparencies. Photographers should provide résumé, business card, promotional literature and tearsheets to be kept on file.
Terms: Pays authors royalty of 5-15% based on retail price. Offers advances of $800-1,600. Pays illustrators royalty of 3-10% based on retail price. Photographers paid royalty of 5-15% based on retail price. Sends galleys to authors; dummies to illustrators. Book catalog available for 9×12 SAE and 2 first-class stamps.
Tips: Looks for "an energetic, hands-on approach for kids to gain an appreciation for the variety and depth of their American cultural heritage."

THE PRESS OF MACDONALD & REINECKE, Imprint of Padre Productions, Box 840, Arroyo Grande CA 93421-0840. (805)473-1947. Book publisher. Estab. 1974. Editor: Lachlan P. MacDonald. 80% of books by first-time authors; 5% of books from agented authors.
Fiction: Middle readers, young adults: folktales, history, nature. No fantasy, mystery, detective, westerns, romances. Average length: middle reader—120-140 pages.
Nonfiction: Middle readers, young adults: history, nature/environment. Average length: middle readers—120 pages.
How to Contact/Writers: Fiction: Submit outline/synopsis and sample chapters. Nonfiction: Submit complete ms. Reports on queries in 2 weeks; on mss in 4 months. Publishes a book 1 year after acceptance. Will consider simultaneous submissions.
Illustration: Works with 8-12 illustrators/year. Editorial will review ms/illustration packages.
How to Contact/Illustrators: Illustrations only: Tearsheets. Reports on art samples only if interested.

Terms: Pays authors in royalties based on retail price. Illustrators paid by the project. Sends galleys to authors; dummies to illustrators. Book catalogs for 9 × 12 SAE and 52¢ in first-class postage. Ms guidelines/artist's guidelines for #10 SASE.
Tips: Writers: "Concentrate on nonfiction that recognizes changes in today's audience and includes minority and gender considerations without tokenism. The Press of Mac-Donald & Reinecke is devoted to highly selected works of drama, fiction, poetry and literary nonfiction. Juveniles must be suitable for 140-page books appealing to both boys and girls in the 8-14 year range of readers." Illustrators: "There is a desperate lack of realism by illustrators who can depict proportionate bodies and anatomy. The flood of torn-paper and poster junk is appalling." Looks for: "A book of historical nonfiction of U.S. regional interest with illustrations that have 19th Century elegance and realistic character representations, about topics that still matter today."

PRICE STERN SLOAN, 11150 Olympic Blvd., Los Angeles CA 90064. (310)477-6100. Book publisher. Imprints: Troubador Press. Contact: Editor-in-Chief. Publishes 0-4 picture books/year; 20-40 young reader titles/year; 10-20 middle reader titles/year; 0-2 young adult titles/year. 35% of books by first-time authors; 65% of books from agented writers; 50% from packagers.
Fiction: Picture books, young readers, middle readers, young adults: adventure, animal, contemporary, health-related, history, nature/environment, sports, suspense/mystery. Recently published *Pick-a-Tales*, by Keith Faulkner (ages 2-6, novelty board story book); *Still More Scary Stories for Sleep-overs*, by Q.L. Pierce (ages 6-10, scary short stories); *Big Busy Building*, by Chuck Reasoner and Cary Phillo Lasser (ages 2 and up, novelty board book with moveable parts).
Nonfiction: Picture books, young readers, middle readers, young adults: activity books, animal, hobbies, music/dance, nature/environment, sports. No religious books. Recently published *I Can't Believe It's History!*, by Donna Guthrie and Katy Keck Arnsteen (ages 7-12, history); *Picture Perfect Board Books*, by Judy Ostarch and Anthony Nex (ages 6 months-2 years, photographic board books); *Number Munch!*, by Chuck Reasoner (ages 1-6, board book).
How to Contact/Writers: Fiction/nonfiction: Query; submit outline/synopsis and 1-2 sample chapters. Reports on queries/mss in 2-3 months. Publishes a book 1 year after acceptance. Will consider simultaneous submissions and previously published work.
Illustration: Will review ms/illustration packages. Editorial will review artwork for future assignments.
How to Contact/Illustrators: Ms/illustration packages: Query; submit 1-2 chapters of ms with 1-2 pieces of final art (color copies—no original work). Illustrations only: Query with samples; provide résumé, promo sheet, portfolio, tearsheets to be kept on file. Reports in 2-3 months.
Photography: Contact: Art Director. Buys stock and assigns work. Model/property release required.
Terms: Pays authors royalty or work purchased outright. Offers advances. Pays illustrators by the project. Photographers paid by the project or per photo. Book catalog available for 9 × 12 SAE and 5 first-class stamps. Ms/artist's guidelines available.
Tips: "We don't have closed doors on any type of book. If it's good or special enough, we'll buy it. Parents are now willing to spend money on books to enhance the information a child would normally get in school."

PROMETHEUS BOOKS, 700 E. Amherst St., P.O. Box 570, Buffalo NY 14215-0570. Book publisher. Editor: Mary A. Read. Publishes 1-2 titles/year. 40% of books by first-time authors; 50% of books from agented writers. Publishes books on moral education, critical thinking, skepticism."
Nonfiction: All levels: sex education, moral education, critical thinking, science, skepticism. Average word length: picture books—2,000; young readers—10,000; middle read-

Filling the Gaps in Children's Literature

When Candy Dawson Boyd, then a fifth grade teacher, decided to write books for children, she began as such a writer should, by reading every children's book she could get her hands on. Dismayed to find precious few whose characters were African-American and fewer still portraying her race as anything other than gun-carrying gang members, Boyd matter-of-factly says there were some very big holes that needed to be filled. And she encourages today's beginning writers to look for similar gaps in children's literature.

Candy Dawson Boyd

"I grew up in a 'ghetto' on the south side of Chicago, and like the poet Nikki Giovanni says, I didn't know it was a ghetto until someone told me when I was much older. It was a neighborhood, a place where people worked hard. My brothers wanted to go to Cub Scouts and I worried about passing division tests, what I would wear to a party and whether a certain boy would like me. I did not see books that addressed these ordinary aspects of life for Black children, and it's the ordinary core of life that's extraordinary for most human beings," Boyd says.

With a Ph.D. in education, six years of experience teaching fifth graders and a vivid recollection of her early years, Boyd had no trouble knowing what she wanted to say to children. It was the craft of writing, the structure of storytelling, that she needed to work on. So she enrolled in children's writing courses at U.C. Berkeley Extension. Then she would have nine years of rejection ahead of her.

But Boyd never forgot the importance of persistence. During talks she gives to young students throughout the country, invariably, Boyd says, she is asked how she dealt with all of that rejection. "Well, I cried," she responds, "and I got mad, and I called all those people in New York bad names. I just fell apart. I felt like an absolute failure. But I pulled myself together and thought there had to be someone in New York that had sense enough to know I'm a good writer. So I tried again, and this time I wrote a story that came straight out of my heart. That was *Circle of Gold*." Written for 9- to 11-year-old children, it was published by Scholastic Inc. in 1984, went on to win the Coretta Scott King Award, and will be published by Scholastic in a special hardcover edition this year.

With her newfound confidence as a writer, Boyd then turned to a manuscript that had been rejected during those nine years, *Breadsticks and Blessing Places*. It was a story she felt compelled to write after overhearing a conversation between educators "about the fact that children didn't experience death or grieve as deeply as adults do. I was just horrified to hear that. I had lost my best friend when I was in fourth grade, and I didn't have another best friend until high school." So Boyd set about the painstaking process of revision.

After studying the comments in her rejection letters, she began to solve the "serious problems" in her manuscript, namely the minimal development of one character, a weak plot, and a lack of focus on the story she wanted to tell. She reread William Sloan's *The Craft of Writing*, as she always does before beginning a new book, and began the research and compilation of her notebook.

Through this system she creates a very detailed outline with tabbed sections for each character and chapter and a history of everything that happened up to the point where the book begins. It's a procedure she always goes through before beginning the actual writing—and one she strongly recommends. In its revised form, *Breadsticks* was accepted by Macmillan Children's Books. Since then Macmillan has published some of her other books, such as *Charlie Pippin*, the paperback rights to which were bought by Puffin Books.

As with *Breadsticks* and *Circle of Gold*, *Charlie Pippin* was spurred by Boyd's desire to set the record straight on a particular issue, in this case the war in Vietnam. Ten years after the war ended, she says, she was struck by the revisionist manner in which it was being presented by the media—as a war fought for the most part by Caucasians. In this book, Charlie, a young girl, volunteers to do a school research project on the war, which not only provides insight into her Vietnam veteran father, with whom she is having conflict, but also politicizes her.

Boyd urges writers not to overlook the fact that children need to deal with such large issues as war, pollution and the nuclear threat. While children may keep their anxieties about these things to themselves, they feel them nonetheless and can only diminish their fears by talking about the issues and taking some kind of action, such as participating in a march or writing a letter to their representatives in Congress, she says.

Ultimately, says Boyd, try to create "a safe place" for young readers, a place where characters, through struggle and the support of family—be it the immediate family, the extended family or the community of family—successfully deal with conflict and come out winners. For Boyd "the elder" plays a key role. "In every book I write," she says, "I have an elder, which I define as a person who has earned the honor and privilege of helping children due to his or her life experience and willingness to engage in life, to persist and remain positive, and to respect and care for children."

Through her books Boyd tries to meet her responsibilities as an African-American elder. "We know children are impacted by what they read," she says. "The vast number of children I do author talks for are Caucasian, and they read the books I write. They're not dumb. They know the characters are Black. But, at the same time, the characters are human." Books for children should help to show that we are all human, no matter how we look, she says. "For the more human and humane we become, the closer we'll be."

—*Lauri Miller*

ers—20,000; young adult/teens—60,000. Published *Wonder-workers! How They Perform the Impossible*, by Joe Nickell (ages 9-14, skepticism); *How Do You Know It's True?*, by Hy Ruchlis (ages 12-15, critical thinking); *Maybe Right, Maybe Wrong*, by Dan Barker (ages 7-12, moral education); *The Tree of Life: The Wonders of Evolution*, by Ellen Jackson (ages 4-9, science).

How to Contact/Writers: Nonfiction: Submit complete ms with sample illustrations (b&w). Reports on queries in 1-2 months; mss in 2-3 months. Publishes a book 12-18 months after acceptance.

Illustration: Works with 2 illustrators/year. Editorial will review ms/illustration packages.

How to Contact/Illustrators: "Prefer to have full work (manuscript and illustrations); will consider any proposal." Include résumé, photocopies.

Terms: "Contract terms vary with projects." Pays authors royalties; author hires illustrator. Sends galleys to author. Book catalog is free on request.

Tips: "Book should reflect secular humanist values, stressing nonreligious moral education, critical thinking, logic and skepticism. Authors should examine our book catalog to learn what sort of manuscripts we're looking for."

PUMPKIN PRESS PUBLISHING HOUSE, P.O. Box 139, Shasta CA 96087. (916)244-3456. Book publisher. President: Dick Bozzi. Or contact: Susan Olson Higgins. Publishes 2-3 picture books/year; 2-3 young readers/year; 1-2 middle readers/year.

Fiction: All levels: adventure, animal, concept, contemporary, fantasy, folktales, health, history, humor, multicultural, nature/environment, poetry, sports.

Nonfiction: All levels: activity books, animal, biography, concept, geography, history, music/dance, nature/environment, religion, science, social issues.

How to Contact/Writers: Submit complete ms. Reports on queries in 3 weeks; on mss in 3 months.

Illustration: Works with 3 illustrators/year. Will review ms/illustration packages. Will review artwork for future assignments. Contact: Design Dept.

How to Contact/Illustrators: Ms/illustration packages: Submit ms with dummy. Original artwork returned at job's completion.

Terms: Work purchased outright from authors. Pays illustrators by the project. Book catalog available for SASE. Ms/artist's guidelines not available.

Tips: "Fresh, fun, original manuscripts focused on pre-school to third-grade children."

G.P. PUTNAM'S SONS, 200 Madison Ave., New York NY 10016. (212)951-8700. Imprint of Putnam and Grosset Group. Book publisher. Executive Editor: Refna Wilkin. Art Director: Nanette Stevenson. Publishes 25 picture books/year; 3 middle readers; 5 young adult titles/year. 5% of books by first-time authors; 50% of books from agented authors.

Fiction: Picture books: adventure, concept, contemporary, folktales, humor. Young readers: adventure, contemporary, folktales, history, humor, special needs, suspense/mystery. Middle readers: adventure, contemporary, history, humor, special needs, suspense/mystery. Young adults: contemporary, humor, problem novels, special needs. "Multicultural books should reflect different cultures accurately but unobtrusively." Regarding special needs, "stories about physically or mentally challenged children should portray them accurately and without condescension." No series, romances, sports fiction. Very little fantasy. Average word length: picture books—200-1,500; middle readers—10,000-30,000; young adults—40,000-50,000. Recently published *Mirette on the High Wire*, by Emily Arnold McCully; *Mayfield Crossing*, by Vaunda Nelson; *Herbie Jones and the Dark Attic*, by Suzy Kline.

Nonfiction: Picture books: multicultural. Young readers: biography, history, multicultural. Middle readers and young adults: biography, history, multicultural, social issues. No hard science, series. Average word length: picture books—200-1,500; middle read-

ers: 10,000-30,000; young adults: 30,000-50,000. Recently published *Freedom's Children*, by Ellen Levine; *Speaking Out*, by Susan Kuklin; *The Tainos*, by Francine Jacobs.
How to Contact/Writers: Fiction/nonfiction: Query; submit outline/synopsis and 3 sample chapters. No unsolicited mss. Reports on queries in 1 month; mss in 8-10 weeks. Publishes a book two years after acceptance. Will consider simultaneous submissions on queries only.
Illustration: Works with 40 illustrators/year. Will review ms/illustration packages. Will review artwork for future assignments.
How to Contact/Illustrators: Query. Reports in 6-8 weeks. Samples returned with SASE; samples filed. Original artwork returned at job's completion.
Terms: Pays authors royalty based on retail price. Pays illustrators by the project or royallty. Sends galleys to authors. Books catalog and ms guidelines available for SASE.

QUARRY PRESS, P.O. Box 1061, Kingston, Ontario K7L 4Y5 Canada. (613)548-8429. Book publisher. Publisher: Bob Hilderley. Publishes 4 picture books/year. 50% of books by first-time authors.
Fiction: Picture books: folktales. Recently published *The Cat Park*, by Mary Alice Downie (grades 1-6); *The Storm Wife*, by Bob Barton (grades 1-6, folklore).
How to Contact/Writers: Fiction: Query; submit outline/synopsis and sample chapters. Reports on queries/mss in 3 months. Publishes a book 6 months-1 year after acceptance. Will consider electronic submissions via disk or modem.
Illustration: Will review ms/illustration packages. Will review artwork for future assignments. Contact: Bob Hilderley, publisher.
How to Contact/Illustrators: Ms/illustration packages: Query; submit 10 pieces of art. Illustration only: Query with samples. Reports in 3 months. Original artwork returned at job's completion.
Terms: Pays authors royalty based on retail price. Pay for illustrators varies. Sends galleys to authors; dummies to illustrators. Book catalog available for 9 × 12 SAE and IRC or 2 first-class Canadian stamps.
Tips: "Make it easy on us. We are inundated with material, so send a clear, easy-to-read letter/manuscript. Include name, address and phone number. Make sure proposals are clear and well organized."

RANDOM HOUSE BOOKS FOR YOUNG READERS, 201 E. 50th St., New York NY 10022. (212)940-7742. Random House, Inc. Book publisher. Vice President/Editor-in-Chief: Kate Klimo. Vice President/Executive Art Director: Cathy Goldsmith. 100% of books published through agents; 2% of books by first-time authors.
Fiction: Picture books: animal, easy-to-read, history, sports. Young readers: adventure, animal, easy-to-read, history, sports, suspense/mystery. Middle readers: adventure, history, science, sports, suspense/mystery.
Nonfiction: Picture books: animal. Young readers: animal, biography, hobbies. Middle readers: biography, history, hobbies, sports.
How to Contact/Writers: Fiction/nonfiction: Submit through agent only. Publishes a book 12-18 months after acceptance. Will consider simultaneous submissions.
Illustration: Will review ms/illustration packages (through agent only). Will review an illustrator's work for possible future assignments.
Terms: Pays authors in royalties; sometimes buys mss outright. Sends galleys to authors. Book catalog free on request.

■**READ'N RUN BOOKS**, P.O. Box 294, Rhododendron OR 97049. (503)622-4798. Subsidiary of Crumb Elbow Publishing. Book publisher. Publisher: Michael P. Jones. Publishes 3 picture books/year; 5 young reader titles/year; 2 middle reader titles/year; 5 young adult titles/year. 50% of books by first-time authors; 8% of books from agented writers; 12% subsidy published.

Fiction: Will consider all categories for all age levels. Word length: "Open."
Nonfiction: Will consider all categories for all age levels. Word length: "Open."
How to Contact/Writers: For fiction and nonfiction: Query. Reports on queries/mss in 2 months "or sooner depending upon work load." Publishes a book about 8 months to a year after acceptance depending on workload and previously committed projects. Will consider simultaneous submissions.
Illustration: Works with 25 illustrators/year. Reviews ms/illustration packages. Publisher, Michael P. Jones, will review illustrator's work for possible future assignments. "Black & white, 8×10 or 5×7 illustrations. No color work for finished artwork, but color work is great to demonstrate the artist's talents."
How to Contact/Illustrators: Query with entire ms and several pieces of the artwork. Query with samples; provide portfolio, slides and tearsheets. Reports on ms/art samples in 1-2 months. Original artwork returned at job's completion.
Photography: Purchases photos from freelancers. Contact: Michael P. Jones. Buys stock and assigns work. Looking for wildlife, history, nature. Model/property releases required; photo captions optional. Publishes photo essays and photo concept books. Uses 5×7 or 8×10 b&w prints; 4×5 or 35mm transparencies. To contact, photographers should query with samples.
Terms: Pays in published copies only. Sends galleys to authors; dummies to illustrators. Book catalog available for $2. Ms/artists' guidelines available for 1 first-class stamp and #10 SAE.
Tips: "Don't give up. The field can seem cruel and harsh when trying to break into the market. Roll with the punches." Wants natural history and historical books. Sees trend toward "more computer generated artwork."

THE ROSEN PUBLISHING GROUP, 29 E. 21st St., New York NY 10010. (212)777-3017. Book publisher. Estab. 1950. Editorial Contact: Gina Strazzabosco. Publisher: Roger Rosen. Publishes 25 middle reader titles/year; 50 young adult titles/year. 35% of books by first-time authors; 3% of books from agented writers.
Nonfiction: Young adults: careers, hi-lo, multicultural, special needs, psychological self-help. No fiction. Average word length: middle readers—10,000; young adults—40,000. Published *Everything You Need to Know When a Parent is in Jail*, (hi-lo, young adult, The Need to Know Library); *The Value of Trust*, by Rita Milios (young adult, The Encyclopedia of Ethical Behavior); *Careers as an Animal Rights Activist*, by Shelly Field (young adult, The Career Series).
How to Contact/Writers: Nonfiction: Submit outline/synopsis and sample chapters. Reports on queries/mss in 1-2 months. Publishes a book 9 months after acceptance.
Photography: Purchases photos from freelancers. Contact: Roger Rosen. Works on assignment only.
Terms: Pays authors in royalties or work purchased outright. Sends galleys to authors. Book catalog free on request.
Tips: "Target your manuscript to a specific age group and reading level and write for established series published by the house you are approaching."

*WILLIAM H. SADLIER, INC., 9 Pine St., New York NY 10005. (212)227-2120. Textbook publisher. President: William S. Dinger. "We publish texts for Roman Catholic religious studies. We are looking for writers whose stories might be used in our religious education programs."
Fiction: All levels: religion. "Multicultural themes are important."
Nonfiction: All levels: religious education textbooks. Average word length: 25-30 words per lesson in each text for all age levels.
Terms: Pays authors "fee for stories" (work for hire).
Tips: "We are looking for engaging stories that will involve the child especially primary grades, ages 3-8."

ST. ANTHONY MESSENGER PRESS, 1615 Republic St., Cincinnati OH 45210. (513)241-5615. Fax: (513)241-0399. Book publisher. Managing Editor: Lisa Biedenbach. 25% of books by first-time authors. "All books nurture and enrich Catholic Christian life. We also look for books for parents and religious educators."
Nonfiction: Middle readers and young adults: religion. No fiction.
How to Contact/Writers: Nonfiction: Query; submit outline/synopsis and sample chapters. Reports on queries in 2-4 weeks; mss in 4-6 weeks. Publishes a book 12-18 months after acceptance.
Illustration: Works with 2 illustrators/year. Editorial will review ms/illustration packages. Will review artwork for future assignments. "We design all covers and do most illustrations in-house." Uses primarily b&w artwork.
How to Contact/Illustrators: Ms/illustration packages: Query with samples; résumé.
Photography: Purchases photos from freelancers. Contact Julie Lonneman, art director. Buys stock and assigns work.
Terms: Pays authors royalties of 10-12% based on net receipts. Offers average advance payment of $600. Pays illustrators by the project. Sends galleys to authors. Book catalog, ms guidelines free on request.
Tips: "We're looking for programs to be used in Catholic schools and parishes—programs that have successful track records."

ST. PAUL BOOKS AND MEDIA, 50 St. Paul's Ave., Jamaica Plain MA 02130. (617)522-8911. Daughters of St. Paul. Book publisher. Estab. 1934. Children's Editor: Sister Anne Joan, fsp. Art Director: Sister Mary Joseph. Publishes 1-2 picture books/year; 1-2 young reader titles/year. 20% of books by first-time authors.
Fiction: All levels: contemporary, religion. Average word length: picture books—150-300; young readers—1,500-5,000.
Nonfiction: All levels: biography (saints), devotionals, religion. Average word length: picture books—200; young readers—1,500-5,000; middle readers—10,000; young adults—20,000-50,000.
How to Contact/Writers: Fiction/nonfiction: Submit outline/synopsis and sample chapters. Reports on queries in 3-8 weeks; on mss in 3 months. Publishes a book 2-3 years after acceptance. No simultaneous submissions.
Illustration: Works with 20 illustrators/year. Will review ms/illustration packages. Will review artwork for future assignments. Style/size of illustration "varies according to the title."
How to Contact/Illustrators: Ms/illustration packages: "Outline first with art samples." Illustrations only: Query with samples; send promo sheets or tearsheets. Reports on art samples in 3-8 weeks.
Photography: Contact: Sister Annette Margaret. Buys stock images. Looking for children, animals—active interaction. Uses 4×5 or 8×10 b&w prints; 35mm or 4×5 transparencies.
Terms: Pays authors in royalties of 4-12% based on gross sales. Illustrations paid by the project. Photographers paid by the project, $15-200. Book catalog for 9×12 SAE and 5 first-class stamps. Manuscript guidelines for legal-size SAE and 1 first-class stamp.
Tips: "We are a Roman Catholic publishing house looking for devotional material for all ages (traditional and contemporary prayer-forms); obviously, material should be consonant with Catholic doctrine and spirituality!"

*SCHOLASTIC HARDCOVER, Imprint of Scholastic Inc., 555 Broadway, New York NY 10012. (212)343-6100. Book publisher. Editorial Director, Jean Feiwel. Executive Editor: Dianne Hess. Editorial contacts are as follows: picture books: Jean Feiwel, Dianne Hess, Grace Maccarone; young readers: Dianne Hess; middle readers: Jean Feiwel and Regina Griffin; young adult tales: Jean Feiwel and Regina Griffin. Publishes 40+ (in hardcover) picture books/year; 20+ young reader titles/year; 20+ middle reader titles/

year; 20+ young adult titles/year. 5% of books by first-time authors; 50% of books from agented authors.

Fiction: Picture books, young readers, middle readers, young adults: animal, contemporary, humor, easy-to-read, fantasy, history, problem novels, romance, science fiction, sports, spy/mystery/adventure.

Nonfiction: Picture books, young readers, middle readers, young adults: animal, biography, education, history, hobbies, music/dance, nature/environment, religion, sports.

How to Contact/Writers: Fiction (for picture book and young reader): Submit complete mss with SASE; (for young adult and middle reader): query or submit outline/synopsis and sample chapters. Nonfiction: Query or submit outline/synopsis and sample chapters. Reports on queries in 4-6 weeks; mss in 6-8 weeks. Publishes a book 1 year after acceptance.

Illustrations: Editorial will review ms/illustration packages. "It is not necessary for authors to supply art." Dianne Hess, executive editor, or Claire Counihan, art director, will review an illustrator's work for possible future assignments.

How to Contact/Illustrators: Illustrations only: Send tearsheets or slides. Reports in 6-8 weeks. Original artwork returned at job's completion.

Terms: Pays authors in royalties of 10% (5% if split with artist) based on retail price. Sends galleys to author; dummies to illustrator. Book catalog for postage and mailing label.

Tips: Writers: "Attend writing workshops, learn your craft, don't be afraid to revise. Illustrators: Create a finished dummy of any story and one piece of finished art to show an editor how you work."

SCIENTIFIC AMERICAN BOOKS FOR YOUNG READERS, W.H. Freeman and Company, 41 Madison Ave., New York NY 10010. (212)576-9400. Fax: (212)689-2383. Book publisher. Publisher, Children's Books: Jacqueline Ball. Executive Editor: Mark Gave. Approximately 30 titles/year. 25% of books from agented authors. Publishes science, social science, math subjects.

Fiction: "We consider fiction with a scientific slant if there is a real purpose in presenting the material in a fictionalized context." Recently published *Mathnet Casebooks— the Unnatural*, by David D. Ganell, illustrated by Danny O'Leary (novelization of popular PBS television show featuring detectives who solve crimes using math).

Nonfiction: Middle readers and young adults: biography, health, nature/environment, science, math, social science. All material should have a scientific slant. No books that are too similar to textbooks. Average word length: middle readers—8,000, young adult/teens—10,000. Recently published *One Small Square—Backyard*, by Donald M. Silver, illustrated by Patricia J. Wayne (ages 7-12, ecosystem); *Mission to Deepspace*, by William E. Burrows (ages 9-14, space exploration); *Aquarium: Bringing the Seas Inside*, by Linda Capus Riley, photos by Michael Baytoff (ages 9-14); *Wolf Island*, by Celia Godkin (ages 4-8, picture book).

How to Contact/Writers: Fiction/nonfiction: Query. Reports on queries in 1 month; reports on mss in 2 months. Will consider simultaneous submissions.

Illustration: Will review ms/illustration packages. Will review artwork for future assignments. Contact: Maria Epes, art director, children's books.

How to Contact/Illustrators: Ms/illustration packages: Query. Illustrations only: Query with samples (reply only upon request); submit portfolio for review; provide tearsheets. Reports in 1 month.

Always include a self-addressed stamped envelope (SASE) or a self-addressed envelope (SAE) and International Reply Coupons (IRCs) with submissions.

Photography: Contact: Maria Epes, art director, children's books. Uses scientific subjects. Model/property release required. Interested in stock photos. May publish photo essays. Uses 35mm transparencies. Photographers should query with samples; submit portfolio for review; provide tearsheets.

Terms: Pays authors royalty based on net sales receipts. Offers advances. Pays illustrators by the project or royalty. Photographers paid by the project or per photo. Sends galleys to authors. Book catalog available. Ms and art guidelines available for SASE.

Tips: "Study the publishers' lists to find out who is publishing what. Don't send anything out to a publisher without finding out if the publisher is interested in receiving such material." Looking for "well-researched, well-written, thoughtful but lively books on a focused aspect of science, social science (anthropology, psychology—not politics, history), with lots of kid interest, for ages 4-14."

CHARLES SCRIBNER'S SONS, 866 Third Ave., New York NY 10022. (212)702-7885. Imprint of Macmillan Publishing Co. Book publisher. Senior Vice President/Editorial Director: Clare Costello. 35% of books from agented writers.

- In November, 1993, all imprints of the Macmillan Children's Book Group and all other divisions of Macmillan were sold to Paramount Communications. This could affect future editorial policies, so watch *Publishers Weekly* and other trade journals for details.

Fiction: Picture books, young readers: adventure, animal, contemporary, fantasy, folktales, nature/environment, science. Middle readers, young adults: adventure, animal, contemporary, fantasy, folktales, history, nature/environment, problem novels, science fiction, sports, suspense/mystery. Recently published *Moose and Friends*, by Jim Latimer (picture book); *The Legend of Slappy Hooper*, by Aaron Shepard (picture book).

Nonfiction: Picture books: animal, nature/environment. Young readers: animal, history, nature/environment. Middle readers, young adults/teens: animal, biography, history, nature/environment. Recently published *Jackal Woman*, by Laurence Pringle (science); *Starting Home: The Story of Horace Pippan* and *Stitching Stars: The Story Quilts of Harriet Powers*, both by Mary E. Lyons (biographies).

How to Contact/Writers: Fiction: Submit outline/synopsis and sample chapters. Nonfiction: Query. Reports on queries in 1 month; mss in 10-14 weeks. Publishes a book 12-18 months after acceptance, "picture books longer." Will consider simultaneous submissions (if specified when submitted).

Illustrations: Editorial will review ms/illustration packages.

How to Contact/Illustrators: Ms/illustration packages: "Query first." Illustrations only: Send tearsheets. Reports back only if interested. Original artwork returned at job's completion.

Terms: Pays authors in royalties based on retail price. Sends galleys to authors; dummies to illustrators. Book catalog for 8×10 SAE; ms guidelines for legal-size SASE.

SEACOAST PUBLICATIONS OF NEW ENGLAND, Suite 165, 2800A Lafayette Rd., Portsmouth NH 03801. Book publisher. Founder: Paul Peter Jesep. Publishes 1-3 young readers/year. 100% of books by first-time authors. Mss "*must* have New England theme."

Fiction: Young readers, middle readers: adventure, animal, contemporary, fantasy, folktales, history, nature/environment. Fiction must be related to New England. Average word length: young readers—1,400. Recently published *Lady-Ghost of the Isles of Shoals*, illustrated by John Bowdren (ages 5-8); *A December Gift from the Shoals*, illustrated by John Bowdren; *I Saw A Whale!*, by Virginia Kroll.

Nonfiction: Young readers, middle readers: animal, biography, geography, history, nature/environment. Average word length: 1,400. "SPNE wants manuscripts that 'celebrate' New England's heritage, culture, folklore and mind-set."

How to Contact/Writers: Fiction/nonfiction: Query. Reports on queries in 2 months; on mss in 4 months. Publishes a book 9 months after acceptance. Will consider simultaneous submissions.

Illustrations: Works with 1-2 illustrators/year. Will review ms/illustration packages. Will review artwork for future assignments. Uses primarily b&w artwork.

How to Contact/Illustrators: Ms/illustration packages: Submit ms with 2 pieces of final art. Illustrations only: Query with samples; provide résumé and client list. Reports in 6 weeks. Samples returned with SASE. Originals not returned.

Photography: Purchases photos from freelancers. Contact: Paul Peter Jesep. Buys stock and assigns work. Wants photos of scenic New England. Model/property releases required; captions required. Uses b&w prints. Photographers should send cover letter and résumé.

Terms: Work purchased outright (range $100-400). Pays illustrators by the project (range: $100-300). Photographers paid per photo ($25 minimum). Ms/artist's guidelines available for SASE.

Tips: Wants "a very unique New England theme—will consider most short children's manuscripts on any of the six New England states, particularly stories about pirates, ghosts, marine life and 18th and 19th century historical figures. The first book issued by Seacoast Publications of New England was about a group of islands off the Maine-New Hampshire coast called the Isles of Shoals. Although the Shoals are rich in pirate lore, ghost stories and New England history, there are few children's books on the topic." No phone calls.

HAROLD SHAW PUBLISHERS, P.O. Box 567, 388 Gundersen Dr., Wheaton IL 60189. (708)665-6700. Book publisher. Estab. 1967. Director of Editorial Services: Ramona Cramer Tucker. Publishes 2 young adult titles/year. 10% of books by first-time authors; 5% of books from agented writers.

Fiction: Young adults: adventure, problem novels. Average length: young adults—112-250 pages. Published *The Sioux Society*, by Jeffrey Asher Nesbit (ages 13 and up, novel); *Light at Summer's End*, by Kimberly M. Ballard (ages 13 and up, novel).

How to Contact/Writers: Reports on queries in 2-4 weeks; mss in 4-6 weeks. Publishes a book 1 year after acceptance. Will consider simultaneous submissions.

Terms: Pays authors in royalties of 5-10% based on retail price. Sends pages to authors. Book catalog available for SAE and $1.25; ms guidelines for SASE.

Tips: "We no longer accept illustrator or photographer packages. At this time we are not accepting any unsolicited manuscripts."

*SILVER MOON PRESS, 126 Fifth Ave., New York NY 10011. (212)242-6499. Book publisher. Managing Editor: Matthew DeBord. Publishes 2 picture books/year; 10 young readers/year; 10 middle readers; 2 young adults titles/year. 25% of books by first-time authors; 10% of books from agented authors.

Fiction: All levels: "We'll look at anything except hi-lo." Average word length: picture books—2,500-5,000; young readers, middle readers, young adults—varies. Recently published *Golden Quest*, by Bonnie Bader (ages 8-13, historical novel); *Drums at Saratoga*, by Lisa Banim (ages 8-13, historical novel); *Voyage of the Half Moon*, by Tracey West (ages 8-13, historical novel).

Nonfiction: All levels: "We'll look at just about anything of quality." Does not want to see activity books, hi-lo. Average word length: picture books—2,500-5,000; young readers, middle readers, young adults—varies. Recently published *Family Celebrations*, by Diana Patrick and Michael Bryant (ages 8-13, family); *Police Lab*, by Robert Sheely (ages 8-13, forensic science).

How to Contact/Writers: Fiction/nonfiction: Query. Reports on queries in 2-4 weeks; mss in 1-2 months. Publishes a book 1-2 years after acceptance. Will consider simultaneous submissions, electronic submissions via disk or modem, previously published work.

How to Contact/Illustrators: Ms/illustration packages: Query. Illustrations only: Query with samples, résumé, client list, arrange personal portfolio review. Reports only if interested. Samples returned with SASE. Original artwork returned at job's completion.

Photography: Purchases photos from freelancers. Buys stock and assigns work. Uses archival, historical, sports photos. Captions required. Uses color, b&w prints; 35mm, 2¼×2¼, 4×5, 8×10 transparencies. Photographers should submit cover letter, résumé, published samples, client list, promo piece.

Terms: Pays authors royalty or work purchased outright. Pays illustrators by the project, royalty. Pays photographers by the project, paid per photo, royalty. Sends galleys to authors; dummies to illustrators. Book catalog available for SAE; ms and art guidelines not available.

SIMON & SCHUSTER CHILDREN'S BOOKS, 15 Columbus Circle, New York NY 10023. (212)373-8500. Imprints: Little Simon, Simon & Schuster Books for Young Readers, Green Tiger Press. Editor-in-Chief: Willa Perlman. Art Director: Lucille Chomowicz. Publishes 100 picture books/year; 8 young readers/year; 25 middle readers/year; 10 young adult titles/year.

Fiction: Picture books: adventure, animal, concept, contemporary, fantasy, folktales, health, humor, multicultural, nature/environment, poetry, sports. Young readers: animal, contemporary, humor, mystery. Middle readers: adventure, animal, anthology, contemporary, fantasy, folktales, history, multicultural, nature/environment, science fiction, sports, mystery. Young adults: anthology, contemporary, fantasy, sports, suspense/mystery. Does not want to see horror, straight romance, mass market series ("Sweet Valley High" type). Average word length: picture books—wordless to 600 words; young readers—1,500; middle readers—2,000; young adult/teens—over 2,000. Published *Me And The End of the World*, by William Corbin (ages 8-12, middle-grade fiction); *Eamily Eyefinger*, by Duncan Ball and George Ulrich (ages 6-9, chapter book); *You Must Kiss a Whale*, by David Skinner (ages 11 and up, young adult).

Nonfiction: Picture books: animal, arts/crafts, biography, concept, geography, history, multicultural, nature/environment, science, social issues. Young readers: activity books, animal, biography, concept, geography, history, multicultural, music/dance, nature/environment, science, social issues. Middle Readers: activity books, animal, biography, concept, geography, history, multicultural, music/dance, nature/environment, science, social issues. Young adults: activity books, animal, biography, concept, geography, history, multicultural, music/dance, nature/environment, social issues. Does not want to see self-help books or poorly written manuscripts. Average word length: picture books—1,000; young readers—1,500; middle readers—2,000. Published *Antarctica*, by Laurence Pringle (ages 9 and up, geography); *Penguins*, by The Cousteau Society (preschool, picture book).

How to Contact/Writers: Fiction: Query; submit complete ms; submit through agently only. Nonfiction: Query; submit through agent only. Reports on queries in 3 weeks; reports on mss in 3 months. Publishes book 2 years after acceptance. Will consider simultaneous submissions and previously published work.

Illustration: Works with 35 illustrators/year. Will review ms/illustration packages only if illustrator is author. "Do not submit original art; copies only." Will review artwork for future assignments. Uses both b&w and color artwork. "No mural-size art, please."

How to Contact/Illustrators: Ms/illustration packages: Query; submit ms with dummy; submit ms with 2-3 pieces of final art. Illustrations only: Query with samples; provide portfolio, slides, tearsheets, arrange personal portfolio review, through agent. Reports only if interested. Samples returned with SASE; samples filed.

Photography: Purchases photos from freelancers. Works on assignment only. Model/property releases required. Uses 35 mm transparencies. Photographers should send cover letter, résumé, published samples, slides, promo piece in color or b&w.

Terms: Pays authors royalty (varies). Pays illustrators royalty. Photographers paid royalty. Sends galleys to authors. Book catalog for 10×13 SAE; ms guidelines available. No artist's guidelines available.

Tips: "Present your manuscript as polished and professionally as possible." Sees trend toward "multicultural, multi-ethnic and multi-generational" books.

SOUNDPRINTS, 165 Water St., P.O. Box 679, Norwalk CT 06856. (203)838-6009. Book publisher. Assistant Editor: Dana Meachen. Publishes 12 picture books/year. 10% of books by first-time authors; 10% of books from agented authors. Subjects published include North American wildlife and habitats.

Fiction: Picture books: animal, nature/environment. No fantasy or anthropomorphic animals. Average word length: picture books—800. Recently published *Swan Flyway*, by Dana Limpert, illustrated by Jo-Ellen Bosson (grages K-3, picture book); *Puffin's Homecoming*, by Darice Bailer, illustrated by Katie Lee (grades, K-3, picture book); *Summer Coat, Winter Coat: TheStory of a Snowshoe Hare*, by Doe Boyle, illustrated by Allen Davis (grades K-3, picure book); *Gray Wolf Pup*, by Doe Boyle, illustrated by Jeff Domm (grades K-3, picture books); *Prairie Dog Town*, by Bettye Rogers, illustrated by Deborah Howland (grades K-3, picture book).

Nonfiction: Picture books: animal, nature/environment. No anthropomorphic animals or pets. Average word length: picture books—800; young readers—1,500. Published *After Columbus: The Horse's Return To America*, by Herman J. Viola with illustrations by Deborah Howland (ages 7-11, history picture book).

How to Contact/Writers: Fiction/nonfiction: Query. Reports on queries/mss in 6-8 weeks. Publishing time "Can vary from one to two years, depending on where it can be fitted into our publishing schedule." Will consider simultaneous submissions.

Illustration: Works with 6-10 illustrators/year. Will review ms/illustration packages "if subject matter is appropriate." Will review artwork for future assignments. Uses color artwork only. Illustrations are usually full bleed two-page spreads.

How to Contact/Illustrators: Ms/illustration packages: Query. Illustrations only: Query with samples; provide résumé, portfolio, promo sheet, slides. "If interest is generated, additional material will be requested." Reports in 1 month. Samples returned with SASE. Original artwork returned at job's completion.

Terms: Pays authors royalty or outright purchase. Offers advances. Pays illustrators by the project or royalty. Book catalog for 8¼×11 SAE and 98¢ postage; ms guidelines for SASE. "It's best to request both guidelines and catalog. Both can be sent in self-addressed envelope at least 8½×11, with 98¢ postage."

Tips: Wants a book that "features North American wildlife and habitats with great accuracy while capturing the interest of the reader/listener."

THE SPEECH BIN, INC., 1965 25th Ave., Vero Beach FL 32960. (407)770-0007. Fax: (407)770-0006. Book publisher. Contact: Jan J. Binney, Senior Editor. Publishes 10-12 books/year. 50% of books by first-time authors; less than 15% of books from agented writers. "Nearly all our books deal with treatment of children (as well as adults) who have communication disorders of speech or hearing or children who deal with family members who have such disorders (e.g., a grandparent with Alzheimer's disease or stroke)."

Fiction: Picture books: animal, easy-to-read, fantasy, health, special needs. Young readers, middle readers, young adult: health, special needs.

Refer to the Business of Children's Writing & Illustrating for up-to-date marketing, tax and legal information.

Nonfiction: Picture books, young readers, middle readers, young adults: activity books, health, textbooks, special needs. Published *Chatty Hats and Other Props*, by Denise Mantione; *Holiday Hoopla: Holiday Games for Language & Speech*, by Michele Rost; *Speech Sports*, by Janet M. Shaw.

How to Contact/Writers: Fiction/nonfiction: Query. Reports on queries in 4-6 weeks; 2-3 months on mss. Publishes a book 10-12 months after acceptance. "Will consider simultaneous submissions *only* if notified; too many authors fail to let us know if ms is simultaneously submitted to other publishers! We *strongly* prefer sole submissions."

Illustration: Works with 4-5 illustrators/year ("usually in-house"). Will review ms/illustration packages. Will review artwork for future assignments.

How to Contact/Illustrators: "Query first!" Submit tearsheets (no original art). Original artwork returned at job's completion.

Photography: Photographers should contact Jan J. Binney, senior editor. Buys stock and assigns work. Looking for scenic shots. Model/property releases required. Uses glossy b&w prints, 35mm or $2\frac{1}{4} \times 2\frac{1}{4}$ transparencies. Photographer should provide résumé, business card, promotional literature or tearsheets to be kept on file.

Terms: Pays authors in royalties based on retail price. Pays illustrators by the project. Photographers paid by the project or per photo. Sends galleys to authors. Book catalog for 3 first-class stamps and 9×12 SAE; manuscript guidelines for #10 SASE.

STANDARD PUBLISHING, 8121 Hamilton Ave., Cincinnati OH 45231. (513)931-4050. Book publisher. Director: Mark Taylor. Children's Editor: Diane Stortz. Creative Director: Coleen Davis. Publishes 4-8 board books/year; 25 picture books/year; 8-10 easy reader titles/year; 8-10 coloring and activity books/year. 25-40% of books by first-time authors; 1% of books from agented writers. Publishes well-written, upbeat books with a Christian perspective.

Fiction: Board/picture books: animal, contemporary, religion (Bible stories). Young readers: adventure, animal, contemporary, religion. Middle readers: adventure, contemporary, religion. Young adults: contemporary, mystery, religion, sports. Average word length: board/picture books—400-1,000; young readers—1,000.

Nonfiction: Board/picture books, young readers: concept, Bible background, nature/environment, sports. Average word length: picture books—400-1,000; young readers—1,000.

How to Contact/Writers: Fiction/nonfiction: Send complete ms. Reports on queries/mss in 2 months. Publishes a book 18 months after acceptance. Will consider simultaneous and electronic submissions via disk or modem.

Illustration: Works with 6-10 illustrators/year. Will review artwork for future assignments. Contact: Coleen Davis, creative director.

How to Contact/Illustrators: Illustrations only: Send cover letter and photocopies. Reports on art samples on if interested.

Terms: Pays authors royalties of 5-12% based on wholesale price or work purchased outright (range $250-1,000). Sends galleys to authors. Book catalog available for $8\frac{1}{2} \times 11$ SAE; ms guidelines for letter-size SASE.

Tips: "We look for manuscripts that help draw children into a relationship with Jesus Christ; help children develop insights about what the Bible teaches; make reading an appealing and pleasurable activity."

STEMMER HOUSE PUBLISHERS, INC., 2627 Caves Rd., Owings Mills MD 21117. (410)363-3690. Fax: (410)363-8459. Book publisher. Estab. 1975. President: Barbara Holdridge. Publishes 1-3 picture books/year. "Sporadic" numbers of young reader, middle reader, young adult titles/year. 60% of books by first-time authors.

Fiction: Picture books: animal, ecology, folktales, multicultural, nature/environment. Young reader, middle reader: history. Does not want to see anthropomorphic characters. Recently published *Grandma's Band*, by Brad Bowles, illustrations by Anthony

Clon (ages 4-6); *The Pied Piper*, by Sharon Chmeloy, illustrations by Pat and Robin DeWitt (ages 4-8); *Why Buffalo Roam*, by L. Michael Kershen, illustrations by Monica Hansen.

Nonfiction: Picture books: young readers: animal, arts/crafts, biography, multicultural, music/dance, nature/environment. Published *The Hawaiian Coral Reef Coloring Book*, by Katherine Orr; *The First Teddy Bear*, by Helen Kay, illustrations by Susan Kranz.

How to Contact/Writers: Fiction/nonfiction: Query; submit outline/synopsis and sample chapters. Reports on queries in 2 weeks; mss in 6 weeks. Publishes a book 18 months after acceptance. Will consider simultaneous submissions.

Illustration: Works with 3 illustrators/year. Will review ms/illustration packages. Will review artwork for future assignments.

How to Contact/Illustrators: Ms/illustration packages: Query first, with several photocopied illustrations. Illustrations only: Send tearsheets and/or slides (with SASE for return). Reports in 2 weeks.

Terms: Pays authors royalties of 4-10% based on wholesale price. Offers average advance payment of $300. Pays illustrators royalty of 4-5% based on wholesale price. Sends galleys to authors. Book catalog for 9 × 12 SASE.

Tips: Writers: "Simplicity, literary quality and originality are the keys." Wants to see ms/illustration packages.

STEPPING STONE BOOKS, 201 E. 50th St., New York NY 10022. (212)940-7682. Series of Random House, Inc. Book publisher. Contact: Stephanie Spinner.

Fiction: Young readers: "There are no restrictions on subject matter—we just require well-written, absorbing fiction." Length: 8,000-9,000 words. Audience: 7-9 year olds.

Illustration: Average number of illustrations used for fiction: young readers—10-15. Prefers b&w drawings.

STERLING PUBLISHING CO., INC., 387 Park Ave. S., New York NY 10016. (212)532-7160. Fax: (212)213-2495. Book publisher. Acquisitions Director: Sheila Anne Barry. Publishes 30 middle reader titles/year. 10% of books by first-time authors.

Nonfiction: Middle readers: activity books, animal, arts/crafts, geography, ghosts, hi-lo, hobbies, how-to, humor, true mystery, nature/environment, reference, science, sports, supernatural incidents. "Since our books are highly illustrated, word length is seldom the point. Most are 96-128 pages." Does not want to see story books or personal narratives. Recently published *Traveler's Guide to the Solar System*, by Patricia Barnes-Svarney (ages 10 and up, an imaginative trip to nine planets and a look at what it would be like to live on them); *World's Best Outdoor Games*, written and illustrated by Glen Vecchione (ages 9 and up); *Paper Action Toys*, by E. Richard Churchill, illustrated by James Michaels (ages 9 and up, easy to follow instructions for making dozens of moving projects with everyday materials).

How to Contact/Writers: Reports on queries/mss in 1-12 weeks. "If we are interested it may take longer." Publishes a book 6-18 months after acceptance. Will consider simultaneous submissions.

Illustration: Works with 7-10 illustrators/year. Will review ms/illustration packages. Will review artwork for future assignments.

How to Contact/Illustrators: Ms/illustration packages: "Query first." Illustrations only: "Send sample photocopies of line drawings; also examples of some color work." Original artwork returned at job's completion "if possible, but usually held for future needs."

Terms: Pays authors in royalties of up to 10% "standard terms, no sliding scale, varies according to edition." Pays illustrators royalty, by the project. Sends galleys to authors. Ms guidelines for SASE.

Tips: Looks for: "Humor, hobbies, science books for middle-school children." Also, "mysterious occurrences, activities and fun and games books."

SUNBELT MEDIA, INC./EAKIN PRESS, P.O. Box 90159, Austin TX 78709. (512)288-1771. Fax: (512)288-1813. Book publisher. Estab. 1978. President: Ed Eakin. Publishes 2 picture books/year; 3 young readers/year; 10 middle readers/year; 2 young adult titles/year. 50% of books by first-time authors; 5% of books from agented writers.

Fiction: Picture books: animal. Middle readers, young adults: history, sports. Average word length: picture books—3,000; young readers—10,000; middle readers—15,000-20,000; young adults—20,000-30,000. "90% of our books relate to Texas and the Southwest."

Nonfiction: Picture books: animal. Middle readers and young adults: history, sports. Recently published *Courage Seed*.

How to Contact/Writers: Fiction/nonfiction: Query. Reports on queries in 2 weeks; mss in 6 weeks. Publishes a book 18 months after acceptance. Will consider simultaneous and electronic submissions via disk.

Illustration: Editorial will review all varieties of ms/illustration packages.

How to Contact/Illustrators: Ms/illustration packages: Query. Illustrations only: Tearsheets. Reports on art samples in 2 weeks.

Terms: Pays authors royalties of 10-15% based on net to publisher. Pays for separate authors and illustrators: "Usually share royalty." Pays illustrators royalty of 10-15% based on wholesale price. Sends galleys to authors. Book catalog, ms/artist's guidelines for SASE.

Tips: Writers: "Be sure all elements of manuscript are included—include bio of author or illustrator." Submit books relating to Texas only.

*SUNDANCE PUBLISHERS & DISTRIBUTORS, P.O. Box 1326 Newtown Rd., Littleton MA 01460. (508)486-9201. Book publisher. Editor-in-Chief: Forrest Stone. Manager, Product and Design: Sarah Kline. Publishes 12 picture books/year. 25% of books by first-time authors; 25% of books from agented authors. Multicultural, usually rhyming books, 300-500 words.

Fiction: Picture books: contemporary, multicultural (all groups, strong narratives). Average word length: picture books—300-500. Recently published *Mei Ling's Tiger*, by Marcia Tullman and Deborah DeRoo; *Manuel, the Portuguese Fisherman*, by Forrest Stone, illustration by Joe Santos; *The Dangerous Journey of Dr. McPain*, by Leon Steinmetz and Gaile Sarma; *What a Wonderful World*, illustrated by Ashley Bryan (all "big books").

Nonfiction: Picture books: biography, geography, multicultural. Young readers, young adults: geography, multicultural. Middle readers: careers, geography, multicultural. Multicultural needs include "all groups; strong, contemporary narratives." Average word length: picture books—300-500; young readers—1,500-4,000; middle readers—10,000-20,000; young adults—15,000-30,000. Recently published *Regalia: Native American Dress & Dance*, by Russell Peters, photos by Richard Haynes (ages preschool-8, "Big Books")

How to Contact/Writers: Fiction: Query (for young readers and up), submit complete ms (for picture books). Nonfiction: Query. Reports on queries in 6-10; mss in 2-3 months. Publishes a book "less than one year" after acceptance.

Illustration: Works with 15-20 illustrators/year. Will review ms/illustration packages. Contact: Forrest Stone, editor-in-chief. Will review artwork for future assignments.

How to Contact/Illustrators: Ms/illustration packages: Query; submit ms with dummy. Illustration only: Query with samples. Reports only if interested. Samples returned with SASE; samples "sometimes" filed. Original artwork "usually" returned.

Photography: Purchases photos from freelancers. Contact Sarah Kline, manager, production and design. Buys stock and assigns work. Uses series of multicultural subjects. Model/property releases required; captions required. Uses 4 × 5 transparencies. Photographers should submit cover letter, résumé, published samples, client list.

Terms: Pays authors royalty of 2½-4½% based on wholesale price, work purchased outright ($250 minimum) or a combination. Offers advances. Pays illustrators by the project ($50 minimum), royalty of 2½-4½% based on wholesale price or a combination. Pays photographers by the project (range: $100-4,000). Sometimes sends galleys to authors; dummies to illustrators. Ms guidelines available for SASE.

Tips: "We're a school publisher. Only submit school material to us."

TAB BOOKS, Blue Ridge Summit PA 17294-0850. (717)794-2191. A division of McGraw-Hill, Inc. Book Publisher. Editor-in-Chief: Kim Tabor. Publishes 6 young reader titles/year; 6 young adult titles/year. 50% of books by first-time authors. 10% of books by agented authors.

Nonfiction: All levels: activity books, geography, multicultural, nature/environment, science. Young adults: geography, nature/environment, science. "We intend to broaden our children's science publishing area by adding books for non-science teachers who are faced with teaching science and envionmental awareness to children in the primary and elementary grades." Recently published *Weather in the Lab: Simulate Nature's Phenomena*, by Thomas Richard Baker (grade 10+, weather experiments); *From Field to Lab: 200 Life Science Experiments for the Amateur Biologist*, by James Witherspoon (grade 10+, life science experiments); *Insect Biology: 49 Science Fair Projects*, by H. Steven Dashefsky (grades 6+, science fair projects).

How To Contact/Writers: Nonfiction: Query; submit outline/synopsis and sample chapters. Reports on queries in 2 months; mss in 3 months. Publishes a book 9-12 months after acceptance. Does not want to see fiction.

Illustration: Works with approximately 8-12 illustrators/year. Will review ms/illustration packages and artwork for future assignments.

How To Contact/Illustrators: Query first; submit résumé, tearsheets, photocopies. Reports back only if interested. Originals returned to artist at job's completion.

Terms: Authors paid royalty of 8-15% based on wholesale price. Illustrators paid by the project. "Terms vary from project to project." Book catalog and manuscript guidelines are free on request.

Tips: Looks for "science topics which are fun and educational and include activities adults and children can work on together. Projects should be designed around inexpensive, household materials and should require under two hours for completion."

TAMBOURINE BOOKS, 1350 Sixth Ave., New York NY 10019. Imprint of William Morrow & Co. Inc. Book publisher. Editor-in-Chief: Paulette Kaufmann. Art Director: Golda Laurens. Publishes 50 picture books/year; 4 middle readers/year; 2 young adult titles/year.

Fiction/Nonfiction: No primary theme for fiction or nonfiction—publishes various categories.

How to Contact/Writers: Fiction/Nonfiction: Submit complete ms. Reports on mss in 1-3 months.

Illustration: Will review ms/illustration packages. Will review artwork for future assignments.

How to Contact/Illustrators: Ms/illustration packages: Submit complete package. Illustrations only: Submit portfolio for review; provide résumé, business card, promotional literature or tearsheets to be kept on file. Original artwork returned at job's completion.

 The asterisk before a listing indicates the listing is new in this edition.

This watercolor illustration by Denny Bond was designed for the cover of The Little Scientist: An Activity Lab, by Jean Stangl, published by Tab Books. Editor-in-Chief Kim Tabor wanted a "fun, playful, non-intimidating" cover for this book of science activities for adults working with children ages 4-6.

Terms: Pays authors royalty based on retail price. Offers advances. Pays illustrators royalty. Sends galleys to authors. Book catalog available for 9 × 12 SASE; ms guidelines available for SASE.

TEXAS CHRISTIAN UNIVERSITY PRESS, Box 30783, Fort Worth TX 76129. (817)921-7822. Fax: (817)921-7822. Book Publisher. Editorial contact: Judy Alter. Art Director: Tracy Row. Publishes 1 young adult title/year. 75% of books by first-time authors. Only publishes historical works set in Texas.
Fiction: Young adults/teens: Texas history. Average word length: 35,000-50,000. Recently published *Josefina and the Hanging Tree*, by Isabelle Ridout Marvin (grades 6-9); *Have Gun — Need Bullets*, by Ruby Tolliver (grades 6-9); *You're an Orphan Mollie Brown!*, by Mary A. Penson (grades 6-9).
Nonfiction: Young adults/teens: Texas biography, Texas history. Average word length: 35,000-50,000.
How To Contact/Writers: Fiction/nonfiction: Query. Reports on queries in 2 weeks; mss in 2 months. Publishes a book 1-2 years after acceptance.
Illustration: Works with 1 illustrator/year. Will review mss/illustraion packages. Editor/Art Director Tracy Row will review artwork for future assignments.
How To Contact/Illustrators: Ms/illustration packages: Query with samples. Reports back to artists within 1 week. Originals returned to artist at job's completion.
Terms: Pays in royalty of 10% based on net price. Pays illustrators flat fee by the project. Book catalog free on request. Ms guidelines free on request.

THISTLEDOWN PRESS LTD., 633 Main St., Saskatoon, Saskatchewan S7H 0J8 Canada. (306)244-1722. Book publisher. Contact: Patrick O'Rourke. Publishes numerous middle reader and young adult titles/year. "Thistledown originates books by Canadian authors only, although we have co-published titles by authors outside Canada. We do not publish children's picture books."
Fiction: Middle readers and young adults: anthology (short stories), mystery/adventure. Average word length: middle readers — 35,000; young adult/teens — 40,000. Published *The Blue Jean Collection*, by various authors (young adult, short story anthology); *Fish House Secrets*, by Kathy Stinson (young adult); *The Mystery of the Missing Will*, by Jeni Mayer (middle reader, mystery series).
How to Contact/Writers: Fiction: Submit outline/synopsis and sample chapters. Reports on queries/mss in 3 months. Publishes a book about one year after acceptance. No simultaneous submissions.
Terms: Pays authors in royalties based on retail price. Sends galleys to authors. Book catalog free on request. Manuscript guidelines for #10 envelope and IRC.

*TICKNOR & FIELDS, Books for Young Readers, 215 Park Ave. S., New York NY 10003. (212)420-5800. Imprint of Houghton Mifflin Company. Book Publisher. Art Director: David Saylor. Publishes 25 picture books/year; 15 young readers/year; 10 middle readers/year; 10 young adult titles/year. 30% of books by first-time authors; 70% of books from agented authors.
Illustration: Works with 60 illustrators/year. Will review ms/illustration packages. Will review artwork for future assignments.
How to Contact/Illustrators: Ms/illustration packages: Submit ms with dummy. Illustrations only: Provide promo sheet, slides or tearsheets. Reports in 1 month. Samples returned with SASE. Samples filed "if we like them." Original artwork returned at job's completion.
Photography: Purchases photos from freelancers. Works on assignment only. Model/property releases required. Uses b&w or color prints; 35mm, 2¼×2¼, 4×5 or 8×10 transparencies. Photographers should send cover letter, published samples, slides or promo piece.
Terms: Pays illustrators by the project or royalty. Photographers paid by the project or royalty.

*TOR BOOKS, 175 Fifth Ave., New York NY 10010. Imprints: Forge, Orb. Book publisher. Director Educational Sales: Kathleen Doherty. Educational Sales Coordinator: Stefan Gerard. Publishes 50 picture books/year; 5-10 young readers/year; 20 middle readers/year; 5-10 young adult titles/year.

Fiction: Young readers, middle readers, young adults: Will consider anything except religious themes and poetry. "We are interested and open to books which tell stories from a wider range of perspectives. We are interested in materials that deal with a wide range of issues." Average word length: picture books—5,000; young readers—20,000; middle readers—10,000; young adults—20,000-40,000. Recently published *The Furious Flycycle*, by Jan Wahl/Ted Erik (ages 6-12, children's, fully illustrated); *The Eyes of Kid Midas*, by Neal Shusterman (ages 10-16, young adult novel).

Nonfiction: Picture books, young readers, middle readers: activity books, animal, arts/crafts, biography, careers, geography, health, history, hobbies, how-to, multicultural, nature/environment, science, social issues, sports. Does not want to see religion, cooking. Recently published *Strange Science: Planet Earth*, by Q.L. Peorce; *Stargazer's Guide*, by Q.L. Peorce (ages 6-12, guide to constellations, illustrated). Average word length: picture books—5,000; young readers—20,000; middle readers—10,000; young adults—40,000.

How to Contact/Writers: Fiction/nonfiction: Submit outline/synopsis and 3 sample chapters. Reports on queries in 1 month; mss in 2 months.

Illustration: Works with 40 illustrators/year. Will review ms/illustration packages. Will review artwork for future assignments. Contact: Stefan M. Gerard, Educational Sales Coordinator.

How to Contact/Illustrators: Ms/illustration packages: Submit ms with dummy. Illustrations only: Query with samples. Reports only if interested. Samples returned with SASE; samples kept on file.

Terms: Pays authors royalty. Offers advances. Pays illustrators by the project. Book catalog available for 9 × 12 SAE and 3 first-class stamps.

Tips: "Get an agent. Allow him/her to direct you to publishers who are most appropriate. It saves time and effort."

TREASURE CHEST PUBLICATIONS, INC., #101, 1802 W. Grant Rd., Tucson AZ 85745. (602)623-9558. Book publisher and distributor. Production Manager: Nancie S. Mahan. Publishes 2 picture books/year; 1 young reader/year; 1 middle reader/year; 1 young adult title/year. All books must pertain to a particular region, Native Americans, Arizona/New Mexico topics, desert living.

Fiction: Picture books, young readers, middle readers and young adults: adventure, animal and multicultural. Does not want to see poetry, novels. Recently published *Patrick Packrat and His Very Old House*, by Martha S. Campbell, illustrated by Sara Light Waller.

Nonfiction: Picture books, young readers: activity books, animal, arts/crafts, multicultural, nature/environment. Middle readers, young adults: activity books, animal, arts/crafts, cooking, hobbies, how-to, multicultural, nature.

How to Contact/Writers: Fiction: Query. Nonfiction: Query; submit outline/synopsis. Reports on queries/mss in 3-4 months. Publishes a book 6-12 months after acceptance "depending on amount of work needed."

Illustration: Works with 3 illustrators/year. Will review ms/illustrations packages. Will review artwork for future assignments.

How to Contact/Illustrators: Ms/illustration packages: Query; submit ms with dummy. Illustrations only: Query with samples; provide résumé. Reports back only if interested. Samples returned with SASE. Copies kept on file.

Terms: Pays authors royalty of 10-15% based on wholesale price; "may split with illustrator." Offers advance (depends on work). Pays illustrators by the project; or royalty of 5-10%; "may split with author." Sends galleys to authors; dummies to illustrators. Book catalog available for SAE.

TROLL ASSOCIATES, 100 Corporate Dr., Mahwah NJ 07430. Book publisher. Editor: Marian Frances.
Fiction: Picture books: animal, contemporary, folktales, history, nature/environment, poetry, sports, suspense/mystery. Young readers: adventure, animal, contemporary, folktales, history, nature/environment, poetry, science fiction, sports, suspense/mystery. Middle readers: adventure, anthology, animal, contemporary, fantasy, folktales, health-related, history, nature/environment, poetry, problem novels, romance, science fiction, sports, suspense/mystery. Young adults: problem novels, romance and suspense/mystery.
Nonfiction: Picture books: activity books, animal, biography, careers, history, hobbies, nature/environment, sports. Young Readers: activity books, animal, biography, careers, health, history, hobbies, music/dance, nature/environment, sports. Middle readers: activity books, animal, biography, careers, health, history, hobbies, music/dance, nature/environment, religion, sports. Young adults: health, music/dance.
How to Contact/Writers: Fiction: Query or submit outline/synopsis and 3 sample chapters. Nonfiction: Query. Reports in 2-4 weeks.
Illustration: Will review ms/illustration packages. Will review artwork for future assignments. Contact: Marian Frances, editor.
How to Contact/Illustrators: Illustrations only: query with samples; arrange a personal interview to show portfolio; provide résumé, promotional literature or tearsheets to be kept on file. Reports in 2-4 weeks.
Photography: Model/property releases required. Interested in stock photos.
Terms: Pays authors royalty or work purchased outright. Pays illustrators by the project or royalty. Photographers paid by the project.

TROPHY BOOKS, 10 E. 53rd St., New York NY 10022. Fax: (212)207-7915. Subsidiary of HarperCollins Children's Books Group. Book publisher. Publishes 6-9 chapter books/year, 25-30 middle grade titles/year, 30 reprint picture books/year, 25-30 young adult titles/year. "Trophy is primarily a paperback reprint imprint. We do not publish original illustrated manuscripts."
Fiction: No subject limitations. Recently published *Maniac Magee*, by Jerry Spinelli; *Prairie Songs*, by Pam Conrad; *El Bronx Remembered*, by Nicholasa Mohr.
Nonfiction: All levels: animal, biography, music/dance, nature/environment. No careers, health, hobbies, religion, textbooks. Recently published *Written for Children*, by John Rowe Townsend; *Voices from the Civil War*, by Milton Meltzer; *Black Music in America*, by James Haskins.
How to Contact/Writers: Submit complete ms (for chapter books); submit outline/synopsis and 3 sample chapters (for middle grade and young adult). Reports on queries in 4-6 weeks; mss in 8-10 weeks. Will consider simultaneous submissions and previously published work.
Photography: Contact Nick Krenitsky, art director. Photo captions required. Photographers should query with samples.
Terms: Sends galleys to authors. Ms guidelines available for SASE.
Tips: "We are developing a new middle grade horror line and a new young adult fiction line."

*TUDOR PUBLISHERS, INC., 3007 Taliaferro Rd., Greensboro NC 27408. Contact: Pam Cocks. Publishes 1 middle readers/year; 2 young adult titles/year. 30% of books by first-time authors. Primarily publishes young adult novels and fiction.
Fiction: Young adults: contemporary, folktales, multicultural (African-American, Native American), problem novels, suspense/mystery. Does not want to see romance. Word

length varies. Recently published *The Mean Lean Weightlifting Queen*, by Mark Emerson (young adult novel).

Nonfiction: Middle readers, young adults: biography, multicultural (folklore, history), reference, science, social issues, sports, textbooks. Average word length: middle readers—10,000-12,000; young adults—15,000-25,000. Recently published *Bill Clinton: President From Arkansas*, by Gene L. Martin and Aaron Boyd (young adult, biography).

How to Contact/Writers: Fiction: Submit outline/synopsis and 3 sample chapters. Nonfiction: Submit outline/synopsis and 1-3 sample chapters. Reports on queries in 2 weeks; mss in 1 month. Publishes a book 9-12 months after acceptance.

Terms: Pays authors royalty of 8-10% based on wholesale price. Offers "occasional modest advance." Sends galleys to authors. Book catalog available for #10 SAE and 1 first-class stamp.

TYNDALE HOUSE PUBLISHERS, INC., 351 Executive Dr., P.O. Box 80, Wheaton IL 60189. (708)668-8300. Book publisher. Children's editorial contact: Marilyn Dellorto. Children's illustration contact: Marlene Muddell. Publishes approximately 20 children's titles/year.

Fiction/Nonfiction: Currently overstocked in all categories. Send queries only. Not accepting unsolicited mss for review.

Illustration: Full-color for book covers, b&w or color spot illustrations for some nonfiction.

How to Contact/Illustrators: Illustrations only: Send photocopies (color or b&w) of samples, résumé.

Terms: Pay for authors and illustrators: variable fee or royalty.

Tips: "All accepted manuscripts will appeal to Evangelical Christian children and parents."

*UNIVERSITY CLASSICS, LTD. PUBLISHERS, One Bryan Rd., P.O. Box 2301, Athens OH 45701. (614)592-4543. Book publisher. President: Albert H. Shuster. Publishes 1 young reader/year; 1 middle reader/year; 1 young adult title/year. 50% of books by first-time authors.

Fiction: Picture books: animal, concept, health, nature/environment. Young readers: concept, health, nature/environment, special needs. Middle readers: health, nature/environment, problem novels, special needs. Young adults: health, nature/environment, special needs. Average word length: young readers—1,200; middle readers—5,000. Recently published *Toodle D. Poodle*, by Katherine Oaha/Dorathyre Shuster (grades 4-6, ages 10-12); *The Day My Dad and I Got Mugged*, by Howard Goldsmith (grades 5-8, ages 12-15).

Nonfiction: Picture books: activity books, animal, arts/crafts, concept, health, nature/environment, self help, special needs. Young readers: activity books, animal, arts/crafts, concept, health, nature/environment, self help, special needs, textbooks. Middle readers, young adults: arts/crafts, concept, health, nature/environment, self help, special needs, textbooks. Average word length: young readers—1,200; middle readers—5,000. Recently published *Fitness and Nutrition: The Winning Combination*, by Jane Buch (ages 13-17, textbook); *The Way We Live: Practical Economics*, by John Shaw (ages 13-adult, textbook); *Ride Across America: An Environmental Committment*, by Lucian Spataro (ages 13-17, trade).

How to Contact/Writers: Fiction: Submit outline/synopsis and 5 sample chapters. Nonfiction: Submit outline/synopsis and 5 sample chapters. Reports on queries/mss in 1 month. Publishes a book 6 months after acceptance. Will consider electronic submissions via disk or modem.

Illustration: Works with 2 illustrators/year. Will review ms/illustration packages.
How to Contact/Illustrators: Ms/illustration packages: Submit ms with 2 pieces of final art. Illustrations only: Send résumé. Reports in 1 month. Samples returned with SASE; samples not filed. Originals not returned.
Terms: Pays authors royalty of 5-15% based on retail price. Pays illustrators flat rate by the project. Sends galleys to authors. Book catalog available for #10 SAE and 2 first-class stamps.
Tips: "Consumers are looking more for educational than fictional books, and this will continue."

***■UNIVERSITY EDITIONS, INC.**, Subsidiary of Aegina Press, Inc., 59 Oak Lane, Spring Valley, Huntington WV 25704. (304)429-7204. Book publisher. Managing Editor: Ira Herman. Art Coordinator: Claire Nudd. Publishes 3 picture books/year; 4 young readers/year; 4 middle readers/year; 4 young adult titles/year. 40% of books by first-time authors; 5% of books from agented authors; more than 50% subsidy published.
Fiction: Picture books, young readers: adventure, animal, fantasy, history, poetry, science fiction, suspense/mystery. Middle readers: adventure, animal, fantasy, history, nature/environment, poetry, romance, science fiction, suspense/mystery. Young adults: adventure, animal, fantasy, nature/environment, romance, science fiction, suspense/mystery. Average word length: picture books—1,000; young readers—2,000; middle readers—10,000; young adults—20,000. Recently published *The Black Cat Inn*, by Brandy O'Shea, illustrated by Bronwyn O'Shea (ages 8-10, animal story); *Coyoacan Hill*, by Carol W. Hazelwood (ages 10-12, fantasy); *Hostage at Hamilton High*, by Diane S. Colvin (ages 10-14, suspense).
Nonfiction: Picture books: animal, history, nature/environment, religion. Young readers: animal, biography, history, religion, science, sports. Middle readers: animal, biography, history, nature/environment, religion, science, sports. Young adults: animal, careers, history, nature/environment, religion, science, sports. Average word length: picture books—1,000; young readers—2,000; middle readers—10,000; young adults—20,000. Recently published *A Young Colonel from Virginia*, by Jane Lipsomb (ages 8-12, history).
How to Contact/Writers: Fiction/nonfiction: Submit complete ms. Reports on queries in 1 week; mss in 1 month. Publishes a book 6 months after acceptance.
Illustration: Works with 15 illustrators/year. Will review ms/illustration packages. Contact: Ira Herman, managing editor. Will review artwork for future assignments.
How to Contact/Illustrators: Ms/illustration packages: Submit ms with dummy or submit ms with 5 pieces of final art. Illustrations only: Query with samples. Reports in 1 month. Cannot return samples; samples not filed. Originals not returned.
Terms: Pays authors royalty of 10-15% based on retail price, "negotiated individually for each book." Pays illustrators by the project ($60 minimum); "pays artists per project, negotiated individually for each book." Sends galleys to authors. Book catalog available for $2, 10×13 SAE and 4 first-class stamps; ms guidelines available for SASE.

VICTOR BOOKS, Scripture Press, 1825 College Ave., Wheaton IL 60187. (708)668-6000. Fax: (708)668-3806. Book publisher. Children's Editor: Liz Duckworth. Publishes 9 picture books/year; 6 middle readers/year. "No young readers at this point, but open to them." 20% of books by first-time authors; 10% of books from agented authors. All books are related to Christianity.
Fiction: Picture books: adventure, animal, contemporary, religion. Young readers: adventure, animal, contemporary, religion, science fiction, sports, suspense/mystery. Middle readers: adventure, contemporary, history, religion, sports, suspense/mystery. Does not want to see stories with "Christian" animals; no holiday legends. Recently published *What Twos Can Do*, by Jane Morton (ages 1-3, board book); *The Morning of the World*, by Bob Hartman (ages 4-7, picture book); *Wings of an Angel*, by Sigmund Browner

(ages 8-12, middle reader); *The Hair-Pulling Bear Dog,* by Lee Roddy (ages 8-12, middle reader).

Nonfiction: Picture books: biography, religion. Young readers: biography, history, religion. Middle readers: biography, history, religion, sports. No ABC books or biographies of obscure/not well-known people.

How to Contact/Writers: Fiction/nonfiction: Submit complete ms for picture books. Submit outline/synopsis and 2 sample chapters for middle readers. Reports on queries in 2 months; mss in 3 months. Publishes a book 1½ years after acceptance. Will consider simultaneous submissions.

Illustration: Will review ms/illustration packages. Will review artwork for future assignments. Contact: Paul Higdon, art director.

How to Contact/Illustrators: Ms/illustration packages: Submit complete package. Illustrations only: Submit portfolio for review. Provide résumé, promotional literature or tearsheets to be kept on file. Reports back only if interested. Originals not returned.

Photography: Contact: Paul Higdon, art director. Uses photos of children. Model/property releases required. Interested in stock photos. Photographers should submit portfolio for review; provide résumé, promotional literature or tearsheets to be kept on file.

Terms: Pays authors royalty of 5-10% based on wholesale price, outright purchase $125-2,500. Offers advance "based on project." Pays illustrators by the project, royalty of 5% based on wholesale price. Photographers paid by the project, per photo. Sends galleys to authors. Book catalog available for 9 × 12 SAE and 2 first-class stamps. Ms guidelines available for SASE.

Tips: "In general children's books I see trends toward increasingly high quality. It's a crowded field, so each idea must be fresh and unique. Ask yourself, 'Does this book belong primarily on the shelf of a *Christian* bookstore?' That's how we distribute so your answer should reflect that."

VICTORY PUBLISHING, 3504 Oak Dr., Menlo Park CA 94025. (415)323-1650. Book publisher. Publisher: Yolanda Garcia. 95% of books by first-time authors. "All books pertain to instruction of elementary age children — specifically bilingual — Spanish/English."

Fiction: Picture books, young readers: concept, poetry. Middle readers: poetry. No fantasy, mystery, religion, sports.

Nonfiction: Picture books, young readers, middle readers: activity books, arts/crafts, concept, cooking, how-to, self help. No animals.

How to Contact/Writers: Fiction/nonfiction: Query. Submit outline/synopsis and 2 sample chapters. "Must send SASE." Reports on queries in 3 weeks; reports on mss in 1 month. Publishes a book 1 year after acceptance.

Illustration: Works with 1-2 illustrators/year. Will review ms/illustration packages. Will review artwork for future assignments. Contact: Veronica Garcia, Illustrator.

How to Contact/Illustrators: Ms/illustration packages: Query. Illustration only: Query with samples; provide résumé, promo sheet to be kept on file. Reports on queries in 3 weeks; mss in 1 month. Samples returned with SASE (if requested); samples filed. "Originals are purchased."

Terms: Work purchased outright from authors (average amount: $100-500). Pays illustrators by the project or set amount per illustration depending on complexity. Sends dummies to illustrators. Ms/artist guidelines not available.

Tips: Wants "teacher resources for elementary school — bilingual Spanish/English activity books."

VOLCANO PRESS, Box 270, Volcano CA 95689. (209)296-3345. Fax: (209)296-4515. Book publisher. President: Ruth Gottstein. Published 1 picture book in 1989; 3 in 1990. **Fiction:** All levels: animals, folktales, multicultural, nature/environment, poetry, history. Recently published *Berchick*, by Esther Silverstein Blanc, illustrated by Tennessee Dixon; *Mighty Mountain and the Three Strong Women*, by Irene Hedlund; *African Animal Tales*, by Rogério Andrade Barbosa (folk talkes). **Nonfiction:** All levels: animal, health, history, multicultural, nature/environment, self help. Will consider feminist, Pacific-rim related (Asian) material for picture books, young readers and middle readers. Sees too much "fiction, trite fantasy, didactic and moralistic material, bad fairy tales, anthropomorphic male animal heroes." Recently published *Save My Rainforest*, by Monica Zak, illustrated by Bengt-Arne Runnerström. **How to Contact/Writers:** Nonfiction: Submit outline/synopsis and sample chapters. Reports on queries in 2-3 weeks; mss in 4-6 weeks. Publishes a book 1 year after acceptance. "Please always enclose SASE." **Illustration:** Works with 2-3 illustrators/year. Will review ms/illustration packages. Will review artwork for future assignments. **How to Contact/Illustrators:** Illustrations only: brief query with samples. **Terms:** Pays authors royalty. Pays illustrators by the project (range: $100-200). Sends galleys to authors; dummies to illustrators. Book catalog for #10 SASE. **Tips:** Considers "non-racist, non-sexist types of books that are empowering to women."

■**W.W. PUBLICATIONS**, P.O. Box 373, Highland MI 48357-0373. (813)585-0985. Subsidiary of American Tolkien Society. Independent book producer. Editorial Contact: Phil Helms. 75% of books by first-time authors. Subsidy publishes 75%. **Fiction/Nonfiction:** All ages: fantasy, Tolkien-related. **How to Contact/Writers:** Fiction: Query. Submit outline/synopsis of complete ms. Reports on queries in 4-6 weeks; 2-3 months on mss. Publishes a book 3-6 months after acceptance. Will consider simultaneous submissions. **Illustrations:** Reviews all illustration packages. Prefers 8½ × 11 b&w and ink. **How to Contact/Illustrators:** Query with samples. Reports on ms/art samples in 3 months. Original artwork returned at job's completion if requested. **Terms:** Pays author free copies. Sends galleys to author if requested; dummies to illustrators. Book catalog for 1 first-class stamp and #10 SAE. **Tips:** "Tolkien oriented only."

WALKER AND CO., 720 Fifth Ave., New York NY 10019. (212)265-3632. Division of Walker Publishing Co. Inc. Book publisher. Estab. 1959. Editor: Mary Rich. Publishes 3-5 picture books/year; 10-15 middle readers/year; 15 young adult titles/year. 10-15% of books by first-time authors; 65% of books from agented writers. **Fiction:** Picture books: fantasy, history. Young readers: animal, history, fantasy. Middle readers: fantasy, science fiction, history. Young adults: fantasy, history, science fiction. Recently published *Steam Train Ride*, by E.C. Mott (picture book); *Brother Night*, by V. Keller (young adult); *Red Dirt Jessie*, by Anna Myers (middle grade). **Nonfiction:** Picture books, young readers, middle readers, young adults: animal, biography, education, history, hobbies, music/dance, nature/environment, religion, science, sports. Published *The Story of Things*, by S. Morrow (picture book history); *America*

Fights the Tide: 1942, by John Devaney (young adult history).

How to Contact/Writers: Fiction/nonfiction: Submit outline/synopsis and sample chapters. Reports on queries/mss in 2-3 months. Will consider simultaneous submissions.

Illustration: Editorial will review ms/illustration packages.

How to Contact/Illustrators: Ms/illustration packages: 5 chapters of ms with 1 piece of final art, remainder roughs. Illustrations only: Tearsheets. Reports on art samples only if interested. Original artwork returned at job's completion.

Terms: Pays authors in royalties of 5-10% based on wholesale price "depends on contract." Offers average advance payment of $2,000-4,000. Pays illustrators by the project (range: $500-5,000); royalties from 50%. Sends galleys to authors. Book catalog available for 9 × 12 SASE; ms guidelines for SASE.

Tips: Writers: "Don't take rejections personally and try to consider them objectively. We receive more than 20 submissions a day. Can it be improved?" Illustrators: "Have a well-rounded portfolio with different styles." Looks for "science and nature series for young and middle readers."

*WARD HILL PRESS, P.O. Box 04-0424, Staten Island NY 10304. (718)816-9449. Editorial Assistant: Loretta Dunlap. Publishes 3-6 middle readers/year; 3-6 young adult titles/year. 90% of books by first-time authors.

Fiction: Middle readers, young adults: folktales. Average word length: middle readers—20,000; young adults—20,000.

Nonfiction: Middle readers, young adults: biography, history, multicultural, social issues. Multicultural needs include biographies of figures from diverse cultures. Does not want to see biographies of mainstream personalities or pop entertainers. Average word length: middle readers—20,000; young adults—20,000. Recently published *Zora Neale Hurston: A Storyteller's Life*, by Janelle Yates, illustrated by David Adams (ages 10 and up, biography).

How to Contact/Writers: Fiction/nonfiction: Query. Reports on queries in 4-6 weeks; mss in 6-8 weeks. Publishes a book 1 year after acceptance. Will consider previously published work.

Illustration: Works with 3-6 illustrators/year.

How to Contact/Illustrators: Ms/illustration packages: Query. Illustrations only: Query with samples; provide résumé. Reports in 1-2 months. Samples returned with SASE; samples filed. Originals not returned.

Terms: Pays authors royalty of 5-8% based on retail price. Offers advances (Average amount: $800). Pays illustrators royalty of 3-5% based on retail price. Sends galleys to authors; dummies to illustrators. Book catalog available for 4 × 9½ SAE and 1 first-class stamp. "We send manuscript guidelines only after seeing query."

WATERFRONT BOOKS, 85 Crescent Rd., Burlington VT 05401. (802)658-7477. Book publisher. Publisher: Sherrill N. Musty. Some books by first-time authors.

Fiction: "Special issues for children only." Picture books, young readers, middle readers, young adults: mental health, family/parenting, health, special issues involving barriers to learning in children.

Nonfiction: "Special issues for children only." Picture books, young readers, middle readers, young adults: education, guidance, health, mental health, social issues. "We publish books for both children and adults on any subject that helps to lower barriers to learning in children: mental health, family/parenting, education and social issues. We are now considering books for children on bettering the environment."

How to Contact/Writers: Fiction/nonfiction: Query. Reports on queries in 2 weeks; mss in 6 weeks. Publishes a book 6 months after acceptance.

Illustration: Will review ms/illustration packages.
How to Contact/Illustrators: Ms/illustration packages: Query first. Illustrations only: Résumé, tearsheets. Reports on art samples only if interested.
Terms: Pays authors in royalties of 10-15% based on wholesale price. Pays illustrators by the job. Sends galleys to authors; dummies to illustrators. Book catalog available for #10 SAE and 1 first-class stamp.
Tips: "Have your manuscript thoroughly reviewed and even copy edited, if necessary. If you are writing about a special subject, have a well-qualified professional in the field review it for accuracy and appropriateness. It always helps to get some testimonials before submitting it to a publisher. The publisher then knows she/he is dealing with something worthwhile."

WEIGL EDUCATIONAL PUBLISHERS, 2114 College Ave., Regina, Saskatchewan S4P 1C5 Canada. (306)569-0766. Book publisher. Publisher: Linda Weigl.
Fiction: Middle readers: folktales, multicultural, nature/environment.
Nonfiction: Young reader, middle reader, young adult: resources involving activity books, careers, education, health, history, nature/environment, social studies. Average word length: young reader, middle reader, young adult—64 pages. Recently published *Career Connection: Alberta, Its People in History*; *Alberta Our Province*; *Citizenship in Action*; *Strategies for Career and Life Management—Student Journal*.
How to Contact/Writers: Nonfiction: Submit query and résumé. Reports on queries in 3 weeks; mss in 6 months. Publishes a book 2 years after acceptance. Will consider simultaneous submissions.
Illustration: Will review ms/illustration packages. Will review artwork for future assignments.
How to Contact/Illustrators: Ms/illustration packages: Query first. Illustrations only: Query with samples. Reports back only if interested or when appropriate project comes in.
Photography: Purchases photos from freelancers. Buys stock and assigns work. Wants political, juvenile, multicultural photos.
Terms: Pays authors royalty or work purchased outright. Pays illustrators by the project. Sends galleys to author; sends dummies to illustrator. Book catalog free on request.
Tips: Looks for "a manuscript that answers a specific curriculum need, or can be applied to a curriculum topic with multiple applications (eg. career education)."

WHITEBIRD BOOKS, 200 Madison Ave., New York NY 10016. Putnam and Grosset Group. Book publisher. Executive Editor: Arthur Levine. Publishes 2 picture books/year. 50% of books by first-time authors.
Fiction: Picture books: folktales. Average word length: picture books—750. Recently published *The Singing Fir Tree: A Swiss Folktale*, by Marti Stone, illustrations by Barry Root (ages 4-8, picture book); *Magic Spring: A Korean Folktale*, by Nami Rhee; *Quail Song: A Pueblo Indian Folktale*, by Valerie Carey, illustrations by Ivan Barnett (ages 4-8, picture book).
How to Contact/Writers: Fiction: Query. Reports on queries in 2 weeks; mss in 2-3 months. Publishes a book 1½-2 years after acceptance.
Illustration: Will review ms/illustration packages. Will review artwork for future assignments. Uses color artwork only.
How to Contact/Illustrators: Ms/illustration packages: Submit ms with dummy; submit ms with 2-3 pieces of final art. Illustrations only: Query with samples; provide résumé, promo sheet, portfolio, tearsheets. Reports back only if interested. Samples returned with SASE; samples filed. Original artwork returned at job's completion.
Terms: Pays authors royalty based on retail price. Offers advances. Pays illustrators royalty based on retail price. Sends galleys to authors; dummies to illustrators. Book catalog available for SASE.

Tips: "In a word: *Research!* If you'd like to be published by Whitebird, read all the Whitebird titles you can get your hands on (a catalog will list these titles) but don't stop there—read dozens of folktales published recently by other companies to get a feeling for contemporary styles." Illustrators should submit "a gorgeously illustrated folktale from a culture that Whitebird has not yet explored. I am particularly interested in writers whose own ethnicity is reflected in their work."

ALBERT WHITMAN & COMPANY, 6340 Oakton St., Morton Grove IL 60053-2723. (708)581-0033. Book publisher. Editor-in-Chief: Kathleen Tucker. Publishes 30 picture books/year; 3 middle readers/year. 15% of books by first-time authors; 15% of books from agented authors. "We publish various categories, but we're mostly known for our concept books—books that deal with children's problems or concerns."
Fiction: Picture books: adventure, animal, contemporary, fantasy, folktales, health, nature/environment, poetry. Young readers and middle readers: adventure, animal, contemporary, fantasy, folktales, health, history, multicultural, nature/environment, poetry, problem novels, special needs, sports, suspense/mystery. Does not want to see "religion-oriented, ABCs, pop-up, romance, counting or any book that is supposed to be written in." Recently published *Two of Everything*, by Lily Toy Hong (picture book); *Kathy's Hats*, by Trudy Krisher (ages 7-10, concept).
Nonfiction: Picture books, young readers and middle readers: animal, careers, health, history, hobbies, multicultural, music/dance, nature/environment, special needs, sports. Does not want to see "religion, any books that have to be written in, biographies of living people." Recently published *Space Probes to the Planets*, by Fay Robinson (grades 1-3); *Theodore Roosevelt Takes Charge*, by Nancy Whitelaw (ages 8 and up).
How to Contact/Writers: Fiction/nonfiction: Submit complete ms. Reports on queries in 4-6 weeks; mss in 2 months. Publishes a book 18 months after acceptance. Will consider simultaneous submissions "but let us know if it is one" and previously published work "if out of print."
Illustration: Will review ms/illustration packages. Will review artwork for future assignments. Contact Editorial. Uses more color art than b&w.
How to Contact/Illustrators: Ms/illustration packages: Submit all chapters of ms with any pieces of final art. Illustrations only: Query with samples. Send slides or tearsheets. Reports back only if interested. Original artwork returned at job's completion.
Photography: Photographers should contact editorial. Publishes books illustrated with photos but not stock photos—desires photos all taken for project. "Our books are for children and cover many topics; photos must be taken to match text. Books often show a child in a particular situation (e.g., a first communion, a sister whose brother is born prematurely.)" Photographers should query with samples; send unsolicited photos by mail.
Terms: Pays authors royalty. Pays illustrators royalty. Offers advances. Sends galleys to authors; dummies to illustrators. Book catalog available for 9 × 12 SAE and 5 first-class stamps. Ms guidelines available for SASE.
Tips: "In both picture books and nonfiction, we are seeking stories showing life in other cultures and the variety of multicultural life in the US. We also want fiction and nonfiction about mentally or physically challenged children—some recent topics have been AIDS, asthma, cerebral palsy."

WILLIAMSON PUBLISHING CO., Box 185, Charlotte VT 05445. (802)425-2102. Fax: (802)425-2199. Book publisher. Editorial Director: Susan Williamson. Publishes 8 young readers titles/year. 80% of books by first-time authors; 20% of books from agented authors. Publishes "very successful nonfiction series (Kids Can! Series) on subjects such as nature, creative play, arts & crafts, geography."
Nonfiction: Picture books, young readers: activity books, animal, arts/crafts, biography, careers, cooking, geography, health, history, hobbies, how-to, multicultural, music/

dance, nature/environment, science, self-help. No textbooks. "We are looking for books which help children embrace other cultures with curiosity and respect." Recently published *Kids Make Music!*, by Avery Hart and Paul Mantell; *Eco Art!*, by Laurie Carlson (earth-friendly art and craft experiences for 3- to 9-year-olds); *Hands Around the World: 365 Ways to Build Cultural Awareness and Global Respect*, by Susan Milord.

How to Contact/Writers: Nonfiction: Query; submit outline/synopsis and 2 sample chapters. Reports on queries/mss in 3-4 months. Publishes book, "depending on graphics, about 12 months" after acceptance. Will consider simultaneous submissions.

Illustration: Will review artwork for future assignments. Uses primarily b&w artwork only.

Photography: Contact: Susan Williamson, editorial director. Buys stock and assigns work.

Terms: Pays authors royalty based on wholesale price. Offers advances. Sends galleys to authors. Book catalog available for 6×9 SAE and 4 first-class stamps; ms guidelines available for SASE.

Tips: Interested in "creative, packed-with-interesting information, interactive learning books written for young readers ages 4-8. In nonfiction children's publishing, we are looking for authors with a depth of knowledge shared with children through a warm, embracing style—a respite in a rough world that tells not only how, but affirms that children can."

WILLOWISP PRESS, 801 94th Ave. N., St. Petersburg FL 33702-2426. Division PAGES, Inc. Book publisher. Writers contact: Acquisitions Editor. Illustrators contact: Art Director. Publishes 15-20 picture books/year; 6-8 young readers/year. 6-8 middle readers/year. 25% of books by first-time authors.

Fiction: Picture books: adventure, animal, contemporary, folktales, history, humor, multicultural, nature/environment, rhymes. Young readers: adventure, animal, contemporary, fantasy, folktales, history, humor, multicultural, nature/environment, sports, suspense/mystery. Middle readers: adventure, animal, anthology, contemporary, folktales, history, humor, multicultural, nature/environment, problem novels, romance, sports, suspense/mystery. Young adults: adventure, animal, anthology, contemporary, folktales, history, humor, multicultural, nature/environment, problem novels, romance, sports, suspense/mystery. No religious or violence. Average word length: picture books—350-1,000; beginning chapter books—3,000-4,000; middle readers—14,000-18,000; young adult—20,000-24,000. Recently published *Earthquake!*, by Alida E. Young (grades 5 and up, novel); *The Haunted Underwear*, by Janet Adele Bloss, grades 3-5, novel; *Daddy Fixed the Vacuum Cleaner* by Robert Scotellaro (grades K-2 picture book).

Nonfiction: Picture books: activity books, animal, biography, geography, history, how-to, multicultural, nature/environment, reference, science. Young readers: activity books, animal, arts/crafts, biography, geography, history, how-to, multicultural, nature/environment, reference, science, sports. Middle readers: activity books, animal, biography, careers, geography, history, hobbies, how-to, multicultural, nature/environment, reference, science, social issues, sports. Young adults: animal, biography, careers, concept, geography, history, hobbies, how-to, multicultural, nature/environment, reference, science, social issues, sports. No religious. Recently published *A Look Around Rain Forests*, by Ed Perez (ages K-3, environment); *People Who Shape Our World: Mother Teresa*, by Margaret Holland (grades 3 and up, biography); *Really Reading: When Dinosaurs Ruled the Earth*, by Martha Morss (grades 1-3, animal).

How to Contact/Writers: Fiction: Query. Submit outline/synopsis and 2 sample chapters. Nonfiction: Query. Submit outline/synopsis and 1 sample chapter. "Only *one* manuscript at a time! Do *not* send original work when querying." Reports on queries/mss in 6-8 weeks. Publishes a book 6-12 months after acceptance. Will consider simultaneous submissions (if so noted). "SASE a must."

Illustration: Works with 10-12 illustrators/year. Will review ms/illustration packages "though almost all art is assigned independent of manuscript." Will review artwork for future assignments.

How to Contact/Illustrators: Ms/illustration packages: Query; submit ms with dummy. Illustrations only: Query with samples that can be kept on file; provide résumé. Reports in 2-3 months. Samples returned with SASE (and on request). Original artwork not returned at job's completion.

Photography: Purchases photos from freelancers. Contact: Acquisitions Editor. Buys stock and assigns work. Seeking photos related to environment, sports, animals. Photo captions required. Uses color slides. To contact, photographers should submit cover letter, résumé, published samples, stock photo list.

Terms: Pays authors royalty or work purchased outright. Offers advance. Pays illustrators by the project. Photographers paid by the project or per photo. "Our terms are highly variable, both in reference to royalties and outright purchase." Book catalog available for 9 × 12 SAE and 5 first-class stamps. Ms guidelines available for SASE. Art guidelines not available.

Tips: "Make sure the adult tone is not in evidence."

■**WINSTON-DEREK PUBLISHERS, INC.**, P.O. Box 90883, Nashville TN 37209. (615)321-0535. Book publisher. Estab. 1972. Editorial contact as follows: picture books: Matalyn Rose Peebles; young reader titles: Maggie Staton; middle reader/young adult titles: Kim Wohlenhaus. Publishes 35-40 picture books/year; 25-30 young reader titles/year; 10-15 middle reader titles/year; 10-15 young adult titles/year. 50% of books by first-time authors; 5% of books from agented authors; 20% of books subsidy published.

Fiction: Picture books: contemporary, folktales, history, religion. Young readers: adventure, folktales, history, religion. Middle readers: adventure, contemporary, folktales, history, religion, suspense/mystery. Young adults: adventure, contemporary, folktales, history, problem novels, religion, suspense/mystery. Average word length: picture book—600-1200; young reader—3,000-5,000; middle reader—2,000; young adult—10,000-40,000. Recently published *The Color of My Fur*, by Nanette Brophy; *The Other Little Angel*, by Fred Crump; *Mystery at Loon Lake*, by Michele Biernot.

Nonfiction: Picture books: biography, careers, religion, textbooks. Young readers, middle readers and young adults: biography, careers, history, religion, textbooks/basal readers, African-American biographies. Average word length: picture book—600-800; young readers—2,500-4,000; middle reader—1,000-2,500; young adult—10,000-30,000.

How to Contact/Writers: Fiction: Query or submit outline/synopsis and sample chapters. Nonfiction: Submit complete ms. Reports on queries in 6 weeks; mss in 8 weeks. Publishes a book 1 year after acceptance. Will consider simultaneous submissions.

Illustration: Will review ms/illustration packages. Will review work for possible assignments. Contact: J.W. Peebles, editor. Usese b&w artwork only.

How to Contact/Illustrators: Ms/illustration packages: Submit 3 chapters of ms with 1 piece of final art. Illustrations only: Send résumé and tearsheets. Reports in 3 weeks. Original artwork returned at job's completion.

Terms: Pays authors royalties of 10-15% based on wholesale price. Also pays in copies and offers some subsidy arrangements. Separate authors and illustrators: 12½% royalty to writer and 2½% royalty to illustrator. Pays illustrators $30-150 or 2½-8½% royalty. Sends galleys to author; dummies to illustrator. Book catalog for SASE; ms/artist's guidelines free on request.

Tips: In illustration, looks for "action, good work and variety of subjects such as male/female." In manuscripts, looks for "educational, morally sound subjects, multi-ethnic; historical facts."

WOMEN'S PRESS, 233-517 College Street, Toronto, Ontario M6G 4A2 Canada. (416)921-2425. Book publisher. Editorial Contact: Anne Decter and Martha Ayim. Publishes 1-2 picture books/year; 0-1 middle reader titles/year; 0-1 young adult titles/year. 60% of books by first-time authors. "We give preference to authors who are Canadian citizens or those living in Canada."
Fiction: Picture books: contemporary, social issues, health and family problems. Young readers, middle readers and young adults: contemporary, problem novels. Average word length: picture books—24 pages; young readers—70-80 pages; middle readers—60-70 pages; young adult/teens—80-150 pages. Published *Asha's Mums*, by Elwin & Paulse (4-8, picture-issue).
Nonfiction: Picture books: environment. Young adults: sex, health.
How to Contact/Writers: Fiction/Nonfiction: Query. Reports on queries in 3 months (minimum); mss in 3-6 months. Publishes a book 1 year after acceptance.
Illustration: Editorial will review ms/illustration packages (Canadian only).
Terms: Pays authors in royalties of 10% min. based on retail price. Sends galleys to authors; dummies to illustrators. Book catalog and/or ms guidelines free on request.

WOODBINE HOUSE, 5615 Fishers Lane, Rockville MD 20852. (301)468-8800. Book publisher. Editor: Susan Stokes. Production Manager: Robin Dhawan. Publishes 0-2 picture books/year; 0-2 young adult titles/year. 100% of books by first-time authors. "All children's books are for or about children with disabilities."
Fiction: Picture books: health-related and special needs (disability-related). "No fiction unless disability-related." Average length: picture books—24 pages. Published *Charlie's Chuckle*, by Clara Berkus (ages 5-11); *My Brother, Matthew*, by Mary Thompson (ages 5-11).
Nonfiction: All levels: special needs (disabilities). Does not want to see anything other than subjects about disabilities; "books written *primarily* to impart messages about people with disabilities to people without disabilities—e.g., 'Everyone is different and that's OK!' "
How to Contact/Writers: Fiction/nonfiction: Submit complete ms. Reports on queries in 3 weeks; reports on mss in 2-3 months. Publishes a book 18 months after acceptance. Will consider simultaneous submissions and previously published work.
Illustration: Works with 0-2 illustrators/year. Will review ms/illustration packages. Will review artwork for future assignments.
How to Contact/Illustrators: Ms/illustration packages: Submit entire ms with 2-3 pieces of art (color photocopies OK). Illustrations only: Query with samples; provide promo sheet, tearsheets. Reports back only if interested.
Terms: Pays authors royalty of 10-12% based on wholesale price. Pays illustrators by the project. Sends galleys to authors. Book catalog available for 6×9 SAE and 3 first-class stamps. Ms guidelines available for SASE.
Tips: "Try your book out on a couple of kids (not your own) and see whether it grabs and holds their interest." Submit books dealing with disability/chronic illness issues.

YMAA PUBLICATION CENTER, 38 Hyde Park Ave., Jamaica Plain MA 02130. (617)524-8892. Book publisher. Director Sales/Marketing: David Ripianzi. Publishes 2 middle readers/year. Publishes "morality stories, i.e., folktales (cultural themes)."
Fiction: All levels: folktales, multicultural, sports. Multicultural needs include "books that identify the lifestyles and virtues of a particular culture." No science fiction, humor, poetry, religion, suspense or mystery.
Nonfiction: All levels: health, multicultural, sports.
How to Contact/Writers: Fiction/nonfiction: Query; submit outline/synopsis. Reports on queries/mss in 1 month. Publishes a book 18 months after acceptance. Will consider simultaneous submissions, electronic submissions via disk and previously published work.

Illustration: Works with one illustrator/year. Will review ms/illustration packages. Will review artwork for future assignments. Uses color artwork only.
How to Contact/Illustrators: Ms/illustration packages: Query; submit ms with dummy. Illustrations only: Query with samples, résumé. Reports in 1 month. Samples returned with SASE. Originals not returned.
Terms: Payment for authors negotiated. Payment for illustrators negotiated. Book catalog available.
Tips: Wants multicultural folktales/sports/health.

JANE YOLEN BOOKS See Harcourt Brace & Co.

Book Publishers/'93-'94 changes

The following markets are not included in this edition of *Children's Writer's & Illustrator's Market* for the reasons indicated within parentheses. If there is no reason given, it means the market did not respond to our requests for updated information for a 1994 listing.

Arcade Publishing
Back to the Bible
Bancroft-Sage Publishing, Inc.
Breakwater Books
Candlewick Press (removed per request)
Colormore Inc.
Fifth House Publishers (not soliciting children's material)
Friendship Press
Gage Educational Publishing Company (no longer publishing children's books)
Gibbs Smith, Publisher
Gospel Light Publications (no longer publishing children's books)
Green Tiger Press, Inc. (not accepting unsolicited mss)
Harbinger House, Inc. (removed per request)
Joy Street Books (imprint discontinued)
Kruza Kaleidoscopix, Inc. (removed per request)
Liguori Publications (no longer publishing children's books)
Lion Publishing
Oddo Publishing, Inc.
Open Hand Publishing
Perfection Learning (inadequate submissions)
Clarkson N. Potter, Inc. (no longer publishing children's books)
Redbud Books (no longer seeking mss)
Sagebrush Books
Shoestring Press (removed per request)
Star Books, Inc.
Starburst Publishers (not accepting unsolicited mss)
Troubador Books (removed per request)
The Vanitas Press

Magazines

For writers and illustrators who lack previous publication, magazines are an ideal place to break into the business. Collecting bylines and illustration credits is essential in building credibility in the children's field. And, while many magazine editors are partial to working with established writers and illustrators, room still exists for newcomers who have not yet made their marks in the publishing industry.

The good news, in fact, is that the number of juvenile magazines which writers and illustrators may approach has increased. As Nina Link, senior vice-president of the Children's Television Workshop magazine group, said in the October 18, 1993 *Publishers Weekly*, "There has been an absolute explosion of children's magazines. ... There are now over 150 magazines for kids that are as diverse as their adult counterparts." More than 100 of these magazines—about two dozen of which are new to this edition—are listed in this section.

Increasing popularity

Juvenile magazines are not only increasing in number, but also in popularity. One reason, perhaps, is that children are simply finding today's offerings more appealing. Like television, current magazines are visually-oriented. Unlike television, they offer a more hands-on experience. Issues may be perused over and over again. And parents prefer to see their children reading instead of watching TV.

Just as magazines serve as a bridge to books for writers and illustrators, many believe they may also serve as a bridge for young readers. While some children may not be patient enough to conquer whole books, they are often willing to flip through the pages of a magazine until something catches their eye. The hope is that once children view reading as enjoyable, they will seek other materials.

More important, however, is that publishers have acknowledged that children—and their interests—are as varied as adults. In this section, for instance, you'll find magazines targeting boys and magazines targeting girls—just as you might find newsstand publications specifically for men or women. Magazines for youngsters affiliated with almost every religious denomination are also listed here, as are periodicals devoted to certain animals or sports.

Another plus for the children's magazine industry is that teachers are utilizing fact-based educational publications—such as those teaching history, math or science—as supplements in their classrooms. As a result, it's not unusual for children to want summer subscriptions, or even their own personal subscriptions, after initially being exposed to the magazines at school.

Above all, children today are more worldly and desire to know what's going on around them. Since magazines have the advantage of timeliness, they can relay information about current events or interests in much less time than books—and at less cost. The average one-year subscription, in fact, is about the same as the cost of one hardcover picture book.

Market concerns

While some of the listings in this section are religious-oriented or special interest publications, others are general interest magazines. And a few are adult magazines with special children's sections. What you are not likely to find here, however, are those periodicals that serve as little more than promotions for toys, movies or television programs. The latter publications use licensed characters and are mostly produced inhouse. As some of these magazines are primarily interested in generating revenue, rather than enriching a young mind, they concentrate more on product advertisement than literary or educational content.

Though the large circulation, ad-driven publications will generally offer a better pay rate than religious or nonprofit magazines, smaller magazines are more open to reviewing the work of newcomers. They also provide an excellent vehicle for you to compile clippings as you work your way toward more lucrative markets.

It's not uncommon, however, for juvenile magazines to purchase all rights to both stories and artwork. Though work for hire is generally frowned upon among freelancers, selling all rights may prove to be advantageous in the end. All of the magazines at the Children's Better Health Institute, for example, buy all rights, as does *Highlights for Children*. Yet these magazines are very reputable, and any clips acquired through them will be valuable.

Classic subjects considered by magazines include stories and/or features about the alphabet, outer space, computers and animals (even dinosaurs). As with books, nonfiction features—especially photo features—are very popular right now, and many magazines are devoting more room to such material. Sports stories and articles describing how things work are also marketable. Current needs in the general interest magazine field include historical fiction, retold folktales, mysteries, science fiction and fantasy.

As efforts to supply readers with stories and artwork which include ethnic diversity remain strong, so does the need for multicultural material. In fact, editors can't seem to find enough of it! And you will notice that some publishers have indicated specific needs in their listings.

While the demand for multicultural material is not expected to subside any-time soon, writers and illustrators should consider creating stories and artwork about groups with only marginal representation in the literature. If you're not a member of the group you are interested in portraying, however, make sure to properly research your subject to insure authenticity. For more information about multicultural trends, read the introduction to Book Publishers on page 33 and Writing and Illustrating from Another Culture's Tradition on page 11.

Do your homework

No matter what the trends in the industry, writers and illustrators must know what appeals to today's youth and target their material appropriately. To insure that your work will interest youngsters—and thus editors—find out what kids are talking about. If in doubt about the relevance of your article or story, read the material to children and see how they respond. By learning what appeals to today's youth, you may find yourself at the beginning of a trend instead of the end.

You must not only know the current interests of children, however, you must also know the topics typically covered by various children's magazines. To help you match your work with the right magazines, we have added a Subject Index at the back of this book. This index lists both book and magazine publishers by the fiction and nonfiction subjects they are seeking. Use this index in conjunction with the Age-Level Index and you will hone the list of markets for your work even further.

Yet, don't just rely on the indexes. Study both the listings and the actual publications. Each magazine has a different editorial philosophy. Language usage also varies between periodicals, as does the length of feature articles and the use of artwork and photographs. Reading the juvenile magazines you are considering submitting to is the best way to determine if your material is appropriate. As many kids' magazines sell subscriptions via direct mail or schools, you may not be able to find a particular publication at the bookstore or newsstand. Most listings in this section, however, have sample copies available and will be glad to send them upon request.

Once you have determined which magazines are potential markets, take another look at their listings to review the preferred method of receiving submissions. Some may wish to see an entire manuscript; others may wish to see a query letter and outline, especially for nonfiction articles (with which accompanying photographs are generally welcome). If you're an artist, review the listing for the types of samples you should send to the art director.

Finally, be sure to submit your best work. Though the magazine market is a good way for children's writers and illustrators to break in, it is by no means a junkyard for "less-than-your-best" material.

*THE ADVOCATE, PKA Publication, 301A Rolling Hills Park, Prattsville NY 12468. (518)299-3103. Articles/Fiction Editor: Remington Wright. Art Director/Photo Editor: CJ Karlie. Bimonthly tabloid. Estab. 1987. Circ. 12,000. "*The Advocate* advocates good writers and quality writings. We publish art, fiction, photos and poetry. *The Advocate*'s submitters are talented people of all ages who do not earn their livings as writers. We wish to promote the arts and to give those we publish the opportunity to be published through a for-profit means rather than in a not-for-profit way. We do this by selling advertising and offering reading entertainment."

Fiction: Middle readers and young adults/teens: animal, contemporary, fantasy, folktales, humorous, nature/environment, romance, science fiction, suspense/mystery. Looks for "well written, entertaining work, whether fiction or nonfiction." Buys approximately 42 mss/year. Average word length: 1,500. Byline given.

Nonfiction: Middle readers and young adults/teens: animal, arts/crafts, biography, careers, cooking, fashion, games/puzzles, history, hobbies, how-to, humorous, interview/profile, nature/environment. Buys 10 mss/year. Average word length: 1,500. Byline given.

Poetry: Reviews any length poetry.

How to Contact/Writers: Fiction/nonfiction: Send complete ms. Reports on queries in 2 weeks/mss in 2 months. Publishes ms 2-18 months after acceptance.

Illustration: Uses b&w artwork only. Reviews ms/illustration packages; reviews artwork for future assignments.

How to Contact/Illustrators: Ms/illustration packages: Submit complete package with final art. Illustrations only: "Send previous unpublished art with SASE, please." Reports in 2 months. Samples returned with SASE; samples not filed. Original work returned upon job's completion. Credit line given.

Photography: Model/property releases required. Uses color and b&w prints. Photographers should send unsolicited photos by mail with SASE. Reports in 2 months.

Terms: Buys first rights for mss. Purchases first rights for artwork and photographs. Pays in copies or other premiums. Photographers paid in contributor's copies. Sample copies for $3. Writer's/illustrator's/photo guidelines for SASE.

Tips: "Artists and photographers should keep in mind that we are a b&w paper."

AIM MAGAZINE, America's Intercultural Magazine, P.O. Box 20554, Chicago IL 60620. (312)874-6184. Articles Editor: Ruth Apilado. Fiction Editor: Mark Boone. Photo Editor: Betty Lewis. Quarterly magazine. Circ. 8,000. Readers are high school and college students, teachers, adults interested in helping, through the written word, to create a more equitable world. 15% of material aimed at juvenile audience.

Fiction: Young adults: history, multicultural, "stories with social significance." Wants stories that teach children that people are more alike than they are different. Does not want to see religious fiction. Buys 20 mss/year. Average word length: 1,000-4,000. Byline given.

Nonfiction: Young adults: interview/profile, multicultural, "stuff with social significance." Does not want to see religious nonfiction. Buys 20 mss/year. Average word length: 500-2,000. Byline given.

How to Contact/Writers: Fiction: Send complete ms. Nonfiction: Query with published clips. Reports on queries/mss in 1 month. Will consider simultaneous submissions.

Illustration: Buys 20 illustrations/issue. Preferred theme: Overcoming social injustices through nonviolent means. Reviews ms/illustration packages; reviews artwork for future assignments.

How to Contact/Illustrators: Ms/illustration packages: Query first. Illustrations only: Query with tearsheets. Reports on art samples in 2 months. Original artwork returned at job's completion "if desired." Credit line given.

Photography: Wants "photos of activists who are trying to contribute to social improvement."

Terms: Pays on publication. Buys first North American serial rights. Pays $15-25 for stories/articles. Pays in contributor copies if copies are requested. Pays $5-25/b&w cover illustration. Photographers paid by the project (range: $10-15). Sample copy $3.50.

Tips: "We need material of social significance, stuff that will help promote racial harmony and peace and (illustrate) the stupidity of racism."

AMERICAN GIRL, Pleasant Company, P.O. Box 984, Middleton WI 53562-0984. (608)836-4848. Articles/Fiction Editor: Michelle Watkins. Editor-in-Chief: Nancy Holyoke. Bimonthly magazine. Estab. 1992. Circ. 150,000. "For girls ages 7-11. We run fiction and nonfiction, historical and contemporary."

Fiction: Middle readers: contemporary, historical, multicultural, suspense/mystery, good fiction about anything. No preachy, moralistic tales or stories with animals as protagonists. Only a girl or girls as characters—no boys. Buys approximately 6 mss/year. Average word length: 1,000-3,000. Byline given.

Nonfiction: Buys 3-10 mss/year. Average word length: 600. Byline sometimes given.

How to Contact/Writers: Fiction: Send complete ms. Nonfiction: Query with published clips. Reports on queries/mss in 4-6 weeks. Will consider simultaneous submissions.

Illustration: Works on assignment only.

Terms: Pays on acceptance. Buys first North American serial rights. Pays $500 minimum for stories; $300 minimum for articles. Sample copies for $3.95 and SAE with $1.90 in postage (send to Editorial Department Assistant). Writer's guidelines free for SASE.

Tips: "Keep (stories and articles) simple but interesting. Kids are discriminating readers, too. They won't read a boring or pretentious story."

*ANIMAL TRAILS, Tellstar Productions, P.O. Box 1264, Huntington WV 25714. Editor: Shannon Bridget Murphy. Semiannual magazine. Estab. 1993. Circ. 500. "A magazine for people of all ages who like to read fiction and true stories about animals, animal issues. Suitable for all ages."

Fiction: All levels: animal, nature/environment. "Would like to see more material written by young people and college students." Buys 4-10 mss/year. Average word length: 1,000-7,000. Byline given.

Nonfiction: All levels: animal, how-to, nature/environment, science. Looks for good, well thought-out plots with animals as the primary focus of interest; stories that communicate animal/human relationship. Buys 4-10 mss/year. Average word length: 1,000-7,000. Byline given.

Poetry: Reviews poetry. Multiple submissions accepted.

How to Contact/Writers: Fiction/nonfiction: Send complete ms. Reports in 6 weeks. Will consider simultaneous submissions and electronic submissions via disk or modem.

Illustration: "Country themes are highly desirable. Use imagination and be creative." Reviews ms/illustration packages; reviews artwork for future assignments.

How to Contact/Illustrators: Ms/illustration packages: Submit complete package with final art, ms with rough sketches. Illustrations only: Submit slides, illustrations. Reports in 6 weeks. Samples returned with SASE; filed with permission from artist. Credit line given.

Photography: Photo captions preferred. Uses color, b&w prints; 35mm, 8×10 transparencies. To contact, photographers should send unsolicited photos by mail, provide business card, promotional literature or tearsheets. Reports in 6 weeks.

Terms: Pays on publication. Buys first rights, one-time rights. Additional payment for ms/illustration packages and when photos accompany articles. Photographers paid by the project or per photo. Sample copies for $7. Writer's/illustrator's/photo guidelines for SASE.

*APPALACHIAN BRIDE, Tellstar Productions, P.O. Box 1264, Huntington WV 25714. Editor: Shannon Bridget Murphy. Triannual magazine. Estab. 1993. Circ. 500. "*Appalachian Bride* focuses on brides and traditions in the Appalachian states." 40% of publication aimed at juvenile market.

Fiction: All levels: folktales, multicultural. Multicultural needs include: work based on Appalachian family life or traditions. Buys approximately 6-12 mss/year. Average word length: 500-3,000. Byline given.

Nonfiction: All levels: multicultural. Multicultural needs include: work related to Appalachian family life or traditions. Buys 6-12 mss/year. Average word length: 500-3,000. Byline given.

Poetry: Reviews poetry. Multiple submissions welcome.

How to Contact/Writers: Fiction/nonfiction: Send complete ms. Reports in 6 weeks. Will consider simultaneous submissions, electronic submissions via disk or modem.

Illustration: "Preferred themes are country and Amish." Reviews ms/illustrations packages; reviews artwork for future assignment.

How to Contact/Illustrators: Ms/illustration packages: Submit complete package with final art, ms with rough sketches. Illustrations only: Submit promo sheet, slides. Reports

 The asterisk before a listing indicates the listing is new in this edition.

in 6 weeks. Samples returned with SASE; samples filed with permission of artist. Credit line given.

Photography: Looks for interesting photographs that feature Appalachian brides, weddings and family life. Uses color, b&w prints; 35mm, 8×10 transparencies. To contact, photographers should query with samples; send unsolicited photos by mail; provide business card, promotional literature or tearsheets. Reports in 6 weeks.

Terms: Pays on publication. Buys first rights, one-time rights. Sometimes pays in copies or other premiums. Additional payment for ms/illustration packages and when photos accompany articles. Writer's/illustrator's/photo guidelines for SASE.

Tips: "Writers, artists and photographers are encouraged to submit work with country or Amish themes. Writers should be creative and imaginative. Children, young people and college students are encouraged to submit work as well."

ASPCA ANIMAL WATCH, ASPCA, 424 E. 92nd St., New York NY 10128. (212)876-7700, ext. 4441. Visual Arts Editor: Dave McMichael. Quarterly magazine. Estab. 1951. Circ. 130,000. Focuses on animal issues. 15% of publication aimed at juvenile market.

Illustration: Buys 4 illustrations/issue; 16 illustrations/year. Reviews ms/illustration packages; reviews artwork for future assignments; works on assignment only.

How to Contact/Illustrators: Illustrations only: Send tearsheets, quality photocopies to hold on file. Reports back only if interested. Samples kept on file. Originals returned upon job's completion. Credit line given.

Photography: Looking for animal care, animal abuse and animal protection shots. Model/property releases required. Uses 8×10, glossy color/b&w prints; 35mm, 2¼×2¼ and 4×5 transparencies. Photographers should send stock list. Reports in 2 months.

Terms: Buys one-time rights for artwork/photographs. Pays illustrators $100-150/color cover; $50-100 color inside. Photographers paid per photo (range: $50-100). Sample copies for 9×12 SASE. Writer's guidelines not available. Illustrator's/photo guidelines for SASE.

Tips: Trends include "more educational, more interactive" material.

Illustrator Michael Fleishman sought to create whimsical, humorous animals and "to capture the bright, bold colors of the rainforest" in this illustration (one of three) assigned to accompany a story in ASPCA Animal Watch magazine. "I love to do animals—never drew a sloth before!!" Fleishman says. The artist combined pen and ink with watercolor wash and colored pencil to mimic the "fun critters" and "lush color" of a rainforest, and received $225 for the entire job.

© 1993 Michael C. Fleishman

ATALANTIK, 7630 Deer Creek Dr., Worthington OH 43085. (614)885-0550. Articles/Fiction Editor: Prabhat K. Dutta. Art Director: Tanushree Bhattacharya. Quarterly magazine. Estab. 1980. Circ. 400. "*Atalantik* is the first Bengali (Indian language) literary magazine published from the USA. It contains poems, essays, short stories, translations, interviews, opinions, sketches, book reviews, cultural information, scientific articles, letters to the editor, serialized novels and a children's section. The special slant may be India and/or education." 10% of material aimed at juvenile audience.

Fiction: Young reader: animal. Middle readers: history, humorous, problem solving, math puzzles, travel. Young adults: history, humorous, problem solving, romance, science fiction, sports, spy/mystery/adventure, math puzzles, travel. Does not want to see: "religious, political, controversial or material without any educational value." Sees too many animal and fantasy stories. Buys 20-40 mss/year. Average word length: 300-1,000. Byline given, "sometimes."

Nonfiction: Middle readers: history, how-to, humorous, problem solving, travel. Young adults: history, how-to, humorous, interview/profile, problem solving, travel, puzzles. Does not want to see: "religious, political, controversial or material without any educational value." Wants to see more educational, math puzzles, word puzzles. Buys 20-40 mss/year. Average word length: 300-1,000. Byline given, "sometimes."

Poetry: Reviews 20-line humorous poems that rhyme; maximum of 5 submissions.

How to Contact/Writers: Fiction/nonfiction: Send complete ms. Reports on queries in 2 weeks; mss in 2-4 months. Will consider simultaneous submissions.

Illustration: Buys 4-20 illustrations/year. Prefers to review juvenile education, activities, sports, culture and recreation. Will review ms/illustration packages, including artwork for future assignments.

How to Contact/Illustrators: Ms/illustration packages: Send "complete manuscript with final art." Illustrations only: Query; send résumé, promo sheet, client list. Reports in 1 month only if interested. Credit line given.

Photography: Purchases photos with accompanying ms only.

Terms: Buys all rights. Usually pays in copies for all circumstances. Sample copy $6. Writer's/illustrator's guidelines free with SAE and 1 first-class stamp.

Tips: Writers: "Let subjects be nature, human beings—not abstract ideas. Be imaginative, thorough, flexible and educational. Most importantly, be a child."

BK NEWS, (formerly Busines$ Kids), %Businesship International, Suite 1400, 1 Alhambra Plaza, Coral Gables FL 33134. Director of Corporate Communications: Michael J. Holmes. Quarterly newsletter. Estab. 1988. Circ. 75,000. "We cover stories about young entrepreneurs, how teens and preteens can become entrepreneurs, and useful information for effective business operation and management. Our goal is to help prepare America's youth for the complex and competitive world of business by sharing with them every possible business experience, the problems *and* the solutions. And while we're *serious* about business, we want them to know that business can be *fun*. 99% of material aimed at juvenile audience with one article aimed at parents in each issue."

Nonfiction: Middle readers and young adult/teens: how-to, interview/profile, problem solving. "All must relate to business"; wants to see "more profiles and photos of kids ages 8-18 who have their own businesses." Buys 15 mss/year. "Our goal is 50% freelance." Average word length: 200-400. Byline: Listed as a contributing writer.

Illustration: Reviews ms/illustration packages.

How to Contact/Writers: Nonfiction: Send complete ms. Reports on mss in 2 months.

Terms: Pays on publication. Buys all rights. Pays 15¢ word/unsolicited articles; $35-50 for puzzles/games; $15-20 for cartoons; $5-10 for b&w/8 × 10 photos. Writer's guidelines and sample copy available for SASE.

Tips: Looking for "any nonfiction pertaining to teens in the business world. How to choose, build, improve, market or advertise a business. When, and how, to hire (or fire) employees. Lots of profiles about successful young entrepreneurs. The latest in *any* field—entertainment, sports, medicine, etc.—where teens are making megabucks (or just movie money!). New products; book reviews on children and money; motivational articles; how-to invest/save money; news releases; tax information; stock market tips;

bonds; banking; precious metals; cartoons; puzzles; poetry; games also sought."

BOYS' LIFE, Boy Scouts of America, 1325 W. Walnut Hill Lane, P.O.Box 152079, Irving TX 75015-2079. (214)580-2000. Editor: Scott Stuckey. Articles Editor: Doug Daniel. Fiction Editor: Kathleen DaGroomes. Director of Design: Joseph P. Connolly. Art Director: Elizabeth Hardaway Morgan. Monthly magazine. Estab. 1911. Circ. 1.3 million. *Boys' Life* is "a general interest magazine for boys 8 to 18 who are members of the Cub Scouts, Boy Scouts or Explorers. A general interest magazine for all boys."
Fiction: Middle readers: animal, contemporary, fantasy, history, humor, problem-solving, science fiction, sports, spy/mystery/adventure. Does not want to see "talking animals and adult reminiscence." Buys 12 mss/year. Average word length: 500-1,200. Byline given.
Nonfiction: Average word length: 500-1,200. Byline given.
How to Contact/Writers: Fiction: Send complete ms. Nonfiction: Query. Reports on queries/mss in 4-6 weeks.
Illustration: Buys 5-7 illustrations/issue; buys 23-50 illustrations/year. Will review ms/illustration packages. Reviews artwork for possible future assignments. Works on assignment only.
How to Contact/Illustrators: Ms/illustration packages: "Query first." Illustrations only: Send tearsheets. Reports on art samples only if interested. Original artwork returned at job's completion. Buys first rights.
Tips: "I strongly urge you to study at least a year's issues to better understand type of material published. All submissions must be accompanied with SASE and adequate postage"

*BREAD FOR GOD'S CHILDREN, Bread Ministries, Inc., P.O. Box 1017, Arcadia FL 33821. (813)494-6214. Articles/Fiction Editor: Anna Lee Carlton. Monthly magazine. Estab. 1972. Circ. 10,000 (US and Canada). "Bread is designed as a teaching tool for Christian families." 85% of publication aimed at juvenile market.
Fiction: Young readers, middle readers, young adults/teens: adventure, animal (no speaking animals), contemporary, history, nature/environment, problem-solving, religous, science fiction, sports, suspense/mystery. Looks for "teaching stories that portray Christian lifestyles without preaching." Buys 20 mss/year. Average word length: 900-1,500 (for teens); 600-900 (for young children). Byline given.
Nonfiction: Preschool-8 years and young readers: arts/crafts, hobbies, how-to, religion. "We do not want anything detrimental of solid family values." Buys 3-4 mss/year. Average word length: 500-800. Byline given.
How to Contact/Writers: Fiction/nonfiction: Send complete ms. Reports on mss in 2 weeks-6 months "if considered for use." Will consider simultaneous submissions and previously published work.
Terms: Pays on publication. Pays $30-40 for stories; $10-20 for articles. Sample copies free for 9 × 12 SAE and 5 first-class stamps (for 3 copies).
Tips: "Know the readership . . . know the publisher's guidelines. Edit carefully for content and grammar."

BRILLIANT STAR, National Spiritual Assembly of the Baha'is of the United States, Bahá'í National Center, Wilmette IL 60091. Managing Editor and Art Director: Pepper Peterson Oldziey. Bimonthly magazine. Estab. 1968. Circ. 2,300. A magazine for Bahá'í children that emphasizes the history, teachings and beliefs of the Bahá'í faith. "We look for sensitivity to multi-racial, multi-cultural audience and a commitment to assisting children in understanding the oneness of the human family." 90% of material aimed at juvenile audience.
Fiction: Young readers, middle readers: contemporary, history, folktales, humorous, multicultural, nature/environment, problem solving, religious, sports, suspense/mystery.

All "should contain analogy or reference to spiritual principles of our faith." Does not want to see material related to traditional Christian holidays or to secular holidays such as Christmas, Easter or Halloween. Nothing that pontificates! Acquires 12-15 mss/year. Average word length: 250-500. Byline given.

Nonfiction: Young readers, middle readers: arts/crafts, biography, cooking, games/puzzles, geography, history, how-to, humorous, interview/profile, multicultural, nature/environment, problem-solving, religion, sports, travel. All "should contain analogy or reference to spiritual principles of our faith." Multicultural needs include material about interracial groups working together. Does not want to see crafts or activities specific to holidays. Accepts 12-15 mss/year. Average word length: 100-250. Byline given.

Poetry: Reviews poetry. Poems "should contain analogy or reference to spiritual principles of our faith." Word/line length open.

How to Contact/Writers: Fiction/nonfiction: Send complete ms. Reports in 2 months. Publishes ms 8-12 months after acceptance. Will consider simultaneous submissions and previously published work.

Illustration: "Illustrations for specific stories on assignment for art director." Reviews ms/illustration packages; reviews artwork for future assignments. Works on assignment only.

How to Contact/Illustrators: Illustrations only: Query; send résumé, promo sheet, tearsheets. Reports on art samples in 2 months. Original artwork returned at job's completion. Credit line given.

Terms: "*Brilliant Star* cannot purchase art or stories at this time." Provides 2 copies of issue in which work appears. Sample copy with 9 × 12 SAE and 5 oz. worth of postage; writer's/illustrator's/photo guidelines free with SASE.

Tips: Writers: "Know the age range and interests of your reader. Read the magazine before you submit. Express a willingness to adapt a story to the editor's needs. A story from real life is always more interesting than what you think children should read. Avoid morals. Any writer who is willing to learn and study the Bahá'í faith in order to write a story from Bahá'í history will be most welcome and encouraged." Illustrators: "Don't be too cute. Get past the one thing you like to draw best and be ready to expand your range. Art director is open to reviewing general submissions. Need artists who can illustrate diversity of peoples without stereotyping, and in a sensitive way that affirms the beauty of different racial characteristics."

CALLIOPE, World History for Young People, Cobblestone Publishing, Inc., 7 School St., Peterborough NH 03458. (603)924-7209. Editor-in-Chief: Carolyn P. Yoder. Art Director: Ann C. Webster. Picture Editor: Francelle Carapetyan. Magazine published 5 times/year. "*Calliope* covers world history (East/West) and lively, original approaches to the subject are the primary concerns of the editors in choosing material."

Fiction: Middle readers and young adults: adventure, folktales, history, biographical fiction. Material must relate to forthcoming themes. Average word length: 800.

Nonfiction: Middle readers and young adults: arts/crafts, biography, cooking, games/puzzles, history. Material must relate to forthcoming themes. Average word length: 300-800.

Poetry: Maximum line length: 100. Wants "clear, objective imagery. Serious and light verse considered."

How to Contact/Writers: "A query must consist of the following to be considered (please use nonerasable paper): a brief cover letter stating subject and word length of the proposed article; a detailed one-page outline explaining the information to be presented in the article; an extensive bibliography of materials the author intends to use in preparing the article; a self-addressed, stamped envelope. Writers new to *Calliope* should send a writing sample with query. If you would like to know if your query has been received, please also include a stamped postcard that requests acknowledgment

of receipt. In all correspondence, please include your complete address as well as a telephone number where you can be reached. A writer may send as many queries for one issue as he or she wishes, but each query must have a separate cover letter, outline, bibliography and SASE. Telephone queries are not accepted. Handwritten queries will not be considered. Queries may be submitted at any time, but queries sent well in advance of deadline *may not be answered for several months*. Go-aheads requesting material proposed in queries are usually sent five months prior to publication date. Unused queries will be returned approximately three to four months prior to publication date."
Illustration: Reviews artwork for future assignments.
How to Contact/Illustrators: Illustrations only: Send tearsheets, photocopies. Original work returned upon job's completion (upon written request).
Photography: Wants photos pertaining to any forthcoming themes. Uses b&w/color prints, 35 mm transparencies. Photographers should send unsolicited photos by mail (on speculation).
Terms: Buys all rights for mss and artwork. Pays 10-17¢/word for stories/articles. Pays illustrators $10-125/b&w inside; $20-210/color inside. "Covers are assigned and paid on an individual basis." Photographers paid per photo (range $15-75). Sample copy for $3.95 and SAE with $1.05 postage. Writer's/illustrator's/photo guidelines for SASE. (See listings for *Cobblestone: The History Magazine for Young People*; *Faces: The Magazine About People*; *Odyssey: Science That's Out of This World*).

CAREER WORLD, Curriculum Innovations Group, 60 Revere Dr., Northbrook IL 60062. (708)205-3000. Fax: (708)564-8197. Articles Editor: Carole Rubenstein. Art Director: Kristi Simkins. Monthly (school year) magazine. Estab. 1972. A guide to careers, for students grades 7-12.
Nonfiction: Young adults: education, how-to, interview/profile, career information. Byline given.
How to Contact/Writers: "We do not want any unsolicited manuscripts." Nonfiction: query with published clips and résumé. Reports on queries in 2 weeks.
Illustration: Buys 5-10 illustrations/year. Reviews ms/illustration packages; reviews artwork for future assignments; works on assignment only.
How to Contact/Illustrators: Query; send promo sheet and tearsheets. Credit line given.
Photography: Purchases photos from freelancers.
Terms: Pays on publication. Buys all rights. Pays $75-250 for articles. Pays illustrators $100-250/color cover; $25-35/b&w inside; $50-75/color inside. Writer's guidelines free, but only on assignment.

CAREERS AND COLLEGES, E.M. Guild, 989 Avenue of the Americas, New York NY 10018. (212)354-8877. Editor-in-Chief: June Rogoznica. Senior Editor: Don Rauf. Art Director: Michael Hofmann. Magazine published 4 times during school year (September, November, January, March). Circ. 500,000. This is a magazine for high school juniors and seniors, designed to prepare students for their futures.
Nonfiction: Young adults: careers, college, health, how-to, humorous, interview/profile, personal development, problem solving, social issues, travel. Wants more celebrity profiles. Buys 30-40 mss/year. Average word length: 1,000-1,250. Byline given.
How to Contact/Writers: Nonfiction: Query. Reports on queries in 3 weeks. Will consider electronic submissions via disk or modem.
Illustration: Buys 10 illustrations/issue; buys 40 illustrations/year. Will review ms/illustration packages. Works on assignment "mostly."
How to Contact/Illustrators: Ms/illustration packages: Query first. Illustrations only: Send tearsheets, cards. Reports on art samples in 3 weeks if interested. Credit line given. Original artwork returned at job's completion.

Terms: Pays on acceptance. Buys first North American serial rights. Pays $250-300 assigned/unsolicited articles. Additional payment for ms/illustration packages "must be negotiated." Pays $500-1,000/color illustration; $300-700 b&w/color (inside) illustration. Sample copy $2.50 with SAE and $1.25 postage; writer's guidelines free with SAE and 1 first-class stamp.

Tips: Make sure queries address the guidelines. Wants articles that are fresh on the subject of careers and colleges and life after high school.

CAT FANCY, The Magazine for Responsible Cat Owners, Fancy Publications, P.O. Box 6050, Mission Viejo CA 92690. (714)855-3045. Articles Editor: Debbie Phillips-Donaldson. Art Director: John Reiss. Monthly magazine. Estab. 1965. Circ. 300,000. "Our magazine is for cat owners who want to know more about how to care for their pets in a responsible manner. We want to see stories and articles showing children relating to or learning about cats in a positive, responsible way. We'd love to see more craft projects for children." 3% of material aimed at juvenile audience.

Fiction: Middle readers: animal, health, problem-solving (all cat-related). Does not want to see stories in which cats talk. Buys 3-9 mss/year. Average word length: 750-1,000. Byline given. Never wants to see work showing cats being treated abusively or irresponsibly or work that puts cats in a negative light. Never uses mss written from cat's point of view.

Nonfiction: Middle readers: animal, arts/crafts, games/puzzles, how-to, health, problem-solving (all cat-related). Buys 3-9 mss/year. Average word length: 450-1,000. Byline given. Would like to see more crafts and how-to pieces for children.

Poetry: Reviews maximum of 64 short-line poems. "No more than 10 poems per submission please."

How to Contact/Writers: Fiction/nonfiction: Send complete ms—query is acceptable too. Reports on queries in 1-2 months; mss in 2-3 months. Publishes ms (juvenile) 4 months after acceptance.

Illustration: Buys 3-6 illustrations/year. "Most of our illustrations are assigned or submitted with a story. We look for realistic images of cats done with pen and ink (no pencil)." Reviews ms/illustration packages; reviews artwork for future assignments.

How to Contact/Illustrators: Query first or send complete ms with final art. "Submit photocopies of work; samples of spot art possibilities." Reports in 2-3 months. Originals returned to artist at job's completion. Credit line given.

Photography: "Cats only, in excellent focus and properly lit. Send SASE for photo needs and submit according to them."

Terms: Pays on publication. Buys first North American serial rights. Buys one-time rights for artwork and photos. Pays $20-75/juvenile articles. Pays additional $45-100 for ms/illustration packages. $35-100/b&w or color (inside). Photographers paid per photo (range: $50-200). Sample copies for $5.50. Writer's/artist's guidelines free for #10 SAE and 1 first-class stamp.

Tips: "Our 'Kids for Cats' department is most open. Perhaps the most important tip I can give is: Consider what 9- to 11-year-olds want to know about cats and what they enjoy most about cats, and address that topic in a style appropriate for them. Writers, keep your writing concise, and don't be afraid to try again after a rejection. Illustrators, we use illustrations mainly as spot art; occasionally we make assignments to illustrators whose spot art we've used before."

*CEMETARY PLOT, Tellstar Productions, P.O. Box 1264, Huntington WV 25714. Editor: Shannon Bridget Murphy. Triannual magazine. Estab. 1993. Circ. 500. *Cemetary Plot* is devoted to horror, suspense, mystery. The material is suitable for all ages. 40% of publication aimed at juvenile market.

Fiction: Picture-oriented material: fantasy, problem-solving, suspense/mystery. Young readers, middle readers: fantasy, horror, problem-solving, suspense/mystery. Young adults: fantasy, horror, suspense/mystery. "Please do not send 'blood and guts' stories." Buys 6-12 mss/year. Average word length: 1,500-3,500. Byline given.

Nonfiction: All levels: how-to, problem-solving. Buys 6-12 mss/year. Average word length: 500-3,500 words. Byline given.

Poetry: Reviews poetry. Multiple submissions welcome. Publishes an annual chapbook of poetry.

How to Contact/Writers: Fiction/nonfiction: Send complete ms. Reports in 6 weeks. Will consider simultaneous submissions, electronic submissions via disk or modem.

Illustration: Reviews ms/illustration packages; reviews artwork for future assignments.

How to Contact/Illustrators: Ms/illustration packages: Submit complete package with final art, ms with rough sketches. Illustrations only: Query; send promo sheet, slides. Reports in 6 weeks. Samples returned with SASE; samples filed (with permission from artist).Credit line given.

Photography: Looks for "imaginative photos; photographs of houses/castles, etc. which would be of interest to *Cemetary Plot*." Model/Property releases required; captions preferred. Uses color, b&w prints; 35mm, 8 × 10 transparencies. To contact, query with samples; send unsolicited photos by mail; provide business card, promotional literature or tearsheets. Reports in 6 weeks.

Terms: Pays on publication. Buys first rights, one-time rights. "Payment depends upon budget. One contributor's copy is provided." Pays photographers per photo. Sample copies for $8. Writer's/illustrator's/photo guidelines for SASE.

Tips: Wants "illustrations with themes of houses, castles, etc; illustrations of children, especially in sets; illustrations that demonstrate the relationship between children and nature or animals with supernatural or mysterious element."

CHALLENGE, (formerly *Pioneer*), Brotherhood Commission, SBC, 1548 Poplar Ave., Memphis TN 38104. (901)272-2461. Articles Editor: Jeno C. Smith. Art Director: Roy White. Monthly magazine. Circ. 30,000. Magazine contains boy interests, sports, crafts, sports personalities, religious.

Nonfiction: Young adults: arts/crafts, games/puzzles, geography, health, hobbies, how-to, humorous, nature/environment, social issues, sports, youth issues. Buys 15 mss/year. Average word length: 700-900. Byline given. Looking for stories on sports heroes with Christian testimony.

How to Contact/Writers: Nonfiction: Send complete ms. Reports on queries/mss in 1 month. Will consider simultaneous submissions.

Illustration: Buys 1-2 illustrations/issue; buys 12 illustrations/year. Reviews ms/illustration packages; reviews artwork for future assignments.

How to Contact/Illustrators: Ms/illustration packages: Send complete ms with final art. Illustrations only: Provide promo sheet to be kept on file. Reports back only if interested. Credit line given.

Photography: Purchases photography from freelancers. Wants b&w photos with youth appeal.

Terms: Pays on acceptance. Buys one-time and reprint rights. Pays $25-50 for articles. Pays illustrators $50-100 for color (cover); $5-20 for b&w (inside); $10-35 for color (inside). Photographers paid per photo (range: $5-100). Sample copy free with #10

SAE and 3 first-class stamps. Writer's/illustrator's guidelines free with SAE and 1 first-class stamp.

Tips: Wants to see "teenagers in sports, nature, health, hobbies—no preachy articles."

CHICKADEE, for Young Children from OWL, Young Naturalist Foundation, Suite 306, 56 The Esplanade, Toronto, Ontario M5E 1A7 Canada. (416)868-6001. Editor: Lizann Flatt. Art Director: Tim Davin. Magazine published 10 times/year. Estab. 1979. Circ: 150,000. *Chickadee* is a "hands-on" publication designed to interest 3-9-year-olds in science, nature and the world around them.

Fiction: Young readers: adventure, animal, fantasy, folktales, humorous, nature/environment, science fiction, sports. Does not want to see religious, anthropomorphic animal, romance material, material that talks down to kids. Buys 8 mss/year. Average word length: 300-800. Byline given. "No religious/antropomorphic material."

Nonfiction: Young readers: animal (facts/characteristics), arts/crafts, cooking, games/puzzles, interview/profile, travel. Does not want to see religious material. Buys 2-5 mss/year. Average word length: 20-200. Byline given.

Poetry: Maximum length: 50 lines. Limit submissions to 5 poems.

How to Contact/Writers: Fiction/nonfiction: Send complete ms. SAE and $1 money order for answer to query and return of ms. Report on mss in 2 months. Will consider simultaneous submissions.

Illustration: Buys 3-5 illustrations/issue; buys 40 illustrations/year. Preferred theme or style: realism/humor (but not cartoons). Reviews ms/illustration packages; reviews artwork for future assignments. Works on assignment only.

How to Contact/Illustrators: Provide promo sheet or tearsheets to be kept on file. Reports on art samples only if interested. Credit line given.

Photography: Looking for animal (mammal, insect, reptile, fish, etc.) photos. Uses 35mm and 2¼ × 2¼ transparencies. Write to request photo package for $1 money order, attention Robin Wilner, photo researcher.

Terms: Pays on acceptance. Buys all rights for mss. Buys one-time rights for photos. Pays $25-210 for stories. Pays illustrators $100-650/color (inside). Photographers paid per photo (range: $100-350). Sample copy $4.50. Writer's guidelines free.

Tips: "Study the magazine carefully before submitting material. Fiction most open to freelancers. Kids should be main characters and should be treated with respect."

CHILD LIFE, Children's Better Health Institute, 1100 Waterway Blvd., Indianapolis IN 46202. (317)636-8881. Editor: Stan Zukowski. Art Director: Janet Moir. Magazine published 8 times/year. Estab. 1923. Circ. 80,000. "Adventure, humor, fantasy and health-related stories with an imaginative twist are among those stories we seek. We try to open our readers' minds to their own creative potential, and we want our stories and articles to reflect and encourage this."

Fiction: Middle readers: adventure, animal, contemporary, fantasy, folktales, health, history, humorous, multicultural, nature/environment, problem-solving, science fiction, sports, suspense/mystery. "Health and fitness is an ongoing need." Buys 30-35 mss/year. Average word length: 850. Byline given.

Nonfiction: Middle readers: animal, arts/crafts, biography, careers, cooking, games/puzzles, geography, health, history, hobbies, how-to, humorous, interview/profile, multicultural, nature/environment, problem solving, science, social issues, sports, travel. Average word length: 800. Byline given.

Poetry: Reviews poetry.

How to Contact/Writers: Fiction/nonfiction: Send complete ms. No queries please. Reports on mss in 8-10 weeks. Will not consider previously published material. Will consider simultaneous submissions. "But be professional—if you sell to another mag, let us know!"

Illustration: Buys 8-10 illustrations/issue; buys 65-80 illustrations/year. Preferred theme: "Need realistic styles especially." Reviews ms/illustration packages; reviews artwork for future assignments. Works on assignment only.

How to Contact/Illustrators: Illustrations only: Send query, résumé and portfolio. Samples must be accompanied by SASE for response and/or return of samples." Reports on art samples only if interested. Credit line given.

Photography: Purchases photos with accompanying ms only.

Terms: Pays on publication. Writers paid 10-15 cents/word for stories/articles. Buys all rights. Illustrators paid $250/color cover; $30-70/b&w inside; $65-140 color inside. For artwork, buys all rights. Photographers paid per photo (range: $25-30). Buys one-time rights for photographs. Writer's/illustrator's guidelines free with SAE and 1 first-class stamp.

Tips: "Writers must be as contemporary as possible in their treatment of modern children's characters. Many stories we receive sound as if they're from the 1950s. Illustrators simply *must* review copies of our magazines — current copies — or they'll not really understand what the individual titles need. Each of our mags is different." Trends include "multiculturalism, definitely. But 'African-Americans' are not the only other cultural group in the US. We'd like to see how *all* cultures have influenced our American culture. Encyclopedic approaches are out. Relay pertinent information through the story — fiction or nonfiction. And for heaven's sake, use some dialogue! Let the characters do the talking — not the author."

CHILDREN'S DIGEST, Children's Better Health Institute, Box 567, Indianapolis IN 46206. (317)636-8881. Articles/Fiction Editor: Elizabeth Rinck. Art Director: Janet Moir. Magazine published 8 times/year. Estab. 1950. Circ. 125,000. For preteens; approximately 33% of content is health-related.

Fiction: Middle readers: animal, contemporary, fantasy, folktales, health, history, humorous, problem solving, science fiction, sports, suspense/mystery/adventure. Buys 25 mss/year. Average word length: 500-1,500. Byline given.

Nonfiction: Middle readers: animal, arts/crafts, biography, cooking, education, games/ puzzles, health, history, how-to, humorous, interview/profile, nature/environment, problem solving, sports, travel. Buys 16-20 mss/year. Average word length: 500-1,200. Byline given.

Poetry: Maximum length: 20-25 lines.

How to Contact/Writers: Fiction/nonfiction: Send complete ms. Reports on mss in 10 weeks.

Illustration: Will review an illustrator's work for possible future assignments. Works on assignment only.

How to Contact/Illustrators: Ms/illustration packages: Query first. Illustrations only: Send résumé and/or slides or tearsheets to illustrate work; query with samples. Reports on art samples in 8-10 weeks.

Photography: Purchases photos with accompanying ms only. Model/property releases required; captions required. Uses 35mm transparencies.

Terms: Pays on acceptance for illustrators, publication for writers. Buys all rights for mss and artwork; one-time rights for photos. Pays 10¢/word for accepted articles. Pays $225/color (cover) illustration; $24-100/b&w (inside); $60-125/color (inside). Photographers paid per photo (range: $10-75). Sample copy $1.25. Writer's/illustrator's guidelines for SAE and 1 first-class stamp.

CHILDREN'S PLAYMATE, Children's Better Health Institute, Box 567, Indianapolis IN 46206. (317)636-8881. Articles/Fiction Editor: Elizabeth Rinck. Art Director: Marty Jones. Magazine published 8 times/year. Estab. 1929. Circ. 135,000. For children between 6 and 8 years; approximately 33% of content is health-related.

Fiction: Young readers: animal, contemporary, fantasy, folktales, history, humorous, science fiction, sports, suspense/mystery/adventure. Buys 25 mss/year. Average word length: 200-700. Byline given.
Nonfiction: Young readers: animal, arts/crafts, biography, cooking, games/puzzles, health, history, how-to, humorous, sports, travel. Buys 16-20 mss/year. Average word length: 200-700. Byline given.
Poetry: Maximum length: 20-25 lines.
How to Contact/Writers: Fiction/nonfiction: Send complete ms. Reports on mss in 8-10 weeks.
Illustration: Will review an illustrator's work for possible future assignments. Works on assignment only.
How to Contact/Illustrators: Ms/illustration packages: Query first. Illustrations only: Query with samples. Reports on art samples in 8-10 weeks.
Photography: Purchases photos with accompanying ms only. Model/property releases required; captions required. Uses 35mm transparencies. Send completed ms with transparencies.
Terms: Pays on acceptance for illustrators, publication for writers. Buys all rights for mss and artwork; one-time rights for photos. Pays 15¢/word for assigned articles. Pays $225/color (cover) illustration; $25-100/b&w (inside); $60-125/color (inside). Photographers paid per photo (range: $10-75). Sample copy $1.25. Writer's/illustrator's guidelines for SAE and 1 first-class stamp.

*CHOICES, The Magazine for Personal Development and Practical Living Skills, Scholastic, Inc. 555 Broadway, New York NY 10012. (212)343-6100. Editor: Lauren Tarshis. Art Director: Joan Michaels. Monthly magazine. Estab. 1986 as *Choices* (formerly called *Coed*). "We go to teenagers in home economics and health classes. All our material has curriculum ties: Personal Development, Family Life, Careers, Food & Nutrition, Consumer Power, Child Development, Communications, Health."
Nonfiction: Buys 30 mss/year. Word length varies. Byline given (except for short items).
How to Contact/Writers: Nonfiction: Query with published clips "We don't want unsolicited manuscripts." Reports on queries in 2 weeks.
Illustration: Works on assignment only. "All art is *assigned* to go with specific articles." Pays on acceptance. Sample copy for 9×12 SAE and 2 first-class stamps.
Tips: *"Read* the specific magazines. We receive unsolicited manuscripts and queries that do not in any way address the needs of our magazine. For example, we don't publish poetry, but we get unsolicited poetry in the mail."

CLUBHOUSE, Your Story Hour, P.O. Box 15, Berrien Springs MI 49103. (616)471-3701. Articles/Fiction Editor, Art Director: Elaine Trumbo. Bimonthly magazine. Estab. 1949. Circ. 6,000.
Fiction: Middle readers, young adults: animal, contemporary, health, history, humorous, problem solving, religious, sports. Does not want to see science fiction/fantasy/Halloween or Santa-oriented fiction. Buys 30 mss/year. Average word length: 800-1,300. Byline given.
Nonfiction: Middle readers, young adults: how-to. "We do not use articles except 200-500 word items about good health: anti—drug, tobacco, alcohol; pro—nutrition." Buys 6 mss/year. Average word length: 200-400. Byline given.
How to Contact/Writers: Fiction/nonfiction: Send complete ms. Reports on queries/mss in 6 weeks. Will consider simultaneous submissions.
Illustration: Buys 20-25 illustrations/issue; buys 120+ illustrations/year. Uses b&w artwork only. Will review artwork for future assignments. Works on assignment only.
How to Contact/Illustrators: Illustrations only: Send photocopies, tearsheets or prints of work to be kept on file. Reports on art samples in 6 weeks. Originals usually not returned at job's completion, but they can be returned if desired.

Terms: Pays "about 6 months" after acceptance for authors, within 2 months for artwork. Buys first and one-time rights for mss and artwork. Pays $25-35 for articles. "Writers and artists receive 2 copies free in addition to payment." Pays $30/b&w (cover) illustration; $7.50-25/b&w (inside). Sample copy for business SAE and 3 first-class stamps; writer's/illustrator's guidelines free for business SAE and 1 first-class stamp.
Tips: Writers: "Take children seriously—they're smarter than you think! Respect their sense of dignity, don't talk down to them and don't write stories about 'bad kids.' Illustrators: "Keep it clean, vigorous, fresh—whatever your style. Send samples we can keep on file. Black & white line art is best."

COBBLESTONE, The History Magazine for Young People, Cobblestone Publishing, Inc., 7 School St., Peterborough NH 03458. (603)924-7209. Fax: (603)924-7380. Editor: Samuel A. Mead. Picture Editor: Francelle Carapetyan. Magazine published 10 times/year. Circ. 42,000. "*Cobblestone* is theme-related. Writers should request editorial guidelines which explain procedure and list upcoming themes. Queries must relate to an upcoming theme. Fiction is not used often, although a good fiction piece offers welcome diversity. It is recommended that writers become familiar with the magazine (sample copies available)."
Fiction: Middle readers, young adults: history. "Authentic historical and biographical fiction, adventure, retold legends, etc., relating to the theme." Buys 6-10 mss/year. Average word length: 800. Byline given.
Nonfiction: Middle readers, young adults: activities, biography, games/puzzles (no word finds), history, interview/profile, travel. All articles must relate to the issue's theme. Buys 120 mss/year. Average word length: 800. Byline given.
Poetry: Up to 100 lines. "Clear, objective imagery. Serious and light verse considered." Pays on an individual basis. Must relate to theme.
How to Contact/Writers: Fiction/nonfiction: Query. "A query must consist of all of the following to be considered (please use nonerasable paper): a brief cover letter stating the subject and word length of the proposed article; a detailed one-page outline explaining the information to be presented in the article; an extensive bibliography of materials the author intends to use in preparing the article; a self-addressed stamped envelope. Writers new to *Cobblestone* should send a writing sample with query. If you would like to know if your query has been received, please also include a stamped postcard that requests acknowledgment of receipt. In all correspondence, please include your complete address as well as a telephone number where you can be reached. A writer may send as many queries for one issue as he or she wishes, but each query must have a separate cover letter, outline, bibliography and SASE. Telephone queries are not accepted. Handwritten queries will not be considered. Queries may be submitted at any time, but queries sent well in advance of deadline *may not be answered for several months.* Go-aheads requesting material proposed in queries are usually sent five months prior to publication date. Unused queries will be returned approximately three to four months prior to publication date."
Illustration: Buys 3 illustrations/issue; buys 36 illustrations/year. Preferred theme or style: Material that is simple, clear and accurate but not too juvenile. Sophisticated sources are a must. Reviews ms/illustration packages; reviews artwork for future assignments; works on assignment only.
How to Contact/Illustrators: Illustrations only: Send photocopies, tearsheets, or other nonreturnable samples. "Illustrators should consult issues of *Cobblestone* to familiarize themselves with our needs." Reports on art samples in 1-2 months. Original artwork returned at job's completion (upon written request).
Photography: Contact: Francelle Carapetyan, picture editor. Photos must relate to upcoming themes. Send transparencies and/or color/b&w prints. Submit on speculation.
Terms: Pays on publication. Buys all rights to articles and artwork. Pays 10¢/word for assigned articles. Pays $10-125/b&w (inside) illustration; $20-210 for color (inside) illus-

tration. Photographers paid $15-75. Sample copy $3.95 with 7½×10½ SAE and 5 first-class stamps; writer's/illustrator's/photographer's guidelines free with SAE and 1 first-class stamp.

Tips: Writers: "Submit detailed queries which show attention to historical accuracy and which offer interesting and entertaining information. Be true to your own style. Study past issues to know what we look for. All feature articles, recipes, activities, fiction and supplemental nonfiction are freelance contributions." Illustrators: "Submit b&w samples, not too juvenile. Study past issues to know what we look for. The illustration we use is generally for stories, recipes and activities." (See listings for *Faces: The Magazine About People; Calliope: The World History Magazine for Young People; ODYSSEY: Science That's Out of This World.*)

COCHRAN'S CORNER, Cochran's Publishing Co., Box 2036, Waldorf MD 20604. (301)843-0485. Articles Editor: Ada Cochran. Fiction Editor/Art Director: Debby Thompkins. Quarterly magazine. Estab. 1986. Circ. 1,000. "Our magazine is open to most kinds of writing that is wholesome and suitable for young children to read. It is 52 pages, 8½×11, devoted to short stories, articles and poems. Our children's corner is reserved for children up to the age of 14. *Right now we are forced to limit our acceptance to subscribers only.*" 30% of material aimed at juvenile audience.

Fiction: Picture-oriented material: religious. Young readers: animal, fantasy, humorous, problem solving, religious. Middle readers: religious. Young adults: contemporary, history, religious, romance, science fiction. Does not want to see "anything that contains bad language or violence." Buys 150 mss/year. Maximum word length: 1,000.

Nonfiction: Picture-oriented material: religious, travel. Young readers: animal, how-to, problem solving, religious, travel. Middle readers: religious, travel. Young adults: history, humorous, interview/profile, religious, travel. Does not want to see "editorials or politics." Buys 100 mss/year. Average word length: 150. Byline given.

Poetry: Reviews 20-line poetry on any subject.

How to Contact/Writers: Fiction/nonfiction: Send complete ms. Reports on queries/mss in 2 weeks. Will consider simultaneous submissions.

Illustration: Revies ms/illustration packages; reviews work for future assignments.

How to Contact/Illustrators: Reports only if interested. Credit line given.

Terms: "Payment is one contributor's copy, but we hope as we grow to begin paying." Sample copy $5 with 9×11 SASE. Writer's guidelines free for SASE.

Tips: Must subscribe to be published in this market ($20/1 year; $30/2 years).

*COUNSELOR, Scripture Press Pub., Inc., Box 632, Glen Ellyn IL 60138. (708)668-6000. Articles/Fiction Editor: Janice K. Burton. Art Director: Blake Ebel. Newspaper distributed weekly; published quarterly. Estab. 1940. "Audience: children 8-12 years. Papers designed to present everyday living stories showing the difference Christ can make in a child's life. Correlated with Scripture Press Sunday school curriculum."

Fiction: Middle readers: adventure, animal, nature/environment, sports (all with Christian context). "Actually, true stories preferred by far. I appreciate well-written fiction that shows knowledge of our product. I suggest people write for samples." Buys approximately 24 mss/year. Average word length: 900-1,000. Byline given.

Nonfiction: Middle readers: animal, arts/crafts, biography, history, how-to, nature/environment, problem-solving, religion, social issues. Buys 24 mss/year. Average word length: 900-1,000. Byline given.

How to Contact/Writers: Fiction/nonfiction: send complete ms. Reports on mss in 8-10 weeks. Publishes ms 1-2 years after acceptance (we work a year in advance). Will consider previously published work.

Illustration: Buys 24-40 illustrations/year. Reviews ms/illustration packages, but not often; reviews artwork for future assignments.

Photography: Purchases photos from freelancers.
Terms: Pays on acceptance. Buys first rights, one-time rights, or all rights for mss. Pays 5-10¢/word for stories or articles. Additional payment for ms/illustration packages. Sample copies for #10 SAE and 2 first-class stamps. Writers/photo guidelines for SASE.
Tips: "Send copy that is as polished as possible. Indicate if story is true. Indicate rights offered. Stick to required word lengths."

CRICKET, THE MAGAZINE FOR CHILDREN, Carus Corporation, P.O. Box 300, Peru IL 61354. (815)224-6656. Articles/Fiction Editor-in-Chief: Marianne Carus. Art Director: Ron McCutchan. Monthly magazine. Estab. 1973. Circ. 100,000. Children's literary magazine for ages 7-14.

● At press time, the Carus Corporation, publisher of *Cricket* and *Ladybug* magazine (see listing in this section), launched *Spider*, a monthly magazine for 6- to 9-year-olds. Send a SAE and 1 first-class stamp for writer's/illustrator's guidelines.

Fiction: Middle readers, young adult: adventure, animal, contemporary, fantasy, folk and fairy tales, history, humorous, multicultural, nature/environmental, science fiction, sports, suspense/mystery/adventure. Buys 180 mss/year. Maximum word length: 1,500. Byline given.
Nonfiction: Animal, arts/crafts, biography/interview/profile, cooking, environment, geography, history, hobbies, how-to, humorous, multicultural, natural science, problem solving, science and technology, space, sports, travel. Also experiments, games/puzzles. Multicultural needs include articles on customs and cultures. Buys 180 mss/year. Average word length: 1,000. Byline given.
Poetry: Reviews poems, 1-page maximum length. Prefers 5 or less submissions.
How to Contact/Writers: Send complete ms. Do not query first. Reports on mss in 2-3 months. Does not like but will consider simultaneous submissions. SASE required for response.
Illustration: Buys 35 illustrations (14 separate commissions)/issue; 425 illustrations/year. Uses b&w and full-color work. Original artwork returned at job's completion. Preferred theme or style: "strong realism; strong people, especially kids; good action illustration; no cartoons. All media, but prefer other than pencil." Will review ms/illustration packages "but reserves option to re-illustrate."
How to Contact/Illustrators: Ms/illustration packages: Send complete ms with sample and query. Illustrations only: Provide tearsheets or good quality photocopies to be kept on file. SASE required for response/return of samples. Reports on art samples in 2 months.
Photography: Purchases photos with accompanying ms only. Model/property releases required. Uses color transparencies, b&w glossy prints.
Terms: Pays on publication. Buys first publication rights in the English language. Buys first publication rights plus promotional rights for artwork. Pays up to 25¢/word for unsolicited articles; up to $3/line for poetry. Pays $500/color cover; $75-150/b&w inside. Writer's/illustrator's guidelines free with SAE and 1 first-class stamp.
Tips: Writers: "Read copies of back issues and current issues. Adhere to specified word limits. *Please* do not query." Illustrators: "Edit your samples. Send only your best work and be able to reproduce that quality in assignments. Put name and address on *all*

Always include a self-addressed stamped envelope (SASE) or a self-addressed envelope (SAE) and International Reply Coupons (IRCs) with submissions.

samples. Know a publication before you submit—is your style appropriate?"

This illustration in acrylic is one of three by Kevin Hawkes that accompanied an article on the history of Colonial American printing in Cricket magazine entitled "The Printer's Apprentice." Since the illustration appeared in the first issue of Cricket to include full color in the interior, Art Director Ron McCutchan wanted "an illustrator whom I knew could deliver a stunning illustration. Kevin has been a frequent contributor for the past few years, but mainly for whimsical or fantastic stories or poems," McCutchan explains. "I wanted something a bit livelier and softer for this article, and I was interested in seeing what Kevin could do with the subject matter."

© 1993 Kevin Hawkes

CRUSADER, Calvinist Cadet Corps, P.O. Box 7259, Grand Rapids MI 49510. (616)241-5616. Editor: G. Richard Broene. Art Director: Robert DeJonge. Magazine published 7 times/year. Circ. 13,000. "Our magazine is for members of the Calvinist Cadet Corps—boys aged 9-14. Our purpose is to show how God is at work in their lives and in the world around them."

Fiction: Middle readers, young adults: adventure, contemporary, humorous, nature/environment, problem solving, religious, sports, suspense/mystery. Does not want to see fantasy, science fiction. Buys 12 mss/year. Average word length: 800-1,500.

Nonfiction: Middle readers, young adults: animal, arts/crafts, biography, games/puzzles, hobbies, humorous, interview/profile, religious, science, sports. Buys 6 mss/year. Average word length: 400-900.

How to Contact/Writers: Fiction/nonfiction: Send complete ms. Reports on queries/mss in 3-5 weeks. Will consider simultaneous submissions.

Illustration: Buys 1 illustration/issue; buys 6 illustrations/year. Works on assignment only. Credit line given.

Terms: Pays on acceptance. Buys first North American serial rights; first rights; one-time rights; reprint rights. Pays 2-5¢/word for stories/articles. Sample copy free with 9×12 SAE and 3 first-class stamps.

Tips: Publication is most open to fiction: write for a list of themes (available yearly in January).

CURRENT HEALTH I, The Beginning Guide to Health Education, 60 Revere Dr., Northbrook IL 60062-1563. (708)205-3000. Monthly (during school year September-May) magazine. "For classroom use by students, this magazine is curriculum specific and requires experienced educators who can write clearly and well at fifth grade reading level."

Nonfiction: Middle readers: health, nature/environment, problem solving. Buys 60-70 mss/year. Average word length: 1,000. "Credit given in staff box."

How to Contact/Writers: Nonfiction: Query with published clips and résumé. Publishes ms 6-7 months after acceptance.

Terms: Pays on publication. Buys all rights. Pays $100-150, "more for longer features." Writer's guidelines available only if writer is given an assignment.
Tips: Needs material about drug education, nutrition, fitness and exercise.

CURRENT HEALTH II, The Continuing Guide to Health Education, 60 Revere Dr., Northbrook IL 60062-1563. (708)205-3000. Monthly (during school year September-May). "For classroom use by students, this magazine is curriculum specific and requires experienced educators who can write clearly and well at a ninth grade reading level."
Nonfiction: Young adults/teens: health, nature/environment, problem-solving, sports. Buys 70-90 mss/year. Average word length: 1,000-2,500. Byline given.
How to Contact/Writers: Nonfiction: Query with published clips and résumé. Reports on queries in 2 months. Publishes ms 6-7 months after acceptance.
Terms: Pays on publication. Buys all rights. Pays $100-150 for assigned article, "more for longer features." Writer's guidelines available only if writers are given an assignment.
Tips: Needs articles on drug education, nutrition, fitness and exercise.

DAY CARE AND EARLY EDUCATION, Suite 330, 351 Pleasant St., Northampton MA 01060. Articles/Fiction Editor: Randa Nachbar. Art Director: Bill Jobson. Quarterly magazine. Circ. 2,500. Magazine uses material "involving children from birth to age 7." 5% of material aimed at juvenile audience.
Fiction: Picture material and young readers: contemporary, fantasy, humorous, problem solving. Average word length: 1,000-3,000. Byline given.
Nonfiction: Picture material and young readers: animal, how-to, humorous, problem solving. Average word length: 1,000-3,000. Byline given.
How to Contact/Writers: Fiction/nonfiction: Send complete ms. Reports on queries in 1 month; mss in 2-3 months.
Illustration: Will review ms/illustration packages.
How to Contact/Illustrators: Ms/illustration packages: Send complete ms with final art. Reports on art samples only if interested. Original artwork returned at job's completion.
Terms: Pays in 2 copies. Free sample copy; free writer's guidelines.

DISCOVERIES, Children's Ministries, 6401 The Paseo, Kansas City MO 64131. (816)333-7000. Editor: Latta Jo Knapp. Executive Editor: Mark York. Weekly tabloid. *Discoveries* is a leisure reading piece for third and fourth graders. It is published weekly by the Department of Children's Ministries of the Church of the Nazarene. "The major purposes of *Discoveries* are to provide a leisure reading piece which will build Christian behavior and values and to provide reinforcement for Biblical concepts taught in the Sunday School curriculum. The focus of the reinforcement will be life-related, with some historical appreciation. *Discoveries*'s target audience is children ages 8-10 in grades three and four. The readability goal is third to fourth grade."
Fiction: Young readers, middle readers: adventure, contemporary, problem-solving, religious. "Fiction — stories should vividly portray definite Christian emphasis or character-building values, without being preachy. The setting, plot and action should be realistic." Average word length: 500-700. Byline given.
How to Contact/Writers: Fiction: Send complete ms. Reports on mss in 6-8 weeks.
Illustration: "*Discoveries* publishes a wide variety of artistic styles, i.e. cartoon, realistic, montage, etc., but whatever the style, artwork must appeal to 8-10-year-old children. It should not simply be child-related from an adult viewpoint. All artwork for *Discoveries* is assigned on a work for hire basis. Samples of art may be sent for review.
How to Contact/Illustrators: Illustrations only: send résumé, portfolio, client list, tearsheets. Reports back only if interested. Credit line given.
Terms: Pays "approximately one year before the date of issue." Buys multi-use rights. Pays 5¢/word. Pays illustrators $75/color (cover). Contributor receives 4 complimentary

Entertaining Kids with Stories of Adventure

"The purpose of *Disney Adventures* is definitely to *entertain*, not to teach," says Suzanne Harper. "Articles must be fascinating, exciting and adventurous first. Education should be secondary."

Harper is managing editor of the full-color monthly founded in 1990 by The Walt Disney Company. The magazine—complete with comics—aims to do what Disney movies have done for years: entertain kids. And it does so with stories of adventure interwoven with fascinating facts. Though *Disney Adventures* appeals to boys and girls ages 7 to 14, the primary audience is 10- to 12-year-olds.

"Our philosophy is to show the adventure in life, whether it's in the kids' daily lives—as in 'Is Your Pet Nuts?' which explains why animals ex-

Suzanne Harper

hibit behaviors we might think odd—or in the accounts of adults who have fascinating adventures—as in articles on explorers, scientists who chase tornadoes, detectives, race car drivers or paleontologists," Harper explains.

The magazine also focuses on the latest in television, movies, music, books, comics and videos. "We cover entertainment in a very behind-the-scenes way, thanks to our location near Los Angeles," says Harper. "We often visit movie sets and celebrity softball games."

The entertainment section and "Big Adventures" (which has focused on such topics as dinosaurs, the Wild West and death-defying photographers) are mostly staff-written, but the areas of science, sports, fiction and puzzles are open to freelancers. Though they seldom publish unsolicited nonfiction manuscripts, a writer who submits in this way might be offered another story assignment, Harper says. "We assign 20 to 30 stories a year based on queries. In general, a good query is much more likely to get you an assignment than an unsolicited article."

In reviewing queries, they look for unusual angles, evidence of research, and a strong sense of exactly what the article will cover. "We see too many vague, general ideas," says Harper. "For example, *books* have been written about the Arctic. What, specifically, will *you* focus on?"

Before even sending a query (and clips, if available), writers should read at least two issues of the magazine to become familiar with the regular features, the length of nonfiction articles (usually 150 to 650 words), and how facts should be incorporated into material. Sending for the writer's guidelines is also helpful.

"As a rule," the guidelines state, "a 200- to 400-word article should contain at least five fascinating facts or bits of information. However, the presentation of those facts is just as important as the information itself. Kids should be able to visualize an idea, especially if it involves quantity or statistics." For instance, the Big Adventures article on dinosaurs in the July 1993 *Disney Adventures* says, "The neck of a Mamenchisaurus was longer than a tennis court is wide."

In fiction Harper looks for the same qualities sought by other fiction editors: a strong hook, excellent writing, a fresh story, lively dialogue, a unique voice and memorable characters. "I see far too many stories—about 99.9 percent—that are simply too young for our audience. Stories should be aimed at the upper end of the middle grade spectrum," she says.

Of course, she's primarily seeking stories that are adventurous—as opposed to relationship or "problem" stories. Though fiction (which may range from 1,500 to 1,800 words) is not used as frequently, any genre—mystery, science fiction, fantasy—is acceptable. "I'm not interested in fiction stories that are thinly veiled nonfiction articles. Again, the fiction should entertain," cautions Harper.

In terms of artwork, she says, "We have found that our readers respond very well to more sophisticated images and palettes—not everything aimed at kids has to be cartoony or pastel." And all of the illustrations used by *Disney Adventures* are assigned. "The illustrators we work with have been featured in illustration annuals and usually have published extensively in other magazines."

Harper advises illustrators to mail promotional pieces to art directors or buy a page in a directory of illustration samples, such as *The Workbook* or *American Showcase*. As for writers, "Focus your time and attention on studying the market, researching story ideas, and making sure each query is as well-written and thought-provoking as possible. An excellent query is the best marketing tool around."

—*Christine Martin*

To illustrate the magazine's focus on entertainment, the cover of Disney Adventures *usually features a celebrity and an animated character. Pictured here is Joey Lawrence from the TV sitcom* Blossom. *The character trying to swipe Joey's apple is Abu, from the Disney movie* Aladdin.

copies of publication. Writer's/artist's guidelines free with #10 SAE.

Tips: "*Discoveries* is committed to reinforcement of the Biblical concepts taught in the Sunday School curriculum. Because of this, the themes needed are mainly as follows: faith in God, obedience to God, putting God first, choosing to please God, accepting Jesus as Savior, finding God's will, choosing to do right, trusting God in hard times, prayer, trusting God to answer, Importance of Bible memorization, appreciation of Bible as God's Word to man, Christians working together, showing kindness to others, witnessing." (See listing for *Power and Light*.)

DISNEY ADVENTURES, The Walt Disney Company, 500 S. Buena Vista St., Burbank CA 91521. (818)973-4333. Fiction Editor: Suzanne Harper. Senior Editors/Nonfiction: Allison Lassieur and Debbie Barnes. Monthly Magzine. Estab. 1990. Circ. 350,000.

Fiction: Middle readers: adventure, contemporary, fantasy, humorous, science fiction, sports, suspense/mystery. Buys approximately 6-10 mss/year. Averge word length: 1,500-2,000. Byline given.

Nonfiction: Middle readers: animal, biography, games/puzzles, interview/profile, nature/environment and sports. Buys 100-150 mss/year. Average word length: 250-750. Byline given.

How to Contact/Writers: Fiction: Send complete ms. Nonfiction: Query with published clips. Reports in 1 month. Publishes ms 6-12 months after acceptance. Will consider simultaneous submissions and electronic submissions via disk or modem.

Illustration: Buys approx. 20 illustrations/issue; 250 illustrations/year. Reviews ms/illustration packages; reviews artwork for future assignments; works on assignment only.

How to Contact/Illustrators: Illustrations only: Provide résumé, business card, promotional literature or tearsheets to be kept on file. Reports only if interested. Does not return original artwork.

Photography: Purchases photos separately. Model/property releases required; captions required. Send "anything but originals—everything sent is kept on file." Photographers should provide résumé, business card, promotional literature or tearsheets to be kept on file. Reports only if interested.

Terms: Pays on acceptance. Buys all rights. Purchases all rights for artwork, various rights for photographs. Pays $250-750 for assigned articles. Pays illustrators $50 and up. Photographers paid $100 minimum per project, or $25 minimum per photo. Sample copies: "Buy on newsstand or order copies by calling 1-800-435-0715." Writer's guidelines for SASE.

DOLPHIN LOG, The Cousteau Society, Suite 402, 870 Greenbrier Circle, Chesapeake VA 23320-2641. (804)523-9335. Editor: Elizabeth Foley. Bimonthly magazine for children ages 7-13. Circ. 80,000. Entirely nonfiction subject matter encompasses all areas of science, natural history, marine biology, ecology and the environment as they relate to our global water system. The philosophy of the magazine is to delight, instruct and instill an environmental ethic and understanding of the interconnectedness of living organisms, including people. Of special interest are articles on ocean- or water-related themes which develop reading and comprehension skills.

Nonfiction: Middle readers, young adult: animal, games/puzzles, geography, interview/profile, nature/environment, science, ocean. Multicultural needs include indigenous peoples, lifestyles of ancient people, etc. Does not want to see talking animals. No dark or religious themes. Buys 10 mss/year. Average word length: 500-700. Byline given.

How to Contact/Writers: Nonfiction: Query. Reports on queries in 1 month; mss in 2 months.

Illustration: Buys 1 illustration/issue; buys 6 illustrations/year. Preferred theme: Biological illustration. Will review ms/illustration packages; will review artwork for future assignments.

How to Contact/Illustrators: Illustrations only: Query; send résumé, promo sheet, slides. Reports on art samples in 8 weeks only if interested. Credit line given to illustrators.

Photography: Wants "sharp, colorful pictures of sea creatures. The more unusual the creature, the better."

Terms: Pays on publication. Buys first North American serial rights; reprint rights. Pays $25-150 for articles. Pays $25-200/color photos. Sample copy $2 with 9 × 12 SAE and 3 first-class stamps. Writer's/illustrator's guidelines free with #10 SAE and 1 first-class stamp.

Tips: Writers: "Write simply and clearly and don't anthropomorphize." Illustrators: "Be scientifically accurate and don't anthropomorphize. Some background in biology is helpful, as our needs range from simple line drawings to scientific illustrations which must be researched for biological and technical accuracy."

DYNAMATH, Scholastic Inc., 555 Broadway, New York NY 10012-3999. (212)343-6461. Fiction Editor: Jackie Glasthal. Art Director: Pam Mitchell. Monthly magazine. Estab. 1981. Circ. 300,000. Purpose is "to make learning math fun, challenging and uncomplicated for young minds in a very complex world."

Fiction: Middle readers, young adults: Anything related to math and science topics, specifically problem-solving books. Byline given.

Nonfiction: All levels: careers, cooking, games/puzzles, how-to, interview/profile, math, problem-solving, science, sports—all must relate to math and science topics.

How to Contact/Writers: Fiction/nonfiction: Query with published clips, send ms. Reports on queries in 1 month; mss in 6 weeks. Publishes ms 4 months after acceptance. Will consider simultaneous submissions.

Illustration: Buys 4 illustrations/issue. Reviews ms/illustration packages; reviews artwork for future assignments.

How to Contact/Illustrators: Query first. Reports back on submissions only if interested. Originals returned to artist at job's completion.

Terms: Pays on acceptance. Pays artists $800-1,000/color cover illustration; $100-800/color inside illustration. Pays photographers $300-1,000/project. Buys first North American serial rights.

EXPLORING, Boy Scouts of America, P.O. Box 152079, 1325 W. Walnut Hill Lane, Irving TX 75015-2079. (214)580-2365. Executive Editor: Scott Daniels. Art Director: Joe Connally. Photo Editor: Brian Payne. Magazine published "4 times a year—not quarterly." *Exploring* is a 12-page, 4-color magazine published for members of the Boy Scouts of America's Exploring program. These members are young men and women between the ages of 14-21. Interests include careers, computers, life skills (money management, parent/peer relationships, study habits), college, camping, hiking, canoeing.

Nonfiction: Young adults: interview/profile, problem solving, travel. Buys 12 mss/year. Average word length: 600-1,200. Byline given.

How to Contact/Writers: Nonfiction: Query with published clips. Reports on queries/mss in 1 week.

Illustration: Buys 3 illustrations/issue; buys 12 illustrations/year. Will review artwork for future assignments. Works on assignment only.

How to Contact/Illustrators: Reports on art samples in 2 weeks. Original artwork returned at job's completion.

Terms: Pays on acceptance. Buys first North American serial rights. Pays $300-500 for assigned/unsolicited articles. Pays $1,000/color (cover); $250-500/b&w (inside); $500-800/color (inside). Sample copy with 8½ × 11 SAE and 5 first-class stamps. Free writer's/illustrator's guidelines.

Tips: Looks for "short, crisp career profiles of 1,000 words with plenty of information to break out into graphics."

FACES, The Magazine About People, Cobblestone Publishing, Inc., 7 School St., Peterborough NH 03458. (603)924-7209. Fax: (603)924-7380. Editor-in-Chief: Carolyn P. Yoder. Art Director: Ann C. Webster. Picture Editor: Francelle Carapetyan. Magazine published 9 times/year (September-May). Circ. 15,000. "Although *Faces* operates on a by-assignment basis, we welcome ideas/suggestions in outline form. All manuscripts are reviewed by the American Museum of Natural History in New York before being accepted. *Faces* is a theme-related magazine; writers should send for theme list before submitting ideas/queries."

Fiction: Middle readers, young adults: anthropology, contemporary, folktales, history, multicultural, religious. Does not want to see material that does not relate to a specific upcoming theme. Buys 9 mss/year. Maximum word length: 800. Byline given.

Nonfiction: Middle readers, young adults: anthropology, arts/crafts, games/puzzles, history, interview/profile, religious, travel. Does not want to see material not related to a specific upcoming theme. Buys 63 mss/year. Average word length: 300-800. Byline given.

How to Contact/Writers: Fiction/nonfiction: Query with published clips and 2-3 line biographical sketch. "Ideas should be submitted six to nine months prior to the publication date. Responses to ideas are usually sent approximately four months before the publication date."

Illustration: Buys 3 illustrations/issue; buys 27 illustrations/year. Preferred theme or style: Material that is meticulously researched (most articles are written by professional anthropologists); simple, direct style preferred, but not too juvenile. Reviews ms/illustration packages; reviews artwork for future assignments; works on assignment only.

How to Contact/Illustrators: Ms/illustration packages: Illustration is done by assignment. Roughs required. Illustrations only: Send samples of b&w work. "Illustrators should consult issues of *Faces* to familiarize themselves with our needs." Reports on art samples in 1-2 months. Original artwork returned at job's completion (upon written request).

Photography: Wants photos relating to forthcoming themes.

Terms: Pays on publication. Buys all rights for mss and artwork. Pays 10¢/word for assigned articles. Pays $10-125/b&w (inside) illustration. Covers are assigned and paid on an individual basis. Pays photographers $15-75/photo. Sample copy $3.95 with 7½×10½ SAE and 5 first-class stamps. Writer's/illustrator's/photo guidelines free with SAE and 1 first-class stamp.

Tips: "Writers are encouraged to study past issues of the magazine to become familiar with our style and content. Writers with anthropological and/or travel experience are particularly encouraged; *Faces* is about world cultures. All feature articles, recipes and activities are freelance contributions." Illustrators: "Submit b&w samples, not too juvenile. Study past issues to know what we look for. The illustration we use is generally for retold legends, recipes and activities." (See listing for *Cobblestone: The History Magazine for Young People; Calliope: The World History Magazine for Young People; ODYSSEY: Science That's Out of This World.*)

FAITH 'N STUFF, The Magazine For Kids, Guideposts Associates, Inc., 16 E. 34th St., New York NY 10016. Editor: Mary Lou Carney. Articles Editor: Sailor Metts. Fiction Editor: Lurlene McDaniel. Art Director: Mike Lyons. Photo Editor: Mary Ann Tanner. Bimonthly magazine. Estab. 1990. Circ. 120,000. "*Faith 'n Stuff, The Magazine for Kids* is published bimonthly by Guideposts Associates, Inc. for kids 7-12 years old (emphasis on upper end of that age bracket). It is a Bible-based, direct mail magazine that is *fun*

Refer to the Business of Children's Writing & Illustrating for up-to-date marketing, tax and legal information.

to read. It is *not* a Sunday school take-home paper or a miniature *Guideposts*."

Fiction: Middle readers: adventure, animal, contemporary, fantasy, historical, humorous, multicultural, problem-solving, science fiction, sports, suspense/mystery. Multicultural needs include: Kids in other cultures—school, sports, families. Does not want to see preachy fiction. "We want real stories about real kids doing real things—conflicts our readers will respect; resolutions our readers will accept. Problematic. Tight. Filled with realistic dialogue and sharp imagery. No stories about 'good' children always making the right decision. If present at all, adults are minor characters and *do not* solve kids' problems for them." Buys approximately 10 mss/year. Average word length: 500-1,500. Byline given.

Nonfiction: Middle readers: animal, interview/profile. "Make nonfiction issue-oriented, controversial, thought-provoking. Something kids not only *need* to know, but *want* to know as well." Buys 10 mss/year. Average word length: 200-1,300. Bylines sometimes given.

How to Contact/Writers: Fiction: Send complete ms. Nonfiction: Query. Reports on queries in 6 weeks; on ms in 2 months.

How to Contact/Illustrators: Send promo sheet, tearsheets. Reports back only if interested. Credit line given.

Photography: Looks for "spontaneous, *real* kids in action shots."

Terms: Pays on acceptance. Buys all rights for mss. "Features range in payment from $150-350; fiction from $150-250. We pay higher rates for stories exceptionally well-written or well-researched. Regular contributors get bigger bucks, too." Additional payment for ms/illustration packages "but we prefer to acquire our own illustrations." Sample copies are $3.25. Writer's guidelines free for SASE.

Tips: "Make your manuscript good, relevant and playful. No preachy stories about Bible-toting children. *Faith 'n Stuff* is not a beginner's market. Study our magazine. (Sure, you've heard that before—but it's *necessary*!) Neatness *does* count. So do creativity and professionalism. SASE essential."

*FALCON MAGAZINE, Falcon Press, 48 Last Chance Gulch, P.O. Box 1718, Helena MT 59624. (406)442-6597. Executive Editor: Kay Morton Ellerhoff. Associate Editor: Carolyn Zieg Cunningham. Design Director: Bryan Knaff. Bimonthly magazine. Estab. 1993. Circ. 55,000. "A magazine for young conservationists."

Nonfiction: Middle readers: animal, arts/crafts (nature oriented), cooking (outdoor), nature/environment. Maximum word length: 800. Byline given.

How to Contact/Writers: Nonfiction: Query. Reports in 2 months. Publishes ms 6 months after acceptance.

Illustration: Buys 6 illustrations/issue; 75 illustrations/year. Reviews ms/illustration packages; reviews artwork for future assignments. Prefers to work on assignment.

How to Contact/Illustrators: Illustrations only: Query; send slides, tearsheets. Reports in 2 months. Samples returned with SASE; samples sometimes filed. Original work returned upon job's completion. Credit line given.

Photography: *Must* be submitted in 20-slide sheets and individual protectors. Looks for "children outdoors—camping, fishing, doing 'nature' projects." Model/property releases required. Photo captions required. Uses 35mm transparencies. To contact photographers should query with samples. Reports in 2 months.

Terms: Pays on publication. Buys one-time rights for mss and photographs. Pays $200 minimum for articles. Additional payment for ms/illustration packages. Pays illustrators $40 b&w inside; $250 color cover; $50-100 color inside. Photographers paid by the project ($50 minimum); per photo (range: $50-100). Sample copies for 8½×11 SAE. Writer's/illustrator's/photo guidelines for SASE.

FFA NEW HORIZONS, The Official Magazine of the National FFA Organization, 5632 Mt. Vernon Memorial Hwy., Alexandria VA 22309. (703)360-3600. Fax: (703)360-5524. Articles Editor: Andrew Markwart. Bimonthly magazine. Estab. 1952. Circ. 400,000. *"FFA New Horizons* strives to strengthen the aims and purposes of FFA by bringing to our readers living examples of how these are being fulfilled daily by individual FFA members."

Nonfiction: Young adults: animal, biography, careers, education, health, hobbies, how-to, humorous, interview/profile, nature/environment, problem-solving, sports. "All stories must be directed toward teens and have an FFA connection. Does not want to see stories that have no FFA connection at all." Average word length: 600-1,000.

How to Contact/Writers: Nonfiction: Query with published clips. Send complete ms. Reports on queries/mss in 1 month. Publishes ms 2-4 months after acceptance. Will consider simultaneous submissions and electronic submissions via disk or modem.

Illustration: Buys 6 illustrations/year. Reviews ms/illustration packages; reviews artwork for future assignments; works on assignment only.

How to Contact/Illustrators: Ms/illustration packages: Query. Illustrations only: Query with samples. Reports in 1 month. Original work not returned.

Photography: Looking for "photos that show the FFA member and illustrate the story." Uses 5×7 color and b&w prints; 35mm transparencies. Reports in 1 month.

Terms: Pays on acceptance. Buys all rights for mss, artwork and photographs. Pay varies. Photographers paid per photo. Sample copies for 9×12 SAE and 5 first-class stamps. Writer's/illustrator's/photo guidelines for SASE.

*FOCUS ON THE FAMILY CLUBHOUSE; FOCUS ON THE FAMILY CLUBHOUSE JR., Focus on the Family, 8605 Explorer Dr., Colorado Springs CO 80920. (719)531-3400. Editor: Linda Piepenbrink. Assistant Editor: Lisa Brock. Art Director: Timothy Jones. Monthly magazine. Estab. 1987. Combined circulation is 250,000. *"Focus on the Family Clubhouse* is a 16-page Christian magazine, published monthly, for children ages 8-12. Similarly, *Focus on the Family Clubhouse Jr.* is published for children ages 4-8. We want fresh, exciting literature that promotes biblical thinking, values and behavior in every area of life, not just in the 'religious' arena."

Fiction: Picture-oriented material and young readers: adventure, animal, contemporary, folktales, religious. Middle readers: adventure, animal, contemporary, folktales, history, humorous, nature/environment, religious. Buys 6-10 mss/year. Average word length: *Clubhouse,* 500-1,400; *Clubhouse Jr.,* 250-1,100. Byline given on all fiction; not on puzzles.

Nonfiction: Picture-oriented material and young readers: animal, arts/crafts, cooking, games/puzzles, hobbies, how-to, nature/environment, religion, science. Middle readers: animal, arts/crafts, biography, cooking, games/puzzles, history, hobbies, how-to, humorous, interview/profile, nature/environment, religion, science, social issues, sports. Buys 3-5 mss/year. Average word length: 200-1,000. Byline given.

Poetry: Wants to see "humorous or biblical" poetry. Maximum length: 25 lines.

How to Contact/Writers: Fiction/nonfiction: send complete ms. Reports in 4-6 weeks. Publishes ms 4-6 months after acceptance.

Illustration: "Most illustrations are done on assignment." Reviews ms/illustration packages; reviews artwork for future assignments; works on assignment mostly.

How to Contact/Illustrators: Ms/illustration packages: submit ms with rough sketches. Illustrations only: send résumé, promo sheet, portfolio and tearsheets. Samples returned with SASE; samples kept on file. Original work returned at job's completion. Credit line given.

Photography: Uses 35mm transparencies. Photographers should query with samples; provide résumé and promotional literature or tearsheets. Reports in 2 months.

Terms: Pays on acceptance. Buys first North American serial rights and reprint rights (occasionally) for mss. Purchases first rights for artwork and photographs. Additional payment for ms/illustration packages. Photographers paid by the project or per photo. Sample copies for 9×12 SAE and 3 first-class stamps. Writers'/illustrator/photo guidelines for SASE.

Tips: "The best stories avoid moralizing or preachiness, and are not written *down* to children. They are the products of writers who share in the adventure with their readers, exploring the characters they have created without knowing for certain where the story will lead. And they are not always explicitly Christian, but are built upon a Christian foundation (and, at the very least, do not contradict biblical views or values)."

FOR SENIORS ONLY, Campus Communications, Inc., 339 N. Main St., New City NY 10956. (914)638-0333. Articles/Fiction Editor: Judi Oliff. Art Director: Randi Wendelkin. Semiannual magazine. Estab. 1971. Circ. 350,000. Publishes career-oriented articles for high school students; college-related articles, and feature articles on travel, etc.

Fiction: Young adults: health, humorous, sports, travel. Byline given.

Nonfiction: Young adults: careers, games/puzzles, health, how-to, humorous, interview/profile, social issues, sports, travel. Buys 4-6 mss/year. Average word length: 1,000-2,500. Byline given.

How to Contact/Writers: Fiction/nonfiction: Query; query with published clips; send complete ms. Publishes ms 2-4 months after acceptance. Will consider simultaneous submissions, electronic submissions via disk or modem and previously published work.

Illustration: Reviews ms/illustration packages; reviews artwork for future assignments.

How to Contact/Illustrators: Ms/illustration packages: Query; submit complete package with final art; submit ms with rough sketches. Illustrations only: Query; send slides. Reports back only if interested. Samples not returned; samples kept on file. Original work returned upon job's completion. Credit line given.

Photography: Model/property release required. Uses 5½×8½ and 4⅞×7⅜ color prints; 35mm and 8×10 transparencies. Photographers should query with samples; send unsolicited photos by mail. Reports back only if interested.

Terms: Pays on publication. Buys exclusive magazine rights. Payment is byline credit. Writer's/illustrator's/photo guidelines for SASE.

*FREEWAY, Scripture Press Publications, Inc., Box 632, Glen Ellyn IL 60138. (708)688-6000. Articles/Fiction Editor: Amy J. Cox. Art Director: Blake Ebel. Quarterly in weekly issues. Estab. 1973. "*FreeWay* is a Sunday School take-home paper aimed at high school and college age Christian youth. It's primary objective is to show how biblical principles for Christian living can be applied to everyday life."

Fiction: Young adults/teens: contemporary, humorous, problem-solving, religious, sports. "Stories must have a clear, spiritual 'take-away' value based on a biblical principle. Please no tacked-on morals or unrealistic conclusions." Buys approximately 45 mss/year. Average word length: 400-1,200. Byline given.

Nonfiction: Young adults/teens: how-to, humorous, interview/profile, multicultural (missionaries, personal experience, teens in other cultures), problem-solving, puzzles, religion, social issues, sports. "We're looking for true stories—personal experience, profiles, and 'as told to.' We also buy articles on teen issues: dating, peer pressure, family relationships, daily Bible study and prayer, etc. All must have clear, biblical basis." Buys approximately 75 mss/year. Average word length: 400-1,200. Byline given.

Poetry: Maximum length: 25 lines. Limit submissions to 5 poems.

How to Contact/Writers: Fiction/nonfiction: Send complete ms. Reports on mss in 2-3 months. Publishes ms at least one year after acceptance. Will consider simultaneous submissions and previously published work.

Illustration: Buys 15 illustrations/year. Uses b&w artwork only. Reviews artwork for future assignments; works on assignment only.

How to Contact/Illustrators: Illustrations only: Send résumé and promo sheet. Reports only if interested. Original work returned at job's completion. Credit line given.

Photography: Looks for "action shots, minorities, mood shots, relationship shots, sports, school, teen hangouts, etc. Modest clothing, jewelry, etc." Model/property releases required. Uses b&w 8 × 10 or 5 × 7 prints. Photographers should query with samples. Reports only if interested.

Terms: Pays on acceptance. Buys one-time rights for mss. Purchases one-time rights for artwork and photographs. Pays $25-150 for stories; $25-150 for articles. Payment for illustrations negotiated with designer. Sample copies for #10 SAE and 1 first-class stamp. Writer's/photo guidelines for SASE.

Tips: "*FreeWay* is a great break-in point. We rely heavily upon freelancers. Each weekly issue contains at least 2 freelance-written features plus at least 2 photographs or illustrations. However, we have a narrow audience. We want stories and articles which will help our readers grow in the Christian faith—without being unrealistic or preachy."

THE FRIEND MAGAZINE, The Church of Jesus Christ of Latter-day Saints, 50 E. North Temple, Salt Lake City UT 84150. (801)240-2210. Managing Editor: Vivian Paulsen. Art Director: Richard Brown. Monthly magazine. Estab. 1971. Circ. 350,000. Magazine for 3-11-year-olds.

Fiction: Picture material, young readers, middle readers: adventure, animal, contemporary, folktales, history, humorous, problem-solving, religious, ethnic, sports, suspense/mystery. Does not want to see controversial issues, political, horror, fantasy. Average word length: 400-1,000. Byline given.

Nonfiction: Picture material, young readers, middle readers: animal, arts/crafts, biography, cooking, games/puzzles, history, how-to, humorous, problem-solving, religious, sports. Does not want to see controversial issues, political, horror, fantasy. Average word length: 400-1,000. Byline given.

Poetry: Reviews poetry. Maximum line length: 20.

How to Contact/Writers: Fiction/nonfiction: Send complete ms. Reports on mss in 2 months.

How to Contact/Illustrators: Illustrators only: Query with samples; arrange personal interview to show portfolio; provide résumé and tearsheets for files.

Terms: Pays on acceptance. Buys all rights for mss. Pays 9-11¢/word for unsolicited articles. Contributors are encouraged to send for free sample copy with 9 × 11 envelope and $1.00 postage. Free writer's guidelines.

Tips: "The *Friend* is published by The Church of Jesus Christ of Latter-day Saints for boys and girls up to twelve years of age. All submissions are carefully read by the *Friend* staff, and those not accepted are returned within two months when a self-addressed, stamped envelope is enclosed. Submit seasonal material at least eight months in advance. Query letters and simultaneous submissions are not encouraged. Authors may request rights to have their work reprinted after their manuscript is published."

THE GOLDFINCH, Iowa History for Young People, State Historical Society of Iowa, 402 Iowa Ave., Iowa City IA 52240. (319)354-3916. Fax: (319)335-3924. Editor: Deborah Gore Ohrn. Quarterly magazine. Estab. 1980. Circ. 2,500. "The award-winning *Goldfinch* consists of 10-12 nonfiction articles, short fiction, poetry and activities per issue. Each magazine focuses on an aspect or theme of history that occurred in or affected Iowa."

Fiction: Middle readers: adventure, animal, folktales, history. Fiction only on spec. Buys approximately 4 mss/year. Average word length: 500-1,500. Byline given.

Nonfiction: Middle readers: arts/crafts, biography, games/puzzles, history, how-to, interview/profile, travel. Uses 20-30 mss/year. Average word length: 500-1,500. Byline given.

Poetry: Reviews poetry. No minimum or maximum word length; no maximum number of submissions.

How to Contact/Writers: Fiction/nonfiction: Query with published clips. Reports on queries/mss in 2-4 weeks. Publishes ms 1 month-1 year after acceptance. Will consider electronic submissions via disk or modem.

Illustration: Buys 4 illustrations/issue; 20 illustrations/year. Uses b&w artwork only. Prefers cartoon, line drawing. Reviews ms/illustration packages; reviews artwork for future assignments; works on assignment only.

How to Contact/Illustrators: Ms/illustration packages: Query. Illustrations only: Query with samples. Reports in 2-4 weeks. Original work returned upon job's completion.

Photography: Types of photos used vary with subject. Model/property releases required with submissions. Uses b&w prints; 35mm transparencies. Query with samples. Reports in 2-4 weeks.

Terms: Pays on acceptance (artwork only). Buys all rights. Payment for mss is in copies at this time. Pays illustrators $10-150. Photographers paid per photo (range: $10-100). Sample copies are $3. Writer's/illustrator's/photo guidelines free for SASE.

Tips: "The editor researches the topic and determines the articles. Writers, most of whom live in Iowa, work from primary and secondary research materials to write pieces. The presentation is aimed at children 8-14 and the writing of E.B. White is a model for the prose."

GUIDE MAGAZINE, Review and Herald Publishing Association, 55 W. Oak Ridge Dr., Hagerstown MD 21740. (301)791-7000. Articles Editor: Jeannette Johnson. Art Director: Bill Kirstein. Weekly magazine. Estab. 1953. Circ. 40,000. "Ours is a weekly Christian journal written for middle readers and young adults, presenting true stories relevant to the needs of today's young person, emphasizing positive aspects of Christian living."

Fiction: Middle readers, young adults: adventure, animal, character-building, contemporary, history, humorous, nature/environment, problem solving, religious, sports, suspense/mystery. "We like 'true-to-life,' that is, based on true happenings." No violence. No articles. "We always need humorous adventure stories."

Nonfiction: Middle readers, young adults: animal, biography, character-building, games/puzzles, history, how-to, humorous, nature/environment, problem solving, religious, social issues, sports. Does not want to see violence, hunting. Buys 300 mss/year. Average word length: 500-600 minimum, 1,000-1,200 maximum. Byline given.

How to Contact/Writers: Nonfiction: Send complete ms. Reports in 1-2 weeks. Will consider simultaneous submissions. "We can only pay half of the regular amount for simultaneous submissions." Reports on queries/mss in 1 week. Credit line given.

Illustration: Buys 4-6 illustrations/issue; buys 350 illustrations/year. Reviews artwork for future assignments. Works on assignment only.

How to Contact/Illustrators: Ms/illustration packages: "Art is by assignment only. Glad to look at portfolios." Illustrations only: Send tearsheets. Reports back only if interested. Original artwork returned at job's completion. Credit line given.

Photography: Purchases photos by assignment only.

Terms: Pays on acceptance. Buys first North American serial rights; first rights; one-time rights; second serial (reprint rights); simultaneous rights. Pays $125-300 for stories and articles. "Writer receives several complimentary copies of issue in which work appears." Pays illustrators $150-250/b&w (cover); $175-300/color (cover); $125-175/b&w (inside); $150-175/color (inside). Photographers paid per photo (range: $50-175). Sample copy free with 5×9 SAE and 2 first-class stamps; writer's/illustrator's guidelines for SASE.

Tips: Children's magazines "want mystery, action, discovery, suspense and humor—no matter what the topic."

HICALL, Gospel Publishing House, 1445 Boonville Ave., Springfield MO 65802-1894. (417)862-2781, ext. 4359. Articles/Fiction Editor: Tammy Bicket. Art Director: Richard Harmon. Quarterly newsletter (Sunday school take-home paper). Estab. 1920. Circ. 80,000. "Slant articles toward the 15- to 17-year-old teen. We are a Christian publication, so all articles should focus on the Christian's responses to life. Fiction should be realistic, not syrupy nor too graphic. Fiction should have a Christian slant also."

Fiction: Young adults: adventure, contemporary, fantasy, history, humorous, problem-solving, religious, romance, sports. Also wants fiction based on true stories. Buys 100 mss/year. Average word length 1,000-1,500. Byline given.

Nonfiction: Young adults: "thoughtful treatment of contemporary issues (i.e. racism, preparing for the future); interviews with famous Christians who have noteworthy stories to tell." Buys 50 mss/year. "Looking for more articles and fewer stories." Average word length: 1,000. Byline given.

How to Contact/Writers: Fiction/nonfiction: Send complete ms. Do *not* send query letters. Reports on mss in 4-6 weeks. Will consider simultaneous submissions.

Illustration: Buys 10-30 illustrations/year. Uses color artwork only. "Freelance art used only when in-house art department has a work overload." Prefers to review "realistic, cartoon, youth-oriented styles." Will review artwork for future assignments. Works on assignment only. "Any art sent will be referred to the art department. Art department will assign freelance art."

How to Contact/Illustrators: Illustrations only: Query with samples; send "tearsheets, slides, photos. Résumé helpful." Reports in 4-6 weeks.

Photography: "Teen photos that look spontaneous. Ethnic and urban photos urgently needed." Uses color prints, 35mm, 2¼×2¼, 4×5 transparencies. To contact, send unsolicited photos by mail.

Terms: Pays on acceptance. For mss, buys first North American serial rights, first rights, one-time rights, second serial (reprint rights), simultaneous rights. For artwork, buys one-time rights for cartoons, all rights for assigned illustrations; one-time rights for photos. Pays 2-4¢/word for articles. Pays $35/b&w cover photo; $50/color cover photo; $25/b&w inside photo; $35/color inside photo. Sample copy free with 6×9 SASE. Writer's guidelines free with SASE.

HIGH ADVENTURE, Assemblies of God, 1445 Boonville Ave., Springfield MO 65802. (417)862-2781, Ext. 4181. Fax: (417)862-0416. Editor: Marshall Bruner. Quarterly magazine. Circ. 86,000. Estab. 1971. Magazine is designed to provide boys with worthwhile, enjoyable, leisure reading; to challenge them in narrative form to higher ideals and greater spiritual dedication; and to perpetuate the spirit of Royal Rangers through stories, ideas and illustrations. 75% of material aimed at juvenile audience.

Fiction: Buys 100 mss/year. Average word length: 1,000. Byline given.

Nonfiction: Articles: Christian living, devotional, Holy Spirit, salvation, self-help; biography; missionary stories; news items; testimonies, inspirational stories based on true-life experiences.

How to Contact/Writers: Fiction/nonfiction: Send complete ms. Reports on queries in 6-8 weeks. Will consider simultaneous submissions. Will review ms/illustration packages.

How to Contact/Illustrators: Ms/illustration packages: Send complete ms with final art. Illustrations only: "Most of our artwork is done in-house."

Terms: Pays on acceptance. Buys first and second rights. Pays 2-3¢/word for articles. Sample copy free with 9×12 SASE. Free writer's/illustrator's guidelines for SASE.

HIGHLIGHTS FOR CHILDREN, 803 Church St., Honesdale PA 18431. (717)253-1080. Manuscript Coordinator: Beth Troop. Art Director: Rosanne Guararra. Monthly (July-August issue combined) magazine. Estab. 1946. Circ. 2.8 million. Our motto is "Fun With a Purpose." We are looking for quality fiction and nonfiction that appeals to children, encourages them to read, and reinforces positive values. All art is done on assignment.

Fiction: Picture-oriented material: animal, contemporary, fantasy, folktales, history, humorous, problem solving. Young readers, middle readers: animal, contemporary, fantasy, history, humorous, problem solving, science fiction, sports, mystery/adventure. Does not want to see: war, crime, violence. Would like to see more: stories/articles with world culture settings, sports pieces, action/adventure. Buys 150 mss/year. Average word length: 400-800. Byline given.

Nonfiction: Picture-oriented material: animal, history, how-to, humorous, problem solving. Young readers, middle readers: animal, arts, foreign, history, how-to, humorous, interview/profile, nature, problem solving, science, sports. Does not want to see: trendy topics, fads, personalities who would not be good role models for children, guns, war, crime, violence. Buys 75 mss/year. Maximum word length: 900. Byline given.

How to Contact/Writers: Send complete ms. Reports on queries in 4 weeks; mss in 4-6 weeks.

Illustration: Preferred theme or style: Realistic, some stylization, cartoon style acceptable. Works on assignment only.

How to Contact/Illustrators: Ms/illustration packages: Art is done on assignment only. Illustrations only: Photocopies, tearsheets, or slides. Résumé optional. Reports on art samples in 4 weeks.

Terms: Pays on acceptance. Buys all rights. Pays 14¢/word and up for unsolicited articles. "Illustration fees vary on size of job. Median range: $350-600. Pays more for covers." Writer's/illustrator's guidelines free on request.

Tips: Writers: "Analyze several issues of the magazines you want to write for. Send for writer's guidelines." Illustrators: "Fresh, imaginative work presented in a professional portfolio encouraged. Flexibility in working relationships a plus. Illustrators presenting their work need not confine themselves to just children's illustrations as long as work can translate to our needs. We also use animal illustrations, real and imaginary. We need party plans, crafts and puzzles—any activity that will stimulate children mentally and creatively. We are always looking for imaginative cover subjects."

*HOB-NOB, 994 Nissley Rd., Lancaster PA 17601. (717)898-7807. Articles/Fiction/Poetry Editor, Art Director: M. K. Henderson. Semiannual magazine. Circ. 350. *Hob-Nob* began as a "family" publication and prefers to avoid any material that could or should not be read by younger readers. There is now a separate "Family Section" in the magazine, approximately 20 pages of material for young children to teens. 30% of prose in current issue aimed at juvenile audience.

Fiction: Picture-oriented material (preschool-8 years): animal, fantasy, humorous, multicultural. Young readers: adventure, animal, folktales, humorous, nature/environment. Middle readers: adventure, animal, contemporary, fantasy, folktales, history, humorous, nature/environment, problem-solving, science fiction, sports, suspense/mystery. Young adults: adventure, contemporary, fantasy, history, humorous, nature/environment, problem solving, religious, romance, science fiction, sports, spy/mystery/adventure, suspense. Does not want to see religious proselytizing material geared to specific denominations or categories of denominations (i.e., "fundamentalist"); "clean" only, no bathroom language. Buys 100 mss/year (all age levels; juvenile—18 in current issue). Maximum word length: 2,000. Byline given.

Nonfiction: Picture-oriented material: arts/crafts, games/puzzles, hobbies, how-to, humorous. Young readers: animal, arts/crafts, biography, games/puzzles, humorous, hobbies, how-to, nature/environment. Middle readers: animal, arts/crafts, biography, careers, hobbies, humorous, interview/profile, nature/environment, problem-solving, science, sports. Young adults: animal, arts/crafts, biography, careers, hobbies, humorous, interview/profile, nature/environment, problem solving, science, sports. Buys 15-20 mss/year, (all ages; juvenile—4 in current issue). Maximum word length: 1,000. Byline given.

How to Contact/Writers: Fiction/nonfiction: Send complete ms. SASE (IRC) for answer to query/return of ms. Reports on queries/mss in 2 months or less. Will consider photocopied and computer printout submissions.

Illustration: "I don't have space for large illustrations so I use cuts, suitable drawings from miscellaneous small ones sent by certain readers." Uses b&w artwork only, no intermediate values. Will review ms/illustration packages. Will review small picture(s) appropriate to a submitted ms.

How to Contact/Illustrators: Ms/illustration packages: Send complete ms and final b&w drawing, small size. Reports on art samples in 2 months or less. Original artwork returned at job's completion if requested and SASE supplied.

Terms: Acquires first or one-time rights. Pays in contributor copies. Sample copy for $3. Writer's guidelines free or sent with sample if requested. $5 paid for illustrations used to illustrate stories (serendipitously found!); $10 prize per issue for best children's story (or poem) as selected by readers.

Tips: Will consider short poetry (up to 16 lines) by and for juveniles. "Write what children will enjoy—test out on your own children if possible." Looks for: "shorter fiction, especially humor or whimsy. First time contributors may submit only in January and February; established contributors may submit September through February only." Publication most open to "cartoons." Current minimum of two years before new contributors' work can appear.

HOBSON'S CHOICE, P.O. Box 98, Ripley OH 45167. (513)392-4549. Editor: Susannah C. West. Monthly magazine. Estab. 1974. Circ. 2,000. "*Hobson's Choice* is a science fiction magazine which also publishes science and technology-related nonfiction along with the stories. Although the magazine is not specifically aimed at children, we do number teenagers among our readers. Such readers are the type who might enjoy reading science fiction (both young adult and adult), attending science fiction conventions, using computers, and be interested in such things as astronomy, the space program, etc."

Fiction: Young adults: fantasy, folktales, science fiction. Buys 12-15 mss/year. Average word length 2,000-10,000. Does not want to see horror or cyberpunk.

Nonfiction: Young adults: biography, careers, education, how-to (science), informational science book review, interview/profile, math, science. Does not want to see crafts. Buys 8-10 mss/year. Average word length: 1,500-5,000. Byline given.

How to Contact/Writers: Fiction: Send complete ms. Nonfiction: query first. Reports on queries/mss in 2-3 months. ("After 16 weeks, author should feel free to withdraw ms from consideration.") Will consider submissions via disk (Macintosh MacWrite, WriteNow, IBM PC or compatible on 3½ disks).

Illustration: Buys 2-5 illustrations/issue; buys 20-30 illustrations/year. Uses b&w artwork only. Prefers to review "science fiction, fantasy or technical illustration." Reviews ms/illustration packages; reviews artwork for future assignments.

How to Contact/Illustrators: Ms/illustration packages: "Would like to see clips to keep on file (b&w only, preferably photocopies)." Illustrations only: Query with tearsheets to be kept on file. "If we have an assignment for an artist, we will contact him/her with the ms we want illustrated. We like to see roughs before giving the go-ahead for final artwork." Reports in 2-3 months. Original artwork returned at job's completion,

The asterisk before a listing indicates the listing is new in this edition.

"sometimes, if requested. We prefer to retain originals, but a high-quality PMT or Velox is fine if artist wants to keep artwork." Credit line given.

Photography: Purchases photos with accompanying ms only. Uses b&w prints. Wants photos for nonfiction.

Terms: Pays 50% on acceptance (for art), 50% on publication. Pays 25% on acceptance (for writing), 75% on publication. Buys first North American serial rights; second serial (reprint rights). Buys first rights for artwork and photographs. Pays $20-100 for stories/articles. Pay illustrators $5-25/b&w inside. Sample copy $2.25; writer's/illustrator's guidelines free with business-size SAE and 1 first-class stamp. "Specify fiction or nonfiction guidelines, or both." Tip sheet package for $1.25 and business-size envelope with 1 first-class stamp (includes all guidelines and tips on writing science fiction and science nonfiction).

Tips: Writers: "Read lots of children's writing in general, especially specific genre if you're writing a genre story (science fiction, romance, mystery, etc.). We list upcoming needs in our guidelines; writers can study these to get an idea of what we're looking for." Illustrators: "Study illustrations in back issues of magazines you're interested in illustrating for, and be able to work in a genre style if that's the type of magazine you want to publish your work. Everything is open to freelancers, as almost all our artwork is done out-of-house. (We occasionally use public domain illustrations, copyright-free illustrations and photographs.)"

*THE HOME ALTAR, Meditations for Families with Children, Augsburg Fortress, 426 S. Fifth St., Box 1209, Minneapolis MN 55440. Articles/Fiction Editor: Carol A. Burk. Quarterly magazine. Circ. 70,000. This is a booklet of daily devotions, used primarily by Lutheran families. Each day's reading focuses on a specific Bible passage. 98% of material aimed at juvenile audience.

Fiction: Young readers, middle readers: contemporary, folktales, problem-solving, religious. Buys 365 mss/year. Average word length: 125-170. Byline given.

Nonfiction: Young readers, middle readers: interview/profile, problem solving, religious. Average word length: 125-170. Byline given.

How to Contact/Writers: Fiction/nonfiction: Query with published clips.

Illustration: Buys 100 illustrations/year. Works on assignment only.

How to Contact/Illustrators: Reports on art samples only if interested.

Terms: Pays on acceptance. Buys all rights. Pays $10 for assigned articles. Free writer's guidelines for 6×9 SAE and 98¢ postage.

HOPSCOTCH, The Magazine for Girls, The Bluffton News Publishing and Printing Company, 103 N. Main St., Bluffton OH 45817. (419)358-4610. Editor: Marilyn Edwards. Bimonthly magazine. Estab. 1989. Circ. 9,000. For girls ages 6-12, featuring traditional subjects—pets, games, hobbies, nature, science, sports etc.—with an emphasis on articles that show girls actively involved in unusual and/or worthwhile activities."

Fiction: Young readers and middle readers: adventure, animal, contemporary, fantasy, folktales, health, history, humorous, multicultural, nature/environment, problem solving, sports, suspense/mystery. Does not want to see stories dealing with dating, sex, fashion, hard rock music. Buys 24 mss/year. Average word length: 300-1,000. Byline given.

Nonfiction: Young readers and middle readers: animal, arts/crafts, biography, careers, cooking, games/puzzles, health, history, hobbies, how-to, humorous, interview/profile, math, multicultural, nature/environment, problem solving, science. Does not want to see pieces dealing with dating, sex, fashion, hard rock music. "Need more nonfiction with quality photos about a *Hopscotch*-age girl involved in a worthwhile activity." Buys 46 mss/year. Average word length: 400-1,000. Byline given.

Poetry: Reviews traditional, wholesome, humorous poems. Maximum word length: 400; maximum line length: 40. Will accept 6 submissions/author.

How to Contact/Writers: Fiction: Send complete ms. Nonfiction: Query, send complete ms. Reports on queries in 3 weeks; on mss in 2 months. Publishes ms 1-2 years after acceptance. Will consider simultaneous submissions.

Illustration: Buys 8-12 illustrations/issue; buys 50-60 illustrations/year. "Generally, the illustrations are assigned after we have purchased a piece (usually fiction). Occasionally, we will use a painting—in any given medium—for the cover, and these are usually seasonal." Uses b&w artwork only for inside; color for cover. Will review ms/illustration packages. Will review artwork for future assignments.

How to Contact/Illustrators: Ms/illustration packages: Query first or send complete ms with final art. Illustrations only: Send résumé, portfolio, client list and tearsheets. Reports on art samples in 2 weeks. Original artwork returned at job's completion. Credit line given.

Photography: Purchases photos separately (cover only) and with accompanying ms. Prefers photos to accompany articles. Model/property releases required. Uses 5×7, b&w prints; 35mm transparencies. Black & white photos should go with ms. Should have girl or girls age 6-12.

Terms: For mss, pays a few months ahead of publication. For mss, artwork and photos, buys first North American serial rights; second serial (reprint rights). Pays $30-100 for stories/articles. "We always send a copy of the issue to the writer or illustrator." Text and art are treated separately. Pays $100-150/color cover; $5-15/b&w inside. Photographers paid per photo (range: $5-15; $150 for color cover photo). Sample copy for $3. Writer's/illustrator's guidelines free for #10 SASE.

Tips: "Please look at our guidelines and our magazine . . . and remember, we use far more nonfiction than fiction. If decent photos accompany the piece, it stands an even better chance of being accepted. We believe it is the responsibility of the contributor to come up with photos. Please remember, our readers are 6-12 years—most are 7-10— and your text should reflect that. Many magazines try to entertain first and educate second. We try to do the reverse of that. Our magazine is more simplistic like a book, to be read from cover to cover."

HUMPTY DUMPTY'S MAGAZINE, Children's Better Health Institute, 1100 Waterway Blvd., P.O. Box 567, Indianapolis IN 46206. (317)636-8881. Editor: Christine French Clark. Art Director: Lawrence Simmons. Magazine published 8 times/year—January/ February; March; April/May; June; July/August; September; October/November; December. *HDM* is edited for kindergarten children, approximately ages 4-6. It includes fiction (easy-to-reads; read alouds; rhyming stories; rebus stories), nonfiction articles (some with photo illustrations), poems, crafts, recipes and puzzles. Much of the content encourages development of better health habits. We especially need material promoting fitness. "All but 2 pages aimed at the juvenile market. The remainder may be seasonal and/or more general."

Fiction: Picture-oriented material: animal, contemporary, fantasy, health-related, humorous, sports. Young readers: animal, contemporary, fantasy, humorous, science fiction, sports, suspense/mystery/adventure, health-related. Does not want to see bunny-rabbits-with-carrot-pies stories! Also, talking inanimate objects are very difficult to do well. Beginners (and maybe everyone) should avoid these. Buys 35-50 mss/year. Maximum word length: 700. Byline given.

Nonfiction: Picture-oriented material, young readers: animal, how-to, health-related, humorous, interview/profile. Does not want to see long, boring, encyclopedia rehashes. "We're open to almost any subject (although most of our nonfiction has a health angle), but it must be presented creatively. Don't just string together some facts." Looks for a fresh approach. Buys 6-10 mss/year. Prefers very short nonfiction pieces—500 words maximum. Byline given.

How to Contact/Writers: Send complete ms. Nonfiction: Send complete ms with bibliography if applicable. "No queries, please!" Reports on mss in 8-10 weeks.

Illustration: Buys 13-16 illustrations/issue; buys 90-120 illustrations/year. Preferred style: Realistic or cartoon. Will review ms/illustration packages. Will review artwork for future assignments. Works on assignment only.

How to Contact/Illustrators: Ms/illustration packages: Send slides, printed pieces or photocopies. Illustrations only: Send slides, printed pieces or photocopies. Reports on art samples only if interested.

Terms: Writers: Pays on publication. Artists: Pays within 6-8 weeks. Buys all rights. "One-time book rights may be returned if author can provide name of interested book publisher and tentative date of publication." Pays about 10-20¢/word for stories/articles; payment varies for poems and activities. Up to 10 complimentary issues are provided to author with check. Pays $250/color cover illustration; $30-70 per page b&w (inside); $55-110/2-color (inside); $65-140/color (inside). Sample copy for $1.25. Writer's/illustrator's guidelines free with SASE.

Tips: Writers: "Study current issues and guidelines. Observe, especially, word lengths and adhere to requirements. It's sometimes easier to break in with recipe or craft ideas, but submit what you do best. Don't send your first, second, or even third drafts. Polish your piece until it's as perfect as you can make it." Illustrators: "Please study the magazine before contacting us. Your art must have appeal to three- to seven-year-olds."

*INSIGHTS, NRA News for Young Shooters, National Rifle Association of America, 1600 Rhode Island Ave. NW, Washington DC 20036. (202)828-6075. Articles Editor: John Robbins. Monthly magazine. Estab. 1980. Circ. 56,000. *"InSights* promotes the shooting sports. We teach the safe and responsible use of firearms for competition shooting, hunting or recreational shooting. Our articles are instructional yet entertaining. We teach but don't preach. We emphasize safety."

Fiction: Young adults: animal, history, humorous, sports. "Fiction that does not relate to the shooting sports or positively promote the safe and ethical use of firearms will not be considered." Buys 12 mss/year. Average word length: 600-1,500. Byline given.

Nonfiction: Young adults: animal, history, how-to, humorous, interview/profile, sports. "All these categories must involve the shooting sports." Buys 40 mss/year. Average word length: 600-1,500. Byline given.

How to Contact/Writers: Fiction/nonfiction: Query, send complete ms. Include Social Security number with submission. Reports on queries/mss in 2 months.

Illustration: Buys 1 illustration/issue; buys 7 illustrations/year. Will review ms/illustration packages submitted by authors with illustrations done by separate artists. Works on assignment only.

How to Contact/Illustrators: Ms/illustration packages: Query first. Illustrations only: "Tearsheets or slides would be great! Illustrator should have technical knowledge of firearms and shooting."

Terms: Pays on acceptance. Buys first North American serial rights, second serial (reprint rights). Pays $200 for assigned/unsolicited articles. Additional payment for ms/illustration packages: $300. Pays $150-200 b&w (inside) illustration. Sample copy free with 10 × 12 SAE and 3 first-class stamps; writer's/illustrator's guidelines free with business SAE and 1 first-class stamp.

Tips: Writers: "You have to know your subject. Kids are smart and quickly pick up on inaccuracies. As an authority, your credibility is then zilch. Material should instruct without sounding preachy. We do not buy material that shows shooting in a bad light. We show our readers the correct, safe and ethical way to use a firearm." Illustrators: "When illustrating a story, stick to the description in the plot. We find young readers don't like illustrations when they differ from the story. Forego creative license this time. Wildlife art must be anatomically and environmentally correct. Shooting scenes must be safe and instructionally correct. We sponsor a wildlife art contest for our readers. Entrants must be in 12th grade or below."

INTERNATIONAL GYMNAST, Paul Zierst and Associates, 225 Brooks, Box 2450, Oceanside CA 92054. (619)722-0030. Editor: Dwight Normile. Published 10 times/year. "We are a magazine about gymnasts for ages 9 and up."
Fiction: Young adults: problem solving and sports stories for gymnasts.
Nonfiction: Young adults: biography, health, interview/profile, sports. Gymnastics material only.
How to Contact/Writers: Query with published clips. Will consider simultaneous submissions (please advise).
Illustration: Will review ms/illustration packages. Uses b&w artwork only, but "very rarely." Usually prefers cartoons—8½ × 11 camera ready.
How to Contact/Illustrators: Ms/illustration packages: Query. Illustrations only: Send slides or prints.
Photography: Looking for clear action/personality photos. Photo captions required. Uses 5 × 7 or 8 × 10, b&w, glossy prints; 35mm transparencies. To contact, send unsolicited photos by mail.
Terms: Pays on publication by arrangement. Buys one-time rights for mss, artwork and photos. Pays $15-25 for articles. Pays illustrators per b&w inside illustration (range: $10-15). Photographers paid per photo (range: $5-50).
Tips: "For us, gymnastics knowledge is necessary. Standard kidstuff with tenuous gym orientation doesn't cut it."

JACK AND JILL, Children's Better Health Institute, 1100 Waterway Blvd., Indianapolis IN 46206. (317)636-8881. Articles, Fiction Editor: Steve Charles. Art Director: Ed Cortese. Magazine published 8 times/year. Estab. 1938. Circ. 360,000. "Write entertaining and imaginative stories *for* kids, not just *about* them. Writers should understand what is funny to kids, what's important to them, what excites them. Don't write from an adult 'kids are so cute' perspective. We're also looking for health and healthy lifestyle stories and articles, but don't be preachy."
Fiction: Young readers: animal, contemporary, fantasy, history, humorous, problem solving. Middle readers: contemporary, humorous. Buys 30-35 mss/year. Average word length: 900. Byline given.
Nonfiction: Young readers: animal, history, how-to, humorous, interview/profile, problem solving, travel. Buys 8-10 mss/year. Average word length: 1,000. Byline given.
Poetry: Reviews poetry.
How to Contact/Writers: Fiction/nonfiction: Send complete ms. Reports on queries in 2 weeks; mss in 8-10 weeks. Will consider simultaneous submissions.
Terms: Pays on publication; minimum 10¢/word. Buys all rights.

JUNIOR TRAILS, Gospel Publishing House, 1445 Boonville Ave., Springfield MO 65802. (417)862-2781. Articles/Fiction Editor: Sinda S. Zinn. Art Director: Leonard Bailey. Quarterly magazine. Circ. 70,000. *Junior Trails* is an 8-page take-home paper for fifth and sixth graders. "Its articles consist of fiction stories of a contemporary or historical nature. The stories have a moral slant to show how modern-day people can work out problems in acceptable ways, or give examples in history from which we can learn."
Fiction: Middle readers: adventure, animal, contemporary, history, humorous, nature/environment, problem solving, religious, suspense/mystery. Does not want to see science fiction, mythology, ghosts and witchcraft. Wants to see more stories about "kids struggling with a problem in Christian living and solving it through biblical principles." Buys 100 mss/year. Average word length: 800-1,500. Byline given.
Nonfiction: Middle readers: animal, games/puzzles, history, how-to, problem solving, religious. Buys 30 mss/year. Average word length: 300-800. Byline given.
Poetry: Wants to see poetry with a religious emphasis.
How to Contact/Writers: Fiction/nonfiction: Send complete ms. Reports on mss in 2-4 weeks. Will consider simultaneous submissions.

Illustration: Uses color artwork only. Reviews artwork for future assignments.
How to Contact/Illustrators: Illustrations only: provide résumé, promo sheet or tear-sheets to be kept on file; or arrange personal interview to show portfolio. Reports only if interested. Credit line sometimes given.
Photography: Uses 2¼ × 2¼ transparencies. To contact, photographers should query with samples; provide résumé, promo sheet or tearsheets to be kept on file. Wants photos of "children involved with activity or with other people."
Terms: Pays on acceptance. For mss, buys one-time rights. Buys all rights to artwork; one-time rights to photographs. Pays 2-3¢/word for articles/stories. Pays illustrators $150-200/color (cover). Photographers paid per photo (range: $30-100). Sample copy free with 9 × 12 SASE.
Tips: "Make the characters and situations real. The story should unfold through their interaction and dialogue, not narration. Don't fill up space with unnecessary details. We are always in need of good fiction stories." Looks for: "fiction that presents believable characters working out their problems according to Bible principles. Present Christianity in action without being preachy; articles with reader appeal, emphasizing some phase of Christian living, presented in a down-to-earth manner; biography or missionary material using fiction technique; historical, scientific or nature material with a spiritual lesson; fillers that are brief, purposeful, usually containing an anecdote, and always with a strong evangelical emphasis."

KEYNOTER, Key Club International, 3636 Woodview Trace, Indianapolis IN 46268. (317)875-8755. Articles Editor: Julie A. Carson. Art Director: James Patterson. Monthly magazine. Estab. 1915. Circ. 133,000. "As the official magazine of the world's largest high school service organization, we publish nonfiction articles that interest teenagers and will help our readers become better students, better citizens, better leaders."
Nonfiction: Young adults: how-to, humorous, problem solving. Does not want to see first-person accounts; short stories. Buys 15 mss/year. Average word length: 1,500-1,800. Byline given.
How to Contact/Writers: Nonfiction: Query. Reports on queries/mss in 1 month. Will consider simultaneous submissions.
Illustration: Buys 2-3 illustrations/issue; buys 15 illustrations/year. Will review ms/illustration packages. Works on assignment only.
How to Contact/Illustrators: Ms/illustration packages: "Because of our publishing schedule, we prefer to work with illustrators/photographers within Indianapolis market." Reports on art samples only if interested. Original artwork returned at job's completion if requested.
Terms: Pays on acceptance. Buys first North American serial rights. Pays $150-300 for assigned/unsolicited articles. Sample copy free with 8½ × 11 SAE and 65¢ postage. Writer's guidelines free with SAE and 1 first-class stamp.
Tips: "We are looking for light or humorous nonfiction, self-help articles." Also looking for articles about education reform, national concerns and trends, teen trends in music, fashion, clothes, ideologies, etc.

KIDS TODAY MINI-MAGAZINE, Today Publishing, Inc., 2724 College Park Rd., Allison Park PA 15101. Editor: Don DiMarco. Art/Photo Director: Deborah Brimner. Quarterly mini-magazine in newsletter format. Estab. 1988. Circ. 15,000. "The mini-magazine is intended for children, targeting but not limited to, grades 3, 4 and 5. The purpose of the publication is to stimulate within our young readership an interest and appreciation for the ability to communicate, learn and entertain through reading, writing and artistic skills. This is accomplished through an appealing mix of fiction nonfiction, poetry, puzzles, games, contests and activities."
Fiction: Young readers, middle readers: adventure, contemporary, history, humorous, science fiction, sports. "Material that is preachy in tone or focuses on violence, war,

drugs or sex is not accepted. Material reflecting racial, religious or gender bias is inappropriate." Average word length: 300-600. Byline given.

Nonfiction: Young readers: arts/crafts, biography, games/puzzles, history, interview/profile, nature/environment, sports. Middle readers: arts/crafts, games/puzzles, history, interview/profile, nature/environment, travel, sports. "We want material that will make a kid say, 'WOW!' Of particular interests are articles about famous people, especially those who serve as ideal role models for children; articles about kids (unusual accomplishments—talents etc.); short pieces about inventions, sports, historical events and biographical sketches." Average word length: 200-500. Byline given.

Poetry: Featured in "Spotlight" section—for *young authors only*.

How to Contact/Writers: Fiction/nonfiction: Send complete ms. Reports on mss in 3 weeks. Publishes ms 6 months after acceptance. Reviews ms/illustration packages.

How to Contact/Illustrators: "Submit illustrations only with manuscript." Reports in 3 weeks. Does not return artwork.

Photography: Purchases photos with accompanying ms only. Model/property releases required. Uses b&w prints. Reports in 3 weeks.

Terms: Pays on publication. "For the most part we prefer to purchase all rights." Pays $10-25 for articles. "Some of our writers forego payment in lieu of multiple copies of publication." Sample copies for $1. Writer's guidelines for SASE.

Tips: "Our readership enjoys short articles and stories about a variety of subjects. Many publications offer complex layouts with commercial integration. Many disadvantaged children cannot afford the cost. *Kids Today* is different. It is distributed free and without advertising. It is simple and clean. The editorial philosophy of *Kids Today Mini-Magazine* is to recognize and celebrate imagination, creativity, distinctiveness and worth of all people, with particular emphasis on *all children*. All mss submitted are carefully reviewed. All material must be original and previously unpublished. Writer's should consider the nature of our mission prior to submitting material. The length of all material must be short. We are particularly interested in mss that are creatively devised to stimulate children to read, think and write. Subscriptions are mailed to any location in the US for a contribution of $5 or more per 3 issues annually. *Kids Today* is produced and distributed by Today Publishing, Inc., a nonprofit, tax-exempt organization."

*THE KILN, A Magazine for Christian Teens, Earthen Vessel Teen (EVT) Ministries, P.O. Box 5763, Vancouver WA 98668. Articles Editor/Art Director: Greg Zschomler. Quarterly magazine. Estab. 1986. "Our theme is teenage discipleship issues."

Fiction: "No fiction—unless it makes a brief, extremely profound statement that couldn't be made by nonfiction and would cause growth in Christ."

Nonfiction: Young adults/teens: arts/crafts, biography, humorous, religion, social issues, sports. Buys approximately 4 mss/year. Average word length: 300-1,400. Byline given.

How to Contact/Writers: Fiction/nonfiction: Query. Reports on queries in 3 weeks/mss in 1 week. Publishes ms 1 quarter after acceptance. Will consider simultaneous, electronic and previously published submissions.

Illustration: Uses b&w artwork only. Reviews ms/illustration packages.

How to Contact/Illustrators: Ms/illustration packages: Query. Illustrations only: Query. Reports in 3 weeks. Samples returned with SASE. Credit line given.

A bullet has been placed within some listings to introduce special comments by the editor of Children's Writer's & Illustrator's Market.

Photography: Wants journalistic action—teens involved. Model/property releases required. Uses b&w glossy prints. Photographers should query with samples. Reports in 3 weeks.

Terms: Pays on publication. Buys first North American serial rights, first rights, one-time rights, reprints rights and all rights (maybe) for mss. Pays $12-15 for stories/articles. Additional payment for ms/illustration packages. Pays illustrators $3 minimum for b&w (cover and inside). Photographers paid by the project or per photo. Sample copies for 5×9 SAE and 2 first-class stamps. Writer's guidelines for SASE.

LADYBUG, THE MAGAZINE FOR YOUNG CHILDREN, P.O. Box 300, 315 Fifth Street, Peru IL 61354. (815)224-6643. Editor-in-Chief: Marianne Carus. Associate Editor: Paula Morrow. Art Director: Ron McCutchan. Monthly magazine. Estab. 1990. Circ. 130,000. Literary magazine for children 2-6, with stories, poems, activities, songs and picture stories.

- At press time, the Carus Corporation, publisher of *Ladybug* and *Cricket* magazine (see listing in this section), launched *Spider*, a monthly magazine for 6- to 9-year-olds. Send a SAE and 1 first-class stamp for writer's/illustrator's guidelines.

Fiction: Picture-oriented and young readers: adventure, animal, contemporary, fantasy, humorous, nature/environment, problem solving, sports suspense/mystery. "Open to any easy fiction stories." Buys 50 mss/year. Average word length 300-750 words. Byline given.

Nonfiction: Picture-oriented and young readers: activities, animal, arts/crafts, concept, games/puzzles, humorous, math, multicultural, nature/environment, problem solving. Buys 35 mss/year.

Poetry: Reviews poems, 20-line maximum length; limit submissions to 5 poems. Uses lyrical, humorous, simple language.

How to Contact/Writers: Fiction/nonfiction: Send complete ms. Queries not accepted. Reports on mss in 3 months. Publishes ms up to 2 years after acceptance. Does not like, but will consider simultaneous submissions.

Illustration: Buys 12 illustrations/issue; 145 illustrations/year. Original artwork returned at job's completion. Uses color artwork only. Prefers "bright colors; all media, but use watercolor and acrylics most often; same size as magazine is preferred but not required." Reviews ms/illustration packages.

How to Contact/Illustrators: Ms/illustrations packages: Submit promo sheet, slides, tearsheets. Reports on art samples in 2 months.

Terms: Pays on publication. For mss, buys first publication rights; second serial (reprint rights). Buys first publication rights plus promotional rights for artwork. Pays up to 25¢/word. Pays $500-750 for color (cover) illustration, $50-100 for b&w (inside) illustration, $150-250 for color (inside) illustration. Sample copy for $2. Writer's/illustrator's guidelines free for SAE and 1 first-class stamp.

Tips: Writers: "Get to know several young children on an individual basis. Respect your audience; don't condescend. Set your manuscript aside for at least a month, then reread critically." Illustrators: "Include examples, where possible, of children, animals, and—most important—action and narrative (i.e., several scenes from a story, showing continuity and an ability to maintain interest)."

LISTEN, Celebrating Positive Choices, 1350 N. Kings Rd., Nampa ID 83687. (208)465-2500. Monthly magazine. Circ. 70,000. *Listen* offers positive alternatives to drug use for its teenage readers.

Fiction: Young adults: contemporary, health, humorous, nature/environment, problem solving activities, sports. Buys 12 mss/year. Average word length: 1,200-1,500. Byline given.

Maryann Cocca-Leffler's first assignment for Ladybug was six illustrations to accompany a story entitled "Puffy and Pink." "It's always great to have my work included in Ladybug with the company of more well-known illustrators," Cocca-Leffler says. "It has good reproduction quality and serves as great promotion."

Nonfiction: Young adults: how-to, interview/profile, problem solving activities. Wants to see more factual articles on drug abuse. Buys 50 mss/year. Average word length: 1,200-1,500. Byline given.

How to Contact/Writers: Fiction/nonfiction: Send complete ms. Reports on queries/mss in 2 months.

Illustration: Reviews ms/illustration packages; reviews work for future assignments.

How to Contact/Illustrators: Query, send promo sheet and slides. Reports in 1 month. Credit line given.

Photography: Purchases photos from freelancers. Looks for "youth oriented—action, personality photos."

Terms: Pays on acceptance. Buys exclusive magazine rights for ms. Pays $40-150 for stories/articles. Pays illustrators $150-500 for color (cover); $50-150 for b&w (inside); $75-250 for color (inside). Photographers paid by the project (range: $200-500) or per photo (range: $50-500). Sample copy for $1 and SASE. Writer's guidelines free with SASE.

Tips: "*Listen* is a magazine for teenagers. It encourages development of good habits and high ideals of physical, social and mental health. It bases its editorial philosophy of primary drug prevention on total abstinence from alcohol and other drugs. Because it is used extensively in public high school classes, it does not accept articles and stories with overt religious emphasis. Four specific purposes guide the editors in selecting materials for *Listen*: 1) To portray a positive lifestyle and to foster skills and values that will help teenagers deal with contemporary problems, including smoking, drinking and using drugs. This is *Listen*'s primary purpose. 2) To offer positive alternatives to a lifestyle of drug use of any kind. 3) To present scientifically accurate information about the nature and effects of tobacco, alcohol and other drugs. 4) To report medical research, community programs and educational efforts which are solving problems connected with smoking, alcohol and other drugs. Articles should offer their readers activities that increase one's sense of self-worth through achievement and/or involvement in helping others. They are often categorized by three kinds of focus: 1) Hobbies. 2) Recreation. 3) Community Service."

THE MAGAZINE FOR CHRISTIAN YOUTH!, United Methodist Publishing House, Box 801, 201 Eighth Ave. S., Nashville TN 37202. (615)749-6319. Articles Editor: Tony Peterson. Art Director/Photo Editor: Phil Francis. Monthly magazine. Estab. 1985. Circ. 35,000. "*Youth!* is a leisure reading magazine whose purpose is to help teenagers develop Christian identity and live the Christian faith in their contemporary culture."

Fiction: Young adults: adventure, animal, contemporary, fantasy, health, history, humorous, multicultural, nature/environment, problem-solving, religious, romance, science fiction, sports, suspense/mystery. "We appreciate fiction that allows people of color to be main characters. We do not want occultic fiction. We appreciate realistic fiction that also takes Christian faith seriously." Buys 5-10 mss/year. Average word length: 500-2,000. Byline given.

Nonfiction: Young adults: animal, arts/crafts, biography, careers, concept, health, history, hobbies, how-to, humorous, interview/profile, multicultural, nature/environment, problem-solving, religion, science, social issues, sports, travel. Buys 10-30 mss/year. Average word length: 500-2,000. Byline given.

How to Contact/Writers: Fiction/nonfiction: Query; send complete ms. Reports on queries in 2 months; mss in 3 months. Will consider simultaneous and electronic submissions via disk or modem and previously published work.

Illustration: Reviews ms/illustration packages; reviews artwork for future assignments.

How to Contact/Illustrators: Ms/illustration packages: Query; submit ms with rough sketches. Illustrations only: Query; send promo sheet, portfolio, slides and tearsheets. Reports in 2 months. Samples returned with SASE. Samples filed. Original work returned upon job's completion. Credit line given.

Photography: Purchases photography from freelancers. Model/property release required. Uses b&w glossy prints; 35mm, 2¼ × 2¼ transparencies. Photographers should query with samples; send unsolicited photos by mail; submit portfolio for review; provide business card, promotional literature and tearsheets. Reports in 2 months.

Terms: Buys first North American serial rights, first rights, one-time rights, reprint rights or all rights for mss. Purchases all rights for artwork; user rights for photographs. Pays $35-125. Additional payment for ms/illustation packages. Pays illustrators $50-150/ b&w cover; $25-50 b&w inside; $150-300/color cover; $50-150 color inside. Photographers paid per photo (range: $25-300). Writer's/illustrator's/photo guidelines for SASE.

Tips: "Refrain from talking down to teens, use 'your' instead of 'they' language. We rarely print fiction from adults."

*MAGIC REALISM, Pyx Press, P.O. Box 620, Orem UT 84059-0620. Editor-in-Chief: C. Darren Butler. Editor: Julie Thomas. Managing Editor: Heather McNamee. Submissions Editor: Patricia Hatch. Magazine published 3 times/year. Estab. 1990. Circ. 1,200. "We publish magic, realism, exaggerated realism, literary fantasy; glib fantasy of the sort found in folktales, fables, myth." 10-20% of publication aimed at juvenile market.
Fiction: Middle readers and young adults: fantasy, folktales. Sees too much of wizards, witches, card readings, sword-and-sorcery, silly or precious tales of any sort, sleight-of-hand magicians. Buys approximately 25 mss/year. Average word length: 4,000. Byline given.
Poetry: Reviews poetry. Length: prefers 3-30 lines. Limit submissions to 3-8 poems.
How to Contact/Writers: Fiction: Send complete ms. Reports on queries in 1 month; mss in 2-4 months. Publishes ms 4 months-2 years after acceptance. Will consider simultaneous submissions.
Illustration: Uses b&w artwork only. Reviews ms/illustration packages; reviews work for future assignments.
How to Contact/Illustrators: Ms/illustration packages: Query; submit complete package with final art or submit ms with rough sketches. Illustrations only: Query or send résumé and portfolio. Reports in 3 month. Samples returned with SASE. Original work returned at job's completion. Credit line given.
Photography: "We consider photos, but have received very few submissions." Model/property releases preferred. Photographers should query with samples and résumé of credits; submit portfolio for review.
Terms: Pays on publication. Buys first North American serial rights or one-time rights and reprints rights for ms, artwork and photographs; also buys worldwide Spanish language rights for Spanish edition published one year after English edition. Pays $2-30 for stories. Pays illustrators $10 for b&w (cover); $1-3 for b&w (inside). Photographers paid per photo (range: $1-10). Sample copies for $4.95. Writer's guidelines for SASE.
Tips: "Only a fraction of the material we publish is for children. We rarely use anthropomorphic tales. Most material for children is related to folklore."

MY FRIEND, A Magazine for Children, Daughters of St. Paul/St. Paul Books and Media, 50 St. Paul's Ave., Jamaica Plain, Boston MA 02130. (617)522-8911. Articles/Fiction Editor: Sister Anne Joan, fsp. Art Director: Sister M. Joseph, fsp. Magazine published 10 times/year. Estab. 1979. Circ. 12,000. "*My Friend* is a magazine of inspiration and entertainment for a predominantly Catholic readership. We reach ages 6-12."
Fiction: Young readers and middle readers: adventure, contemporary, history, humorous, religious, suspense/mystery. Does not want to see poetry, animals as main characters in religious story, stories whose basic thrust would be incompatible with Catholic values. Buys 50 mss/year. Average word length: 450-750. Byline given.
Nonfiction: Young readers: arts/crafts, games/puzzles, health, history, hobbies, humorous, religious. Middle readers: arts/crafts, games/puzzles, health, history, hobbies, how-to, humorous, interview/profile, nature/environment, problem solving, religion, science, sports. Does not want to see material that is not compatible with Catholic values; no "New Age" material. Buys 10 mss/year. Average word length: 450-750. Byline given.
How to Contact/Writers: Fiction/nonfiction: Send complete ms. Reports on queries in 1 month; mss in 1-2 months.
Illustration: Buys 8 illustrations/issue; buys 60-80 illustrations/year. Preferred theme or style: Realistic depictions of children, but open to variety! "We'd just like to hear from more illustrators who can do *humans*! (We see enough of funny cats, mice, etc.)" Looking for a "Bible stories" artist, too. Reviews ms/illustration packages; reviews artwork for future assignments.

How to Contact/Illustrators: Ms/illustration packages: Send complete ms with copy of final art. Illustrations only: Send résumé, promo sheet and tearsheets. Reports on art samples only if interested. Original artwork returned at job's completion. Credit line given.

Photography: Wants photos of "children at play or alone; school scenes."

Terms: Pays on acceptance for mss. Buys one-time rights for mss, artwork and photos. Pays $20-150 for stories/articles. Pays illustrators $50-100/b&w (inside); $50-175/color (inside). Sample copy $1 with 9×12 SAE and 4 first-class stamps. Writer's/illustrator's guidelines free with SAE and 1 first-class stamp.

Tips: Writers: "Right now, we're especially looking for science articles and stories that would appeal to boys. We are not interested in poetry unless it is humorous." Illustrators: "Please contact us! For the most part, we need illustrations for fiction stories."

THE MYTHIC CIRCLE, Mythopoeic Society, P.O. Box 6707, Altadena CA 91001. Editor: Tina Cooper and Christine Lowentrout. Art Director: Lynn Maudlin. Magazine published three times annually. Circ. 150. Fantasy writer's workshop in print featuring reader comments in each issue. 5% of publication aimed at juvenile market.

Nonfiction: How-to, interview/profile. "We are just starting with nonfiction—dedicated to how to write and publish." Buys maximum of 2 mss/year. Average word length: 250-2,000. Byline given.

How to Contact/Writers: Fiction: Send complete ms. Nonfiction: Query. SASE (IRC) for answer to query and return of ms. Reports on queries/mss in 2 months. Will consider photocopied, computer printout (dark dot matrix) and electronic submissions via disk (query for details). Submissions by subscribers favored.

Illustration: Buys 10 illustrations/issue; buys 30 illustrations/year. Preferred theme or style: fantasy, soft science fiction.

How to Contact/Illustrators: Reports on art samples in 3-6 weeks. Original artwork returned at job's completion (only if postage paid).

Terms: Pays on publication. Buys one-time rights. Pays in contributor copies. Sample copy $6.50. Writer's guidelines free with SAE and 1 first-class stamp.

Tips: "We are a good outlet for a story that hasn't sold but 'should' have—good feedback and tips on improvement."

*NATIONAL GEOGRAPHIC WORLD, National Geographic Society, 17th and M Streets NW, Washington DC 20036. (202)857-7000. Editor: Susan M. Tejada. Illustrations Director: Chuck Herron. Art Director: Ursula Vosseler. Monthly magazine. Circ. 1.2 million. "*National Geographic World* features factual stories on outdoor adventure, natural history, sports, science and history for children ages 8 and older. Full-color photographs are used to attract young readers and the text easily guides them through the story." Does not publish fiction.

Nonfiction: Picture material: animal, history, how-to, travel. Middle readers, young adults: animal, history, humorous, multicultural, nature/environment, sports. "*World* does not publish manuscripts from outside writers. Story ideas that lend themselves to photo stories will be considered. All writing is done by staff." Average word length: 90-600.

How to Contact/Writers: Nonfiction: Query only—no ms please. Reports on queries in 6-8 weeks.

Illustration: Assignment only.

How to Contact/Illustrators: Illustrations only: Query with samples; arrange personal interview to show portfolio.

Photography: Purchases photos separately. Looking for "imaginative, eye-catching action transparencies." Model/property releases and photo captions required. Uses 35mm transparencies. To contact, photographers should query with proposal and outline of photo possibilities.

Terms: Pays on publication. Buys one-time rights for mss, artwork and photos. Pays $600 for color (cover), $100-300 for color (inside) photos. Photographers are paid per published page. Free sample copy; contributor's guidelines available free.

Tips: "All *World* stories are written by staff. For *World*, the story proposal is the way to break in. Think through the focus of the story and outline what action photos are available. Keep in mind that *World* is a visual magazine. A story will work best if it has a very tight focus and if the photos show children interacting with their surroundings as well as with each other."

NATURE FRIEND MAGAZINE, Pilgrim Publishers, 22777 State Road 119, Goshen IN 46526. (219)534-2245. Articles Editor: Stanley Brubaker. Monthly magazine. Estab. 1983. Circ. 9,500. "See our writer's guidelines *before* submitting articles."

Nonfiction: All levels: animal, nature. Does not want to see evolutionary material. Buys 50-80 mss/year. Average word length: 350-1,500. Byline given.

How to Contact/Writers: Nonfiction: Send complete ms. Reports on mss in 1-4 months. Will consider simultaneous submissions.

Illustration: Buys 60 illustrations/year. See samples of magazine for styles of art used. Will review ms/illustration packages.

Terms: Pays on publication. Buys one-time rights. Pays $15-75. Payment for ms/illustration packages: $15-40. Payment for illustrations: $15-80/b&w inside. Two sample copies for $4 with 7×10 SAE and 85¢ postage. Writer's/illustrator's guidelines for $1.

Tips: Looks for "main articles, puzzles and simple nature and science projects."

NEW ERA MAGAZINE, Official Publication for Youth of the Church of Jesus Christ of Latter-Day Saints, 50 E. North Temple Street, Salt Lake City UT 84150. (801)240-2951. Articles/Fiction Editor: Richard M. Romney. Art Director: B. Lee Shaw. Monthly magazine. Estab. 1971. Circ. 200,000. General interest religious publication for youth ages 12-18 who are members of The Church of Jesus Christ of Latter-Day Saints (Mormons).

Fiction: Young adults: adventure, contemporary, fantasy, humorous, problem solving, religious, romance, science fiction, sports. "All material must relate to Mormon point of view. Does not want to see formula pieces, stories not sensitive to an LDS audience." Buys 20 mss/year. Average word length: 250-2,500. Byline given.

Nonfiction: Young adults: biography, careers, education, fashion, games/puzzles, humorous, interview/profile, problem solving, religion, travel, sports; "general interest articles by, about and for young Mormons. Would like more about Mormon youth worldwide. Does not want to see formula pieces, articles not adapted to our specific voice and our audience." Buys 150-200 mss/year. Average word length: 250-2,000. Byline given.

Poetry: Reviews poems, 30-lines maximum. Limit submissions to 10 poems.

How to Contact/Writers: Fiction/nonfiction: Query. Reports on queries/mss in 2 months. Publishes ms 1 year or more after acceptance. Will consider electronic submissions via disk.

Illustration: Buys 5 illustrations/issue; buys 50-60 illustrations/year. "We buy only from our pool of illustrators. We use all styles and mediums." Works on assignment only.

How to Contact/Illustrators: Illustrations only: Submit portfolio for review; provide résumé, business card, promotional literature and tearsheets to be kept on file. Reports on art samples in 2 months. Original artwork returned at job's completion. Credit line given.

Terms: Pays on acceptance. For mss, buys first rights; right to publish again in other church usage (rights reassigned on written request). Buys all or one-time rights for artwork and photos. Pays $25-375 for stories; $25-350 for articles. Pays illustrators and photographers "by specific arrangements." Sample copy for $1. Writer's guidelines free for #10 SAE and 1 first-class stamp.

Tips: Open to "first-person and true-life experiences. Tell what happened in a conversational style. Teen magazines are becoming more brash and sassy. We shy away from the outlandish and trendy, but still need a contemporary look."

NOAH'S ARK, A Newspaper for Jewish Children, #250, 8323 Southwest Freeway, Houston TX 77074. (713)771-7143. Articles/Fiction Editor: Debbie Israel Dubin. Monthly tabloid. Circ. 450,000. All submissions must have Jewish content and positive Jewish values. The newspaper is sent to more than 400 religious schools and submissions must be appropriate for educational use as well.
Fiction: Young readers, middle readers: contemporary, fantasy, folktales, health, history, humorous, nature/environment, religious, sports. Does not want to see Christian and secular material. Buys 3 mss/year. Average word length: 650. Byline given.
Nonfiction: Young readers, middle readers: arts/crafts, biography, cooking (Jewish recipes), games/puzzles, history, how-to, interview/profile, nature/environment, religious, social issues. Does not want to see secular, Christian nonfiction. Buys 1 ms/year, "only because more are not submitted." Average word length: 500. Byline given.
How to Contact/Writers: Fiction/nonfiction: Send complete ms. Report on mss 6-8 weeks.
Terms: Pays on acceptance. Buys first North American serial rights. Pays 5¢/word for stories/articles. Sample copy free with #10 SAE and 1 first-class stamp. Writer's guidelines free with SASE.
Tips: "Send appropriate material. We receive mostly inappropriate submissions; very few submissions have Jewish values as required."

ODYSSEY, Science That's Out of This World, Cobblestone Publishing, Inc., 7 School St., Peterborough NH 03458. (603)924-7209. Editor: Elizabeth E. Lindstrom. Editor-in-Chief: Carolyn P. Yoder. Art Director: Ann C. Webster. Picture Editor: Francelle Carapetyan. Magazine published 10 times/year. Estab. 1979. Circ. 40,000. Magazine covers astronomy and space exploration for children ages 8-14. All material must relate to the theme of a specific upcoming issue in order to be considered.
Fiction: Middle readers and young adults: adventure, folktales, history, biographical fiction. Does not want to see anything not theme-related. Average word length: 750 maximum.
Nonfiction: Middle readers and young adults: arts/crafts, biography, cooking, games/puzzles (no word finds), science. Don't send anything not theme-related. Average word length: 200-750, depending on section article is used in.
How to Contact/Writers: "A query must consist of all of the following to be considered (please use nonerasable paper): a brief cover letter stating the subject and word length of the proposed article; a detailed one-page outline explaining the information to be presented in the article; an extensive bibliography of materials the author intends to use in preparing the article; SASE. Writers new to *Odyssey* should send a writing sample with query. If you would like to know if your query has been received, please also include a stamped postcard that requests acknowledgment of receipt. In all correspondence, please include your complete address as well as a telephone number where you can be reached. A writer may send as many queries for one issue as he or she wishes, but each query must have a separate cover letter, outline, bibliography, and SASE. Telephone queries are not accepted. Handwritten queries will not be considered. Queries may be submitted at any time, but queries sent well in advance of deadline *may not be answered for several months*. Go-aheads requesting material proposed in queries are usually sent five months prior to publication date. Unused queries will be returned approximately three to four months prior to publication date."
Illustration: Reviews artwork for future assignments.
How to Contact/Illustrators: Illustrations only: Send tearsheets, photocopies. Original artwork returned upon job's completion (upon written request).

Photography: Wants photos pertaining to any of our forthcoming themes. Uses b&w and color prints; 35mm transparencies. Photographers should send unsolicited photos by mail (on speculation).
Terms: Buys all right for mss and artwork. Pays 10-17¢/word for stories/articles. "Covers are assigned and paid on an individual basis. Pays illustrators $10-125/b&w inside; $20-210/color (inside). Photographers paid per photo (range: $15-75). Sample copy for $3.95 and SASE with $1.05 postage. Writer's/illustrator's/photo guidelines for SASE.

ON THE LINE, Mennonite Publishing House, 616 Walnut Ave., Scottdale PA 15683. (412)887-8500. Editor: Mary Clemens Meyer. Magazine published "monthly in weekly parts." Estab. 1970. Circ. 10,000.
Fiction: Young adults: contemporary, history, humorous, problem-solving, religious, sports and suspense/mystery. "No fantasy or fiction with animal characters." Buys 60 mss/year. Average word length: 900-1,200. Byline given.
Nonfiction: Middle readers, young adults: animal, arts/crafts, biography, cooking, games/puzzles, health, history, hobbies, how-to, humorous, nature/environment, problem-solving. Does not want to see articles written from an adult perspective. Average word length: 200-600. Byline given.
Poetry: Wants to see light verse, humorous poetry. Maximum length: 24 lines.
How to Contact/Writers: Fiction/nonfiction: Send complete ms. Reports on queries/mss in 1 month. Will consider simultaneous submissions.
Illustration: Buys 1-2 illustrations/issue; buys 52 illustrations/year. "Illustrations are done on assignment only, to accompany our stories and articles—our need for new artists is very limited."
How to Contact/Illustrators: Illustrations only: "Prefer samples they do not want returned; these stay in our files." Reports on art samples only if interested. Original art work returned at job's completion.
Photography: Looking for photography showing ages 12-14, both sexes, good mix of races, wholesome fun. Uses 8×10 glossy b&w prints. Photographers should send unsolicited photos by mail.
Terms: Pays on acceptance. For mss buys one-time rights; second serial (reprint rights). Buys one-time rights for artwork and photos. Pays 2-5¢/word for assigned/unsolicited articles. Pays $25-50/color (inside) illustration. Photographers are paid per photo, $15-50 (cover). Sample copy free with 7×10 SAE. Free writer's guidelines.
Tips: "We will be focusing on the 12-13 age group of our age 0-14 audience. (Focus was somewhat younger before.)"

*OTTERWISE, for kids who are into saving animals and the environment, P.O. Box 1374, Portland ME 04104. (207)871-7214. Articles/Fiction Editor: Cheryl Miller. Quarterly newsletter. Estab. 1987. "*Otterwise* is designed to promote a love and respect for animals and the natural world among children age 8-13."
Fiction: Young readers, middle readers, young adults: animal, health (vegetarianism), nature/environment. "We'd like to see material that gives children ideas on how they can help animals and the environment. It should not be preachy or 'talk down' to kids." Acquires a maximum of four mss/issue. All work must be *free* as we are nonprofit, all-volunteer. Byline given.
Nonfiction: Young readers, middle readers and young adults: animal, cooking (vegetarian), health (vegetarianism), nature/environment. "We see too many cute animal stories that don't contain any message." Acquires maximum of four mss/issue. Work must be *free*. Length: 500-1,000. Byline given.
How to Contact/Writers: Fiction/nonfiction: Query. Reports on queries in 1 month/mss in 1 month. Publishes ms 1-2 months after acceptance. Will consider simultaneous submissions and previously published work.
Terms: "If a writer's/artist's work is published, we do send complimentary issues."

OWL MAGAZINE, The Discovery Magazine for Children, Young Naturalist Foundation, Stuite 306, 56 The Esplanade, Toronto, Ontario M5E 1A7 Canada. (416)868-6001. Editor: Debora Pearson. Managing Editor: Nyla Ahmad. Art Director: Tim Davin. Magazine published 10 times/year. Circ. 160,000. *"OWL* helps children over eight discover and enjoy the world of science and nature. We look for articles that are fun to read, that inform from a child's perspective, and that motivate hands-on interaction. *OWL* explores the reader's many interests in the natural world in a scientific, but always entertaining, way."

Fiction: Middle readers, young adults: animal, contemporary, fantasy, humorous, science fiction, sports, suspense/mystery/adventure. Does not want to see romance, religion, anthropomorphizing. Average word length: 500-1,000. Byline given. "We publish only 3-4 pieces of fiction per year."

Nonfiction: Middle readers, young adults: animal, biology, high-tech, humor, interview/profile, travel. Does not want to see religious topics, anthropomorphizing. Buys 20 mss/year. Average word length: 200-1,500. Byline given.

How to Contact/Writers: Fiction/nonfiction: Query with published clips. Report on queries in 4-6 weeks; mss in 6-8 weeks.

Illustration: Buys 3-5 illustrations/issue; buys 40-50 illustrations/year. Uses color artwork only. Preferred theme or style: lively, involving, fun, with emotional impact and appeal. "We use a range of styles." Works on assignment only.

How to Contact/Illustrators: Illustrations only: Send tearsheets and slides. Reports on art samples only if interested. Original artwork returned at job's completion.

Photography: Looking for shots of animals and nature. "Label the photos." Uses 2¼ × 2¼ and 35mm transparencies. Photographers should query with samples.

Terms: Pays on acceptance. For mss, artwork and photos buys first North American and world rights. Pays $200-500 (Canadian) for assigned/unsolicited articles. Pays up to $650 (Canadian) for illustrations. Photographers are paid per photo. Sample copy $4.28. Free writers' guidelines.

Tips: Writers: "Talk to kids and find out what they're interested in; make sure your research is thorough and find good consultants who are doing up-to-the-minute research. Be sure to read the magazine carefully to become familiar with *OWL*'s style."

POCKETS, Devotional Magazine for Children, The Upper Room, 1908 Grand, P.O. Box 189, Nashville TN 37202. (615)340-7333. Articles/Fiction Editor: Janet R. McNish. Art Director: Chris Schechner, Stuite 207, 3100 Carlisle Plaza, Dallas TX 75204. Magazine published 11 times/year. Estab. 1981. Circ. 72,000. "Stories should help children 6 to 12 experience a Christian lifestyle that is not always a neatly wrapped moral package, but is open to the continuing revelation of God's will."

Fiction: Young readers, middle readers: contemporary, fantasy, history, religious, "retold Bible stories." Does not want to see violence. Buys 26-30 mss/year. Average word length: 800-2,000. Byline given.

Nonfiction: Young readers, middle readers: history, interview/profile, religious, "communication activities." Does not want to see how-to articles. "Our nonfiction reads like a story." History is in form of role-model stories as is profile. Buys 10 mss/year. Average word length: 800-2,000. Byline given.

How to Contact/Writers: Fiction/nonfiction: Send complete ms. "Prefer not to deal with queries." Report on mss in 2-4 weeks. Will consider simultaneous submissions.

Always include a self-addressed stamped envelope (SASE) or a self-addressed envelope (SAE) and International Reply Coupons (IRCs) with submissions.

Illustration: Buys 30 illustrations/issue. Preferred theme or style: varied; both 4-color and 2-color. Will review artwork for future assignments. Works on assignment only.
How to Contact/Illustrators: Illustrations only: Send tearsheets and slides to Chris Schechner. Reports on art samples only if interested. Original artwork returned at job's completion. Credit line given.
Photography: Purchases photography from freelancers.
Terms: Pays on acceptance. Buys first North American rights for mss; one-time rights for artwork and photos. Pays 12-15¢/word for stories/articles. Pays $500-600/color (cover) illustration; $50-400/color (inside); $50-250 (2-color). Pays $25 for color transparencies accompanying articles; $500 for cover photos. Sample copy free with 8 × 10 SAE and 4 first-class stamps. Writer's/illustrator's guidelines free with SAE and 1 first-class stamp.
Tips: "Ask for our themes first. They are set yearly in the fall. Also, we are looking for articles about real children involved in environment, peace or similar activities."

POWER AND LIGHT, Children's Ministries, 6401 The Paseo, Kansas City MO 64131. (816)333-7000. Editor: Beula Postlewait. Executive Editor: Mark York. Weekly story paper. "*Power and Light* is a leisure reading piece for fifth and sixth graders. It is published weekly by the Department of Children's Ministries of the Church of the Nazarene. The major purposes of *Power and Light* are to provide a leisure reading piece which will build Christian behavior and values; provide reinforcement for Biblical concepts taught in the Sunday School curriculum. The focus of the reinforcement will be life-related, with some historical appreciation. *Power and Light*'s target audience is children ages 11-12 in grades five and six."
Fiction: Middle readers: adventure, contemporary, nature/environment, multicultural, problem-solving, religious. "Avoid fantasy, science fiction, abnormally mature or precocious children, personification of animals. Also avoid extensive cultural or holiday references, especially those with a distinctly American frame of reference. Our paper has an international audience. We need stories involving multicultural teens in realistic settings dealing with realistic problems with God's help." Average word length: 500-700. Byline given.
How to Contact/Writers: Send complete ms. Reports on queries in 1 month; mss in 2 months. Publishes ms 2 years after acceptance.
Illustration: Illustrations only: Query with résumé, promo sheet, and portfolio. *Power and Light* publishes a wide variety of artistic styles, i.e., cartoon, realistic, montage, etc., but whatever the style, artwork must appeal to 11-12 year old children. Reviews artwork for future assignments.
How to Contact/Illustrators: Illustrations only: Query; send résumé, portfolio. Reports back only if interested. Credit line given.
Photography: Buys "b&w archeological/Biblical for inside use and color preteen/contemporary/action for cover use."
Terms: Pays on publication. "Payment is made approximately one year before the date of issue." Buys one-time rights, all rights and multiple use rights for ms. Purchases all rights and first/one-time rights for artwork and photographs. Pays 3.5-5¢/word for stories/articles. Pays illustrators $40/b&w (cover); $75/color (cover); $40/b&w (inside); $50-75/color (inside). Photographers paid per photo (range: $35-45; $200 maximum for cover color photo). Writer's/illustrator's guidelines for SASE.
Tips "Themes and outcomes should conform to the theology and practices of the Church of the Nazarene, Evangelical Friends, Free Methodist, Wesleyan and other Bible-believing Evangelical churches." Looks for "bright, colorful illustrations; concise, short articles and stories." (See listing for *Discoveries*.)

*PRIMARY DAYS, Scripture Press Pub., Inc., Box 632, Glen Ellyn IL 60138. (708)668-6000. Articles/Fiction Editor: Janice K. Burton. Art Director: Blake Ebel. Distributed weekly; published quarterly. Estab. 1935. "Our audience is children 6-8 years old."
Fiction: Young readers: adventure, animal, problem-solving, sports (Christian concepts only). Average word length: 600-700.
Nonfiction: Young readers: animal, arts/crafts, history, hobbies, how-to, nature/environment, problem-solving, religion, social issues (appropriate to age). Average word length: 600-700.
How to Contact/Writers: Fiction/nonfiction: Send complete ms. Reports on mss in 8-10 weeks. Publishes ms 1-2 years after acceptance. Will consider previously published work.
Illustration: Buys 24-40 illustrations/year. Credit line given.
Terms: Pays on acceptance. Buys first rights and one-time rights for ms. Pays 5-10¢/word for stories. Additional payment for ms/illustration packages. Sample copies for #10 SASE and 2 first-class stamps. Writer's/photo guidelines for SASE.

RACING FOR KIDS, Griggs Publishing Company Inc., P.O. Box 500, Concord NC 28026. (704)786-7132. Editor: Donna Cox. Monthly magazine. Estab. 1990. Circ. 10,000. Publication caters to kids interested in racing.
Nonfiction: Young readers: auto racing, health, nature/environment, multicultural, science, sports. Middle readers and young adults: animal, arts/crafts, cooking, fashion, health, history, hobbies, interviews/profile, math, multicultural, nature/environment, science, sports — all as they relate to auto racing. Multicultural needs include: sensitivity to minorities in racing — women and African-Americans; with foreign drivers, tell a little about their home country. Buys 12-20 mss/year. Average word length: 400-1,200. Byline given.
How to Contact/Writers: Nonfiction: Query. Reports on queries in 2 months only if interested. Publishes ms 6-12 months after acceptance.
Terms: Pays on publication. Buys exclusive magazine rights for mss. Pays $50-150 for stories, $50-150 for articles. Additional payment for photos that accompany article.
Tips: "Know the subject matter, study publication. All stories are racing-related. We like stories about NASCAR, NHRA and Monster Truck drivers. No fiction please."

R-A-D-A-R, Standard Publishing, 8121 Hamilton Ave., Cincinnati OH 45231. (513)931-4050. Editor: Margaret Williams. Weekly magazine. Circ. 120,000. *R-A-D-A-R* is a weekly take-home paper for boys and girls who are in grades 3-6. "Our goal is to reach these children with the truth of God's Word, and to help them make it the guide of their lives. Many of our features, including our stories, now correlate with the Sunday school lesson themes. Send for a quarterly theme list and sample copies of *R-A-D-A-R*. Keep in mind that others will be submitting stories for the same themes — this is not an assignment."
Fiction: Middle readers: animal, contemporary, history, humorous, problem solving, religious, sports, suspense/mystery/adventure. Does not want to see fantasy or science fiction. Buys 150 mss/year. Average word length: 400-1,000. Byline given.
Nonfiction: Middle readers: animal, history, how-to, humorous, interview/profile, problem solving, religious, travel. Buys 50 mss/year. Average word length: 400-1,000. Byline given.
Poetry: Reviews poetry. Maximum line length: 16.
How to Contact/Writers: Fiction/nonfiction: Send complete ms. Reports on queries/mss in 6-8 weeks. Will consider simultaneous submissions (but prefers not to). Reprint submissions must be retyped.
Illustration: Will review all illustration packages. "Works on assignment only; there have been a few exceptions to this."

Respect for Wildlife Key at *Ranger Rick*

Cougars, kingfishers and cockroaches—these are just a few of the subjects covered in an issue of *Ranger Rick*. Published monthly by the National Wildlife Federation, this long-running magazine is dedicated to teaching children respect for wildlife.

"*Ranger Rick* was born in 1967 of the belief that people conserve only what they love," explains Editor Gerald Bishop. "Kids who learn to love and appreciate wildlife will grow to become its staunchest defenders. That belief drives our editorial mission today."

With a monthly circulation of nearly 900,000, *Ranger Rick* features both fiction and nonfiction articles covering all aspects of nature, outdoor adventure and wildlife. The articles are presented in a fun yet informative way, accompanied by incred-

Gerald Bishop

ibly sharp, colorful, up-close photos. The writing style conveys warmth and respect toward whatever subject may be covered, be it a cute, fuzzy bear cub or a lizard with a face only its mother could love.

Ranger Rick publishes about 20-30 freelance pieces each year, and many come from a small stable of established writers. "It's difficult for most freelance writers and illustrators to get their work into *Ranger Rick*," Bishop says. "At any given time, we have found ourselves buying most of our material from only a dozen or so writers and illustrators. And of that number, only a few get the great majority of assignments. But we're not snobs about it—we'll buy a piece from an unpublished beginner as readily as from a well-established pro." And Bishop should know—he sold his very first story to the magazine he now works for.

"Getting published in *Ranger Rick* was one of the biggest thrills of my life," Bishop explains. "At the time (1971), I was in San Francisco fooling around as a freelance nature photographer. The mother of a friend, who happened to work for the magazine and who knew of my interest in nature and the environment, suggested I write a biographical sketch of renowned naturalist John Muir for an upcoming issue."

It seemed to be more a friendly gesture than a rational suggestion because Bishop had never written for publication before and had never even thought about writing for kids. He went to the public library to see what he could learn, and with a few books about Muir and one called *How to Write a Biography for Children*, he got to work.

MORE BOOKS TO HELP YOU GET PUBLISHED!

The Children's Writer's Word Book
This handy reference book offers everything you need to ensure your writing speaks to your young audience, including word lists, a thesaurus of listed words and reading levels for a variety of synonyms. You'll also find samples of writing for each reading level, and guidelines for sentence length, word usage and theme at each level. 352 pages/$19.95/hardcover

Writing for Children & Teenagers
Filled with practical know-how and step-by-step instruction, including how to hold a young reader's attention, where to find ideas, and vocabulary lists based on age level. This third edition provides all the tips you need to flourish in today's children's literature market. 265 pages/$12.95/paperback

How to Write & Illustrate Children's Books
A truly comprehensive guide that demonstrates how to bring freshness and vitality to children's text and pictures. Numerous illustrators, writers, and editors contributed their expert advice. 143 pages/$22.50/hardcover

1994 Guide to Literary Agents & Art/Photo Reps
Interviews with top reps and agents in the field answer the most often asked questions about getting representation; then over 500 listings of literary and script agents, and art/photo reps will help you find one that's right for you. 240 pages/$18.95/paperback

1994 Artist's Market
The 2,500 listings of art buyers listed, along with helpful interviews from top professionals in the art field, make this the ultimate marketing tool for illustrators, designers, and fine artists. 672 pages/$22.95/hardcover

Use the coupon on the other side to order these books today!

"Six weeks later a letter arrived, congratulating me on my first sale. I quickly sold my second article to the magazine, and not too long afterward I was headed out East to begin a new job as a *Ranger Rick* associate editor," he says.

Bishop's story may sound like a fairy tale to many aspiring writers, but he's managed to keep a level head about it. "My painless entry into writing for children could have left me with a distorted perspective," he says. "But I quickly saw, in the sad ratio of rejections to acceptances given hopeful freelancers, that writing successfully for kids is far from easy."

One important trait Bishop looks for in writers for *Ranger Rick* is a sensitivity to the audience. "There's no showing off allowed in this business," he says. "You need to be aware of young kids' needs and their limitations and to structure your writing accordingly. Children's writer Russell Freedman is right: The easier it is to read, the harder it is to write. If you follow the old adage and 'write for yourself,' you may indeed find yourself with an audience of one."

A passion for their subject—a true love of nature and the environment—is also vital for writers wanting to be published here. "Our writers use their passion to bring all the sounds, smells, colors and textures of life to their words," Bishop explains. "Their copy scratches and squeals and smells of wet fur."

Since *Ranger Rick* is an educational magazine, writers must be knowledgeable about their subjects and carefully research all facts. "Successful *Ranger Rick* writers share an allegiance to truthfulness," Bishop adds, "whether they're writing fiction or nonfiction. They worry over getting things right. One such author recently wrote to apologize for making a slight factual error in her *query letter!*"

But acute attention to detail doesn't mean the material in *Ranger Rick* must read like a textbook. It's up to the writer to bring life and excitement to articles that are designed to teach and inform. "With all the discipline and care shown by our best writers," Bishop observes, "they still have a hell of a good time. Their joy brings joy to their readers. And that, in the end, is the whole story."

—Cindy Laufenberg

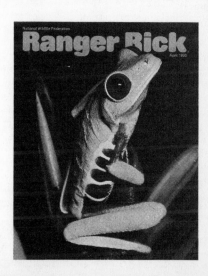

By teaching children respect for wildlife, the staff of Ranger Rick hopes they will grow to become its staunchest defenders. Pictured here is a red-eyed tree frog from the rainforest of Central America. This close-up photo was taken under controlled conditions by Michael and Patricia Fogden.

How to Contact/Illustrators: Illustrations only: Send résumé, tearsheets or promo sheets; samples of art can be photocopied. Reports on art samples only if interested.

Photography: Purchases photos from freelancers. Model/property releases required. Send résumé, business card, promotional literature or tearsheets to be kept on file.

Terms: Pays on acceptance. Buys first rights, one-time rights, second serial, first North American rights for mss. Purchases all rights for artwork. Pays 3-7¢/word for unsolicited articles few are assigned. Contributor copies given "not as payment, but all contributors receive copies of their art/articles." Pays $70-125 for color illustrations; $125-150 for color cover; $40-60 for line art only. Photographers paid $125 maximum per photo. Sample copy and writer's guidelines free with 9⅜ × 4¼ SAE and 1 first-class stamp.

Tips: "Write about current topics, issues that elementary-age children are dealing with. Keep illustrations/photos current." (See listing for *Straight*.)

RANGER RICK, National Wildlife Federation, 8925 Leesburg Pike, Vienna VA 22184. (703)790-4000. Editor: Gerald Bishop. Design Director: Donna Miller. Monthly magazine. Circ. 890,000. "Our audience ranges from ages six to twelve, though we aim the reading level of most material at nine-year-olds or fourth graders."

Fiction: Middle readers: animal (wildlife), fantasy, humorous, science fiction. Buys 4-6 mss/year. Average word length: 900. Byline given.

Nonfiction: Middle readers: animal (wildlife), conservation, outdoor adventure, humorous. Buys 20-30 mss/year. Average word length: 900. Byline given.

How to Contact/Writers: Fiction: Query with published clips; send complete ms. Nonfiction: Query with published clips. Reports on queries/mss in 6 weeks.

Illustration: Buys 6-8 illustrations/issue; buys 75-100 illustrations/year. Preferred theme: nature, wildlife. Will review artwork for future assignments. Works on assignment only.

How to Contact/Illustrators: Illustrations only: Send résumé, tearsheets. Reports on art samples in 6 weeks. Original artwork returned at job's completion.

Terms: Pays on acceptance. Buys all rights (first North American serial rights negotiable). Pays up to $575 for full-length of best quality. For illustrations, buys one-time rights. Pays $250-1,000 for color (inside, per page) illustration. Sample copy $2. Writer's guidelines free with SASE.

Tips: "Fiction and nonfiction articles may be written on any aspect of wildlife, nature, outdoor adventure and discovery, domestic animals with a 'wild' connection (such as domestic pigs and wild boars), science, conservation or related subjects. To find out what subjects have been covered recently, consult our annual indexes and the *Children's Magazine Guide*. These are available in many libraries. The National Wildlife Federation (NWF) discourages the keeping of wildlife as pets, so the keeping of such pets should not be featured in your copy. Avoid stereotyping of any group. For instance, girls can enjoy nature and the outdoors as much as boys can, and mothers can be just as knowledgeable as fathers. The only way you can write successfully for *Ranger Rick* is to know the kinds of subjects and approaches we like. And the only way you can do that is to read the magazine. Recent issues can be found in most libraries or are available from our office for $2 a copy."

SASSY, 230 Park Ave., New York NY 10169. (212)551-9554. Fiction Editor: Christina Kelly. Art Director: Karmen Lizzul. Monthly magazine. Estab. 1988. Circ. 650,000. Audience is teenage girls.

Fiction: Young Adults: quality fiction. Buys approx. 11 mss/year. Average word length: 1,000-2,000. Byline given.

How to Contact/Writers: Send complete ms. Reports in 3 months. Will consider simultaneous submissions.

SCHOLASTIC MATH MAGAZINE, Scholastic, Inc., 555 Broadway, New York NY 10012-3999. (212)343-6100. Editor: Tracey Randinelli. Senior Designer: Leah Bossio. Art Director: Joan Michael. Magazine published 14 times/year, September-May. Estab. 1980. Circ. 265,000. "We are a math magazine for seventh-, eighth- and ninth-grade classrooms. We present math in current, relevant, high-interest topics. Math skills we focus on include whole number, fraction and decimal computation, percentages, ratios, proportions, geometry."

Nonfiction: Young adults: animal, arts/crafts, careers, cooking, fashion, games/puzzles, geography, health, history, hobbies, how-to, humorous, interview/profile, math, multicultural, nature/environment, problem solving, science, social issues, sports, travel. No fiction. Does not want to see "anything dealing with *very* controversial issues — e.g., teenage pregnancy, etc." Buys 20 mss/year. Byline given.

How to Contact/Writers: Query. Reports on queries in 2 months. Will consider simultaneous submissions.

Illustration: Buys 4 illustrations/issue; 56 illustrations/year. Prefers to review "humorous, young adult sophistication" types of art. Will review ms/illustration packages. Works on assignment only.

How to Contact/Illustrators: Ms/illustration packages: Query first. Illustrations only: Query with samples; submit portfolio for review. Reports back only if interested. Original artwork returned at job's completion.

Terms: Pays on publication. Buys all rights for mss. Pays $25 for puzzles and riddles; maximum of $350 for stories/articles. Photographers are paid by the project.

Tips: "For our magazine, stories dealing with math concepts and applications in the real world are sought."

SCHOOL MATES, USCF's Magazine For Beginning Chess Players, United States Chess Federation, 186 Rt. 9W, New Windsor NY 12553. (914)562-8350. Fax: (914)561-CHES. Editor-in-Chief: Jennie Simon. Art Director: Jami Anson. Bimonthly magazine. Estab. 1987. Circ. 18,000. Magazine for beginning chess players. Offers instructional articles, features on famous players, scholastic chess coverage, games, puzzles, occasional fiction, listing of chess tournaments.

Fiction: Middle readers: problem-solving (chess related). Average word length: 1,000-5,000 words.

Nonfiction: Middle readers: games/puzzles, chess. "No *Mad Magazine* type humor. No sex, no drugs, no alcohol, no tobacco. No stereotypes. We want to see chess presented as a wholesome, non-nerdy activity that's fun for all. Good sportsmanship, fair play, and 'thinking ahead' in chess as in life are extremely desirable in articles. Also, celebrities who play chess."

Poetry: Infrequently published. Must be chess related.

How to Contact/Writers: Send complete ms. Reports on queries/mss in 3 months

Illustration: Buys 2-3 illustrations/year. Prefers b&w and ink; cartoons OK. Reviews ms/illustration packages; reviews artwork for future assignments.

How to Contact/Illustrators: Query first. Reports back only if interested. "Typically, a cover is credited while an illustration inside gets only the artist's signature in the work itself."

Photography: Purchases photos from freelancers. Wants "action shots of chess games, well-done portraits of popular chess players."

Terms: Pays on publication. Buys one-time rights for mss, artwork and photos. For stories/articles, pays $40/1,000 words. Pays illustrators $50-75/b&w cover; $25-45/b&w inside. Pays photographers per photo (range: $25-75). Sample copies free for 9 × 12 SAE and 2 first-class stamps. Writer's guidelines free on request.

Tips: Writers: "Lively prose that grabs and sustains kids' attention is desirable. Don't talk down to kids or over their heads. Don't be overly 'cute.' " Illustration/photography: "Whimsical shots are often desirable."

SCIENCE WEEKLY, Science Weekly Inc., Suite 202, 2141 Industrial Pkwy., Silver Spring MD 20904. (301)680-8804. Fax: (301)680-9240. Editor: Deborah Lazar. Magazine published 16 times/year. Estab. 1984. Circ. 250,000.
Nonfiction: Young readers, middle readers, (K-8th grade): education, problem-solving, science/math education. "Author must be within the greater DC area, VA, MD."
Terms: Pays on publication. Prefers people with education, science and children's writing background. *Send résumé.*

SCIENCELAND, To Nurture Scientific Thinking, Scienceland Inc., #2108, 501 Fifth Ave., New York NY 10017-6102. (212)490-2180. Fax: (212)490-2187. Editor/Art Director: Al Matano. Magazine published 8 times/year. Estab. 1977. Circ. 16,000. This is "a content reading picture-book for K-3rd grade to encourage beginning readers; for teachers and parents."
Nonfiction: Picture-oriented material, young readers: animal, art/crafts, biography, careers, cooking, education, games/puzzles, health, history, how-to, nature/environment, problem solving. Does not want to see unillustrated material.
Poetry: Reviews poetry. Maximum length: 12 lines.
How to Contact/Writers: *Must* be picture or full-color illustrated stories.
Illustration: Prefers to review "detailed, realistic, full color art. No abstracts." Uses "predominantly" color artwork. Will review ms/illustration packages; reviews artwork for future assignments.
How to Contact/Illustrators: Ms/illustration packages: "Query first." Illustrations only: Send unsolicited art by mail; provide résumé, promotional literature or tearsheets to be kept on file. Reports back in 3-4 weeks. Original artwork returned at job's completion, "depending on material."
Photography: Wants to see "physical and natural science photos with children in scenes whenever possible." Model/property release and photo captions required. Uses 35mm transparencies. Photographer should submit portfolio for review; provide résumé, promotional literature or tearsheets to be kept on file.
Terms: Pays on publication. Buys first rights for mss, artwork and photos. Payment for ms/illustration packages: $50-500. Payment for illustrations: $25-300 color cover; $25-300 color inside. Photographers paid by the project. Sample copy free with 9 × 12 SASE.
Tips: "Must be top notch illustrator or photographer. No amateurs."

SEVENTEEN MAGAZINE, K-III Magazines, 850 Third Ave., New York NY 10022. (212)759-8100. Executive Editor: Catherine Cavender. Fiction Editor: Joe Bargmann. Senior Editor: Eileen Livers. Art Director: Shem Law. Monthly magazine. Estab. 1944. Circ. 1,750,000. "General interest magazine for teenage girls."
Fiction: Young adults: adult, contemporary, fantasy, humorous, religious, romance, science fiction, sports, spy/mystery/adventure. "We consider all good literary short fiction." Buys 12-20 mss/year. Average word length: 900-3,000. Byline given.
Nonfiction: Young adults: how-to, humorous, interview/profile, problem solving, reporting, social issues. Buys 150 mss/year. Word length varies from 800-1,000 words for short features and monthly columns to 2,500 words for major articles. Byline given.
Poetry: Reviews poetry "only by writers younger than 21."
How to Contact/Writers: Fiction: Send complete ms. Nonfiction: Query with published clips or send complete ms. Reports on queries/mss in 3 weeks. Will consider simultaneous submissions.
Illustration: Uses 1 illustration per short story. Will review ms/illustration packages. Pays illustrators by the project. Writer's guidelines for business-size envelope and 1 first-class stamp.

Refer to the Business of Children's Writing & Illustrating for up-to-date marketing, tax and legal information.

SHARING THE VICTORY, Fellowship of Christian Athletes, 8701 Leeds, Kansas City MO 64129. (816)921-0909. Fax: (816)921-8755. Articles/Photo Editor: John Dodderidge. Art Director: Frank Grey. Monthly magazine. Estab. 1982. Circ. 55,000. "Purpose is to present to coaches and athletes, and all whom they influence, the challenge and adventure of receiving Jesus Christ as Savior and Lord."

Nonfiction: Young adults: interview/profile, sports. Buys 20-25 mss/year. Average word length: 400-900. Byline given.

Poetry: Reviews poetry. Maximum word length 50-75.

How to Contact/Writers: Nonfiction: Query with published clips. Reports in 3 weeks. Publishes ms 3 months after acceptance. Will consider simultaneous submissions, electronic submissions via disk or modem and previously published work.

Photography: Purchases photos separately. Looking for photos of sports action. Uses color, b&w prints and 35mm transparencies.

Terms: Pays on publication. Buys first rights and second serial (reprint rights). Pays $50-250 for assigned and unsolicited articles. Photographers paid per photo (range: $50-300). Sample copies for 9×12 SASE and $1. Writer's/photo guidelines for SASE.

Tips: "Be specific—write short. Take quality photos that are useable." Wants interviews and features. Interested in colorful sports photos.

SHOFAR, 43 Northcote Dr., Melville NY 11747. (516)643-4598. Managing Editor: Gerald H. Grayson. Magazine published monthly Oct. through May—double issues Dec./Jan. and April/May. Circ. 17,000. For Jewish children ages 9-13.

Fiction: Middle readers: cartoons, contemporary, humorous, poetry, religious, sports. All material must be on a Jewish theme. Buys 10-20 mss/year. Average word length: 500-700. Byline given.

Nonfiction: Middle readers: history, humorous, interview/profile, puzzles, religious. Buys 10-20 mss/year. Average word length: 500-1,000. Byline given.

How to Contact/Writers: Fiction/nonfiction: Send complete ms (preferred). Queries welcome. Submit holiday theme pieces at least 4 months in advance. Will consider simultaneous and electronic submissions via disk or modem (only Macintosh).

Illustration: Buys 3-4 illustrations/issue; buys 15-20 illustrations/year. Works on assignment only.

How to Contact/Illustrators: Ms/illustration packages: Query first. Illustrations only: Send tearsheets. Works on assignment only. Reports on art samples only if interested. Original artwork returned at job's completion.

Terms: Buys first North American serial rights or first serial rights. Pays on publication. Pays 10¢/word plus 5 contributor's copies. Photos purchased with mss at additional fees. Pays $25-100/b&w cover illustration; $50-150/color (cover). Sample copy free with 9×12 SAE and 3 first-class stamps. Free writer's/illustrator's guidelines.

THE SINGLE PARENT, Journal of Parents Without Partners, Inc., 401 N. Michigan Ave., Chicago IL 60611. (312)644-6610, ext. 3226. Fax: (312)245-1082. Articles/Fiction Editor/Art Director: Mercedes Vance. Quarterly magazine. Estab. 1957. Circ. 90,000. Members of PWP are single parents who are divorced, widowed or never married. "*The Single Parent* looks at the positive side of the single parent's situation and is interested in all aspects of parenting, and the particular situation of single parenting." 10% of material aimed at juvenile audience.

Fiction: Young readers, middle readers, young adults: contemporary, humorous, problem solving, suspense/mystery/adventure (only stories with single parent angle). No sad stories or sports, romance or religious material. Buys commissioned and noncommissioned mss. Average word length: 800-1,500. Accompanying photos/graphics strongly encouraged. Byline given.

Nonfiction: Primarily for adult readers: careers, cooking, education, health, history, humorous, interview/profile, problem-solving. Does *not* want to see material unrelated to single-parent children and families. Average word length: 800-1,500. Buys commissioned and noncommissioned mss. Byline given.

How to Contact/Writers: Fiction/nonfiction: Send complete ms with accompanying photos/graphics and author photo and bio. Mss must be submitted in WordPerfect/ASCII format on 3.5 disk with hardcopy. Mss nonreturnable. Editor contacts *only* those authors whose mss will be published. *TSP* reserves copyright for all published articles.

SKIPPING STONES, A Multicultural Children's Magazine, P.O. Box 3939, Eugene OR 97403. (503)342-4956. Editor: Arun N. Toké. Publishes 5 issues bimonthly during the school year. Estab. 1988. Circ. 3,000. "*Skipping Stones* is a multi-cultural nonprofit children's magazine designed to encourage cooperation, creativity and celebration of cultural and environmental richness. We encourage submissions by minorities and under-represented populations."

Fiction: All levels: multicultural, nature/environment. Multicultural needs include: bilingual or multilingual pieces; use of words from other languages; settings in other cultures or multi-ethnic communities.

Nonfiction: All levels: animal, biography, games/puzzles, history, humorous, interview/profile, multicultural, nature/environment, problem-solving, religion and cultural celebrations, sports, travel, multicultural and environmental awareness. Does not want to see preaching or abusive language; no poems by authors over 18 years old; no suspense or romance stories for the sake of the same. Average word length: 500. Byline given.

How to Contact/Writers: Fiction: Query. Nonfiction: Send complete ms. Reports on queries in 2 months; ms in 4 months. Will consider simultaneous submissions. Please include your name on each page.

Illustration: Prefers b&w drawings especially by young adults. Will consider all illustration packages.

How to Contact/Illustrators: Ms/illustration packages: Query; submit complete ms with final art. Submit tearsheets. Reports back in 4 months (only if interested). Original artwork returned at job's completion. Credit line given.

Photography: Black & white photos preferred, but color photos will be considered.

Terms: Pays in copies. Acquires one-time rights. Sample copy for $4 with SAE and 4 first-class stamps. Writer's/illustrator's guidelines for 1 first-class stamp and 4×9 SAE.

Tips: "Think, live and write as if you were a child. Let the 'inner child' within you speak out—naturally, uninhibited." Wants "material that gives insight on cultural celebrations, lifestyle, custom and tradition, glimpse of daily life in other countries and cultures. Photos, songs, artwork are most welcome if they illustrate/highlight the points. Translations are welcome if your submission is in a language other than English. In 1994, our themes will include homeless and street children, world religions and cultures, African-American experiences, Japan, bilingual issue, indigenous architecture, songs from various cultures, Reduce, Reuse and Recycle, nutrition and foods from around the world, hospitality, death and loss, substance abuse, . ."

*SLEUTH, Tellstar Productions, P.O. Box 1264, Huntington WV 25714. Articles Editor: Shannon Bridget Murphy. Semiannual magazine. Estab. 1993. Circ. 500. "Mystery magazine for children/young adult readers."

Fiction: All levels: problem-solving, suspense/mystery. "Please do not send stories too complex for children or young readers. I would like to see children's stories that feature children." Average word length: 500-1,500.

Nonfiction: All levels: problem-solving. "I would like to see practical problem-solving nonfiction articles." Average word length: 500-1,500. Byline given.

Poetry: Reviews poetry. Multiple poetry submissions welcome.

How to Contact/Writers: Fiction/nonfiction: Send complete ms. Reports in 6 weeks. Will consider simultaneous submissions, electronic submissions via disk or modem.

Illustration: Looks for illustrations that feature children; illustrations of children in sets. Reviews ms/illustration packages; reviews artwork for future assignments.
How to Contact/Illustrators: Ms/illustration packages: Submit complete package with final art; submit ms with rough sketches. Illustration only: Query; send portfolio, slides. Reports in 6 weeks. Samples returned with SASE; samples filed with permission of artist. Original work returned upon job's completion. Credit line given.
Photography: Model/property releases required. Uses color, b&w prints; 35mm, 8 × 10 transparencies. To contact, photographers should query with samples; send unsolicited photos by mail; provide business card, promotional literature or tearsheets.
Terms: Pays on publication. Buys first rights, one-time rights for mss. Additional payment for ms/illustration packages and when photos accompany articles. Sample copies for $7. Writer's/illustrator's/photo guidelines for SASE.
Tips: "Work of young writers and college students welcome."

STORY FRIENDS, Mennonite Publishing House, 616 Walnut Ave., Scottdale PA 15683. (412)887-5181. Fax: (412)887-3111. Editor: Marjorie Waybill. Art Director: Jim Butti. Magazine published monthly in weekly issues. Estab. 1905. Circ. 9,000. Story paper that reinforces Christian values for children ages 4-9.
Fiction: Young readers: contemporary, humorous, problem solving, religious, relationships. Buys 45 mss/year. Average word length: 300-800. Byline given.
Nonfiction: Picture-oriented and young readers: interview/profile, nature/environment. Buys 10 mss/year. Average word length: 300-800. Byline given.
Poetry: "I like variety—some long story poems and some four-lines."
How to Contact/Writers: Fiction/nonfiction: Send complete ms. Reports on mss in 2-3 weeks. Will consider simultaneous submissions.
Illustration: Works on assignment only.
Terms: Writer's guidelines free with SAE and 2 first-class stamps.

STRAIGHT, Standard Publishing, 8121 Hamilton Ave., Cincinnati OH 45231. (513)931-4050. Articles/Fiction Editor: Carla J. Crane. Magazine published quarterly in weekly parts. Circ. 60,000. *Straight* is a magazine designed for today's Christian teenagers.
Fiction: Young adults: adventure, contemporary, health, humorous, nature/environment, problem solving, religious, sports. Does not want to see science fiction, fantasy, historical. Buys 100-115 mss/year. Average word length: 1,100-1,500. Byline given.
Nonfiction: Young adults: careers, concept, health, how-to, humorous, interview/profile, nature/environment, problem solving, religious, science, social issues. Does not want to see devotionals. Buys 24-30 mss/year. Average word length: 500-1,000. Byline given.
Poetry: Reviews poetry from teenagers only.
How to Contact/Writers: Fiction/nonfiction: Query or send complete ms. Reports on queries in 1-2 weeks; mss in 4-6 weeks. Will consider simultaneous submissions.
Illustration: Buys 40-45 illustrations/year. Uses color artwork only. Preferred theme or style: Realistic, cartoon (full-color only). Reviews ms/illustration packages "on occasion." Reviews artwork for future assignments. Works on assignment only.
How to Contact/Illustrators: Ms/illustration packages: Query first. Illustrations only: Submit portfolio or tearsheets. Reports back only if interested. Credit line given.
Photography: Purchases photos from freelancers. Looking for contemporary teenagers. Model/property release required. Uses 5 × 7 or 8 × 10 b&w prints and 35mm transparencies. Photographer should send unsolicited photos by mail.
Terms: Pays on acceptance. Buys first North American rights and second serial (reprint rights) for mss. Buys full rights for artwork; one-time rights for photos. Pays 3-7¢ per word for stories/articles. Pays illustrators $150-250/color inside. Photographers paid per photo (range: $50-125). Sample copy free with business SASE. Writer's/illustrator's guidelines free with business SASE.

Tips: "The main characters should be contemporary teens who cope with modern-day problems using Christian principles. Stories should be uplifting, positive and character-building, but not preachy. Conflicts must be resolved realistically, with thought-provoking and honest endings. Accepted length is 1,100 to 1,500 words. Nonfiction is accepted. We use devotional pieces, articles on current issues from a Christian point of view and humor. Nonfiction pieces should concern topics of interest to teens, including school, family life, recreation, friends, part-time jobs, dating and music." (See listing for *R-A-D-A-R*.)

STREET TIMES, Outside In, 1236 SW Salmon, Portland OR 97205. Editor: Louis Folkman. Monthly newsletter. Estab. 1987. Circ. 800. Contains "resources, street life stories, poetry and art—designed as a pre-employment training tool for Portland street youth." 70% of publication aimed at juvenile market.
Nonfiction: Wants experiences of "other street youth or former street youth; difficulties of getting off the street."
Poetry: Reviews poetry.
How to Contact/Writers: Nonfiction: Send complete ms. Will consider simultaneous submissions and previously published work.
Illustration: Uses b&w artwork only.
How to Contact/Illustrators: Samples not returned; samples kept on file. Originals not returned.
Terms: Sample copies free for SASE.

*STUDENT LEADERSHIP JOURNAL, InterVarsity Christian Fellowship, P.O. Box 7895, Madison WI 53707. (608)274-9001, ext. 425. Editor: Jeff Yourison. Quarterly magazine. Estab. 1988. Circ. 11,000.
Fiction: Young adults: multicultural, religious. Multicultural themes include: forming campus fellowships that reflect the ethnic makeup of the campus and demonstrating *reconciliation* beyond celebrating difference. "I see too much aimed at young teens. Our age group is 18-30 years old." Buys 4 mss/year. Average word length: 300-1,800. Byline given.
Nonfiction: Young adults/teens: history, interview/profile, multicultural, nature/environment, religion, social issue. Multicultural themes include: affirming the need for ethnic validation and reconciliation. "We don't affirm all lifestyles—therefore we are promoting multi-ethnicity but not full-orbed multiculturalism. We prefer articles on issues, leadership, spiritual growth, sexual healing, dysfunctionality, etc." Buys 6-8 mss/year. Average word length: 1,100-2,200. Byline given.
Poetry: Wants to see free verse; lots of good imagery. Maximum length: 18 lines. Limit submissions to 5 poems.
How to Contact/Writers: Fiction/nonfiction: Send complete ms. Reports on queries/mss in 6 months. Publishes ms 1-2 years after acceptance. Accepts IBM compatible word processing files on diskettes.
Illustration: Buys 5 illustrations/issue; 20 illustrations/year. Uses b&w line art only. Prefers cartoon pen & ink 5×7 or 8×10 stand alone campus/religious humor. Reviews artwork for future assignments.
How to Contact/Illustrators: Illustrations only: Send promo sheet, portfolio and tearsheets. Reports only if interested. Samples not returned; samples kept on file. Original work returned at job's completion. Credit line given.
Photography: Looks for campus shots—all types: single faces, studying, thinking, "mood"—pairs and groups: praying, studying, talking, playing. 18-22-year-old subjects or professor-types. Model/property release preferred. Uses color and b&w 5×7 glossy prints; 2¼×2¼, 4×5 or 35mm transparencies. Photographers should query with samples; send unsolicited photos by mail; provide business card, promotional literature

or tearsheets. "Send photocopies I can keep. I'll call for the print." Reports only if interested.

Terms: Pays on acceptance for ms; on publication for photos and cartoons. Buys first North American serial rights, first rights and reprint rights for ms. Purchases first rights for artwork; one-time rights for photographs. Pays $50-75 for stories; $50-125 for articles; and contributor's copies. Pays illustrators $50-100 for b&w (cover); $25-75 for b&w (inside). Photographers paid per photo (range: $25-50). Sample copies for $3. Writer's/illustrator's/photo guidelines for SASE.

Tips: "Please write and photograph according to the audience. Research the age group and the subculture. Older teens are really sensitive to tokenism and condescension toward their generation. They want to be treated as sophisticated even though they are frequently uninformed and hurting. To reach this audience requires credibility, vulnerability, transparency and confidence!"

SUPERSCIENCE BLUE, Scholastic, Inc., 555 Broadway, New York NY 10012-3099. (212)343-6100. Editor: Kathy Burkett. Art Director: Susan Kass. Monthly (during school year) magazine. Estab. 1989. Circ. 375,000. "News and hands-on science for children in grades 4-6. Designed for use in a class setting; distributed by teacher. Articles make science fun and interesting for a broad audience of children. Issues are theme-based."

Nonfiction: Middle readers: animal, how-to (science experiments), nature/environment, problem solving, science topics. Does not want to see "general nature stories. Our focus is science with a *news* or *hands-on* slant. To date we have never purchased an unsolicited manuscript. Instead, we assign articles based on clips—and sometimes queries." Write for editorial calendar. Average word length: 250-800. Byline sometimes given.

How to Contact/Writers: Nonfiction: Query with published clips. (Most freelance articles are assigned.) Reports on queries in 4-6 weeks. Publishes ms 4 months after acceptance.

Illustration: Buys 2-3 illustrations/issue; 10-12 illustrations/year. Works on assignment only.

How to Contact/Illustrators: Illustrations only: Send résumé and tearsheets. Reports on art samples only if interested. Original artwork returned at job's completion.

Terms: Pays on acceptance. Buys all rights. Pays $100-600. Illustrations only: $75 minimum/b&w (inside); $150-1,200/color (inside) (complicated spreads only). Writer's guidelines free on request.

Tips: Looks for "news articles and photo essays. Good journalism means always going to *primary* sources—interview scientists in the field, for example, and *quote* them for a more lively article."

TEEN POWER, Scripture Press Publications, Inc., P.O. Box 632, Glen Ellyn IL 60138. (708)668-6000. Editor: Amy J. Cox. Quarterly magazine. Estab. 1965. "*Teen Power* is an eight-page Sunday School take-home paper aimed at 11-16-year-olds in a conservative Christian audience. Its primary objective is to help readers see how principles for Christian living can be applied to everyday life."

Fiction: Young adults: contemporary, humorous, problem solving, religious, sports. Does not want to see "unrealistic stories with tacked-on morals. Fiction should be true-to-life and have a clear, spiritual take-away value." Buys 50 mss/year. Average word length: 400-1,200. Byline given.

Nonfiction: Young adults: how-to, humorous, interview/profile, multicultural, problem-solving, puzzles, religion, social issues. Multicultural themes include: Christian teens in foreign countries, missions, missionary kids, ethnic Christian teens in US and Canada. Does not want to see "articles with no connection to Christian principles." Buys 30 mss/year. Average word length: 250-700. Byline given.

How To Contact/Writers: Fiction/nonfiction: Send complete ms. Reports on mss in 2-3 months. Publishes ms "at least one year" after acceptance, Will consider simultaneous submissions.

Illustration: Reviews artwork for future assignments.

How to Contact/Illustrators: Send résumé, promo sheet. Reports back only if interested. Credit line given.

Photography: Looks for mood shots: teen fads and hang outs; sport and school activities shots.

Terms: Pays on acceptance. Buys one-time rights. Pays $25-75 for stories; $20-120 for articles. Negotiates illustrators' fees. Photographers paid per photo. Sample copies and writer's guidelines for #10 SAE and 1 first-class stamp.

Tips: "Take-home papers are a great "break-in" point. Each weekly issue contains at least 2 freelance-written featuers. However, we are very specific about the type of material we are looking for. We want stories and articles to reinforce our Sunday School lessons and help our readers apply what they learned in Sunday School throughout the week."

*TEENAGE CHRISTIAN MAGAZINE, Christian Publishing Inc., P.O. Box 1438, Murfreesboro TN 37133-1438. Articles/Fiction Editor: Marty Dodson. Photo Editor: Shana Pounders. Bimonthly magazine. Circ. 14,000. "We publish articles that challenge Christian teenagers to grow in their Christian faith."

Fiction: Young adults/teens: adventure, contemporary, humorous, problem-solving, religious, sports, suspense/mystery. "We see too many articles where adult writers use "cool" teen slang. We also get too many articles about perfect people where everything works out in the end. We like to see real-life stories." Buys 15-20 mss/year. Average word length: 1,000-1,750. Byline sometimes given.

Nonfiction: Young adults/teens: animal, arts/crafts, biography, careers, games/puzzles, health, history, hobbies, how-to, humorous, interview/profile, problem-solving, religion, social issues, sports, travel. "Work needs to be in touch with evangelical Christian teen perspective." Buys 20 mss/year. Average word length: 500-2,000. Byline sometimes given.

Poetry: Reviews religious teen-oriented poetry. Maximum length: 20-25 lines. Limit submissions to 3 poems.

How to Contact/Writers: Fiction: Query. Nonfiction: Send complete ms. Reports on queries in 1 month/mss in 2 months. Publishes ms 4-6 months after acceptance. Will consider simultaneous and previously published submissions.

Terms: Pays on publication. Buys one-time rights for ms. Pays $15-25 (occasionally more) for stories/articles. Sample copies for 9 × 12 SAE and 98¢ postage.

Tips: "We look at anything that would help our audience. It is obvious when writers have read the magazine and when they have not. We use freelance writers almost exclusively for fiction. We use well-written pieces on nonfiction topics such as: dating, alcohol, finding jobs, etc."

3-2-1 CONTACT, Children's Television Workshop, One Lincoln Plaza, New York NY 10023. (212)595-3456. Articles Editor: Curtis Slepian. Art Director: Gretchen Grace. Magazine published 10 times/year. Estab. 1979. Circ. 440,000. This is a science and technology magazine for 8- to 14-year-olds. Features all areas of science and nature.

Fiction: "Our fiction piece is an on-going series called 'The Time Team.' It is written in-house."

Nonfiction: Middle readers, young adults: animal, health, how-to, interview/profile, multicultural, nature/environment, science. Multicultural needs include: how kids live in other countries (with a science hook; profiles of minority scientists). Does not want to see religion, travel or history. "We see too many research reports on the life of a toad. We'd like to see more articles about scientists doing exciting work (in the field)

with lots of quotes." Buys 20 mss/year. Average word length: 750-1,000. Byline given.
How to Contact/Writers: Query with published clips. Reports on queries in 3 weeks.
Illustration: Buys 15 illustrations/issue; buys 150 illustrations/year. Works on assignment only.
How to Contact/Illustrators: Illustrations only: Send tearsheets, portfolio. Reports on art samples only if interested. Original artwork returned at job's completion. Credit line given.
Terms: Pays on acceptance. Buys all rights for mss (negotiable). Purchases one-time rights for photos unless on assignment. Pays $100-600 for assigned/unsolicited articles. Pays $500-1,000/color (cover) illustration; $150-300/b&w (inside); $175-500/color (inside). Photographers paid per photo (range: $150-750). Sample copy for $1.75 and 8 × 14 SASE; writer's/illustrator's guidelines free with 8½ × 11 SASE.
Tips: Looks for "features. We do not want articles based on library research. We want on-the-spot interviews about what's happening in science now."

TOUCH, Calvinettes, Box 7259, Grand Rapids MI 49510. (616)241-5616. Editor: Joanne Ilbrink. Managing Editor: Carol Smith. Art Director: Chris Cook. Monthly (with combined issues May/June, July/August) magazine. Circ. 16,000. *"Touch* is designed to help girls ages 9-14 see how God is at work in their lives and in the world around them."
Fiction: Middle readers, young adults: animal, contemporary, history, humorous, problem solving, religious, romance. Does not want to see unrealistic stories and those with trite, easy endings. Buys 40 mss/year. Average word length: 400-1,000. Byline given.
Nonfiction: Middle readers, young adults: how-to, humorous, interview/profile, problem solving, religious. Buys 5 mss/year. Average word length: 200-800. Byline given.
How to Contact/Writers: Send for biannual update for publication themes. Fiction/nonfiction: Send complete ms. Reports on mss in 2 months. Will consider simultaneous submissions.
Illustration: Buys 1-2 illustrations/issue; buys 10-15 illustrations/year. Prefers illustrations to go with stories. Works on assignment only.
How to Contact/Illustrators: Ms/illustration packages: "We would prefer to consider finished art with a ms."
Terms: Pays on publication. Buys first North American serial rights; first rights; second serial (reprint rights); simultaneous rights. Pays $20-50 for assigned articles; $5-30 for unsolicited articles. "We send complimentary copies in addition to pay." Pays $25-50/b&w (cover) illustration; $15-25/b&w (inside) illustration. Writer's guidelines free with SASE.
Tips: Writers: "The stories should be current, deal with adolescent problems and joys, and help girls see God at work in their lives through humor as well as problem solving."

TURTLE MAGAZINE, For Preschool Kids, Children's Better Health Institute, P.O. Box 567, Indianapolis IN 46206. (317)636-8881. Editor: Christine Clark. Art Director: Bart Rivers. Monthly/bimonthly magazine, January/February, March, April/May, June, July/August, September, October/November, December. Circ. 550,000. *Turtle* uses read-aloud stories, especially suitable for bedtime or naptime reading. Also used are poems, simple science experiments, and health-related articles. All but 2 pages aimed at juvenile audience.
Fiction: Picture-oriented material: adventure, animal, contemporary, folktales, health-related, seasonal stories with holiday themes, humorous, nature/environment, problem-solving, sports. "Need adaptations of folktales for 'Pokey Toes Theatre,' a regular feature starring the Turtle character, Pokey Toes. Also needs action rhymes to foster creative movement." Does not want to see stories about monsters or scary things. Avoid stories in which the characters indulge in unhealthy activities like eating junk food. Buys 50 mss/year. Average word length: 200-600. Byline given.

Nonfiction: Picture-oriented material: animal, arts/crafts, games/puzzles, health, multicultural, nature/environment, science, sports. Buys 20 mss/year. Average word length: 200-600. Byline given.

How to Contact/Writers: Fiction/nonfiction: Send complete ms. "No queries, please." Reports on mss in 8-10 weeks.

Illustration: Buys 20-25 illustrations/issue; 160-200 illustrations/year. Prefers "realistic and humorous illustration." Reviews artwork for future assignments.

How to Contact/Illustrators: Illustrations only: Send promo sheet, slides, tearsheets. Reports back only if interested. Credit line given.

Photography: Purchases photos from freelancers with accompanying ms only.

Terms: Pays on publication. Buys all rights for mss/artwork; one-time rights for photographs. Pays 10-20¢/word for articles, depending upon length and quality. Pays $250/color (cover) illustration, $30-70/b&w (inside); $65-140/color (inside). Sample copy $1.25. Writer's/illustrator's guidelines free with SAE and 1 first-class stamp.

Tips: "We're beginning to edit *Turtle* more for the very young preschooler, so we're looking for stories and articles that are written more simply than those we've used in the past. Our need for health-related material, especially features that encourage fitness, is ongoing. Health subjects must be age-appropriate. When writing about them, think creatively and lighten up! Fight the tendency to become boringly pedantic. Nobody—not even young kids—likes being lectured. Always keep in mind that in order for a story or article to educate preschoolers, it first must be truly entertaining—warm and engaging, exciting, or genuinely funny. Understand that writing for *Turtle* is a difficult challenge."

2 HYPE AND HYPE HAIR, Word Up Publication, Suite 230, 63 Grand Ave., River Edge NY 07661. (201)487-6124. Art Director: Stuart Koban. Bimonthly magazine. Estab. 1990. Publishes articles about music (rap and R&B)—fashion, hair trends, health, grooming, games, contests—all dealing with music.

Nonfiction: Young adults: careers, fashion, games/puzzles, health, hobbies, how-to, interview/profile, problem-solving. Byline given.

How to Contact/Writers: Nonfiction: Query with published clips. Publishes ms 5 months after acceptance. Will consider electronic submissions via disk or modem.

Illustration: Buys 10 illustrations/issue. Illustrations should be done on 8½ × 11 paper. Reviews ms/illustration packages; reviews artwork for future assignments; works on assignment only.

How to Contact/Illustrators: Ms/illustration packages: Submit complete package with final art. Illustrations only: Send promo sheet, portfolio, tearsheets. Reports back only if interested. Samples not filed. Original work returned upon job's completion. Credit line given.

Photography: Model/property releases and photo captions required. Uses b&w and color prints. Photographers should send unsolicited photos by mail. Reports back only if interested.

Terms: Pays on publication. Buys one-time rights to mss. Pays $75-100 for articles. Additional payment for ms/illustration packages. Pays illustrators $50-75. Photographers paid per photo (range $35-150). Writer's/illustrator's/photo guidelines free for SASE.

Tips: "Send fun ideas for people with short attention spans."

U.S. KIDS, Children's Better Health Institute, P.O. 567, Indianapolis IN 46202. (317)636-8881. Editor: Steve Charles. Art Editor: Mary Pesce. Magazine published 8 times a year. Estab. 1987. Circ. 250,000.

Fiction: Young readers and middle readers: adventure, animal, contemporary, health, history, humorous, multicultural, nature/environment, problem-solving, sports, suspense/mystery. "I see too many stories with no real story line. I'd like to see more mysteries and contemporary humor stories." Buys 8-16 mss/year. Average word length: 500-800. Byline given.

Nonfiction: Young readers and middle readers: animal, arts/crafts, cooking, games/puzzles, health, history, hobbies, how-to, humorous, interview/profile, multicultural, nature/environment, science, social issues, sports, travel. Wants to see interviews with kids' ages 5-11, who have done something unusual or different. Buys 30-40 mss/year. Average word length: 500-600. Byline given.

Poetry: Maximum length: 32 lines.

How tc Contact/Writers: Fiction: Send complete ms. Nonfiction: Query. Reports on queries and mss in 1 month. Publishes ms 6 months after acceptance. Will consider simultaneous submissions, electronic submissions via disk or modem and previously published work.

Illustration: Buys 8 illustrations/issue; 70 illustrations/year. Color artwork only. Reviews ms/illustration packages; reviews artwork for future assignments; works on assignment only.

How to Contact/Illustrators: Ms/illustration packages: Query. Illustrations only: Send résumé and tearsheets. Reports back only if interested. Samples returned with SASE; samples kept on file. Does not return originals. Credit line given.

Photography: Purchases photography from freelancers. Looking for photos that pertain to children ages 5-11. Model/property release required. Uses color and b&w prints; 35mm, 2¼ × 2¼, 4 × 5 and 8 × 10 transparencies. Photographers should provide résumé, business card, promotional literature or tearsheets to be kept on file. Reports back only if interested.

Terms: Pays on publication. Buys all rights for mss. Purchases all rights for artwork. Purchases one-time rights for photographs. Pays 10¢/word minimum. Additional payment for ms/illustration packages. Pays illustrators $140/page for color (inside). Photographers paid by the project or per photo (negotiable). Sample copies for $2.50. Writer's/illustrator/photo guidelines for SASE.

Tips: "Write clearly and concisely without preaching or being obvious."

VENTURE, Christian Service Brigade, P.O. Box 150, Wheaton IL 60189. (708)665-0630. Articles/Fiction Editor: Deborah Christensen. Art Director: Robert Fine. Bimonthly magazine. Estab. 1937. Circ. 19,000. The magazine is designed "to speak to the concerns of boys from a biblical perspective. To provide wholesome, entertaining reading for boys."

Fiction: Middle readers, young adults: adventure, contemporary, humorous, nature/environment, problem-solving, religious, sports, suspense/mystery. Does not want to see fantasy, romance, science fiction or anything without Christian emphasis. "We see too much 'new kid in town' stories. We'd like to see more humor." Buys 12 mss/year. Average word length: 1,000-1,500. Byline given.

Nonfiction: Middle readers, young adults: animal, geography, humorous, nature/environment, problem solving, religious, science, social issues. Buys 6 mss/year. Average word length: 1,000-1,500. Byline given.

How to Contact/Writers: Fiction/nonfiction: send complete ms. Reports on queries/mss in 1-2 weeks. Will consider simultaneous submissions.

Illustration: Buys 3 illustrations/issue; 18 illustrations/year. Reviews ms/illustration packages; reviews artwork for future assignments.

How to Contact/Illustrators: Ms/illustration packages: Send complete ms. Illustrations only: Send promo sheets or tearsheets. Reports on art samples only if interested. Original artwork returned at job's completion. Credit line given.

Photography: Purchases photography from freelancers. Wants photos of boys 10-15 years old.

Terms: Pays on publication for mss, artwork and photos. Buys first North American serial rights; first rights; second serial (reprint rights). Pays $30-120 for stories/articles.

Pays $75-125/b&w (cover) illustration—usually photos only; $35-250/b&w (inside) illustration (includes photos). Sample copy $1.85 with 9 × 12 SAE and 98¢ postage. Writer's/illustrator's guidelines free with SAE and 1 first-class stamp.

Tips: "Know kids and their language. Too many writers use the vernacular of their childhood instead of contemporary language. I've seen illustrations and stories become more wild and exciting. Kids like movement."

WITH, Faith & Life Press, Mennonite Publishing House, 722 Main, P.O. Box 347, Newton KS 67114. (316)283-5100. Editors: Eddy Hall, Carol Duerksen. Published 8 times a year. Circ. 6,100. Magazine published for teenagers, ages 15-18, in Mennonite congregations. "We deal with issues affecting teens and try to help them make choices reflecting an Anabaptist-Mennonite faith."

Fiction: Young adults: contemporary, fantasy, folktales, humorous, multicultural, nature/environment, problem solving, religious, sports. Multicultural needs include: race relations, first-person stories featuring teens of ethnic minorities. "Would like to see more humor and parables/allegories." Buys 10 mss/year. Average word length: 1,000-2,000. Byline given.

Nonfiction: Young adults: first-person teen personal experience (as-told-to), humorous, nature/environment, problem-solving, religious, social issues. Buys 15-20 mss/year. Average word length: 500-1,500. Byline given.

Poetry: Wants to see religious, humorous, nature. "We're cutting back on poetry." Maximum length: 50 lines.

How to Contact/Writers: Send complete ms. Query on first-person teen personal experience stories and how-to articles. Reports on queries in 1 month; mss in 2 months. Will consider simultaneous submissions.

Illustration: Buys 6-8 illustrations/issue; buys 50-60 illustrations/year. Uses b&w and 2-color artwork only. Preferred theme or style: Candids/interracial. Will review ms/illustration packages. Reviews artwork for future assignments.

How to Contact/Illustrators: Ms/illustration packages: Query first. Illustrations only: Query with portfolio (photocopies only) or tearsheets. Reports on art samples only if interested. Original artwork returned at job's completion upon request. Credit line given.

Photography: Looking for teens (ages 15-18), ethnic minorities, candids. Uses 8 × 10 b&w glossy prints. Photographers should send unsolicited photos by mail.

Terms: Pays on acceptance. For mss buys one-time rights; second serial (reprint rights). Buys one-time rights for artwork and photos. Pays 4¢/word for unpublished manuscripts; 2¢/word for reprints. Will pay more for assigned as-told-to stories. Pays $25-50/b&w (cover) illustration; $20-35/b&w (inside) illustration. Photographers are paid per photo (range: $20-50 cover only). Sample copy for 9 × 12 SAE and $1.21 postage. Writer's/illustrator's guidelines free with SASE.

Tips: "We're hungry for stuff that makes teens laugh—fiction, nonfiction and cartoons. It doesn't have to be religious, but must be wholesome."

WONDER TIME, Beacon Hill Press, 6401 The Paseo, Kansas City MO 64131. (816)333-7000. Editor: Lois Perrigo. Weekly magazine. Circ. 45,000. "*Wonder Time* is a full-color story paper for first and second graders. It is designed to connect Sunday School learning with the daily living experiences and growth of the primary child. Since *Wonder Time's* target audience is children ages six to eight, the readability goal is to encourage begin-

---

A bullet has been placed within some listings to introduce special comments by the editor of Children's Writer's & Illustrator's Market.

ning readers to read for themselves. The major purposes of *Wonder Time* are to: Provide a life-related paper which will build Christian values and encourage ethical behavior and provide reinforcement for the biblical concepts taught in the Word Action Sunday School curriculum."

Fiction: Young readers: contemporary, problem-solving, religious. Buys 52 mss/year. Average word length: 300-400. Byline given.

Nonfiction: Young readers: religious.

Poetry: Reviews religious poetry of 4-8 lines.

How to Contact/Writers: Fiction/nonfiction: Send complete ms. Reports on queries/mss in 4 weeks. Will consider simultaneous submissions.

Illustration: Buys 100 illustrations/year. Will review illustration packages. Works on assignment only.

How to Contact/Illustrators: Ms/illustration packages: Ms with sketch. Illustrations only: Samples of work. Reports on art samples only if interested. Credit line given.

Terms: Pays on publication. Pays $25 per story for rights which allow the publisher to print the story multiple times in the same publication without repayment. Pays illustrators $40 for b&w (cover or inside); $75 for color (cover or inside). Photographers paid per photo (range: $25-75). Sends complimentary contributor's copies of publication. Sample copy and writer's guidelines with 9½ × 12 SAE and 2 first-class stamps.

Tips: "Basic themes reappear regularly. Please write for a theme list."

*WRITER'S OPEN FORUM, Bristol Publishing, P.O. Box 516, Tracyton WA 98393. Bimonthly magazine. Estab. 1990. Up to 25% aimed at juvenile market.

Fiction: Young readers, middle readers and young adults: adventure, animal, contemporary, fantasy, folktales, humorous, nature/environment, problem-solving, science fiction, suspense/mystery. "No experimental formats. We see too many anthropomorphic characters. We would like to see more mysteries, problem-solving and adventures." Buys approximately 25-42 mss/year. Average word length: 400-2,000. Byline given.

Nonfiction: Young readers, middle readers and young adults: biography, geography, history, hobbies, how-to, humorous, nature/environment, travel. "We do not print articles about writing." Buys 6 mss/year. Average word length: 500-1,500.

How to Contact/Writers: Fiction/nonfiction: Reports on mss in 2 months. Publishes ms 4 months after acceptance.

Terms: Pays on acceptance. Buys first North American serial rights. Pays $5 minimum for stories/articles. Sample copies for $3.

Tips: "All the stories and articles accepted for publication in Writer's Open Forum are critiqued by our readers. Many of our readers write for children and/or are school teachers. The most often noted critique on our children's pieces is that writers fail to clearly write for specific age group. Determine your audience's age, then write every word, description and action to that audience. Our 'Writer to Writer' column uses tips on the writing process and is our most open area; limit is 300 words and payment is one contributor copy. For stories and articles, the shorter the manuscript the better the chance of acceptance."

*YOUNG CHRISTIAN, Tellstar Productions, P.O. Box 1264, Huntington WV 25714. Articles Editor: Shannon Bridget Murphy. Semiannual magazine. Estab. 1993. Circ. 500. "We publish Christian based stories aimed at a young audience."

Fiction: All levels: religious. Average word length: 500-1,500. Byline given.

Nonfiction: All levels: religion. Average word length: 500-1,500. Byline given.

Poetry: Reviews poetry. Multiple poetry submissions welcome.

How to Contact/Writers: Fiction/nonfiction: Send complete ms. Reports in 6 weeks. Will consider simultaneous submissions; electronic submissions via disk or modem.

Illustration: Reviews ms/illustration packages; reviews artwork for future assignments.
How to Contact/Illustrators: Ms/illustration packages: Submit complete package with final art; submit ms with rough sketches. Illustrations only: Send promo sheet, portfolio, slides. Reports in 6 weeks. Samples returned with SASE; samples filed with permission of artist. Original work returned upon job's completion. Credit line given.
Photography: Looks for photographs that feature children in religious or nature oriented settings. Uses color, b&w prints; 35mm, 8 × 10 transparencies. To contact, photographers should query with samples; send unsolicited photos by mail; provide business card, promotional literature or tearsheets. Reports in 6 weeks.
Terms: Pays on publication. Buys first rights, one-time rights. Additional payment for ms/illustration packages and when photos accompany articles. Sample copy for $7. Writer's/illustrator's/photo guidelines for SASE.
Tips: "Work of young writers and college students welcome."

YOUNG NATURALIST FOUNDATION See listings for Chickadee, Owl.

YOUNG SALVATIONIST, The Salvation Army, 615 Slaters Lane, P.O. Box 269, Alexandria VA 22313. (703)684-5500. Editor: Lt. Deborah Sedlar. Monthly magazine. Estab. 1984. Circ. 50,000. "We accept material with clear Christian content written for high school age teenagers. *Young Salvationist* is published for teenage members of The Salvation Army, a fundamental, activist denomination of the Christian Church."
Fiction: Young adults: multicultural, religious, sports (with Christian perspective). Buys 12-20 mss/year. Average word length: 750-1,200. Byline given.
Nonfiction: Young adults: religious—hobbies, how-to, interview/profile, multicultural, nature/environment, problem-solving, social issues. Buys 40-50 mss/year. Average word length: 750-1,200. Byline given.
Poetry: Reviews 16-20 line poetry dealing with a Christian theme. Send no more than 6 submissions.
How to Contact/Writers: Fiction/nonfiction: Query with published clips or send complete ms. Reports on queries in 2-3 weeks; mss in 1 month. Will consider simultaneous submissions.
Illustrations: Buys 2-3 illustrations/issue; 20-30 illustrations/year. Reviews ms/illustration packages; reviews artwork for future assignments.
How to Contact/Illustrators: Ms/illustration packages: Query or send ms with art. Illustrations only: Query; send resumé, promo sheet, portfolio, tearsheets. Reports on artwork in 2-3 weeks (with SASE). Original artwork returned at job's completion "if requested." Credit line given.
Photography: Purchases photography from freelancers. Looking for teens in action.
Terms: Pays on acceptance. For mss, buys first North American serial rights, first rights, one-time rights, second serial (reprint rights). Purchases one-time rights for artwork and photographs. For mss, pays 10¢/word. Pays $100-150 color (cover) illustration; $50-100 b&w (inside) illustration; $100-150 color (inside) illustration. Sample copy for 9 × 12 SAE and 3 first-class stamps. Writer's/illustrator's guidelines free for #10 SASE.
Tips: "Ask for theme list/sample copy! Write 'up,' not down to teens. Aim at young *adults*, not children." Wants "less fiction, more 'journalistic' nonfiction."

YOUTH UPDATE, St. Anthony Messenger Press, 1615 Republic St., Cincinnati OH 45210. (513)241-5615. Articles Editor: Carol Ann Morrow. Art Director: Julie Lonneman. Monthly newsletter. Estab. 1982. Circ. 30,000. "Each issue focuses on one topic only. *Youth Update* addresses the faith and Christian life questions of young people and is designed to attract, instruct, guide and challenge its audience by applying the gospel to modern problems and situations. The students who read *Youth Update* vary in their religious education and reading ability. Write for average high school students. These students are 15-year-olds with a C+ average. Assume that they have paid attention to religious instruction and remember a little of what 'sister' said. Aim more toward 'table talk' than 'teacher talk.' "

Nonfiction: Young adults/teens: religious. Buys 12 mss/year. Average word length: 2,300-2,400. Byline given.

How to Contact/Writers: Nonfiction: Query. Reports on queries/mss in 6 weeks. Will consider computer printout and electronic submissions via disk.

Terms: Pays on acceptance. Buys first North American serial rights. Pays $325-400 for articles. Sample copy free with #10 SAE and 1 first-class stamp. Writer's guidelines free on request.

Tips: "Read the newsletter yourself—3 issues at least. In the past, our publication has dealt with a variety of topics including: dating, Lent, teenage pregnancy, baptism, loneliness, rock and roll, confirmation and the Bible. When writing, use the *New American Bible* as translation. More interested in church-related topics."

Magazines/'93-'94 changes

The following markets are not included in this edition of *Children's Writer's & Illustrator's Market* for the reasons indicated within parentheses. If there is no reason given, it means the market did not respond to our requests for updated information for a 1994 listing.

Marion Zimmer Bradley's Fantasy Magazine (not a children's market)
Equilibrium [10]
The Fun Zone (ceased publication)
I.D.
Instructor Magazine

Kid City
Lighthouse
Pets Today (ceased publication)
School Magazine, Blast Off!, Countdown, Orbit, Touchdown
Spark! Creative Fun for Kids

(suspended publication)
Take 5 (ceased publication)
'Teen Magazine
TQ, Teen Quest (ceased publication)
The Young Crusader
Young Judean

Audiovisual Markets

Video products are no longer sidelines in the children's market. Videocassette recorders (VCRs) can now be found in millions of homes, as well as thousands of schools, and with them comes a new means of entertaining and educating children.

Video stores used to be the only places to buy videos, but now such items are prominent in book and toy stores as well. Also, people are purchasing reasonably-priced videos rather than renting them, and children's videos make up a major percentage of these purchases.

Though children's entertainment videos can be considered "babysitters," parents are equally interested in the educational advantages. For example, the mass market audience has responded strongly to interactive videos, or read-alongs, for children. One such series is the Bank Street Read-Along Story Videos, which combine live action with computer animation. In these videos, each story is told twice. The second telling includes words printed on the screen so kids can read along.

New in this ever-expanding technological field are laser videodiscs, which are as much a threat to videotapes as compact discs were to records. They have clearer pictures than videotapes and digital sound. Laser videodiscs do not wear out, and therefore are good for repeated playing and are virtually childproof. They're used alone or in conjunction with a personal computer, making for an interactive teaching system.

The prognosis is good for the future of children's audiovisual products. Video production companies are recognizing the profit potential of the children's market. Many such production companies are included in this section and have a range of writing and animation needs that include educational and entertainment subjects. Educational films may not pay quite as much as those destined for entertainment distribution, but they are a good way to break in. If you haven't done so already, read Getting Started in the Educational Market on page 15 for more information.

Video isn't the only format produced by production houses, by the way. Interested writers and illustrators may find themselves working on film projects, filmstrips or multi-media productions.

Be aware, however, that audiovisual media rely more on the "visual" to tell the story. The script itself plays a secondary role and explains only what the visual message doesn't make clear to viewers. Thus, these markets may be more open to work-for-hire artists with specific skills, such as in animation, storyboarding and video graphics.

*AERIAL IMAGE VIDEO SERVICES, 137 W. 19th St., New York NY 10011. (212)229-1930. Fax: (212)229-1929. President: John Stapsy. Estab. 1979. Type of company: Video production and post production, and audio production, post production, and computer-based program production. Uses videotapes and audio. (For list of recent productions consult the Random House catalog of children's videos.)
Children's Writing: Does not accept unsolicited material. Submissions returned with proper SASE. Reports in "days."

Illustration/Animation: Does not accept unsolicited material. Hires illustrators for computer and hand animation, storyboarding, live action and comprehensives. Types of animation produced: cel animation, clay animation, stop motion, special effects, 3-D, computer animation, video graphics, motion control and live action. To submit, send cover letter, résumé and demo tape. Art samples returned with proper SASE. Reports in "weeks." Pays "per project."
Tips: When reviewing a portfolio/samples, looks for "application to a project, general talent and interests based on examples."

ARTICHOKE PRODUCTIONS, 4114 Linden St., Oakland CA 94608. (510)655-1283. Producer/Director: Paul Kalbach. Estab. 1981. Production House (live action and computer graphics/animation). Audience: General. Produces films, videotapes.
Children's Writing: To submit, query with synopsis. Submissions returned with proper SASE. Reports back only if interested. Pay depends on project.
Illustration/Animation: Hires illustrators for character development. Animation produced: stop motion, special effects, cel and computer animation, video graphics, live action. Art samples returned with proper SASE. Reports back only if interested.

BENNU PRODUCTIONS INC., 626 McLean Ave., Yonkers NY 10705. (914)964-1828. Fax: (914)964-2914. Producer: Wayne J. Keeley. Estab. 1985. Film and video production house. Audience: General public, businesses, schools, etc. Uses multimedia productions, films and videotapes. Children's productions: "Say No to Strangers," written by Wayne J. Keeley (video safety program for children); "Save Our Planet," written by Wayne J. Keeley/Chris Austermann (environmental eductional video for junior to senior high). 25% of writing is by freelancers; 25% of illustrating/animating is by freelancers.
Children's Writing: Needs educational material on all relevant topics for all age levels. Subjects include: substance abuse, environment, history, health, science, art, etc. To submit, query. Submissions returned with proper SASE. Reports back only if interested. Pay varies.
Illustration/Animation: Hires illustrators for animation (computer and graphic), storyboarding, character development, live action, comprehensives, pencil testing. Types of animation produced: special effects, computer animation, video graphics, live action. To submit, send cover letter, résumé, demo tape (VHS) and business card. Art samples returned with proper SASE. Reports back only if interested. Pay varies.
Tips: "Educationally stimulating material should be submitted." Looks for "creativity, innovation, flexibility."

*BES CREATIVE, a division of BES Teleproductions, 6829-E Atmore Rd., Richmond VA 23225. (804)276-5110. Executive Producer: Carolyn McCulley. Director of Animation: Ed Lazor. Estab. 1973. Full service production company within digital post-production facility. Uses films, videotapes. "We simply produce the creative concepts developed by others."
Illustration/Animation: Types of animation produced: cel animation, clay animation, special effects, computer animation, video graphics, live action. To submit, send cover letter, demo tape, proposal. Pays varies per project.

BROADCAST QUALITY, INC., #316, 5701 Sunset Dr., South Miami FL 33143. (305)665-5416. President: Diana Udel. Estab. 1978. Video production and post production house. Produces videotapes. Children's productions: "It's Ours to Save—Biscayne National

 The asterisk before a listing indicates the listing is new in this edition.

Park," written by Jack Moss, produced by Diana Udel/BQI, Betacam SP/1" Master, (Environmental awareness for grades 4-7); "The Wildlife Show at Parrot Jungle," written by Amy Smith, produced by BQI, Betacam SP/1" Master, (Hands on to Florida's Wildlife for K-8th grade). Uses 2-5 freelance writers/year; purchases various projects/year.
Tips: "Send a résumé and demo reel. Seeks variety, knowledge of subject and audience."

*CENTRE COMMUNICATIONS, Suite #207, 1800 30th St., Boulder CO 80301. (303)444-1166. Contact: Ronald C. Meyer. Estab. 1975. Production and distribution company. Audience: schools, libraries and television. Produces films and videotapes. Recent children's productions: "Harry the Dirty Dog," written by Gene Zion; "Pepper and All the Legs," written by Dick Gackenbach. Uses 2-3 freelance writers/year; purchases 5-6 writing projects/year.
Children's Writing: Needs: educational material, documentaries and live action. "We only commission work or distribute finished products." Buys material outright.
Illustration: Hires illustrators for character development and live action. To submit, send cover letter and demo tape (VHS). "Payment is subject to negotiations."

*CHESHIRE CORP., P.O. Box 61109, Denver CO 80206. (303)333-9729. Fax: (303)333-4037. Scriptwriters contact: Paul Lalley. Illustrator/animators contact: Ray Happel. Estab. 1985. Educational publisher. Audience: elementary and middle school market. Produces filmstrips and videotapes. Recent children's productions: "Life Stories: Introducing Biographies," written by Paul Lalley (video aimed at middle school); "Beyond The Stacks: Finding Fun In The Library," written by Paul Lalley (video aimed at middle school). Uses 2 freelance artists/year.
Children's Writing: To submit, query. Submissions cannot be returned.
Illustration: Hires illustrators for storyboarding. Types of animation produced: video graphics. To submit, send cover letter and résumé.

CLEARVUE/eav, 6465 N. Avondale, Chicago IL 60631. (312)775-9433. Editor/Producer: Mary Watanabe. Estab. 1969. Type of company: production and distribution house. Audience: educational pre-school through high school. Uses filmstrips, slide sets, CD-ROM, videodiscs, videotapes. 70% of illustrating/animating is by freelancers.
Children's Writing: "At this time we are only accepting for review *finished* video projects that we will consider for distribution." Query with résumé. Reports back only if interested. Pays 5-10% royalty.
Illustration/Animation: Hires illustrators for computer animation of company-owned filmstrips. Send cover letter, résumé, demo tape (VHS). Reports in 2 weeks only if interested. Video samples returned. Guidelines/catalog free. Pay: "open."
Tips: "Programs must be designed for educational market—not home or retail. We are looking for good animators with equipment to scan in our filmstrips and animate the characters and action according to prepared directions that allow for artistic variations."

DIMENSION FILMS, 15007 Gault St., Van Nuys CA 91405. (818)997-8065. President: Gary Goldsmith. Estab. 1962. Production house. Audience: schools and libraries. Uses filmstrips, films, videotapes. 10% of writing is by freelancers; 100% of illustrating/animating is by freelancers.
Children's Writing: Needs: educational material and documentaries for kindergarten-12th-grade audience. To submit, query. Submissions filed. Reports "in a matter of weeks. Call for guidelines." Pays in accordance with Writer's Guild standards.
Illustration/Animation: Hires illustrators for storyboarding, comprehensives. Types of animation produced: cel animation, video graphics, live action. Submission method: send cover letter and résumé. Reports "in a matter of weeks. Call for guidelines." Pays $30-60/frame.

Tips: Illustrators/animators: looking for "imagination, clarity and purpose." Portfolio should show "strong composition; action in stillness."

EDUCATIONAL VIDEO NETWORK, 1401 19th St., Huntsville TX 77340. (409)295-5767. Editor: Gary Edmondson. Estab. 1954. Production house. Audience: educational (school). Uses videotapes. 20% of writing by freelancers; 20% of illustrating/animating is by freelancers.

Children's Writing: Needs: "Educational material" for ages 9-11 and 12-18. To submit, send script with video or animation. Submissions returned with proper SASE. Reports in 1 month. Guidelines/catalog free. Pays writers in royalties or buys material outright.

Illustration/Animation: Hires illustrators for: acetate cels, animation. Types of animation produced: cel animation stills, video graphics, live action. To submit, send cover letter and VHS demo tape. Art samples returned with proper SASE. Reports in 1 month. Guidelines/catalog free.

Tips: "Materials should fill a curriculum need in grades 6-12." Writers/scriptwriters: "Work must be of professional quality adaptable to video format." Illustrators/animators: Looks for "creativity. More live-action is being demanded. Go to school library and ask to review most popular AV titles."

FILM CLASSIC EXCHANGE, 143 Hickory Hill Circle, Osterville MA 02655. (508)428-7198. President: J.H. Aikman. Estab. 1916. Distribution/production house. Audience: Pre-school through college. Produces films, videotapes. Recent children's productions: "The Good Deed," written by William P. Pounder, illustrated by Karen Losaq (film on family values aimed at preschool); "Willie McDuff's Big Day," written and illustrated by Joe Fleming (Film on anti-drug aimed at ages 12+). Uses 6 freelance writers and artists/year. Purchase 6 writing and 6 art projects/year.

Children's Writing: Needs: Preschool. Subjects include: Anti-drug. Query with synopsis or submit completed script. Submissions are returned wtih proper SASE. Reports back only if interested. Buys material outright.

Illustration/Animation: Hires illustrators for cel/video animation, storyboarding, character development, live action, comprehensives, pencil testing. Types of animation produced: cel animation, clay animation, stop motion, special effects, computer animation, video graphics, motion control, live action. To submit, send cover letter, résumé, demo tape (VHS), color print samples. Art samples returned with proper SASE. Reports back only if interested.

Tips: "Keep sending updated résumés/samples of work."

FINE ART PRODUCTIONS, 67 Maple St., Newburgh NY 12550. (914)561-5866. Director: Richie Suraci. Estab. 1989. "We cover every aspect of the film, video, publishing and entertainment industry." Audience: All viewers. Uses filmstrips, films, slide sets, videotapes, multimedia productions, any format needed. Children's productions: "1991 Great Hudson River Revival," illustrated by various artists (35mm film and print on environment, clearwater sailing ship); "Wheel and Rock to Woodstock Bike Tour," written and illustrated by various artists (film, print, video on exercise, health, music and volunteerism). Percent of freelance illustrators/animators used varies.

Children's Writing: To submit, query with synopsis, or submit synopsis/outline, completed script, résumé. Submissions are filed, or returned with proper SASE. Reports in 1 month if interested. Pay is negotiated.

Illustration/Animation: Hires illustrators for animation, storyboarding, character development, live action, comprehensives, pencil testing. Types of animation produced: cel animation, clay animation, stop motion, special effects, computer animation, video graphics, motion control, live action. To submit, send cover letter, résumé, demo tape (VHS or ¾"), b&w print samples, color print samples, tearsheets, business card. Art samples are filed, or returned with proper SASE. Reports in 1 month if interested. Guidelines/catalog for SAE. Pay is negotiated.

HOME, INC., 731 Harrison Ave., Boston MA 02118. (617)266-1386. Director: Alan Michel. Estab. 1974. Nonprofit video production and post production facility which produces some teen television programming for the local Boston market. Audience: teenagers, teachers, instructors, education administrators, parents, social workers and court intervention professionals. Uses videotapes. Children's productions: "Going to Court," written by Ken Cheeseman, graphics by Alan Michel (¾" videotape puppet drama explaining the court for ages 3 through teens); "Stand Back from Crack," written by Young Nation, graphics by Alan Michel (¾" videotape, anti-drug public service video for teen and pre-teen). 90% of writing is by freelancers; 15% of illustrating/animating is by freelancers.

Children's Writing: Needs: scripts, curriculum, educational support material for videos, proposal writing for elementary through high school. Subjects include social or cultural content/sometimes career or health care oriented. To submit, send synopsis/outline and résumé. Submissions are filed and cannot be returned. Reports back only if interested. Payment negotiated/commissioned.

Illustration/Animation: Hires illustrators for storyboarding and graphics. Types of animation produced: special effects, computer animation and video graphics. To submit send cover letter, résumé, VHS demo tape, b&w and color print samples. Samples are filed and not returned. Reports back only if interested. Payment negotiated. Pays $250-4,000/project for specialized animation.

Tips: "We look for cooperative associates who have a commitment to quality and to their profession. This includes their presentation and follow-through in their dealings with us prior to project engagement."

I.N.I. ENTERTAINMENT GROUP, INC., Suite 700, 11150 Olympic Blvd., Los Angeles CA 90064. (310)479-6755. Fax: (310)479-3475. Chairman of the Board/CEO: Irv Holender. President: Michael Ricci. Director of Advertising: Linda Krasnoff. Estab. 1985. Producer/International Distributor. Audience: children of all ages. Uses films. Children's productions: "The Adventures of Oliver Twist," screenplay written by Fernando Ruiz (updated version of the Dickens tale for ages 4-12); "Alice Through the Looking Glass," screenplay written by James Brewer (updated and upbeat version of Carroll's book for ages 4-12). 100% of writing is by freelancers; 100% of illustrating/animating is by freelancers.

Children's Writing: Needs: animation scripts. "Anything from fantasy to fable." To submit, query with synopsis. Submit synopsis/outline, completed script, résumé. Submissions returned with proper SASE. Reports back only if interested. Pay varies.

Illustration/Animation: Type of animation produced: computer animation. To submit, send cover letter, résumé, demo tape (VHS), color print samples, business card. Art samples are filed, returned with proper SASE or not returned. Reports back only if interested.

Tips: "We are gearing to work with fairytales or classic stories. We look for concise retelling of older narratives with slight modifications in the storyline, while at the same time introducing children to stories that they would not necessarily be familiar with. We are currently in production doing 'International Family Classics, Part II.' We don't hire illustrators for animation. We hire the studio. The illustrators that we hire are used to create the advertising art."

JEF FILMS, 143 Hickory Hill Circle, Osterville MA 02655. (508)428-7198. President: Jeffrey H. Aikman. Estab. 1973. Production house. Audience: schools/libraries/video retailers. Produces slide sets, multimedia productions, films, videotapes. Children's productions: "The Reward," written and illustrated by Dennis Chatfield (film on animation aimed at pre-school); "Kiddy Kartoon Korner," written by Carolyn Elckoff, illustrated by Bill Wicksdorf (35mm film on animation aimed at ages 5-8.) Uses 20-24 freelance writers/year; purchases 20-24 writing projects/year. Uses 20-24 freelance artists/year; purchases 20-24 art projects/year.

Children's Writing: Needs: animation scripts for ages 5-8. Subjects include: tales with messages. To submit, send synopsis/outline. Submissions returned with proper SASE. Reports in 2 months. Buys outright.

Illustration/Animation: Hires illustrators for cel/video/clay animation, storyboarding, character development, live action, comprehensives, pencil testing. Types of animation produced: cel animation, clay animation, stop motion, special effects, video graphics, motion control, live action. To submit, send cover letter, résumé, demo tape (VHS), b&w print samples, color print samples, tearsheets, slides, promo sheet. Samples returned with proper SASE; samples filed. Reports in 2 months.

Tips: "Be persistent. We receive a great number of inquiries and cannot always use everyone who submits work. Keep us updated on all new projects. Everything sent to us is kept on file. We look for unique styles unlike other works on market."

*KDOC-TV, 1730 S. Clementine, Anaheim CA 92802. (714)999-5000. Fax: (714)999-1218. Program Manager: Lisa Starr. Promotion Manager: Steve Schaub. Estab. 1982. TV station. Audience: All viewers. Uses videotapes. "Always open to new ideas."

Children's Writing: Needs: scripts, documentaries. To submit, query with synopsis. Submissions filed. Reports in 3-4 weeks. Writers paid in accordance with Writer's Guild standards.

Illustration/Animation: Hires illustrators for animation (computer, video graphics). Types of animation produced: video graphics. To submit, send ¾″ demo tape. Art samples are filed. Reports in 3-4 weeks. Pay is "open."

KENSINGTON FALLS ANIMATION, Suite 200, 2921 Duss Ave., Ambridge PA 15003. (412)266-0329. Fax: (412)266-4016. Producer: Michael Schwab. Estab. 1979. Animation studio. Audience: Entertainment, educational. Uses filmstrips, slide sets, films, videotapes. 100% of writing is by freelancers; 100% of illustrating/animating is by freelancers. Uses 5-20 freelance writers/year; purchases 5-20 writing projects/year. Uses 1-10 freelance artists/year.

Children's Writing: Needs: animation scripts, educational material. To submit, query with résumé. Submissions are filed. Reports back only if interested. Guidelines/catalog free on request. Writers paid in accordance with Writer's Guild standards.

Illustration/Animation: Hires illustrators for character animation, storyboarding, character development, pencil testing, background illustration, ink and paint production. Types of animation produced: cel animation, computer animation, video graphics. To submit, send cover letter, résumé, demo tape (VHS or ¾″). Art samples returned with proper SASE. Guidelines/catalog free on request. Pays: $10-50/hour for storyboarding/comp work; $20-50/hour for animation work.

Tips: "We offer apprenticeships."

KIDVIDZ: Special Interest Video for Children, 618 Centre St., Newton MA 02158. (617)965-3345. Partner: Jane Murphy. Estab. 1987. Home video publisher. Audience: pre-school and primary-age children, 2-12 years. Produces videotapes. Recent children's productions: "Paws, Claws, Feathers and Fins: A Kids Video Guide to Pets," "Piggy Banks to Money Markets: A Kids Video Guide to Dollars and Sense," "Hey, What About Me: A Kids Video Guide for Brothers and Sisters of New Babies," "Kids Get Cooking: The Egg." Uses 2 freelance writers/year. Uses 3 freelance artists/year. Submissions filed.

KJD TELEPRODUCTIONS, 30 Whyte Dr., Voorhees NJ 08043. (609)751-3500. Fax: (609)751-7729. President: Larry Scott. Creative Director: Kim Davis. Estab. 1989. Location production services (Betacam Sp) plus interformat edit and computer animation. Audience: industrial and broadcast. Uses slide sets, multimedia productions, videotapes. Children's productions: "Kidstuff," written by Barbara Daye, illustrated by Larry Scott (educational vignettes for ages 6-16). 10% of writing is by freelancers; 25% of animating/illustrating by freelancers.
Children's Writing: Needs: animation. To submit, query. Submissions are filed. Reports in 2 weeks. Pays royalty or buys material outright.
Illustration/Animation: Hires illustrators for animation. Types of animation produced: computer animation. To submit, send cover letter, résumé, demo tape (VHS or ¾"), b&w print samples, tearsheets, business card. Art samples are filed. Reports in 2 weeks. Pay varies.

*LANDYVISION, 11 Hill 99, Woodstock NY 12498. (914)679-9016. Vice President: Diana Oestreich. President: Elliott Landy. Estab. 1990. Production/distribution company. Audience varies. Produces slide sets, multimedia productions and videotapes. Recent children's productions: "Table Manners," written by Diana Oestreich (videotape, ages 4 and up); "Grokgazer," written and illustrated by Todd Rungren (videotape for all ages). Uses 2 freelance writers/year; purchases 2 writing projects/year. Uses 1 freelance artist/year.
Children's Writing: Needs: entertainment and education for all ages. To submit, send completed script. Submissions cannot be returned; submissions not filed. Reports in 1 month. Guidelines/catalog free on request. Payment varies depending on situation.
Illustration: Hires illustrators for books in association with videos.
Tips: Supply good ideas and scripts for commercial, entertaining and educational purposes for children of all ages. "Videos are becoming an important format for teaching through entertainment. Find good writing workshops, college classes or producers who develop projects."

MARSHMEDIA, P.O. Box 8082, Shawnee Mission KS 66208. (816)523-1059. Fax: (816)333-7421. Production Director: Joan K. Marsh. Estab. 1969. Production and marketing house. Audience: grades K-12. 100% of writing is by freelancers; 100% of illustrating/animating is by freelancers.
Children's Writing: Needs: educational materials, self-esteem stories for K-3: animal protagonist, significant geographical setting, strong non-sexist self-esteem message, 1,500 words. To submit, query with synopsis and submit completed scripts, résumé. Submissions returned with proper SASE. Buys material outright.
Illustration/Animation: To submit, send résumé and VHS demo tape. Art samples returned with proper SASE. Reports in 1 month.

NATIONAL GALLERY OF ART, Education Dept., Washington DC 20565. Fax: (202)789-2681. Head, Dept. of Teacher and School Programs: Kathy Walsh-Piper. Estab. 1941. Museum. Audience: teachers and students. Uses filmstrips, slide sets, videotapes, reproductions. Children's productions: "The Magic Picture Frame," written by Maura Clarkin (reproductions of paintings for NGA Museum Guide for ages 7-10). 50% of writing is by freelancers.
Children's Writing: Needs: educational material for all levels. Subjects include knowledge of art-making and art history. To submit, send résumé. Submissions are filed. Reports back only if interested. Guidelines/catalog not available. Buys material outright.

NEW & UNIQUE VIDEOS, 2336 Sumac Dr., San Diego CA 92105. (619)282-6126. Fax: (619)283-8264. Acquisitions Managers: Candy Love, Mark Schulze. Estab. 1985. Video production and distribution services. "Audience varies with each title." Uses films and videotapes. Children's productions: "Battle at Durango: The First-Ever World Mountain Bike Championships," written by Patricia Mooney, produced by Mark Schulze (VHS video mountain bike race documentary for 12 and over); "John Howard's Lessons in Cycling," written by John Howard, direction and camera by Mark Schulze (VHS video on cycling for 12 and over). 50% of writing is by freelancers; 85% of illustrating/animating is by freelancers.

Children's Writing: Needs: video scripts and/or completed videotape productions whose intended audiences may range from 1 and older. "Any subject matter focusing on a special interest that can be considered 'new and unique.'" To submit, query. Submissions are returned with proper SASE. Reports in 2-3 weeks. Payment negotiable.

Illustration/Animation: Hires illustrators for film or video animation. Types of animation produced: computer animation and video graphics. To submit, send cover letter. Art samples returned with proper SASE. Reports back in 2-3 weeks. Payment negotiable.

Tips: "As more and more video players appear in homes across the world, and as the interest in special interest videos climbs, the demand for more original productions is rising meteorically."

TOM NICHOLSON ASSOC., INC., 8th Floor, 295 Lafayette St., New York NY 10012. (212)274-0470. Estab. 1987. Interactive multimedia developer. Audience: children ages 6-13. Produces multimedia. Recently produced a worldwide series of multi-discipline educational titles (CD-ROM and floppy disk for ages 6-13). Uses 6-10 freelance writers/year. Uses 6-10 freelance artists/year.

Children's Writing: Needs: documentary film, animation scripts, educational/entertainment. Subjects include: science, humanities, nature, etc. To submit, query. Reports back only if interested. Pay is negotiable.

Illustration/Animation: Hires illustrators for animation, storyboarding, character development, live action, comprehensives. Types of animation produced: cel animation, computer animation. To submit, send VHS demo tape, tearsheets, promo sheets. Art samples not returned; samples filed. Reports back only if interested.

Tips: "Samples of past projects are essential and are the basis for all hiring decisions." Looks for "ability to present educational information in a clear, yet highly engaging manner."

NTC PUBLISHING GROUP, 4255 W. Touhy Ave., Lincolnwood IL 60646. (708)679-5500. Fax: (708)679-2494. Art Director: Karen Christoffersen. Estab. 1960. Type of company: publisher. Audience: all ages. Uses film strips, multimedia productions, videotapes, books and audiocassettes. Children's production: *Let's Learn English Picture Dictionary*, (versions in Spanish, French, German and Italian); illustrations by Marlene Goodman. For ages 7-11. 40% of writing is by freelancers; 50% of illustrating/animating is by freelancers.

Children's Writing: Needs: educational material for ages 5-14. Subjects include: "mostly foreign language, travel and English." To submit, include synopsis/outline, completed script, résumé and samples. Submission returned with proper SASE only. Reports in 2 months. Guidelines/catalog free. Pays writers in royalties or buys material outright—"depends on project."

Illustration/Animation: Hires illustrators for character development, comprehensives, pencil testing. Types of animation produced: stop motion, video graphics. To submit, send cover letter, résumé, color print samples, tearsheets, business card. Art samples returned with proper SASE. Reports in 8 weeks. Guidelines/catalog free.

Tips: Looking for "experienced professionals only with proven track record in the *educational* field."

OLIVE JAR ANIMATION, 44 Write Place, Brookline MA 02146. (617)566-6699. Fax: (617)566-0689. Executive Producer: Matthew Charde. Estab. 1984. Animation studio. Audience: all ages. Uses films, videotapes. 75% of writing is by freelancers; 75% of illustrating/animating is by freelancers.
Illustration/Animation: Hires illustrators for animation (all types), storyboarding, pencil testing, design, ink paint, sculpture, illustration. Types of animation produced: cel and clay animation, stop motion, special effects. To submit, send cover letter, résumé, demo tape, b&w print samples, color print samples, tearsheets, business card. Art samples are filed. Reports back only if interested. Pays flat rate according to job.
Tips: Looks for "someone who is really good at a particular style or direction as well as people who work in a variety of mediums. Attitude is as important as talent. The ability to work with others is very important."

*MICHAEL SAND INC., 157 Aspinwall Ave., Brookline MA 02146. (617)566-5599. Fax: (617)566-3966. President: Michael Sand. Estab. 1964. Museum planning consultants. Audience: museum visitors. Produces multimedia productions, films, videotapes and interactive video disks. Recent children's productions: "The Big Dig," written by Doug Smith, illustrated by Robert Barner (hands-on highway planning for upper elementary-adult); "Whale Discover Center," written by Richard Ellis, illustrated by Tom Vann-Bishop (computer games on marine ecology for lower elementary-adult). Uses 4 freelance writers/year; purchases 12 writing projects/year. Uses 8 freelance artists/year; purchases 30 art projects/year.
Children's Writing: Needs: animation scripts, educational material, documentaries (ages 5-8, 9-11, 12 and older). Subjects include: history, science, art. To submit, query with synopsis, completed script, résumé, samples. Submissions are returned with proper SASE; submissions sometimes filed. Reports in 1 month. Guidelines/catalog not available. Buys material outright (pay varies).
Illustration: Hires illustrators for computer-based animation, storyboarding, character development, comprehensives, pencil testing, exhibit renderings, models, 3-D illustration. Type of animation produced: cel animation, stop motion, special effects, computer animation, video graphics, motion control, live action. To submit, send cover letter, résumé, demo tape (VHS), b&w print samples, color print samples, tearsheets, slides, promo sheet. Samples somtetimes filed. Reports in 1 month if interested. Guidelines/catalog not available. Pays minimum $25/hour.

SEA STUDIOS, INC., 810 Cannery Row, Monterey CA 93940. (408)649-5152. Fax: (408)649-1380. Office Manager: Cindy Ignacio. Estab. 1985. Natural history video production company. Audience: general. Uses multimedia productions, videotapes. 50% of writing is by freelancers; 50% of illustrating/animating is by freelancers.
Children's Writing: Needs: educational material—target age dependent on project. To submit, send résumé (no phone calls please). Submissions returned with proper SASE. Reports back only if interested. Pay negotiable.
Illustration/Animation: To submit, send cover letter, résumé (no phone calls please). Art samples returned with proper SASE. Reports back only if interested.

Market conditions are constantly changing! If you're still using this book and it is 1995 or later, buy the newest edition of Children's Writer's & Illustrator's Market *at your favorite bookstore or order directly from* Writer's Digest Books.

SHADOW PLAY RECORDS & VIDEO, P.O. Box 180476, Austin TX 78718. (512)345-4664. Fax: (512)345-9734. President: Peter J. Markham. Estab. 1984. Children's music publisher. Audience: families with children ages 3-10. Uses videotapes. Children's productions: "Joe's First Video," written by Joe Scruggs, illustrated by various artists (VHS children's music videos for preschool-10 years). 5% of writing is by freelancers; 100% of illustrating/animating by freelancers.
Children's Writing: Needs: poems or lyrics for children's songs. To submit, send query. "No unsolicited submissions accepted!" Submissions returned with proper SASE. Reports in 6 weeks. Pays royalty or buys material outright.
Illustration/Animation: Hires illustrators for animation, storyboarding, live action, pencil testing. Types of animation produced: cel animation, clay animation, stop motion, special effects, computer animation, video graphics, live action. To submit, send cover letter, résumé, demo tape (VHS), color print samples, business card. Art samples returned with proper SASE. Reports in 6 weeks. Pay varies by project and ability of artist.

SISU HOME ENTERTAINMENT, Suite 202, 20 W. 38th St., New York NY 10018. (212)768-2197. Fax: (212)768-7413. President: Haim Scheinger. Estab. 1988. Video and audio manufacturers (production, distribution). Audience: Children (educational videos and entertainment videos). Uses videotapes and audio. Children's productions: "Lovely Butterfly—Chanuka," written by IETV (Israel Educational TV), illustrated by IETV (Jewish holiday-program for ages 2-5). 25% of writing is by freelancers.
Children's Writing: Needs are for publicity writing—all ages. To submit, arrange interview.
Illustration/Animation: Types of animation produced: clay animation, video graphics. To submit, send résumé. Art samples filed. Reports back only if interested.

STILES-BISHOP PRODUCTIONS INC., 3255 Bennett Dr., Los Angeles CA 90068. (213)883-0011. Fax: (213)466-5496. Contact: Katy Bishop. Estab. 1974. Production house. Audience: children. Uses videotapes and books. Children's productions: "The Cinnamon Bear" (audiotape and books of children's Christmas story for ages 2-10). 50% of writing is by freelancers; 100% of illustrating/animating is by freelancers.
Children's Writing: Needs: children's fiction for ages 2-11. Subjects include: all genres. To submit, send synopsis/outline, completed script, résumé, book. Submissions cannot be returned. Reports back only if interested. Pays negotiable royalty.
Illustration/Animation: Hires illustrators for animation and books. Types of animation produced: cel animation, computer animation, live action. To submit, send cover letter, résumé, VHS or ¾" demo tape, color print samples. Art samples are not returned. Reports back only if interested. Payment negotiable.

TREEHAUS COMMUNICATIONS, INC., P.O. Box 249, 906 W. Loveland Ave., Loveland OH 45140. (513)683-5716. President: Gerard A. Pottebaum. Estab. 1968. Production house. Audience: preschool through adults. Uses filmstrips, multimedia productions, videotapes. Children's productions: *Seeds of Self-Esteem* series, written by Dr. Robert Brooks, Jane Ward and Gerard A. Pottebaum, includes two books for teachers, four in-service teacher training videos and 27 posters for children from primary grades through junior high school, distributed by American Guidance Service, Inc. 30% of writing is by freelancers; 30% of illustrating/animating is by freelancers.
Children's Writing: Needs: educational material/documentaries, for all ages. Subjects include: "social studies, religious education, documentaries on all subjects, but primarily about people who live ordinary lives in extraordinary ways." To submit, query with synopsis. Submissions returned with proper SASE. Reports in 1 month. Guidelines/catalog for SAE. Pays writers in accordance with Writer's Guild standards.

Tips: Illustrators/animators: "Be informed about movements and needs in education, multi-cultural sensitivity." Looks for "social values, originality, competency in subject, global awareness."

*VIRTUAL MOUNTAIN, INC., P.O. Box 239, Fitzwilliam NH 03347. (603)585-3094. Creative Director: Bruce Carroll. Estab. 1992. Animation studio, interactive programming, audio recording studio. Audience: children of all ages. Produces multimedia productions. Recent children's productions: "Posty," written by Bruce Carroll, illustrated by Lenni Armstrong (multimedia interactive children's play and discovery for all ages); "Understanding the Maya," written and illustrated by Bruce Carroll (multimedia on the Maya indians of Central America for age 5 and up). Uses 2 freelance writers/year; purchases 4 writing projects/year. Uses 4 freelance artists/year; purchases 8 art projects/year.

Children's Writing: To submit, query. Submissions returned with proper SASE; submissions not filed. Reports only if interested. Guidelines/catalog not available. Pay varies with project.

Illustration: Hires illustrators for animation. Types of animation produced: cel animation, special effects, computer animation, video graphics. To submit, send cover letter, demo tape (VHS). Art samples returned with proper SASE. Sample not filed. Reports back only if interested. Guidelines/catalog not available. Pays minimum $25/hour.

Audiovisual Markets/'93-'94 changes

The following markets are not included in this edition of *Children's Writer's & Illustrator's Market* for the reasons indicated within parentheses. If there is no reason given, it means the market did not respond to our requests for updated information for a 1994 listing.

Ball & Chain
Gateway Productions, Inc.
Grey Falcon House (removed
    per request)
The Partnership Works

Audiotapes

Efforts to promote children's audiovisual products, both spoken-word and musical, have paid off. Today, children's cassettes and book/cassette packages make up a significant presence in most bookstore and library inventories. And, according to a report in the January 11, 1993 *Publishers Weekly*, audiotapes are the best-selling non-book item in children's-only bookstores.

Indications are the popularity of audiotapes is more than a passing fad. The art of storytelling is becoming more popular, so much so that large storytelling festivals are held annually throughout the country—the largest being each October in Jonesborough, Tennessee. And most large publishers house audio departments and produce cassettes from their own backlists.

Spoken word cassette/book packages are loved by children who enjoy having stories read to them (with today's two-career families, parents don't have as much time to read to their kids). Book/cassette packages also expedite the development of reading skills among children by allowing them to read books while simultaneously listening to recorded narrations. Though story tapes aren't intended to replace reading, they do make an excellent supplement. One trend in story tapes is for celebrities to do the narrations. Also, established authors are recording their own creations.

As for the children's music market, this past year industry professionals gained media attention as they gathered for the first-ever Kids' Music Seminar, held as part of the annual New Music Seminar. While participants celebrated their growing business, they also expressed concern over major labels turning away from live performing artists and toward licensed characters.

Though it is too early to tell how this trend will affect the rest of the children's music industry, producers looking for contemporary material from live artists still exist. And seminar participants suggested making a play for the educational market as well. (See Getting Started in the Educational Market on page 15 for more information.)

Overall, flashier packaging is evident in audiocassettes, to make them more appealing. Also, with the presence of compact disc players in households nationwide, it is expected that the majority of children's audio packages will soon be available on compact disc. To learn more about trends in children's audiotapes, read *Billboard* magazine's Child's Play column.

In this section are 48 book publishers, sheet music publishers and recording companies looking for good story material or unique children's music to record. Some are interested in reviewing both. And 22 of the listings are *new* to this edition. Study each listing to determine what subject matter is preferred and to what age levels material should be targeted. Pay rates will, for the most part, be based on royalties for writers and songwriters or, for recording musicians, on recording contracts.

ALISO CREEK PRODUCTIONS, INC., P.O. Box 8174, Van Nuys CA 91409. (818)787-3203. President: William Williams. Record company, book publisher. Estab. 1987.
Music: Releases 2 LPs-cassettes; 2 CDs/year. Records 20 children's songs/year. Works with composers, lyricists, team collaborators. For songs recorded pays musicians/artists

on record contract and songwriters on royalty contract. Call first and obtain permission to submit material. Submit 3-5 songs with lyric sheets on demo cassette. SASE/IRC for return of submission. Reports in 3 weeks. Recorded songs: "Brontosaurus Stomp," by Bob Menn and William Williams, recorded on Aliso Creek Records label (dixieland music for ages 3-8); "What Make a Car Go, Dad?," by Bob Menn and William Williams, recorded on Aliso Creek Records label (Gilbert & Sullivan type of music for ages 3-8).

Music Tips: "We're looking for music in a variety of styles that doesn't talk down to children or isn't preachy, but does convey positive values or educate."

Stories: Publishes 2 book/cassette packages/year; 2 cassettes/CDs/year. 100% of stories are fiction. Will consider all types of fiction, but story and songs must be related. "We publish musical plays on cassette aimed at ages 3-8." Will consider all types of nonfiction aimed at ages 3-8. Authors are paid negotiable royalty based on retail price; work purchased outright. Submit both cassette tape and ms. Reports on queries in 3 weeks. Catalog for #10 SAE and 1 first-class stamp. Recently published: *Take a Trip with Me*, by Bob Menn and William Williams, narrated by Kevin Birkbeck and Katy Morkri (ages 3-8); *Move!*, by Bob Men and William Williams, narrated by Katy Morkri (ages 3-8, a family adjusts to moving to a different city).

Story Tips: "We publish song and story cassettes with an illustrated lyric book so we need writers and illustrators to create a unified product."

AMERICAN MELODY, P.O. Box 270, Guilford CT 06437. (203)457-0881. President: Phil Rosenthal. Music publisher, record company (American Melody), recording studio, book publisher. Estab. 1985.

Music: Releases 4 LPs/year. Member of BMI. Publishes 20 children's songs/year; records 30 children's songs/year. Works with composers, lyricists, team collaborators. For music published pays standard royalty of 50%; for songs recorded pays musicians/artists on record contract, musicians on salary for inhouse studio work, and songwriters on royalty contract. Call first and obtain permission to submit material. Submit demo cassette. SASE/IRC for return of submission. Reports in 1 month. Recorded songs: "The Bremen Town Song," by Max Showalter and Peter Walker, recorded by Max Showalter on American Melody label (folk music for ages 2-10); "Calico Pie," by Phil Rosenthal, recorded by Phil Rosenthal on American Melody label (bluegrass music for ages 1-8).

Music Tips: "Submit as nice a demo as possible, with lyrics understandable."

Stories: "Plan to publish 2 book/cassette packages/year." 100% of stories are fiction. Will consider all kinds of genres for ages 2-10. For nonfiction, considers biography and history. Authors are paid royalties based on wholesale price. Submit both cassette tape and manuscript. Reports on queries/mss in 1 month. Catalog is free on request. Recorded story tapes: *The Gold Dog*, by Lev Ustinov, narrated by Max Showalter (fairy tales for ages 4-12); *Tales from the First World*, written and narrated by Sylvia and Jeff McQuillan (adaptations of folktales for ages 2-12).

ART AUDIO PUBLISHING COMPANY/TIGHT HI-FI SOUL MUSIC, Dept. CWIM, 9706 Cameron Ave., Detroit MI 48211. (313)893-3406. President: Albert M. Leigh. Music publisher. Estab. 1962.

Music: Works with composers and lyricists. For music published pays standard royalty of 50%. Submit demo tape by mail; unsolicited submissions OK. Submit demo cassette with 1-3 songs, lyric and/or lead sheet. SASE/IRC for return of submission. Reports in 2 weeks.

Music Tips: "We are looking for songs with a strong hook, strong words. We are looking for hits, such as 'Little Teddy Bear,' 'Duckey Lucky' or 'Chicken Little.' Can be songs or musical stories for movie sound tracks. All lyrics are up-front: Words are clearly understandable."

BRENTWOOD MUSIC, INC., 316 Southgate Court, Brentwood TN 37027. (615)373-3950. Fax: (615)373-8612. Creative Director: Ed Kee. Music publisher, book publisher, record company, children's video. Estab. 1980.
Music: Releases 40 cassettes/year; 24-30 CDs/year. Member of ASCAP, BMI and SESAC. Publishes 60-120 children's songs/year. Works with composers. Pays standard royalty of 50% of net receipts for music published. Submit demo cassette tape by mail; unsolicited submissions OK; 2 songs and lyric sheet or lead sheet. "No music can be returned unless you include a self-addressed, stamped envelope. Do not send stamps or postage only. If you want it back, send an *envelope* big enough to hold all material with the *proper* postage affixed. No exceptions." Reports in 3-6 months. Recently recorded songs: "Once Upon an Orchestra," by Don and Lorie Marsh on Designer Music label (orchestral story—like "Peter & The Wolf," ages 3-7); "It's A Cockadoodle Day," by Janet McMahan-Wilson, Tom McBryde, Mary Jordan on Brentwood Kids Co. label (sing along for ages 2-7).
Stories: Will consider fictional animal, fantasy or adventure aimed at preschool through 3rd or 4th grades. Author's pay is negotiable, depending on project. Query. Reports in 3 months. Recently recorded story tapes: *The Leap Year Frog*, by Freddy Richardson, narrated by Mother Goose (ages 2-6, birthday); *How the Donkey Got His Tail*, by Freddy Richardson, narrated by Mother Goose (ages 2-6, birthday).
Tips: "Songs and stories with a Christian or Bible theme fill more of our product development needs than other topics or themes."

*BRIDGER PRODUCTIONS, INC., 4150 Gloryview, P.O. Box 8131, Jackson WY 83001. (307)733-7871. Contact: Mike Emmer. Music publisher, film and video production corporation. Estab. 1990.
Music: Releases 2 singles/year. Publishes 1 children's song/year. Hires staff writers for children's music. Works with composers and lyricists, team collaborators. Pays contracted price. Submit demo tape by mail; unsolicited submissions OK. Submit demo cassette, VHS or ¾" SP videocassette if available with 3 songs. Include lyric sheet, lead sheet. Cannot return material. Reports in 3 weeks. "We've recorded mostly adults' music lately but we are interested in contracting artists to record in our studios—we pay a one time (buyout) fee."
Music Tips: "Songs must be in conjunction with a film/video project for us to be interested."
Stories: Publishes 1 book/cassette package/year. 100% of stories are nonfiction. Will consider all genres of nonfiction. Pays contracted price. Reports on queries/ms in 3 weeks.
Story Tips: "Stories must be in conjunction with a film/video paying project."

*BROADCAST PRODUCTION GROUP, 1901 S. Bascom Ave., Campbell CA 95008. (408)559-6309. Fax: (408)559-6382. Creative Director: Dan Korb. Video and film production group. Estab. 1986.
Music: Hires staff writers for children's music. Works with composers and/or lyricists, team collaborators. "Our projects are on a single-purchase basis." Pays per project for songs recorded. Submit demo tape by mail; unsolicited submissions okay. Submit demo cassette, résumé and videocassette if available. Not necessary to include lyric or lead sheets. Reports in 3 weeks.

CENTER FOR THE QUEEN OF PEACE, Suite 412, 3350 Highway 6, Houston TX 77478. Music publisher, book publisher and record company. Record labels include Cosmotone Records, Cosmotone Music. Estab. 1984.
Music: Releases 1 single, 1 12-inch single and 1 LP/year. Member of ASCAP. Works with team collaborators. Pays negotiable royalty for music published; for songs recorded pays musicians on salary for inhouse studio work, songwriters on royalty contract. Write

for permission to submit material. "Will respond only if interested."

CHILDREN'S MEDIA PRODUCTIONS, P.O. Box 40400, Pasadena CA 91114. (818)797-5462. President: C. Ray Carlson. Video publisher. Estab. 1983.
Music: Works with composers and/or lyricists. For songs recorded pays musicians/artists on record contract. Write for permission to submit material.
Tips: "We use only original music and songs for videos. We serve markets worldwide and must often record songs in foreign languages. So avoid anything provincially *American*. Parents choose videos that will *'teach* for a lifetime' (our motto) rather than entertain for a few hours. State concisely what the 'message' is in your concept and why you think parents will be interested in it. How will it satisfy new FCC regulations concerning 'educational content?' We like ethnic and/or multi-racial stories and illustrations."

THE CHRISTIAN SCIENCE PUBLISHING SOCIETY, One Norway Street, Boston MA 02115. (617)450-2033. Fax: (617)450-2017. General Publications Product Manager: Rhoda M. Ford. Book publisher "but we do issue some recordings." Estab. 1898.
Music: Works with team collaborators on audiocassettes. Submit query letter with proposal, references, résumé. Does not return unsolicited submissions unless requested. Reports in 3-4 months.
Stories: 100% of stories are nonfiction. Will consider nonfiction for beginning readers, juveniles, teens based on the Bible (King James Version). Authors are paid royalty or work purchased outright, "negotiated with contract." Submit query letter with proposal, references and résumé. Include Social Security number. Reports on queries in 3-4 months. Trade Kit available.
Tips: "Since we are part of The First Church of Christ, Scientist, all our publications are in harmony with the teachings of Christian Science."

*CREDENCE CASSETTES, 115 E. Armour Blvd., Kansas City MO 64111. (816)531-0538. Fax: (816)531-7466. Director: Clarence Thomson. Religious/spoken word recording company. Estab. 1973.
Stories: Publishes 20 book/cassette packages/year. 10% of stories are fiction; 90% non-fiction. Will consider religious kindergarten-adult. Authors are paid 10% royalty based on retail price. Submit cassette tape or story. Reports on queries in 3 weeks. Catalog free on request. Ms guidelines not available. Recently recorded story tapes: *The Friendship Song*, by Karen Blomgren/C. Thomson, narrated by Karen Blomgren (ages 6-12, story of bird who couldn't sing); *The Pine Tree's Christmas Dream*, by C. Thomson, narrated by Karen Blomgren (ages 4-10, a pine tree becomes Christmas tree).
Tips: Looks for "religious, but symbolic — not fundamentalist, 15-20 minutes long. We're just starting into children's fiction (we've done adult Christian material for 20 years)."

*CRYSTAL SOUND RECORDING, INC., 220 W. 19th St., New York NY 10011. (212)255-6745. Fax: (212)255-8931. President: Larry Buksbaum. Music production and narration production company. Estab. 1987.
Music: Records 30 children's songs/year. Hires staff writers for children's music. Works with composers and/or, lyricists, teams collaborators. Pays musicians/artists on record contract, musicians on salary for inhouse studio work, songwriters on royalty contract. Books studio time (discount for children's songwriters). Recently recorded songs: "Tyco Toys," recorded by Jerry Plotkin (toy commercial jingle); *My First Nature Video*, recorded by Peter Calandra (children's video music underscore).

*DERCUM AUDIO, P.O. Box 1425, West Chester PA 19380. (215)430-8889. Fax: (215)430-8891. Contact: Amy Lewis. Audio book producer. Estab. 1985.
Stories: Recently produced story tapes: *Culpepper Adventure Series*, by Gary Paulsen, narrated by Bill Fantini (ages 8-14, adventure).

DISCOVERY MUSIC, 5554 Calhoun Ave., Van Nuys CA 91401. (818)782-7818. Fax: (818)782-7817. Chief Creative Officer: David Wohlstadter. Record company (Discovery Music). Estab. 1985.
Music: Releases 2-3 LPs and 2-3 CDs/year. Records approximately 45 songs/year. For songs recorded pays musicians/artists on record contract, musicians on salary for in-house studio work, songwriters on royalty contract (percentage royalty). Submit demo tape by mail; unsolicited submissions OK. Submit demo cassette with cover letter. Cannot return material. Reporting on submissions "varies." Recorded songs: "Put Yourself Together, Humpty and Jack & Jill's Better Scheme," both by Dennis Hysom, recorded by Discovery Music on Discovery Music label (children's music for ages 3-8).

DOVE AUDIO, Suite 301 N. Cañon Dr., Beverly Hills CA 90210. (310)273-7722. Fax: (310)273-0365. Customer Service Supervisor: Maryann Camarillo. Audio book publisher. Estab. 1985.
Stories: Publishes approximately 100/year (audiotapes only). 50% of stories are fiction; 50% nonfiction. Submit through agent only. Reports in 2 weeks. Catalog is free on request. Recently recorded story tapes include *Enchanted Tales*, narrated by Audrey Hepburn (ages 5 and up); *Rap, Rap, Rapunzel*, narrated by Patti Austin (ages 3 and up).

DUTTON CHILDREN'S BOOKS, 375 Hudson St., New York NY 10014. (212)366-2600. Fax: (212)366-2011. President and Publisher: Christopher Franceschelli. Book publisher.
Stories: Publishes 3 book/cassette packages/year. 100% of stories are fiction. Will consider animal and fantasy. Story tapes aimed at ages 2-10. Authors are paid 5-12% royalties based on retail price; outright purchase of $2,000-20,000; royalty inclusive. Average advance $3,000. Submit outline/synopsis and sample chapters through agent. Reports on queries in 3 weeks; on mss in 6 months. Catalog is available for 8×11 SAE and 8 first-class stamps. Ms guidelines available for #10 SAE and 1 first-class stamp. Children's story tapes include *Noah's Ark*, narrated by James Earl Jones.
Tips: "Do not call publisher. Get agent. Celebrity readers sell."

*ROY EATON MUSIC INC., 595 Main St., Roosevelt Island NY 10044. (212)980-9046. Fax: (212)980-9068. President: Roy Eaton. Music publisher, TV and radio music production company. Estab. 1982.
Music: Member of BMI. Hires staff writers for children's music. Works with composers, lyricists, team collaborators. For music published pays standard royalty of 50%. Write or call for permission to submit material. Submit demo cassettte with lyric sheet.
Tips: "Primarily interested in commericals for children."

MARTIN EZRA & ASSOCIATES, 45 Fairview Ave., Lansdowne PA 19050. (215)622-1600. President: Martin Ezra. Producer. Estab. 1968.
Music: Submit demo tape by mail; unsolicited submissions OK. Submit demo cassette (VHS videocassette if available). Lyric or lead sheets not necessary.
Stories: Will consider all types of fiction and nonfiction. Submit cassette tape of story.

FINE ART PRODUCTIONS, 67 Maple St., Newburgh NY 12550. (914)561-5866. Contact: Richie Suraci. Music publisher, record company, book publisher. Estab. 1989.
Music: Member of ASCAP and BMI. Publishes and records 1-2 children's songs/year. Hires staff writers for children's music. Works with composers, lyricists, team collabora-

---

Always include a self-addressed stamped envelope (SASE) or a self-addressed envelope (SAE) and International Reply Coupons (IRCs) with submissions.

tors. For music published pays standard royalty of 50% or other amount; for songs recorded pays musicians/artists on record contract, musicians on salary for inhouse studio work, songwriters on varying royalty contract. Submit ½" demo tape by mail; unsolicited submissions OK. Submit demo cassette. Not neccessary to include lyric or lead sheets. SASE/IRC for return of submission. Reports in 3-4 months.
Stories: Publishes 1 book/cassette package and 1 audiotape/year. 50% of stories are fiction; 50% nonfiction. Will consider all genres for all age groups. Authors are paid varying royalty on wholesale or retail price. Submit both cassette tape and ms. Reports in 3-4 months. Catalog is not available. Ms guidelines free with SASE.

*PAUL FRENCH & PARTNERS, INC., 503 Gabbettville Rd., LaGrange GA 30240. (706)882-5581. Fax: (706)882-3004. Vice Presidents: Lee Davis and Charles Hall. Video producer. Estab. 1978.
Music: Member of AFTRA, SAG. Pays musicians/artists on record contract; songwriters on royalty contract. Submit demo tape by mail; unsolicited submissions OK. Submit ¾-½" VHS videocassette if available. Not necessary to include lyric or lead sheets. SASE/IRC for return of submission. Reports in 3 weeks.
Stories: 90% of stories are fiction; 10% nonfiction. Work purchased outright. Query. Reports on queries/ms in 3 weeks. Submission guidelines not available.

GORDON MUSIC CO. INC./PARIS RECORDS, P.O. Box 2250, Canoga Park CA 91306. (818)883-8224. Owner: Jeff Gordon. Music publisher, record company. Estab. 1950.
Music: Releases 3-4 CDs/year. Member of ASCAP and BMI. Publishes 6-8 children's songs/year; records 10-15 children's songs/year. Works with composers, lyricists, team collaborators. For music published pays standard royalty of 50%; for songs recorded, arrangement made between artist and company. Call first and obtain permission to submit. Submit 3-4 videocassette tapes, lyric and lead sheets. Does not return unsolicited submissions. Recorded children's songs: "Izzy, the Pest of the West," recorded by Champ on Paris label.

*HIGH WINDY AUDIO, 260 Lambeth Walk, Fletcher NC 28732. (704)628-1728. Fax: (704)628-4435. Owner: Virginia Callaway. Record company.
Music: Releases 2 LPs-cassettes/year; 2 CDs/year. Member of BMI, AFTRA. Records 12 children's songs/year. Works with storytellers, musicians. Pays musicians/artists on record contract plus one time studio work.
Stories: Publishes 2 CDs/year. 100% of stories are fiction. Will consider animal, fantasy, history, scary, sports, spy/mystery/adventure. Authors are paid royalty based on retail price. Query. Reports on queries in 3 weeks. Catalog free on request. Submission guidelines not available. Recently recorded story tapes: *Hairyman*, narrated by David Holt (ages 4-adult, folktale); *The Boy Who Loved Frogs*, narrated by Jay O'Callahan (ages 4-adult, animal story).
Tips: "Call first."

*KKDS-AM 1060–THE IMAGINATION STATION, P.O. Box 57760, Salt Lake City UT 84157. (801)262-5624. Fax: (801)266-1510. Program Director: Sue Chamberlin. Radio Station. Estab. 1967.
Music: Member of ASCAP, BMI, SESAC. Write for permission to submit material. Submit demo cassette. Send finished cassette to station.
Tips: "We play children's stories on storytime each day. Play music that fits the station. Call first."

*LISTENING LIBRARY, INC., One Park Ave., Old Greenwich CT 06870. (203)637-3616. Fax: (203)698-1998. Contact: Editorial Review Committee. Spoken word recording company.

Stories: Purchases material outright. Submit completed script. SASE/IRC for return of submission. Reports in 2 months. Recently recorded books: *A Wrinkle in Time*, by Madeleine L'Engle (ages 5-12); *Superfudge*, by Judy Blume (ages 5-12).
Tips: "We primarily produce works that are already published. However, we occasionally find that an audio project will arise out of original material submitted to us."

*MEDICINE SHOW MUSIC, INC., 19 Beech Court, Fishkill NY 12524. (914)896-9359. Fax: (914)896-9359. President: Karan Bunin. Estab. 1991.
Music: Member of BMI. Publishes and records 12 children's songs/year. Hires staff writers for children's music. Works with composers and/or lyricists, team collaborators. Pay varies with projects. Submit demo tape by mail; unsolicited submissions OK. Submit demo cassette (videocassette if available), press kits. Include lyric sheet. Cannot return material. Recently recorded songs: "Skating On The Moon," by Karan Bunin and Jeff Waxman, recorded by Karan & The Musical Medicine Show on 200M Express/BMG Kidz (children's music for ages preschool-adult); "Coming To Your Town," by Karan Bunin, recorded by Karan & The Musical Medicine Show on 200M Express/BMG Kidz (Children's music for ages preschool-adults).
Tips: Send tapes with information about project and intentions (goals). Follow up with phone call 2 weeks after sending.

MELODY HOUSE, INC., 819 NW 92nd St., Oklahoma City OK 73114. (405)840-3383. Fax: (405)840-3384. President: Stephen Fite. Record company. Estab. 1972.
Music: Releases 6 LPs/year. Records 72 children's songs/year. Works with composers, lyricists, team collaborators. For songs recorded pays musicians on salary for inhouse studio work or standard mechanical royalty per song. Submit demo tape by mail; unsolicited submissions OK. Submit demo cassette (5 songs or more) with lyric and lead sheets. SASE/IRC for return of submission. Reports in 2 months. Recorded songs: "Blues for My Blue Sky," by Stephen Fite, recorded by Al Rasso on Melody House label (rhythm and blues for ages 4-8); "What A Beautiful World," by Al Rasso, recorded by Stephen Fite on Melody House label (ballad for ages 4-8).
Tips: "The music and the lyrics should reach out and grab the child's attention. Children are much more sophisticated in their listening than their parents were at the same age. Children's music is definitely taking on the characteristics of the pop market with the sounds and even the hype in some cases. Even some of the messages are now touching on issues such as divorce/separation, the environment and social consciousness, both in the U.S. and the world."

*MUSIC FOR LITTLE PEOPLE, P.O. Box 1460, Redway CA 95560. (707)923-3991. Fax: (707)923-3241. Contact: Barbara Ellis. Record company.
Music: Releases 6-12 cassettes/year; 6-12 CDs/year. Records 40 children's songs/year. Works with composers and/or lyricists, team collaborators. Pays musicians/artists on record contract. Write for permission to submit material. Cannot return material. Reports in 2-6 months. Recently recorded songs: "Water From Another Time," by John McCutcheon, recorded by Scott Petito (folk for ages 3-8); "Three Little Birds," by Bob Marley, recorded at Banquet Studios—Santa Rosa on Music for Little People (reggae, ages 3-8).
Stories: Publishes 2-6 book/cassette packages/year. 100% nonfiction. For nonfiction, considers cultural and musical history; biography (ages 3-8). Work purchased outright, $500 minimum. Query. Reports on queries in 2-6 months. Catalog is free on request. Submission guidelines not available.

*NATIVE AMERICAN PUBLIC BROADCASTING CONSORTIUM, INC., P.O. Box 83111, Lincoln NE 68501. (402)472-3522. Fax: (402)472-8675. Public television and radio production and distribution. Estab. 1977.

Music: Call first and obtain permission to submit material. Submit demo cassette, VHS videocassette if available. Reports in 3 months.
Stories: Will consider anything about Native Americans for all audiences. Catalog free on request. Submission guidelines not available.
Story Tips: "We are looking for programs that can be aired on public radio and on the American Indian Radio On Satellite Network (AIROS) and by or about Native Americans. There is a growing demand for good multicultural programs as well as quality children's multicultural programs. With more and more states passing legislation that mandates multicultural programs be incorporated into the school curriculums, the demand has become tremendous."

OAK STREET MUSIC, 1067 Sherwin Rd., Winnipeg, Manitoba R3H 0T8 Canada. (204)957-0085. Record company. Estab. 1987.
Music: Releases 8 LPs-cassettes/year; 3 CDs/year. Member of SOCAN and PROCAN. Records 30 children's songs/year. Works with team collaborators. For songs recorded pays musicians/artists on record contract; songwriters on royalty contract. Submit demo tape by mail; unsolicited submissions OK. Include demo cassette (VHS videocassette if available); minimum 2-5 songs; not necessary to include lyric or lead sheets. SASE/IRC for return of submission. Recently recorded songs: "You Can Count On Me," by Sammy Cahn, recorded by Fred Penner on Oak Street Music label (children's music for ages 2-10); "Oo Babba Loo," by Markus, recorded by Fred Penner on Oak Street Music label (children's music for ages 2-10).
Stories: Publishes 2 book/cassette packages/year. 50% of stories are fiction; 50% nonfiction. Interested in all types of fiction for "older" children (ages 5-8). Interested in all types of nonfiction. Submit both cassette tape and ms.
Tips: "Listen to our products for an idea of what we need or choose a specific artist like Fred Penner to write for."

PETER PAN INDUSTRIES, 88 St. Francis St., Newark NJ 07105. (201)344-4214. Fax: (201)344-0465. Vice President of Sales: Shelly Rudin. Music publisher, record company. Record labels include Parade Music, Compose Music, Peter Pan. Estab. 1927.
Music: Releases 20 singles/year; 10 12-inch singles; 45 LPs/year; 45 CDs/year. Member of ASCAP and BMI. Publishes 50 children's songs/year; records 80-90 songs/year. Works with composers, lyricists, team collaborators. For music published pays standard royalty of 50%; for songs recorded pays musicians/artists on record contract, songwriters on royalty contract. Submit a 15 IPS reel-to-reel demo tape or VHS videocassette by mail—unsolicited submissions OK. SASE (or SAE and IRCs) for return of submissions. Reports in 4-6 weeks.
Stories: Publishes 12 book/cassette packages/year. 90% of stories are fiction; 10% nonfiction. Will consider all genres of fiction and nonfiction aimed at 6-month to 9-year-olds. Authors are paid in royalties based on wholesale price. Query. Reports on queries in 4-6 weeks. Book catalog, ms guidelines free on request.
Tips: "Tough business but rewarding. Lullabys are very popular."

*PRAKKEN PUBLICATIONS, INC., Suite 1, 275 Metty Dr., P.O. Box 8623, Ann Arbor MI 48103. (313)769-1211. Fax: (313)769-8383. Publisher: George Kennedy. Magazine publisher. Estab. 1934.
Stories: Publishes 4 book/cassette packages/year. 100% of stories nonfiction. Will consider any genre of nonfiction (ages 3-8). Authors are paid 10% royalty based on net sales. Other payment negotiable. Advance not standard practice but possibly negotiable. Submit outline/synopsis and sample chapters. Reports on queries in 2 weeks; on mss in 6 weeks if return requested and SASE enclosed. Catalog free on request. Submission free with SASE.

Tips: "We are presently a publisher of magazines and books for educators. We now seriously seek to expand into such areas as children's books and other-than-print media."

*PRODUCTIONS DIADEM INC., C.P. 33 Pointe-Gatineau, Québec J8T 4Y8 Canada. (819)561-4114. President: Denyse Marleau. Record company. Record label Jouvence. Estab. 1982.
Music: Releases 1-2 LPs/year; 1-2 CDs/year. Member of CAPAC. Records 16-20 songs/year. Works with composers, lyricists. For songs recorded pays musicians/artists on record contract, musicians on salary for inhouse studio work, songwriters on 10% royalty contract. Making contact: Write first and obtain permission to submit a cassette tape with 3 songs and a lyric sheet. SASE (or SAE and IRCs). Reports in 1 month. Recorded songs: "Vive l'hiver," by Marie Marleau, (children's contemporary music); "Chers grands-parents," by Denyse Marleau, (children's contemporary music); "Mon ami l'ordinateur," (children's popular music), all recorded by DIADEM on the Jouvence label.

QUIET TYMES, INC., Suite 521, 2121 S. Oneida St., Denver CO 80224. (303)757-5545. Fax: (303)757-3679. Vice President: Cathy Gavend. Record company. Estab. 1987.
Music: "We've released 2 audiocassette tapes since our company began. We are now working on our third." Works with composers, teams collaborators. Pays royalties for music published; pays musicians/artists on record contract. Write for permission to submit material. Submit demo tape. SASE/IRC for return of submission. Reports in 6 weeks. Recently recorded songs: "Sleepy Angels," by Jim Oliver (age 10-adult mothers-to-be, but enjoyed by all); "The Baby Soother," by Roger Wannell (sounds for infants to 1½ years).

RHYTHMS PRODUCTIONS/TOM THUMB MUSIC, P.O. Box 34485, Los Angeles CA 90034. President: R.S. White. Record company, cassette and book packagers. Record label, Tom Thumb—Rhythms Productions. Estab. 1955.
Music: Member of ASCAP. Works with composers and lyricists. For songs recorded pays musicians/artists on record contract, songwriters on royalty contract. Submit a cassette demo tape or VHS videotape by mail—unsolicited submissions OK. Requirements: "We accept musical stories. Must be produced in demo form, and must have educational content or be educationally oriented." Reports in 2 months. Recorded *Adventures of Professor Whatzit & Carmine Cat*, by Dan Brown and Bruce Crook (6 book and cassette packages); and *First Reader's Kit* (multimedia learning program); all on Tom Thumb label.

CHARLES SEGAL MUSIC, 16 Grace Rd., Newton MA 02159. (617)969-6196. Fax: (617)969-6114. Contact: Charles Segal. Music publisher and record company. Record labels include Spin Record. Estab. 1980.
Music: Publishes 36 children's songs/year. Works with composers and/or lyricists, team collaborators. For music published pays standard royalty of 50%; for songs recorded pays musicians/artists on record contract. Submit demo tape by mail.; unsolicited submissions OK. Submit demo cassette if available with 1-3 songs and lyric or lead sheets. Reports in 6-7 weeks. Recorded songs: "Animal Concert," by Colleen Hay, recorded by Concert Kids on CBS label (sing along for ages 4-13); "Everyday Things," recorded by Charles Segal on MFP label (kids pop music for ages 6-15).
Music Tips: "Must be of educational value, entertaining easy listening. The lyrics should not be focused on sex, killing, etc."
Stories: Publishes 6 book/cassette packages/year. 50% of stories are fiction; 50% nonfiction. Will consider all genres aimed at ages 6-15. For nonfiction, considers all aimed at ages 6-15. Authors are paid royalty. Submit complete ms or submit both cassette tape and ms. Reports on queries in 6 weeks; mss in 2 months.

Story Tips: "I always look for the experienced writer who knows where he's going and not beating around the bush; in other words, has a definite message—a simple, good storyline."

*SMARTY PANTS AUDIO/VIDEO, Suite #2, 15104 Detroit, Lakewood OH 44107. (216)221-5300. Fax: (216)221-5348. President: S. Tirk. Music publisher, book publisher, record company. Record labels include Smarty Pants, High Note, S.P.I. Estab. 1988.
Music: Releases 25 LPs/year; 25 CDs/year. Member of BMI. Publishes 5-10 songs/year; records 10-20 songs and stories/year. Hires staff writers for children's music. Works with composers, lyricists, team collaborators. Purchases all rights to material. Call first and obtain permission to submit material. Submit demo cassette and videocassette if available; 3 or 4 songs and lyric sheet. Material must be copyrighted. SASE/IRC for return of submission. Reports in 2 weeks. Recently recorded songs: "Nice & Easy," by S. Tirk/ Kathy Garver, recorded by Kathy Garver on the Smarty Pants label (children's music for ages 3-7); "Trip Trott," by S. Tirk/Kathy Garver, recorded by Kathy Garver on the Smarty Pants label (children's music for ages 3-7).
Music Tips: "Keep it upbeat, topical and clear." Sees big name artists trying to crack children's market.
Stories: Publishes 8 book/cassette packages/year; 2 cassettes/CDs/year. 100% of stories are fiction. Considers animal, fantasy aimed at ages 3-8. Work purchased outright. Submit both cassette tape and manuscript. Reports on queries/mss in 2 weeks. Catalog free on request. Call for guidelines. Recently published and recorded story tapes: *Tale of Peter Rabbit*, by Beatrix Potter, narrated by Kathy Garver (ages 3-8); *The Real Mother Goose*, by Blanche Fisher Wright, narrated by Kathy Garver (ages 3-8).

SONG WIZARD RECORDS; SONG WIZARD MUSIC (ASCAP), P.O. Box 931029, Los Angeles CA 90093. (213)461-8848. Fax: (213)461-0936. Owner: Dave Kinnoin. Music publisher, record company. Record label Song Wizard Records. Estab. 1987.
Music: Releases 1 cassette/year. Member of ASCAP. Records 12 songs/year. Publishes 20 songs/year. Works with composers, lyricists and team collaborators. For music published pays negotiable royalty; for songs recorded pays songwriters on royalty contract (negotiable). Write for permission to submit material. Submit demo cassette with 3 songs and lyric sheet. "Put name, address, phone number and copyright notice on all pieces of submission." SASE/IRC for return of submission. Reports within 6 weeks. Recorded songs: "Dunce Cap Kelly," written and recorded by Dave Kinnoin on Song Wizard Records label (pop rock for ages 7-12); "Daring Dewey," written and recorded by Dave Kinnoin on Song Wizard Records label (pop rock for ages 5-12).
Tips: "Be startlingly fresh with true rhymes and poetic devices that live happily with singability. Songs have to be extra-good because competition is strong. If someone sends me a song that is so amazing I can't ignore it, I'll use it or pass it on to someone else who may."

SOUND PUBLICATIONS, INC., Suite 108, 10 E. 22nd St., Lombard IL 60148. (708)916-7071. President: Cheryl Basilico. Music publisher, record company. Record labels include Sound Publications. Estab. 1991.
Music: Releases 10 LPs/year. Publishes and records 50 children's songs/year. For music published pays standard royalty of 50%; songs recorded on joint venture. Call or write for permission to submit material. Submit demo cassette with 3-5 songs, lyric sheet. "Music is to be educational." SASE/IRC for return of submission. Reports in 3 months.

Refer to the Business of Children's Writing & Illustrating for up-to-date marketing, tax and legal information.

SOUNDPRINTS, a Division of Trudy Management Corporation, P.O. Box 679, 165 Water St., Norwalk CT 06856. (203)838-6009. Assistant Editor: Dana Meacher. Book publisher. Estab. 1988.
Stories: Publishes 6-7 book/cassette packages/year. Almost 100% of stories are fiction. Will consider realistic animal stories for preschool-3rd grade. Query with SASE. Reports on queries in 2 weeks; mss in 1 month. Catalog free on request. Ms guidelines free with SASE. Published and recorded story tapes: *Jackrabbit and the Prairie Fire*, by Susan Saunders, narrated by Peter Thomas (black-tailed jackrabbit on the Great Plains for preschool-3rd grade); *Seasons of a Red Fox*, by Susan Saunders, narrated by Peter Thomas (the first year in the life of a red fox for preschool-3rd grade).
Tips: "Be realistic. Much of what I get is not worth reading."

*TREEHOUSE RADIO®, Station A, Box 2334, Champaign IL 61825. (217)356-2400. Executive Producer: Cherie Lyn. Weekly children's radio show hosted by kids. Estab. 1990.
Tips: "We give priority to songs done from a kids' perspective, and/or written by kids."

*TVN-THE VIDEO NETWORK, 31 Cutler Dr., Ashland MA 01721. (508)881-1800. Fax: (508)881-3532. Producer: Gregg C. McAllister. Video publisher. Estab. 1986.
Music: Member of ASCAP and BMI. Publishes and records 8 children's songs/year. Hires staff writers for children's music. Pays on a work-for-hire basis. Pays musicians on salary for inhouse studio work. Submit demo cassette, VHS videocassette if available. "Reports on an as needed basis only." Recently recorded "My Dad and Me."

*UPSTREAM PRODUCTIONS, 35 Page Ave., P.O. Box 8843, Asheville NC 28814. (704)258-9713. Fax: (704)258-9727. Owner: Steven Heller. Music composer and producer and record company. Estab. 1982.
Music: Releases 1-3 LPs and 1-3 CDs/year. Member of ASCAP and BMI. Publishes and records 5-8 children's songs/year. Works with composers and lyricists. For music published pays standard royalty of 50%. "Submit letter first for cassette request. Cassettes should have 1-3 songs." Cassettes not returned.

WATCHESGRO MUSIC PUBLISHING CO., Watch Us Climb, #1234, 4185 Paradise Rd., Las Vegas NV 89109-6513. (702)792-9891. President: Eddie Lee Carr. Music publisher, record company. Record labels include Interstate 40 Records, Tracker Records. Estab. 1970.
Music: Releases 10 singles/year; 5 12-inch singles/year; 1 LP/year; 1 CD/year. Member of BMI and ASCAP. Publishes 15 children's songs/year; records 4 children's songs/year. Works with composers, lyricists. For music published pays standard royalty of 50%; for songs recorded pays musicians/artists on record contract, musicians on salary for inhouse studio work. Write or call first and obtain permission to submit a cassette tape. Does not return unsolicited material. Reports in 1 week.

WE LIKE KIDS!, produced by KTOO-FM, 224 4th St., Juneau AK 99801. (907)586-1670. Fax: (907)586-3612. Producer: Jeff Brown. Producer of nationwide children's radio show.
Music: Releases 50 programs/year. Member of Children's Music Network; National Association for the Preservation and Perpetuation of Storytelling. Submit demo tape by mail; unsolicited submissions OK. Submit demo cassette, vinyl, CD.
Music Tips: "The best advice we could give to anyone submitting songs for possible airplay is to make certain that you give your best performance and record it in the best way possible. A mix of well-honed songwriting skills, an awareness of a variety of international musical styles, and the advent of home studios have all added up to a delightful abundance of quality songs and stories for children."

Stories: "Our show is based on themes most of the time. Send us your *recorded* stories. We play an average of one story per show, *all* from pre-recorded cassettes, LPs and CDs. Please do not send us *written* stories. Several storytellers have discovered We Like Kids! as a way of sharing their stories with a nationwide audience. Most recently, storyteller Margaret Wolfson sent her tape of 2 stories; one of which we just used! She found out about WLK! through the *Children's Writer's & Illustrator's Market!*"

WORLD LIBRARY PUBLICATIONS INC., 3815 N. Willow Rd., Schiller Park IL 60176. (708)678-0621. General Editor: Nicholas T. Freund. Music publisher. Estab. 1945.
Music: Publishes 10-12 children's songs/year. Works with composers. For music published pays 10% of sales. Making contact: Submit demo cassette tape and lead sheet by mail; unsolicited submissions OK. "Should be liturgical. We are primarily a Roman Catholic publisher." Reports in 3 months. Published children's songs: "Let the Children Come to Me," written and recorded by James V. Marchconda on WLP cassette 7845 label (religious/catechetical); "Gather You Children," written by Peter Finn and James Chepponis (religious/catechetical); and "Mass of the Children of God," written by James V. Marchionda on WLP Cassette 7664 label (liturgical).

*WUVT-FM; HICKORY DOCK SHOW, P.O Box 99, Pilot VA 24138. (703)382-4975. Producer: Linda DeVito. Radio producer of children's show which features music, stories, poems. Estab. 1989.
Music: Submit demo cassette. SASE/IRC for return of submission.
Music Tips: "Write material that the whole family can enjoy. Sing-songy is out. Current topics and acoustic/folk melodies are great!"
Stories: Will consider animal, fantasy, sports, adventure. For nonfiction, considers animal, sports (ages 4-10).

*WXPN-FM; KID'S CORNER, 3905 Spruce St., Philadelphia PA 19104. (215)898-6677. Fax: (215)573-2152. Host/Producer: Kathy O'Connell. Radio program. Estab. 1988.
Music: Member of Children's Music Network, National Federation of Community Broadcasters, National Association of Independent Record Distributors. Submit demo tape by mail; unsolicited submissions OK. Submit demo cassette, CD, include lyric sheet. Cannot return material. Recently played songs: "Mine," by Idlet/Grimwood, recorded by Trout Fishing in America on Trout Records (rock/folk/children's, ages 7 and up); "Nobody," by Idlet/Grimwood, recorded by Trout Fishing in America on Trout Records (children's, ages 7 and up).
Tips: "Make it funny! Make it appealing to adults. Better production! Funnier/wittier lyrics!"

Audiotapes/'93-'94 changes

The following markets are not included in this edition of *Children's Writer's & Illustrator's Market* for the reasons indicated within parentheses. If there is no reason given, it means the market did not respond to our requests for updated information for a 1994 listing.

The Cutting Corporation
Frontline Music Group/FMG Books
Home, Inc.
Mama-T Artists/The Folk-
tellers
New Day Press
Planetary Playthings
A.J. Shalleck Productions, Inc. (out of business)
Trenna Productions
Zack Press, Stiles-Bishop Productions, Inc.

Scriptwriter's Markets

Rumors suggest children are less discriminating than adults, and therefore not as picky about the plays they view. The reality is children are about the cruelest critics there are. Most adults will sit patiently and watch a dull play just to be polite, but kids, for the most part, are less inhibited about visibly expressing their dissatisfaction. One way to assure against a bored audience is to use plenty of rhythm, repetition and effective dramatic action. Also, avoid using subplots, which will lengthen the play. Most plays for children average less than an hour.

"Fourth wall" plays, or plays where actors perform as if they are not aware of the audience, are still the standard in this field. But because of the competition of movies and television, interactive plays which involve the audience are gaining more acceptance.

The U.S. population is comprised of a multitude of ethnic subcultures. Be aware of this when writing plays for children. You might have a better chance at selling a script if it reflects racial diversity.

Since many theater groups produce plays with limited budgets, scripts containing elaborate staging and costumes might not meet their needs. Also, many children's plays are touring productions that consist of three to six actors. More characters might exist in your play than available actors, so think about how the roles can be doubled up. Also, touring theaters want simple sets that can be easily transported. To become more familiar with the types of plays the listed markets are seeking, contact them about their specific needs. Some will have catalogs available.

Plays using adult roles *and* plays with children's roles are being solicited by the markets in this section. Note the percentages of how many plays produced are for adult roles, and how many are for children's roles.

Finally, payment for playwrights usually comes in the form of royalties, outright payments or a combination of both. The pay scale isn't going to be quite as high as screenplay rates, but playwrights *do* benefit by getting to see their work performed live by a variety of groups using a multitude of interpretations.

A.D. PLAYERS, 2710 W. Alabama, Houston TX 77098. (713)526-2721. Literary Manager: Martha Doolittle. Estab. 1967. Produces 4-5 children's plays/year in new Children's Theatre Series; 1-2 musical/year. Produces children's plays for professional productions. 99-100% of plays/musicals written for adult roles; 1-0% for juvenile roles. "Cast must utilize no more than 4 actors. Need minimal, portable sets for proscenium or arena stage with no fly space and no wing space." Produced plays: *Secret Passwords*, by Gillette Elvgren, Jr. — teaching children to say no to wrong touching for ages 5-12; *The Promise Comes After*, by Sharla R. Boyce — Noah and his floating 200 for ages 5-100. Does not want to see large cast or set requirements or New Age themes. Will consider simultaneous submissions and previously performed work. Submission method: Query with synopsis, character breakdown and set description; no tapes until requested. Reports in 6 months-1 year. Purchases some residual rights. Pay negotiated. Submissions returned with SASE.
Tips: "Children's musicals tend to be large in casting requirements. For those theaters with smaller production capabilities, this can be a liability for a script. Try to keep it

small and simple, especially if writing for theaters where adults are performing for children. We are interested in material that reflects family values, emphasizes the importance of responsibility in making choices, encourages faith in God and projects the joy and fun of telling a story."

*AMERICAN STAGE, P.O. Box 1560, St. Petersburg FL 33731. (813)823-1600. Artistic Director: Victoria Holloway. Estab. 1977. Produces 5 children's plays/year; 2 children's musicals/year. Produces children's plays for professional children's theatre program, mainstage, school tour, performing arts halls. Limited by budget and performance venue. Subject matter: Classics and original work for children (ages K-12) and families. Recently produced plays: *The Diary of Anne Frank*, by Francis Goodrich and Albert Hackett (grades 7-12); *Charlotte's Web*, by E.B. White (grades K-6). Does not want to see plays that look down on children. Approach must be that of the child or fictional beings or animals. Will consider previously performed work. Submission method: Submit complete ms; query with synopsis, character breakdown. Reports in 6 months. Purchases "professional rights." Pays writers in royalties (6-8%); $25-35/performance. SASE for return of submission.
Tips: Sees a move toward basic human values and relationships, and multicultural communities in plays.

ART EXTENSIONS THEATER, 11144 Weddington, N. Hollywood CA 91601. (818)760-8675. Fax: (818)508-8613. Artistic Director: Maureen Kennedy Samuels. Estab. 1991. Produces 2 plays/year; 1 musical/year. Small budget. Equity waiver. 90% of plays/musicals written for adult roles; 10% for juvenile roles. Produced plays: *Working without Annette*, by Debbie Devine—about fear of change. Will consider simultaneous submissions and previously performed work. Submission method: Query with synopsis, character breakdown and set description; submit complete ms and score. Reports in 6 weeks. Pays writers in royalties of 5-10%; pays $10-25/performance. SASE for return of submission.

ARTREACH TOURING THEATRE, 3074 Madison Rd., Cincinnati OH 45209. (513)871-2300. Fax: (513)871-2501. Artistic Director: Kathryn Schultz Miller. Estab. 1976. "ArtReach has cast requirement of 3—2 men and 1 woman. Sets must look big but fit in large van." Professional theater. Produced plays: *Young Cherokee*, by Kathryn Schultz Miller—history and culture of early Cherokee tribe as seen through the eyes of a young brave, for primary students and family audiences; *The Trail of Tears*, by Kathryn Schultz Miller—a companion play to *Young Cherokee* depicting story of Cherokee removal and unjust destruction of their culture, for intermediate through adult audiences. Does not want to see musicals, holiday plays, TV type scripts (about drugs, child abuse etc.) or fractured fairy tales. Will consider simultaneous submissions and previously performed work. Submission method: Query with synopsis, character breakdown and set description. Reports in 10 days to 6 weeks. Author retains rights. Pays writers in royalties. SASE for return of submission.
Tips: "Type script in professional form found in *The Writer's Digest Guide to Manuscript Formats*. Do not submit plays that are less than 45 pages long. Look to history, culture or literature as resources."

BAKER'S PLAYS, 100 Chauncy St., Boston MA 02111. (617)482-1280. Fax: (617)482-7613. Associate Editor: Raymond Pape. Estab. 1845. Publishes 5-8 children's plays/year; 2-4 children's musicals/year. 80% of plays/musicals written for adult roles; 20% for juvenile roles. Subject matter: "Touring shows for 5-8 year olds, full lengths for family audience and full lengths and one act plays for teens." Submission method: Submit complete ms, score and tape of songs. Reports in 3-8 months. Obtains worldwide rights. Pays writers in royalties (amount varies).

Tips: "Know the audience you're writing for before you submit your play anywhere. 90% of the plays we reject are not written for our market."

BOARSHEAD: MICHIGAN PUBLIC THEATER, 425 S. Grand Ave., Lansing MI 48933. (517)484-7800. Artistic Director: John Peakes. Estab. 1966. Produces 4 children's plays/ year. Produces children's plays for professional production. Majority of plays written for adult roles. Produced plays: *1,000 Cranes*, by Amy Schultz—radiation death years after Hiroshima, for ages 6-15; *Charlotte's Web*, by E.B. White—pigs 'n stuff for ages 6-12. Does not want to see musicals. Will consider previously performed work. Submission method: Query with synopsis, character breakdown and set description. Include 10 pages of representative dialogue. Reports in 2 weeks on queries; 4 months on submissions. Pays writers $15-25/performance. Submissions returned with SASE. If no SASE, send self-addressed, stamped postcard for reply.

CHILDREN'S STORY SCRIPTS, Baymax Productions, Suite 130, 2219 W. Olive Ave., Burbank CA 91506. (818)563-6105. Fax: (818)563-2968. Editor: Deedra Bebout. Estab. 1990. Produces 3-10 children's scripts/year. "Except for small movements and occasionally standing up, children remain seated in Readers Theatre fashion." Publishes scripts sold to schools, camps, churches, scouts, hotels, cruise lines, etc.; wherever there's a program to teach or entertain children. "All roles read by children except K-2 scripts, where kids have easy lines, leader helps read the narration." Subject matter: Scripts on all subjects. Targeted age range—K-8th grade, 5-13 years old. Recently published plays: *I Won't Stand For It!*, by Elliot L. Markson—recreates Rosa Parks refusing to give up her seat on a 1955 Montgomery, Alabama bus, for grades 1, 2, 3; *The Song of the Tree Frogs*, by Mary Macdonald—Australian aboriginal legend which explains why the tree frogs sing through the night, for grades 3-8. No stories that preach a point; stories about catastrophic disease or other terribly heavy topics; theatrical scripts with no narrative prose to move the story along; stories that have only one speaking character. Accepts simultaneous submissions and previously performed work (if rights are available). Submission method: Submit complete ms. Reports in 2 weeks. Purchases all rights; authors retain copyrights. Pays writers in royalties; 10-15% on sliding scale, based on number of copies sold. SASE for reply and return of submission.
Tips: "We are not currently publishing new titles. When we will resume publishing depends on when we become better known in the marketplace. When we see a story which might work for us, we contact the author, but urge him or her to try to sell elsewhere. If the story is available when we resume publishing new titles, great—if not, maybe he or she can write something else for us. In any case, we do not want any author to pass up a hard sale waiting for us. We just don't know when we will be able to publish new works. However, we are always interested in seeing submissions." Writer's guidelines packet available for business-sized SASE with two first-class stamps. Guidelines explain what Children's Story Scripts are, give four-page examples from two different scripts, give list of suggested topics for scripts.

THE CHILDREN'S THEATRE COMPANY, 2400 Third Ave. S., Minneapolis MN 55404. (612)874-0500. Artistic Director: Jon Cranney. Estab. 1965. Produces 9 children's plays/ year; 1-3 children's musicals/year. Produces children's plays for professional, not-for-profit productions. 60% of plays/musicals written for adult roles; 40% for juvenile roles in all productions. Produced plays: *Ramona Quimby*, by Len Jenkin—family life of the Quimbys for all ages; *On the Wings of the Hummingbird: Tales of Trinidad*, by Beverly Smith-Dawson—life in Trinidad during carnival for all ages. Does not want to see plays written for child performers only. Will consider simultaneous submissions and previously performed work. Submission method: Submit complete ms and score (if a musical). Reports in 2-6 months. Rights negotiable. Pays writers in royalties (2%). Submissions returned with SASE.

Tips: "The Children's Theatre Company rarely (if ever) produces unsolicited manuscripts; we continue a long tradition of producing new works commissioned to meet the needs of our audience and catering to the artistic goals of a specific season. Though the odds of us producing submitted plays are very slim, we always enjoy the opportunity to become acquainted with the work of a variety of artists, particularly those who focus on young audiences."

CIRCA '21 DINNER THEATRE, P.O. Box 3784, Rock Island IL 61204-3784. (309)786-2667. Producer: Dennis Hitchcock. Estab. 1977. Produces 2-3 children's plays/year; 3 children's musicals/year. "Prefer a cast no larger than 10." Produces children's plays for professional productions. 95% of plays/musicals written for adult roles; 5% written for juvenile roles. Submission method: Query with synopsis, character breakdown, tape and set description. Reports in 3 months. Payment negotiable.

I.E. CLARK, INC., P.O. Box 246, Schulenburg TX 78956. Fax: (409)743-4765. Estab. 1956. Publishes 3 children's plays/year; 1 or 2 children's musicals/year. Medium to large casts preferred. Publishes plays for all ages. Published plays: *Wind of a Thousand Tales*, by John Glore—about a young girl who doesn't believe in fairy tales for ages 5-12; *Rock'n'Roll Santa*, by R. Eugene Jackson—Santa's reindeer form a rock band for ages 4-16. Does not want to see plays that have not been produced. Will consider simultaneous submissions and previously performed work. Submission method: Submit complete ms and audio or video tape. Reports in 6-8 months. Purchases all rights. Pays writers in negotiable royalties. SASE for return of submission.
Tips: "We publish only high quality literary works."

COMMUNITY CHILDREN'S THEATRE OF KANSAS CITY INC., 8021 E. 129th Terrace, Grandview MO 64030. (816)761-5775. Contact: Blanche Sellens. Estab. 1951. Produces 5 children's plays/year. Prefer casts of between 6-8. Produces children's plays for amateur productions for ages K-6. Produced play: *Red Versus the Wolf*, by Judy Wolferman—musical for K-6 audience. Submission method: Query first then submit complete ms. Reports in a matter of months. "Winning script is performed by one of the units for two years."
Tips: "Write for guidelines and details for The Margaret Bartle Annual Playwriting Award."

CONTEMPORARY DRAMA SERVICE, Division of Meriwether Publishing Ltd., 885 Elkton Dr., Colorado Springs CO 80907. (719)594-4422. Fax: (719)594-9916. Editor: Arthur Zapel. Estab. 1979. Publishes 45 children's plays/year; 5 children's musicals/year. 15% of plays/musicals written for adult roles; 85% for juvenile roles. Recently published plays: *Stormin' The Teacher's Lounge*—a comedy about high school hi-jinks; *Be Yourself*—a collection of playlets about self-esteem and peer group pressure for high school performers; *Yo, Daniel!*, by Walter K. Davis—a Bible story for Sunday School kids. "We do not publish plays for elementary level except for church plays for Christmas and Easter. All of our secular plays are for teens or college level." Does not want to see "full-length, 3-act plays (unless they have production history) or plays with dirty language." Will consider simultaneous submissions or previously performed work. Submission method: Query with synopsis, character breakdown and set description; "query first if a musical." Reports in 1 month. Purchases all first rights. Pays either 10% royalty or buys material outright for $100-1,000. SASE for return of submission.

THE COTERIE, 2450 Grand, Kansas City MO 64108. (816)474-6785. Fax: (816)474-6785. Artistic Director: Jeff Church. Estab. 1979. Produces 7 children's plays/year; 1 children's musical/year. "Prefer casts of between 5-7, no larger than 15." Produces children's plays for professional productions. 80% of plays/musicals written for adult roles; 20% for juvenile roles. "We do *not* produce puppet shows, although we may use puppets in our plays. We produce original plays, musicals and literary adaptations for ages 5 through adult." Produced plays: *Amelia Lives*, by Laura Annawyn Shamas—one-woman show on Amelia Earhart for 6th grade through adult; *Dinosaurus*, by Ed Mast and Lenore Bensinger—Mobil Oil workers discover cavern of dinosaurs, for ages 5 through adult. "We do *not* want to see 'camp' adaptations of fairytales." Submission method: Query with synopsis, sample scene, character breakdown and set description. Reports in 4-6 months. Rights purchased "negotiable." Pays writers in royalties per play of approximately $500-1,500. SASE for return of submission.
Tips: "We're interested in adaptations of classic literature with small casts, simple staging requirements, strong thematic, character and plot development, and also multicultural topics. There is a need for non-condescending material for younger age groups (5-8) and for middle school (ages 9-13)."

CREEDE REPERTORY THEATRE, P.O. Box 269, Creede CO 81130. (719)658-2541. Fax: (719)658-2343. Artistic Director: Richard Baxter. Estab. 1966. Produces 1-2 children's plays/year. Limited to 4-6 cast members and must be able to tour. Produces children's plays for summer, school or professional productions. 100% of plays/musicals written for adult roles. Publishes plays for ages K-12. Recently produced plays: *Wiley and the Hairy Man*, by Susan Zedec—young man faces fears for ages K-6; *Greater Tuna*, by Williams, Sears, Howard—Texas for 6-adult. Does not want to see historical plays. Will consider simultaneous submissions and previously performed work. Submission method: Query first, submit complete ms and score, or query with synopsis, character breakdown and set description. Reports in 12 months. Pays writers in 5% royalties; pays $25-30 per performance.

DRAMATIC PUBLISHING, INC., 311 Washington St., Woodstock IL 60098. (815)338-7170. Fax: (815)338-8981. Estab. 1885. Publishes 105 plays/year, 110 musicals/year children and young adults. Published plays: *Secret Garden*, by Pamela Sterling—newly published adaptation with optional underscoring for elementary to adult; *Johnny Tremain*, by Lola H. and Coleman A. Jennings—portrays turbulent times of Revolutionary Boston, adapted from Esther Forbes' book for middle elementary to adults. Will consider simultaneous submissions and previously performed work. Submission method: Query with synopsis, character breakdown and set description; send script, (with a cassette if a musical) and include an SASE if wish to have submission returned. Reports in 3-4 months. Pays writers in royalties.
Tips: "Scripts should be from ½ to 1½ hours long, and not didactic or condescending. Original plays dealing with hopes, joys and fears of today's children are preferred to adaptations of old classics."

ELDRIDGE PUBLISHING CO. INC., P.O. Box 1595, Venice FL 34284. (813)496-4679. Fax: (813)496-9680. Editor: Nancy Vorhis. Estab. 1906. Publishes approximately 25 children's plays/year (5 for elementary; 20 for junior and senior high); 2-3 high school musicals/year. Prefers simple staging; flexible cast size. We "publish for middle, junior and high school, all genres." Published plays: *Dirty Dealings in Dixie*, by Craig Sodaro—parody on Gone With The Wind, a hilarious melodrama for high school age; *Fly Away*

Home, by Peg Sheldrick—effects of divorce on a teen's family at Christmas, for junior and senior high school audience. Submission method: Submit complete ms, score and tape of songs (if a musical). Reports in 2 months. Purchases all dramatic rights. Pays writers royalties of 35-50%; buys material outright for $150-500.

Tips: "We're always on the lookout for large-cast comedies which provide a lot of fun for our customers. But other more serious topics which concern teens, as well as intriguing mysteries, and children's theater programs are of interest to us as well. We know there are many new talented playwrights out there and we look forward to reading their fresh scripts."

ENCORE PERFORMANCE PUBLISHING, P.O. Box 692, Orem UT 84059. (801)225-0605. Estab. 1978. Publishes 10-20 children's plays/year; 8-15 children's musicals/year. Prefers equal male/female ratio if possible. Adaptations for K-12 and older. 60% of plays written for adult roles; 40% for juvenile roles. Recently published plays: *Yushi and The Dragon*, by Chuck Hudson—a fabulous Japanese myth brought to life on the stage in traditional Japanese fashion for ages 7-15; *Las Fabulas Chistosas De Esopo (Aesop's Funny Fables)*, by Patricia Barry Rumble and Alicia Mena—Aesops Fables in action-packed fun-filled entertainment for bilingual audiences preschool through 6th grades. Will only consider previously performed work. Looking for issue plays and unusual fairy tale adaptations. Submission method: Query first with synopsis, character breakdown and set description. Purchases all publication and production rights. Author retains copyright. Pays writers in royalties (50%). SASE for return of submission.

Tips: "Give us issue and substance, be controversial without offence. Use a laser printer! Don't send old manuscript. Make yours look the most professional."

FLORIDA STUDIO THEATRE, 1241 N. Palm Ave., Sarasota FL 34236. (813)366-9017. Artistic Director: Richard Hopkins. Estab. 1980. Produces 3 children's plays/year; 1-3 children's musicals/year. Produces children's plays for professional productions. 50% of plays/musicals written for adult roles; 50% for juvenile roles. "Prefer small cast plays that use imagination more than heavy scenery." Will consider simultaneous submissions and previously performed work. Submission method: Query with synopsis, character breakdown and set description. Reports in 3 months. Rights negotiable. Pay negotiable. Submissions returned with SASE.

Tips: "Children are a tremendously sophisticated audience. The material should respect this."

THE FREELANCE PRESS, P.O. Box 548, Dover MA 02030. (508)785-1260. Estab. 1979. Produces 3 musicals and/or plays/year. Casts are comprised of young people, ages 8-15, and number 25-30. "We publish original musicals on contemporary topics for children and adaptations of children's classics (e.g., Velveteen Rabbit, Rip Van Winkle)." Published plays: *Velveteen Rabbit*, based on story of same name for ages 8-11; *Monopoly*, 3 young people walk through board game, the winner gets to choose where he/she wants to live (ages 11-15). No plays for adult performers. Will consider simultaneous submissions and previously performed work. Submission method: Submit complete ms and score with SASE. Reports in 3 months. Pays writers 10% royalties. SASE for return of submission.

SAMUEL FRENCH, INC., 45 W. 25th St., New York NY 10010. (212)206-8990. Fax: (212)206-1429. Editor: Lawrence Harbison. Estab. 1830. Publishes 2 or 3 children's plays/year; "variable number of musicals." Subject matter: "All genres, all ages. No puppet plays. No adaptations of any of those old 'fairy tales.' No 'Once upon a time, long ago and far away.' No kings, princesses, fairies, trolls, etc." Submission method: Submit complete ms and demo tape (if a musical). Reports in 2-8 months. Purchases "publication rights, amateur and professional production rights, option to publish next

3 plays." Pays writers "book royalty of 10%; professional production royalty of 90%; amateur production royalty of 80%." SASE for return of submissions.
Tips: "Children's theater is a very tiny market, as most groups perform plays they have created themselves or have commissioned."

EMMY GIFFORD CHILDREN'S THEATER, 3504 Center St., Omaha NE 68105. Artistic Director: James Larson. Estab. 1949. Produces 9 children's plays/year; 1 children's musical/year. Produces children's plays for professional productions. 100% of plays/musicals written for adult roles. Need plays with small casts, no fly space necessary. Produced plays: *Pippi Longstocking*; *Bye Bye Birdie*. Does not want to see adult plays. Will consider simultaneous submissions, electronic submissions via disk or modem, or previously performed work. Submission method: Query first. Reports in 6 months. Pays writers in royalties (6%). Submissions returned with SASE.

THE GREAT AMERICAN CHILDREN'S THEATRE COMPANY, P.O. Box 92123, Milwaukee WI 53202. (414)276-4230. Fax: (414)276-2214. Artistic Director: Teri Solomon Mitze. Estab. 1975. Produces 2 children's plays/year. Produces children's plays for professional productions; 100% written for adult roles. Produced plays: *The Secret Garden*, by Brett Reynolds—children's classic for grades K-8; *Charlie & the Chocolate Factory*, by Richard R. George—children's classic for grades K-8. Will consider previously performed work. Submission method: Query with synopsis, character breakdown and set description. Reports in weeks. Rights and payment negotiable.

HAYES SCHOOL PUBLISHING CO. INC., 321 Pennwood Ave., Wilkinsburg PA 15221. (412)371-2373. Fax: (412)371-6408. Estab. 1940. Produces 1-2 children's plays/year. Wants to see supplementary teaching aids for grades K-12. Will consider simultaneous and electronic submissions or previously performed work. Submission method: Query first with synopsis, character breakdown and set description, or with complete ms and score. Reports in 3-4 weeks. Purchases all rights. Work purchased outright. SASE for return of submissions.

HONOLULU THEATRE FOR YOUTH, 2846 Ualena St., Honolulu HI 96819. (808)839-9885. Fax: (808)839-7018. Artistic Director: Pamela Sterling. Estab. 1955. "Cast size should be limited to 10; 6 is ideal." Produces 6 children's plays/year. Subject matter: Looks for plays "celebrating cultures of the Pacific Rim, especially. Also, plays that deal with issues of concern to today's young audiences (varying in age from 6-18)." Produced plays: *The Council*, by William S. Yellow Robe, Jr.—man's relationship with the environment for age 10 through adult; *The Giant's Baby*, by Allan Ahlberg—"modern" fairytale for ages 5 years through adult. Will consider simultaneous submissions and previously performed work. Submission method: Query first with cast requirements and synopsis. SASE required for each script requested. Pays writers in royalties (4%) and by commission fee ($2,000-5,000).
Tips: "Obviously, I look for smaller casts, less technical machinery, more imaginative use of resources. I have to balance a season with some 'title' recognition, i.e. adaptations of well-known books of fairy-tales, but I am more interested in good, *original* theatrical literature for young audiences."

INDIANA REPERTORY THEATRE, 140 W. Washington, Indianapolis IN 46204. (317)635-5277. Artistic Director: Libby Appel. Estab. 1971. Produces 3 children's plays/year. Produces children's plays for professional productions. 100% of plays written for adult roles. "Limit 8 in cast, 75 min. running time." Recently produced plays: *Tales from the Arabian Nights*, by Michael Dixon; *Red Badge of Courage*, adaptation by Thomas Olson. Does not want to see preschool and K-4 material. Will consider previously performed work. Submission method: Query with synopsis, character breakdown and set description to Janet Allen, Assoc. Artistic Director. Reports in 6 months. Pays writers negotiable royalty (6%) or commission fee. Submissions returned with SASE.

THE MUNY STUDENT THEATRE, 560 Trinity, St. Louis MO 63130. (314)862-1255. Artistic Director: Christopher Limber. Estab. 1979. Produces 5 children's plays/year; 1 or 2 children's musicals/year. "We produce a touring and mainstage season September-May and offer extensive theater classes throughout the entire year." 100% of plays/musicals written for adult roles; 40% for juvenile roles. Prefers cast of four or five equity actors, children's parts unlimited. "Tour sets are limited in size." Produced plays: *Flat Stanley*, by Jeff Brown/adapted by Larry Pressgrove—based on children's book for ages K-3; *BOCON!*, written by Lisa Loomer—a young boy's travels from El Salvador to Los Angeles for ages 4-6. Will consider simultaneous submissions and previously performed work. Submission method: Query with synopsis, character breakdown and set description. Rights negotiable.
Tips: "We emphasize diverse ethnic and cultural backgrounds. Tour shows should fit into the school curriculum. The Muny Student Theatre's mission is to introduce theater to young people, to encourage creative learning and to develop future theater audiences. The company is now one of the most comprehensive theater education programs in Missouri. Each year the company reaches more than 100,000 students through its resident touring company, professional story tellers, mainstage productions and theater classes."

THE NEW CONSERVATORY CHILDREN'S THEATRE COMPANY & SCHOOL, 25 Van Ness Ave., San Francisco CA 94102. (415)861-4914. Fax: (415)861-6988. Executive Director: Ed Decker. Estab. 1981. Produces 6-10 children's plays/year; 1-2 children's musicals/year. Limited budget. Produces children's plays as part of "a professional theater arts training program for youths ages 4-19 during the school year and two summer sessions. The New Conservatory also produces educational plays for its touring company." 100% written for juvenile roles. "We do not want to see any preachy or didactic material." Submission method: Query with synopsis, character breakdown and set description, or submit complete ms and score. Reports in 3 months. Rights purchased negotiable. Pays writers in royalties. SASE for return of submission.
Tips: Trends: "Addressing socially relevant issues for young people and their families."

NEW PLAYS INCORPORATED, P.O. Box 5074, Charlottesville VA 22905. (804)979-2777. Artistic Director: Patricia Whitton. Estab. 1964. Publishes 4 plays/year; 1 or 2 children's musicals/year. Publishes "generally material for kindergarten through junior high." Published *Play With Shakespeare*, by Linda Buyson—scenes and adaptations for junior high and high school performers for junior high and high school teachers and students; *Cinderella: The World's Favorite Fairy Tale*, by Lowell Swortzell—dramatizations of Cinderella in China, Russia and American Indian folklore for elementary school. Does not want to see "adaptations of titles I already have. No unproduced plays; no junior high improvisations." Will consider simultaneous submissions and previously performed work. Submissions method: Submit complete ms and score. Reports in 2 months. Purchases exclusive rights to sell acting scripts. Pays writers in royalties (50% of production royalties; 10% of script sales). SASE for return of submission.

NEW YORK STATE THEATRE INSTITUTE, 155 River St., Troy NY 12180. (518)274-3200. Fax: (518)274-3815. Producing Director: Patricia B. Snyder. Estab. 1976. Produces 1-2 children's plays/year; 1-2 children's musicals/year. Produces family plays for professional theater. 90% of plays/musicals are written for adult roles; 10% for juvenile roles. Does not want to see plays for children only. Recently produced plays: *The Secret Garden*, adapted by Thomas W. Olson—for all ages; *To Kill a Mockingbird*, adapted by Christopher Sergel—for grade 8 and up. Will consider simultaneous submissions and previously performed work. Submission method: Query with synopsis, character breakdown and set description; submit complete ms and tape of songs (if a musical). Reports in 2-3 months on submissions; 1 month for queries. SASE for return of submission.

Tips: Writers should be mindful of "audience *sophistication*. We do not wish to see material that is childish. Writers should submit work that is respectful of young people's intelligence and perception — work that is appropriate for families, but that is also challenging and provocative."

THE OPEN EYE: NEW STAGINGS, 270 W. 89th St., New York NY 10024. (212)769-4143. Fax: (212)595-0336. Artistic Director: Amie Brockway. Estab. 1972 (theater). Produces plays for a family audience. Most productions are with music, but are not musicals. "Casts are usually limited to six performers because of economic reasons. Technical requirements are kept to a minimum for touring purposes." Produces professional productions using members of Actor's Equity Association. Most plays/musicals written for adult roles. Recently produced plays: *The Wise Men of Chelm*, by Sandra Fenichel Asher — weaving of several Jewish folk tales for ages 8 through adult; *Freedom is my Middle Name*, by Lee Hunkins — unsung African-American heroes for ages 8 through adult. "No videos or cassettes. We accept only one script per playwright per year; no queries or synopses." Will consider previously performed work. Submit complete ms and score and résumé. Reports in 3-6 months. Rights agreement negotiated with author. Pays writers one time fee or royalty negotiated with publisher. SASE for return of submission.

Tips: "We are seeing a trend toward plays that are appropriate for a family audience and that address today's multicultural concerns."

PIONEER DRAMA SERVICE, P.O. Box 4267, Englewood CO 80155. (303)779-4035. Fax: (303)779-4315. Producer: Steven Fendrich. Artistic Director: Elizabeth Berry. Estab. 1960. Publishes 7 children's plays/year; 2 children's musicals/year. Subject matter: Publishes plays for ages 9-high school. Recently published plays/musicals: *Bang Bang Your Dead*, by Tim Kelly — gun control/safety for ages 12-adult; *Ezekial Saw the What?*, by Kirk Brown — religious for high school-adult. Does not want to see "script, scores, tapes, pics and reviews." Will consider simultaneous submissions, electronic submissions via disk or modem, previously performed work. Submission method: Query with synopsis, character breakdown and set description. Submit complete ms and score (if a musical). Reports in 2 months. Purchases all rights. Pays writers in royalties (10% on sales, 50% royalties on productions); or buys material outright for $200-1,000.

PLAYERS PRESS, INC., P.O. Box 1132, Studio City CA 91614-0132. (818)789-4980. Vice President: R. W. Gordon. Estab. 1965. Publishes 5-25 children's plays/year; 2-15 children's musicals/year. Subject matter: "We publish for all age groups." Published plays/musicals: *Rapunzel N' the Witch*, by William-Alan Landes — musical for grades 4-12. Submission method: query with synopsis, character breakdown and set description; include #10 SASE with query. Reports on query in 2-4 weeks; submissions in 6-9 months. Purchases stage, screen, TV rights. Payment varies; work purchased possibly outright upon written request.

Tips: "Entertainment quality is on the upswing and needs to be directed at the world, no longer just the US."

THE PLAYHOUSE JR., 222 Craft Ave., Pittsburgh PA 15213. (412)621-4445. Fax: (412)687-3606. Director: Wayne Brinda. Estab. 1949. Produces 5 children's plays/year; 1 children's musical/year. Produces children's plays for semi-professional production with a college theater department. 100% of plays/musicals written for adult roles. Recently produced plays: *The Three Musketeers*, by Bruce Hurlbut — adaptation of Dumas' classic for age 3-middle school; *Jack and the Beantree*, by Paul Laurakas — musical, Appa-

lachian adaptation of the fairytale for grades K-4. Does not want to see "strong social problem plays." Will consider simultaneous submissions or previously produced work. Submission method: Query with synopsis, character breakdown and set description; first drafts. Reports in 1 month. Purchases performance rights; negotiable. Pays writers commission/royalty. SASE for return of submission.
Tips: Looks for "clearly developed plot lines, imaginative use of the space, rather than realistic interiors. Plays should stimulate the imaginations of the director/producer, casts, designers and, ultimately, the audiences."

PLAYS FOR YOUNG AUDIENCES, P.O. Box 4267, Englewood CO 80155. (303)779-4035. Fax: (303)779-4315. Producer: Steven Fendrich. Artistic Director: Elizabeth Berry. Estab. 1989. Publishes 7 children's plays/year; 1 children's musical/year. Subject matter: Publishes plays for preschool-12th grade audience. Recently produced plays: *Bang Bang Your Dead*, by Tim Kelley—gun safety for ages 12-adult; *It's a Bird, It's a Plane*, by Craig Sodaro—comedy for ages 10-adult. Does not want to see "script, score, tape, pictures and reviews." Will consider simultaneous submissions, electronic submissions via disk or modem, previously performed work. Submission method: query first; query with synopsis, character breakdown and set description. Reports in 2 months. Purchases all rights. Pays writers in royalties of 10% in sales, 50% on productions.

PLAYS, THE DRAMA MAGAZINE FOR YOUNG PEOPLE, 120 Boylston St., Boston MA 02116-4615. (617)423-3157. Managing Editor: Elizabeth Preston. Estab. 1941. Publishes 70-75 children's plays/year. "Props and staging should not be overly elaborate or costly. Our plays are performed by children in school." 100% of plays written for juvenile roles. Subject matter: Audience is lower grades through junior/senior high. Published plays: *Moonlight Is When*, by Kay Arthur, about a shy young researcher who finds romance in an unexpected place—the Museum of Natural History; *Express to Valley Forge*, by Earl J. Dias, about a courageous patriot who saves the day for George Washington's army; and *Kidnapped*, a dramatization of the Herman Melville classic, adapted by Adele Thane. Send "nothing downbeat—no plays about drugs, sex or other 'heavy' topics." Submission methods: query first on adaptations of folk tales and classics; otherwise submit complete ms. Reports in 2-3 weeks. Rights obtained on mss: all rights. Pay rates vary, on acceptance. Guidelines available; send SASE. Sample copy $3.50.
Tips: "Above all, plays must be entertaining for young people with plenty of action and a satisfying conclusion."

ST. LOUIS BLACK REPERTORY COMPANY, Suite 10 F, 634 N. Grand Blvd., St. Louis MO 63103. (314)534-3807. Artistic Director: Ron Himes. Estab. 1976. Produces 6 children's plays; 2-3 children's musicals/year. Produces children's plays for professional productions. "The St. Louis Black Rep is a professional production company which includes a mainstage and touring component. The touring component produces 3-4 plays per year for young audiences." Produces "African and African-American stories for preschoolers-adults." 100% of plays/musicals written for adult roles. "The touring shows are designed to be flexible and totally self-contained." Recently produced/published *The Eighth Voyage of Sinbad*, by Patton Hasegawa—story of Sinbad's greatest and most dangerous journey for grades K-6; *A Long Hard Journey*, by Patricia McKissack, adapted by Eric Wilson—a fascinating train ride brings to life the story of the men who brought the system to its knees by yelling "No more!" for grade 6-adult. Will consider previously performed work. Submission method: Submit complete ms; query with synopsis, character breakdown and set description; submit complete ms and score (if musical). Rights are mutually agreed upon via contract. Pays writers per performance ($20-35). Submissions returned with SASE.

Tips: "Our touring company consists of 4-5 actors, therefore we need plays written for at least four or a maximum of five characters. If a play calls for more than five roles, the actors must be able to double and interchange them."

STAGE ONE: THE LOUISVILLE CHILDREN'S THEATRE, 425 W. Market, Louisville KY 40202. (502)589-5946. Fax: (502)589-5779. Producing Director: Moses Goldberg. Estab. 1946. Produces 10 children's plays/year; 1-3 children's musicals/year. Stage One is an Equity company producing children's plays for professional productions. 100% of plays/ musicals written for adult roles. "Sometimes we do use students in selected productions." Produced plays: *Bridge to Terabithia*, by Katherine Paterson, Stephanie Tolan, music by Steven Leibman—deals with friendship and the acceptance of tragedy, for ages 9-adult; *Babar*, by Thomas Olson (adaptation)—story about the adventures of an elephant for ages 4-12. Submission method: Submit complete ms, score and tape of songs (if a musical); include the author's résumé if desired. Reports in 3-4 months. Pays writers in royalties or per performance.
Tips: Looking for "stageworthy and respectful dramatizations of the classic tales of childhood, both ancient and modern; plays relevant to the lives of young people and their families; and plays directly related to the school curriculum."

TADA!, 120 W. 28th St., New York NY 10001. (212)627-1732. Artistic Director: Janine Trevens. Estab. 1984. Produces 3-4 children's plays/year; 3-4 children's musicals/year. "All actors are children, ages 6-17." Produces children's plays for professional, year-round theater. 100% of plays/musicals written for juvenile roles. Recently produced plays: *The Little House of Cookies*, adapted by Janine Nina Trevens, music/lyrics by Joel Gelpe—about a house with special powers, making new friends and people working together to make dreams come true for ages 2-adult; *Wide-Awake Jake*, book by Alice Elliott, music by Robby Merkin, lyrics by Faye Greenburg—join Jake on his magical journey to meet the Yami of Yawn, who teaches him how easy falling asleep can be. Submission method: Query with synopsis, character breakdown and set description; submit complete ms, score and tape of songs (if a musical). Reports in 3 months. Rights purchased "Depends on the piece." Pays writers in royalties. SASE for return of submissions.
Tips: "Too many authors are writing productions, not plays. Our company is multiracial and city-oriented. We are not interested in fairy tales."

THEATRE FOR YOUNG AMERICA, 7428 Washington St., Kansas City MO 64114. (816)333-9200. Artistic Director: Gene Mackey. Estab. 1974. Produces 10 children's plays/year; 3-5 children's musicals/year. "We use a small cast (4-7), open thrust stage." Theatre for Young America is a professional equity company. 90% of plays/musicals written for adult roles; 10% for juvenile roles. Produced plays: *The Wizard of Oz*, by Jim Eiler and Jeanne Bargy—for ages 6 and up; *A Partridge in a Pear Tree*, by Lowell Swortzell—deals with the 12 days of Christmas, for ages 6 and up; *Three Billy Goats Gruff*, by Gene Mackey and Molly Jessup—Norwegian folk tales, for ages 6 and up. Submission method: Query with synopsis, character breakdown and set description. Will consider simultaneous submissions and previously performed work. Reports in 2 months. Purchases production rights, tour rights in local area. Pays writers in royalties or $10-50/ per performance.
Tips: Looking for "cross-cultural material that respects the intelligence, sensitivity and taste of the child audience."

THEATREWORKS/USA, 890 Broadway, New York NY 10003. (212)677-5959. Artistic Director: Jay Harnick. Estab. 1960. Produces 2 children's plays/year; 8 children's musicals/year. Cast of 5 or 6 actors. Play should be 1 hour long, tourable. Professional children's theatre comprised of adult equity actors. 100% of musicals are written for

adult roles. Recently produced plays: *Curious George*, book and lyrics by Thomas Toce, music by Tim Brown—adaptation for grades K-3; *Little Women*, by Allan Knee (non-musical), incidental music by Kim Olen and Alison Hubbard—adaptation for grades 4-8. No fractured, typical "kiddy theatre" fairy tales or shows written strictly to teach or illustrate. Will consider previously performed work. Submission method: Query first with synopsis, character breakdown and set description. Reports in 6 months. Pays writers royalties of 6%. SASE for return of submission.
Tips: "Plays should be not only entertaining, but 'about something.' They should touch the heart and the mind. They should not condescend to children."

WEST COAST ENSEMBLE, 6240 Hollywood Blvd., Hollywood CA 90028. (213)871-8673. Artistic Director: Les Hanson. Estab. 1982. Produces 2 children's plays/year; 1 children's musical/year. "We operate under an Equity Theatre for Young Audiences contract or under the Los Angeles 99-seat Theatre Plan." 90% of plays/musicals written for adult roles; 10% for juvenile roles. Prefer simple sets; casts of no more the eight. There are no limits on style or subject matter. Will consider simultaneous submissions (no more than two) and previously performed work. Submission method: Submit complete ms, submit complete ms and score (if a musical). Purchases exclusive rights to perform play/musical in Southern California. Pays writers per performance ($25-50). Submissions returned with SASE.

THE YOUNG COMPANY, P.O. Box 225, Milford NH 03055. (603)673-4005. Producing Director: Blair Hundertmark. Estab. 1984. Produces 5-8 children's plays/year; 1-2 children's musicals/year. "Scripts should not be longer than an hour, small cast preferred; very small production budgets, so use imagination." The Young Company is a professional training program associated with American Stage Festival, a professional theater. Produced plays/musicals: *Dancing on the Ceiling*, by Austin Tichenor—adaptation of Kafka's *Metamorphosis* for ages 7 and up; *High Pressure Zone*, music by Andrew Howard, book and lyrics by Austin Tichenor—musical about addictive behavior for middle school and older audience; *The First Olympics*, by Eve Muson and Austin Tichenor—deals with mythology/Olympic origins for 6 year old through adult audience. Does not want to see condescending material. Submission method: Query with synopsis, character breakdown and sample score. Purchases first production credit rights on all future materials. Pays small fee and housing for rehearsals.
Tips: Looks for "concise and legible presentation, songs that further dramatic action. Develop material with strong marketing possibilities. See your work in front of an audience and be prepared to change it if your audience doesn't 'get it.' Don't condescend to your audience. Tell them a *story*."

Special Markets

Over 90% of children's-only bookstores carry a variety of ancillary products. In fact, posters, coloring books, activity books, stickers, greeting cards, giftwrap, puzzles and games may all be found on store shelves. The reason is simple: Booksellers have discovered that such sidelines are valuable.

First, these products act as bait to lure customers who might not visit the bookstore if it only carried books. Prominently displayed sidelines increase the visual attractiveness and enhance the image of a bookstore. As a result, the more inviting atmosphere is more likely to draw customers—an important factor in these days of increased competition. Second, booksellers like selling sidelines because they offer a higher margin of profit than books, therefore making them a good source of supplemental revenue. Bookstore owners are especially interested in products which are book-related or education-oriented.

What follows is a list of special markets that produce various sidelines for children and are interested in using the services of freelancers. As sidelines consist of a potpourri of products, needs among these markets vary greatly. Read through listings carefully to determine desired subjects and methods of submission. If more specific guidelines are available from companies, write to request them. As in other areas of the children's market, remember that the materials created must not only appeal to children but also to the adults who will purchase them. Finally, see the interview with Paula Carlson, president of Handprint Signature, on page 264, for a closer look at a special market.

ALEF JUDAICA, 3384 Motor Ave., Los Angeles CA 90034. (310)202-0024. Owner: Guy Orner. Greeting card and paper products company. Publishes Judaica card line, Judaica gift wrap and party goods. Publishes greeting cards (Hanukkah card line), books and novelties (Hanukkah party goods).
Writing: Needs freelance writing for children's greeting cards and books. Makes 50 writing assignments/year. To contact, send cover letter and writing samples. Reports only if interested. For greeting cards, pays flat fee of $100-200. For other writing, pays by the project (range: $1,000-5,000). Pays on publication. Purchases all rights and exclusive product rights. Credit line given.
Illustration: Needs freelance illustration for children's greeting cards and party goods. Makes about 50 illustration assignments/year. To contact, send published samples, photocopies and portfolio. Reports only if interested. Keeps materials on file. For children's greeting cards, pays flat fee of $100-200. For other artwork, pay "depends on how complicated the project is." Pays on publication. Buys all rights, exclusive product rights. Credit line sometimes given.
Tips: 25% of products are made for kids or have kids' themes. Seasonal material should be submitted 1 year in advance.

AMCAL, #500, 2500 Bisso Lane, Concord CA 94520. (415)689-9930. Fax: (415)689-0108. Art Director: Barbara Trannie. Estab. 1975. Greeting cards, calendars, desk diaries, boxed Christmas cards, limited edition prints.
Illustration: Buys 30 freelance projects/year; receives 150 submissions/year. "AMCAL publishes high quality full color, narrative and decorative art for a wide market from traditional to contemporary. We are currently seeking delightful illustrations for greeting cards. Juvenile illustration should have some adult appeal. We don't publish cartoon,

humorous or gag art, or bold graphics. We sell to small, exclusive gift retailers. Submissions are always accepted for future lines." To contact, send samples, photocopies, slides. Reports in 1 month. Pays on publication. Pay negotiable/usually advance on royalty. Rights purchased negotiable. Guideline sheets for #10 SASE and 1 first-class stamp.

AMERICAN ARTS & GRAPHICS, INC., 10915 47th Ave. W., Mukilteo WA 98275. (206)353-8200. Licensing Director: Shelley Lampman. Estab. 1948. Paper products company. Publishes and distributes posters "for many large retail chains, specialty stores, bookstores and independent accounts."
Writing: Needs posters. Makes 1-3 writing assignments/month; 12-20/year. To contact, send cover letter, pieces suited for children's posters. Reports in "weeks." Pays $250-1,000 advance against 10% royalties. Pays on acceptance. Purchases exclusive product rights. Credit line given.
Illustration: Needs freelance illustration for children's posters. Makes 1-3 illustration assignments/month; 12-20/year. "Prefers airbrush (bright colors), to fit a 22″×34″ format—fantasy, cute or funny animals, other popular children and teen subjects." Uses color artwork only. To contact, send cover letter, color photocopies, portfolio, promo pieces, slides. Reports in "weeks." Returns material with SASE. Materials sometimes filed. Pay is negotiable—usually $500-1,000 against 10% royalty for 2-3 years. Pays on acceptance. Buys exclusive product rights. Credit line given. Artist's guidelines available for SASE.
Photography: Purchases photography from freelancers. Buys stock and assigns work. Buys 30 stock images/year; makes 12 assignments/year. Wants "exotic sports cars, cute and/or funny animals, wildlife (especially tigers, panthers), sports." Uses 2¼×2¼ and 4×5 transparencies. To contact, send cover letter, slides and portfolio. Reports in "weeks." Materials returned with SASE. Materials sometimes filed. Pays $500-1,000 advance against 10% royalties. Pays on acceptance. Buys exclusive product rights. Credit line given. Photographer's guidelines available for SASE.

AMPERSAND PRESS, Bldg. #5A, 8040 North East Dr. W., Bainbridge Island WA 98110. (415)663-9163. Creative Director: Tim Lowell. Estab. 1973. Publisher of games, puzzles, books, etc.—"science and environmental stuff. Specializing in educational games for children." Publishes coloring books, puzzles, games and posters.
Illustration: Needs freelance illustration for games, puzzles, books, (nature related). Makes 2-6 illustration assignments/year. To contact, send cover letter and promo piece. To query with specific ideas, write to request disclosure form first. Reports back only if interested. Returns materials with SASE. Materials filed. "We pay differently for each component of the project." Pays on acceptance or publication. Buys one-time rights, reprint rights or all rights. Credit line sometimes given.
Photography: Purchases photography from freelancers. Buys stock images. Buys 2-10 stock images/year. To contact, send cover letter with promo piece. Reports back only if interested. Materials returned with SASE. Materials filed. Pays on usage. Buys one-time rights. Credit line sometimes given. Photographer's guidelines not available.
Tips: 90% of products are made for kids or have kids' themes. Seasonal material should be submitted 10-12 months in advance.

ARISTOPLAY, LTD., P.O. Box 7529, Ann Arbor MI 48107. (313)995-4353. Fax: (313)995-4611. Product Development Director: Lorraine Hopping Egan. Estab. 1979. Produces educational board games and card decks, activity kits—all educational subjects.
Illustration: Needs freelance illustration and graphic designers (including art directors) for games and card decks. Makes 2-6 illustration assignments/year. To contact, send cover letter, résumé, published samples or color photocopies. Reports back only if inter-

ested. For artwork, pays by the project, $500-5,000. Pays on acceptance (½-sketch, ½-final). Buys all rights. Credit line given.

Tips: "Creating board games requires a lot of back and forth in terms of design, illustration, editorial and child testing; the more flexible you are, the better. Also, factual accuracy is important." Target age group 4-14. "We are an educational game company. Writers and illustrators working for us must be willing to research the subject and period of focus."

A/V CONCEPTS CORP., 30 Montauk Blvd., Oakdale NY 11769. (516)567-7227. Fax: (516)567-8745. Editor: Laura Solimene. President: Philip Solimene. Estab. 1969. "We are an educational publisher. We publish books for the K-12 market—primarily language arts and math and reading."

Writing: Needs freelance writing for classic workbooks only: adaptations from fine literature. Makes 5-10 assignments/year. To contact, send cover letter and writing samples. Reports in 2 weeks. For other writing assignments, pays by the project ($1,000 maximum). Pays on publication. Buys all rights. No credit line given.

Illustration: Needs freelance illustration for classic literature adaptations, fine art, some cartoons, super heros. Makes 25 illustration assignments/year. Needs "super hero-like characters in four-color and b&w." To contact, send cover letter and photocopies. Reports back in 2 weeks. For other artwork, pays by the project (range: $25-750). Buys all rights. No credit line given.

THE AVALON HILL GAME CO., 4517 Harford Rd., Baltimore MD 21214. (301)254-9200. Fax: (301)254-0991. President: Jack Dott. Editor: A. Eric Dott. Art Director: Jean Baer. Estab. 1958. 50% of material written and illustrated by freelancers. Buys 50 freelance projects/year; receives 500 submissions annually. Produces comic books (*Tales From the Floating Vagabond*), magazine for girls ages 7-14 and an extensive line of games.

Writing: Makes 6 writing assignments/month; 36/year. To contact send cover letter, résumé, client list, writing samples. Reports back only if interested. Pays on publication. Buys all rights. Credit line sometimes given.

Illustration: Makes 2-3 illustration assignments/month; 30/year. Prefers styles pertaining to general interest topics for girls. To contact send cover letter, résumé, published samples, portfolio. Reports in 1 month. Pays on acceptance. Buys all rights. Credit line sometimes given.

AVANTI PRESS, INC., 2500 Penobscot Bldg., Detroit MI 48226. (313)961-0022. Submit images to this address: Avanti, Suite 602, 84 Wooster, New York NY 10012. (212)941-9000. Picture Editor: Nathalie Goldstein. Estab. 1979. Greeting card company. Publishes photographic greeting cards—nonseasonal and seasonal.

Photography: Purchases photography from freelancers. Buys stock and assigns work. Buys approximately 50-75 stock images/year. Makes approximately 20-30 assignments/year. Wants "narrative, storytelling images, graphically strong and colorful!" Uses b&w/color prints; 35mm, 2¼ × 2¼ and 4 × 5, transparencies. To contact, "Call for submission guidelines—no originals!!" Reports in 2 weeks. Returns materials with SASE. "We pay either a flat fee or a royalty which is discussed at time of purchase." Pays on acceptance. Buys exclusive product rights (world-wide card rights). Credit line given. Photographer's guidelines for SASE.

Tips: At least 50% of products have kids' themes. Submit seasonal material 9 months-1 year in advance. "All images submitted should express some kind of sentiment which either fits an occasion or can be versed and sent to the recipient to convey some feeling."

bePUZZLED/LOMBARD MARKETING, INC., 22 E. Newberry Rd., Bloomfield CT 06002. (203)769-5707. Fax: (203)769-5799. Editor/Art Director: Luci Seccareccia. New Product Development: Susan Braun. Estab. 1987. Publishes jigsaw puzzle mysteries, mystery games, mystery word puzzles, mystery entertainment.
Writing: Needs freelance writing for short mystery stories. Makes 10-15 writing assignments/year. To contact, send cover letter and writing samples. Reports back only if interested. Pays by the project (range: $200-1,000). Pays on publication. Buys all rights. No credit line given.
Illustration: Needs freelance illustration for mystery jigsaw puzzles. Makes 25-30 illustration assignments/year. Preferences announced when needed. To contact, send cover letter, résumé, client list and color promo pieces. Reports back only if interested. Pays by the project ($50). Pays on publication. Buys all rights. No credit line given.
Tips: "Send SASE for guidelines. Submissions should be short and include idea of writing style, and an outline of ideas for visual and literal clues (6 each, some with red herrings)."

RUSS BERRIE & COMPANY, INC., 111 Bauer Dr., Oakland NJ 07436. (201)337-9000. Director, Greeting Cards: Angelica Urra. Estab. 1963. Greeting card and paper products company. Manufactures "all kinds of paper products and impulse gifts—photo frames, mugs, buttons, trolls, baby gift products, cards, plush, ceramics, toys, bibs, booties, etc."
Writing: Needs freelance writing for children's greeting cards and other children's products (T-shirts, buttons, bookmarks, stickers, diaries, address books, plaques, perpetual (undated) calendars). "We are also beginning to review material for children's books looking for strong story lines with characters that can effectively stand alone as plush, dolls, toys, ceramics, etc." Makes 10-50 writing assignments/month. Tired of children's greeting card writing which talks down to kids. To contact, send writing samples. Reports in 2-3 months. Materials returned with SASE. Files materials "if we think there may be interest later." For greeting cards, pays flat fee of $50-100 per piece of copy. For other writing, pays by the project. Pays on acceptance. Buys all rights or exclusive product rights. Writer's guidelines for SASE.
Illustration: Needs freelance illustration for children's greeting cards and other children's products. Makes 10-50 illustration assignments/month. Artwork should be "contemporary, eye catching, colorful—professional. Because we also do products for parents and parents-to-be, we seek both juvenile *and* adult looks in products about children." To contact, send client list, published samples, photocopies, slides and/or promo piece. To query with specific ideas, send tight roughs. Reports in 2 months. Returns material with SASE. Files material "if future interest is anticipated." For greeting cards, pays flat fee of $250-500. Pays on acceptance. Buys all rights or exclusive product rights. Credit line sometimes given. Artist's guidelines for SASE.
Photography: Purchases photography from freelancers. Buys stock and assigns work. Buys 100 stock images/year. Makes 100 assignments/year. Photos should be "humorous with animals or children; unusual, eye catching, interesting, contemporary—not too arty." Uses b&w prints; 35mm, 2¼×2¼, 4×5 and 8×10 transparencies. To contact, send slides, client list, published samples, promo piece, portfolio, prints. Reports in 2 months. Materials returned with SASE. Files photos "if there will be future interest." Pays per photo or by the project. Pays on acceptance. Buys all rights or exclusive product rights. Credit line sometimes given. Photographer's guidelines for SASE.
Tips: "One third of our products are made for kids or have kids' themes. Seasonal material should be submitted 18 months in advance. We're using more freelance illustrators and freelance writers who can submit a concept rather than single piece of writing. We are upbeat, with a large, diverse baby/children's line. Send all material to greeting card director—if it is for another product it will be passed along to the appropriate department."

BRILLIANT ENTERPRISES, 117 W. Valerio St., Santa Barbara CA 93101. Art Director: Ashleigh Brilliant. Estab. 1967. Publishers greeting cards—a wide range of humorous concepts; unrhymed.
Writing/Illustration: Reports in 3 weeks. Purchases all rights. Pays on acceptance. Pay for greeting cards $40 minimum. Writer's/illustrator's guideline sheet for $2 and SAE.

BURGOYNE INC., 2030 E. Byberry Rd., Philadelphia PA 19116. (215)677-8000. Art Studio Manager: Mary Beth Burgoyne. Creative Director: Jeanna Lane. Estab. 1907. Greeting card company. Publisher of Christmas and everyday cards.
Illustration: Interested in illustrations for children's greeting cards. To contact, send cover letter. To query with specific ideas, send slides, published samples or original art. Reports in 2 months. Materials filed. Pays on acceptance. Buys greeting card US and worldwide rights. Credit line sometimes given. Artist's guidelines for SASE.
Tips: "We are looking for new traditional Christmas artwork with a detailed children's book look. We are also looking for juvenile birthday and all-occasion artwork year round."

CONTEMPORARY DESIGNS, 213 Main St., Gilbert IA 50105. (515)232-5188. Fax: (515)232-3380. Editor and Art Director: Sallie Abelson. Estab. 1977. 25% of material is written by freelancers; 20% illustrated by freelancers. Buys 50 freelance projects/year; receives 150 submissions/year. Publishes greeting cards, coloring books and puzzles and games. "Greeting cards should be funny—for children who go to camp."
Writing/Illustration: Submit seasonal material 1 year in advance. SASE. Reports in 1 month. Buys all rights on accepted material. Pays on acceptance. Pays $40 for greeting cards; negotiable amount for coloring books and puzzles. Writer's/illustrator's guidelines for SASE.
Tips: "Greeting cards for campers and Jewish markets only. Puzzles, games and coloring books should be Judaic."

CREATE-A-CRAFT, P.O. Box 330008, Fort Worth TX 76163-0008. Contact: Editor. Estab. 1967. Produces greeting cards, giftwrap, games, calendars, posters, stationery and paper tableware products for all ages.
Illustration: Works with 3 freelance artists/year. Buys 3-5 designs/illustrations/year. Prefers artists with experience in cartooning. Works on assignment only. Buys freelance designs/illustrations mainly for greetings cards and T-shirts. Also uses freelance artists for calligraphy, P-O-P displays, paste-up and mechanicals. Considers pen & ink, watercolor, acrylics and colored pencil. Prefers humorous and "cartoons that will appeal to families. Must be cute, appealing, etc. No religious, sexual implications or off-beat humor." Produces material for all holidays and seasons; submit 6 months before holiday. Contact only through artist's agent. Some samples are filed. Samples not filed are not returned. Reports only if interested. Write to schedule an appointment to show a portfolio, which should include original/final art, final reproduction/product, slides, tearsheets, color and b&w. Original artwork is not returned. "Payment depends upon the assignment, amount of work involved, production costs, etc. involved in the project." Buys all rights. For guidelines and sample cards, send $2.50 and #10 SASE.
Tips: "Demonstrate an ability to follow directions exactly. Too many submit artwork that has no relationship to what we produce."

Always include a self-addressed stamped envelope (SASE) or a self-addressed envelope (SAE) and International Reply Coupons (IRCs) with submissions.

DESIGN DESIGN INC., P.O. Box 2266, Grand Rapids MI 49501. (616)774-2448. President: Don Kallil. Creative Director: Lisa Tallarico-Robertson. Estab. 1986. Greeting card company.

Writing: Needs freelance writing for children's greeting cards. For greeting cards, prefers both rhymed and unrhymed verse ideas. To contact, send cover letter and writing samples. Reports in 3 weeks. Materials returned with SASE. Materials not filed. Pay varies. Buys all rights or exclusive product rights; negotiable. No credit line given. Writer's guidelines for SASE.

Illustration: Needs freelance illustration for children's greeting cards, notecards, wrapping paper. Makes 30 illustration assignments/month. Uses color artwork only. To contact, send cover letter, published samples, color or b&w photocopies color or b&w promo pieces and slides. Reports in 3 weeks. Returns materials with SASE. Materials not filed. Pay varies. Buys all rights or exclusive product rights; negotiable. No credit line given. Artist's guidelines available for SASE.

Photography: Purchases photography from freelancers. Buys stock and assigns work. Uses 4×5 transparencies or high quality 35mm slides. To contact, send cover letter with slides, stock photo list, published samples and promo piece. Reports in 3 weeks. Materials returned with SASE. Materials not filed. Pays per photo or royalties. Pays on usage. Buys all rights or exclusive product rights; negotiable. No credit line given. Photographer's guidelines for SASE.

ECLIPSE COMICS, P.O. Box 1099, Forestville CA 95436. (707)887-1521. Fax: (707)887-7128. Editor-in-Chief: Catherine Yronwode. "Publishes comic books, graphic albums, trading cards, books and posters for young adult and adult market. Most are fictional, but we also have factual, educational lines." Estab. 1978.

Writing: Makes approximately 100 writing assignments/year. To contact, send cover letter, writing samples and short proposal or query. Reports in 2 months. Payment varies—"impossible to answer as books, comic books, trading cards all have different rates. We always pay an advance and royalty." Pays on acceptance. Rights negotiable. Credit line given.

Illustration: Makes approximately 100 illustration assignments/year. To contact, send cover letter, published samples, photocopies, portfolio and promo piece. "See our artist's guidelines first—send SASE #10 envelope." Reports in 2 months. "Pay varies by project—all jobs pay an advance plus royalty." Pays on acceptance. Rights negotiable. Credit line given.

Tips: "Send for writers'/artists' guidelines before submitting work. Painters interested in remaining on file for trading cards, send slides, promo pieces—color only."

EPHEMERA BUTTONS, P.O. Box 490, Phoenix OR 97535. Estab. 1980. 90% of material written and 10% illustrated by freelancers. Buys over 200 freelance projects/year; receives over 2,000 submissions/year. Novelty pin back buttons with slogans and art. Need simple and bold line art that would work on a button.

Writing/Illustration: SASE for return of submission. Reports in 3 weeks. Material copyrighted. Pays on publication. Pays $25 per slogan or design. Guideline sheets for #10 SAE and 1 first-class stamp.

Tips: Looks for "very silly and outrageously funny slogans. We also are looking for provocative, irreverent and outrageously funny *adult* humor, and politically correct/incorrect slogans."

EVERYTHING PERSONALIZED, INC., P.O. Box 650610, Vero Beach FL 32965. Vice President: Jim St. Clair. Estab. 1981. Personalized wood toy manufacturer. Specializes in personalized puzzles, games, accessories. Manufactures novelties (coat hangers and stools), puzzles and games.

Illustration: Makes 1-3 illustration assignments/year. Prefers screen pattern designs for puzzles and games. Uses both b&w and color artwork. To contact, send cover letter, published samples, photocopies, promo piece. To query with specific ideas, send cover letter or call. Reports only if interested. Returns materials if accompanied with SASE. Pays a flat fee or royalties. For other artwork, pays by the project (range: negotiable). Pays on acceptance. Rights negotiable. Credit line given. Artist's guidelines not available.

FAX-PAX USA, INC., 37 Jerome Ave., Bloomfield CT 06002. (203)242-3333. Fax: (203)242-7102. Editor: Stacey L. Savin. Estab. 1990. Buys 1 freelance project/year. Publishes educational picture cards. Needs include US history, natural history.
Writing/Illustration: Buys all rights. Pays on publication. Cannot return material.
Tips: "Well written, interesting US history sells best."

FOTOFOLIO/ARTPOST, 536 Broadway, New York NY 10012. (212)226-0923. Editorial Director: Ron Schick. Estab. 1976. Greeting card company. Also publishes fine art and photographic postcards, notecards, posters, calendars. New children's line.
Illustration: Needs freelance illustration for children's greeting cards, calendars and coloring books. To contact, send cover letter, published samples, photocopies, slides, promo piece. Reports back only if interested. Returns materials with SASE. Materials not filed. Rights negotiable. Credit line given. Artist's guidelines not available.
Photography: Purchases photography from freelancers. Buys stock images. To contact, send cover letter, slides, stock photo list, published samples and promo piece. Reports back only if interested. Returns material with SASE. Pays on usage. Rights negotiable. Credit line given. Photographer's guidelines not available.

GALISON BOOKS, Suite 910, 36 W. 44th St., New York NY 10036. (212)354-8840. Editorial Director: Wendy Missan. Estab. 1978. Paper products company. Publishes museum-quality gift products, including notecards, journals, address books and jigsaw puzzles. Publishes children's greeting cards and puzzles.
Illustration: Needs freelance illustration for adults and children's greeting cards, jigsaw puzzles. Makes 30 illustration assignments/year. Uses color artwork only. To contact, send cover letter, published samples and color promo piece. To query with specific ideas, write to request disclosure form first. Reports back only if interested. Returns materials with SASE. Materials filed. For greeting cards, pays flat fee (range: $250-1,000). Pays on publication. Buys one-time rights; negotiable. Credit line given. Artist's guidelines not available.
Photography: Purchases photography from freelancers. Buys stock images. Buys 40 stock images/year. Uses 35mm, 2¼×2¼ and 4×5 transparencies. To contact, send cover letter, stock photo list, published samples and color promo piece. Reports back only if interested. Returns materials with SASE. Materials filed. Pays $250/photo. Pays on publication. Buys one-time rights; negotiable. Credit line given. Photographer's guidelines available for SASE.
Tips: 10% of products are made for kids or have kids' themes. Seasonal material should be submitted 6 months in advance.

THE GIFT WRAP COMPANY, 28 Spring Ave., Revers MA 02151. (617)284-6000. Produce Development and Marketing Coordinator: Betsey Cavallo. Estab. 1904. Paper products company. "We manufacture gift wrap and ribbons. Also sell greeting cards (Christmas only)/gift bags."
Illustration: Needs freelance illustration for gift wrap and gift bag designs. Number of illustration assignments "depends on our needs"—20 maximum/year. Looking for baby prints, juvenile birthday, wedding and shower. Uses color artwork only. To contact, send cover letter, résumé, color photocopies and non-returnable art. Reports back only if

Combining Kids, Art and Correspondence

When Paula Carlson saw a homemade card signed with her baby granddaughter's handprint, the wheels in her mind began turning. "I loved the idea. That was the only way she could give of herself. And I knew it would touch others, too," she says. Carlson then turned the creative idea into a thriving business.

In 1988, she established Handprint Signature, a line of greeting cards for babies, toddlers and preschoolers to sign and send. The cards, sold in museum, toy, gift and stationery stores, are marketed with an easy-cleaning, nontoxic, powdered paint packet. Kids use the paint to sign the cards with their handprints or footprints.

Not only are the cards fun for kids to make and send, but they also become treasured keepsakes

Paula Carlson

for parents and grandparents. "I think it's important to teach children to be thoughtful, kind and respectful, and greeting cards give children one way in which to learn these values," explains Carlson.

While Handprint Signature's line includes artwork of carousels, dinosaurs and ballet slippers in vivid primary colors, Carlson is open to a variety of subjects rendered in a bright, simple palette. "I ask artists to look back into their own childhoods and choose what delighted them—and then present that idea with the same freshness of spirit." As president of the Portland, Oregon company, she urges illustrators to keep in mind that the ultimate card buyer is the parent, who must also be attracted to the artwork.

Using the work of six local freelancers, Handprint Signature now offers 21 cards and eight paint colors, and is ready to grow and see work from artists around the country. Besides design additions to the current handprint series, Carlson says, "I'm looking for art for grade-school-age kids to color, cards children can invest in emotionally and personalize by adding their own artistic element." Although Handprint Signature's current needs for freelance writing are limited, Carlson likes to receive text suggestions along with art submissions.

"A new artist has as much chance with us as an established artist," she says. And Carlson plans to purchase up to 12 design pieces for publication this year. "After an artist has viewed our product and is sure he or she has something to offer, I would like to see examples of existing work. As long as an artist understands our cards' purpose, the work samples in the portfolio do not necessarily have to be specifically suited to our card line.

"For example, I chose one artist after viewing several sales pieces, one of which was a map of Oregon wine country. On the map she had included a whimsical dolphin and seahorse. Viewing these elements, I was certain she could create a card for our line," she says.

Carlson cautions, however, "The biggest mistake an artist can make in submitting work to me is thinking that a beautiful, technically correct image with a childhood theme is appropriate." Instead, she prefers images that are simple, honest and not necessarily "perfect."

Once the buying public responds favorably to a particular artist, that artist may become eligible for royalties on future projects. The industry itself has already responded favorably to Handprint Signature—two cards were nominated for the National Greeting Card Association's 1992-1993 "Louie" Award. This honor inspires Carlson to continue her work in creating the perfect card, one that will come, "when the design and text are from the heart."

—Amy Tirk

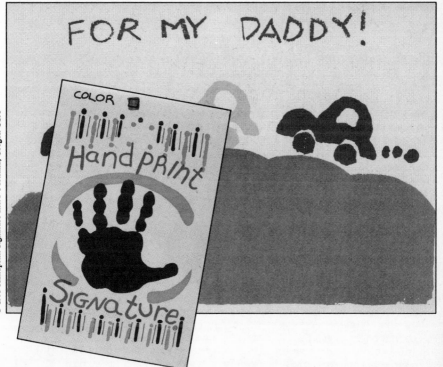

© 1993 Handprint Signature Inc.® Portland, Oregon USA

Paula Carlson published this card by Jennifer Lawson because of the "genuine feeling captured in both design and text." Inside the card—along with the paint packet shown on the left—it reads: "He picks me up when I feel bad. He makes me laugh when I am sad. He's my Daddy and I love him!!"

interested. Returns materials with SASE. Materials filed. Pays by the project (range: $150-300). Pays on acceptance. Buys all rights. No credit line given.
Tips: 20-30% of products are made for kids or have kids' themes. Seasonal material should be submitted 4 months in advance. "We look for general designs that will fill our mass market and upscale lines."

GREAT AMERICAN PUZZLE FACTORY, INC., 16 S. Main St., S. Norwalk CT 06854. (203)838-4240. Fax: (203)838-2065. Art Director: Pat Duncan. Estab. 1976. Produces puzzles.
Illustration: Buys 30 freelance projects/year. Not interested in seasonal. SASE. Reports in 2 weeks. Rights vary. Pays on publication. Pay varies.
Tips: Wants "whimsical, fantasy" material. Target age group: 4-12.

GREAT SEVEN, INC., #202, 3838 Del Amo Blvd., Torrance CA 90503. (310)371-4555. Vice President: Ronald Chen. Estab. 1984. Paper products company. Publishes educational and fun stickers for children and teenager market.
Illustration: Needs freelance illustration for children's fun stickers. Makes 120 illustration assignments/year. Wants "kid themes." To contact, send published samples and b&w photocopies. To query with specific ideas, write to request disclosure form first. Reports back only if interested. Returns material with SASE. Materials filed. Pays on acceptance. Buys all rights. No credit line given. Artist's guidelines not available.
Tips: 100% of products are made for kids or have kids' themes. Seasonal material should be submitted 10 months in advance.

HANDPRINT SIGNATURE, INC., P.O. Box 22682, Portland OR 97269. (503)295-1925. Fax: (503)295-3673. President: Paula Carlson. Greeting card company. "Manufacturer of greeting cards especially designed for kids to send. Each card to be 'signed' with a child's handprint or footprint."
Illustration: Needs freelance illustration for children's greeting cards. "All art must tie in with general theme of Handprint Signature — cards for kids to send. Pure colors." To contact, send cover letter, résumé, published samples and acknowledgement that he/she has seen and understands Handprint Signature card line. Reports in 1 month. Returns materials with SASE. Materials not filed. For greeting cards, pays advance and 4% royalty for national/life of card. Pays on publication. No credit line given. Artist's guidelines not available.
Tips: "100% of products are made for kids or have kids' themes. I need a line of cards for kids to color for ages 4 and up. Even though this artist's work must tie in with other artists already published, the design and presentation must stand out as his or her own unique interpretation. The card design and the text should be harmonious and always conscious that even though the parent (adult) is buying the card, the card is from a child."

INTERCONTINENTAL GREETINGS LTD., 176 Madison Ave., New York NY 10016. (212)683-5830. Contact: Robin Lipner. Estab. 1964. 100% of material freelance written and illustrated. Produces greeting cards, scholastic products (notebooks, pencil cases), novelties (gift bags, mugs), tin gift boxes, shower and bedding curtains.
Writing: Needs "humorous writing for greeting cards only. Greeting card (style) artwork in series of three or more. We use very little writing except for humor." Makes 4 writing assignments/year. To contact, send cover letter, résumé, client list and writing samples. Reports in 4-6 weeks. Pays advance of $20-100 and royalty of 20% for life. Pays on publication. Purchases exclusive product rights. Credit line sometimes given.
Illustration: Needs children's greeting cards, notebook cover, photo albums, gift products. Makes 15 illustration assignments/mongh. Prefers primarily greeting card subjects, suitable for gift industry. To contact, send cover letter, résumé, client list, published

samples, photocopies, slides and promo piece. Reports in 4-6 weeks. For greeting cards pays advance of $75 against 20% royalty for life. For other artwork pays 20% royalty for life. Pays on publication. Buys exclusive product rights. Credit line sometimes given. **Tips:** Target group for juvenile cards: ages 1-10. Illustrators: "Use clean colors, not muddy or dark."

JILLSON & ROBERTS GIFTWRAP, INC., 5 Watson Ave., Irvine CA 92718. (714)859-8781. Art Director: Max Bromwell. Estab. 1973. Paper products company. Makes giftwrap/giftbags.
Illustration: Needs freelance illustration for children's giftwrap. Makes 6-12 illustration assignments/year. Wants children/baby/juvenile themes. To contact, send cover letter. To query with specific ideas, write to request disclosure form first. Reports in 1 week. Returns material with SASE. Materials filed. For wrap and bag designs, pays flat fee of $250. Pays on publication. Rights negotiable. No credit line given. Artist's guidelines for SASE.
Tips: 20% of products are made for kids or have kids' themes. Seasonal material should be submitted up to 1 month in advance. "We produce two lines of giftwrap per year: 1 everyday line and 1 Christmas line. The closing date for everyday is June 30th and Christmas is September 15."

*KINGDOM PUZZLES, 7231 Vanalden Ave., Reseda CA 91335-2580. (818)705-4572. Fax: (818)705-2580. Owner: M. Oldenkamp. Estab. 1987. Produces puzzles. Submit seasonal puzzles 1 year in advance. SASE. Reports in 2 months. Pay varies.
Tips: Wants "wildlife, nature" material for children and adults.

LUCY & COMPANY, 7711 Lake Ballinger Way NE, Edmonds WA 98925. (206)775-8826. Art Director: Noelle Rigg. Estab. 1977. Paper products company. Publishes greeting cards, calendars, books, gift items, tote bags, announcements, invitations. Publishes children's greeting cards (Lucy & Me line), magnets, coloring books, posters, calendars, children's stories, scrapbooks.
Writing: Needs freelance writing for children's greeting cards and books. Makes 2 writing assignments/month; 24/year. For greeting cards, prefers unrhymed verse ideas. Looks for greeting card writing which is sweet and slightly humorous. Tired of greeting card writing which is mushy. Other needs for freelance writing include children's stories. To contact, send client list and writing samples. To query with specific ideas, write to request disclosure form first. Reports back only if interested. Materials returned with SASE. Materials filed. Pays on publication. Buys reprint rights; negotiable. Credit line sometimes given. Writer's guidelines not available.
Illustration: Needs freelance illustration for children's greeting cards, wrap, bags, invitations, books. Makes 6 illustration assignments/month. Needs "ecological, detailed, animals, characters." Uses color artwork only. To contact, send client list, published samples, photocopies and promo piece. To query with specific ideas, write to request disclosure form first. Reports back only if interested. Returns materials with SASE. Materials filed. Pays flat fee or by the project. Pays on publication. Rights negotiable. Credit line given. Artist's guidelines for SASE.
Tips: 80% of products are made for kids or have kids' themes. Seasonal material should be submitted 6 months in advance.

MAGIC MOMENTS GREETING CARDS, 10 Connor Lane, Deer Park NY 11729. (516)595-2300 ext. 1206. Art Director: A. Braunstein. Estab. 1938. Greeting card company. Publish and wholesale greeting cards.
Illustration: Needs freelance illustration for children's greeting cards. Uses color artwork only. To contact, send color photocopies and slides. Reports in 1 week. Returns materials with SASE. Materials not filed. For greeting cards, pays flat fee of $75-135.

Pays on acceptance. Buys exclusive product rights. No credit line given. Artist's guidelines not available.

MAYFAIR GAMES, 5641 Howard St., Niles IL 60714. (708)647-9650. Fax: (708)647-0939. Editorial Director: Ray Winninger. Art Director: Maria Paz Cabardo. Estab. 1981. Produces games under DC Heroes license and role playing and strategy games for teens and adults. 100% of material is written and illustrated by freelancers.
Writing: Buys 25 freelance projects/year; receives 100 submissions/year. SASE. Reports in 2 months. Pays on acceptance and publication. Writer's guideline sheet for SASE.
Tips: Target age group: 14- to 40-years-old.

*MU PRESS, 5014-D Roosevelt Way NE, Seattle WA 98105. (206) 525-0632. Editor: Dennis Weber. Art Director: Diana Vick. Estab. 1980. 96% of material freelance written and illustrated. Bought 8 freelance projects last year. Receives more than 100 submissions annually. Produces alternative b&w comics and graphic albums.
Writing/Illustration: Submit seasonal/holiday comic book material in mid-late summer. Reports in 1-2 months. Purchases first world serial rights. Pays $100-2,000/issue for comic books. Writer's/illustrator's guidelines for #10 SAE and 1 first-class stamp.

NATIONAL POLY CONSUMER PRODUCTS, (formerly United Plastic Products), 211 3rd Ave., Mankato MN 56001. Vice President Marketing: Ronald Smith. Estab. 1960. Plastic products manufacturer. Prints plastic table covers, table skirting, aprons, bibs (adult and child), gloves and boots. Manufactures children's bibs (printed with animals).
Illustration: Makes 3-4 illustration assignments/year. Uses b&w artwork only. To contact, send cover letter, photocopies, slides. To query with specific ideas, write to request disclosure from first. Reports in 2 weeks. For artwork, pays by the project (range $150-2,000). Material not filed. Pays on acceptance. Buys one-time rights. Credit line given.
Tips: About 3% of the products are made for kids or have kids' themes. Seasonal material should be submitted 6 months in advance.

P.S. GREETINGS/FANTUS PAPER PRODUCTS, 4459 W. Division St., Chicago IL 60651. (312)384-0909. Art Director: Kevin Lahvic. Greeting card company. Publishes boxed and individual counter cards. Publishes greeting cards (Kards for Kids—counter; Kids Kards—boxed; Christmas).
Writing: Needs freelance writing for children's greeting cards. Makes 1-10 writing assignments/year. Looks for writing which is "appropriate for kids to give to relatives." To contact, send writing samples. Reports in 6 months. Material returned only if accompanied with SASE. Materials filed. For greeting cards, pays flat fee. Pays on acceptance. Buys all rights. Credit line sometimes given. Writer's guidelines for SASE.
Illustration: Needs freelance illustration for children's greeting cards. Makes 50-100 illustration assignments/year. "Open to all mediums, all themes—use your creativity!" To contact, send published samples (up to 20 samples of any nature) and photocopies. Reports in 6 months. Returns materials with SASE. Materials filed. For greeting cards, pays flat fee. Pays on acceptance. Buys all rights. Credit line sometimes given. Artist's guidelines for SASE.
Photography: Purchases photography from freelancers. Buys stock images. Buys 10-20 stock images/year. Wants florals, animals, seasonal (Christmas, Easter, Valentines, etc.). Uses transparencies (any size). To contact, send slides. Reports in 6 months. Materials returned with SASE. Materials filed. Pays on acceptance. Buys all rights. Credit line sometimes given. Photographer's guidelines for SASE.
Tips: "Only 7% of products are made for kids or have kids' themes, so it needs to be great stuff!" Seasonal material should be submitted 6 months in advance. "We are open to all creative ideas—generally not fads, however. All mediums are considered equally. We have a great need for 'cute' Christmas subjects."

*PAINTED HEARTS & FRIENDS, (formerly David Mekelburg & Friends), 1222 N. Fair Oaks Ave., Los Angeles CA 91103. (818)798-3633. Fax: (818)793-7385. Editor: Richard Crawford. Estab. 1988. Material produced includes greeting cards.
Illustration: Buys 5 freelance projects/year. Material returned with SASE. Reports in 1 week. Pays on publication.
Tips: Submit seasonal material 1 year in advance.

PALM PRESS, INC., 1442A Walnut St., Berkeley CA 94709. (510)480-0502. Assistant Photo Editor: Theresa McCormick. Estab. 1980. Greeting card company. Publishes high quality blank and greeting cards from photos.
Photography: Purchases photography from freelancers. Buys stock images. Buys 15 stock images/year. Wants unusual images for birthday cards, new baby, friendship, get well, Valentines, Mother's Day, Christmas. Uses 35mm, 2¼ × 2¼ and 4 × 5 transparencies. Reports in 2 weeks. Materials returned with SASE. Pays per photo (range $150-1,000) or royalties of 6½%. Pays on usage. Buys exclusive product rights. Credit line given. Photographer's guidelines for SASE.
Tips: 15% of products are made for kids or have kids' themes. Seasonal material should be submitted 1½ years in advance.

PEACEABLE KINGDOM PRESS, 1051 Folger Ave., Berkeley CA 94710. (510)644-9801. Fax: (510)644-9805. Art Director: Olivia Hurd. Estab. 1983. Produces posters and greeting cards. Uses images from classic children's books.
Illustration: Needs freelance illustration for children's greeting cards and posters. Makes 5 illustration assignments/month; 60/year. To contact, send cover letter and color photocopies. Submit seasonal posters and greeting cards 6 months in advance. Reports in 3 weeks. Buys rights to distribution worldwide. Pays on publication with advance. Pays 5-10% of wholesale for greeting cards.
Tips: "We only choose from illustrations that are from published children's book illustrators, or commissioned art by established children's book illustrators."

PEACOCK PAPERS, INC., 273 Summer St., Boston MA 02210. New Product Manager: Mia Miranda. Estab. 1982. Manufactures children's T-shirts and sweatshirts, wrappings (papers, bags).
Writing: Needs freelance writing for apparel (Ts and sweats). Makes 8-10 writing assignments/year. To contact, send cover letter. To query with specific ideas, submit on 8½ × 11 paper, double spaced. Reports in 3 weeks. Materials returned with SASE. Materials filed. Pays $50 for 1st use. Pays on acceptance. Buys exclusive product rights. No credit line given. Writer's guidelines for SASE.
Tips: "Send only *original*, one-liners (quick reads) that relate to *all* children."

*PORTAL PUBLICATIONS, LTD., 770 Tamalpais Dr., Corte Madera CA 94925. (415)924-5652. Art Director: Wendy Lagerström. Photo/Art Director: Patricia Collette. Estab. 1955. Publisher and distributor of posters, cards, calendars, art prints, gift bags and T-shirts.
Illustration: Needs freelance illustration for children's greeting cards and posters. Makes 200-300 illustration assignments/year. Prefers animals. Uses color artwork only. To contact, send published samples, slides (not originals). Reports in 2-3 months. Returns materials if accompanied with SASE. Materials filed. For greeting cards pays flat fee of $200-350, royalty of 5% for 4 years or life of card or advance of $100-200 against

---

Refer to the Business of Children's Writing & Illustrating for up-to-date marketing, tax and legal information.

5% royalty for life of card. For other artwork, pays $500-800 flat fee or $400-600 advance against 5% royalty. Pays on publication. Buys first rights. Credit line given. Artist's guidelines available.

Photography: Purchases photography from freelancers. Buys stock and assigns work. Buys 150-250 stock images/year. Makes 200-250 assignments/year. Uses transparencies of all sizes. To contact, send slides (not originals), published samples and promo piece. Materials returned with SASE. Pays per photo (range: $150-1,500 flat fee for photo), or royalties of 3-5%. Pays on usage. Buys first rights. Credit line given. Photographer's guidelines for SASE.

Tips: Ten percent of products are made for kids. Seasonal material should be submitted 9 months in advance. "Contemporary decor colors and trends are important to our products – e.g. cows, wolves, pigs, dogs, cats and whales are popular; sunflowers and environmental themes too."

RIVERCREST INDUSTRIES, P.O. 771662, Houston TX 77215. (713)789-5394. Fax: (713)789-9666. Editor: Harry Capers. Produces games and books. Estab. 1981.

Illustration: 100% of material airbrushed by freelancers. Buys 2 freelance projects/year. Interested in someone to handle airbrush on completed illustrations. SASE. Pays on acceptance.

Tips: Produces holiday games and juvenile books. Target age groups 2-7 for books; 6-adult for games.

RUBBER STAMPEDE, 967 Stanford, Oakland CA 94608. (510)843-8910. Fax: (510)843-5906. Art Director: Rita Wood. Estab. 1978. Produces puzzles. Themes: nature, Victorian, teddy bears, cute animals, fantasy.

Writing/Illustration: 50% of material written by freelancers; 50% illustrated by freelancers. Buys 25 freelance projects/year; receives 50 submissions/year. Reports in a month. Buys all rights. Pays on acceptance.

Tips: Target age group 3 to 103. Submit seasonal special games, puzzles or comic books 4 months in advance.

SHULSINGER SALES, INC., 50 Washington St., Brooklyn NY 11201. (718)852-0042. Art Director: Patty Segovia. Estab. 1950. Greeting card and paper products company. "We are a Judaica company, distributing products such as greeting cards, books, paperware, puzzles, games, novelty items – all with a Jewish theme." Publishes greeting cards, novelties, coloring books and puzzles.

Writing: Looks for greeting card writing which can be sent by children to adults and sent by adults to children (of all ages). To contact, send cover letter. To query with specific ideas, write to request disclosure form first. Reports in 2 weeks. Materials returned with SASE. Materials filed. For greeting cards, pays flat fee (this includes artwork). Pays on acceptance. Buys exclusive product rights. Writer's guidelines not available.

Illustration: Needs freelance illustration for children's greeting cards, books, novelties, games. Makes 10-20 illustration assignments/year. "The only requirement is a Jewish theme." To contact, send cover letter and photocopies, color if possible. To query with specific ideas, write to request disclosure form first. Reports in 2 weeks. Returns materials with SASE. Materials filed. For children's greeting cards, pays flat fee (this includes writing). For other artwork, pays by the project. Pays on acceptance. Buys exclusive product rights. Credit line sometimes given. Artist's guidelines not available.

Tips: 40% of products are made for kids or have kids' themes. Seasonal material should be submitted 6 months in advance.

STANDARD PUBLISHING, 8121 Hamilton Ave., Cincinnati OH 45231. (513)931-4050. Fax: (513)931-0904. Director: Mark Taylor. Children's Editor: Diane Stortz. Estab. 1866. Publishes children's books and teacher helps for the religious market. Publishes board books, easy readers, coloring books, puzzles, games and activity books.
Writing: Needs freelance writing for children's books. Makes 6-12 writing assignments/year. Reports in 2 months. Pays on acceptance. Buys all rights. Credit line given.
Illustration: Needs freelance illustration for puzzle, activity books, teacher helps. Makes 6-10 illustration assignments/year. Freelance artwork needed for activity books, etc. (b&w line art). To contact, send cover letter and photocopies. Reports back only if interested. Pays on acceptance. Buys all rights. Credit line given.
Tips "We look for upbeat manuscripts with a Christian perspective."

THE STRAIGHT EDGE, INC., 296 Court St., Brooklyn NY 11231. (718)643-2794. President: Amy Epstein. Estab. 1983. Manufactures placemats, puzzles, rugs on educational theme for children, ages 6 months and up.
Illustration: Needs freelance illustration for placemats and puzzles. Makes approximately 6-10 illustration assignments/year. Wants "line art; no rendering; realistic drawings with a sense of humor." Uses color artwork only. To contact, send cover letter and b&w photocopies. Reports back only if interested. Does not return materials. Materials filed. For artwork, pays by the project (range: $350-400 per mechanical per design). Pays on completion of mechanical. Buys exclusive product rights. No credit line given.

SUNRISE PUBLICATIONS, INC., P.O. Box 4699, Bloomington IN 47402. (812)336-9900. Fax: (812)336-8712. Editors: Lori Teesch/Sheila Gerber. Art Review Coordinator: Laurie Hoover. Estab. 1974. Buys 600 freelance projects/year. Receives 1,000/year. Greeting card lines: general greetings, holidays, note cards. Greeting cards: unrhymed verse.
Writing/Illustration: Submit seasonal greeting cards 6-8 months in advance. Reports in 10 weeks. Material copyrighted. Pays on acceptance. Pay for greeting cards $40-125 (versing); $350 per design. Guideline sheets for #10 SAE and 1 first-class stamp.
Tips: Looks for "bright, festive, not-too-wordy versing; occasion specific illustration.

TLC GREETINGS, 615 McCall Rd., Manhattan KS 66502. (913)776-4041. Creative Director: Michele Johnson. Estab. 1986. Greeting card company. Publishes greeting cards and gift items for children's, women's and college markets. "We do a few children's cards—working at doing more children's gift items/products."
Writing: Needs freelance writing for children's greeting cards and products. Makes 15 writing assignments/year. Prefers unrhymed verse ideas. Looks for writing with new, innovative approaches. Other need for freelance writing includes iron-on transfers, mugs, notepads. To contact, send cover letter and writing samples. To query with specific ideas, write to request disclosure form first. Reports in 1 month. Materials returned with SASE. For ideas, pays flat fee (range: $35-75). For other writing, pays by the project (range $100-500). Pays on acceptance. Buys all rights. Credit line sometimes given. Writer's guidelines for SASE.
Illustration: Needs freelance illustration for children's greeting cards and products. "We are now just looking to publish children's cards; our company is diversifying, so we are looking at everything." Uses color artwork only. To contact, send cover letter and b&w or color photocopies. To query with specific ideas, write to request disclosure form first. Reports in 1 month. Returns materials with SASE. Materials filed. For greeting cards, pays flat fee (range $35-75), royalty of 5% (2 years; negotiable) or advance of $200 (against 5% royalty for 2 years). For artwork, pays by the project (range $200-1,000). Pays on publication. Buys all rights. Credit line given. Artist's guidelines for SASE.
Tips: 10% of products are made for kids or have kids' themes (but looking to expand). Seasonal material should be submitted 6 months in advance. "We are beginning to work

more and more with freelancers, developing lines around a style."

WARNER PRESS, P.O. Box 2499, Anderson IN 46018. Product Editorial Manager: Cindy Maddox. Product Editor: Robin Fogle. Art Department Manager: Roger Hoffman. Photo Editor: Millie Corzine. Estab. 1880. Publishes children's greeting cards, coloring and activity books and posters, all religious-oriented. "Need fun, up-to-date stories for coloring books, with religious emphasis. Also considering activity books for Sunday school classroom use."
Writing: Needs freelance writing for children's greeting cards, coloring and activity books. To contact, request guidelines first. Reports in 4-6 weeks. For greeting cards, pays flat fee (range: $20-30). Pays on acceptance. Buys all rights. Credit line sometimes given.
Illustration: Needs freelance illustration for children's greeting cards, coloring and activity books. Wants religious, cute illustrations. To contact, send published samples, photocopies and promo pieces (all non-returnable). Reports in 1 month. For greeting cards, pays flat fee (range: $250-350). Pays on acceptance. Buys all rights. Credit line given.
Tips: Write for guidelines before submitting. Looking for "high quality art illustrated on flexible material for scanning. Meeting deadlines is very important for children's illustrations. We publish simple illustration styles. Unsolicited material that does not follow guidelines will not be reviewed."

Special Markets/'93-'94 changes

The following markets are not included in this edition of *Children's Writer's & Illustrator's Market* for the reasons indicated within parentheses. If there is no reason given, it means the market did not respond to our requests for updated information for a 1994 listing.

Collector's Gallery
English Cards, Ltd.
Fantagraphics Books, Inc.
For Kids' Sake Publishers (un-able to locate)
The Fun Zone, Activity Books (ceased publication)
Paper Impressions (removed per request)
Pieces of the Heart
Red Farm Studio

Young Writer's & Illustrator's Markets

As young writers and illustrators trying to tackle the markets in this section, many of you won't exactly fit the mold of a typical freelancer. You probably have not received the litany of rejection letters that most writers collect over time. You won't have years of experience to draw upon when seeking topics to write about. For that matter, most of you have not received a high school diploma let alone special art training. The 49 listings in this section (11 of which are new this year) are special, however, because they seek work from talented youths.

Some of the magazines in this section are exclusively for children; others are adult magazines that have set aside special sections to feature the work of younger writers and illustrators. Since most juvenile magazines are distributed through schools, churches and home subscriptions, some of the smaller, literary magazines here may not be easily found in the bookstore or library. In such a case, you may need to contact the magazine to see if a sample copy is available, and what the cost might be. It is important for writers and artists to be familiar with the editorial needs of magazines before submitting material.

Be advised that it is also important to send a self-addressed, stamped envelope (SASE) with proper postage affixed with each submission. This way, if the market is not interested in your work, they will send it back to you. If you do not send a SASE with your submission, you probably will not get your work returned. Refer to the Business of Children's Writing & Illustrating at the beginning of this book for more information about what steps to take when submitting.

If your material is rejected the first time you send it out, rest assured you are not the only one this has happened to. Many of our best known writers and artists were turned down more times than they can count at the beginning of their careers. The key to becoming published lies in persistence as well as talent. Keep sending out stories and artwork as you continue to improve your craft. Someday, an editor may decide your work is just what he needs.

To locate competitions open to young writers and illustrators, turn to Contests & Awards. Listings in that section which are designated by a double dagger (‡) are contests specifically for students.

Additional opportunities for writers can be found in the *Market Guide for Young Writers* by Kathy Henderson. The fourth edition of that book, published by Writer's Digest Books in 1993, not only includes markets for young writers, but also features Stephen King's first published story—written when he was about 13—and an interview with Michael Crichton, author of *Jurassic Park*.

THE ACORN, 1530 7th St., Rock Island IL 61201. (309)788-3980. Newsletter. Estab. 1989. Audience consists of "kindergarten-12th grade, teachers and other adult writers." Purpose in publishing works for children: to expose children's manuscripts to others and provide a format for those who might not have one. Children must be K-12 (put grade on manuscripts). Accepts submissions by adult authors who slant mss to K-12. Guidelines available for SASE.

Magazines: 50% of magazine written by children. Uses 6 fiction pieces (500 words), 6 nonfiction pieces (500 words), 20 pieces of poetry (32 lines). No payment; purchase of a copy isn't necessary to be printed. Sample copy $2. Subscription $10 for 6 issues. Submit mss to Betty Mowery, editor. Send complete ms. Will accept typewritten, legibly handwritten and/or computer printout. SASE. Reports in 1 week.

Artwork/Photography: Publishes artwork by children. Looks for "all types; size 4 × 5. Use black ink in artwork." No payment. Submit artwork either with manuscript or separately to Betty Mowery. SASE. Reports in 1 week.

Tips: "My biggest problem is not having names on the manuscripts. If the manuscript gets separated from the cover letter, there is no way to know whom to respond to. Also, adults who submit will often go over word limit—we are a small publication and cannot handle more than wordage previously stated. I will use fiction or nonfiction by adults, but it must relate to something that will help children with their writing—submitting or publishing, as well as just entertain. Manuscripts without SASE will not be returned."

AMERICAN GIRL, P.O. Box 984, Middleton WI 53562-0984. (608)836-4848. Bimonthly magazine. Audience consists of girls ages 7-12 who are joyful about being girls. Must be 7-12 years old, no proof needed of original work. Writer's guidelines not available.

Magazines: 5% of magazine written by young people. "Only two pages of each issue are set aside for children and articles are answers to a question or request that has appeared in a previous issue of *American Girl*." Pays in copies. Submit to Harriet Braun, editor. Will accept legibly handwritten ms. SASE. Reports in 2 months.

*THE APPRENTICE WRITER, % Gary Fincke, Susquehanna University, Selinsgrove PA 17870. (717)372-4164. Magazine. Published annually. "Writing by high school students and for high school students." Purpose in publishing works by young people: to provide quality writing by students which can be read for pleasure and serve as a text for high school classrooms. Work is primarily from eastern and northeastern states, but will consider work from other areas of US. Students must be in grades 9-12. Writer's guidelines available for SASE.

Magazines: Uses 15 short stories (prefers under 5,000 words); 15 nonfiction personal essays (prefers under 5,000 words); 60 poems (no word limit) per issue. Pays in copies to writers and their schools. Submit mss to Gary Fincke, editor. Submit complete ms. Will accept typewritten mss. SASE. Submit ms by March 15. Responds by May of each year.

Artwork/Photography: Publishes artwork and photography by children. Looks for b&w. Pays in copies to artists and their schools. Submit originals or high quality copies. Submit art and photographs to Gary Fincke, editor. SASE. Submit artwork by March 15. Responds by May of each year.

BEYOND WORDS PUBLISHING, INC., 13950 NW Pumpkin Ridge Rd., Hillsboro OR 97124. (503)647-5109. Book publisher. Publishes 1-2 books by children per year. Looks for "books that encourage creativity and an appreciation of nature in children." Wants to "encourage children to write, create, dream and believe that it is possible to be published. The books must be unique, be of national interest and the child must be personable and promotable."

Books: Publishes stories and joke books. Publisher not accepting unsolicited ms at this time.

BOODLE, P.O. 1049, Portland IN 47371. (219)726-8141. Magazine published quarterly. "Each quarterly issue offers children a special invitation to read stories and poems written by others. Children can learn from the ideas in these stories and the techniques of sharing ideas in picures and written form. Audience is ages 6-12. We hope that publishing children's writing will enhance the self-esteem of the authors and motivate other children to try expressing themselves in this form." Submission requirements: "We ask that authors include grade when written, current grade, name of school, and a statement from parent or teacher that the work is original."

Magazines: 95% of magazine written by children. Uses 12 short stories (100-500 words), 1 mostly animal nonfiction piece (100-500 words), 25 poems (50-500 words), 2 puzzles and mazes (50-500 words). Pays 2 copies of issue. Submit mss to Mavis Catalfio, editor. Submit complete ms. Will accept typewritten and legibly handwritten mss. Include SASE.

Artwork/Photography: Wants "mazes, cartoons, drawings of animals or seasons or sports which will likely match a story or poem we publish." Pays 2 copies of issue. "Drawings should be done in black ink or marker." Submit artwork to Mavis Catalfio, editor. Reports in 2 months.

Tips: "Submit seasonal materials at least 6 months in advance. We love humor and offbeat stories. We seldom publish sad or depressing stories about death or serious illness."

BOYS' LIFE, P.O. Box 152079, 325 W. Walnut Hill Lane, Irving TX 75015-2079. (214)580-2366. Magazine published monthly. Audience consists of children ages 7-17. *Boys' Life* is published by the Boy Scouts of America to make available to children ages 7-17 the highest caliber of fiction and nonfiction, to stimulate an interest in good reading and to promote the principles of scouting. Must be 18 or under to submit.

Magazines: Small percentage of magazine written by young people. Uses hobby and collecting tips for "Hobby Hows" and "Collecting" columns. Pays $5/tip. Uses jokes for "Think & Grin" column. Pays choice of $2 or copy of *Scout Handbook* or *Scout Fieldbook*/joke. Several times/year uses personal stories (500 words maximum) for "Readers' Page." Pays $25. Submit mss to column. Submit complete ms. Will accept typewritten and legibly handwritten mss.

CHICKADEE MAGAZINE, Suite 306, 56 The Esplanade, Toronto, Ontario M5E 1A7 Canada. (416)868-6001. Magazine published 10 times/year. "*Chickadee* is for children ages 3-9. It's purpose is to entertain and educate children about science, nature and the world around them. We publish children's drawings to give readers the chance to express themselves. Drawings must follow the topics that are given in the 'Chirp' section of each issue." Children are asked to provide their age and return address. No payment given.

Artwork/Photography: Publishes artwork by children. Mail submissions with name, age and return address for thank you note. Submit to Mitch Butler, Chirp editor. Reports in 3 months.

CHILDREN'S DIGEST, P.O. Box 567, Indianapolis IN 46206. (317)636-8881. Magazine. Published 8 times/year. Audience consists of preteens. Purpose in publishing works by children: to encourage children to express themselves through writing. Requires proof of originality before publishing stories. Writer's guidelines available on request.

Magazines: 10% of magazine written by children. Uses 1 fiction story (about 200 words), 6-7 poems, 15-20 riddles, 7-10 letters/issue. "There is no payment for manuscripts submitted by readers." Submit mss to *Children's Digest*, Elizabeth A. Rinck, editor. Submit complete ms. Will accept typewritten, legibly handwritten and computer

 The asterisk before a listing indicates the listing is new in this edition.

printout mss. "Readers whose material is accepted will be notified by letter. Sorry, no materials can be returned."

CHILDREN'S PLAYMATE, P.O. Box 567, Indianapolis IN 46206. (317)636-8881. Magazine. Estab. 1928. Audience consists of children between 6 and 8 years of age. Purpose in publishing works by children: to encourage children to write. Writer's guidelines available on request.
Magazines: 10% of magazine written by children. Uses 6-7 poems, 8-10 jokes, 8-10 riddles/issue. "There is no payment for manuscripts submitted by children." Submit mss to *Children's Playmate*, Elizabeth A. Rinck, editor. Submit complete ms. Will accept typewritten, legibly handwritten, computer printout mss. "If a child's work is published, he/she will be notified by a letter. No material may be returned."
Artwork/Photography: Publishes artwork by children. "Prefers dark-colored line drawings on white paper. No payment for children's artwork published." Submit artwork to *Children's Playmate*, Elizabeth A. Rinck, editor.

CLUBHOUSE, P.O. Box 15, Berrien Springs MI 49103. (616)471-9009. Director of Publications: Elaine Trumbo. Magazine. Estab. 1949. Published monthly. Occasionally publishes items by kids. "Audience consists of kids ages 9-14; philosophy is God loves kids, kids are neat people." Purpose in publishing works by children: encouragement; demonstration of talent. Children must be ages 9-14; must include parent's note verifying originality.
Magazines: Uses adventure, historical, everyday life experience (fiction/nonfiction-1,200 words); health-related short articles; poetry (4-24 lines of "mostly mood pieces and humor"). Pays in prizes for children, money for adult authors. Query. Will accept typewritten, legibly handwritten and computer printout mss. "Will not be returned without SASE." Reports in 6 weeks.
Artwork/Photography: Publishes artwork by children. Looks for all types of artwork—white paper, black pen. Pays in prizes for kids. Send b&w art to Elaine Trumbo, editor. "Won't be returned without SASE."
Tips: "All items submitted by kids are held in a file and used when possible. We normally suggest they do not ask for return of the item."

CREATIVE KIDS, P.O. Box 6448, Mobile AL 36660. (205)478-4700. Editor/Publisher: Fay L. Gold. Magazine published 8 times/year (October-May). Estab. 1979. "All of our material is by children, for children." Purpose in publishing works by children: "to create a product that is good enough for publication and to offer an opportunity for children to see their work in print." Writers ages 5-18 must have statement by teacher or parent verifying originality. Writer's guidelines available on request with SASE.
Magazines: Uses "about 6" fiction stories (200-750 words); "about 6" nonfiction stories (200-750 words); poetry, plays, ideas to share 200-750 words/issue. Pays "free magazine." Submit mss to Fay L. Gold, editor. Will accept typewritten, legibly handwritten mss. SASE. Reports in 1 month.
Artwork/Photography: Publishes artwork by children. Looks for "any kind of drawing, cartoon, or painting." Pays "free magazine." Send original or a photo of the work to Fay L. Gold, editor. No photocopies. SASE. Reports in 1 month.
Tips: "*Creative Kids* is a magazine by kids, for kids. The work represents children's ideas, questions, fears, concerns and pleasures. The material never contains racist, sexist or violent expression. The purpose is to encourage youngsters to create a product that is good enough for publication. A person may submit one or more pieces of work. Each piece must be labeled with the student's name, birth date, grade, school, home address and school address. Include a photograph, if possible. Recent school pictures are best. Material submitted to *Creative Kids* must not be under consideration by any other publication. Items should be carefully prepared, proofread and double checked. All activities

requiring solutions must be accompanied by the correct answers. We're looking for current topics of interest: nutrition, ecology, cleaner environment, etc."

CREATIVE WITH WORDS, *We Are Writers, Too!*, Creative With Words Publications, P.O. Box 223226, Carmel CA 93922. Editor: Brigitta Geltrich. Semiannual anthology. Estab. 1975. "We publish the creative writing of children." Audience consists of children, schools, libraries, adults, reading programs. Purpose in publishing works by children: to offer them an opportunity to get started in publishing. "Work must be of quality, original, unedited, and not published before; age must be given (up to 19 years old)." SASE must be enclosed with all correspondence and mss. Writer's guidelines available on request.
Books: Considers all categories except those dealing with death and murder. Uses fairy tales, folklore items (1,000 words) and poetry (not to exceed 20 lines, 46 characters across). Published *We Are Writers, Too!* (anthology, children and adults); *A Scary Halloween!* (children and adults); *A CWW Easter!* and *Seasons and Holidays!* (anthology, children and adults); *Tall Tales and Fairy Tales* (children and adults). Pays 20% discount on each copy of publication in which fiction or poetry by children appears. Submit mss to Brigitta Geltrich, editor. Query; teacher or parent must submit; teacher and/or parents must verify originality of writing. Will accept typewritten and/or legibly handwritten mss. SASE. Reports in 2 months after deadline.
Artwork/Photography: Publishes artwork and computer artwork by children (language artwork). Pays 20% discount on every copy of publication in which work by children appears. Submit artwork to Brigitta Geltrich, editor.

FAMILYFUN, P.O. Box 929, North Hampton MA 01060. (413)585-0444. Magazine. Purpose in publishing works by young people: entertainment. Must be 5-15 years old, will call to verify proof of original work. Writer's guidelines not available.
Magazines: 5% of magazine written by young people. Uses 1 fiction story (about 100-200 words), 30 nonfiction stories (length varies)/issue. Submit mss to Greg Lauzon, senior editor. Submit complete ms. Will accept legibly handwritten mss. SASE. Reports in 2 months.
Artwork/Photography: Publishes artwork and photography by children. Pays with certificate of recognition and one issue. Reports in 2 months.

FREE SPIRIT PUBLISHING INC., Suite 616, 400 First Ave. North, Minneapolis MN 55401. (612)338-2068. "Our first book by a child will be released this year." Published 8-12 books/year since starting in 1983. "We specialize in SELF-HELP FOR KIDS®. Our main interests include the development of self-esteem, self-awareness, creative thinking and problem solving abilities, assertiveness, and making a difference in the world. Children have a lot to share with each other. They also can reach and teach each other in ways adults cannot. "We accept submissions from young people ages 14 and older. Plese send a letter from a parent/guardian/leader verifying originality." Writer's guidelines available on request (specify student guidelines).
Books: Publishes psychology, self-help, how-to, education. Pays advance and royalties. Submit mss to M.E. Salzmann, editorial assistant. Send query. Will accept typewritten mss. SASE. Reports in 3-4 months.

FUTURIFIC, INC., the Foundation for Optimism, Futurific, T-3, 150 Haven Ave., New York NY 10032. Publisher: B. Szent-Miklosy. (212)297-0502. Magazine published monthly. Audience consists of people interested in an accurate report of what is ahead. "We do not discriminate by age. We look for the visionary in all people. They must say what will be. No advice or 'may-be.' We've had 18 years of accurate forecasting." Sample copy for $5 postage and handling. Writer's guidelines available on request.

Magazines: Submit mss to B. Szent-Miklosy, publisher. Will accept typewritten, legibly handwritten, computer printout, 5.25 inch Word Perfect diskette mss.
Artwork/Photography: Publishes artwork by children. Looks for "what the future will look like." Pay is negotiable. Send b&w drawings or photos. Submit artwork to B. Szent-Miklosy, publisher.

THE GOLDFINCH, 402 Iowa Ave., Iowa City IA 52240. (319)335-3916. Magazine published quarterly. Audience is fifth and sixth graders. "Magazine supports creative work by children: research, art, writing." Submitted work must go with the historical theme of each issue.
Magazines: 10-20% written by children. Uses at least 1 nonfiction essay, poem, story/issue (500 words). Pays complimentary copies. Submit mss to Deborah Gore Ohrn, editor. Submit complete ms. Will accept typewritten, legibly handwritten, computer disk (Apple) mss. Reports in 1 month.
Artwork/Photography: Publishes artwork/photographs by children. Art and photos must be b&w. Pays complimentary copies. Query first to Deborah Gore Ohrn.

HIGH SCHOOL WRITER, P.O. Box 718, Grand Rapids MN 55744. (218)326-8025. Magazine published monthly during the school year. "The *High School Writer* is a magazine written by students *for* students. All submissions must exceed usual and customary standards of decency." Purpose in publishing works by children: "To provide a real audience for student writers—and text for study." Submissions by junior high and middle school students accepted for our junior edition. Senior high students' works are accepted for our senior high edition. Students attending schools that subscribe to our publication are eligible to submit their work." Writer's guidelines available on request.
Magazines: Uses fiction, nonfiction (1,000 words maximum) and poetry. Submit mss to Roxanne Kain, editor. Submit complete ms (teacher must submit). Will accept typewritten, computer generated (good quality) mss.
Tips: "Submissions should not be sent without first obtaining a copy of our guidelines. Also, submissions will not be considered unless student's school subscribes."

HIGHLIGHTS FOR CHILDREN, 803 Church St., Honesdale PA 18431. (717)253-1080. Magazine published monthly. "We strive to provide wholesome, stimulating, entertaining material that will encourage children to read. Our audience is children ages 2-12." Purpose in publishing works by children: to encourage children's creative expression. Age limit is 15 to submit.
Magazines: 15-20% of magazine written by children. Features which occur occasionally: "What Are Your Favorite Books?" (8-10/year), "Recipes" (8-10/year), "Science Letters" (15-20/year). Special features which invite children's submissions on a specific topic: "Tell the Story" (15-20/year), "You're the Reporter" (8-10/year), "Your Ideas, Please" (8-10/year), "Endings to Unfinished Stories" (8-10/year). Submit complete mss to the editor. Will accept typewritten, legibly handwritten and computer printout mss. Responds in 3-6 weeks.
Artwork/Photography: Publishes artwork by children. No cartoon or comic book characters. No commercial products. Submit b&w or color artwork for "Our Own Pages." Features include "Creatures Nobody Has Ever Seen" (5-8/year) and "Illustration Job" (18-20/year). Responds in 3-6 weeks.

*HOW ON EARTH!, Teens supporting compassionate, ecologically sound living, P.O. Box 3347, West Chester PA 19381. (717)529-8638. Newsletter. Published quarterly. Youth audience. "*How On Earth!* strives to provide a voice for youth concerned about animals and the earth and provide a forum where young people can share ideas, experiences, feelings and concerns." Must be ages 13-20 and work must be original. Articles well-referenced. "Please send a SASE with 1 first-class stamp."

Magazines: 95% of publication written by teenagers. Uses 1-2 creative writing stories, 2-5 research or informative articles, interviews, food articles, 4-5 poems. Submit mss to: Sally Clinton, coordinator. Query for fiction. Submit complete ms for nonfiction. Will accept typewritten and legibly handwritten mss or 3½" disk (Macintosh). SASE "only if they want it returned." Reports in 2 months.

Artwork/Photography: Publishes artwork and photographs by children. "We accept anything depicting nature, animals, ecology, activism, vegetarian food and anything concerning issues related to these topics. Cartoons welcome as well. Pen & ink or dark pencil only." No pay: "All volunteer at this point." Submit artwork and photos to: Sally Clinton, coordinator. SASE "only if they want it returned." Reports in 2 months.

*IOWA WOMAN, P.O. Box 680, Iowa City IA 52244. (319)987-2879. Published quarterly. "We publish quality fiction, essays, interviews, poetry, book reviews and feature articles for women everywhere. We welcome submissions by girls and young women to encourage them to communicate and share their creative work. If work is by children, we prefer it not be rewritten by an adult. We welcome drawings and visual art, too." Guidelines available for SASE.

Magazines: Less than 1% of magazine written by young people ("we hardly ever get submissions"). Last year, used 1 nonfiction personal essay about relationship with mother (1,200 words); 2 poetry departments (varying word lengths). Submit mss to Rebecca Childers, managing editor. Submit complete ms. Will accept typewritten mss (diskette if accepted). SASE. Reports in 6 weeks-3 months.

Artwork/Photography: Publishes artwork and photography by children. Looks for "specific illustrations for fiction and essays we've accepted; illustration by child for her own written work." Pays $15 for illustration per story, any genre (b&w only). "Ask to be on artist list or send photocopy samples." Submit art and photographs to Marianne Abel, editor. SASE. Reports in 3 weeks.

Tips: "We welcome submissions for 'under 21' a column/department open to any genre of work by younger writers."

KIDS TODAY MINI-MAGAZINE, 2724 College Park Rd., Allison Park PA 15101. A mini-magazine in newsletter format. Quarterly. Targets kids in grades 3-5. Purpose in publishing works by young people: "to recognize and celebrate imagination, creativity, distinctiveness and worth of all people, with particular emphasis on *all* children; to stimulate within our young readership an interest and appreciation for the ability to communicate, learn and entertain through reading, writing and artistic skills." The Spotlight feature is reserved for publication of creative writing submitted by children ages 6-11. Writer's guidelines available on request.

Magazines: 25% of magazine written by young people. Uses 2 short stories (150-250 words), 12 poems (up to 100 words) per issue. Pays certificate of publication and contributor copies. Submit mss to Don DiMarco, editor. Submit complete ms. Will accept typewritten and legibly handwritten mss. SASE if author wants work returned. Reports in 3 weeks.

Artwork/Photography: Publishes artwork only when submitted with written work. Two children may submit as a team. Photos should be 8½×11 b&w.

Tips: "We respond to all young writers, offering positive reinforcement, even if work is not accepted. Children must state their age."

KIDSART, P.O. Box 274, Mt. Shasta CA 96067. (916)926-5076. Newsletter published quarterly. Publishes "hands-on art projects, open-ended art lessons, art history, lots of child-made art to illustrate." Purpose in publishing works by children: "to provide achievable models for kids—give young artists a forum for their work. We always phone before publishing works to be sure it's OK with their folks, name is spelled correctly, etc."

Artwork/Photography: Publishes artwork/photographs by children. Any submissions by children welcomed. Pays free copies of published work. Submit artwork/photos to Kim Solga, editor. "Your originals will be returned to you in 4-6 weeks." SASE desired, but not required. Free catalog available describing KidsArt newsletter. Sample copy $3.

*KOPPER BEAR PRESS, P.O. Box 19454, Boulder CO 80308-2454. (303)786-9808. Publishes as material is available. "We believe that young people have important things to say—to everyone!" Purpose in publishing works by young people: to give young people another outlet for their feelings/ideas. Must be 13-21 years old. Must be able to prove work is original. Guidelines available on request.
Books: Publishes stories, poetry, essays, novels. Will review any length. Pay depends on work. For poems, short stories, would like copyright outright. For longer works, advance and royalty. Submit mss to Howard Bashinski. Submit complete ms. Will accept typewritten and legibly handwritten mss. Reports in 1 month.

*THE LOUISVILLE REVIEW—CHILDREN'S CORNER, Dept. of English, University of Louisville, 315 Bingham Humanities, Louisville KY 40292. (502)588-6801. Semiannual magazine. "We are a contemporary literary journal." Purpose in publishing works by young people: to encourage children to write with fresh images and striking metaphors. Must supply SASE and permission slip from parent stating that work is original and giving permission to publish if accepted.
Magazines: 10-20% of magazine written by children. Uses 10-25 pages of poetry any length. Pays in copies. Submit mss to Children's Corner. Submit complete ms. Will accept typewritten mss. SASE. Reports in 3 months.

MERLYN'S PEN: The National Magazines of Student Writing, P.O. Box 1058, East Greenwich RI 02818. (401)885-5175. Magazine. Published every 2 months during the school year, September-May. "We publish a Senior Edition (grades 9-12) and an Intermediate Edition (grades 7-10) including 150 manuscripts annually by students in grades 7-12. The entire magazine is dedicated to young adults' writing. Our audience is classrooms, libraries and students from grades 7-12." Writers must be in grades 7-12 and must follow submission guidelines for preparing their mss. When a student is accepted, he/she, a parent and a teacher must sign a statement of originality.
Magazines: Uses 25 short stories (less than 4,000 words), plays; 8 nonfiction essays (less than 3,000 words); 10 pieces of poetry; letters to the editor; editorials; reviews of previously published works; and reviews of books, music, movies. Pays for ms in 3 copies of the issue and a paperback copy of *The Elements of Style* (a writer's handbook). Also, a discount is offered for additional copies of the issue. Submit complete ms. Will only accept typewritten mss. "All rejected manuscripts receive an editor's constructive critical comment in the margin." Reports in 11 weeks.
Artwork/Photography: Publishes artwork by young adults, grades 7-12. Looks for b&w line drawings, cartoons, color art for cover. Pays in 3 copies of the issue to the artist, and a discount is offered for additional copies. Send unmatted original artwork. SASE. Reports in 11 weeks.
Tips: "All manuscripts and artwork must be submitted with a cover sheet listing: name, age and grade, home address, home phone number, school name, school phone number, school address, teacher's name and principal's name. SASE must be large enough and carry enough postage for return."

MY FRIEND, 50 St. Paul's Ave., Jamaica Plain, Boston MA 02130. (617)522-8911. Magazine published 10 times/year. Audience consists of children ages 6-12, primarily Roman Catholics. Purpose in publishing works by children: to stimulate reader participation and to encourage young Catholic writers. Requirements to be met before work is published: accepts work from children ages 6-16. Requirements regarding originality in-

We've just made getting your words published a little easier

Subscribe to WRITER'S DIGEST now, and get this invaluable guide, *Getting Published: What Every Writer Needs to Know*, FREE with your paid subscription.

SPECIAL FREE GIFT OFFER!

INSIDE: How to write irresistible query letters and prepare polished manuscripts. How to give an editor nothing to do—except buy your work. Where to find ideas. And the "test" every editor gives...14 questions you can use to evaluate your freelancing savvy.

Use the card below to start your subscription today!

No other source offers so much information and instruction...

on writing...

WRITER'S DIGEST is packed with advice from the experts that can make you a better writer. Whatever your challenge...from generating plot ideas to overcoming writer's block. Whatever your specialty...from writing poetry to children's stories.

and selling what you write!

Learn the secrets of top-dollar freelancers. How to slant your writing for multiple sales and negotiate contracts with editors and publishers. How to make and keep contacts that help your career. Find out what markets are hot for your work right now, how much they're paying, and how to get in touch with the right people.

Subscribe today and save 46% off the newsstand price!

We've just made getting your words published a little easier

Getting Published:
What Every Writer Needs to Know

Writer's DIGEST

Subscribe to
WRITER'S DIGEST
now, and get this
invaluable guide,
*Getting Published: What
Every Writer Needs to Know,*
FREE with your paid subscription.

SPECIAL FREE GIFT OFFER!

INSIDE: How to write irresistible
query letters and prepare polished
manuscripts. How to give an editor
nothing to do—except buy your work.
Where to find ideas. And the "test"
every editor gives...14 questions you can
use to evaluate your freelancing savvy.

**Use the card below to start
your subscription today!**

No other source offers so much information and instruction...

on writing...

WRITER'S DIGEST is packed with advice from the experts that can make you a better writer. Whatever your challenge...from generating plot ideas to overcoming writer's block. Whatever your specialty...from writing poetry to children's stories.

and selling what you write!

Learn the secrets of top-dollar freelancers. How to slant your writing for multiple sales and negotiate contracts with editors and publishers. How to make and keep contacts that help your career. Find out what markets are hot for your work right now, how much they're paying, and how to get in touch with the right people.

Subscribe today and save 46% off the newsstand price!

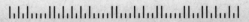

cluded in guidelines. Writer's guidelines available for SASE.

Tips: "Our 'Junior Reporter' feature gives young writers the chance to do active research on a variety of topics. Children may ask for an 'assignment' or suggest topics they'd be willing to research and write on. This would be mainly where our interest in children's writing would lie."

*NATIONAL GEOGRAPHIC WORLD, 17th and M St. NW, Washington DC 20036. (202)857-7000. Magazine published monthly. Picture magazine for ages 8 and older.

Artwork/Photography: Publishes art, letters, poems, games, riddles, jokes and craft ideas by children in mailbag section only. Send by mail to: Mailbag. "Sorry, but *World* cannot acknowledge or return your contributions."

THE PIKESTAFF FORUM, P.O. Box 127, Normal IL 61761. (309)452-4831. Magazine published annually; "We hope to eventually get out two issues per year. The basic audience of *The Pikestaff Forum* is adult; in each issue we have a Young Writers feature publishing writing and artwork by young people aged 7-17. Purpose in publishing works by children: Our purpose is twofold: (1) to put excellent writing by young people before the general public, and (2) to encourage young people in developing their self-confidence and powers of literary expression. Work must be by young people aged 7-17; it must be original, previously unpublished, and submitted by the authors themselves (we do *not* wish parents or teachers to submit the work); the person's age at the time the piece was written must be stated and SASE must be included." Writer's guidelines available on request.

Magazines: 10% of magazine written by children. Uses 1-3 fiction stories, 7-10 poems/ issue. Poetry always welcome. Author or artist receives 3 copies of the issue in which work appears, and has option of purchasing additional copies at 50% discount. Submit complete mss to Robert D. Sutherland, editor/publisher. Will accept typewritten, legibly handwritten, computer printout mss. SASE. Reports in 3 months.

Artwork/Photography: Publishes artwork by children. No restrictions on subject matter; "should be free-standing and interesting (thought-provoking). *Black & white only* (dark image); we cannot handle color work with our format." Artist receives three free copies of the issue in which the work appears, and has the option of purchasing additional copies at a 50% discount off cover price. In b&w, clearly mark with artist's name, address and age at the time the work was created. Submit artwork to Robert D. Sutherland, editor/publisher. Reports in 3 months. "We do not wish teachers to submit for their students, and we do not wish to see batches of works which are simply the product of school assignments."

SHOFAR MAGAZINE, 43 Northcote Dr., Melville NY 11747. (516)643-4598. Magazine published 6 times/school year. Audience consists of American Jewish children age 9-13.

Magazines: 10-20% of magazine written by young people. Uses fiction/nonfiction (500-750 words), Kids Page items (50-150 words). Submit mss to Gerald Grayson, managing editor. Submit complete ms. Will accept typewritten, legibly handwritten mss and computer disk (Mac only). SASE. Reports in 1-2 months.

Artwork/Photography: Publishes artwork and photography by children. Pays "by the piece, depending on size and quantity." Submit original with SASE. Reports in 1-2 months.

SKIPPING STONES, Multicultural Children's Magazine, P.O. Box 3939, Eugene OR 97403. (503)342-4956. Articles/Fiction Editor: Arun N. Toké. Publishes 5 issues bimonthly during the school year. Estab. 1988. Circulation 3,000. "*Skipping Stones* is a multicultural, nonprofit, children's magazine to encourage cooperation, creativity and celebration of cultural and environmental richness. It offers itself as a creative forum for communication among children from different lands and backgrounds. We prefer

Creating an Outlet for Children of All Cultures

Skipping Stones magazine's logo depicts the earth with two people skipping stones across continents and oceans, making a connection between cultures of the world. The logo accurately illustrates what the bimonthly publication is about—the interconnectedness of all people, from a child's perspective.

"It is a unique multicultural publication wading the waters that separate people and nature, cultures and generations. Gentle and positive in its outlook, *Skipping Stones* does not shy away from addressing difficult issues like war and peace, homelessness, or death and loss," says Arun Narayan Toké, founder and executive editor.

Arun Narayan Toké

The magazine, based in Eugene, Oregon, has a readership primarily of 8- to 15-year-olds, as well as their parents and teachers. *Skipping Stones* received the 1993 EdPress Award for Excellence in Educational Journalism. And about 50-60 percent of the material published is created by children.

Items are printed in the writer's native language and accompanied by an English translation. "It's a multilingual magazine," says Toké. "We're truly global in our approach and contents. We want to be a forum for young people from all over to communicate with each other. We welcome art and writing by kids of *all* backgrounds."

Like the magazine he established, Toké is also multilingual. Though born in India, he's experienced many other cultures, including those of Asia, Europe, and Central and North America. "I saw a need for multicultural resources for youth, so I founded *Skipping Stones*. We're seeking a world with appreciation and respect for diversity," he explains.

The most rewarding part of his job, says Toké, is reading exceptional, creative writing by children, seeing it in print, and getting letters of appreciation—"and we get them by the dozens—from parents, teachers and kids. We hope to be a resource in schools and libraries, but *Skipping Stones* is a labor of love, not a money-making venture. Knowing that each one of us is making a contribution in our own way to society is important to us and our satisfaction."

The magazine is produced by a multicultural team of volunteers. Interns screen the 45 to 60 manuscripts received each month, and two editors conduct a final screening. Keep in mind that when evaluating manuscripts, Toké says editors look for originality, multicultural awareness, nature themes, ecological understanding, kindness toward other beings, social responsibility and poetic expression.

Accepted pieces are usually published in three to six months. Occasionally, the staff produces issues centered around specific themes. However, theme issues are only published when enough related material is received. So it may take awhile for a theme piece to appear, says Toké. Writers and illustrators can obtain a list of upcoming topics by referring to page 34 of any issue or by sending the staff a self-addressed, stamped envelope (SASE).

Toké advises children submitting articles or stories to "be natural in your style. Be yourself. Put your feelings, your own self, in your writing. Don't follow someone else's style. Be specific. Don't drag on. We prefer 'short' pieces so that we can publish a variety of writings from many children. Also, include information about your cultural background and where your family came from."

As for illustrations, the staff prefers black & white (pen and ink) drawings. "We do accept color photos and paintings, however, and transfer them to black & white halftones for publication. Often, we use illustrations submitted by one child to complement writing by someone else," says Toké. When submitting illustrations, send the original and a photocopy with a SASE. "You might wish to send several works of art to us," he adds. "Chances are good that we might like one specific piece due to its subject matter."

When sending *any* material to *Skipping Stones*, Toké says, "Remember our future depends on how we understand nature, how we take care of our ecological riches and on our understanding of each other's customs, cultures, languages and thinking. Our differences and diversity are our assets — to be respected, cherished and promoted."

— *Donna Collingwood*

Skipping Stones *is a multicultural publication that accepts material from children around the world, and occasionally produces theme issues. The theme of the issue pictured here is "Thinking of All Beings," and readers were asked to focus on their relationship to animals, says Editor Arun N. Toké. The cover art, entitled "The Spirit of the Northwest," was created by German Nieto-Maquehue, a Mapuche Native from Chile.*

Skipping Stones
A Multicultural Children's Quarterly
Volume 5, No. 2   US $ 4.00

Thinking Of All Beings

"The Spirit of the Northwest"
The great spirit is constantly watching over the endangered natural balance. I drew this mask as a homage to my Native brothers and sisters of the Northwest.
—German Nieto-Maquehue, Mapuche from Chile, South America

work by children up to 17-18 year olds. International, minorities and under represented populations receive priority, multilingual submissions encouraged."

Magazines: 50-60% written by children. Uses 10 fiction short stories (500-900 words); 5 nonfiction articles, letters, history, descriptions of celebrations (500-900 words); 15-20 poetry, jokes, riddles, proverbs (200 words or less) per issue. Pays in contributor's copies. Submit mss to Arun Toké, editor. Query for non-fiction; submit complete ms for fiction or other work; teacher may submit; parents can also submit their contributions. Will accept typewritten, legibly handwritten and computer/word processor mss. SASE. Responds in 3 months. Accepts simultaneous submissions.

Artwork/Photography: Will review all varieties of ms/illustration packages.Wants b&w or color — 8 × 10 or 4 × 6 photos; any size artwork. Subjects include children, people, celebrations, nature, ecology, multicultural.

Terms: "*Skipping Stones* is a labor of love. No cash payment. You'll receive 1-4 copies depending on the length of your contribution and illustrations." Reports back to artists in 3 months. Sample copy for $4 and 8½ × 11 SAE with 4 first-class stamps.

Tips: "Let the 'inner child' within you speak out — naturally, uninhibited." Wants "material that gives insight on cultural celebrations, lifestyle, custom and tradition, glimpse of daily life in other countries and cultures. Photos, songs, artwork are most welcome if they illustrate/highlight the points. Upcoming features: African-American experience, drugs and substance abuse, religions and cultures from around the world, death and loss, Spanish-English bilingual issue, Japan, street children, the world in 2025AD, songs and foods from around the world, resource conservation and sustainable lifestyles, indigenous architecture, family, women and young girls in various cultures, etc."

SKYLARK, 2200 169th St., Hammond IN 46323. (219)989-2262. Editor: Pamela Hunter. Young Writer's Editor: Kathy Natiello. Annual magazine. Circ. 500-750. 15% of material aimed at juvenile audience. Presently accepting material *by* children. "*Skylark* wishes to provide a vehicle for creative writing of all kinds, by all ages, particularly ages five through eighteen, especially in our area, which has not ordinarily provided such an outlet. Children need a place to have their work published alongside that of adults." Proof or originality is required from parents or teachers for authors 18 and under. Writer's guidelines available upon request.

Magazines: 15% of magazine written by young people. Uses animals, friends, families, life experiences, mystery. Does not want to see material about Satan worship, graphic sex. Uses 1-3 fiction stories (1,200 words max.), 1-3 nonfiction story (1,200 words max.), 25 poems, (20 lines max.). Pay in contributor's copies. Submit ms to Kathy Natiello, young writers' editor. Submit complete ms. Will accept typewritten ms only. SASE. Reports in 3 months. Byline given.

Artwork/Photography: Publishes artwork/photos by children. Looks for "photos of animals, landscapes and sports, and artwork to go along with text." Pay in contributor's copies. All artwork and photos must be b&w, 8½ × 11, unlined paper. Do not use pencil and no copyrighted characters. Submit artwork/photos to Kathy Natiello, Young Writers' Editor. SASE. Reports in 6 months.

*SNAKE RIVER REFLECTIONS, 1863 Bitterroot Dr., Twin Falls ID 83301. (208)734-0746. Newsletter. Publishes 10 times/year (not published in October or December). Proof of originality required with submissions. Guidelines available on request.

Magazines: 5% of magazine written by children. Uses poetry (30 lines maximum). Pays in copies only. Submit mss to William White, editor. Submit complete ms. Will accept typewritten and legibly handwritten mss. SASE. Reports in 1 month.

THE SOW'S EAR POETRY REVIEW, 19535 Pleasant View Dr., Abingdon VA 24210-6827. (703)628-2651. Magazine published quarterly. "Our editorial philosophy is to serve contemporary literature by publishing the best poetry we can find. Our audience includes serious poets throughout the US. We publish school-aged poets in most issues to encourage young writers and to show our older audience that able young poets are writing. We request young poets to furnish age, grade, school and list of any previous publication." Writer's guidelines available on request.
Magazines: 3% of magazine written by children. Uses 2-3 poems (1 page) per issue. Pays 1 copy. Submit complete ms. Will accept typewritten, legibly handwritten mss. SASE. Reports in 3 months.
Artwork/Photography: Publishes artwork by children. "Prefer line drawings. Any subject or size that may be easily reduced or enlarged. Must be b&w." Pays 1 copy. Submit artwork to Mary Calhoun, graphics editor. SASE. Reports in 4 months.

SPRING TIDES, 824 Stillwood Dr., Savannah GA 31419. (912)925-8800. Annual magazine. Audience consists of children 5-12 years old. Purpose in publishing works by children: to encourage writing. Requirements to be met before work is published: must be 5-12 years old. Writers guidelines available on request.
Magazines: Uses 12-24 pieces of material per issue. Submit complete ms. Will accept typewritten mss. SASE.
Artwork/Photography: Publishes artwork by children. "We have so far used only local children's artwork because of the complications of keeping and returning pieces."

STONE SOUP, The Magazine by Children, Children's Art Foundation, P.O. Box 83, Santa Cruz CA 95063. (408)426-5557. Articles/Fiction Editor, Art Director: Ms. Gerry Mandel. Magazine published 5 times/year. Circ. 17,000. "We publish fiction, poetry and artwork by children through age 13. Our preference is for work based on personal experiences and close observation of the world." Purpose in publishing works by children: to encourage children to read and to express themselves through writing and art. Writer's guidelines available upon request.
Magazines: 100% of magazine written by children. Uses animal, contemporary, fantasy, history, problem solving, science fiction, sports, spy/mystery/adventure fiction stories. Uses 5-10 fiction stories (100-2,500 words), 5-10 nonfiction stories (100-2,500 words), 2-4 poems per issue. Does not want to see classroom assignments and formula writing. Buys 65 mss/year. Byline given. Pays on acceptance. Buys all rights. Pays $10 each for stories and poems, $15 for book reviews. Contributors also receive 2 copies. Sample copy $2. Free writer's guidelines. "We don't publish straight nonfiction, but we do publish stories based on real events and experiences." Send complete ms. Will accept typewritten and legibly handwritten mss. SASE. Reports in 1 month.
Artwork/Photography: Publishes any type, size or color artwork/photos by children. Pays $8 for b&w illustrations. Contributors receive 2 copies. Sample copy $2. Free illustrator's guidelines. Send originals if possible. SASE. Reports in 1 month. Original artwork returned at job's completion. All artwork must be by children through age 13.

STRAIGHT MAGAZINE, Standard Publishing, 8121 Hamilton Ave., Cincinnati OH 45231. (513)931-4050. Magazine published weekly. Estab. 1951. Magazine includes fiction pieces and articles for Christian teens 13-19 years old to inform, encourage and uplift them. Purpose in publishing works by children: to provide them with an opportunity to express themselves. Children must submit their birth dates and Social Security numbers (if they have one). Writer's guidelines available on request, "included in regular guidelines."
Magazines: 15% of magazine written by children. Uses fiction (500-1,000 words), personal experience pieces (500-700 words), poetry (approx. 1 poem per issue). Pays flat fee for poetry; per word for stories/articles. Submit mss to Carla J. Crane, editor.

Submit complete ms. Will accept typewritten and computer printout mss. Reports in 4-6 weeks.

Artwork/Photography: Publishes artwork by children. Looks for "anything that will fit our format." Pays flat rate. Submit artwork to Carla Crane, editor. Reports in 4-6 weeks.

TEXAS HISTORIAN, Texas State Historical Association, 2/306 Sid Richardson Hall, University Station, Austin TX 78731. (512)471-1525. Articles Editor: David De Boe. Magazine published 4 times a year in February, May, September and November. "The *Texas Historian* is the official publication of the Junior Historians of Texas. Articles accepted for publication must be written by members of the Junior Historians of Texas." **Magazines:** Uses history articles aimed at young adults (about 2500 words). Does not accept unsolicited mss.

THUMBPRINTS, 928 Gibbs St., Caro MI 48723. (517)673-6653. Newsletter published monthly. "Our newsletter is designed to be of interest to writers and allow writers a place to obtain a byline." Purpose in publishing works by children: to encourage them to seek publication. Statement of originality required. Writer's guidelines available on request, "same guidelines as for adults."
Newsletters: Percentage of newsletter written by children "varies from month to month." Pays in copies. Submit ms to Janet Ihle, editor. Submit complete ms or have teacher submit. Will accept typewritten and computer printout mss. Reports in 6-8 weeks.
Artwork/Photography: Publishes artwork by children. Looks for art that expresses our monthly theme. Pays in copies. Send pencil or ink line drawings no larger than 3×4. Submit artwork to Janet Ihle, editor. SASE. Reports in 3 months.
Tips: "We look forward to well written articles and poems by children. It's encouraging to all writers when children write and are published."

TURTLE, Ben Franklin Literary & Medical Society, Children's Better Health Institute, P.O. Box 567, 1100 Waterway Blvd., Indianapolis IN 46206. (317)636-8881. Magazine. "*Turtle* is a health-related magazine geared toward children from ages 2-5." Purpose in publishing works by children: "we enjoy giving children the opportunity to exercise their creativity." Publishes artwork or pictures that children ages 2-5 have drawn or colored all by themselves. Writer's guidelines available on request.
Artwork/Photography: Publishes artwork by children. There is no payment for children's artwork. All artwork must have the child's name, age and complete address on it. Submit artwork to Christine Clark, editorial director. "No artwork can be returned."

*TYKETOON PUBLISHING COMPANY, 7417 Douglas Lane, Fort Worth TX 76180. (817)581-2876. Publishes 8 books/year by children. "We are looking for books written and illustrated by elementary and middle school students. Our audience is the same age readers. We believe authors should write for their own age level." Purpose in publishing works by young people: to provide incentives to write, to publish models of good writing, to use our published books as teaching tools." Must be ages 6-14. Guidelines available for SASE. Publishes all types of fiction and nonfiction. Publishes poetry in book format

---

Market conditions are constantly changing! If you're still using this book and it is 1995 or later, buy the newest edition of Children's Writer's & Illustrator's Market *at your favorite bookstore or order directly from* Writer's Digest Books.

with illustrations—one author's collection of poetry or a collaboration from two or more authors (same grade level). Word length: under 5,000. Pays scholarship check. Submit mss to Ms. Marty Kusmierski, publisher. Submit complete ms with SASE. Will accept typewritten and legibly handwritten mss or any readable format. Reports in 3 months.

VIRGINIA WRITING, Longwood College, 201 High St., Farmville VA 23909. (804)395-2160. Magazine published twice yearly. "*Virginia Writing* publishes prose, poetry, fiction, nonfiction, art, photography, music and drama from Virginia high school students and teachers. The purpose of the journal is to publish 'promise.' The children must be attending a Virginia high school, preferably in no less than 9th grade (though some work has been accepted from 8th graders). Originality is strongly encouraged. The guidelines are also in the front of our magazine." No profanity or racism accepted.
Magazines: 85% of magazine written by children. Uses approximately 5 fiction and nonfiction short stories, 56 poems and prose pieces per issue. Submit mss to Billy C. Clark, founder and editor. Submit complete ms. Will accept typewritten mss. Reports as soon as possible.
Artwork/Photography: Publishes artwork by children. All types of artwork, including that done on computer. Color slides of artwork are acceptable. All original work is returned upon publication in a non-bendable, well protected package. Submit artwork to Billy C. Clark. Reports as soon as possible.
Tips: "All works should be submitted with a cover letter describing student's age, grade and high school currently attending."

VOICES OF YOUTH, Voices of Youth, Inc., P.O. Box 1869, Sonoma CA 95476. (707)938-8314. Publishes 4 magazines/school year of work by high school youths. Purpose in publishing works by young people: to provide a forum for expression and acknowledge ideas and great work of high school students across the country. Our audience is high school students and anyone else interested in what high school students are doing. Must be in grades 9-12 to submit, does not insist upon proof of original work. Writer's guidelines available on request.
Magazines: Uses 40-50 pieces of student writing (length varies) including fiction, nonfiction, poetry and prose per issue. Pays with complimentary copy when article appears. Submit mss to editor. Submit complete ms. Will accept typewritten mss. SASE.
Artwork/Photography: Publishes artwork and photography by children on "any subject of interest to high school students." Prefers b&w. Pays in copies. Send a copy of artwork. Submit art and photos to editor. SASE. Reports in 3-6 weeks.

WHOLE NOTES, P.O. Box 1374, Las Cruces NM 88004. (505)382-7446. Magazine published twice yearly. "We look for original, fresh perceptions in writing poems that demonstrate skill in using language effectively, with carefully chosen images, clear ideas and fresh perceptions. Our audience (general) loves poetry. We try to recognize excellence in creative writing by children as a way to encourage and promote imaginative thinking." Writer's guidelines available for SASE.
Magazines: Every fourth issue is 100% by children. Writers should be 21 years old or less. Uses 30 poems/issue (length open). Pays complimentary copy. Submit mss to Nancy Peters Hastings, editor. Submit complete ms. Will accept typewritten and legibly handwritten mss. SASE. Reports in 3 weeks.
Artwork/Photography: Publishes artwork and photographs by children. Looks for b&w line drawings which can easily be reproduced; b&w photos. Pays complimentary copy. Send clear photocopies. Submit artwork to Nancy Peters Hastings, editor. SASE. Reports in 3 weeks.
Tips: Sample issue is $3.

WOMBAT: A JOURNAL OF YOUNG PEOPLE'S WRITING AND ART, 365 Ashton Dr., Athens GA 30606. (706)549-4875. Published 4 times a year. "Illiteracy in a free society is an unnecessary danger which can and must be remedied. *Wombat*, by being available to young people and their parents and teachers, is one small incentive for young people to put forth the effort to learn to read and write (and draw) better, to communicate better, to comprehend better and—hopefully—consequently, to someday possess greater discernment, judgment and wisdom as a result." Purpose in publishing works by children: to serve as an incentive, to encourage them to work hard at their reading, writing and—yes—drawing/art skills, to reward their efforts. Writers must be ages 6-16, from any geographic region and include a statement that work is original.

Magazines: 95% of magazine written by children. Have one 2-4 page "Guest Adult Article" in most issues/when available (submitted). Uses poetry; any kind of fiction (3,000 words maximum, shorter preferred) but avoid extreme violence, religion or sex (approaching pornography); any kind of nonfiction of interest to 6-16 year olds (3,000-4,000 words); cartoons, puzzles and solutions, jokes and games and solutions. Pays in copies and frameable certificates. Submit mss to Jacquelin Howe, publisher. Submit complete ms. Teacher can submit; parents, librarians, students can submit. Will accept typewritten, legibly handwritten, computer printout mss. Responds in 1-2 weeks with SASE; up to 1 year with seasonal or holiday works (past season or holiday). Written work is not returned. SASE permits *Wombat* to notify sender of receipt of work.

Artwork/Photography: Publishes artwork by children. Looks for works on paper, not canvas. Photocopies OK if clear and/or reworked for clarity and strong line definition by the artist. Pays in copies and frameable certificates. Submit artwork to Jacquelin Howe, publisher. "Artwork, only, will be returned if requested and accompanied by appropriate sized envelope, stamped with sufficient postage."

Tips: *"Wombat* is, unfortunately, on 'hold' probably throughout this entire school year; therefore, we are asking people to please query as to when/if we will resume publication, before subscribing or submitting works to *Wombat* right now."

*WORD DANCE, Playful Productions, Inc., 435R Hartford Turnpike, Vernon CT 06066. (203)870-8614. Magazine. Published quarterly. "We're a magazine of creative writing and art that is for *and* by children in kindergarten through grade 8."

Magazines: Uses adventure, fantasy, humor, etc. (fiction); travel stories and stories based on real life experiences (nonfiction). Publishes 250 total pieces of writing/year; length: 3 pages. Publishes Haiku, free verse and other forms of poetry. Pays on publication. Submit mss to Stuart Ungar, articles editor. Submit complete ms with permission slip. SASE. Reports in 6-8 months.

Artwork/Photography: Illustrations accepted from young people in kindergarten through grade 8. Accepts illustrations of specific stories or poems or other artwork. Must be high contrast. Query. Submit complete package with final art to Karen Rosser, art director. SASE. Reports in 6-8 months.

*WRITERS' OPEN FORUM, P.O. Box 516, Tracyton WA 98393. Magazine published bimonthly. Purpose in publishing works by young people: to assist young writers by publishing stories, articles and essays which are then critiqued by readers. Our international readership offers a wide scope of opinions and helpful tips. Guidelines available on request; same as for adults, however. Please state age in cover letter.

Magazines: Part of each issue is written by children (amount varies). Uses up to 4 fiction short stories, any genre (400-2,000 words); 2 nonfiction articles (500-1,500 words); 2 essays (one 500-1,000 words, one under 500 words)/issue. Pays $5 minimum on acceptance. Submit mss to Sandra E. Haven, editorial director. Submit complete ms with cover letter stating author's age. Will accept typewritten mss. SASE. Reports in 2 months.

THE WRITERS' SLATE, (The Writing Conference, Inc.), P.O. Box 664, Ottawa KS 66067. (913)242-1059. Magazine. Publishes 3 issues/year. *The Writers' Slate* accepts original poetry and prose from students enrolled in Kindergarten-12th grade. The audience is students, teachers and librarians. Purpose in publishing works by young people: to give students the opportunity to publish and to give students the opportunity *to read* quality literature written by other students. Writer's guidelines available on request.
Magazines: 90% of magazine written by young people. Uses 10-15 fiction, 1-2 nonfiction, 10-15 other mss per issue. Submit mss to Carlee N. Vieux, editor, P.O. Box 734, Garden City, KS 67846. Submit complete ms. Will accept typewritten mss. Reports in 1 month.
Artwork/Photography: Publishes artwork by young people. Bold, b&w, student artwork may accompany a piece of writing. Submit to Carlee N. Vieux, editor. Reports in 1 month.

*WRITING, 60 Revere Dr., Northbrook IL 60062. (708)205-3000. Magazine published monthly September-May. Purpose in publishing work by young people: "to teach students to write and write well; grades 7-12. Should indicate age, address, school and teacher with submission. No formal guidelines; but letter is sent if request received."
Magazines: Small percentage of magazine written by children. Uses 1-10 mss/issue. No pay for student writing. Submit mss to Alan Lenhoff, editor. Submit complete ms; include student's age, address, school and teacher with submission; either child or teacher may submit. Prefers typewritten mss. SASE.

YOUNG VOICES MAGAZINE, P.O. Box 2321, Olympia WA 98507. (206)357-4683. Magazine published bimonthly. "*Young Voices* is by elementary and middle school/junior high students for people interested in their work." Purpose in publishing work by young people: to provide a forum for their creative work. Send age, grade and school with submission. "Home schooled writers *definitely* welcome, too." Writer's guidelines available on request.
Magazines: Uses 20 fiction stories, 5 reviews, 5 essays and 20 poems per issue (lengths vary). Pays $3-5 on acceptance (more depending on the length and quality of the writing). Submit mss to Steve Charak, publisher or Char Simons, editor. Submit complete ms. Will accept typewritten and legibly handwritten mss. SASE. Reports in 3 months.
Artwork/Photography: Publishes artwork and photography by children. "Prefer work that will show up in black and white; anything but tanks and horses." Pays $3-5 on acceptance. Submit artwork to Steve Charak or Char Simons. SASE. Reports in 3 months.

Young Writer's & Illustrator's Markets/'93-'94 changes

The following markets are not included in this edition of *Children's Writer's & Illustrator's Market* for the reasons indicated within parentheses. If there is no reason given, it means the market did not respond to our requests for updated information for a 1994 listing.

Chalk Talk Magazine
Children's Album, Kids Creative Fun Magazine (ceased publication)
Essential News for Kids (unable to locate)
The Fun Zone (ceased publication)
The McGuffey Writer
Spark! Creative Fun for Kids
(suspended publication)
Sunshine Magazine (suspended publication)

Contests & Awards

Publication is not the only way to get your work recognized. Contests can also be viable vehicles to gain recognition in the industry. Placing in a contest or winning an award validates the time spent writing and illustrating. Even for those who don't place, many competitions offer the chance to obtain valuable feedback from judges and other established writers or artists.

Not all of the contests here are strictly for professionals. Many are designed for "amateurs" who haven't yet been published. Still others are only open to students. You will find contests for students marked with a double dagger (‡).

When considering contests, be sure to study the guidelines and requirements. Regard entry deadlines as gospel and note whether manuscripts and artwork should be unpublished or previously published. Also, be aware that awards vary. Where one contest may award a significant monetary amount, another may award a certificate or medal instead of money.

You will notice that some contests require nominations. For published authors, competitions provide an excellent way to promote your work. If your book is eligible for a contest or award, have the appropriate people at your publishing company nominate or enter your work for consideration. Then make sure enough copies of your book are sent to the contest judges and any other necessary people affiliated with the competition.

To select potential contests for your work, read through the listings that interest you, then send for more information about the types of written or illustrated material considered and any other details you should know about, such as who retains the rights to prize-winning material.

JANE ADDAMS CHILDREN'S BOOK AWARD, Jane Addams Peace Association, % Judith Volc, 2015 Bluebell, Boulder CO 80302. (303)442-3578. Contest/Award Director: Judith Volc. Annual award. Estab. 1953. Purpose of the award: "The Jane Addams Children's Book Award is presented annually for a book that most effectively promotes the cause of peace, social justice, world community, and the equality of the sexes and all races." Previously published submissions only; year previous to year the award is presented. Deadline for entries: April 1. SASE for contest/award rules and entry forms. No entry fee. Awards a certificate to the author and seals for book jackets to the publisher (at cost). A separate award will be given for a picture book. Judging by a committee of children's librarians and teachers. Works displayed at an award ceremony.

AIM Magazine Short Story Contest, P.O. Box 20554, Chicago IL 60620. (312)874-6184. Contest Directors: Ruth Apilado, Mark Boone. Annual contest. Estab. 1983. Purpose of the contest: "We solicit stories with social significance. Youngsters can be made aware of social problems through the written word and hopefully they will try solving them." Unpublished submissions only. Deadline for entries: August 15. SASE for contest rules and entry forms. SASE for return of work. No entry fee. Awards $100. Judging by editors. Contest open to everyone. Winning entry published in fall issue of *AIM*. Subscription rate $10/year. Single copy $3.50

*‡AMERICA & ME ESSAY CONTEST, Farm Bureau Insurance, Box 30400, 7373 W. Saginaw, Lansing MI 48909. (517)323-7000. Contest Coordinator: Lisa Fedewa. Annual contest. Estab. 1968. Purpose of the contest: to give Michigan 8th graders the opportunity to express their thoughts/feelings on America and their roles in America. Unpublished submissions only. Deadline for entries: mid-November. SASE for contest rules and entry forms. "We have a school mailing list. Any school located in Michigan is eligible to participate." Entries not returned. No entry fee. Awards savings bonds and plaques for state top 10 ($500-1,000), certificates and plaques for top 3 winners from each school. Judging by home office employee volunteers. Requirements for entrants: "Participants must work through their schools or our agents' sponsoring schools. No individual submissions will be accepted. Top 10 essays and excerpts from other essays are published in booklet form following the contest. State capitol/schools receive copies."

*‡AMHAY LITERARY CONTEST, American Morgan Horse Association Youth, P.O. Box 960, Shelburne VT 05482. (802)985-4944. Contest Director: Lisa Peterson. Annual contest. The contest includes categories for both poetry and essays. The 1993 theme was "Morgans and Youth—Breaking the Mold." Entrants should write to receive the 1994 entry form and theme. Unpublished submissions only. Submissions made by author. Deadline for entries: December 1. SASE for contest rules and entry forms. No entry fee. Awards $50 cash and ribbons to up to 5th place. "Winning entry will be published in 'The Morganizer,' a quarterly youth newsletter."

‡ARTS RECOGNITION AND TALENT SEARCH (ARTS), National Foundation for Advancement in the Arts, 3915 Biscayne Blvd., Miami FL 33137. (305)573-0490. Contact: Sherry Thompson. Open to students/high school seniors or 17- and 18-year-olds. Annual award. Estab. 1981. "Created to bring exceptional young artists to a higher plateau of excellence, Arts Recognition and Talent Search (ARTS) is an innovative national program of the National Foundation for Advancement in the Arts (NFAA). ARTS touches the lives of gifted young people across the country, providing financial support, scholarships and goal-oriented artistic, educational and career opportunities. Each year, from a pool of 5,000-7,500 applicants, an average of 250 ARTS awardees are chosen for NFAA support by panels of distinguished artists and educators. Each ARTS applicant, generally a high school senior, has special talent in music, dance, theater, visual arts or creative writing." Submissions made by the student. Deadline for entries: June 1 and October 1 (late). SASE for award rules and entry forms. Entry fee is $25/35 (late) Fee waivers available based on need. Awards $150/$500/$1,500 and $3,000—unrestricted cash grants. Judging by a panel of authors and educators recognized in the field. Rights to submitted/winning material: NFAA/ARTS retains the right to duplicate work in an anthology or in Foundation literature unless otherwise specified by the artist. Works will be published in an anthology distributed during ARTS Week, the final adjudication phase which takes place in Miami.

‡BAKER'S PLAYS HIGH SCHOOL PLAYWRITING CONTEST, Baker's Plays, 100 Chauncy St., Boston MA 02111. (617)482-1280. Contest Director: Raymond Pape. Annual contest. Estab. 1990. Purpose of the contest: "To acknowledge playwrights at the high school level and to insure the future of American Theatre by encouraging and supporting those who are its cornerstone: young playwrights." Unpublished submissions only. Deadline for entries: January 31. SASE for contest rules and entry forms. No entry fee. Awards $500 to the first place playwright and Baker's Plays will publish the play under the Best Plays from the High School Series; $250 to the second place playwright

The double dagger before a listing indicates the contest is for students.

with an honorable mention; and $100 to the third place playwright with an honorable mention in the series. Judged anonymously. Open to any high school student. The first place playwright will have his/her play published in an acting edition the September following the contest. The work will be described in the Baker's Plays Catalogue, which is distributed to 50,000 prospective producing organizations. "Plays must be accompanied by the signature of a sponsoring high school drama or English teacher, and it is recommended that the play receive a production or a public reading prior to the submission. Please include a SASE."

MARGARET BARTLE ANNUAL PLAYWRITING AWARD, Community Children's Theatre of Kansas City, 8021 E. 129th Terrace, Grandview MO 64030. (816)761-5775. Chairperson: Blanche Sellens. Annual contest. Estab. 1947. "Community Children's Theatre of Kansas City, Inc. was organized in 1947 to provide live theater for elementary aged children. We are now recognized as being one of the country's largest organizations providing this type of service." Unpublished submissions only. Deadline for entries: end of January. SASE for award rules and entry forms. SASE for return of entries. No entry fee. Awards $500. Judging by a committee of five. "CCT reserves the right for one of the units to produce the prize winning play for two years. The plays are performed before students in elementary schools. Although our 5- to 12-year-old audiences are sophisticated, gratuitous violence, mature love stories, or slang are not appropriate — cursing is *not acceptable*. In addition to original ideas, subjects that usually provide good plays are legends, folklore, historical incidents, biographies and adaptations of children's classics."

BAY AREA BOOK REVIEWER'S ASSOCIATION (BABRA), % Chandler & Sharp, 11A Commercial Blvd., Novato CA 94949. (415)883-2353. Fax: (415)883-4280. Contact: Jonathan Sharp. Annual award for outstanding book in children's literature, open to Bay Area authors, northern California from Fresno north. Annual award. Estab. 1981. "BABRA presents annual awards to Bay Area (northern California) authors annually in fiction, nonfiction, poetry and children's literature. Purpose is to encourage Bay Area writers and stimulate interest in books and reading." Previously published submissions only. Submissions nominated by publishers; author or agent could also nominate published work. Deadline for entries: December. Send 3 copies of the book to Jonathan Sharp. No entry fee. Awards $100 honorarium and award certificate. Judging by voting members of the Bay Area Book Reviewer's Association. Books that reach the "finals" (usually 3-5 per category) displayed at annual award ceremonies (spring).

THE IRMA S. AND JAMES H. BLACK BOOK AWARD, Bank Street College of Education, 610 W. 112th St., New York NY 10025. (212)222-6700. Contact: Linda Greengrass. Annual award. Estab. 1972. Purpose of the award: "The award is given each spring for a book for young children, published in the previous year, for excellence of both text and illustrations." Entries must have been published during the previous calendar year. Deadline for entries: January 1. "Publishers submit books to us by sending them here to me at the Bank Street library. Authors may ask their publishers to submit their books. Out of these, three to five books are chosen by a committee of older children and adults. These books are then presented to children in selected second, third and fourth grade classes here and at a few other cooperating schools on the East Coast. These children are the final judges who pick the actual award. A scroll (one each for the author and illustrator, if they're different) with the recipient's name and a gold seal designed by Maurice Sendak are awarded in May."

*BOOK OF THE YEAR FOR CHILDREN, Canadian Library Association, Suite 602, 200 Elgin St., Ottawa, Ontario K2P 1L5 Canada. (613)232-9625. Chairperson, Canadian Association of Children's Librarians. Annual award. Estab. 1947. "The main purpose of the award is to encourage writing and publishing in Canada of good books for children up to and including age 14. If, in any year, no book is deemed to be of award calibre, the award shall not be made that year. To merit consideration, the book must have been published in Canada and its author must be a Canadian citizen or a permanent resident of Canada." Previously published submissions only; must be published between January 1 and December 1 of the previous year. Deadline for entries: January 1. SASE for award rules and entry forms. Entries not returned. No entry fee. Awards a medal. Judging by committee of members of the Canadian Association of Children's Librarians. Requirements for entrants: Contest open only to Canadian authors or residents of Canada. Winning books are on display at CLA headquarters.

BOOK PUBLISHERS OF TEXAS, Children's/Young People's Award, The Texas Institute of Letters, P.O. Box 9032, Wichita Falls TX 76308-9032. (817)689-4123. Contact: James Hoggard. Send to above address for list of judges to whom entries should be submitted. Annual award. Purpose of the award: "To recognize notable achievement by a Texas writer of books for children or young people or by a writer whose work deals with a Texas subject. The award goes to the author of the winning book, a work published during the calendar year before the award is given. Judges list available each October. Deadline is first postally operative day of January." Previously published submissions only. SASE for award rules and entry forms. No entry fee. Awards $250. Judging by a panel of three judges selected by the TIL Council. Requirements for entrants: The writer must have lived in Texas for two consecutive years at some time, or the work must have a Texas theme.

THE BOSTON GLOBE-HORN BOOK AWARDS, The Boston Globe & The Horn Book, Inc., The Horn Book, 14 Beacon St., Boston MA 02108. (617)227-1555. Award Directors: Stephanie Loer and Anita Silvey. Writing Contact: Stephanie Loer, children's book editor for *The Boston Globe*, 298 North St., Medfield MA 02052. Annual award. Estab. 1967. "Awards are for picture books, nonfiction and fiction. Up to two honor books may be chosen for each category." Books must be published between July 1, 1993 and June 30, 1994. Deadline for entries: May 15. "Publishers usually nominate books. Award winners receive $500 and silver engraved bowl, honor book winners receive a silver plate." Judging by three judges involved in children's book field who are chosen by Anita Silvey, editor-in-chief for *The Horn Book Magazine* and Stephanie Loer, children's book editor for *The Boston Globe*. "*The Horn Book Magazine* publishes speeches given at awards ceremonies. The book must be available/distributed in the US. The awards are given at the fall conference of the New England Library Association."

*‡ANN ARLYS BOWLER POETRY CONTEST, *Read* Magazine, 245 Long Hill Rd., Middletown CT 06457. (203)638-2406. Contest/Award Director: Kate Davis. Annual contest. Estab. 1988. Purpose of the contest/award: to reward young adult poetry. Unpublished submissions only. Submissions made by the author or nominated by a person or group of people. Must include signature of teacher and parent or guardian. Deadline for entries: December. SASE for contest rules and entry forms. No entry fee. Awards 6 winners $100 each and publication. Judging by *Read* editorial staff. "Entrant understands that prize will include publication, but sometimes pieces are published in other issues. A story may be bought later." Requirements for entrants: the material must be original. Winning entries will be published in the April issue of *Read* (all-student issue).

 The asterisk before a listing indicates the listing is new in this edition.

BUCKEYE CHILDREN'S BOOK AWARD, State Library of Ohio, 65 S. Front St., Columbus OH 43266-0334. (614)644-7061. Nancy Short, Chairperson. Correspondence should be sent to Floyd C. Dickman at the above address. Award every two years. Estab. 1981. Purpose of the award: "The Buckeye Children's Book Award Program was designed to encourage children to read literature critically, to promote teacher and librarian involvement in children's literature programs, and to commend authors of such literature, as well as to promote the use of libraries. Awards are presented in the following three categories: grades K-2, grades 3-5 and grades 6-8." Previously published submissions only. Deadline for entries: February 1. "The nominees are submitted by this date during the even year and the votes are submitted by this date during the odd year. This award is nominated and voted upon by children in Ohio. It is based upon criteria established in our bylaws. The winning authors are awarded a special plaque honoring them at a banquet given by one of the sponsoring organizations. The BCBA Board oversees the tallying of the votes and announces the winners in March of the voting year in a special news release and in a number of national journals. The book must have been written by an author, a citizen of the United States and originally copyrighted in the US within the last three years preceding the nomination year. The award-winning books are displayed in a historical display housed at the Columbus Metropolitan Library in Columbus, Ohio."

‡BYLINE MAGAZINE STUDENT PAGE, P.O. Box 130596, Edmond OK 73013. (405)348-5591. Contest Director: Marcia Preston, publisher. Estab. 1981. "We offer student writing contests on a monthly basis, September through June, with cash prizes and publication of top entries." Previously unpublished submissions only. Deadline for entries varies. "Entry fee usually $1." Awards cash and publication. Judging by qualified editors and writers. "We publish top entries in student contests. Winners' list published in magazine dated 3 months past deadline." Send SASE for details.

CALDECOTT AWARD, Association for Library Service to Children, Division of the American Library Association, 50 E. Huron, Chicago IL 60611. (312)280-2163. Executive Director ALSC: Susan Roman. Annual award. Estab. 1938. Purpose of the award: to honor the artist of the most distinguished picture book for children published in the US (Illustrator must be US citizen or resident.) Must be published year preceding award. Deadline for entries: December. SASE for contest/award rules and entry forms. Entries not returned. No entry fee. "Medal given at ALA Annual Conference during the Newbery/Caldecott Banquet."

CALIFORNIA BOOK AWARDS, The Commonwealth Club of California, 595 Market St., San Francisco CA 94105. (415)597-6700. Directors: James L. Coplan and Annie Hayflick. Annual award. Estab. 1931. Purpose of the award: to promote "the encouragement and production of literature in California." Previously published submissions only. Submissions made by the author or the author's agent. Must be published between January and December of the previous year. Deadline for entries: January 31. SASE for award rules. No entry fee. Award is presentation of a medal. Judging by club jury members, comprised of men and women prominent in academia and other areas related to writing. Illustration is judged in conjunction with prose. Announcement of winners published in Club newsletter. Works displayed at award ceremony.

CALIFORNIA WRITERS' CONFERENCE AWARDS, California Writers' Club, 2214 Derby St., Berkeley CA 94705. (510)841-1217. "Ask for contest rules before submitting entries." Award offered every two years. Next conference, July 1995. Purpose of the award: "To encourage writers." Categories: adult short stories, adult novels, adult nonfiction, juvenile fiction, poetry and scripts. Unpublished submissions only. SASE for contest/award rules and entry forms. SASE for return of entries. Fee possible, but not yet determined. Awards cash prizes and certificates in all categories. Judging by "published writer-members of California Writers' Club. Open to all."

‡CALIFORNIA YOUNG PLAYWRIGHTS CONTEST, Playwrights Project, Suite 215, 1450 Frazee Rd., San Diego CA 92108. (619)298-9242. Director: Deborah Salzer. Open to Californians under age 19. Annual contest. Estab. 1985. "Our organization, and the contest, are designed to nurture promising young writers. We hope to develop playwrights and audiences for live theater. We also teach playwriting." Submissions required to be unpublished and not produced professionally. Submissions made by the author. Deadline for entries: usually April 1. "Call for exact date." SASE for contest rules and entry form. No entry fee. Award is professional productions of 3-5 short plays each year, participation of the writers in the entire production process, with a royalty award of $100 per play. Judging by professionals in the theater community, a committee of 5-7; changes somewhat each year. Works performed "in San Diego at the Cassius Carter Centre Stage of the Old Globe Theatre. Writers submitting scripts of 10 or more pages may receive a detailed script evaluation letter if requested."

*CANADA COUNCIL GOVERNOR GENERAL'S LITERARY AWARDS, P.O. Box 1047, 99 Metcalfe St., Ottawa, Ontario K1P 5V8 Canada. (613)598-4376. Officer, Writing and Publishing Section: Josiane Polidori. Annual award. Estab. 1937. Purpose of award: to encourage Canadian authors and illustrators of books for young people as well as to recognize the importance of their contribution to literary activity. Award categories include children's text and children's illustration. Must be published between October 1 and September 30. Eligible books are submitted by publishers (3 copies must be sent to Canada Council). All entries (books or bound galleys) must be received by August 31. (If the submission is in the form of a bound galley, the actual book must be published and received at the Canada Council no later than September 30.) Submission forms available on request. Entries not returned. No entry fee. Awards $10,000 (Canadian). Judging by practicing writers, illustrators or critics. Contest open to Canadian writers and illustrators only.

*‡CHICKADEE COVER CONTEST, Chickadee Magazine, Suite 306, 56 The Esplanade, Toronto, Ontario M5E 1A7 Canada. (416)868-6001. Contest Director: Mitch Butler, Chirp Editor. Annual contest. There is a different theme published each year. The 1993 contest asked readers to send a drawing of an animal "you'd like to be for a day." Unpublished submissions only. Submissions are submitted by readers. Deadline for entries: November. Announcement published each October issue. No entry fee. Winning drawing published on cover of February issue. Judging by staff of *Chickadee*. Requirements for entrants: Must be 3- to 9-year-old readers.

*‡CHICKADEE'S GARDEN EVENT, Chickadee Magazine, Suite 306, 56 The Esplanade, Toronto, Ontario M5E 1A7 Canada. (416)868-6001. Contest/Award Director: Mitch Butler, Chirp Editor. Annual. *Chickadee* readers are asked "to grow a favorite fruit or vegetable (anything as long as you can eat it) and submit a photo or drawing of you and your plant, and tell us why you chose the plant you did, and who helped you to care for it." Unpublished submissions only. Deadline for entries: September. Announcement published in January issue. Judging by staff of *Chickadee*. Requirements for entrants: Must be 3- to 9-year-old readers.

CHILDREN'S BOOK AWARD, Federation of Children's Book Groups, 30 Senneleys Park Rd., Northfield Birmingham B31 1AL England. (021)427-4860. Coordinator: Jenny Blanch. Purpose of the contest/award: "The C.B.A. is an annual prize for the best children's book of the year judged by the children themselves." Categories: (I) picture books, (II) short novels, (III) longer novels. Estab. 1980. Previously unpublished submissions only. Deadline for entries: December 31. SASE for contest rules and entry forms. Entries not returned. Awards "a magnificent silver and oak trophy worth over $6,000 and a portfolio of children's work." Silver dishes to each category winner. Judging by children. Requirements for entrants: Work must be fiction and published during the current year (poetry is ineligible). Work will be published in our current "Pick of the Year" publication.

CHILDREN'S READING ROUND TABLE AWARD, Children's Reading Round Table of Chicago, #1507, 3930 N. Pine Grove, Chicago IL 60613. (312)477-2271. Annual award. Estab. 1953. "Annual award to individual who has made outstanding contributions to children's books. Individual is nominated by membership, and selected by a committee from the membership, and finalized by a special committee of members, as well as nonmembers of CRRT." Awards a recognition certificate and stipend of $250. Award recipients have been authors, editors, educators and illustrators. "Note that our award recognizes *contributions* to children's literature. This includes people who are neither writers nor illustrators."

*CHILDREN'S WRITER WRITING CONTESTS, 95 Long Ridge Rd., West Redding CT 06896. (203)792-8600. Contest offered every 4 months. Purpose of the contest/award: To promote higher quality children's literature. "Each contest has its own theme. Our last three were: (1) A nonfiction treatment of any subject in any form appropriate for a 4- to 6-year-old. 400 words. (2) A contemporary story on any subject for 6- to 8-year-olds. 500 words. (3) A profile of an interesting person for 8- to 10-year-olds. The article may profile someone well-known or unknown, contemporary or historical, but will be judged on interest, factual accuracy, age appropriateness, use of research and quality of writing." Unpublished submissions only. Submissions made by the author. Deadline for entries: Last Friday in February, June and October. "We charge a $10 entry fee for non-subscribers only, which is applicable against a subscription to *Children's Writer*." Awards 1st place—$100, a certificate and publication in *Children's Writer*; 2nd place—$50 and certificate; 3rd-5th places—$25 and certificates. Judging by a panel of five selected from the staff of the Institute of Children's Literature. "We acquire First North American Serial Rights (to print the winner in *Children's Writer*), after which all rights revert to author." Open to any writer. Entries are judged on age targeting, originality, quality of writing and, for nonfiction, how well the information is conveyed and accuracy. "Submit clear photocopies only, not originals; submission will *not* be returned. Manuscripts should be typed double-spaced. No pieces containing violence or derogatory, racist or sexist language or situations will be accepted, at the sole discretion of the judges."

THE CHRISTOPHER AWARD, The Christophers, 12 E. 48th St., New York NY 10017. (212)759-4050. Christopher Awards Coordinator: Peggy Flanagan. Annual award. Estab. 1969 (for young people; books for adults honored since 1949). "The award is given to works, published in the calendar year for which the award is given, that have achieved artistic excellence, affirming the highest values of the human spirit. They must also enjoy a reasonable degree of popular acceptance." Previously published submissions only; must be published between January 1 and December 31. "Books should be submitted all year." Entries not returned. No entry fee. Awards a bronze medallion. Books are judged by both reading specialists and young people. Requirements for entrants: "only published works are eligible and must be submitted during the calendar year in which they are first published."

CITY OF FOSTER CITY WRITERS' CONTEST, Foster City Arts and Culture Committee, 650 Shell Blvd., Foster City CA 94404-2501. Chairman: John Hauer. Annual contest. Estab. 1974. Contest open to all writers—no age or geographic limit. Categories include

Best Story for Children—2,000 word limit. Unpublished submissions only. Submissions made by the author. "Include a 3×5 card with your name, address, phone number, manuscript title and category written in the upper left hand corner. Your manuscript must be typed, double-spaced on white 8½×11 paper with the pages numbered at the top right corner. Your name should not appear on your manuscript; judging is done blind. No illustrated manuscripts." SASE for contest rules and entry form. Entry fee $10/entry. Awards $250 in each category. Judging by Peninsula Press Club—California.

*CHRISTOPHER COLUMBUS SCREENPLAY DISCOVERY AWARDS, Christopher Columbus Society of the Creative Arts, #600, 433 N. Camden Dr., Beverly Hills CA 90210. (310)288-1988. Contest/Award Director: Mr. Carlos Abreu. Annual and monthly awards. Estab. 1990. Purpose of contest/award: To discover new screenplay writers. Unpublished submissions only. Submissions are made by the author or author's agent. Deadline for entries: November 1st and monthly (last day of month). Entry fee is $45. Awards: 1. Feedback—development process with industry experts. 2. Financial rewards—option moneys up to $10,000. 3. Access to key decision makers. Judging by entertainment industry experts, producers and executives.

THE COMMONWEALTH CLUB'S BOOK AWARDS CONTEST, The Commonwealth Club of California, 595 Market St., San Francisco CA 94105. (415)597-6700. Executive Director: James D. Rosenthal. Annual contest. Estab. 1932. Purpose of the contest is the encouragement and production of literature in California. Juvenile category included. Previously published submission; must be published from January 1 to December 31. Deadline for entries: January 31. SASE for contest rules and entry forms. No entry fee. Awards gold and silver medals. Judging by the Book Awards Jury. The contest is only open to California writers/illustrators. "The award winners will be honored at the Annual Book Awards Program."

‡CRICKET LEAGUE, *Cricket*, the Magazine for Children, 315 Fifth St., Peru IL 61354. (815)224-6643. Monthly. Estab. 1973. "The purpose of Cricket League contests is to encourage creativity and give children an opportunity to express themselves in writing, drawing, painting or photography. There are two contests each month. Possible categories include story, poetry, art or photography. Each contest relates to a *specific theme* described on each *Cricket* issue's Cricket League page. Entries which do not relate to the current month's theme cannot be considered." Unpublished submissions only. Deadline for entries: the 25th of each month. Cricket League rules, contest themes and submission deadline information can be found in the current issue of *Cricket*. "We prefer that children who enter the contests subscribe to the magazine, or that they read *Cricket* in their school or library." No entry fee. Awards certificate suitable for framing and children's books or art/writing supplies. Judging by *Cricket* Editors. Obtains right to print prize-winning entries in magazine. Requirements for entrants: Must be 14 or younger. Restrictions of mediums for illustrators: Usually artwork must be b&w only. Refer to contest rules in current *Cricket* issue. Winning entries are published on the Cricket League pages in the *Cricket* magazine 3 months subsequent to the issue in which the contest was announced.

MARGUERITE DE ANGELI PRIZE, Bantam Doubleday Dell Books for Young Readers, 1450 Broadway, New York NY 10036. Estab. 1992. Annual Award. Purpose of the award: To encourage the writing of fiction for children that examines the diversity of the American experience in the same spirit as the works of Marguerite de Angeli; to encourage unpublished writers in the field of middle grade fiction. Unpublished submissions only. Submissions made by author or author's agent. Deadline for entries: October 29. SASE for award rules and entry forms. No entry fee. Awards a $1,500 cash prize plus a hardcover and paperback book contract with a $3,500 advance against a royalty to be negotiated. Judging by Bantam Doubleday Dell Books for Young Readers editorial staff. Open to US and Canadian writers who have not previously published a novel for middle-grade readers. Works published in an upcoming Bantam Doubleday Dell Books for Young Readers list.

DELACORTE PRESS PRIZE FOR A FIRST YOUNG ADULT NOVEL, Delacorte Press, Books for Young Readers Department, 1540 Broadway, New York NY 10036. (212)354-6500. Annual award. Estab. 1982. Purpose of the award: To encourage the writing of contemporary young adult fiction. Previously unpublished submissions only. Mss sent to Delacorte Press may not be submitted to other publishers while under consideration for the prize. "Entries must be submitted between Labor Day and New Year's Day of the year following publication. The real deadline is a December 31 postmark. Early entries are appreciated." SASE for award rules. No entry fee. Awards a $1,500 cash prize and a $6,000 advance against royalties on a hardcover and paperback book contract. Judged by the editors of the Books for Young Readers Department of Delacorte Press. Rights acquired "only if the entry wins or is awarded an Honorable Mention." Requirements for entrants: The writer must be American or Canadian and must *not* have previously published a young adult novel. He may have published anything else. "Books (manuscripts) should have a contemporary setting and be suitable for ages 12-18, and be between 100 and 224 pages long. *Summaries are urgently requested.*"

VIOLET DOWNEY BOOK AWARD, National Chapter of Canada IODE, Suite 254, 40 Orchard View Blvd., Toronto, Ontario M5R 1B9 Canada. (416)487-4416. Award Director: Helen Dick. Annual award. Estab. 1985. Purpose of the award: To name the best children's book, by a Canadian, published in Canada for ages 5-13, over 500 words. Previously published submissions only. Submissions made by author, author's agent; anyone may submit. Must have been published during previous calendar year. Deadline for entries: January 31. SASE for award rules and entry forms. No entry fee. Awards $3,000. Judging by a panel of six, four IODE members and two professionals.

DREXEL CITATION, Drexel University, College of Information Studies, Philadelphia PA 19104. (215)895-2447. Director: Shelley G. McNamara. Annual award. Purpose of the award: "The Drexel citation is an award that was established in 1963 and has been given at irregular intervals since that time to honor Philadelphia authors, illustrators, publishers or others who have made outstanding contributions to literature for children in Philadelphia. The award is co-sponsored by The Free Library of Philadelphia. The recipient is selected by a committee representing both the College of Information Studies and The Free Library of Philadelphia. There is only one recipient at any given time and that recipient is recognized at an annual conference on children's literature presented each year in the spring on the Drexel campus. The recipient receives an individually designed and hand-lettered citation at a special award luncheon during the conference."

SHUBERT FENDRICH MEMORIAL PLAYWRIGHTING CONTEST, Pioneer Drama Service, Inc., P.O. Box 22555, Denver CO 80222. (303)759-4297. Director: Steven Fendrich. Annual contest. Estab. 1990. Purpose of the contest: "To encourage the development of quality theatrical material for educational and community theater." Previously unpublished submissions only. Deadline for entries: March 1st. SASE for contest rules and entry forms. No entry fee. Awards $1,000 royalty advance and publication. Judging by Editors. All rights acquired when work is published. Restrictions for entrants: Any writers currently published by Pioneer Drama Service are not eligible.

*CAROLYN W. FIELD AWARD, Pennsylvania Library Association, 1919 N. Front St., Harrisburg PA 17102. (717)233-3113. Executive Director: Margaret S. Bauer, CAE. Annual award. Estab. 1983. Purpose of the award: "To honor outstanding Pennsylvania children's authors/illustrators." Previously published submissions only; must be published January-December of year of award." Deadline for entries: March 1. SASE for contest rules and entry forms. SASE for return of entries. No entry fee. Awards a medal and citation and holds a luncheon honoring award winner. Judging by "children's librarians." Requirements for entrants: "Writer/illustrator must be a Pennsylvania resident." Works displayed at PLA annual conference each fall.

DOROTHY CANFIELD FISHER CHILDREN'S BOOK AWARD, Vermont Department of Libraries, Vermont State PTA and Vermont Congress of Parents and Teachers, % Southwest Regional Library, Pierpoint Ave., Rutland VT 05701. (802)773-5879. Chairman (currently): Barbara Ellingson. Annual award. Estab. 1957. Purpose of the award: to encourage Vermont children to become enthusiastic and discriminating readers by providing them with books of good quality. Previously published entries are not eligible. Deadline for entries: "January of the following year." SASE for award rules and entry forms. No entry fee. Awards a scroll presented to the winning author at an award ceremony. Judging is by the children grades 4-8. They vote for their favorite book. Requirements for entrants: "The book must be copyrighted in the current year. It must be written by an American author living in the U.S."

‡FLORIDA STATE WRITING COMPETITION, Florida Freelance Writers Assoc., Maple Ridge Rd., North Sandwich NH 03259. (603)284-6367. Juvenile Chairman: Jean Pollack. Annual contest. Estab. 1984. Picture Books/under 6-year-old readers: 400 words maximum. Short Fiction: all age groups judged together/ages 7-10—400-900 words; ages 12 and up—2,000 words maximum. Previously published category new for 1994. Book Chapter, fiction or nonfiction: ages 7-10—1,000 words maximum; ages 12 and up—3,000 words maximum. Entry fee is $5 (members), $7 (non-members). Awards $100 first prize, certificates for second through fifth prizes. Judging by teachers, editors and published authors. Judging criteria: Interest and readability within age group, writing style and mechanics, originality, salability. Deadline: March 15. For copy of official entry form, send #10 SASE.

‡4-H ESSAY CONTEST, American Beekeeping Federation, Inc., P.O. Box 1038, Jesup GA 31545. (912)427-8447. Contest Director: Troy H. Fore. Annual contest. Purpose of contest: To award the best essay discussing "Products of the Hive and Their Uses." Unpublished submissions only. Deadline for entries: before March 1. No entry fee. Awards 1st place: $250; 2nd place: $100; 3rd place: $50. Judging by American Beekeeping Federation's Essay Committee. "All National entries become the property of the American Beekeeping Federation, Inc., and may be published or used as it sees fit. No essay will be returned. Essayists *should not* forward essays directly to the American Beekeeping Federation office. Each state 4-H office is responsible for selecting the state's winner and should set its deadline so state judging can be completed at the state level in time for the winning state essay to be mailed to the ABF office before March 1, 1994. The National Winner will announced by May 1, 1994."

DON FREEMAN MEMORIAL GRANT-IN-AID, Society of Children's Book Writers and Illustrators, #106, 22736 Vanowen St., West Hills CA 91307. (818)888-8760. Estab. 1974. Purpose of award: to "enable picture book artists to further their understanding, training and work in the picture book genre."Applications and prepared materials will be accepted between January 15 and February 15. Grant awarded and announced on June 15. SASE for award rules and entry forms. SASE for return of entries. No entry fee. Annually awards one grant of $1,000 and one runner-up grant of $500. "The Grant-

In-Aid is available to both full and associate members of the SCBWI who, as artists, seriously intend to make picture books their chief contribution to the field of children's literature."

GOLD MEDALLION BOOK AWARDS, Evangelical Christian Publishers Association, Suite 101, 3225 S. Hardy Dr., Tempe AZ 85282. (602)966-3998. Fax: (602)966-1944. Director: Doug Ross. Annual contest/award. Estab. 1978. Categories include Preschool Children's Books, Elementary Children's Books, Youth Books. "All entries must be evangelical in nature and cannot be contrary to ECPA's Statement of Faith (stated in official rules)." Deadlines for entries: December 1. SASE for contest/award rules and entry form. "The work must be submitted by the publisher." Entry fee is $250 for non-members. Awards a Gold Medallion plaque.

GOLDEN KITE AWARDS, Society of Children's Book Writers and Illustrators, #106, 22736 Vanowen St., West Hills CA 91307. (818)888-8760. Coordinator: Sue Alexander. Annual award. Estab. 1973. "The works chosen will be those that the judges feel exhibit excellence in writing, and in the case of the picture-illustrated books—in illustration, and genuinely appeal to the interests and concerns of children. For the fiction and nonfiction awards, original works and single-author collections of stories or poems of which at least half are new and never before published in book form are eligible—anthologies and translations are not. For the picture-illustration awards, the art or photographs must be original works (the texts—which may be fiction or nonfiction—may be original, public domain or previously published). Deadline for entries: December 15. SASE for award rules. Self-addressed mailing label for return of entries. No entry fee. Awards statuettes and plaques. The panel of judges will consist of two children's book authors, a children's book artist or photographer (who may or may not be an author), a children's book editor and a librarian." Requirements for entrants: "Must be a member of SCBWI." Winning books will be displayed at national conference in August. Books to be entered, as well as further inquiries, should be submitted to: The Society of Children's Book Writers and Illustrators, above address.

HIGHLIGHTS FOR CHILDREN FICTION CONTEST, 803 Church St., Honesdale PA 18431. (717)253-1080. Mss should be addressed to Fiction Contest. Editor: Kent L. Brown Jr. Annual contest. Estab. 1980. Purpose of the contest: to stimulate interest in writing for children and reward and recognize excellence. Unpublished submissions only. Deadline for entries: February 28; entries accepted after January 1 only. SASE for contest rules. SASE for return of entries. No entry fee. Awards 3 prizes of $1,000 each in cash (or, at the winner's election, attendance at the Highlights Foundation Writers Workshop at Chautauqua). Judging by *Highlights* editors. Winning pieces are purchased for the cash prize of $1,000 and published in *Highlights*. Requirements for entrants: contest open to any writer. Winners announced in June. "This year's contest is for action/adventure stories for children. Length up to 900 words. Stories for beginning readers should not exceed 500 words. Stories should be consistent with *Highlights* editorial requirements. No violence, war, crime or derogatory humor."

‡HOOT AWARDS, WRITING CONTEST, PHOTO CONTEST, POETRY CONTEST, COVER CONTEST, *Owl Magazine,* 56 The Esplanade, Toronto, Ontario M4V 1G2 Canada. (416)868-6001. Annual contest. Purpose of contest: "to encourage children to contribute and participate in the magazine. The Hoot Awards recognize excellence in an individual or group effort to help the environment." Unpublished submissions only. Deadlines change yearly. Prizes/awards "change every year. Often we give books as prizes." Winning entries published in the magazine. Judging by art and editorial staff. Entries become the property of the Young Naturalist Foundation (*Owl Magazine*). "The contests and awards are open to children up to 14 years of age."

AMELIA FRANCES HOWARD-GIBBON MEDAL, Canadian Library Association, Suite 602, 200 Elgin St., Ottawa, Ontario K2P 1L5 Canada. (613)232-9625. Contact: Chairperson, Canadian Association of Children's Librarians. Annual award. Estab. 1971. Purpose of the award: "To honor excellence in the illustration of children's book(s) in Canada. To merit consideration the book must have been published in Canada and its illustrator must be a Canadian citizen or a permanent resident of Canada." Previously published submissions only; must be published between January 1 and December 31 of the previous year. Deadline for entries: February 1. SASE for award rules and entry forms. Entries not returned. No entry fee. Awards a medal. Judging by selection committee of members of Canadian Association of Children's Librarians. Requirements for entrants: illustrator must be Canadian or Canadian resident. Winning books are on display at CLA Headquarters.

INDIAN PAINTBRUSH BOOK AWARD, Wyoming Library Association, P.O. Box 1387, Cheyenne WY 82003. (307)632-7622. Award Director: Laura Grott. Annual award. Estab. 1986. Purpose of award: to encourage the children of Wyoming to read good books. Previously published submissions only. Deadline for entries: April 1. Books can only be submitted for the nominations list by the children of Wyoming. No entry fee. Awards a watercolor painting. Judging by the children of Wyoming (grades 4-6) voting from a nominations list of 20. Requirements for entrants: only Wyoming children may nominate; books must be published in last 5 years, be fiction, have good reviews; final list chosen by a committee of librarians.

INTERNATIONAL READING ASSOCIATION CHILDREN'S BOOK AWARD, 3203 Buffalo Run Rd., Bellefonte PA 16823. Annual award. "The IRA Children's Book Awards will be given for a first or second book, either fiction or nonfiction, in 2 categories (younger readers: ages 4-10; older readers: ages 10-16 +) to 2 authors who show unusual promise in the children's book field." To submit a book for consideration, send 10 copies to: Mary Dupuis, above address. Must be published during the calendar year. Deadline for entries: December 1 of each year. SASE for award rules and entry forms. Awards a $1,000 stipend and a medal. Award is presented each year at annual convention.

IOWA CHILDREN'S CHOICE AWARD, Iowa Educational Media Association, 106 Lord Ave., Muscatine IA 52761. (319)262-8219. Chair: Beth Elshoff. Annual award. Estab. 1979. Purpose of the award: to encourage children to read more and better books; to provide an avenue for positive dialogue between teacher, parent and children about books and authors; to give recognition to those who write books for children. "Writers and illustrators *do not 'enter'* their works themselves. A committee of teachers, librarians and students choose the books that are on the list each year. The list is narrowed down to 20-25 books based on set criteria." The award is unique in that it gives children an opportunity to choose the book to receive the award and to suggest books for the yearly reading list. Deadline for entries: February 15. "Students in grades 3-6 throughout Iowa nominate." Awards a brass-plated school bell. Judging by "students in grades 3-6 throughout Iowa."

IOWA TEEN AWARD, Iowa Educational Media Association, 306 E. H Ave., Grundy Center IA 50638. (319)824-6788. Contest Director: Don Osterhaus. Annual award. Estab. 1983. Previously published submissions only. Purpose of award: to allow students to read high quality literature and to have opportunity to select their favorite from this list. Must have been published "in last 3-4 years." Deadline for entries: August 1. SASE for award rules/entry forms. No entry fee. "Media specialists, teachers and students nominate possible entries." Awards a brass apple. Judging by Iowa students in 6-9th grades. Requirements: Work must be of recent publication, so copies can be ordered for media center collections and to be nominated by media specialists on a scale of 1-5. Works displayed "at participating schools in Iowa."

IUPUI YOUTH THEATRE PLAYWRITING COMPETITION AND SYMPOSIUM, Indiana University-Purdue University at Indianapolis, 525 N. Blackford St., Indianapolis IN 46202. (317)274-2095. Director: Dorothy Webb. Entries should be submitted to W. Mark McCreary, Literary Manager. Contest every two years. Estab. 1983. Purpose of the contest: "To encourage writers to create artistic scripts for young audiences. It provides a forum through which each playwright receives constructive criticism of his/her work and, where selected, writers participate in script development with the help of professional dramaturgs, directors and actors." Unpublished submissions only. Submissions made by author. Deadline for entries: September 1. SASE for contest rules and entry forms. No entry fee. "Awards will be presented to the top ten finalists. Four cash awards of $1,000 each will be received by the top four playwrights of whose scripts will be given developmental work culminating in polished readings showcased at the symposium held on the IUPUI campus. Major publishers of scripts for young audiences, directors, producers, critics and teachers attend this symposium and provide useful reactions to the plays. If a winner is unable to be involved in preparation of the reading and to attend the showcase of his/her work, the prize will not be awarded. Remaining finalists will receive certificates." Judging by professional directors, dramaturgs, publishers, university professors. Write for guidelines and entry form.

*‡KENTUCKY STATE POETRY SOCIETY ANNUAL CONTEST, Kentucky State Poetry Society, 5018 Wabash Place, Louisville KY 40214. (502)366-8900. Contest Director: Miriam Woolfolk. Annual contest. Estab. 1966. Unpublished submissions only. Deadline for entries: July 10. SASE for contest rules and entry forms. Categories 2-6 are free, all others $1. $5 for grand prix. Awards certificates of merit and cash prizes from $1 to $100. Sponsors pick judges. "One-time printing rights acquired for publication of first prizes in *Pegasus*, our annual journal." Contest open to all. "No illustrations, please." "First place winners will be published in *Pegasus* and all other winners will be displayed at our annual awards banquet."

KERLAN AWARD, Kerlan Collection, 109 Walter Library, 117 Pleasant St. SE, University of Minnesota, Minneapolis MN 55455. (612)624-4576. Curator: Karen Nelson Hoyle. Annual award. Estab. 1975. "Given in recognition of singular attainments in the creation of children's literature and in appreciation for generous donation of unique resources to the Kerlan Collection." Previously published submissions only. Deadline for entries: November 1. Anyone can send nominations for the award, directed to the Kerlan Collection. No materials are submitted other than the person's name. No entry fee. Award is a laminated plaque. Judging by the Kerlan Award Committee—three representatives from the University of Minnesota faculty (from the College of Education, the College of Human Ecology and the College of Liberal Arts); one representative from the Kerlan Collection (ex officio); one representative from the Kerlan Friends; one representative from the Minnesota Library Association. Requirements for entrants: open to all who are nominated. Anyone can submit names. "For serious consideration, entrant must be a published author and/or illustrator of children's books (including young adult fiction) and have donated original materials to the Kerlan Collection."

CORETTA SCOTT KING AWARD, Coretta Scott King Task Force, Social Responsibility Round Table, American Library Association, 50 E. Huron St., Chicago IL 60611. "The Coretta Scott King Award is an annual award for a book (one for text and one for illustration) that conveys the spirit of brotherhood espoused by M.L. King, Jr.—and also speaks to the Black experience—for young people. There is an award jury that judges the books—reviewing over the year—and making a decision in January. A copy of an entry must be sent to each juror. Acquire jury list from SRRT office in Chicago."

JANUSZ KORCZAK AWARDS, Joseph H. and Belle R. Braun Center for Holocaust Studies, Anti-Defamation League, 823 United Nations Plaza, New York NY 10017. (212)490-2525. Fax: (212)867-0779. Award Director: Dr. Dennis B. Klein. Contest/ award usually offered every two years. Estab. 1980. Purpose of award: "The award honors books about children which best exemplify Janusz Korczak's principles of self-lessness and human dignity." Previously published submissions only; for 1994, books must have been published in 1992 or 1993. SASE for award rules and entry forms. No entry fee. Awards $1,000 cash and plaque (first prize); plaque (Honorable Mention). Judging by an interdisciplinary committee of leading scholars, editors, literary critics and educators. Requirements for entrants: Books must meet entry requirements and must be published in English. No entries are returned. They become the property of the Braun Center. Press release will announce winners.

LANDERS THEATRE CHILDREN'S PLAYWRITING AWARD, Landers Theatre, 311 E. Walnut, Springfield MO 65806. (417)869-3869. Contact: Mick Denniston. Award offered every two years. Estab. 1992. Purpose of the award: to produce full-fledged mainstage production of new musicals for young audiences. Unpublished submissions only. Submissions made by the author. Deadline for entries: November 1, 1994. SASE for award rules and entry forms. No entry fee. Awards $5,000 plus full production. Judging by theater artistic staff and panel. Winning play performed in a Spring, 1995 production.

‡ELIAS LIEBERMAN STUDENT POETRY AWARD, Poetry Society of America, 15 Gramercy Park, New York NY 10003. (212)254-9628. Award Director: Elise Paschen. Annual award. Purpose of the award: To honor the best unpublished poem by a high or preparatory school student (grades 9-12) from the US and its territories. Unpublished submissions only. Deadline for entries: December 22. SASE for award rules and entry forms. Entries not returned. No entry fee. Award: $100. Judging by a professional poet. Requirements for entrants: Contest open to all high school and preparatory students from the US and its territories. School attended, as well as name and address, should be noted. Line limit: none. "The award-winning poem will be included in a sheaf of poems that will be part of the program at the award ceremony, and sent to all PSA members."

MAGAZINE MERIT AWARDS, Society of Children's Book Writers and Illustrators, #233, 4912 Verdugo Way, Camarillo CA 93012. (805)646-4337. Award Coordinator: Dorothy Leon. Annual award. Estab. 1988. Purpose of the award: "To recognize outstanding original magazine work for young people published during that year and having been written or illustrated by members of SCBWI." Previously published submissions only. Entries must be submitted between January 31 and December 15 of the year of publication. SASE for award rules and entry forms. No entry fee. Must be a SCBWI member. Awards plaques and honor certificates for each of the three categories. Judging by a magazine editor and two "full" SCBWI members. "Every magazine work for young people by an SCBWI member—writer, artist or photographer—is eligible during the year of original publication. In the case of co-authored work, both authors must be

SCBWI members. Members must submit their own work." Requirements for entrants: 4 copies each of the published work and proof of publication (may be contents page) showing the name of the magazine and the date of issue. Brochures may be obtained by writing to the address above. The SCBWI is a professional organization of writers and illustrators and others interested in children's literature. Membership is open to the general public at large.

‡MANNINGHAM POETRY TRUST STUDENT CONTESTS, National Federation of State Poetry Societies, Inc., Box 607, Green Cove Springs FL 32043. (904)284-0505. Chairman: Robert E. Dewitt. Estab. 1980. Two separate contests are held each year: grades 6-8; grades 9-12. Poems may have been printed and may have won previous awards. Deadline for entries: April 9, 1994. Submit one poem neatly typed on standard typewriter paper. Submit one original and one copy. On copy only, type: (1) name (2) complete home mailing address (3) school (4) grade. Awards $50, 1st place; $30, 2nd place; $20, 3rd place; and five honorable mentions of $5 each. Winners will be announced at the 1994 NFSPS convention, and checks will be mailed shortly beforehand. Send SASE if you wish to receive a winner's list.

VICKY METCALF BODY OF WORK AWARD, Canadian Authors Association, Suite 500, 275 Slater St., Ottawa, Ontario K1P 5H9 Canada. (613)233-2846. Fax: (613)235-8237. Attn: Awards Chair. Annual award. Estab. 1963. Purpose: to honor a body of work inspirational to Canadian youth. Deadline for entries: December 31. SASE for award rules and entry forms. Entries not returned. No entry fee. Awards $10,000 and certificate. Judging by panel of CAA-appointed judges including past winners. "The prizes are given solely to stimulate writing for children by Canadian writers," said Mrs. Metcalf when she established the award. "We must encourage the writing of material for Canadian children without setting any restricting formulas."

*‡MICHIGAN STUDENT FILM & VIDEO FESTIVAL, Detroit Area Film and Television, Harrison High School, 29995 W. 12 Mile Rd., Farmington Hills MI 48334. (313)489-3491. Contest/Award Director: Margaret Culver. Open to students in grades K-12; *entrants must be Michigan residents*. Annual contest/award. Estab. 1968. Film entries must be 8mm or 16mm; categories for video entries are teleplay, commercials, music, documentary, series, artistic, general entertainment, sports, news, editing, unedited, drug awareness (public service announcement), instructional and animation. Submissions made by the author. Deadline for entries is usually in February. Contest/award rules and entry form available with SASE. Entry fee required. Prizes include ribbons or medals for all winners; prizes for Best of Show award range from cameras to scholarships. Judging is done by adults in media, education and production of film and video. The festival reserves the right to use the material for educational or promotional purposes. Work will be shown at the Detroit Film Theater, Detroit Institute of Arts.

*MILKWEED PRIZE FOR CHILDREN'S LITERATURE, Milkweed Editions, Suite 400, 430 First Ave. N., Minneapolis MN 55401-1473. (612)332-6192. Contest/Award Director: Emilie Buchwald, publisher/editor. Annual contest/award. Estab. 1993. Purpose of the contest/award: to encourage writers to turn their attention to readers in the 8-14 age group. Unpublished submissions only "in book form." Submissions made by the author. Deadline for entries is March 15, 1994. Contest/award rules and entry form available with SASE. No entry fee required. Prizes include publication by Milkweed Editions and a cash advance of $3,000 against royalties. Judging is done by Milkweed Editions. Winners announced in June. Requirements of entrants: writers of English who have previously published a book of fiction or nonfiction for children or adults, or a minimum of three short stories or articles in nationally distributed magazines for children or adults. Manuscript should be 110-350 pages in length, typed double-spaced on good quality white paper.

THE MILNER AWARD, Atlanta-Fulton Public Library/Friends of the Atlanta Fulton Public Library, One Margaret Mitchell Square, Atlanta GA 30303. (404)730-1710. Executive Director: Charlene P. Shucker. Annual award. Estab. 1983. Purpose of the award: "The Milner Award is an annual award to a living American author of children's books. Selection is made by the children of Atlanta voting for their favorite author during Children's Book Week." Previous winners not eligible. "The winning author is awarded a specially commissioned work of the internationally famous glass sculptor, Hans Frabel, and a $1,000 honorarium." Requirements for entrants: "Winner must be an American author, able to appear personally in Atlanta to receive the award at a formal program." *No submission process.*

‡MISSISSIPPI VALLEY POETRY CONTEST, North American Literary Escadrille, P.O. Box 3188, Rock Island IL 61204. (309)786-8041. Director: Sue Katz. Annual contest. Estab. 1971. Purpose of the contest: "To provide children, students, adults, Sr. Citizens, ethnic groups and teachers the opportunity to express themselves in verse and poetry on a regional and national scale." Categories for adults, and high school, junior high and elementary students include The Mississippi Valley, senior citizen, jazz, religious, humorous, rhyming, ethnic, history. Unpublished submissions only. Deadline for entries: September 15. SASE for contest rules and entry forms. Entry fee of $3 student, $5 adult will cover up to 5 poems submitted. Awards cash from $50-175. Open to any student or adult poet, writer or teacher. "Prizes are presented during a special awards night in October at the Butterworth Center, a grand old mansion in Molie, Illinois. Winning poems are read by professional readers, and event is widely publicized. Those not present are notified by mail and prizes forwarded. Contest is nonprofit and registered as such in the state of Illinois."

NATIONAL JEWISH BOOK AWARD FOR CHILDREN'S LITERATURE, JCCA Jewish Book Council, 15 E. 26th St., New York NY 10010. (212)532-4949. Awards Coordinator: Dr. Marcia W. Posner. Annual award. Estab. 1950. Previously published submissions only; must be published in 1993 for 1994 award. Deadline for entries: November 19. SASE for award rules and entry forms. Entries not returned. No entry fee. Awards $750. Judging by 3 authorities in the field. Requirements for entrants: Jewish children's books, published only for ages 8-14 only. Books will be displayed at the awards ceremony in NYC in June.

NATIONAL JEWISH BOOK AWARD—PICTURE BOOKS, (Marcia & Louis Posner Award), Jewish Book Council, 15 E 26th St., New York NY 10010. (212)532-4949. Awards Coordinator: Dr. Marcia W. Posner. Annual award. Estab. 1980. Previously published submissions only; must be published the year prior to the awards ceremony— 1993 for 1994 award. Deadline for entries: November 19. SASE for award rules and entry forms. Entries not returned. No entry fee. Awards $750. Judging by 3 authorities in the field. Requirements for entrants: subject must be of Jewish content, published. Works displayed at the awards ceremony.

‡NATIONAL PEACE ESSAY CONTEST, For High School Students, United States Institute of Peace, Suite 700, 1550 M St. NW, Washington DC 20005-1708. (202)429-3846. Contest Director: Heidi Schaeffer. Annual contest. Estab. 1987. "The contest gives students the opportunity to do valuable research, writing and thinking on a topic of importance to international peace and conflict resolution. Submissions, instead of being published, can be a classroom assignment." Previously published entries must have appeared between September 1 and February 1 previous to the contest deadline. Deadline for entries: February 1 (postmark deadline). "The opening and closing dates vary only slightly. Interested students, teachers and others may write or call to receive free contest kits. Please do not include SASE." No entry fee. State Level Awards are college scholarships in the following amounts: 1st place $500; 2nd place $250; 3rd place $100. National winners are selected from among the 1st place state winners. National winners receive scholarships in the following amounts: 1st place $10,000; 2nd $5,000; 3rd $3,500. Judging is conducted by education professionals from across the country and by the Board of Directors of the United States Institute of Peace. "All submissions become property of the U.S. Institute of Peace to use at its discretion. The U.S. Institute of Peace may use, at its discretion and without royalty or any limitation, any winning essay. Grades 9-12 in the U.S., its territories and overseas schools may submit essays for review by completing the application process. Please — no illustrations. National winning essays for each competition will be published by the U.S. Institute of Peace for public consumption."

‡THE 1994 NATIONAL WRITTEN & ILLUSTRATED BY . . . AWARDS CONTEST FOR STUDENTS, Landmark Editions, Inc., P.O. Box 4469, Kansas City MO 64127. (816)241-4919. Contest Director: Teresa Melton. Annual awards contest with three published winners. Estab. 1986. Purpose of the contest: to encourage and celebrate the creative efforts of students. There are three age categories (ages 6-9, 10-13 and 14-19). Unpublished submissions only. Deadline for entries: May 1. Contest rules available for self-addressed, business-sized envelope, stamped with 58¢ postage. "Need to send a self-addressed, sufficiently stamped book mailer with book entry for its return." Entry fee is $1. Awards publication of book. Judging by national panel of educators, editors, illustrators and authors. "Each student winner receives a publishing contract allowing Landmark to publish the book. Copyright is in student's name and student receives royalties on sale of book. Books must be in proper contest format and submitted with entry form signed by a teacher or librarian. Students may develop their illustrations in any medium of their choice, as long as the illustrations remain two-dimensional and flat to the surface of the paper." Works will be published in 1995 in Kansas City, Missouri, for distribution nationally and internationally.

THE NENE AWARD, Manoa Public Library, 2716 Woodlawn Dr., Honolulu HI 96822. (808)988-6655. Award Director: Janet Yap. Estab. 1964. "The Nene Award was designed to help the children of Hawaii become acquainted with the best contemporary writers of fiction, become aware of the qualities that make a good book and choose the best rather than the mediocre." Previously published submissions only. Books must have been copyrighted not more than six years prior to presentation of award. Work is nominated. Awards Koa plaque. Judging by the children of Hawaii. Requirements for entrants: books must be fiction, written by a living author, copyrighted not more than six years ago and suitable for children in grades 4, 5 and 6.

*‡NEW ERA WRITING WRITING, ART, PHOTOGRAPHY & MUSIC CONTEST, The Church of Jesus Christ of Latter-day Saints, 50 E. North Temple, Salt Lake City UT 84150. (801)240-2951. Managing Editor: Richard M. Romney. Annual contest. Estab. 1971. Purpose of the contest: To feature the creative abilities of young Latter-day Saints. Unpublished submissions only. Submissions made by the author. Deadline for entries: December 31. SASE for contest rules and entry forms. No entry fee. Awards partial scholarships to LDS colleges, cash prizes. Judging by *New Era* editors. All rights, reassigned to author upon written request. Requirements for entrants: Must be an active member of the LDS Church, ages 12-23. Winning entries published in each August's issue.

NEWBERY MEDAL AWARD, Association for Library Service to Children—Division of the American Library Association, 50 E. Huron, Chicago IL 60611. (312)280-2163. Executive Director, ALSC: Susan Roman. Annual award. Estab. 1922. Purpose of the award: To recognize the most distinguished contribution to American children's literature published in the US. Previously published submissions only; must be published prior to year award is given. Deadline for entries: December. SASE for award rules and entry forms. Entries not returned. No entry fee. Medal awarded at banquet during annual conference. Judging by Newbery Committee.

THE NOMA AWARD FOR PUBLISHING IN AFRICA, Kodansha Ltd., % Hans Zell Associates, P.O. Box 56, 11 Richmond Rd., Oxford 0X1 3EL England. (0865)511428. Telex: 94012872ZELLG. Fax: (0865)793298 or (0865)311534. Secretary of the Managing Committee: Hans M. Zell. Annual award. Estab. 1979. Purpose of award: To encourage publications of works by African writers and scholars in Africa, instead of abroad, as is still too often the case at present. Books in the following categories are eligible: scholarly or academic, books for children, literature and creative writing, including fiction, drama and poetry. Previously published submissions only. 1994 Award given for book published in 1993. Deadline for entries: end of February 1994. Submissions must be made through publishers. Conditions of entry and submission forms are available from the secretariat. Entries not returned. No entry fee. Awards $5,000. Judging by the Managing Committee (jury): African scholars and book experts and representatives of the international book community. Chairman: Professor Abiola Irele. Requirements for entrants: Author must be African, and book published in Africa. "Winning titles are displayed at appropriate international book events."

THE SCOTT O'DELL AWARD FOR HISTORICAL FICTION, 1418 E. 57th St., Chicago IL 60637. Award Director: Mrs. Zena Sutherland. Annual award. Estab. 1981. Purpose of the award: "To promote the writing of historical fiction of good quality." Previously published submissions only; must be published between January 1 and December 31 previous to deadline. Deadline for entries: December 31. "Publishers send books, although occasionally a writer sends a note or a book." SASE for award rules and entry forms. No entry fee. Awards $5,000. Requirements for entrants: "Must be published by a U.S. publisher in the preceding year; must be by an American citizen; must be set in North or South America; must be historical fiction."

‡OHIO GENEALOGICAL SOCIETY ESSAY/ART CONTEST, Ohio Genealogical Society, P.O. Box 2625, Mansfield OH 44906. (419)522-9077. Education Chairperson: Julie Overton. Annual contest. Estab. 1985. "The purpose is to foster an interest in the child's ancestry and heritage. The essay division requires knowledge of proper research techniques, documentation, proper grammar and footnoting. The art division includes paintings, songs, poetry, needlework, photography, etc. and is designed to encourage creativity involving a family's heritage. Please write to OGS before submitting to be sure contest is still in existence." Unpublished submissions only. Deadline for entries: March 1. SASE for contest rules and entry forms. No entry fee. Monetary awards. OGS reserves the right to print winning essays and photographs of winning art entries. Contestants retain all rights to copyright or any material submitted. Requirements for entrants: "Children submitting entries must be a member of OGS, or child/grandchild/great grandchild of an OGS member if living out of state. All children living in Ohio are eligible to enter, regardless of OGS membership." There are 2 divisions—junior division includes students in third grade through the age of 13; senior division open to students over 13 through seniors in high school.

 The double dagger before a listing indicates the contest is for students.

OHIOANA BOOK AWARDS, Ohioana Library Association, State Departments Bldg., Suite 1105, 65 S. Front St., Columbus OH 43215. (614)466-3831. Director: Linda R. Hengst. Annual award. "The Ohioana Book Awards are given to books of outstanding literary quality. Up to 6 Book Awards are given each year. Awards may be given in the following categories: fiction, nonfiction, children's literature, poetry and books about Ohio or an Ohioan. Books must be received by the Ohioana Library during the calendar year prior to the year the Award is given and must have a copyright date within the last two calendar years." Deadline for entries: December 31. SASE for award rules and entry forms. No entry fee. Winners receive citation and glass sculpture. "Any book that has been written or edited by a person born in Ohio or who has lived in Ohio for at least five years" is eligible.

HELEN KEATING OTT AWARD FOR OUTSTANDING CONTRIBUTION TO CHILDREN'S LITERATURE, Church and Synagogue Library Association, P.O. Box 19357, Portland OR 97280. (503)244-6919. Chair of Committee: Lillian Koppin. Annual award. Estab. 1980. "This award is given to a person or organization that has made a significant contribution to promoting high moral and ethical values through children's literature." Deadline for entries: February 1. "Recipient is honored in July during the conference." Awards certificate of recognition and a conference package consisting of registration, meals and housing and a complementary 1-year membership. "A nomination for an award may be made by anyone. It should include the name, address and telephone number of the nominee plus the church or synagogue relationship where appropriate. Nominations of an organization should include the name of a contact person. A detailed description of the reasons for the nomination should be given, accompanied by documentary evidence of accomplishment. The person(s) making the nomination should give his/her name, address and telephone number and a brief explanation of his/her knowledge of the nominee's accomplishments. Elements of creativity and innovation will be given high priority by the judges."

PEN CENTER USA WEST LITERARY AWARD FOR CHILDREN'S LITERATURE, PEN Center USA West, Suite 41, 672 S. Lafayette Park Place, Los Angeles CA 90057. (213)365-8500. Contact: Chair of the Awards Committee. Open to published authors. Annual award. Estab. 1982. Purpose of the award: "To recognize the work of published writers who live west of the Mississippi. The 1994 awards are for books published in 1993." Categories include Children's Literature. Previously published submissions only. Submissions made by the author, author's agent or publishers. Deadline for entries: December 31. SASE for award rules. Cash award, at least $500, and plaque. Judging by awards committee.

*PEN/NORMA KLEIN AWARD FOR CHILDREN'S FICTION, PEN American Center, 568 Broadway, New York NY 10012. (212)334-1660. Awarded in odd-numbered years. Estab. 1990. "In memory of the late PEN member and distinguished children's book author Norma Klein, the award honors new authors whose books demonstrate the adventuresome and innovative spirit that characterizes the best children's literature and Norma Klein's own work." Previously published submissions only. "Candidates may not nominate themselves. We welcome all nominations from authors and editors of children's books." Deadline for entries: December 31. Awards $3,000 which will be given in May, 1995. Judging by a panel of three distinguished children's book authors. Nominations open to authors of books for elementary school to young adult readers. "It is strongly recommended that the nominator describe in some detail the literary character of the candidates work and how it promises to enrich American literature for children."

PLEASE TOUCH MUSEUM BOOK AWARD, Please Touch Museum, 210 N. 21st St., Philadelphia PA 19103. (215)963-0667. Child Development Specialist: Marzy Sykes, Ph.D. Annual award. Estab. 1985. Purpose of the award: "To recognize and encourage the publication of books for young children by first-time American authors that are of the highest quality and will aid them in enjoying the process of learning through books. Awarded to a picture book that is particularly imaginative and effective in exploring a concept or concepts with children 36 months or younger." Previously published submissions only. "To be eligible for consideration a book must: (1) Explore and clarify an idea for young children. This could include the concept of numbers, colors, shapes, sizes, senses, feelings, etc. There is no limitation as to format. (2) Be distinguished in both text and illustration. (3) Be published within the last year by an American publisher. (4) Be the first book written by an American author." Deadline for entries: end of February (submissions may be made throughout the year). SASE for award rules and entry forms. No entry fee. Judging by selected jury of children's literature experts, librarians and early childhood educators. Education store purchases books for selling at Book Award Celebration Day and throughout the year. Receptions and autographing sessions held in bookstores, the main branch of Philadelphia's library and at the museum.

EDGAR ALLAN POE AWARD, Mystery Writers of America, Inc., 6th Floor, 17 E. 47th St., New York NY 10017. (212)888-8171. Executive Director: Priscilla Ridgway. Annual award. Estab. 1945. Purpose of the award: To honor authors of distinguished works in the mystery field. Previously published submissions only. Submissions made by the author, author's agent; "normally by the publisher." Must be published the year of the contest. Deadline for entries: December 1 "except for works only available in the month of December." SASE for award rules and entry forms. No entry fee. Awards ceramic bust of "Edgar" for winner; scrolls for all nominees. Judging by professional members of Mystery Writers of America (writers). Requirements for entrants: Authors "must have been published/produced. Nominee press release sent after first Wednesday in February. Winner press release sent day of Edgar Banquet, held in late April."

*‡THE PRISM AWARDS, The Kids Netword, Unit 16, 390 Edgeley Blvd., Concord, Ontario L4K 3Z6 Canada. (416)889-2957. Award Director: Lucy La Grassa. Annual award. Estab. 1989. Purpose of the award: Children have an opportunity to submit mss for review. Winners are chosen based on originality of ideas and self-expression. Unpublished submissions only. Deadline for entries: January 27, 1994 (new deadline every year). SASE for award rules and entry forms. Entry fee is $2. Award consists of $500 cash and editorial training and possible publication. Judging by more than 40 independent judges. Requirements for entrants: Must be a Canadian or landed immigrant in Canada, ages 7-14; story must be written solely by the submitter. No less than 4 pages, no more than 16 pages. Copyright to winning ms acquired by The Kids Netword upon winning.

‡PUBLISH-A-BOOK CONTEST, Raintree Steck-Vaughn Publishers, P.O. Box 27010, Austin TX 78755. (512)795-3230. Fax: (512)795-3229. Contact: Elaine Johnston. Annual contest. Estab. 1984. Purpose of the contest: To stimulate 4th, 5th and 6th graders to write outstanding stories for children. Unpublished submissions only. Word limits: grades 4-6, 700-900 words; grades 2-3, 300-500 words. Deadline for entries: January 31. SASE for contest rules and entry forms. "Entries must be sponsored by a teacher or librarian." Entries not returned. No entry fee. Grand prizes: Raintree will publish four winning entries. Each winner will receive a $500 advance against an author royalty contract and ten free copies of the published book. The sponsor named on each of these entries will receive 20 free books from the Raintree catalog. Honorable mentions: each of the 20 honorable mention writers will receive $25. The sponsor named on each of these entries will receive ten free books from the Raintree Steck-Vaughn catalog. Judging by an editorial team. Contract issued for Grand Prize winners. Payment and royalties paid. Requirements for entrants: Contest is open only to 4th, 5th and 6th graders enrolled in a school program in the United States or other countries. Books will be displayed and sold in the United States and foreign markets. Displays at educational association meetings, book fairs. "We also have a separate contest for children in grades 2 and 3, established in 1989. All of the above is the same with the exception of the grades, and number of winners will be one."

*‡QUILL AND SCROLL INTERNATIONAL WRITING/PHOTO CONTEST, *Quill and Scroll*, School of Journalism, University of Iowa, Iowa City IA 52242. (319)335-5795. Contest Director: Richard Johns. Annual contest. Previously published submissions only. Submissions made by the author or school newspaper adviser. Must be published February 6, 1993 to February 4, 1994. Deadline for entries: February 5. SASE for contest rules and entry forms. Entry fee is $2/entry. Awards National Gold Key (pin); seniors in high school are eligible for scholarships; each sweepstakes winner receives electric typewriter. Judging by various judges. *Quill and Scroll* acquires the right to publish submitted material in the magazine if it is chosen as a winning entry. Requirements for entrants: Must be students in grades 7-12.

‡THE AYN RAND INSTITUTE'S ANTHEM ESSAY CONTEST, P.O. Box 6099, Dept. DB, Inglewood CA 90312. (310)306-9232. Fax: (310)306-4925. Contest Director: Dr. Michael S. Berliner. Contest Coordinator: Donna Montrezza. Open to students. Annual. Estab. 1992. Purpose of the contest: "To encourage analytical thinking and writing excellence, and to introduce young people to the philosophic meaning of Ayn Rand's novelette *Anthem*." Deadline: March 30. SASE for contest rules and entry forms. No entry fee. Total prizes: $5,000. One 1st prize of $1,000; ten 2nd prizes of $200; twenty 3rd prizes of $100. Judging: All papers are first read by a national testing service in Oakland, CA; semi-finalist and finalist papers are red by a panel of writers, professors and high school teachers. Rights to submitted or winning entries: Entry becomes property of the Ayn Rand Institute and will not be returned. Open to all 9th and 10th graders in high school. The Institute publishes the winning essay in its fall newsletter.

‡THE AYN RAND INSTITUTE'S FOUNTAINHEAD ESSAY CONTEST, The Ayn Rand Institute, P.O. Box 6004, Dept. DB, Inglewood CA 90312. (310)306-9232. Fax: (310)306-4925. Contest Director: Dr. Michael S. Berliner. Annual contest. Estab. 1986. Purpose of the contest: "To introduce high school juniors and seniors to the fiction and nonfiction writings, as well as the ideas, of Ayn Rand, novelist and philosopher. To encourage well-organized, analytic writing; to place issues important to young people, such as independence and integrity, before them." Unpublished submissions only. Deadline for entries: April 15. Contest rules and entry forms available to high school juniors and seniors for SASE. No entry fee. Awards one 1st prize $5,000 cash; five 2nd prizes $1,000 each; ten 3rd prizes $500 each. Judging: entries are read by a national testing service in Oakland, CA; semifinalists and finalists are chosen by a panel of writers, professors and professional people; winner is selected from top entries by a university professor. Submitted or winning entries become property of the Ayn Rand Institute. Entrant must be in last two years of secondary school. The Institute publishes the winning essay in its newsletter.

*‡READ WRITING & ART AWARDS, *Read* magazine, 245 Long Hill Rd., Middletown CT 06457. (203)638-2406. Contest Director: Kate Davis. Annual award. Estab. 1978. Purpose of the award: to reward excellence in writing and art in the categories of short story, essay and art. Unpublished submissions only. Submissions made by the author or nominated by a person or group of people. Must include signature of teacher and parent or guardian. Deadline for entries: December. SASE for contest/award rules and entry forms. No entry fee. Awards 1st prize ($100), 2nd prize ($75), 3rd prize ($50). Prizes are given in each category, plus publication of 1st place winners. Judging by *Read* editorial staff. "Entrant understands that prize will include publication, but sometimes pieces are published in other issues. A story may be bought later." Work must be original. Black and white reproduces best but high-contrast color is OK. Published in April issue of *Read* (all-student issue).

‡ANNA DAVIDSON ROSENBERG AWARD FOR POEMS ON THE JEWISH EXPERIENCE, Judah L. Magnes Museum, 2911 Russell St., Berkeley CA 94705. (510)849-2710. Poetry Award Coordinator: P. Friedman. Annual award. Estab. 1986-87. Purpose of the award: to encourage poetry in English on the Jewish experience. Previously unpublished submissions only. Deadline for entries: August 31. SASE for award rules and entry forms by July 31. SASE for list of winners. Awards $100-1st Prize, $50-2nd Prize, $25-3rd Prize; honorable mention certificates; $25 Youth Commendation (poets under 19). Judging by committee of 3. There will be a reading of winners in December at Museum. Prospective anthology of winning entries. Write for entry form and guidelines *first*; entries must follow guidelines and be accompanied by entry form. *Please do not phone.*

CARL SANDBURG LITERARY ARTS AWARDS, Friends of the Chicago Public Library, Harold Washington Library Center, 400 S. State St., Chicago IL 60605. (312)747-4907. Annual award. Categories: fiction, nonfiction, poetry, children's literature. Published submissions only; must be published between June 1 and May 31 (the following year). Deadline for entries: August 1. SASE for award rules. Entries not returned. No entry fee. Awards medal and $1,000 prize. Judging by authors, reviewers, book buyers, librarians. Requirements for entrants: native born Chicagoan or presently residing in the six county metropolitan area. Two copies must be submitted by August 1. All entries become the property of the Friends.

‡THE SCHOLASTIC ART AWARDS, Scholastic, Inc., 555 Broadway, New York NY 10012. (212)343-6100. Program Manager: Diane McNutt. Director: Susan Ebersole. Annual award. Estab. 1922. Purpose: encouragement and recognition of student achievement in the visual arts. "There are 15 categories: painting, drawing, computer graphics, video, film and animation, 2-D design, 3-D design, mixed media, printmaking, fiber arts and textile design, sculpture, ceramics, jewelry and metalsmithing, photography. Seniors only may submit art and photography portfolios. Awards consist of cash awards, scholarships and prizes. Unpublished submissions only. Some areas have sponsors who conduct a regional preliminary judging and exhibition." SASE for award rules and entry forms. Entry fees and deadlines vary depending on region in which a student lives. Judging by art educators, artists, photographers and art administrators. All publication rights are given to Scholastic, Inc., (for one year). Requirements for entrants: students must be in grades 7-12. National winners work on exhibition during the summer.

‡SCHOLASTIC WRITING AWARDS, Scholastic, Inc., 555 Broadway, New York NY 10012-3999. (212)343-6100. Program Manager: Diane McNutt. Director: Susan Ebersole. Annual award. Estab. 1923. Purpose of award: encouragement and recognition of young writers. Open to students in grades 6-12. Group I (Grades 6, 7, 8, 9). Group II—grades 10,11,12. There are 7 categories: short story, short short story, essay/nonfiction/persuasive writing, dramatic script, poetry, humor and science fiction. Seniors only may submit portfolios representing their best group of writing. Awards consist of cash awards, scholarships and prizes. Selected works will be published in scholastic magazines. Unpublished submissions only. Deadlines are indicated on entry forms. All publication rights are given to Scholastic, Inc. for two years. Send SASE for guidelines and entry forms.

SCIENCE WRITING AWARD IN PHYSICS AND ASTRONOMY, The American Institute of Physics, 1 Physics Ellipse St., College Park MD 20740. (212)661-9404. Contact: Manager, Public Information Division. Annual contest/award. Estab. 1987. Purpose of the award: to stimulate and recognize writing that improves children's understanding and appreciation of physics and astronomy. Previously published submissions only; must be published between October 1 and September 30 (the following year). Deadline for entries: October 10. "Entries may be submitted by the publisher as well as the author." Entries not returned. No entry fee. Awards $3,000 and an engraved chair. Judging by a committee selected by the Governing Board of the AIP. Requirements for entrants: "entries must be articles or books, written in English or English translations, dealing primarily with physics, astronomy or related subjects directed at children, from preschool ages up to age 15. Entries must have been available to and intended for young people. Your signature on submission will constitute your acceptance of the contest rules. Postmarked no later than January 31."

‡SEVENTEEN FICTION CONTEST, 9th Floor, 850 Third Ave., New York NY 10022. Fiction Editor: Joe Bargmann. Annual contest. Estab. 1945. Unpublished submissions only. Deadline for entries: April 30. SASE for contest rules and entry forms; contest rules also published in November issue of *Seventeen*. Entries not returned. No entry fee. Awards cash prize and possible publication in December's *Seventeen*. Judging by "external readers, in-house panel of editors." If first prize, acquires first North American rights for piece to be published. Requirements for entrants: "Our annual fiction contest is open to anyone between the ages of 13 and 21 on April 30. Submit only original fiction that has never been published in any form other than in school publications. Stories should be between 1,500 and 3,000 words in length (six to twelve pages). All manuscripts must be typed double-spaced on a single side of paper. Submit as many original stories as you like, but each story must include your full name, address, birth date and signature in the top right-hand corner of the first page. Your signature on submission will constitute your acceptance of the contest rules."

CHARLIE MAY SIMON BOOK AWARD, Arkansas Elementary School Council, Arkansas Dept. of Education, Room 302B, #4 Capitol Mall, Little Rock AR 72201. (501)682-4371. Award Director: James A. Hester. Annual contest. Estab. 1970. Purpose of award: to promote reading—to encourage reading of quality literature and book discussion. Previously published submissions only; must be published between January 1 and December 31 of calendar year; all books must have recommendations from three published sources. "Books are selected based on being published in previous calendar year from time of committee work; *Horn Book* is used as selection guide." Students in grades 4-6 vote on their favorite book on a reading list; the book with the most votes receives a medallion and runner-up receives a trophy; reading list prepared by committee of 25 people representing cooperating organizations. No entry fee. Contest open to entry by any writer, provided book is printed in year being considered.

*SMOKEBRUSH FESTIVAL OF NEW PLAYS FOR CHILDREN, Smokebrush Center for Arts & Theater, 235 S. Nevada Ave., Colorado Springs CO 80903-1906. (719)444-0884. Fax: (719)444-0566. Artistic Director: Kat Walter. Submit writing entries to Director of Development: Linda Borrell. Annual contest/award. Estab. 1994. Unpublished submissions only. Submissions made by the author or the author's agent. Phone for contest/award rules and entry form. No entry fee. Winning playwright receives an expense paid trip to view a professional production of a Smokebrush play during the season. Judging done by a panel of professionals in the children's writing/theater industry.

SOCIETY OF MIDLAND AUTHORS AWARDS, Society of Midland Authors, % Phyllis Ford-Choyke, 29 E. Division, Chicago IL 60610. (312)337-1482. Annual award. Estab. 1915. Purpose of award: "To stimulate creative literary effort, one of the goals of the Society. There are seven categories, including children's fiction and children's nonfiction." Previously published submissions only. Submissions made by the author or publisher. Must be published during calendar year previous to deadline. Deadline for entries: January 15. SASE for award rules and entry forms. No entry fee. Awards plaque given at annual dinner, cash. Judging by panel of three per category, writers for the most part. "Award is for book published in the awards year or play professionally produced in that year for the first time." Author to be currently residing in the Midlands, i.e., Illinois, Indiana, Iowa, Kansas, Michigan, Minnesota, Missouri, Nebraska, North Dakota, South Dakota, Ohio, or Wisconsin.

GEORGE G. STONE CENTER FOR CHILDREN'S BOOKS RECOGNITION OF MERIT AWARD, George G. Stone Center for Children's Books, The Claremont Graduate School, 131 E. 10th St., Claremont CA 91711-6188. (714)621-8000 ext. 3670. Award Director: Doty Hale. Annual award. Estab. 1965. Purpose of the award: To recognize an author or illustrator of a children's book or a body of work exhibiting the "power to please and expand the awareness of children and teachers as they have shared the book in their classrooms." Previously published submissions only. SASE for award rules and entry forms. Entries not returned. No entry fee. Awards a scroll. Judging by a committee of teachers, professors of children's literature and librarians. Requirements for entrants: "Nominations are made by students, teachers, professors and librarians. Award made at annual Claremont Reading Conference in spring (March)."

JOAN G. SUGARMAN CHILDREN'S BOOK AWARD, Washington Independent Writers Legal and Educational Fund, Inc., #220, 733 15th St. NW, Washington DC 20005. (202)347-4973. Director: Isolde Chapin. Open to residents of D.C., Maryland, Virginia. Award offered every two years. Estab. 1987. Purpose of award: to recognize excellence in children's literature, ages 1-15. Previously published submissions only. Submissions made by the author or author's agent or by publishers. Must be published in the two years preceeding award year. Deadline for entries: January 31. SASE for award rules and entry forms. No entry fee. Awards $500-1,000. Judging by selected experts in children's books. Requirements for entrants: Publication of material; residence in D.C., Maryland or Virginia. Works displayed at reception for award winners.

SYDNEY TAYLOR BOOK AWARD, Association of Jewish Libraries, %National Foundation of Jewish Culture, 330 Seventh Ave., New York NY 10001. Chairman: Claudia Z. Fechter. Annual award. Estab. 1973. Purpose of the award: to "recognize books of quality in the field of Judaic books for children in two categories: picture books for young children, and older children's books." Previously published submissions only. Submissions made by publisher. Must be published January-December of the year being judged. Deadline for entries: February 15. SASE for award rules and entry forms. No entry fee. Awards plaque and $300-500. Judging by a committee of six librarians. Requirements for entrants: "Subject matter must be of Judaic content."

SYDNEY TAYLOR MANUSCRIPT COMPETITION, Association of Jewish Libraries, 15 Goldsmith St., Providence RI 02906. (401)274-1117. Director: Lillian Schwartz. Annual contest. Estab. 1985. Purpose of the contest: "This competition is for unpublished writers of fiction. Material should be for readers aged 8-11 years, with universal appeal that will serve to deepen the understanding of Judaism for all children, revealing positive aspects of Jewish life." Unpublished submissions only. Deadline for entries: January 15. SASE for contest rules and entry forms. No entry fee. Awards $1,000. Judging by qualified judges from within the Association of Jewish Libraries. Requirements for entrants:

Must be an unpublished fiction writer. "AJL assumes no responsibility for publication, but hopes this cash incentive will serve to encourage new writers of children's stories with Jewish themes for all children."

‡TIME EDUCATION PROGRAM STUDENT WRITING AND ART COMPETITION, *TIME* Magazine, Time Education Program, Box 1000, Mt. Kisco NY 10549-0010. (800)882-0852. Annual contest. "The aims of this competition are reflective of *TIME* Magazine's basic mission — to communicate ideas and information with intelligence, style and meaning." Previously unpublished submissions only. Deadlines for entries: February 1 of each year. SASE for contest rules and entry forms. No entry fee. Awards for writing: Grand Prize: $5,000 scholarship; First Prize: $2,500 scholarship; 2 Awards for Excellence: $1,000 scholarship each. Awards for Cover Art: Grand Prize: $5,000; First Prize: $2,500; 2 Awards for Excellence: $1,000 each. Awards for Cartoon Art: Grand Prize: $5,000; First Prize: $2,500; 2 Awards for Excellence; $1,000 each. Judging by *TIME* editorial staffers and educators. Rights to submitted material acquired or purchased. Open to any high school or college student in the U.S. or Canada. "Submissions must be no larger than 11 × 17; original 2 dimensional pieces." Works published in May issue of *TimeLines*.

‡VEGETARIAN ESSAY CONTEST, The Vegetarian Resource Group, P.O. Box 1463, Baltimore MD 21203. (410)366-VEGE. Address to Vegetarian Essay Contest. Annual contest. Estab. 1985. Unpublished submissions only. Deadline for entries: May 1 of each year. SASE for contest rules and entry forms. No entry fee. Awards $50 savings bond. Judging by awards committee. Acquires right for The Vegetarian Resource Group to reprint essays. Requirements for entrants: ages 19 and under. Winning works may be published in Vegetarian Journal, instructional materials for students. "Submit 2-3 page essay on any aspect of vegetarianism, which is the abstinence of meat, fish and fowl. Entrants can base paper on interviewing, research or personal opinion. Need not be vegetarian to enter."

‡VERY SPECIAL ARTS YOUNG PLAYWRIGHTS PROGRAM, Very Special Arts Education Office, The John F. Kennedy Center for the Performing Arts, Washington DC 20566. (202)628-2800. National Programs Coordinator: Avery Beesch. Annual contest. Estab. 1984. "All scripts must address or incorporate some aspect of disability." Unpublished submissions only. Deadline for entries: April 15. Write to Young Playwrights Coordinator for contest rules and entry forms. No entries returned. No entry fee. Judging by Artists Selection Committee. "Very Special Arts retains the rights for videotaping and broadcasting on television and/or radio." Entrants must be students age 12-18. "Script will be selected for production at The John F. Kennedy Center for the Performing Arts, Washington DC. The winning play is presented each October."

‡VFW VOICE OF DEMOCRACY, Veterans of Foreign Wars of the U.S., 406 W. 34th St., Kansas City MO 64111. (816)756-3390. Annual contest. Estab. 1960. Purpose of the contest: to give high school students the opportunity to voice their opinions about their responsibility to our country and to convey them via the broadcast media to all of America. Deadline for entries: November 15. No entry fee. Winners receive awards ranging from $1,000-18,000. Requirements for entrants: "10th, 11th and 12th grade students in public, parochial and private schools in the United States and overseas are eligible to compete. Former national and/or 1st place state winners are not eligible to compete again. Contact your high school counselor or your local VFW Post to enter."

THE STELLA WADE CHILDREN'S STORY AWARD, *Amelia* Magazine, 329 E St., Bakersfield CA 93304. (805)323-4064. Editor: Frederick A. Raborg, Jr. Annual award. Estab. 1988. Purpose of the award: "With decrease in the number of religious and secular magazines for young people, the juvenile story and poetry must be preserved and enhanced." Unpublished submissions only. Deadline for entries: August 15. SASE for award rules. Entry fee is $5 per adult entry; there is no fee for entries submitted by young people under the age of 17, but such entry must be signed by parent, guardian or teacher to verify originality. Awards $125 plus publication. Judging by editorial staff. Previous winners include Maxine Kumin and Sharon E. Martin. "We use First North American serial rights only for the winning manuscript." Contest is open to all interested. If illustrator wishes to enter only an illustration without a story, the entry fee remains the same. Illustrations will also be considered for cover publication. Restrictions of mediums for illustrators: Submitted photos should be no smaller than 5 × 7; illustrations (drawn) may be in any medium. "Winning entry will be published in the most appropriate issue of either *Amelia*, *Cicada* or *SPSM&H*—subject matter would determine such. Submit clean, accurate copy."

WASHINGTON POST/CHILDREN'S BOOK GUILD AWARD FOR NONFICTION, % Patricia Markun, 4405 "W" St. NW, Washington DC 20007. (202)965-0403. Annual contest. Estab. 1977. Purpose of contest: "to encourage nonfiction writing for children of literary quality. Awarded for the body of work of a leading American nonfiction author." No entry fee. Awards $1000 and an engraved crystal cube (paperweight). Judging by a jury of Children's Book Guild librarians and authors and a *Washington Post Book World* editor. "One doesn't enter. One is selected."

‡WE ARE WRITERS, TOO!, Creative with Words Publications, P.O. Box 223226, Carmel CA 93922. Contest Director: Brigitta Geltrich. Annual contest. Estab. 1975. Unpublished submissions only. Deadline for entries: June 15 and December 31. SASE for contest rules and entry forms. SASE for return of entries "if not winning poem." No entry fee. Awards publication is an anthology. Judging by selected guest editors and educators. June 15 contest open to children only (up to and including 19 years old). December 31 contest open to all. Writer should request contest rules. SASE with all correspondence. "Age of child must be stated and manuscript must be verified of its authenticity."

WESTERN HERITAGE AWARDS, National Cowboy Hall of Fame, 1700 NE 63rd St., Oklahoma City OK 73111. (405)478-2250. Director of Public Relations: Dana Sullivant. Annual award. Estab. 1961. Purpose of the award: The WHA are presented annually to encourage the accurate and artistic telling of great stories of the West through 15 categories of western literature, television and film, including fiction, nonfiction, children's books and poetry. Previously published submissions only; must be published the calendar year before the awards are presented. Deadline for entries: December 31. SASE for award rules and entry forms. Entries not returned. No entry fee. Awards a Wrangler award. Judging by a panel of judges selected each year with distinction in various fields of western art and heritage. Requirements for entrants: The material must pertain to the development or preservation of the West, either from a historical or contemporary viewpoint. Historical accuracy is vital. Works recognized during special awards ceremonies held annually third weekend in March at the museum. There is an autograph party preceding the awards. Film clips are shown during the awards presentation. Awards ceremonies are broadcast.

LAURA INGALLS WILDER AWARD, Association for Library Service to Children—A division of the American Library Association, 50 E. Huron, Chicago IL 60611. (312)280-2163. Executive Director, ALSC: Susan Roman. Award offered every 3 years. Purpose of the award: to recognize an author or illustrator whose books, published in the US, have over a period of years made a substantial and lasting contribution to children's literature. Awards a medal presented at banquet during annual conference. Judging by Wilder Committee.

‡PAUL A. WITTY OUTSTANDING LITERATURE AWARD, International Reading Association, Special Interest Group, Reading for Gifted and Creative Learning, School of Education, P.O. Box 32925, Fort Worth TX 76129. (817)921-7660. Award Director: Dr. Cathy Collins Block. Annual award. Estab. 1979. Categories of entries: poetry/prose at elementary, junior high and senior high levels. Unpublished submissions only. Deadline for entries: February 1. SASE for award rules and entry forms. SASE for return of entries. No entry fee. Awards $25 and plaque, also certificates of merit. Judging by 2 committees for screening and awarding. Works will be published in Reading Association publications. "The elementary students' entries must be legible and may not exceed 1,000 words. Secondary students' prose entries should be typed and may exceed 1,000 words if necessary. At both elementary and secondary levels, if poetry is entered, a set of 5 poems must be submitted. All entries and requests for applications must include a self-addressed, stamped envelope."

PAUL A. WITTY SHORT STORY AWARD, International Reading Association, P.O. Box 8139, 800 Barksdale Rd., Newark DE 19714-8139. (302)731-1600. Chair of Committee: Barbara D. Stoodt, 5011 Manning Dr., Greensboro NC 27410. Annual award. Estab. 1986. Purpose of award: The entry must be an original short story appearing in a young children's periodical that regularly publishes short stories for children. (These would be periodicals generally aimed at readers to about age 12.) The short story should serve as a reading and literary standard by which readers can measure other writing and should encourage young readers to read by providing them with enjoyable and profitable reading. Deadline for entries: The entry must have been published for the first time in the eligibility year; the short story must be submitted during the calendar year of publication. Anyone wishing to nominate a short story should send it to the designated Paul A. Witty Short Award Subcommittee Chair by November 1. Deadline for completed entries to the subcommittee chair is December 1. Both fiction and nonfiction writing are eligible; each will be rated according to characteristics that are appropriate for the genre. Send inquiry to Barbara D. Stoodt, above address. Award is $1,000 and recognition at the annual IRA Convention.

ALICE LOUISE WOOD OHIOANA AWARD FOR CHILDREN'S LITERATURE, Ohioana Library Association, Suite 1105, State Department Bldg., 65 S. Front St., Columbus OH 43215. (614)466-3831. Director: Linda R. Hengst. Annual award. Estab. 1991. Purpose of the award: "To recognize an Ohio author whose body of work has made, and continues to make, a significant contribution to literature for children or young adults." SASE for award rules and entry forms. Awards $1,000. Requirements for entrants: "Must have been born in Ohio, or lived in Ohio for a minimum of five years; established a distinguished publishing record of books for children and young people; body of work has made, and continues to make, a significant contribution to the literature for young people; through whose work as a writer, teacher, administrator, or through community service, interest in children's literature has been encouraged and children have become involved with reading."

WORK-IN-PROGRESS GRANTS, Society of Children's Book Writers and Illustrators, #106, 22736 Vanowen St., West Hills CA 91307. (818)347-8188. Annual award. "The SCBWI Work-In-Progress Grants have been established to assist children's book writers in the completion of a specific project." Five categories: (1) General Work-In-Progress Grant. (2) Grant for a Contemporary Novel for Young People. (3) Nonfiction Research Grant. (4) Grant for a work whose author has never had a book published. (5) Grant for a picture book writer. Requests for applications may be made beginning October 1.

Completed applications accepted February 1-May 1 of each year. SASE for applications for grants. In any year, an applicant may apply for any of the grants except the one awarded for a work whose author has never had a book published. (The recipient of this grant will be chosen from entries in all categories.) Five grants of $1,000 will be awarded annually. Runner-up grants of $500 (one in each category) will also be awarded. "The grants are available to both full and associate members of the SCBWI. They are not available for projects on which there are already contracts." Previous recipients not eligible to apply.

*WRITER'S EXCHANGE POETRY CONTEST, R.S.V.P. Press, Box 394, Society Hill SC 29593. (803)378-4556. Contest Director: Gene Boone. Quarterly contest. Estab. 1985. Purpose of the contest: To promote friendly competition among poets of all ages and backgrounds, giving these poets a chance to be published and win an award. Submissions are made by the author. Continuous deadline; entries are placed in the contest closest to date received. SASE for contest rules and entry forms. Entry fee is $1 per poem. Awards 50% of contest proceeds, usually $30-100 varying slightly in each quarterly contest due to changes in response. Judging by Gene Boone or a guest judge such as a widely published poet or another small press editor. "From the entries received, we reserve the right to publish the winning poems in an issue of *Writer's Exchange*, a literary newsletter. The contest is open to any poet." The winning poem and two runners-up will be published in *Writer's Exchange*. "Poems on any subject/theme, any style, to 24 lines, may be entered. Poems should be typed, single-spaced, with the poet's name in the upper left corner."

*WRITER'S OPEN FORUM CONTESTS, Writers' Open Forum, P.O. Box 516, Tracyton WA 98393. Contest Director: Sandra E. Haven. Two contests per year—Summer, 1994; Winter 1994-95. Estab. 1991. Purpose of the contest: To inspire excellence in the traditional short story format. "We like identifiable characters, strong storylines, and crisp, fresh endings. We particularly like helping new writers, writers changing genres and young writers." Unpublished submissions only. Submissions made by the author. Deadline for entries: Summer—July 31, Winter—January 30. SASE for contest rules and entry forms. No entry fee for subscribers; $5 for non-subscribers. Awards $50, 1st place; $25, 2nd place; $10, 3rd place. "We reserve the right to publish 1st, 2nd and 3rd place winners." Please state genre of story and age of intended audience (as "children's story, aged 5-9") in cover letter. Summer Contest winners announced and 1st place published in September/October issue; Winter Contest winners announced and 1st place published in March/April issue. Word count restrictions vary with each contest. Some contests require following a theme or other stipulation. Please request guidelines for contest you want to enter.

*‡WRITING CONFERENCE WRITING CONTESTS, The Writing Conference, Inc., P.O. Box 664, Ottawa KS 66067. (913)242-0407. Contest Director: John H. Bushman. Annual contest. Estab. 1987. Purpose of contest: To further writing by students with awards for narration, exposition and poetry at the elementary, middle school and high school levels. Unpublished submissions only. Submissions made by the author or teacher. Deadline for entires: January 7. SASE for contest rules and entry form. No entry fee. Awards plaque and publication of winning entry in *The Writer's Slate*, March issue. Judging by a panel of teachers. Requirements for entrants: Must be enrolled in school—kindergarten-12th grade.

*‡YEARBOOK EXCELLENCE CONTEST, *Quill and Scroll*, School of Journalism, University of Iowa, Iowa City IA 52242. (319)335-5795. Executive Director: Richard Johrs. Annual contest. Estab. 1987. Previously published submissions only. Submissions made by the author or school yearbook adviser. Must be published before November 1, 1993 and November 1, 1994. Deadline for entries: November 1. SASE for contest rules and entry form. Entry fee is $2 per entry. Awards National Gold Key; sweepstakes winners and high school receive plaque; seniors eligible for scholarships. Judging by various judges. Winning entries may be published in *Quill and Scroll* magazine. Requirements for entrants: Must be in a high school that is a charter member of Quill & Scroll.

*YOUNG ADULT CANADIAN BOOK AWARD, The Canadian Library Association, 602-200 Elgin St., Ottawa, Ontario K2P 1L5 Canada. (613)232-9625. Fax: (613)563-9895. Contact: Committee Chair. Annual award. Estab. 1981. Purpose of award: "To recognize the author of an outstanding English-language Canadian book which appeals to young adults between the ages of 13 and 18 that was published the preceding calendar year. Information is available for anyone requesting. We approach publishers, also send news releases to various journals, i.e. *Quill & Quire*." Entries are not returned. No entry fee. Awards a leather-bound book, sometimes author tour. Requirement for entrants: Must be a work of fiction (novel or short stories), the title must be a Canadian publication in either hardcover or paperback, and the author must be a Canadian citizen or landed immigrant. Award given at the Canadian Library Association Conference.

YOUNG READER'S CHOICE AWARD, Pacific Northwest Library Association, 133 Suzzallo Library, FM-30, University of Washington, Graduate School of Library and Information Science, Seattle WA 98195. (206)543-1897. Secretary: Carol Doll. Award Director: Named annually. Annual award for published authors. Estab. 1940. Purpose of the award: "To promote reading as an enjoyable activity and to provide children an opportunity to endorse a book they consider an excellent story." Previously published submissions only; must be published 3 years before award year. Deadline for entries: February 1. SASE for award rules and entry forms. No entry fee. Awards a silver medal, struck in Idaho silver. "Children vote for their favorite (books) from a list of titles nominated by librarians, teachers, students and other interested persons."

THE ANNA ZORNIO MEMORIAL CHILDREN'S THEATRE PLAYWRITING AWARD, University of New Hampshire Theatre in Education Program, Department of Theatre and Dance, Paul Creative Arts Center, 30 College Rd., University of New Hampshire, Durham NH 03824. Contact: Peggy Rae Johnson. Annual award. Estab. 1979. Purpose of the award: "To honor the late Anna Zornio, an alumna of The University of New Hampshire, for dedication to and inspiration of children's theater playwriting." Unpublished submissions only. Submissions made by the author. Deadline for entries: April 15, 1994. SASE for award rules and entry forms. No entry fee. Awards $250 plus guaranteed production. Judging by faculty committee. Acquires rights to campus production. Requirements for entrants: Open to all playwrights in the US and Canada. Write for details.

Contests & Awards/'93-'94 changes

The following markets are not included in this edition of *Children's Writer's & Illustrator's Market* for the reasons indicated within parentheses. If there is no reason given, it means the market did not respond to our requests for updated information for a 1994 listing.

AIP Science Writing Award

Resources

Clubs & Organizations

Children's writers and illustrators can benefit from contacts made through organizations such as the ones listed in this section. Professional organizations provide a writer or artist with a multitude of educational, business and legal services. Many of these services come in the form of newsletters, workshops or seminars that provide tips about how to be a better writer or artist, types of business records to keep, health and life insurance coverage to carry and/or organizational competitions to consider.

An added benefit to belonging to an organization is the ability to network with those who have similar interests, thus creating a support system to help you through tight creative and financial periods. As in any business, knowing the right people can often help your career, and important contacts can be made through your peers. Membership in a writer's or artist's group also presents to a publisher an image of being serious about your craft. Of course, this provides no guarantee that your work will be published, but it offers an added dimension of credibility and professionalism.

Some of the organizations here welcome anyone with an interest, while others are only open to professionals. Still others, such as the Society of Children's Book Writers & Illustrators, have varying levels of membership. SCBWI offers associate membership to those with no publishing credits, while those who have had work for children published receive full membership. Feel free to write for more information regarding any group that sounds interesting. Be sure to inquire about membership qualifications as well as the various services offered to members.

AMERICAN ALLIANCE FOR THEATRE & EDUCATION, Theatre Department, Arizona State University, Tempe AZ 85287-3411. (602)965-6064. Administrative Director: Katherine Krzys. Purpose of organization: to promote standards of excellence in theater and drama/theater education by providing the artist and educator with a network of resources and support, a base for advocacy, and access to programs and projects that focus on the importance of drama in the human experience. Membership cost: $68 annually for individual in US and Canada, $75 annually for foreign, $95 annually for organization, $38 annually for students, $48 annually for retired people. Annual conference held jointly with the Educational Theatre Association in Tempe AZ, August 4-7, 1994 and in Minneapolis MN, August 1995 (exact date not yet confirmed). Newsletter published quarterly; must be member to subscribe. Contests held for unpublished play reading project and annual awards for best play for K-8 and one for secondary audience. Award plaque and stickers for published playbooks. Published list of unpublished plays deemed worthy of performance in newsletter and press release.

*AMERICAN SOCIETY OF JOURNALISTS AND AUTHORS, 1501 Broadway, New York NY 10036. (212)997-0947. Executive Director: Alexandra Cantor. Qualifications for membership: "Need to be a professional nonfiction writer published 8-10 times in general circulation publications." Membership cost: Initiation fee—$100; annual dues—$145. Group sponsors annual conference; monthly workshops in New York City. Workshops/conferences open to nonmembers. Publishes a newsletter for members that provides confidential information for nonfiction writers.

ARIZONA AUTHORS ASSOCIATION, #117, 3509 E. Shea Blvd., Phoenix AZ 85028-3339. (602)996-9706. President: Gerry Benninger. Purpose of organization: Membership organization offering professional, educational and social opportunities to writers and authors. Membership cost: $40/yr. professional and associate; $50/yr. affiliate; $25/yr. student. Different levels of membership include: Professional—published writers; Associate—writers working toward publication; Affiliate—professionals in publishing industry; student—full-time students. Workshops/conferences: monthly educational workshops; contact office for current calendar. Newsletter provides information useful to writers (markets, book reviews, calendar of meetings and events) and news about members. Non-member subscription $25/yr. Sponsors Annual Literary Contest. Awards include total of $1,000 in prizes in several categories. Contest open to non-members.

ASSITEJ/USA, % The Open Eye, New Stagings, 270 W. 89th St., New York NY 10024. (212)769-4141. Editor, TYA TODAY: Amie Brockway. Purpose of organization: service organization for theaters focused on productions for young audiences. Also serves as US Center for International Association of Theatre for Children and Young People. Membership Cost: $100 for organizations with budgets below $99,999; $200 for organizations with budgets of $100,000-$399,999; $300 for organizatons with budgets over $400,000; $50 annually/individual; $25 students and retirees; $65 for foreign organizations or individuals outside the US; $30 for library rate. Different levels of membership include: organizations, individuals, students, retirees, corresponding, library rates. Sponsors workshops or conferences. Publishes newsletter that focuses on information on field in US and abroad.

THE AUTHORS GUILD, 29th Floor, 330 W. 42nd St., New York NY 10036-6902. (212)563-5904. Executive Director: Robin Davis Miller. Purpose of organization: membership organization of 6,700 members offers services and information materials intended to help authors with the business and legal aspects of their work, including contract problems, copyright matters, freedom of expression and taxation. Qualifications for membership: book author published by an established American publisher within 7 years or any author who has had three works, fiction or nonfiction, published by a magazine or magazines of general circulation in the last 18 months. Associate membership also available. Annual dues: $90. Different levels of membership include: associate membership with all rights except voting available to an author who has work in progress but who has not yet met the qualifications for active membership. This normally involves a firm contract offer from a publisher. Workshops/conferences: "The Guild and Authors League of America conduct several symposia each year at which experts provide information, offer advice, and answer questions on subjects of interest and concern to authors. Typical subjects have been the rights of privacy and publicity, libel, wills and estates, taxation, copyright, editors and editing, the art of interviewing, standards of criticism and book reviewing. Transcripts of these symposia are published and circulated to members." Symposia open to members only. "The *Author's Guild Bulletin*, a quarterly journal, contains articles on matters of interest to writers, reports of Guild activities, contract surveys, advice on problem clauses in contracts, transcripts of Guild and League symposia, and information on a variety of professional topics. Subscription included in the cost of the annual dues."

THE AUTHORS RESOURCE CENTER, Box 64785, Tucson AZ 85728-4785. (602)325-4733. Executive Director: Martha R. Gore. Purpose of organization: to help writers understand the business and professional realities of the publishing world—also have literary agency (opened March 1, 1987) that markets members' books to publishers. Qualifications for membership: serious interest in writing or cartooning. Membership cost: $60 per year for aspiring and published members. The *Tarc Report* is published bimonthly and includes information about markets, resources, legal matters, writers workshops, reference sources, announcement of members' new books, reviews and other news important to members. Subscription included in membership fee. *TARC* was established in 1984. Interested only in multicultural books."

CALIFORNIA WRITERS' CLUB, 2214 Derby St., Berkeley CA 94705. (510)841-1217. Secretary: Dorothy V. Benson. Purpose of organization: "We are a nonprofit professional organization open to writers to provide writing and market information and to promote fellowship among writers." Qualifications for membership: "publication for active members; expected publication in five years for associate members." Membership cost: entry fee $20; annual dues $35. (Entry fee is paid once.) Workshops/conferences: "Biennial summer conference, July 1995, at Asilomar, Pacific Grove, CA; other conferences are held by local branches as they see fit." Conferences open to nonmembers. "Newsletter, which goes out to all CWC members, to newspapers and libraries, publishes the monthly meetings upcoming in the eight branches, plus the achievements of members, and market and contest opportunities." Sponsors contests. CWC's "major contest is every two years, and prizes are cash in each of 5 categories."

CANADIAN AUTHORS ASSOCIATION, #500, 275 Slater St., Ottawa, Ontario K1P 5H9 Canada. (613)233-2846. Fax: (613)235-8237. Contact: National Secretary. Purpose of organization: to help "emerging" writers and provide assistance to professional writers. Membership is divided into two categories for individuals: Member (voting)—Persons engaged in writing in any genre who have produced a sufficient body of work; Associate (non-voting)—Persons interested in writing who have not yet produced sufficient material to qualify for full membership, or those who, though not writers, have a sincere interest in Canadian literature. Persons interested in learning to write may join the Association for one year. Membership cost: $107 members, $107 associates, $107 introductory rate. Workshops/conferences: 73rd Annual Conference, June 23-27, 1994 in Waterloo, Ontario. "The conference draws writers, editors and publishers together in a congenial atmosphere providing seminars, workshops, panel discussions, readings by award-winning authors, and many social events." Open to nonmembers. Publishes a newsletter for members only. Also publishes a quarterly journal and a bienniel writer's guide available to nonmembers. "The Association created a major literary award program in 1975 to honor writing that achieves literary excellence without sacrificing popular appeal. The awards are in four categories—fiction, (for a full-length novel); nonfiction (excluding works of an instructional nature); poetry (for a volume of the works of one poet); and drama (for a single play published or staged). The awards consist of a handsome silver medal and $5,000 in cash; they are funded by Harlequin Enterprises, the Toronto-based international publisher." Contest open to nonmembers. Also contests for writing by students and for young readers (see Vicky Metcalf and Canadian Author awards); sponsors Air Canada Awards.

CANADIAN SOCIETY OF CHILDREN'S AUTHORS, ILLUSTRATORS AND PERFORMERS, (CANSCAIP), Suite 103, 542 Mt. Pleasant Rd., Toronto, Ontario M4S 2M7 Canada. (416)654-0903. Secretary: Nancy Prasad. Purpose of organization: development of Canadian children's culture and support for authors, illustrators and performers working in this field. Qualifications for membership: *Members*—professionals who have been published (not self-published) or have paid public performances/records/tapes to their credit. *Friends*—share interest in field of children's culture. Membership cost: $60 (members dues), $25 (friends dues), $30 (institution dues). Fees due each January. Sponsors workshops/conferences. Publishes newsletter: includes profiles of members; news round-up of members' activities countrywide; market news; news re awards, grants, etc; columns related to professional concerns.

*LEWIS CARROLL SOCIETY OF NORTH AMERICA, 617 Rockford Rd., Silver Spring MD 20902. (301)593-7077. Secretary: M. Schaefer. "We are an organization of Carroll admirers of all ages and interests and a center for Carroll studies." Qualifications for membership: "An interest in Lewis Carroll and a simple love for Alice (or even the Snark)." Membership cost: $20/year. There is also a contributing membership of $50. "We plan to hold a conference in 1994." Publishes a newsletter.

THE CHILDREN'S BOOK COUNCIL, INC., 568 Broadway, New York NY 10012. (212)966-1990. Purpose of organization: "A nonprofit trade association of children's and young adult publishers, CBC promotes the enjoyment of books for children and young adults, and works with national and international organizations to that end. The CBC has sponsored National Children's Book Week since 1945." Qualifications for membership: Trade publishers of children's and young adult books are eligible for membership. Membership cost: "Individuals wishing to receive mailings from the CBC (our semi-annual newsletter, *CBC Features*, and our materials brochures) may be placed on our mailing list for a one-time-only fee of $50. Publishers wishing to join should contact the CBC for dues information." Sponsors workshops and seminars. Publishes a newsletter with articles about children's books and publishing, and listings of free or inexpensive materials available from member publishers.

CHILDREN'S READING ROUND TABLE OF CHICAGO, #1507, 3930 N. Pine Grove, Chicago IL 60613. (312)477-2271. Information Chairperson: Marilyn Singer. Purpose of organization: "to support activities which foster and enlarge children and young adults' interest in reading and to promote good fellowship among persons actively interested in the field of children's books." Qualifications for membership: "Membership is open to anyone interested in children's books. There are no professional qualifications; however, the majority of our members are authors, freelance writers, illustrators, librarians, educators, editors, publishers and booksellers." Membership cost: $15 for year (July 1 through June 30), applicable to members within our Chicago meeting area; Associate Membership $10, limited to persons outside the Metropolican Chicago Area or who are retired. "All members have same privileges, which include attendance at meetings; newsletter, *CRRT Bulletin*; yearbook published biennially; and access to information about CRRT special activities." Workshops/conferences: Children's Reading Round Table Summer Seminar for Writers & Illustrators, given in odd-numbered years. The 2-day seminar, at a Chicago college campus, usually in August, features guest speakers and a variety of profession-level workshops, ms critiquing and portfolio appraisal. Enrollment is open to members and nonmembers; one fee applicable to all. Meals included, housing extra. Also, Children's Reading Round Table Children's Literature Conference, given in even-numbered years. One-day program, at a Chicago college campus, usually in early September. Program includes guest authors and educators, variety of workshops, exhibits, bookstore, lunch. Enrollment open to members and nonmembers; one fee applicable to all. *CRRT Bulletin, Children's Reading Round Table of Chicago* is published seven times a year, in advance of dinner meetings, and contains articles; book reviews; special sections of news about authors and artists, librarians and educators, publishers and booksellers. An Opportunity Column provides information about professional meetings, workshops, conferences, generally in the Midwest area. The *Bulletin* is available to members on payment of dues. Sample copies may be requested. Awards: "We do give an honorary award, the Children's Reading Round Table

Annual Award, *not* for a single book or accomplishment but for long-term commitment to children's literature. Award includes check, lifetime membership, plaque. Nominations can be made *only* by CRRT members; nominees are not limited to membership."

CHRISTIAN WRITERS GUILD, 260 Fern Lane, Hume Lake CA 93628. (209)335-2333. Director: Norman B. Rohrer. Purpose of organization: to offer a 48-unit home study, 3-year correspondence course. Qualifications for membership: the ability to think clearly and a commitment to editorial communication. Membership cost: $495 total: $35 down, $15/month. Different levels of membership. "One can join for $45 annually to receive help on his or her editorial projects." Sponsors workshops and conferences. "Conference held at Hume Lake each year for certain in July, then elsewhere as we have invitations." Publishes a small sheet called the "Quill o' the Wisp."

FLORIDA FREELANCE WRITERS ASSOCIATION, Cassell Network of Writers, Maple Ridge Rd., North Sandwich NH 03259. (603)284-6367. Executive Director: Dana K. Cassell. Purpose of organization: to act as a link between Florida writers and buyers of the written word; to help writers run more effective communications businesses. Qualifications for membership: "None—we provide a variety of services and information, some for beginners and some for established pros." Membership cost: $90/year. Sponsors annual conference held third weekend in May. Publishes a newsletter focusing on market news, business news, how-to tips for the serious writer. Non-member subscription: $39—does not include Florida section—includes national edition only. Sponsors contest: annual deadline March 15. Guidelines available fall of year. Categories: juvenile, adult nonfiction, adult fiction, poetry. Awards include cash for top prizes, certificate for others. Contest open to non-members.

GRAPHIC ARTISTS GUILD, 11 W. 20th St., New York NY 10011. (212)463-7730. Executive Director: Paul Basista. Purpose of organization: "To unite within its membership all professionals working in the graphic arts industry; to improve the economic and social conditions of professional artists and designers; to improve industry standards." Qualification for full membership: 51% of income derived from artwork. Associate members include those in allied fields, students and retirees. Initiation fee: $25. Full memberships $100-175/year. Associate membership $55-95/year. Sponsors "Eye to Eye," a national conference exploring the relationships between artists/artists and artists/clients. Publishes *Graphic Artists Guild Handbook, Pricing and Ethical Guidelines*. "Advocates the advancement and protection of artists' rights and interests."

THE INTERNATIONAL WOMEN'S WRITING GUILD, P.O. Box 810, Gracie Station, New York NY 10028. (212)737-7536. Executive Director and Founder: Hannelore Hahn. IWWG is "a network for the personal and professional empowerment of women through writing." Qualifications: open to any woman connected to the written word regardless of professional portfolio. Membership cost: $35 annually; $45 annually for foreign members. "IWWG sponsors 13 annual conferences a year in all areas of the US. The major conference is held in August of each year at Skidmore College in Saratoga Springs NY. It is a week-long conference attracting more than 300 women interna-

---

Market conditions are constantly changing! If you're still using this book and it is 1995 or later, buy the newest edition of Children's Writer's & Illustrator's Market *at your favorite bookstore or order directly from Writer's Digest Books.*

tionally." Also publishes a 28-page magazine, *Network*, 6 times/year; offers health insurance at group rates.

THE JEWISH PUBLICATION SOCIETY, 1930 Chestnut St., Philadelphia PA 19103-4599. (215)564-5925. Editor-in-Chief: Dr. Ellen Frankel. Children's Editor: Bruce Black. Purpose of organization: "to publish quality Jewish books and to promote Jewish culture and education. We are a non-denominational, nonprofit religious publisher. Our children's list specializes in fiction and nonfiction with substantial Jewish content for preschool through young adult readers." Qualifications for membership: "One must purchase a membership of at least $25 which entitles the member to purchase a certain unit number of our books. Our membership is nondiscriminatory on the basis of religion, ethnic affiliation, race or any other criteria." Levels of membership include: JPS member, $25; Associate, $50; Friend, $100; Fellow, $125; Senior member, $200; Sustaining member, $500. "*The JPS Bookmark* reports on JPS Publications; activities of members, authors and trustees; JPS projects and goals; JPS history; children's books and activities." All members receive *The Bookmark* with their membership.

LEAGUE OF CANADIAN POETS, 24 Ryerson Ave., Toronto, Ontario M5T 2P3 Canada. (416)363-5047. Fax: (416)860-0826. Executive Director: Edita Petrauskaite. President: Blaine Marchand. Inquiries to Administrative Assistant: Manny Goncalzes. The L.C.P. is a national organization of published Canadian poets. Our constitutional objectives are to advance poetry in Canada and to promote the professional interests of the members. Qualifications for membership: full—publication of at least one book of poetry by a professional publisher; associate membership—an active interest in poetry, demonstrated by several magazine/periodical publication credits. Membership fees: full—$175/year, associate—$60. Holds an Annual General Meeting every spring; some events open to nonmembers. "We also organize reading programs in schools and public venues. We publish a newsletter which includes information on poetry/poetics in Canada and beyond. Also publish the books *Poetry Markets for Canadians*; *Who's Who in the League of Canadian Poets*; *When is a Poem* (teaching guide) and its accompanying anthology of Canadian Poetry *Vintage*; plus a series of cassettes. We sponsor a National Poetry Contest, open to Canadians living here and abroad." Rules: Unpublished poems of any style/subject, under 75-lines, typed, with name/address on separate sheet. $6 entry fee (includes GST) per poem. $1,000-1st prize, $750-2nd, $500-3rd; plus best 50 published in an anthology. Inquire with SASE. Contest open to Canadian nonmembers. Organizes two annual awards: The Gerald Lampert Memorial Award for the best first book of poetry published in Canada in the preceding year and The Pat Lowther Memorial Award for the best book of poetry by a Canadian woman published in the preceding year. Deadline for both the poetry contest and award is January 31 each year. Send SASE for more details.

NATIONAL STORY LEAGUE, #6, 3516 Russell, St. Louis MO 63104. (314)773-5555. Board Member, Story Art Contributor: E.G. Stirnaman. Purpose of organization: to promote the art of storytelling. Qualifications for membership: the wish to become a good storyteller and to work at it. Annual dues: $15. Publishes a magazine of story art. Non-member subscription: $5. Sponsors storywriting contest (original). Awards include cash and publication. Contest open to nonmembers.

NATIONAL WRITERS ASSOCIATION, (formerly National Writers Club), Suite 424, 1450 S. Havana, Aurora CO 80012. (303)751-7844. Executive Director: Sandy Whelchel. Purpose of organization: association for freelance writers. Qualifications for membership: associate membership—must be serious about writing; professional membership—must be published and paid writer (cite credentials). Membership cost: $50-associate; $60-professional; $15 setup fee for first year only. Workshops/conferences: TV/Screenwriting Workshops, NWA Annual Conferences, Literary Clearinghouse, Editing and Critiquing Services, Local Chapters. National Writer's School. Open to nonmembers. Publishes industry news of interest to freelance writers; how-to articles; market information; member news and networking opportunities. Nonmember subscription $18. Sponsors poetry contest; short story/article contest; novel contest. Awards cash for top three winners; books and/or certificates for other winners; honorable mention certificate places 11-20. Contests open to nonmembers.

NATIONAL WRITERS UNION, Suite 203, 873 Broadway, New York NY 10003. (212)254-0279. Office Manager: Anne Mitchell. Purpose of organization: advocacy for freelance writers. Qualifications for membership: "Membership in the NWU is open to all qualified writers, and no one shall be barred or in any manner prejudiced within the Union on account of race, age, sex, sexual preference, disability, national origin, religion or ideology. You are eligible for membership if you have published a book, a play, three articles, five poems, one short story or an equivalent amount of newsletter, publicity, technical, commercial, government or insitutional copy. You are also eligible for membership if you have written an equal amount of unpublished material and you are actively writing and attempting to publish your work." Membership cost: annual writing income under $5,000, $75/year; annual writing income $5,000-25,000, $125/year; annual writing income over $25,000, $170/year. National union newsletter quarterly, issues related to freelance writing and to union organization. Nonmember subscription: $15.

THE NEBRASKA WRITERS GUILD, P.O. Box 30341, Lincoln NE 68503-0341. (402)477-3804. President: Diane L. Kirkle. Purpose of organization: to provide support and information to professional and aspiring writers. "To be an active member, you must meet at least one of these criteria: have published and placed on sale through regular channels one or more books; have received payment for 5,000 words of prose published in magazines or newspapers of 2,500 circulation or more; have written for television, radio or other media seen or heard by an authenticated audience of 2,500 or more; present evidence of a continuous body of poetry to be judged on the basis of number and quality of publications, regardless of payment or circulation. If you don't qualify as an active member but are interested in the publishing industry, you may join the NWG as an Associate Member." Membership cost: Active and Associate member, $15/year; youth member (has same benefits as Assoc. member but for people under 18), $7/year. Different levels of membership include: Active member—professional writers; Associate member—aspiring writers, editors, publishers, librarians, etc.; Youth member—18 or younger. Holds two conferences/year—between April and October. Provides market and how-to information and news about the Guild and its members.

PEN AMERICAN CENTER, 568 Broadway, New York NY 10012. (212)334-1660. Purpose of organization: "To foster understanding among men and women of letters in all countries. International PEN is the only worldwide organization of writers and the chief voice of the literary community. Members of PEN work for freedom of expression wherever it has been endangered." Qualifications for membership: "The standard qualification for a writer to join PEN is that he or she must have published, in the United States, two or more books of a literary character, or one book generally acclaimed to be of exceptional distinction. Editors who have demonstrated commitment to excellence in their profession (generally construed as five years' service in book editing), translators who have published at least two book-length literary translations, and playwrights whose works have been professionally produced, are eligible for membership. An application form is available upon request from PEN Headquarters in New York. Candidates for membership should be nominated by two current members of PEN. Inquiries about membership should be directed to the PEN Membership Committee. Friends of PEN is also open to writers who may not yet meet the general PEN membership requirements. PEN sponsors more than fifty public events at PEN Headquarters in New York, and at the branch offices in Boston, Chicago, Houston, San Francisco and Portland, Oregon. They include tributes by contemporary writers to classic American writers, dialogues with visiting foreign writers, symposia that bring public attention to problems of censorship and that address current issues of writing in the United States, and readings that introduce beginning writers to the public. PEN's wide variety of literary programming reflects current literary interests and provides informal occasions for writers to meet each other and to welcome those with an interest in literature. Events are all open to the public and are usually free of charge. The Children's Book Authors' Committee sponsors regular public events focusing on the art of writing for children and young adults and on the diversity of literature for juvenile readers. The PEN/Norma Klein Award was established in 1991 to honor an emerging children's book author. National union newsletter covers PEN activities, features interviews with international literary figures, transcripts of PEN literary symposia, reports on issues vital to the literary community. All PEN publications are available by mail order directly from PEN American Center. Individuals must enclose check or money order with their order. Subscription: $8 for 4 issues; sample issue $2. Pamphlets and brochures all free upon request. Sponsors several competitions per year. Monetary awards range from $700-12,750.

THE PLAYWRIGHTS' CENTER, 2301 Franklin Ave. E., Minneapolis MN 55406. (612)332-7481. Outreach Director: Sally MacDonald. Purpose of organization: to serve as a service organization for playwrights, offering development, classes, grants. Qualifications for membership: General members pay $35 fee; Associate and Core members apply for membership through a peer selection panel. Membership cost: $35 annually. Levels of membership include: General—space in calendar, discounts on classes, automatic notification of fellowships and grant opportunities; Associate—a one-year term with access to developmental lab (and all the above); Core—a 7-year term (see above). Sponsors workshops/conferences. Publishes newsletter: Playwrights' Center activities and programs; members' achievements. Sponsors awards: PlayLabs developmental workshops; McKnight, Jerome fellowships; Jones commissions; McKnight Advancement grants; Many Voices programs, exchanges and other opportunities by application. Awards include developmental services, cash awards. Awards open to non-members. Contact: Lisa Stevens, Public Relations/Membership Director.

PUPPETEERS OF AMERICA, INC., #5 Cricklewood Path, Pasadena CA 91107. (818)797-5748. Membership Officer: Gayle Schluter. Purpose of organization: to promote the art of puppetry. Qualifications for membership: interest in the art form. Membership cost: single adult, $35; junior member, $20; retiree, $35 ($25 after member for 5 years); group or family, $55; couple, $45. Sponsors workshops/conferences. Publishes newsletter. *The Puppetry Journal* provides news about puppeteers, puppet theatres, exhibitions, touring companies, technical tips, new products, new books, films, television, and events sponsored by the Chartered Guilds in each of the eight P of A regions. Subscription: $30.

SCIENCE-FICTION AND FANTASY WRITERS OF AMERICA, INC., #1B, 5 Winding Brook Dr., Guilderland NY 12084. (518)869-5361. Executive Secretary: Peter Dennis Pautz. Purpose of organization: to encourage public interest in science fiction literature and provide organization format for writers/editors/artists within the genre. Qualifications for membership: at least one professional sale or other professional involvement within the field. Membership cost: annual active dues—$50; affiliate—$35; one-time installation fee of $10; dues year begins July 1. Different levels of membership include: active—requires three professional short stories or one novel published; affiliate—requires one professional sale or professional involvement. Workshops/conferences: annual awards banquet, usually in April or May. Open to nonmembers. Publishes newsletter. Nonmember subscription: $15 in US. Sponsors SFWA Nebula® Awards for best published science fiction in the categories of novel, novella, novelette and short story. Awards trophy.

SOCIETY OF CHILDREN'S BOOK WRITERS AND ILLUSTRATORS, Suite 106, 22736 Vanowen St., West Hills CA 91307. (818)888-8760. Chairperson, Board of Directors: Sue Alexander. Purpose of organization: to assist writers and illustrators working or interested in the field. Qualifications for membership: an interest in children's literature and illustration. Membership cost: $40/year. Different levels of membership include: full membership—published authors/illustrators; associate membership—unpublished writers/illustrators. Holds 30-40 events (workshops/conferences) around the country each year. Open to nonmembers. Publishes a newsletter focusing on writing and illustrating children's books. Sponsors grants for writers and illustrators who are members.

SOCIETY OF ILLUSTRATORS, 128 E. 63rd St., New York NY 10021. (212)838-2560. Director: Terrence Brown. Purpose of organization: to promote interest in the art of illustration for working professional illustrators and those in associated fields. Membership cost: Initiation fee—$250. Annual dues for Non-Resident members (those living more than 125 air miles from SI's headquarters) are $234. Dues for Resident Artist Members are $396 per year, Resident Associate Members $462. Different levels of membership: *Artist Members* "shall include those who make illustration their profession" and through which they earn at least 60% of their income. *Associate Members* are "those who earn their living in the arts or who have made a substantial contribution to the art of illustration." This includes art directors, art buyers, creative supervisors, instructors, publishers and like categories. "All candidates for membership are admitted by the proposal of one active member and sponsorship of four additional members. The candidate must complete and sign the application form which requires a brief biography, a listing of schools attended, other training and a résumé of his or her professional career." Candidates for *Artist* membership, in addition to the above requirements, must submit examples of their work. Sponsors "The Annual of American Illustration." Awards include gold and silver medals. Open to nonmembers. Deadline: October 1. Sponsors "The Original Art: The Best of Children's Book Illustration." Deadline: mid-July. Call for details.

SOCIETY OF MIDLAND AUTHORS, % Ford-Choyke, 29 E. Division St., Chicago IL 60610. (312)337-1482. President: Phyllis Ford-Choyke. Purpose of organization: create closer association among writers of the Middle West; stimulate creative literary effort; maintain collection of members works; encourage interest in reading and literature by cooperating with other educational and cultural agencies. Qualifications for membership: to be author or co-author of a book demonstrating literary style and published by a recognized publisher or author of published or professionally produced play and be identified through birth or residence with Illinois, Indiana, Iowa, Kansas, Michigan, Minnesota, Nebraska, North Dakota, Ohio, South Dakota or Wisconsin. Membership cost: $25/year dues. Different levels of membership include: regular—published book authors; associate, nonvoting—not published as above but having some connection with literature, such as librarians, teachers, publishers, and editors. Workshops/conferences: program meetings at 410 Club, Chicago, held 5 times a year, featuring authors, publishers, editors or the like individually or on panels. Usually second Tuesday of October, November, January, February and March. Also holds annual awards dinner at 410 Club, Chicago, in May. Publishes a newsletter focusing on news of members and general items of interest to writers. Non-member subscription: $5. Sponsors contests. "Annual awards in 7 categories, given at annual dinner in May. Monetary awards for books published or plays which premiered professionally in previous calendar year. Send SASE to contact person for details." Contest open to non-members.

SOCIETY OF SOUTHWESTERN AUTHORS, P.O. Box 30355, Tucson AZ 85751-0355. President: Don Young. Purpose of organization: to promote fellowship among members of the writing profession, to recognize members' achievements, to stimulate further achievement, and to assist persons seeking to become professional writers. Qualifications for membership: proof of publication of a book, articles, TV screenplay, etc. Membership cost: $25 initiation plus $10/year dues. The Society of Southwestern Authors has annual Writers' Conference, traditionally held the last Saturday of January (write for more information). Publishes a newsletter, *The Write Word*, about members' activities and news of interest to members. Each spring a contest for beginning writers is sponsored. Applications are available in February. Send SASE.

THE WRITERS ALLIANCE, 12 Skylark Lane, Stony Brook NY 11790. (516)571-7080. Executive Director: Kiel Stuart. Purpose of organization: "A support/information group for all types of writers." Membership cost: $15/year, payable to Kiel Stuart. A corporate/group membership costs $25. Publishes newsletter for all writers who use (or want to learn about) computers. Nonmember subscription $15 — payable to Kiel Stuart.

WRITERS CONNECTION, Suite 103, 275 Saratoga Ave., Santa Clara CA 95050-6444. (408)554-2090. Editor: Jan Stiles. Vice President/Program Director: Meera Lester. Purpose of organization: to provide services and resources for writers. Qualifications for membership: interest in writing or publishing. Membership cost: $45/year. Conferences: Selling to Hollywood and various genre conferences, including writing for children. Publishes a newsletter focusing on writing and publishing (all fields except poetry), how-to, markets, contests, tips, etc., included with membership.

Clubs & Organizations/'93-'94 changes

The following markets are not included in this edition of *Children's Writer's & Illustrator's Market* for the reasons indicated within parentheses. If there is no reason given, it means the market did not respond to our requests for updated information for a 1994 listing.

Education Writers Association
San Diego Writers/Editors Guild

Workshops

Writers and illustrators eager to expand their knowledge of the children's industry should consider attending one of the many conferences and workshops held each year. Whether you're a novice or seasoned professional, workshops listed in this section are great places to pick up information on a variety of topics.

Not every workshop included here focuses on juvenile writing or illustrating. Nevertheless, information acquired can be utilized in creating material for children. Illustrators may be interested in general painting and drawing workshops, while writers can learn about techniques and meet editors and agents. Some of these workshops touch on business issues, such as changes in tax and copyright laws.

Artists can find a detailed directory of art workshops annually offered nationwide in the March issue of *The Artist's Magazine*. Writers should consult the May issue of *Writer's Digest* or *The Guide to Writers Conferences* (Shaw Associates, Publishers) for more general conferences.

Listings in this section will provide details about what conference and workshop courses are offered, where and when, and the costs. Some of the national writing and art organizations also offer regional workshops throughout the year. Write to them for information.

ANNUAL ARIZONA CHRISTIAN WRITERS CONFERENCE, P.O. Box 5168, Phoenix AZ 85010. (602)838-4919. Director: Reg Forder. Writer and illustrator workshops geared toward beginner, intermediate and advanced levels. Classes offered include: fiction, nonfiction, poetry, photography, music, etc. Workshops held November 11-13, 1993. Length of each session: 75 minutes. Maximum class size: 30 (approximate). Cost of conference: $119.

*ANTIOCH WRITERS' WORKSHOP, P.O. Box 494, Yellow Springs OH 45387. (513)767-7068. Director: Susan Carpenter. Writers workshop geared toward all levels. Emphasizes "basic poetry, fiction, nonfiction—with some emphasis on genre and on screenwriting; little on children's, but we have one or two informal sessions." Workshops held second week of July. Cost of workshop: $450; includes tuition. Room and board extra.

THE ART & BUSINESS OF HUMOROUS ILLUSTRATION, Cartoon Art Museum, 665 3rd St., San Francisco CA 94107. (415)546-3922. Director: Paola Muggia. Writer and illustrator workshops geared toward professional levels. "Class focus is on cartooning, but we do cover some marketing topics about children's books." Workshops held fall and spring. Length of each session: 10 weeks. Registration limited to 30. Cost of workshop: $145, includes art and writing instruction. Write for more information.

AUTUMN AUTHORS' AFFAIR XI, 1507 Burnham Ave., Calumet City IL 60409. (708)862-9797. President: Nancy McCann. Writer workshop geared toward beginner, intermediate, advanced levels. Emphasizes writing for children and young adults. Annual workshop. Workshops held generally the fourth weekend in October. Cost of workshop: $65 for one day, $100 for weekend. Write for more information.

BE THE WRITER YOU WANT TO BE—MANUSCRIPT CLINIC, Villa 30, 23350 Sereno Court, Cupertino CA 95014. (415)691-0300. Contact: Louise Purwin Zobel. Writer and illustrator workshops geared toward beginner, intermediate, advanced levels. "Participants may turn in manuscripts at any stage of development to receive help with structure and style, as well as marketing advice. Manuscripts receive some written criticism and an oral critique from the instructor, as well as class discussion." Annual workshop. Usually held in the spring. Length of each session: 1-2 days. Registration limited to 20-25. Cost of workshop: $40-65/day, depending on the campus; includes an extensive handout.

BENNINGTON WRITING WORKSHOPS, Bennington College, Bennington VT 05201. (802)442-5401, ext. 320. Assistant Director of Special Programs: Priscilla Hodgkins. Writer and illustrator workshops geared toward beginner, intermediate, advanced and professional levels. Classes offered include fiction, nonfiction and poetry. Annual workshop. Workshops divided into two two-week sessions. Participants can attend one or both. Registration limited to 100-150. Last year's cost of workshop: two weeks tuition $785, room and board $440; four weeks tuition $1,250, room and board $775. Must provide writing sample, résumé of related experience, application form and $25 application fee. Write for more information.

BLUE RIDGE WRITERS CONFERENCE, Roanoke College, 221 College Lane, Salem VA 24153-3794. (703)375-2207. Writer workshops geared toward beginner, intermediate levels. Illustrator workshops geared toward beginner level. Annual workshop. Workshops held first Saturday in October. Length of each session: one day. Registration limited to 200. Cost of conference: $50 includes workshops, lunch, reception and keynote address. No requirements prior to registration unless submitting work for critique. Write for more information (include SASE). "We are a small conference dedicated to inspiring writers and assisting publication. Children's literature is *not* covered every year."

THE BROCKPORT WRITERS FORUM SUMMER WORKSHOPS, Lathrop Hall, State University of New York College at Brockport, Brockport NY 14420. (716)395-5713. Director: Dr. Stan Rubin. Writer workshops geared toward intermediate level. Classes offered include Children's Writing and Writing for Young Adults. Workshops held in July. Length of each session: 6 days. Registration limited to 10-15/genre (60-80 total in all genres offered). Cost of workshop: approximately $400; includes all seminars, readings, guest writers, editors, etc.; access to videotape library; breakfast, some lunches and dinners. Individual conference. Submission of ms in progress or representative finished work required. Write for more information. "Our workshop has run for 12 years drawing participants from New York State and around the U.S. We are a small, pleasant village on the banks of the Erie Canal, 10 miles from Lake Ontario. Our airport is Rochester International." The children's/YA workshop is *not* offered annually. Check with director for schedule.

CAPE LITERARY WORKSHOPS, Cape Cod Writers Center, Route 132, West Barnstable MA 02668. (508)775-4811. Executive Director: Marion Vuilleumier. Writer and illustrator workshops geared toward intermediate, advanced levels. Summer workshops offered in children's book writing and children's book illustration. Workshops held second week in August. Conference held third week in August. Intensive workshops meet Monday-Friday from 9-1. Afternoons and evenings are used to do assignments and enjoy Cape Cod attractions. Class sizes limited. Cost of workshop: $410; includes registration and tuition. Materials, room and board extra. "It is not necessary to have works-in-progress but those who do will find these workshops especially helpful. Participants are encouraged to send current work in advance." Send for brochure for more information on workshops and accommodations.

NINTH ANNUAL CHILDREN'S LITERATURE CONFERENCE, 110 Hofstra University, U.C.C.E., 205 Davison Hall, Hempstead NY 11550. (516)463-5016. Writers/Illustrators Director, Liberal Arts Studies: Lewis Shena. Writer and illustrator workshops geared toward beginner, intermediate, advanced, professional levels. Emphasizes: fiction, nonfiction, poetry, submission procedures, picture books. Workshops held April 23, 1994, 9:30 a.m.-4:30 p.m. Length of each session: one hour. Registration limited to 35/class. Cost of workshop: approximately $50; includes 2 workshops, reception, lunch, panel discussion with guest speakers, e.g. "What An Editor Looks For." Write for more information. Co-sponsored by Society of Children's Book Writers & Illustrators.

CLARION SCIENCE FICTION & FANTASY WRITING WORKSHOP, Lyman Briggs School, E-28 Holmes Hall, Michigan State University, East Lansing MI 48825-1107. (517)353-7196. Administrative Assistant: Mary Sheridan. Writer and illustrator workshop geared toward intermediate levels. Emphasizes science fiction and fantasy. "An intensive workshop designed to stimulate and develop the talent and techniques of potential writers of speculative fiction. Previous experience in writing fiction is assumed. Approximately 20 participants will work very closely together over a six-week period, guided by a series of professional writers of national reputation." 1994 Workshop — June 20-July 30. Length of session: six weeks. Registration limited to 20. Cost of tuition (7 credits of upper-level course work): $500-600 for Michigan resident, $1,300-1,400 for non-Michigan resident (depending on residence and educational status). Lodging (single room) and meal costs are being negotiated. Submission of two mss (up to 2,500 words each) for review, and a completed application form with a $25 application fee required prior to registration. Write for more information.

CREATIVE COLLABORATIVE, P.O. Box 2201, La Jolla CA 92038-2201. (619)459-8897. Director: Penny Wilkes. Writer workshops geared toward intermediate, advanced levels. "Writing topics are geared to stimulating the creative spark and following it through to story development. Sharing of ideas and collaborating to enhance everyone's efforts become the keys to this workshop." Workshops held periodically from October-May. Length of each session: half- to full-day sessions. Registration limited to 20 students. Cost of workshop: $75; includes morning creativity session, afternoon writing and reading. Submission of story (1,500 words) or excerpts not to exceed 5 pages required prior to registration. Write for more information.

*PETER DAVIDSON'S WRITER'S SEMINAR; HOW TO WRITE A CHILDREN'S PICTURE BOOK SEMINAR, (formerly Writer's Seminar), 12 Orchard Lane, Estherville IA 51334. Seminar Presenter: Peter Davidson. Writer's Seminar emphasizes writing fiction, nonfiction, magazine articles, poetry, scripts, children's work, personal experiences, etc. How to Write A Children's Picture Book is for those interested in both writing and illustrating children's material. Seminars are presented year round at community colleges. In 1994, Peter Davidson will present seminars in Colorado, Wyoming, Kansas, Nebraska, Iowa, South Dakota and Minnesota (write for a schedule). Length of each session: one day, 9 am-4 pm. Cost of workshop: varies from $42-59, depending on location; includes approximately 35 pages of handouts. Write for more information.

*DILLMAN'S CREATIVE WORKSHOPS, 3305 Sand Lake Lodge Lane, Lac du Flambeau WI 54538. (715)588-3143. Coordinators: Amber Weldon or Dennis Robertson. "All levels of art workshops (watercolor, acrylics, pastels and oils) geared to all different levels." 1994 schedule includes a wide variety. Write for tentative 1994 schedule. Workshops held mid May through mid October. Length of each session: usually 5 days/6 nights—sometimes weekends. Registration limited to 25/class. Writing and/or art facilities available: 3-4 separate studios—fully equipped. Cost varies from $600-800. This includes room, board and tuition. $100-350 tuition only for people staying off-grounds. Write for brochure (include SASE).

DRURY COLLEGE/SCBWI WRITING FOR CHILDREN WORKSHOP, Drury College, Springfield MO 65802. (417)873-7329. Assistant Director, Continuing Education: Lynn Doke. Writer and illustrator workshop geared toward beginner, intermediate, advanced, professional levels. Emphasizes all aspects of writing for children and teenagers. Classes offered include: "Between Author and Editor: One Editor's View," "Marketing Yourself," "An Editor Works with Illustrators," "No Place for Cowards: Writing Tough Scenes," "Picture Books, or How to Write for Little Bitty Short People," "Digging Up the Bones: Researching the Nonfiction Book," "Children's Interests: What's In It for Me? and Who's In It for You?" and "Skywalking: Poetry that Kids Love." One-day workshop held in October. Length of each session: 1 hour. Ms and portfolio consultations (by appointment only). Registration limited to 25-30/class. $50 registration fee; individual consultations $25. Send SASE for more information.

DUKE UNIVERSITY WRITERS' WORKSHOP, P.O. Box 90703, Durham NC 27708-0703. Director: Marilyn Hartman. "There are various small groups based on level and genre." Writer workshops geared toward beginner, intermediate, advanced, professional levels. Classes offered include short short fiction, creative nonfiction, poetry, youth and young adult fiction, novel, etc. Annual workshop. Workshops held June 19-24, 1994. Length of each session: five days. Registration limited to 10 in each small group. Cost of workshop: $345; includes registration, instruction materials, a few social meals. "Workshop sections are small; participants work a lot. We're low on large-group stuff, high on productivity."

EDUCATION WRITERS ASSOCIATION NATIONAL SEMINAR, 1001 Connecticut Ave. NW, Washington DC 20036. (202)429-9680. Administrative Assistant: Tonya Brice. Writer workshops geared toward beginner, intermediate, advanced and professional levels. Emphasizes topics in education, education writing, investigative reporting in education, narrative writing. Workshops held April, 1994 in Seattle, Washington (annual meeting); regional conferences. Length of each session: 4 days/1 day. Cost of workshop: $195 for annual meeting; includes some meals. Write for more information.

FLORIDA STATE WRITERS CONFERENCE, Cassell Network of Writers, Maple Ridge Rd., North Sandwich NH 03259. (603)284-6367. Executive Director: Dana K. Cassell. Writer workshops geared toward beginner, intermediate, advanced and professional levels. Emphasizes juvenile, novels, books, articles, business management and legal writing. Workshops held third weekend in May. Length of each session: 1 hour. Registration limit varies according to topic. Accommodations are typical hotel facilities. Cost of workshop: varies (single-day through complete packages). Write for more information.

FLORIDA SUNCOAST WRITERS' CONFERENCE, Dept. of English, University of South Florida, Tampa FL 33620. (813)974-1711. Director: Ed Hirshberg. Writer and illustrator workshops geared toward intermediate, advanced, professional levels. Workshops held first weekend in February. Class sizes range from 30-100. Cost of workshop: $95; $75

 The asterisk before a listing indicates the listing is new in this edition.

students; includes all sessions, receptions, panels. Conference is held on St. Petersburg campus of USF.

GREEN LAKE CHRISTIAN WRITERS CONFERENCE, American Baptist Assembly, Green Lake WI 54941-9300. (800)558-8898. Writer workshops geared toward beginner, intermediate and advanced levels. Emphasizes poetry, nonfiction, writing for children, fiction. Classes/courses offered include: same as above plus one-session or two-session presentations on marketing, devotional writing and retelling Bible stories. Workshops held July 9-16, 1994. Length of conference: Saturday dinner through the following Saturday breakfast. Registration limited to 20/class. Writing and/or art facilities available: housing, conference rooms, etc. "No special equipment for writing." Cost of workshop: $80; includes all instruction plus room and meals as selected. Write for more information. "The conference focuses on helping writers to refine their writing skills in a caring atmosphere utilizing competent, caring faculty. This annual conference has been held every year since 1948."

HEART OF AMERICA WRITERS' CONFERENCE, JCCC, 12345 College Blvd., Overland Park KS 66210. (913)469-3838. Director: Judith Choice. Writer workshops geared toward beginner, intermediate, advanced, professional levels. Annual workshop. Workshops held April 29-30, 1994. Length of each session: 1-3 hrs. Registration limited to 250. Cost of workshop: $100; includes lunch, reception. Write for more information.

HIGHLIGHTS FOUNDATION WRITERS WORKSHOP AT CHAUTAUQUA, Dept. CWL, 711 Court St., Honesdale PA 18431. (717)253-1192. Conference Director: Jan Keen. Writer workshops geared toward beginner, intermediate and advanced levels. Classes offered include: "Children's Interests," "Writing Dialogue," "Beginnings and Endings," "Rights, Contracts, Copyrights," "Science Writing." Workshops held July 16-23, 1994, Chautauqua Institution, Chautauqua, NY. Registration limited to 100/class. Write for more information.

HOFSTRA UNIVERSITY SUMMER WRITERS' CONFERENCE, 110 Hofstra University, UCCE, 205 Davison Hall, Hempstead NY 11550-1090. (516)463-5016. Director of Liberal Arts Studies: Lewis Shena. Writer workshops geared toward beginner, intermediate, advanced, professional levels. Classes offered include fiction, nonfiction, poetry, children's literature, stage/screenwriting and other genres. Children's writing faculty has included Pam Conrad, Johanna Hurwitz, Tor Seidler and Jane Zalben, with Maurice Sendak once appearing as guest speaker. Annual workshop. Workshops held July 11-22, 1994. Length of each session: Each workshop meets for 2½ hours daily for a total of 25 hours. Students can register for a maximum of 3 workshops, schedule an individual conference with the writer/instructor and submit a short ms. (less than 10 pages) for critique. Enrollees may register as certificate students or credit students. Cost of workshop: certificate students enrollment fee is approximately $600 plus $26 registration fee; two-credit student enrollment fee is approximately $800 undergraduate and $835 graduate; four-credit student enrollment fee is approximately $1,500 undergraduate and $1,550 graduate. On-campus accommodations for the sessions are available for approximately $300/person. Certificate students may attend any of the five workshops, a private conference and special programs and social events. Credit students may attend only the workshops they have registered for (a maximum of two for two credits each) and the special programs and social events.

INTERNATIONAL WOMEN'S WRITING GUILD, P.O. Box 810, Gracie Station, New York NY 10028. (212)737-7536. Executive Director: Hannelore Hahn. Writer and illustrator workshops geared toward beginner, intermediate, advanced, professional levels. Offers 60 different workshops—some are for children's book writers and illustrators.

Also sponsors 13 other events throughout the US. Annual workshops. Workshops held in August. Length of each session: 1½ hours; sessions take place for an entire week. Registration limited to 400. Cost of workshop: $300. Write for more information. "This workshop always takes place at Skidmore College in Saratoga Springs, NY."

THE IUPUI NATIONAL YOUTH THEATRE PLAYWRITING SYMPOSIUM, 525 N. Blackford St., Indianapolis IN 46202. (317)274-2095. Literary Manager: W. Mark McCreary. "The purpose of the Symposium is to provide a forum in which we can examine and discuss those principles which characterize good dramatic literature for young people and to explore ways to help playwrights and the promotion of quality drama. Publishers, playwrights, directors, producers, librarians and educators join together to examine issues central to playwriting. Playwriting competition held in 1994. Send SASE for guidelines and entry form. Deadline: September 1, 1994.

I'VE ALWAYS WANTED TO WRITE BUT—BEGINNERS' CLASS, Villa 30, 23350 Sereno Ct., Cupertino CA 95014. (415)691-0300. Contact: Louise Purwin Zobel. Writer and illustrator workshops geared toward beginner, intermediate levels. "This seminar/workshop starts at the beginning, although the intermediate writer will benefit, too. There is discussion of children's magazine and book literature today, how to write it and how to market it. Also, there is discussion of other types of writing and the basics of writing for publication." Annual workshops. "Usually several times a year; fall, winter and spring." Sessions last 1-2 days. Cost of workshop: $45-65/day, depending on the campus; includes expensive handout. Write for more information.

*MAINE WRITERS WORKSHOP, 2 Central St., Rockport ME 04856. (207)236-8581. Assistant to Director: Jenni Scidel. Founder and Director, David H. Lyman. "These workshops are for professional writers who have a history of published work. Newspaper writers may wish to develop their craft in writing novels, or to improve their travel writing. Professional travel writers may wish to begin work on their first novel, or need help overcoming a block. Writers without a history of published work are discouraged from attending, but are accepted if samples of their work show talent and dedication. A résumé *must* accompany your application indicating your publishing career." Workshops held in summer and fall. Length of each session: 1 week. Maximum class size: varies. Write for cost information, brochure on workshops and accommodations.

MAPLE WOODS COMMUNITY COLLEGE WRITERS' CONFERENCE, 2601 NE Barry Rd., Kansas City MO 64156. (816)734-4878. Coordinator, Continuing Education: Pattie Smith. Writer workshops geared toward beginner, intermediate levels. Various writing topics and genres covered. Will be held in fall. Length of each session: 1 hour. Registration limited to 150/class. Cost of workshop: $40; includes lunch.

*MARITIME WRITERS' WORKSHOP, Dept. Extension & Summer School, P.O. Box 4400, University of New Brunswick, Fredericton, New Brunswick E3B 5A3 Canada. (506)453-4646. Week-long workshop geared to all levels and held in July. Length of each session: 3 hours per day. Group workshop plus individual conferences, public readings, etc. Registration limited to 10-12/class. Cost of workshop: $250 tuition. Meals and accomodations extra. 10-20 ms pages due before conference (deadline announced). Scholarships available.

MIDLAND WRITERS CONFERENCE, Grace A. Dow Memorial Library, 1710 W. St. Andrews, Midland MI 48640. (517)835-7151. Conference Co-chairs: Margaret Allen and Eileen M. Finzel. Writer and illustrator workshops geared toward beginner, intermediate, advanced and professional levels. "We always have one session each on children's, poetry and basics." Classes offered include: how to write poetry, writing for youth and your literary agent/what to expect. Workshops held June 11, 1994. Length of each session: concurrently, four one-hour and two-hour sessions. Maximum class size: 40. "We are a public library." Cost of workshop: $45; $35 seniors and students. Choice of workshops and the keynote speech given by a prominent author (last year Judith Viorst). Write for more information.

MISSISSIPPI VALLEY WRITERS CONFERENCE, Augustana College, Rock Island IL 61265. (309)762-8985. Conference Director: David R. Collins. Writer workshops geared toward beginner, intermediate, advanced, professional levels. Classes offered include Juvenile Writing—one of nine workshops offered. Annual workshop. Workshops held June 5-10, 1994; usually it is the second week in June each year. Length of each session: Monday through Friday, one hour each day. Registration limited to 20 participants/ workshop. Writing facilities available: college library. Cost of workshop: $25 registration; $40 to participate in one workshop, $70 in two, $30 for each additional; $20 to audit a workshop. Write for more information.

MOUNT HERMON CHRISTIAN WRITERS CONFERENCE, Mount Hermon Christian Conference Center, P.O. Box 413, Mount Hermon CA 95041. (408)335-4466. Director of Public Affairs: David R. Talbott. Writer workshops geared toward beginner, intermediate, advanced and professional levels. Emphasizes religious writing for children via books, articles; Sunday school curriculum; marketing. Classes offered include: Suitable Style for Children; Everything You Need to Know to Write and Market Your Children's Book; Take-Home Papers for Children. Workshops held annually over Palm Sunday weekend: March 25-29, 1994. Length of each session: 5-day residential conferences held annually. Registration limited 45/class, but most are 10-15. Conference center with hotel-style accommodations. Cost of workshop: $450-$560 variable; includes tuition, resource notebook, refreshment breaks, full room and board for 13 meals and 4 nights. Write for more information.

THE NATIONAL WRITERS ASSOCIATION 1994 CONFERENCE, (formerly The National Writers Club Conference), Suite 424, 1450 S. Havana, Aurora CO 80012. (303)751-7844. Executive Director: Sandy Whelchel. Writer workshops geared toward beginner, intermediate, advanced, professional levels. Classes offered include marketing, agenting, "What's Hot in the Market." Annual workshop. Workshops held in June 1994. Length of each session: 50-minute sessions for 2½ days. Write for more information.

CHRISTOPHER NEWPORT UNIVERSITY WRITERS' CONFERENCE, 50 Shoe Lane, Newport News VA 23606-2998. (804)594-7158. Coordinator: Doris Gwaltney. Writer workshops geared toward beginner, intermediate, professional levels. Emphasizes all genres. Length of each session: 2¼ hours. Registration limited to 35/class. Cost of workshop: $65.

101 WAYS TO MARKET YOUR BOOK, P.O. Box 152281, Arlington TX 76015. (817)468-9924. Seminar Director: Mary Bold. Writer workshops geared toward beginner, intermediate levels. Classes offered include heavy emphasis on how books are marketed to the public and how author and publisher can work together in promoting new titles. Annual workshop. Workshops held usually, spring and fall. Length of each session: half day. Cost of workshop: $40-50; includes lunch and materials. No prior requirements. Write for more information. "I am a charter member of the national organization for conference directors, Writers' Conferences & Retreats (WCR). Many of my seminars (for both writers and publishers) are sponsored by area universities and learning centers, as well as by the National Association of Independent Publishers."

OZARK CREATIVE WRITERS, INC. CONFERENCE, 6817 Gingerbread Lane, Little Rock AR 72204. (501)565-8889. President: Peggy Vining. Writer's workshops geared to all levels. "All forms of the creative process dealing with the literary arts. This year we have expanded to songwriting." Always the second weekend in October at Inn of the Ozarks in Eureka Springs AR (a resort town). Morning sessions are given to main attraction author . . . six one-hour satellite speakers during each of the two afternoons. Two banquets. "Approximately 125-150 attend the conference yearly . . . many others enter the creative writing competition." Cost of workshop: $25-30. "This does not include meals or lodging. We do block off fifty rooms prior to September 1 for OCW guests." Write for contest rules for entering competition. "Reserve early."

*PERSPECTIVES IN CHILDREN'S LITERATURE CONFERENCE, 226 Furcolo Hall, University of Massachusetts, Amherst MA 01003. (413)545-4325 or (413)545-1116. Director of Conference: Masha K. Rudman. Writer and illustrator workshops geared to all levels. Emphasis varies from year to year. Workshops held last Saturday in April or first Saturday in May. Length of each session: 9 a.m.-3 p.m. (lunch included). Registration limited to 500. Cost of workshop: about $45. Graduate credit available.

*PORT TOWNSEND WRITER'S CONFERENCE, Centrum, P.O. Box 1158, Port Townsend WA 98368. (206)385-3102. Director: Carol Jane Bangs. Writer workshops geared toward intermediate, advanced and professional levels. Emphasizes writing for children and young adults. Classes offered include: Jane Yolen master class; intermediate/advanced writing for children. Workshops held mid-July. Length of each session: 10 days. Registration limited to 20/class. Writing facilities available: classrooms. Cost of workshop: $360; includes tuition. Publication list for master class. Write for more information. $100 deposit necessary. Applications accepted after December 1 for following July; workshops fill by February.

ROBERT QUACKENBUSH'S CHILDREN'S BOOK WRITING AND ILLUSTRATING WORKSHOP, 460 E. 79th St., New York NY 10021. (212)744-3822. Contact: Robert Quackenbush. Writer and illustrator workshops geared toward beginner, intermediate, advanced, professional levels. Emphasizes picture books from start to finish. Courses offered include: fall and winter courses, extend 10 weeks each—1½ hour/week; July workshop is a full five day (9 a.m.-4 p.m.) extensive course. Workshops held fall, winter and summer. Registration limited to 8/class. Writing and/or art facilities available: work on the premises; art supply store nearby. Cost of workshop: $650 for instruction. Write for more information.

READER'S DIGEST WRITER'S WORKSHOP, Northern Arizona University, P.O. Box 4092, Flagstaff AZ 86011-4092. (602)523-3232. Associate to the President: Ray Newton. Writer workshops geared toward beginner, intermediate, advanced, professional levels. Classes offered include major emphasis on nonfiction magazine articles for major popular publications. Annual workshops in various locations in US. Workshops held June 11-18, 1994 on a Carribean cruise ship and August 19-20, 1994 in Albuquerque, New Mexico. Length of each session: intensive two-day sessions, each approximately 1 hour. Registration limited to 250. Writing facilities available: Usually computers and other writing facilities. Cost of workshop: June—$1,500, includes airfare, cruise, workshop fee and taxes; August—$60 for first day, $90 second day; $140 both days. "Participants will have opportunity for one-on-one sessions with major editors, writers representing national magazines, including the *Reader's Digest*." Write for more information.

SAN DIEGO STATE UNIVERSITY WRITERS' CONFERENCE, The College of Extended Studies, San Diego CA 92182. (619)594-5152. Extension Director: Jan Wahl. Writer workshops geared toward beginner, intermediate and advanced levels. Emphasizes nonfiction, fiction, screenwriting, advanced novel writing. Classes offered include: Learning to Think Like an Editor; Writing for Television and Motion Pictures; Writing Children's Nonfiction and Picture Books. Workshops held third weekend in January each year. Length of each session: 50 minutes. Registration limited to 100/class. Cost of workshop: 1993 fees were $184; included Saturday reception, 2 lunches and all sessions. Write for more information.

SEMINARS FOR WRITERS, % Writers Connection, Suite 103, 275 Saratoga Ave., Santa Clara CA 95050-6664. (408)554-2090. Fax: (408)554-2099. Program Director: Meera Lester. Writer's workshops geared toward beginner, intermediate levels. Length of each session: six-hour session usually offered on a Saturday. Registration limited to 30-35/ class. Occasional seminars on writing for children (approximately 1-2 per year). Bookstore of writing, reference and how-to books. Monthly newsletter with membership only. Write for more information.

SOCIETY OF CHILDREN'S BOOK WRITERS & ILLUSTRATORS – FLORIDA REGION, Apt. F-103, 2000 Springdale Blvd., Palm Springs FL 33461. (407)433-1727. Florida Regional Advisor: Jean Shirley. Writer and illustrator workshops geared toward beginner, intermediate, advanced and professional levels. Subjects to be announced. Workshop held in the meeting rooms of the Palm Springs Public Library, 217 Cypress Lane, Palm Springs FL. Registration limited to 100/class. Cost of workshop: $35 for members, $40 for non-members. Write for more information. "We plan to give one conference a year to be held on the second Saturday in September."

SOCIETY OF CHILDREN'S BOOK WRITERS & ILLUSTRATORS – HAWAII, 2908 Robert Place, Honolulu HI 96816. (808)737-6963. Regional Advisor: Ruth Brantley. Writer and illustrator conferences geared toward beginner, intermediate, advanced, professional levels and others interested in promoting children's literature. Write for more information.

SOCIETY OF CHILDREN'S BOOK WRITERS & ILLUSTRATORS – INDIANA RETREAT, 4810 Illinois Rd., Fort Wayne IN 46804. (219)436-2160. Conference Director: Betsy Storey. Writer and illustrator workshops geared toward beginner, intermediate, advanced, professional levels. Classes offered include "Nuts and Bolts for Beginners"; "First Sales"; "Professionalism, Writing the Picture Book"; and "Nonfiction for Children." All are geared toward children's writers and illustrators. Workshops held annually in June. Length of each session: 45 minutes to 1½ hours. Cost of workshop: approximately $225; includes accommodations, meals and workshops. Write for more information. "Ms and portfolio critiques by published writers and illustrators will be offered at additional charge."

SOCIETY OF CHILDREN'S BOOK WRITERS & ILLUSTRATORS – MID-ATLANTIC WRITERS' ANNUAL CONFERENCE, P.O. Box 1707, Midlothian VA 23112. (804)744-6503. Contact Regional Advisor: Mrs. T.R. Hollingsworth. Writer workshops geared toward all levels. Illustrator workshops geared toward beginner, intermediate levels. Annual workshop. Workshops held in fall of each year. Length of each session: one day. Registration limited to 100. Writing and/or art facilities available: writing contest, display of illustrations. Cost of workshop: $60-70; includes breakfast coffee, luncheon, afternoon soft drinks. Write for more information.

SOCIETY OF CHILDREN'S BOOK WRITERS & ILLUSTRATORS NEW ENGLAND CONFERENCE, RFD #3, Box 627 Putney VT 05346. (802)387-2601. Regional Advisor: Jessie Haas. Writer/illustrator workshops geared toward all levels. Emphasizes writing and illustrating for the children's market. One-day workshop held April 16, 1994 in Brattleboro VT (location varies from year to year) includes keynote speakers and many workshops. Length of each session: 8-5 p.m. Registration limited to 250. "Specific cost yet to be determined; usually includes all-day conference, lunch. Conference is open to both published and unpublished writers and illustrators of children's books (and magazines) and anyone else interested in those aspects of children's books.'

SOCIETY OF CHILDREN'S BOOK WRITERS & ILLUSTRATORS—ROCKY MOUNTAIN CHAPTER SUMMER RETREAT, Franciscan Center, Colorado Springs CO 80919. Conference Director: Mary Peace Finley. Writer workshop geared toward beginner, intermediate, advanced, professional levels. Annual workshop. Workshops held July 29-31, 1994. Length of session: Friday-Sunday. Registration limited to 60. Cost of workshop: approximately $200; includes room, board and all sessions. Participants may submit writing to be critiqued by speakers (additional fee charged). Write for more information.

*SOCIETY OF CHILDREN'S BOOK WRITERS & ILLUSTRATORS—TENNESSEE SPRING CONFERENCE, Box 3342, Clarksville TN 37043-3342. (615)358-9849. Regional Advisor: Cheryl Zach. Writer workshop geared toward beginner, intermediate, advanced and professional levels. Illustrator workshops geared toward beginner, intermediate levels. Emphasizes writing the picture book, writing and selling chapter books and middle grade fiction, young adult fiction, characterization, nonfiction and biography, plotting young adult and middle grade novels. Workshop held in the Spring. Length of each session: one day. Registration limited to 100. Write for more information. "SCBWI-Tennessee's 1994 conference is scheduled for April 30 in Nashville."

SOCIETY OF CHILDREN'S BOOK WRITERS & ILLUSTRATORS—WISCONSIN FOURTH ANNUAL FALL RETREAT, 26 Lancaster Court, Madison WI 53719-1433. (608)271-0433. Regional Advisor: Sheri Cooper Sinykin. Writer workshops geared toward beginner, intermediate, advanced, professional levels. Classes offered include: Pre-publication Secrets; Post-Publication Problems; workshops on craft; author-editor dialogues on the revision process; working relationships; marketing. "The entire retreat is geared *only* to children's book writing." Annual workshop. Workshops held September 30-October 2, 1994. Length of each session: 1-2 hours; retreat lasts from Friday evening to Sunday afternoon. Registration limited to approximately 60. Cost of workshop: usually $160-180 for SCBWI members, higher for non-members; includes room, board, book and program. "We strive to offer an informal weekend with an award-winning children's writer, an illustrator and an editor from a trade house in New York."

SOUTHERN CALIFORNIA SOCIETY OF CHILDREN'S BOOK WRITERS & ILLUSTRATORS; ILLUSTRATORS DAY, #105, 11943 Montana Ave., Los Angeles CA 90049. (310)820-5601. Regional Advisor: Judith Enderle. Illustrator workshops geared toward beginner, intermediate, advanced, professional levels. Emphasizes illustration and illustration markets. Conference includes: presentations by art director, children's book editor and panel of artists/author-illustrators. Workshops held annually in the fall. Length of session: full day. Maximum class size: 100. "Editors and art directors will view portfolios. We want to know if each conferee is bringing a portfolio or not." SCBWI Membership: $40/yr. "This is a chance for illustrators to meet editors/art directors and each other. Writers Day held in the spring. National conference for authors *and* illustrators held every August."

SPLIT ROCK ARTS PROGRAM, University of Minnesota, 306 Wesbrook Hall, 77 Pleasant St. SE, Minneapolis MN 55455. (612)624-6800. Registrar: Vivien Oja. Writer and illustrator workshops geared toward intermediate, advanced, professional levels. Workshops offered in writing and illustrating books for children and young people. 1994 workshops begin July 10. Length of each session: One week intensive, Sunday night to Saturday noon. Two college credits available. Registration limited to 16/class. Workshops held on the University of Minnesota-Duluth campus. Cost of workshop: $290-345; includes tuition and fees. Amounts vary depending on course fee, determined by supply needs, etc. "Moderately priced on-campus housing available." Complete catalogs available March 15. Call or write anytime to be put on mailing list. Some courses fill very early.

STATE OF MAINE WRITERS' CONFERENCE, 16 Colby Ave., Ocean Park ME 04063. (207)934-5034 (summer). (413)596-6734 (winter). Chairman: Richard F. Burns. Writers' workshops geared toward beginner, intermediate, advanced levels. Emphasizes poetry, prose, mysteries, editors, publishers, etc. Annual workshop. Workshops held August 16-19, 1994. Cost of workshop: $70; include all sessions and banquet, snacks, poetry booklet. Write for more information.

MARK TWAIN WRITERS CONFERENCE, 921 Center St., Hannibal MO 63401. (314)221-2462 or (800)747-0738. Director: James C. Hefley. Writers' workshops geared toward beginner, intermediate and advanced levels. Emphasizes fiction, nonfiction, photography. Workshops covering poetry, humor, Mark Twain, newspapers, freelancing, the autobiography and working with an agent. Workshops held in June. Length of each session: 50-90 minutes. Registration limited to 12-20/class. Writing facilities available: computers. Cost of workshop: $395; includes all program fees, room, meals and group photo. Write for more information.

UNIVERSITY OF KENTUCKY WOMEN WRITERS CONFERENCE, 106 Frazee Hall, University of Kentucky, Lexington KY 40506-0031. (606)257-6681. Conference Director: Jane Oaks. Writer workshops geared toward beginner, intermediate, advanced, professional levels. Courses offered include: annual ms workshops for poets, playwrights, children's writers, short fiction writers. Workshops held in October. Length of session: 3 hours. Cost of workshop: $10-25/day; includes registration. Submit ms by deadline, 3 months before conference. 20 pages maximum; 4 poems, maximum 6 pages; essays, maximum 10 pages. "Write to obtain brochure, available mid-August, outlining daily events, visiting writers bio info, registration costs/procedures."

VASSAR INSTITUTE OF PUBLISHING AND WRITING: CHILDREN'S BOOKS IN THE MARKETPLACE, Box 300, Vassar College, Poughkeepsie NY 12601. (914)437-5903. Program Coordinator: Maryann Bruno. Director: Barbara Lucas. Writer and illustrator workshops geared toward beginner, intermediate, advanced, professional levels. Emphasizes "the editorial, production, marketing and reviewing processes, on writing fiction and nonfiction for all ages, creating the picture book, understanding the markets and selling your work." Classes offered include: "Writing Fiction," "The Editorial Process," "How to Write a Children's Book and Get It Published." Workshop held second week of June or July. Length of each session: 3½-hour morning critique sessions, afternoon and evening lectures. Registration limited to 40/class (with three instructors). Cost of workshop: approximately $700, includes room, board and tuition for all critique sessions, lectures and social activities. "Proposals are pre-prepared and discussed at morning critique sessions. Art portfolio review given on pre-prepared works." Write for more information. "This conference gives a comprehensive look at the publishing industry as well as offering critiques of creative writing and portfolio review."

VENTURA/SANTA BARBARA (CA) SPRING MINI-CONFERENCE AND FALL WORK-SHOP, 5777 Summerfield, Camarillo CA 93012. (805)482-9417. Regional Advisor: Jean Stangl. Writer workshops geared toward beginner, intermediate, advanced, professional levels. "We invite editors, authors and author/illustrators. We have had speakers on the picture book, middle grade, YA, magazine, religious markets and photographer for photo essay books. Both fiction and nonfiction are covered." Semiannual workshops. Workshop held in February and October. Length of each session: 9:30 a.m.-4 p.m. on Saturdays. Cost of workshop: $40; includes all sessions and lunch. Write for more information.

WELLS WRITERS' WORKSHOP, 69 Broadway, Concord NH 03301. (603)225-9162. Co-ordinator: Victor Andre Levine. Writer workshops geared toward beginner, intermediate levels. "Sessions focus on careful plot preparation, as well as on effective writing (characterization, dialogue and description), with lots of time for writing." Workshops offered twice a year. Length of each session: 5 days. Registration limited to 5/class. Writing facilities available: space, electrical outlets, resident MS-DOS computer. Cost of workshop: $750; some scholarship money available. Cost includes tuition, housing and food. Write for more information. "I invite interested writers to call or write. I'd be happy to meet with them if they're reasonably close by. Workshop stresses the importance of getting the structure right when writing stories for children."

WESLEYAN WRITERS CONFERENCE, Wesleyan University, Middletown CT 06459. (203)343-3988, ext. 2448. Director: Anne Greene. Writer workshops geared toward beginner, intermediate, advanced and professional levels. "This conference is useful for writers interested in how to structure a story, poem or nonfiction piece. Although we don't always offer classes in writing for children, the advice about structuring a piece is useful for writers of any sort, no matter who their audience is." Classes in the novel, short story, fiction techniques, poetry, journalism and literary nonfiction. Guest speakers and panels offer discussion of fiction, poetry, reviewing, editing and publishing. Individual ms consultations available. Workshops held annually the last week in June. Length of each session: 6 days. "Usually, there are 100 participants at the Conference." Classrooms, meals, lodging and word processing facilities available on campus. Cost of workshop: tuition—$415, room—$85, meals (required of all participants)—$165. "Anyone may register; people who want financial aid must submit their work and be selected by scholarship judges." Write for more information.

WESTERN RESERVE WRITERS AND FREELANCE CONFERENCE, Lakeland Community College, 7700 Clocktower Dr., Mentor OH 44060. (216)953-7080. Coordinator: Lea Leever Oldham. Writer workshops geared toward beginner, intermediate, advanced, professional levels. Emphasizes fiction, photography, greeting card writing, science fiction and fantasy writing, poetry. Classes offered include: Writing For Children in Whole Language & Curriculum. Workshops held in mid-September. Length of each session: 7 hrs. Cost of workshop: $39; includes sessions and lunch. Critiques available at $10 per 10 pages. Other workshops held in late March or early April. Write for more information to #110, 34200 Ridge Rd., Willoughby OH 44094. (216)943-3047.

WILLAMETTE WRITERS ANNUAL WRITERS CONFERENCE, Suite 5A, 9045 SW Barbur Blvd., Portland OR 97219. (503)452-1542. Writer workshops geared toward beginner, intermediate, advanced, professional levels. Emphasizes all areas of writing. Opportunities to meet one-on-one with leading literary agents and editors. Workshops held in August.

*WORKING WRITERS RETREAT—SCBWI NW, 12180 Southwest Ann Place, Tigard OR 97223. (503)639-5754. Retreat Chair: Margaret Bechard. Writer workshop geared toward intermediate, advanced levels. Illustrator workshop geared toward beginner, intermediate levels. "We have craft lectures with published authors who usually discuss how they got started, how they work and how they market. We also have an editor who usually discusses market trends. In the mornings, we have craft lectures. The afternoons are devoted to small groups where participants can critique manuscripts, exchange ideas or meet with the faculty." Retreat held at Silver Falls Conference Center. "We basically go all day. Although participants may choose to not attend everything." Registration limited to 40. Small groups are usually 5-10 people. Cost of workshop: 1991 prices: $255 (members of SCBWI-NW $10/year for membership), $280 (nonmembers); double occupancy room (single $45 more), 5 nights, all meals, all events.

*WRITE TO SELL WRITER'S CONFERENCE, 8465 Jane St., San Diego CA 92129. (619)484-8575. Conference Director: Diane Dunaway. Writer and illustrator workshops geared toward beginner, intermediate, advanced, professional levels. Emphasizes How-to, Trends, Read and Critique; Workshops led by writers, editors and agents. Classes offered include: Writing the Picture Book, Middle Grade, YA, General Fiction, Nonfiction and Screen Writing; Illustrating for Children's Books. Workshops held second weekend in May. Length of each session: 50 minutes. Maximum class size: 100. Conference is held at a local hotel; workshops are held in individual classrooms. Cost of conference: $195. Cost includes Friday evening through Sunday and two lunches. "Just bring chapters and/or artwork." Write for more information.

*WRITERS STUDIO SPRING WRITERS CONFERENCE, 3403 45th St., Moline IL 61265. (309)762-8985. Coordinator, Pro Tem: David R. Collins. Writer workshops geared toward intermediate level. Emphasizes basic writing and mechanics. Workshops held March 26, 1994. Length of each session: 3 hours. Workshop is free. Write for more information.

WRITING BOOKS FOR CHILDREN, Nathan Mayhew Seminars of Martha's Vineyard, P.O. Box 1125, Vineyard Haven MA 02568. (508)693-6603. Director: Cynthia Riggs. Writer and illustrator workshops geared toward intermediate and advanced levels. Annual workshop. Workshops held in mid-August, Friday-Sunday from 9 a.m.-4 p.m. Registration limited to 25. Overnight accommodations available on campus. Cost of workshop: $175. Write for more information.

Workshops/'93-'94 changes

The following markets are not included in this edition of *Children's Writer's & Illustrator's Market* for the reasons indicated within parentheses. If there is no reason given, it means the market did not respond to our requests for updated information for a 1994 listing.

Biola University Writers Institute (institute closed)
Children's Book Publishing: A Comprehensive Book Illustrations Workshop

Children's Book Publishing: An Intensive Writing & Editing Workshop
Southern California Writers Conference * San Diego

Writing for Young People
Writing Multicultural Books for Children and Young Adults (no longer offered)

Recommended Books & Publications

Children's Writer's & Illustrator's Market recommends the following reading materials to stay informed of market trends as well as to find additional names and addresses of buyers of juvenile material. Many of the publications recommended here incorporate business-oriented material with information about how to write or illustrate more creatively and skillfully. Most are available in a library or bookstore or may be ordered directly from the publisher.

Books of interest

THE ART OF WRITING FOR CHILDREN: SKILLS & TECHNIQUES OF THE CRAFT. Epstein, Connie C. Archon Books, 1991.

THE ARTIST'S FRIENDLY LEGAL GUIDE. Conner, Floyd; Karlen, Peter; Perwin, Jean; Spatt, David M. North Light Books, 1991.

GETTING STARTED AS A FREELANCE ILLUSTRATOR OR DESIGNER. Fleishman, Michael. North Light Books, 1990.

GUIDE TO WRITING FOR CHILDREN. Yolen, Jane. The Writer, Inc., 1989.

HOW TO SELL YOUR PHOTOGRAPHS & ILLUSTRATIONS. Gordon, Elliott & Barbara. North Light Books, 1990.

HOW TO WRITE, ILLUSTRATE, AND DESIGN CHILDREN'S BOOKS. Gates, Frieda. Lloyd-Simone Publishing Company, 1986.

HOW TO WRITE & SELL CHILDREN'S PICTURE BOOKS. Karl, Jean. Writer's Digest Books, 1994.

HOW TO WRITE A CHILDREN'S BOOK & GET IT PUBLISHED. Seuling, Barbara. Charles Scribner's Sons, 1991.

HOW TO WRITE AND ILLUSTRATE CHILDREN'S BOOKS. Bicknell, Treld Pelkey; Trotman, Felicity, eds. North Light Books, 1988.

ILLUSTRATING CHILDREN'S BOOKS: A GUIDE TO DRAWING, PRINTING, & PUBLISHING. Hands, Nancy S. Prentice Hall Press, 1986.

MARKET GUIDE FOR YOUNG WRITERS. Henderson, Kathy. Writer's Digest Books, 1993.

THE WRITER'S ESSENTIAL DESK REFERENCE. Neff, Glenda, ed. Writer's Digest Books, 1991.

A WRITER'S GUIDE TO A CHILDREN'S BOOK CONTRACT. Flower, Mary. Fern Hill Books, 1988.

WRITING BOOKS FOR YOUNG PEOPLE. Giblin, James Cross. The Writer, Inc., 1990.

WRITING FOR CHILDREN & TEENAGERS. Wyndham, Lee; Madison, Arnold. Writer's Digest Books, 1988.

WRITING WITH PICTURES: HOW TO WRITE AND ILLUSTRATE CHILDREN'S BOOKS. Shulevitz, Uri. Watson-Guptill Publications, 1985.

Publications of interest

BYLINE. Preston, Marcia, ed. P.O. Box 130596, Edmond OK 73013.

BOOK LINKS. American Library Association, 50 E. Huron St., Chicago IL 60611.

CHILDREN'S BOOK INSIDER. Backes, Laura, ed. P.O. Box 2290, Evergreen CO 80439-2290.

CHILDREN'S WRITER. Susan Tierney, ed. The Institute of Children's Literature, 95 Long Ridge Rd., West Redding CT 06896-1124.

THE FIVE OWLS. 2004 Sheridan Ave. S., Minneapolis MN 55405.

THE HORN BOOK MAGAZINE. Silvey, Anita, ed. The Horn Book, Inc., 14 Beacon St., Boston MA 02108.

THE LION AND THE UNICORN: A CRITICAL JOURNAL OF CHILDREN'S LITERATURE. The Johns Hopkins University Press—Journals Publishing Division, Suite 275, 701 W. 40th St., Baltimore MD 21211-2190.

ONCE UPON A TIME . . . . Baird, Audrey, ed. 553 Winston Court, St. Paul MN 55118.

SOCIETY OF CHILDREN'S BOOK WRITERS AND ILLUSTRATORS BULLETIN. Mooser, Stephen; Oliver, Lin, eds. Society of Children's Book Writers and Illustrators, Suite 106, 22736 Vanowen St., West Hills CA 91307.

Glossary

AAR. Association of Author's Representatives (merger of Society of Author's Representatives and Independent Literary Agents Association, Inc.).

Advance. A sum of money a publisher pays a writer prior to the publication of a book. It is usually paid in installments, such as one-half on signing the contract; one half on delivery of a complete and satisfactory manuscript. The advance is paid against the royalty money that will be earned by the book.

AIMP. Association of Independent Music Publishers.

All rights. The rights contracted to a publisher permitting a manuscript's use anywhere and in any form, including movie and book-club sales, without additional payment to the writer.

Anthropomorphization. To attribute human form and personality to things not human (such as animals).

ASAP. Abbreviation for as soon as possible.

ASCAP. American Society of Composers, Authors and Publishers. A performing rights organization.

B&W. Abbreviation for black & white artwork or photographs.

Backlist. A publisher's list of books not published during the current season but still in print.

Biennially. Once every two years.

Bimonthly. Once every two months.

Biweekly. Once every two weeks.

Bleed. Area of a plate or print that extends beyond the actual trimmed sheet to be printed.

BMI. Broadcast Music, Inc. A performing rights organization.

Book packager. Draws all elements of a book together, from the initial concept to writing and marketing strategies, then sells the book package to a book publisher and/or movie producer. Also known as book producer or book developer.

Business-size envelope. Also known as a #10 envelope, it is the standard size used in sending business correspondence.

Camera-ready. Art that is completely prepared for copy camera platemaking.

Caption. A description of the subject matter of an illustration or photograph; photo captions include names of people where appropriate. Also called cutline.

Clean-copy. A manuscript free of errors and needing no editing; it is ready for typesetting.

Contract. A written agreement stating the rights to be purchased by an editor or art director and the amount of payment the writer or illustrator will receive for that sale.

Contributor's copies. The magazine issues sent to an author or illustrator in which his/her work appears.

Copy. Refers to the actual written material of a manuscript.

Copyediting. Editing a manuscript for grammar usage, spelling, punctuation, and general style.

Copyright. A means to legally protect an author's/illustrator's work. This can be shown by writing ©, your name, and year of work's creation.

Cover letter. A brief letter, accompanying a complete manuscript, especially useful if responding to an editor's request for a manuscript. A cover letter may also accompany a book proposal. See The Business of Children's Writing & Illustrating.

Cutline. See caption.

Disk. A round, flat magnetic plate on which computer data is stored.

Division. An unincorporated branch of a company.

Professional Courses to Help Make You a More Successful, Published Writer

Novel Writing Workshop. A professional novelist helps you iron out your plot, develop your main characters, write the background for your novel, and complete the opening scene and a summary of your novel's complete story. You'll even identify potential publishers and write a query letter.

Nonfiction Book Workshop. You'll work with your mentor to create a book proposal that you can send directly to a publisher. You'll develop and refine your book idea, write a chapter-by-chapter outline of your subject, line up your sources of information, write sample chapters, and complete your query letter.

Writing to Sell Fiction. Learn the basics of writing and selling short stories: plotting, characterization, dialogue, theme, conflict, and other elements of a marketable short story. You'll write one complete short story by the conclusion of your course.

Writing to Sell Nonfiction. Master the fundamentals of writing and selling nonfiction articles: finding article ideas, conducting interviews, writing effective query letters, targeting your articles to the right publications, and other important elements of a salable article. You'll complete one article manuscript and its revision by the end of the course.

Fine Art Courses Designed to Make You a More Confident, More Accomplished Artist

The Fundamentals of Fine Art. A comprehensive program in the basics of drawing and painting. The Fundamentals of Fine Art course provides a solid foundation for beginners and an excellent refresher for artists who want to fine tune their drawing, sketching and composition skills in five easy-to-follow lessons: Observation and Drawing, Form and Perspective, Design and Composition, Materials, and Color.

The Artist's Studio Workshops. Enjoy all the excitement of a painting workshop right in your own studio! You'll concentrate on perfecting your skill in your favorite medium—watercolor, oil or acrylic—as you create 12 original paintings that will be evaluated by your personal art tutor.

For FREE information about these exciting courses, mail the post-paid card below today!

Dummy. Handmade mock-up of a book.

Final draft. The last version of a "polished" manuscript ready for submission to the editor.

First North American serial rights. The right to publish material in a periodical before it appears in book form, for the first time, in the United States or Canada.

Flat fee. A one-time payment.

GAG. Graphic Artists Guild.

Galleys. The first typeset version of a manuscript that has not yet been divided into pages.

Gatefold. A page larger than the trim size of a book which is folded so as not to extend beyond the edges.

Genre. A formulaic type of fiction, such as adventure, mystery, romance, science fiction or western.

Glossy. A black & white photograph with a shiny surface as opposed to one with a non-shiny matte finish.

Gouache. Opaque watercolor with an appreciable film thickness and an actual paint layer.

Halftone. Reproduction of a continuous tone illustration with the image formed by dots produced by a camera lens screen.

Hard copy. The printed copy of a computer's output.

Hi-Lo. Abbreviation for high interest, low reading level, as it pertains mostly to beginning adult readers.

Illustrations. May be artwork, photographs, old engravings. Usually paid for separately from the manuscript.

Imprint. Name applied to a publisher's specific line or lines of books.

IRC. International Reply Coupon; sold at the post office to enclose with text or artwork sent to a foreign buyer to cover his postage cost when replying or returning work.

Keyline. Identification, through signs and symbols, of the positions of illustrations and copy for the printer.

Kill fee. Portion of the agreed-upon price the author or artist receives for a job that was assigned, worked on, but then canceled.

Layout. Arrangement of illustrations, photographs, text and headlines for printed material.

Line drawing. Illustration done with pencil or ink using no wash or other shading.

LORT. League of Resident Theaters.

Mechanicals. Paste-up or preparation of work for printing.

Middle reader. The general classification of books written for readers 9-11 years of age.

Modem. A small electrical box that plugs into the serial card of a computer, used to transmit data from one computer to another, usually via telephone lines.

Ms (mss). Abbreviation for manuscript(s).

One-time rights. Permission to publish a story in periodical or book form one time only.

Outline. A summary of a book's contents in 5-15 double-spaced pages; often in the form of chapter headings with a descriptive sentence or two under each one to show the scope of the book.

Package sale. The editor buys manuscript and illustrations/photos as a "package" and pays for them with one check.

Payment on acceptance. The writer or artist is paid for his work at the time the editor or art director decides to buy it.

Payment on publication. The writer or artist is paid for his work when it is published.

Photocopied submissions. Submitting photocopies of an original manuscript instead of sending the original. Do not assume that an editor who accepts photocopies will also accept simultaneous submissions.

Photostat. Black & white copies produced by an inexpensive photographic process using paper negatives; only line values are held with accuracy. Also called stat.

Picture book. A type of book aimed at the preschool to 8-year-old that tells the story primarily or entirely with artwork.

PMT. Photostat produced without a negative, somewhat like the Polaroid process.

Print. An impression pulled from an original plate, stone, block, screen or negative; also a positive made from a photographic negative.

Proofreading. Reading a manuscript to correct typographical errors.

Query. A letter to an editor designed to capture his/her interest in an article or book you purpose to write.

Reading fee. An arbitrary amount of money charged by some agents and publishers to read a submitted manuscript.

Reprint rights. Permission to print an already published work whose rights have been sold to another magazine or book publisher.

Response time. The average length of time it takes an editor or art director to accept or reject a manuscript or artwork and inform you of the decision.

Rights. What you offer to an editor or art director in exchange for printing your manuscripts or artwork.

Rough draft. A manuscript which has been written but not checked for errors in grammar, punctuation, spelling or content. It usually needs revision and rewriting.

Roughs. Preliminary sketches or drawings.

Royalty. An agreed percentage paid by the publisher to the writer or illustrator for each copy of his work sold.

SASE. Abbreviation for self-addressed, stamped envelope.

SCBWI. Society of Children's Book Writers and Illustrators.

Second serial rights. Permission for the reprinting of a work in another periodical after its first publication in book or magazine form.

Semiannual. Once every six months.

Semimonthly. Twice a month.

Semiweekly. Twice a week.

Serial rights. The rights given by an author to a publisher to print a piece in one or more periodicals.

Simultaneous submissions. Sending the same article, story, poem or illustration to several publishers at the same time. Some publishers refuse to consider such submissions. No simultaneous submissions should be made without stating the fact in your cover letter.

Slant. The approach to a story or piece of artwork that will appeal to readers of a particular publication.

Slush pile. What editors call the collection of submitted manuscripts which have not been specifically asked for.

Software. Programs and related documentation for use with a particular computer system.

Solicited manuscript. Material which an editor has asked for or agreed to consider before being sent by the writer.

SPAR. Society of Photographers and Artists Representatives, Inc.

Speculation (Spec). Writing or drawing a piece with no assurance from the editor or art director that it will be purchased or any reimbursements for material or labor paid.

Stat. See photostat.

Subsidiary rights. All rights other than book publishing rights included in a book contract, such as paperback, book club and movie rights.

Subsidy publisher. A book publisher who charges the author for the cost of typesetting, printing and promoting a book. Also vanity publisher.

Synopsis. A brief summary of a story or novel. If part of a book proposal, it should be a page to a page and a half, single-spaced.

Tabloid. Publication printed on an ordinary newspaper page turned sideways.

Tearsheet. Page from a magazine or newspaper containing your printed art, story, article, poem or ad.

Thumbnail. A rough layout in miniature.

Transparencies. Positive color slides; not color prints.

Unsolicited manuscript. A story, article, poem, book or artwork sent without the editor's or art director's knowledge or consent.

Vanity publisher. See subsidy publisher.

Word length. The maximum number of words a manuscript should contain as determined by the editor or guidelines sheet.

Word processor. A computer that produces typewritten copy via automated typing, text-editing, and storage and transmission capabilities.

Young adult. The general classification of books written for readers ages 12-18.

Young reader. The general classification of books written for readers ages 5-8.

Age-Level Index

This index is designed to help you more quickly locate book and magazine markets geared to the age group(s) for which you write or illustrate. Read each listing carefully and follow the publisher's specific information about the type(s) of manuscript(s) each prefers and the style(s) of artwork each wishes to review.

Book Publishers

Picture books (preschoolers to 8-year-olds). Advocacy Press; Aegina Press/University Editions; Africa World Press; African American Images; Aladdin Books/Collier Books for Young Readers; Alyson Publications, Inc.; American Bible Society; American Education Publishing; Atheneum Publishers; Bantam Doubleday Dell; Barrons Educational Series; Behrman House Inc.; Bess Press; Black Moss Press; Boyds Mills Press; Bradbury Press; Carolina Wren Press/Lollipop Power Books; Carolrhoda Books, Inc.; Chariot Books; Charlesbridge; Children's Book Press; Childrens Press; China Books; Chronicle Books; Clarion Books; Cobblehill Books; Concordia Publishing House; Coteau Books Ltd.; Council for Indian Education; Crocodile Books, USA; Crown Publishers (Crown Books for Children); Crystal River Press; CSS Publishing; Dawn Publications; Dial Books for Young Readers; Discovery Enterprises, Ltd.; Distinctive Publishing Corp.; Dorling Kindersley, Inc.; Dutton Children's Books; Eakin Press; Eerdmans Publishing Company, Wm. B.; Falcon Press Publishing Co.; Farrar, Straus & Giroux; Four Winds Press; Free Spirit Publishing; Geringer Books, Laura; Godine, Publisher, David R.; Golden Books; Greenwillow Books; Grosset & Dunlap, Inc.; Harcourt Brace & Co.; HarperCollins Children's Books; Harvest House Publishers; Hendrick-Long Publishing Company; Holiday House Inc.; Holt & Co., Inc., Henry; Homestead Publishing; Houghton Mifflin Co.; Humanics Limited Publishing Group; Huntington House Publishers; Hyperion Books for Children; Ideals Children's Books; Jalmar Press; Jewish Lights Publishing; Jewish Publication Society; Jordan Enterprises Publishing Co., Inc.; Just Us Books, Inc.; Kabel Publishers; Kar-Ben Copies, Inc.; Knopf Books for Young Readers; Laredo Publishing Co. Inc.; Lee & Low Books, Inc.; Little, Brown and Company; Lodestar Books; Lothrop Lee & Shepard Books; Lucas/Evans Books Inc.; McElderry Books, Margaret K.; Macmillan Children's Books; Mage Publishers Inc.; Magination Press; March Media, Inc.; Metamorphous Press; Millbrook Press, The; Morehouse Publishing Co.; Morris Publishing, Joshua; Muir Publications, Inc, John; NAR Publications; Northland Publishing; NorthWord Press, Inc.; Orca Book Publishers; Orchard Books; Our Child Press; Owen Publishers, Inc., Richard C.; Pacific Press; Parenting Press, Inc.; Paulist Press; Pelican Publishing Co. Inc.; Perspectives Press; Philomel Books; Pippin Press; Pocahontas Press, Inc.; Preservation Press, The; Price Stern Sloan; Prometheus Books; Pumpkin Press Publishing House; Putnam's Sons, G.P.; Quarry Press; Random House Books for Young Readers; Read'n Run Books; Sadlier, Inc., William H.; St. Paul Books and Media; Scholastic Hardcover; Scribner's Sons, Charles; Silver Moon Press; Simon & Schuster Children's Books; Soundprints; Speech Bin, Inc., The; Standard Publishing; Stemmer House Publishers, Inc.; Sunbelt Media, Inc./Eakin Press; Sundance Publishers & Distributors; Tab Books; Tambourine Books; Treasure Chest Publications, Inc.; Troll Associates; Trophy Books; Tyndale House Publishers, Inc.; University Classics, Ltd. Publishers; University Editions, Inc.; Victor Books; Victory Publishing; Volcano Press; Walker and Co.; Whitebird Books; Whitman & Company, Albert; Williamson Publishing Co.; Willowisp Press; Winston-Derek Publishers, Inc.; Women's Press; Woodbine House; YMAA Publication Center

Young readers (5- to 8-year-olds). Addison-Wesley Publishing Co.; Advocacy Press; Aegina Press/University Editions; Africa World Press; African American Images; Aladdin Books/Collier Books for Young Readers; Alyson Publications, Inc.; American Bible Society; American Education Publishing; Appalachian Mountain Club Books; Atheneum Publishers; Bantam Doubleday Dell; Barrons Educational Series; Bess Press; Bethany House Publishers; Bethel Publishing; Boyds Mills Press; Bradbury Press; Bright Ring Publishing; Capstone Press Inc.; Carolina Wren Press/Lollipop Power Books; Carolrhoda Books, Inc.; Chariot Books; Chicago Review Press; Childrens Press; China Books; Chronicle Books; Clarion Books; Cobblehill Books; Concordia Publishing House; Coteau Books Ltd.; Council for Indian Education; Crown Publishers (Crown Books for Children); Crystal River Press; CSS Publishing; Dawn Publications; Denison Co. Inc., T.S.; Dial Books for Young Readers; Discovery Enterprises, Ltd.; Distinctive Publishing Corp.; Dorling Kindersley, Inc.; Dutton Children's Books; Eakin Press; Eerdmans Publishing Company, Wm. B.; Enslow Publishers Inc.; Falcon Press Publishing Co.; Farrar, Straus & Giroux; Franklin Watts, Inc.; Free Spirit Publishing; Geringer Books, Laura; Godine, Publisher, David R.; Golden Books; Greenwillow Books; Grosset & Dunlap, Inc.; Harcourt Brace & Co.; HarperCollins Children's Books; Harvest House Publishers; Hendrick-Long Publishing Company; Herald Press; Holiday House Inc.; Holt & Co., Inc., Henry; Homestead Publishing; Houghton Mifflin Co.; Humanics Limited Publishing Group; Hunter House Publishers; Huntington House Publishers; Hyperion Books for Children; Ideals Children's Books; Incentive Publications, Inc.; Jalmar Press; Jewish Lights Publishing; Jewish Publication Society; Jones University Press/Light Line Books, Bob; Jordan Enterprises Publishing Co., Inc.; Just Us Books, Inc.; Kabel Publishers; Kar-Ben Copies, Inc.; Knopf Books for Young Readers; Laredo Publishing Co. Inc.; Lee & Low Books, Inc.; Little, Brown and Company; Lodestar Books; Look and See Publications; Lothrop Lee & Shepard Books; Lucas/Evans Books Inc.; McElderry Books, Margaret K.; Macmillan Children's Books; Magination Press; March Media, Inc.; Meadowbrook Press; Messner, Julian; Metamorphous Press; Millbrook Press, The; Morehouse Publishing Co.; Morris Publishing, Joshua; NAR Publications; Northland Publishing; NorthWord Press, Inc.; Orca Book Publishers; Orchard Books; Our Child Press; Pacific Press; Parenting Press, Inc.; Paulist Press; Peartree; Pelican Publishing Co. Inc.; Perspectives Press; Philomel Books; Pippin Press; Players Press, Inc.; Pocahontas Press, Inc.; Preservation Press, The; Price Stern Sloan; Prometheus Books; Pumpkin Press Publishing House; Putnam's Sons, G.P.; Random House Books for Young Readers; Read'n Run Books; Sadlier, Inc., William H.; St. Paul Books and Media; Scholastic Hardcover; Scribner's Sons, Charles; Seacoast Publications of New England; Silver Moon Press; Simon & Schuster Children's Books; Speech Bin, Inc., The; Standard Publishing; Stemmer House Publishers, Inc.; Stepping Stone Books; Sunbelt Media, Inc./ Eakin Press; Sundance Publishers & Distributors; Tab Books; Treasure Chest Publications, Inc.; Troll Associates; Trophy Books; Tyndale House Publishers, Inc.; University Classics, Ltd. Publishers; University Editions, Inc.; Victor Books; Victory Publishing; Volcano Press; W.W. Publications; Walker and Co.; Weigl Educational Publishers; Whitman & Company, Albert; Williamson Publishing Co.; Willowisp Press; Winston-Derek Publishers, Inc.; Women's Press; Woodbine House; YMAA Publication Center

Middle readers (9- to 11-year-olds. Addison-Wesley Publishing Co.; Advocacy Press; Aegina Press/University Editions; Africa World Press; African American Images; Aladdin Books/Collier Books for Young Readers; Alyson Publications, Inc.; American Bible Society; American Education Publishing; Appalachian Mountain Club Books; Archway Paperbacks/Minstrel Books; Atheneum Publishers; Avon Books; Bantam Doubleday Dell; Barrons Educational Series; Behrman House Inc.; Bess Press; Bethany House Publishers; Bethel Publishing; Blue Heron Publishing, Inc.; Boyds Mills Press; Bradbury Press; Bright Ring Publishing; Capstone Press Inc.; Carolrhoda Books, Inc.; Chariot Books; Chicago Review Press; Childrens Press; China Books; Chronicle Books; Clarion Books; Cloverdale Press; Cobblehill Books; Concordia Publishing House; Council for Indian Education; Crestwood House; Crown Publishers (Crown Books for Children); Crystal River Press; CSS Publishing; Davis Pubilcations, Inc.; Dawn Publications; Denison Co. Inc., T.S.; Dial Books for Young Readers; Dillon Press, Inc.; Discovery Enterprises, Ltd.; Dutton Children's Books; Eakin Press; Eerdmans Publishing Company, Wm. B.; Enslow Publishers Inc.; Falcon Press Publishing Co.; Farrar, Straus & Giroux; Fawcett Juniper; Four Winds Press; Franklin Watts, Inc.; Free Spirit Publishing; Geringer Books, Laura; Godine, Publisher, David R.; Golden Books; Greenhaven Press; Greenwillow Books; Harcourt Brace & Co.; HarperCollins Children's Books; Harvest House Publishers; Hendrick-Long Publishing Company; Herald Press; Holiday House Inc.; Holt & Co., Inc., Henry; Homestead Publishing; Houghton Mifflin Co.; Hunter House Publishers; Huntington House Publishers; Hyperion Books for Children; Incentive Publications, Inc.; Jalmar Press; Jewish Lights Publishing; Jewish Publication Society; Jones University Press/Light Line Books, Bob; Jordan Enterprises Publishing Co., Inc.; Just Us Books, Inc.; Kabel Publishers; Kar-Ben Copies, Inc.; Knopf Books for Young Readers; Laredo Publishing Co. Inc.; Lee & Low Books, Inc.; Lerner Publications Co.; Little, Brown and Company; Lodestar Books; Look and See Publications; Lothrop Lee & Shepard Books; Lucas/Evans Books Inc.; Lucent Books; McElderry Books, Margaret K.; Macmillan Children's Books; March Media, Inc.; Meadowbrook Press; Meriwether Publishing Ltd.; Messner, Julian; Metamorphous Press; Millbrook Press, The; Misty Hill Press; Morehouse Publishing Co.; Morris Publishing, Joshua; Muir Publications, Inc, John; New Discovery Books; Orca Book Publishers; Orchard Books; Our Child Press; Pacific Press; Pando Publications; Parenting Press, Inc.; Paulist Press; Peartree; Pelican Publishing Co. Inc.; Perspectives Press; Philomel Books; Pippin Press; Players Press, Inc.; Pocahontas Press, Inc.; Preservation Press, The; Press of Macdonald & Reinecke, The; Price Stern Sloan; Prometheus Books; Pumpkin Press Publishing House; Putnam's Sons, G.P.; Random House Books for Young Readers; Read'n Run Books; Sadlier, Inc., William H.; St. Anthony Messenger Press; St. Paul Books and Media; Scholastic Hardcover; Scientific American Books For Young Readers; Scribner's Sons, Charles; Seacoast Publications of New England; Silver Moon Press; Simon & Schuster Children's Books; Speech Bin, Inc., The; Standard Publishing; Stemmer House Publishers, Inc.; Sterling Publishing Co., Inc.; Sunbelt Media, Inc./Eakin Press; Sundance Publishers & Distributors; Tab Books; Tambourine Books; Thistledown Press Ltd.; Treasure Chest Publications, Inc.; Troll Associates; Trophy Books; Tudor Publishers, Inc.; Tyndale House Publishers, Inc.; University Classics, Ltd. Publishers; University Editions, Inc.; Victor Books; Victory Publishing; Volcano Press; W.W. Publications; Walker and Co.; Ward Hill Press; Weigl Educational Publishers; Whitman & Company, Albert; Williamson Publishing Co.; Willowisp Press; Winston-Derek Publishers, Inc.; Women's Press; Woodbine House; YMAA Publication Center

Young adults (ages 12 and up). Addison-Wesley Publishing Co.; Aegina Press/University

Editions; Africa World Press; African American Images; Aladdin Books/Collier Books for Young Readers; Alyson Publications, Inc.; American Bible Society; American Education Publishing; Appalachian Mountain Club Books; Archway Paperbacks/Minstrel Books; Atheneum Publishers; Avon Books/Books for Young Readers; Bandanna Books; Bantam Doubleday Dell; Barrons Educational Series; Behrman House Inc.; Berkley Publishing Group; Bess Press; Bethany House Publishers; Bethel Publishing; Blue Heron Publishing, Inc.; Boyds Mills Press; Bradbury Press; Chariot Books; Chicago Review Press; Childrens Press; Clarion Books; Cloverdale Press; Cobblehill Books; Concordia Publishing House; Council for Indian Education; Crystal River Press; CSS Publishing; Davenport, Publishers, May; Davis Pubilcations, Inc.; Dawn Publications; Dial Books for Young Readers; Discovery Enterprises, Ltd.; Dutton Children's Books; Eakin Press; Eerdmans Publishing Company, Wm. B.; Enslow Publishers Inc.; Facts on File; Farrar, Straus & Giroux; Fawcett Juniper; Franklin Watts, Inc.; Free Spirit Publishing; Geringer Books, Laura; Globe Fearon Educational Publisher; Golden Books; Greenhaven Press; Greenwillow Books; Grosset & Dunlap, Inc.; Harcourt Brace & Co.; HarperCollins Children's Books; Harvest House Publishers; Hendrick-Long Publishing Company; Herald Press; Holt & Co., Inc., Henry; Homestead Publishing; Houghton Mifflin Co.; Hunter House Publishers; Huntington House Publishers; Hyperion Books for Children; Incentive Publications, Inc.; Jalmar Press; Jewish Lights Publishing; Jewish Publication Society; Jones University Press/Light Line Books, Bob; Jordan Enterprises Publishing Co., Inc.; Kabel Publishers; Knopf Books for Young Readers; Lerner Publications Co.; Lion Books, Publisher; Little, Brown and Company; Lodestar Books; Lothrop Lee & Shepard Books; Lucas/Evans Books Inc.; Lucent Books; McElderry Books, Margaret K.; Macmillan Children's Books; Meriwether Publishing Ltd.; Messner, Julian; Metamorphous Press; Millbrook Press, The; Misty Hill Press; Morehouse Publishing Co.; Naturegraph Publisher, Inc.; Orca Book Publishers; Orchard Books; Our Child Press; Pacific Press; Pando Publications; Philomel Books; Players Press, Inc.; Pocahontas Press, Inc.; Preservation Press, The; Press of Macdonald & Reinecke, The; Price Stern Sloan; Prometheus Books; Pumpkin Press Publishing House; Putnam's Sons, G.P.; Read'n Run Books; Rosen Publishing Group, The; Sadlier, Inc., William H.; St. Anthony Messenger Press; St. Paul Books and Media; Scholastic Hardcover; Scientific American Books For Young Readers; Scribner's Sons, Charles; Shaw Publishers, Harold; Silver Moon Press; Simon & Schuster Children's Books; Speech Bin, Inc., The; Standard Publishing; Sunbelt Media, Inc./Eakin Press; Sundance Publishers & Distributors; Tab Books; Tambourine Books; Texas Christian University Press; Thistledown Press Ltd.; Treasure Chest Publications, Inc.; Troll Associates; Trophy Books; Tudor Publishers, Inc.; University Classics, Ltd. Publishers; University Editions, Inc.; Volcano Press; W.W. Publications; Walker and Co.; Ward Hill Press; Weigl Educational Publishers; Williamson Publishing Co.; Willowisp Press; Winston-Derek Publishers, Inc.; Women's Press; Woodbine House; YMAA Publication Center

Magazines

Picture-oriented material (preschoolers to 8-year-olds). Animal Trails; Appalachian Bride; Chickadee; Cochran's Corner; Day Care and Early Education; Focus on the Family Clubhouse; Friend Magazine, The; Highlights for Children; Humpty Dumpty's Magazine; Ladybug, the Magazine for Young Children; National Geographic World; Nature Friend Magazine; Science Weekly; Scienceland; Skipping Stones; Sleuth; Story Friends; Turtle Magazine; Young Christian

Young readers (5- to 8-year-olds). Advocate, The; Animal Trails; Appalachian Bride; ASPCA Animal Watch; Atalantik; Brilliant Star; Chickadee; Children's Playmate; Cochran's Corner; Day Care and Early Education; Discoveries; DynaMath; Focus on the Family Clubhouse; Friend Magazine, The; Highlights for Children; Hob-Nob; Home Altar, The; Hopscotch; Humpty Dumpty's Magazine; Jack and Jill; Kids Today Mini-Magazine; Ladybug, the Magazine for Young Children; My Friend; Nature Friend Magazine; Noah's Ark; Pockets; Racing for Kids; School Mates; Science Weekly; Scienceland; Sharing the Victory; Single Parent, The; Skipping Stones; Sleuth; Story Friends; U.S. Kids; Wonder Time; Writer's Open Forum; Young Christian

Middle readers (9- to 11-year-olds). Advocate, The; American Girl; Animal Trails; Appalachian Bride; ASPCA Animal Watch; Atalantik; BK News; Boys' Life; Brilliant Star; Calliope; Cat Fancy; Child Life; Children's Digest; Clubhouse; Cobblestone; Cochran's Corner; Counselor; Cricket, The Magazine for Children; Current Health I; Discoveries; Disney Adventures; Dolphin Log; DynaMath; Faces; Faith 'n Stuff; Friend Magazine, The; Goldfinch, The; Guide Magazine; High Adventure; Highlights for Children; Hob-Nob; Home Altar, The; Hopscotch; Jack and Jill; Junior Trails; Kids Today Mini-Magazine; Magic Realism; My Friend; National Geographic World; Nature Friend Magazine; Noah's Ark; Odyssey; On The Line; Owl Magazine; Pockets; Power and Light; Racing for Kids; R-A-D-A-R; Ranger Rick; School Mates; Science Weekly; Shofar; Single Parent, The; Skipping Stones; Sleuth; Superscience Blue; 3-2-1 Contact; Touch; U.S. Kids; Venture; Writer's Open Forum; Young Christian

Young adults (ages 12 and up). Aim Magazine; Animal Trails; Appalachian Bride; Atalantik; BK News; Calliope; Career World; Careers And Colleges; Challenge; Clubhouse; Cobblestone; Cochran's Corner; Cricket Magazine; Current Health II; Dolphin Log; DynaMath; Exploring; Faces; FFA New Horizons; For Seniors Only; FreeWay; Guide Magazine; Hicall; High Adventure; Hob-Nob; Hobson's Choice; InSights; Keynoter; Listen; Magazine for Christian Youth!, The; Magic Realism; My Friend; National Geographic World; Nature Friend Magazine; New Era Magazine; Odyssey; On The Line; Owl Magazine; Racing for Kids; Sassy; Scholastic Math Magazine; School Mates; Science Weekly; Seventeen Magazine; Sharing the Victory; Single Parent, The; Skipping Stones; Sleuth; Straight; Street Times; Teen Power; Teenage Christian Magazine; 3-2-1 Contact; Touch; 2 Hype And Hype Hair; Venture; With; Writer's Open Forum; Young Christian; Young Salvationist; Youth Update

Subject Index

Use this index to more quickly locate the book and magazine publishers seeking the fiction and nonfiction subjects you write about and/or illustrate. Read each listing carefully and follow the publisher's specific information about the type(s) of manuscript(s) each prefers and the style(s) of artwork each wishes to review.

Book Publishers: Fiction

Adventure. Aegina Press/University Editions; Africa World Press; American Education Publishing; Archway Paperbacks/Minstrel Books; Avon Books/Books for Young Readers; Bantam Doubleday Dell; Bess Press; Bethany House Publishers; Bethel Publishing; Black Moss Press; Blue Heron Publishing, Inc.; Boyds Mills Press; Childrens Press; Clarion Books; Cobblehill Books; Council for Indian Education; Crystal River Press; Dial Books for Young Readers; Distinctive Publishing Corp.; Dorling Kindersley, Inc.; Dutton Children's Books; Farrar, Straus & Giroux; Geringer Books, Laura; Godine, Publisher, David R.; Grosset & Dunlap, Inc.; HarperCollins Children's Books; Houghton Mifflin Co.; Hyperion Books for Children; Ideals Children's Books; Jewish Publication Society; Jones University Press/Light Line Books, Bob; Jordan Enterprises Publishing Co., Inc.; Just Us Books, Inc.; Knopf Books for Young Readers; Laredo Publishing Co. Inc.; Lee & Low Books, Inc.; Lerner Publications Co.; Little, Brown and Company; Lodestar Books; McElderry Books, Margaret K.; Macmillan Children's Books; Morris Publishing, Joshua; Orca Book Publishers; Orchard Books; Owen Publishers, Inc., Richard C.; Peartree; Philomel Books; Price Stern Sloan; Pumpkin Press Publishing House; Putnam's Sons, G.P.; Random House Books for Young Readers; Scribner's Sons, Charles; Seacoast Publications of New England; Shaw Publishers, Harold; Simon & Schuster Children's Books; Standard Publishing; Thistledown Press Ltd.; Tor Books; Treasure Chest Publications, Inc.; Troll Associates; University Editions, Inc.; Victor Books; Whitman & Company, Albert; Willowisp Press; Winston-Derek Publishers, Inc.

Animal. Advocacy Press; Aegina Press/University Editions; American Education Publishing; Archway Paperbacks/Minstrel Books; Atheneum Publishers; Bantam Doubleday Dell; Barrons Educational Series; Bess Press; Blue Heron Publishing, Inc.; Boyds Mills Press; Bradbury Press; Childrens Press; China Books; Chronicle Books; Clarion Books; Cobblehill Books; Council for Indian Education; Crocodile Books, USA; Crown Publishers (Crown Books for Children); Crystal River Press; Dawn Publications; Dial Books for Young Readers; Distinctive Publishing Corp.; Dutton Children's Books; Farrar, Straus & Giroux; Four Winds Press; Geringer Books, Laura; Godine, Publisher, David R.; Grosset & Dunlap, Inc.; Harcourt Brace & Co.; HarperCollins Children's Books; Holiday House Inc.; Houghton Mifflin Co.; Hyperion Books for Children; Ideals Children's Books; Jones University Press/Light Line Books, Bob; Jordan Enterprises Publishing Co., Inc.; Knopf Books for Young Readers; Laredo Publishing Co. Inc.; Little, Brown and Company; Lodestar Books; Macmillan Children's Books; Morris Publishing, Joshua; Northland Publishing; NorthWord Press, Inc.; Orchard Books; Owen Publishers, Inc., Richard C.; Pando Publications; Peartree; Philomel Books; Pippin Press; Pumpkin Press Publishing House; Random House Books for Young Readers; Scholastic Hardcover; Scribner's Sons, Charles; Seacoast Publications of New England; Simon & Schuster Children's Books; Soundprints; Speech Bin, Inc., The; Standard Publishing; Stemmer House Publishers, Inc.; Sunbelt Media, Inc./Eakin Press; Tor Books; Treasure Chest Publications, Inc.; Troll Associates; University Classics, Ltd. Publishers; University Editions, Inc.; Victor Books; Walker and Co.; Whitman & Company, Albert; Willowisp Press

Anthology. Bess Press; Blue Heron Publishing, Inc.; Council for Indian Education; Crystal River Press; Dutton Children's Books; Farrar, Straus & Giroux; Geringer Books, Laura; HarperCollins Children's Books; Houghton Mifflin Co.; Hyperion Books for Children; Lee & Low Books, Inc.; Macmillan Children's Books; Meriwether Publishing Ltd.; Orchard Books; Simon & Schuster Children's Books; Thistledown Press Ltd.; Troll Associates; Willowisp Press

Concept. Africa World Press; American Education Publishing; Bess Press; Bethany House Publishers; Childrens Press; Dial Books for Young Readers; Farrar, Straus & Giroux; Grosset & Dunlap, Inc.; HarperCollins Children's Books; Herald Press; Holiday House Inc.; Houghton Mifflin Co.; Huntington House Publishers; Ideals Children's Books; Jalmar Press; Laredo Publishing Co. Inc.; Magination Press; Meriwether Publishing Ltd.; Morris Publishing, Joshua; Orchard Books; Pando Publications; Pumpkin Press Publishing House; Putnam's Sons, G.P.; Simon & Schuster Children's Books; Tor Books; University Classics, Ltd. Publishers; Victory Publishing; Women's Press

Contemporary. Africa World Press; American Education Publishing; Archway Paperbacks/Minstrel Books; Atheneum Publishers; Avon Books/Books for Young Readers; Bantam Doubleday Dell;

Barrons Educational Series; Bess Press; Black Moss Press; Blue Heron Publishing, Inc.; Boyds Mills Press; Bradbury Press; Children's Book Press; Childrens Press; China Books; Clarion Books; Cobblehill Books; Coteau Books Ltd.; Council for Indian Education; Crocodile Books, USA; Crystal River Press; Davenport, Publishers, May; Dorling Kindersley, Inc.; Dutton Children's Books; Farrar, Straus & Giroux; Fawcett Juniper; Four Winds Press; Free Spirit Publishing; Geringer Books, Laura; Golden Books; Harcourt Brace & Co.; HarperCollins Children's Books; Harvest House Publishers; Houghton Mifflin Co.; Hyperion Books for Children; Ideals Children's Books; Jewish Publication Society; Jones University Press/Light Line Books, Bob; Just Us Books, Inc.; Knopf Books for Young Readers; Lee & Low Books, Inc.; Lerner Publications Co.; Little, Brown and Company; Lodestar Books; McElderry Books, Margaret K.; Macmillan Children's Books; Mage Publishers Inc.; Northland Publishing; Orca Book Publishers; Orchard Books; Owen Publishers, Inc., Richard C.; Peartree; Price Stern Sloan; Pumpkin Press Publishing House; Putnam's Sons, G.P.; St. Paul Books and Media; Scholastic Hardcover; Scribner's Sons, Charles; Seacoast Publications of New England; Simon & Schuster Children's Books; Standard Publishing; Sundance Publishers & Distributors; Tor Books; Troll Associates; Tudor Publishers, Inc.; Victor Books; Whitman & Company, Albert; Willowisp Press; Winston-Derek Publishers, Inc.

Fantasy. Advocacy Press; Aegina Press/University Editions; American Education Publishing; Archway Paperbacks/Minstrel Books; Atheneum Publishers; Bantam Doubleday Dell; Bradbury Press; China Books; Clarion Books; Crystal River Press; Dial Books for Young Readers; Dutton Children's Books; Eerdmans Publishing Company, Wm. B.; Farrar, Straus & Giroux; Fawcett Juniper; Geringer Books, Laura; Godine, Publisher, David R.; Harcourt Brace & Co.; HarperCollins Children's Books; Harvest House Publishers; Houghton Mifflin Co.; Hyperion Books for Children; Ideals Children's Books; Jordan Enterprises Publishing Co., Inc.; Laredo Publishing Co. Inc.; Little, Brown and Company; McElderry Books, Margaret K.; Macmillan Children's Books; Orchard Books; Peartree; Philomel Books; Pippin Press; Pumpkin Press Publishing House; Scholastic Hardcover; Scribner's Sons, Charles; Seacoast Publications of New England; Simon & Schuster Children's Books; Speech Bin, Inc., The; Tor Books; University Editions, Inc.; Victory Publishing; W.W. Publications; Walker and Co.; Whitman & Company, Albert; Willowisp Press

Folktales. Africa World Press; American Education Publishing; Bess Press; Boyds Mills Press; Carolrhoda Books, Inc.; Childrens Press; China Books; Chronicle Books; Clarion Books; Coteau Books Ltd.; Council for Indian Education; Crystal River Press; Dawn Publications; Dial Books for Young Readers; Dorling Kindersley, Inc.; Dutton Children's Books; Eerdmans Publishing Company, Wm. B.; Farrar, Straus & Giroux; Geringer Books, Laura; Godine, Publisher, David R.; HarperCollins Children's Books; Holiday House Inc.; Houghton Mifflin Co.; Huntington House Publishers; Hyperion Books for Children; Ideals Children's Books; Jewish Publication Society; Jordan Enterprises Publishing Co., Inc.; Laredo Publishing Co. Inc.; Lerner Publications Co.; Little, Brown and Company; Lodestar Books; McElderry Books, Margaret K.; Macmillan Children's Books; Mage Publishers Inc.; Northland Publishing; Orca Book Publishers; Orchard Books; Owen Publishers, Inc., Richard C.; Pando Publications; Pelican Publishing Co. Inc.; Philomel Books; Pippin Press; Press of Macdonald & Reinecke, The; Pumpkin Press Publishing House; Putnam's Sons, G.P.; Quarry Press; Scribner's Sons, Charles; Seacoast Publications of New England; Simon & Schuster Children's Books; Stemmer House Publishers, Inc.; Tor Books; Troll Associates; Tudor Publishers, Inc.; Ward Hill Press; Weigl Educational Publishers; Whitebird Books; Whitman & Company, Albert; Willowisp Press; Winston-Derek Publishers, Inc.; YMAA Publication Center

Health. Barrons Educational Series; Council for Indian Education; Crystal River Press; Dawn Publications; Dial Books for Young Readers; Farrar, Straus & Giroux; Geringer Books, Laura; Houghton Mifflin Co.; Jordan Enterprises Publishing Co., Inc.; Laredo Publishing Co. Inc.; Lerner Publications Co.; Little, Brown and Company; Magination Press; Orchard Books; Pelican Publishing Co. Inc.; Price Stern Sloan; Pumpkin Press Publishing House; Simon & Schuster Children's Books; Speech Bin, Inc., The; Tor Books; Troll Associates; University Classics, Ltd. Publishers; Waterfront Books; Whitman & Company, Albert; Women's Press; Woodbine House

Hi-Lo. Bess Press; Childrens Press; Crystal River Press; Globe Fearon Educational Publisher; HarperCollins Children's Books; Jordan Enterprises Publishing Co., Inc.; Lerner Publications Co.; Peartree; Pumpkin Press Publishing House; Simon & Schuster Children's Books; Tor Books

History. Africa World Press; Bandanna Books; Bess Press; Blue Heron Publishing, Inc.; Boyds Mills Press; Bradbury Press; Carolrhoda Books, Inc.; China Books; Chronicle Books; Clarion Books; Council for Indian Education; Crocodile Books, USA; Crown Publishers (Crown Books for Children); Crystal River Press; Davenport, Publishers, May; Denison Co. Inc., T.S.; Dial Books for Young Readers; Distinctive Publishing Corp.; Dorling Kindersley, Inc.; Dutton Children's Books; Farrar, Straus & Giroux; Four Winds Press; Geringer Books, Laura; Grosset & Dunlap, Inc.; Harcourt Brace & Co.; HarperCollins Children's Books; Hendrick-Long Publishing Company; Herald Press; Holiday House Inc.; Houghton Mifflin Co.; Huntington House Publishers; Hyperion Books for Children; Ideals Children's Books; Jewish

Publication Society; Jones University Press/Light Line Books, Bob; Jordan Enterprises Publishing Co., Inc.; Just Us Books, Inc.; Lee & Low Books, Inc.; Lerner Publications Co.; Little, Brown and Company; Lodestar Books; Macmillan Children's Books; Misty Hill Press; Northland Publishing; Orca Book Publishers; Orchard Books; Pando Publications; Pelican Publishing Co. Inc.; Philomel Books; Press of Macdonald & Reinecke, The; Price Stern Sloan; Putnam's Sons, G.P.; Random House Books for Young Readers; Scholastic Hardcover; Scribner's Sons, Charles; Seacoast Publications of New England; Stemmer House Publishers, Inc.; Sunbelt Media, Inc./Eakin Press; Texas Christian University Press; Troll Associates; University Editions, Inc.; Walker and Co.; Whitman & Company, Albert; Willowisp Press; Winston-Derek Publishers, Inc.

Humor. Aegina Press/University Editions; American Education Publishing; Archway Paperbacks/Minstrel Books; Avon Books/Books for Young Readers; Bantam Doubleday Dell; Bess Press; Black Moss Press; Boyds Mills Press; Childrens Press; Crown Publishers (Crown Books for Children); Crystal River Press; Davenport, Publishers, May; Distinctive Publishing Corp.; Farrar, Straus & Giroux; Four Winds Press; HarperCollins Children's Books; Houghton Mifflin Co.; Hyperion Books for Children; Jordan Enterprises Publishing Co., Inc.; Little, Brown and Company; Lodestar Books; McElderry Books, Margaret K.; Macmillan Children's Books; March Media, Inc.; Meriwether Publishing Ltd.; Orca Book Publishers; Orchard Books; Pippin Press; Pumpkin Press Publishing House; Putnam's Sons, G.P.; Scholastic Hardcover; Simon & Schuster Children's Books; Tor Books; Willowisp Press

Multicultural. Africa World Press; African American Images; Bandanna Books; Barrons Educational Series; Bess Press; Boyds Mills Press; Carolina Wren Press/Lollipop Power Books; Carolrhoda Books, Inc.; Children's Book Press; Childrens Press; China Books; Chronicle Books; Clarion Books; Coteau Books Ltd.; Council for Indian Education; Crystal River Press; Denison Co. Inc., T.S.; Distinctive Publishing Corp.; Dorling Kindersley, Inc.; Dutton Children's Books; Farrar, Straus & Giroux; Free Spirit Publishing; Globe Fearon Educational Publisher; HarperCollins Children's Books; Houghton Mifflin Co.; Hyperion Books for Children; Ideals Children's Books; Jewish Lights Publishing; Jordan Enterprises Publishing Co., Inc.; Just Us Books, Inc.; Kar-Ben Copies, Inc.; Laredo Publishing Co. Inc.; Lee & Low Books, Inc.; Lerner Publications Co.; Little, Brown and Company; Lodestar Books; McElderry Books, Margaret K.; Macmillan Children's Books; Mage Publishers Inc.; Magination Press; March Media, Inc.; Northland Publishing; Orca Book Publishers; Orchard Books; Our Child Press; Owen Publishers, Inc., Richard C.; Peartree; Pelican Publishing Co. Inc.; Philomel Books; Pippin Press; Pumpkin Press Publishing House; Simon & Schuster Children's Books; Stemmer House Publishers, Inc.; Sundance Publishers & Distributors; Tor Books; Treasure Chest Publications, Inc.; Tudor Publishers, Inc.; Weigl Educational Publishers; Whitman & Company, Albert; Willowisp Press; YMAA Publication Center

Nature/Environment. Advocacy Press; American Education Publishing; Barrons Educational Series; Bess Press; Blue Heron Publishing, Inc.; Carolrhoda Books, Inc.; China Books; Clarion Books; Council for Indian Education; Crown Publishers (Crown Books for Children); Crystal River Press; Dawn Publications; Denison Co. Inc., T.S.; Dial Books for Young Readers; Distinctive Publishing Corp.; Dorling Kindersley, Inc.; Dutton Children's Books; Farrar, Straus & Giroux; Geringer Books, Laura; Grosset & Dunlap, Inc.; HarperCollins Children's Books; Houghton Mifflin Co.; Ideals Children's Books; Jordan Enterprises Publishing Co., Inc.; Knopf Books for Young Readers; Laredo Publishing Co. Inc.; Lee & Low Books, Inc.; Lerner Publications Co.; Little, Brown and Company; Lodestar Books; Macmillan Children's Books; Morris Publishing, Joshua; Northland Publishing; NorthWord Press, Inc.; Orca Book Publishers; Orchard Books; Owen Publishers, Inc., Richard C.; Pando Publications; Peartree; Pelican Publishing Co. Inc.; Philomel Books; Pippin Press; Press of Macdonald & Reinecke, The; Price Stern Sloan; Pumpkin Press Publishing House; Scribner's Sons, Charles; Seacoast Publications of New England; Simon & Schuster Children's Books; Soundprints; Stemmer House Publishers, Inc.; Tor Books; Troll Associates; University Classics, Ltd. Publishers; University Editions, Inc.; Weigl Educational Publishers; Whitman & Company, Albert; Willowisp Press

Poetry. Aegina Press/University Editions; Boyds Mills Press; China Books; Council for Indian Education; Crystal River Press; Denison Co. Inc., T.S.; Dutton Children's Books; Geringer Books, Laura; HarperCollins Children's Books; Hyperion Books for Children; Jewish Publication Society; Jordan Enterprises Publishing Co., Inc.; Laredo Publishing Co. Inc.; Lerner Publications Co.; McElderry Books, Margaret K.; Macmillan Children's Books; Orchard Books; Owen Publishers, Inc., Richard C.; Philomel Books; Pumpkin Press Publishing House; Simon & Schuster Children's Books; Troll Associates; University Editions, Inc.; Victory Publishing; Whitman & Company, Albert; Willowisp Press

Problem Novels. Avon Books/Books for Young Readers; Bandanna Books; Berkley Publishing Group; Bess Press; Bethany House Publishers; Cobblehill Books; Crystal River Press; Dial Books for Young Readers; Eerdmans Publishing Company, Wm. B.; Farrar, Straus & Giroux; Geringer Books, Laura; Harcourt Brace & Co.; HarperCollins Children's Books; Harvest House Publishers; Herald Press; Houghton Mifflin Co.; Hyperion Books for Children; Jewish Publication Society; Jones University Press/Light Line Books, Bob; Jordan Enterprises Publishing Co., Inc.; Lee & Low Books, Inc.; Lerner Publications Co.; Macmillan Children's Books; Imagination Press; Orca Book Publishers; Pelican Publishing Co. Inc.; Philomel Books; Putnam's Sons, G.P.; Scholastic Hardcover; Scribner's Sons, Charles; Shaw Publishers, Harold; Troll Associates; Tudor Publishers, Inc.; Whitman & Company, Albert; Willowisp Press; Winston-Derek Publishers, Inc.; Women's Press

Religious. Aegina Press/University Editions; Bethel Publishing; China Books; Concordia Publishing House; Crystal River Press; CSS Publishing; Dial Books for Young Readers; Eerdmans Publishing Company, Wm. B.; Herald Press; Huntington House Publishers; Jewish Lights Publishing; Jewish Publication Society; Kar-Ben Copies, Inc.; March Media, Inc.; Meriwether Publishing Ltd.; Morehouse Publishing Co.; Morris Publishing, Joshua; Orchard Books; Pacific Press; Paulist Press; Pelican Publishing Co. Inc.; Sadlier, Inc., William H.; St. Paul Books and Media; Standard Publishing; Victor Books; Victory Publishing; Winston-Derek Publishers, Inc.

Romance. Aegina Press/University Editions; Archway Paperbacks/Minstrel Books; Avon Books/Books for Young Readers; Bandanna Books; Berkley Publishing Group; Bethany House Publishers; Council for Indian Education; Farrar, Straus & Giroux; Fawcett Juniper; Harcourt Brace & Co.; HarperCollins Children's Books; Harvest House Publishers; Houghton Mifflin Co.; Hyperion Books for Children; Jewish Publication Society; Jordan Enterprises Publishing Co., Inc.; Orchard Books; Scholastic Hardcover; Troll Associates; University Editions, Inc.; Willowisp Press

Science Fiction. Aegina Press/University Editions; American Education Publishing; Bradbury Press; Clarion Books; Crystal River Press; Dial Books for Young Readers; Dutton Children's Books; Farrar, Straus & Giroux; Fawcett Juniper; Harcourt Brace & Co.; HarperCollins Children's Books; Houghton Mifflin Co.; Hyperion Books for Children; Jordan Enterprises Publishing Co., Inc.; Knopf Books for Young Readers; Little, Brown and Company; Macmillan Children's Books; Orchard Books; Scholastic Hardcover; Scribner's Sons, Charles; Simon & Schuster Children's Books; Troll Associates; University Editions, Inc.; Victor Books; Walker and Co.

Special Needs. Alyson Publications, Inc.; Carolrhoda Books, Inc.; Crystal River Press; Free Spirit Publishing; Globe Fearon Educational Publisher; HarperCollins Children's Books; Jordan Enterprises Publishing Co., Inc.; Imagination Press; Orca Book Publishers; Our Child Press; Philomel Books; Putnam's Sons, G.P.; Scholastic Hardcover; Speech Bin, Inc., The; Tor Books; University Classics, Ltd. Publishers; Waterfront Books; Whitman & Company, Albert; Woodbine House

Sports. Aegina Press/University Editions; Archway Paperbacks/Minstrel Books; Avon Books; Bantam Doubleday Dell; Bess Press; Boyds Mills Press; Clarion Books; Cobblehill Books; Council for Indian Education; Crystal River Press; Dial Books for Young Readers; Farrar, Straus & Giroux; Geringer Books, Laura; Golden Books; Grosset & Dunlap, Inc.; Harcourt Brace & Co.; HarperCollins Children's Books; Holiday House Inc.; Houghton Mifflin Co.; Hyperion Books for Children; Ideals Children's Books; Jewish Publication Society; Jones University Press/Light Line Books, Bob; Jordan Enterprises Publishing Co., Inc.; Just Us Books, Inc.; Knopf Books for Young Readers; Lee & Low Books, Inc.; Lerner Publications Co.; Morris Publishing, Joshua; Orchard Books; Pelican Publishing Co. Inc.; Price Stern Sloan; Pumpkin Press Publishing House; Random House Books for Young Readers; Scribner's Sons, Charles; Simon & Schuster Children's Books; Standard Publishing; Sunbelt Media, Inc./Eakin Press; Tor Books; Troll Associates; Victor Books; Victory Publishing; Whitman & Company, Albert; Willowisp Press; YMAA Publication Center

Suspense/Mystery. Aegina Press/University Editions; Archway Paperbacks/Minstrel Books; Avon Books/Books for Young Readers; Bantam Doubleday Dell; Bess Press; Bethany House Publishers; Boyds Mills Press; Bradbury Press; Cobblehill Books; Council for Indian Education; Crocodile Books, USA; Crystal River Press; Davenport, Publishers, May; Dial Books for Young Readers; Distinctive Publishing Corp.; Dutton Children's Books; Farrar, Straus & Giroux; Geringer Books, Laura; Godine, Publisher, David R.; Harcourt Brace & Co.; HarperCollins Children's Books; Holiday House Inc.; Houghton Mifflin Co.; Hyperion Books for Children; Jones University Press/Light Line Books, Bob; Jordan Enterprises Publishing Co., Inc.; Knopf Books for Young Readers; Lee & Low Books, Inc.; Lerner Publications Co.; Little, Brown and Company; Lodestar Books; Macmillan Children's Books; Morris Publishing, Joshua; Orca Book Publishers; Orchard Books; Owen Publishers, Inc., Richard C.; Pelican Publishing Co. Inc.; Pippin Press; Price Stern Sloan; Putnam's Sons, G.P.; Random House Books for Young Readers; Scholastic Hardcover; Scribner's Sons, Charles; Simon & Schuster Children's Books; Thistledown Press Ltd.; Tor Books; Troll Associates; Tudor Publishers, Inc.; University Editions, Inc.; Victor Books; Victory Publishing; Whitman & Company, Albert; Willowisp Press; Winston-Derek Publishers, Inc.; Berkley Publishing Group; Jewish Publication Society

Book Publishers: Nonfiction

Activity Books. American Education Publishing; Appalachian Mountain Club Books; Barrons Educational Series; Bess Press; Boyds Mills Press; Bright Ring Publishing; Chicago Review Press; China

Books; Crown Publishers (Crown Books for Children); Crystal River Press; Davenport, Publishers, May; Davis Pubilcations, Inc.; Denison Co. Inc., T.S.; Dial Books for Young Readers; Enslow Publishers Inc.; Grosset & Dunlap, Inc.; HarperCollins Children's Books; Humanics Limited Publishing Group; Ideals Children's Books; Jalmar Press; Jordan Enterprises Publishing Co., Inc.; Just Us Books, Inc.; Lerner Publications Co.; Lion Books, Publisher; Little, Brown and Company; Lodestar Books; Look and See Publications; Meadowbrook Press; Meriwether Publishing Ltd.; Millbrook Press, The; Morris Publishing, Joshua; Muir Publications, Inc, John; NorthWord Press, Inc.; Pacific Press; Pando Publications; Preservation Press, The; Price Stern Sloan; Pumpkin Press Publishing House; Simon & Schuster Children's Books; Speech Bin, Inc., The; Sterling Publishing Co., Inc.; Tab Books; Treasure Chest Publications, Inc.; Troll Associates; University Classics, Ltd. Publishers; Victory Publishing; Weigl Educational Publishers; Williamson Publishing Co.; Willowisp Press

Animal. Aegina Press/University Editions; American Education Publishing; Archway Paperbacks/ Minstrel Books; Atheneum Publishers; Barrons Educational Series; Boyds Mills Press; Bradbury Press; Capstone Press Inc.; Carolrhoda Books, Inc.; Childrens Press; Chronicle Books; Clarion Books; Cobblehill Books; Council for Indian Education; Crown Publishers (Crown Books for Children); Crystal River Press; Dawn Publications; Denison Co. Inc., T.S.; Dial Books for Young Readers; Dillon Press, Inc.; Distinctive Publishing Corp.; Dorling Kindersley, Inc.; Dutton Children's Books; Enslow Publishers Inc.; Facts on File; Falcon Press Publishing Co.; Four Winds Press; Grosset & Dunlap, Inc.; Harcourt Brace & Co.; HarperCollins Children's Books; Homestead Publishing; Huntington House Publishers; Ideals Children's Books; Jones University Press/Light Line Books, Bob; Jordan Enterprises Publishing Co., Inc.; Knopf Books for Young Readers; Lerner Publications Co.; Little, Brown and Company; Lodestar Books; Macmillan Children's Books; Messner, Julian; Millbrook Press, The; Morris Publishing, Joshua; Muir Publications, Inc, John; Naturegraph Publisher, Inc.; Northland Publishing; NorthWord Press, Inc.; Orca Book Publishers; Orchard Books; Owen Publishers, Inc., Richard C.; Pacific Press; Pando Publications; Pippin Press; Price Stern Sloan; Pumpkin Press Publishing House; Random House Books for Young Readers; Scholastic Hardcover; Scribner's Sons, Charles; Seacoast Publications of New England; Simon & Schuster Children's Books; Soundprints; Stemmer House Publishers, Inc.; Sterling Publishing Co., Inc.; Sunbelt Media, Inc./Eakin Press; Treasure Chest Publications, Inc.; Troll Associates; Trophy Books; University Editions, Inc.; Walker and Co.; Whitman & Company, Albert; Williamson Publishing Co.; Willowisp Press

Arts/Crafts. Boyds Mills Press; Bright Ring Publishing; Chicago Review Press; Childrens Press; China Books; Chronicle Books; Crystal River Press; Davis Pubilcations, Inc.; Denison Co. Inc., T.S.; Grosset & Dunlap, Inc.; HarperCollins Children's Books; Humanics Limited Publishing Group; Jordan Enterprises Publishing Co., Inc.; Lerner Publications Co.; Lion Books, Publisher; Little, Brown and Company; Millbrook Press, The; Muir Publications, Inc, John; Pando Publications; Philomel Books; Simon & Schuster Children's Books; Stemmer House Publishers, Inc.; Sterling Publishing Co., Inc.; Treasure Chest Publications, Inc.; University Classics, Ltd. Publishers; Victory Publishing; Williamson Publishing Co.; Willowisp Press

Biography. American Education Publishing; Atheneum Publishers; Bandanna Books; Bess Press; Boyds Mills Press; Bradbury Press; Carolrhoda Books, Inc.; Childrens Press; China Books; Clarion Books; Cloverdale Press; Council for Indian Education; Crestwood House; Crown Publishers (Crown Books for Children); Crystal River Press; Dial Books for Young Readers; Dillon Press, Inc.; Discovery Enterprises, Ltd.; Distinctive Publishing Corp.; Dorling Kindersley, Inc.; Dutton Children's Books; Eerdmans Publishing Company, Wm. B.; Enslow Publishers Inc.; Facts on File; Falcon Press Publishing Co.; Four Winds Press; Globe Fearon Educational Publisher; Greenhaven Press; Grosset & Dunlap, Inc.; Harcourt Brace & Co.; HarperCollins Children's Books; Holiday House Inc.; Homestead Publishing; Huntington House Publishers; Ideals Children's Books; Jewish Publication Society; Jones University Press/Light Line Books, Bob; Jordan Enterprises Publishing Co., Inc.; Just Us Books, Inc.; Knopf Books for Young Readers; Lee & Low Books, Inc.; Lerner Publications Co.; Lion Books, Publisher; Little, Brown and Company; Lodestar Books; McElderry Books, Margaret K.; Macmillan Children's Books; Messner, Julian; Millbrook Press, The; Muir Publications, Inc, John; New Discovery Books; Orchard Books; Pando Publications; Pelican Publishing Co. Inc.; Philomel Books; Pippin Press; Pocahontas Press, Inc.; Pumpkin Press Publishing House; Putnam's Sons, G.P.; Random House Books for Young Readers; St. Paul Books and Media; Scholastic Hardcover; Scientific American Books for Young Readers; Scribner's Sons, Charles; Seacoast Publications of New England; Simon & Schuster Children's Books; Stemmer House Publishers, Inc.; Sundance Publishers & Distributors; Texas Christian University Press; Troll Associates; Trophy Books; Tudor Publishers, Inc.; University Editions, Inc.; Victor Books; Walker and Co.; Ward Hill Press; Williamson Publishing Co.; Willowisp Press; Winston-Derek Publishers, Inc.

Careers. Barrons Educational Series; Childrens Press; Council for Indian Education; Crestwood House; Crown Publishers (Crown Books for Children); Crystal River Press; Denison Co. Inc., T.S.; Dial Books for Young Readers; Distinctive Publishing Corp.; Enslow Publishers Inc.; Globe Fearon

Educational Publisher; Jordan Enterprises Publishing Co., Inc.; Lerner Publications Co.; Lodestar Books; Millbrook Press, The; Owen Publishers, Inc., Richard C.; Rosen Publishing Group, The; Sundance Publishers & Distributors; Troll Associates; University Editions, Inc.; Weigl Educational Publishers; Whitman & Company, Albert; Williamson Publishing Co.; Willowisp Press; Winston-Derek Publishers, Inc.

Concept. Africa World Press; American Education Publishing; Barrons Educational Series; Bess Press; Childrens Press; Clarion Books; Crystal River Press; Four Winds Press; Grosset & Dunlap, Inc.; HarperCollins Children's Books; Jalmar Press; Jordan Enterprises Publishing Co., Inc.; Just Us Books, Inc.; Little, Brown and Company; Lodestar Books; Magination Press; Millbrook Press, The; Muir Publications, Inc, John; Orchard Books; Pando Publications; Pumpkin Press Publishing House; Simon & Schuster Children's Books; University Classics, Ltd. Publishers; Victory Publishing; Willowisp Press

Cooking. Barrons Educational Series; China Books; Chronicle Books; Cloverdale Press; Crystal River Press; Fiesta City Publishers; Jordan Enterprises Publishing Co., Inc.; Little, Brown and Company; Pando Publications; Pelican Publishing Co. Inc.; Treasure Chest Publications, Inc.; Victory Publishing; Williamson Publishing Co.

Educational. Atheneum Publishers; Waterfront Books

Geography. Bess Press; Boyds Mills Press; Charlesbridge; Chicago Review Press; Childrens Press; China Books; Clarion Books; Crystal River Press; Dillon Press, Inc.; Discovery Enterprises, Ltd.; Distinctive Publishing Corp.; Falcon Press Publishing Co.; HarperCollins Children's Books; Humanics Limited Publishing Group; Lerner Publications Co.; Little, Brown and Company; Lodestar Books; Millbrook Press, The; Orchard Books; Pando Publications; Pumpkin Press Publishing House; Seacoast Publications of New England; Simon & Schuster Children's Books; Sterling Publishing Co., Inc.; Sundance Publishers & Distributors; Tab Books; Williamson Publishing Co.; Willowisp Press

Health. Barrons Educational Series; Childrens Press; Council for Indian Education; Crown Publishers (Crown Books for Children); Crystal River Press; Dawn Publications; Dial Books for Young Readers; Enslow Publishers Inc.; Free Spirit Publishing; Globe Fearon Educational Publisher; Jordan Enterprises Publishing Co., Inc.; Lerner Publications Co.; Lucent Books; Magination Press; Millbrook Press, The; Orchard Books; Pacific Press; Parenting Press, Inc.; Pelican Publishing Co. Inc.; Scientific American Books for Young Readers; Speech Bin, Inc., The; University Classics, Ltd. Publishers; Volcano Press; Waterfront Books; Weigl Educational Publishers; Whitman & Company, Albert; Williamson Publishing Co.; Women's Press; YMAA Publication Center

Hi-Lo. Bess Press; Childrens Press; Crestwood House; Crystal River Press; Globe Fearon Educational Publisher; HarperCollins Children's Books; Jordan Enterprises Publishing Co., Inc.; Lerner Publications Co.; Rosen Publishing Group, The; Sterling Publishing Co., Inc.; Williamson Publishing Co.

History. Aegina Press/University Editions; Africa World Press; Appalachian Mountain Club Books; Atheneum Publishers; Bandanna Books; Barrons Educational Series; Behrman House Inc.; Bess Press; Blue Heron Publishing, Inc.; Boyds Mills Press; Bradbury Press; Carolrhoda Books, Inc.; Childrens Press; China Books; Chronicle Books; Clarion Books; Council for Indian Education; Crestwood House; Crocodile Books, USA; Crown Publishers (Crown Books for Children); Crystal River Press; Denison Co. Inc., T.S.; Dial Books for Young Readers; Dillon Press, Inc.; Discovery Enterprises, Ltd.; Distinctive Publishing Corp.; Dutton Children's Books; Eerdmans Publishing Company, Wm. B.; Enslow Publishers Inc.; Facts on File; Falcon Press Publishing Co.; Four Winds Press; Golden Books; Greenhaven Press; Grosset & Dunlap, Inc.; Harcourt Brace & Co.; HarperCollins Children's Books; Hendrick-Long Publishing Company; Holiday House Inc.; Homestead Publishing; Huntington House Publishers; Ideals Children's Books; Jewish Publication Society; Jones University Press/Light Line Books, Bob; Jordan Enterprises Publishing Co., Inc.; Just Us Books, Inc.; Laredo Publishing Co. Inc.; Lee & Low Books, Inc.; Lerner Publications Co.; Lion Books, Publisher; Little, Brown and Company; Lodestar Books; Look and See Publications; Lucent Books; McElderry Books, Margaret K.; Macmillan Children's Books; March Media, Inc.; Messner, Julian; Millbrook Press, The; Misty Hill Press; New Discovery Books; Orchard Books; Pando Publications; Parenting Press, Inc.; Pelican Publishing Co. Inc.; Philomel Books; Pippin Press; Pocahontas Press, Inc.; Preservation Press, The; Press of Macdonald & Reinecke, The; Pumpkin Press Publishing House; Putnam's Sons, G.P.; Random House Books for Young Readers; Scholastic Hardcover; Scribner's Sons, Charles; Seacoast Publications of New England; Simon & Schuster Children's Books; Sunbelt Media, Inc./Eakin Press; Texas Christian University Press; Troll Associates; University Editions, Inc.; Victor Books; Volcano Press; Walker and Co.; Ward Hill Press; Weigl Educational Publishers; Whitman & Company, Albert; Willowisp Press; Winston-Derek Publishers, Inc.

Hobbies. Addison-Wesley Publishing Co.; American Education Publishing; Avon Books/Books for Young Readers; Bradbury Press; Bright Ring Publishing; Carolrhoda Books, Inc.; Chicago Review Press; Childrens Press; China Books; Council for Indian Education; Crown Publishers (Crown Books for Children); Crystal River Press; Dorling Kindersley, Inc.; Enslow Publishers Inc.; Four Winds Press; Free Spirit

Publishing; Harcourt Brace & Co.; HarperCollins Children's Books; Ideals Children's Books; Jordan Enterprises Publishing Co., Inc.; Lion Books, Publisher; Messner, Julian; Millbrook Press, The; Muir Publications, Inc, John; Orchard Books; Pando Publications; Pocahontas Press, Inc.; Price Stern Sloan; Random House Books for Young Readers; Scholastic Hardcover; Sterling Publishing Co., Inc.; Treasure Chest Publications, Inc.; Troll Associates; Walker and Co.; Whitman & Company, Albert; Williamson Publishing Co.; Willowisp Press

How-to. American Education Publishing; Appalachian Mountain Club Books; Barrons Educational Series; Boyds Mills Press; Chicago Review Press; Childrens Press; Cloverdale Press; Crystal River Press; Dorling Kindersley, Inc.; Herald Press; Jalmar Press; Jordan Enterprises Publishing Co., Inc.; Magination Press; Meriwether Publishing Ltd.; Pando Publications; Pumpkin Press Publishing House; Sterling Publishing Co., Inc.; Tab Books; Treasure Chest Publications, Inc.; Victory Publishing; Willowisp Press

Multicultural. Africa World Press; African American Images; American Bible Society; Bandanna Books; Bess Press; Boyds Mills Press; Carolrhoda Books, Inc.; Childrens Press; China Books; Clarion Books; Council for Indian Education; Crestwood House; Crystal River Press; Davis Pubilcations, Inc.; Denison Co. Inc., T.S.; Dillon Press, Inc.; Dorling Kindersley, Inc.; Dutton Children's Books; Facts on File; Free Spirit Publishing; Globe Fearon Educational Publisher; HarperCollins Children's Books; Humanics Limited Publishing Group; Ideals Children's Books; Jordan Enterprises Publishing Co., Inc.; Just Us Books, Inc.; Laredo Publishing Co. Inc.; Lee & Low Books, Inc.; Lerner Publications Co.; Lion Books, Publisher; Little, Brown and Company; Lodestar Books; Lucent Books; Mage Publishers Inc.; Magination Press; Millbrook Press, The; Muir Publications, Inc, John; Naturegraph Publisher, Inc.; New Discovery Books; Northland Publishing; Orchard Books; Our Child Press; Owen Publishers, Inc., Richard C.; Pando Publications; Parenting Press, Inc.; Pelican Publishing Co. Inc.; Philomel Books; Pippin Press; Preservation Press, The; Putnam's Sons, G.P.; Rosen Publishing Group, The; Scholastic Hardcover; Simon & Schuster Children's Books; Sundance Publishers & Distributors; Tab Books; Treasure Chest Publications, Inc.; Tudor Publishers, Inc.; Volcano Press; Ward Hill Press; Whitman & Company, Albert; Williamson Publishing Co.; Willowisp Press; Winston-Derek Publishers, Inc.; YMAA Publication Center

Music/Dance. Avon Books/Books for Young Readers; Bradbury Press; Bright Ring Publishing; China Books; Council for Indian Education; Crown Publishers (Crown Books for Children); Crystal River Press; Denison Co. Inc., T.S.; Dorling Kindersley, Inc.; Fiesta City Publishers; Four Winds Press; Harcourt Brace & Co.; HarperCollins Children's Books; Humanics Limited Publishing Group; Ideals Children's Books; Jordan Enterprises Publishing Co., Inc.; Lodestar Books; Macmillan Children's Books; Metamorphous Press; Millbrook Press, The; Orchard Books; Pelican Publishing Co. Inc.; Philomel Books; Pippin Press; Players Press, Inc.; Price Stern Sloan; Pumpkin Press Publishing House; Simon & Schuster Children's Books; Stemmer House Publishers, Inc.; Troll Associates; Trophy Books; Walker and Co.; Williamson Publishing Co.

Nature/Environment. Addison-Wesley Publishing Co.; Aegina Press/University Editions; American Education Publishing; Appalachian Mountain Club Books; Archway Paperbacks/Minstrel Books; Barrons Educational Series; Blue Heron Publishing, Inc.; Boyds Mills Press; Bradbury Press; Bright Ring Publishing; Carolrhoda Books, Inc.; Charlesbridge; Childrens Press; China Books; Chronicle Books; Clarion Books; Cobblehill Books; Council for Indian Education; Crestwood House; Crocodile Books, USA; Crown Publishers (Crown Books for Children); Crystal River Press; Dawn Publications; Denison Co. Inc., T.S.; Dial Books for Young Readers; Dillon Press, Inc.; Discovery Enterprises, Ltd.; Dorling Kindersley, Inc.; Dutton Children's Books; Eerdmans Publishing Company, Wm. B.; Enslow Publishers Inc.; Facts on File; Falcon Press Publishing Co.; Four Winds Press; Free Spirit Publishing; Globe Fearon Educational Publisher; Golden Books; Greenhaven Press; Grosset & Dunlap, Inc.; Harcourt Brace & Co.; HarperCollins Children's Books; Holiday House Inc.; Homestead Publishing; Humanics Limited Publishing Group; Ideals Children's Books; Jones University Press/Light Line Books, Bob; Jordan Enterprises Publishing Co., Inc.; Lerner Publications Co.; Little, Brown and Company; Lodestar Books; Lucent Books; Macmillan Children's Books; March Media, Inc.; Messner, Julian; Millbrook Press, The; Morris Publishing, Joshua; Muir Publications, Inc, John; Naturegraph Publisher, Inc.; Northland Publishing; NorthWord Press, Inc.; Orca Book Publishers; Orchard Books; Owen Publishers, Inc., Richard C.; Pacific Press; Pando Publications; Parenting Press, Inc.; Pelican Publishing Co. Inc.; Pippin Press; Pocahontas Press, Inc.; Press of Macdonald & Reinecke, The; Price Stern Sloan; Pumpkin Press Publishing House; Scholastic Hardcover; Scientific American Books for Young Readers; Scribner's Sons, Charles; Seacoast Publications of New England; Simon & Schuster Children's Books; Soundprints; Standard Publishing; Stemmer House Publishers, Inc.; Sterling Publishing Co., Inc.; Tab Books; Treasure Chest Publications, Inc.; Troll Associates; Trophy Books; University Classics, Ltd. Publishers; University Editions, Inc.; Volcano Press; Walker and Co.; Weigl Educational Publishers; Whitman & Company, Albert; Williamson Publishing Co.; Willowisp Press; Women's Press

Reference. American Education Publishing; Barrons Educational Series; Bess Press; Childrens Press; Crystal River Press; Denison Co. Inc., T.S.; HarperCollins Children's Books; Jordan Enterprises Publishing Co., Inc.; Millbrook Press, The; Pando Publications; Sterling Publishing Co., Inc.; Tudor Publishers, Inc.; Willowisp Press

Religious. American Bible Society; Behrman House Inc.; Bethany House Publishers; Bethel Publishing; China Books; Concordia Publishing House; Crown Publishers (Crown Books for Children); Crystal River Press; CSS Publishing; Dial Books for Young Readers; Eerdmans Publishing Company, Wm. B.; Facts on File; Harcourt Brace & Co.; Harvest House Publishers; Herald Press; Huntington House Publishers; Jewish Lights Publishing; Jewish Publication Society; Jordan Enterprises Publishing Co., Inc.; March Media, Inc.; Meriwether Publishing Ltd.; Morehouse Publishing Co.; Morris Publishing, Joshua; Orchard Books; Pacific Press; Paulist Press; Pelican Publishing Co. Inc.; Pumpkin Press Publishing House; Sadlier, Inc., William H.; St. Anthony Messenger Press; St. Paul Books and Media; Scholastic Hardcover; Standard Publishing; Troll Associates; University Editions, Inc.; Victor Books; Walker and Co.; Winston-Derek Publishers, Inc.

Science. Addison-Wesley Publishing Co.; American Education Publishing; Barrons Educational Series; Bright Ring Publishing; Carolrhoda Books, Inc.; Charlesbridge; Chicago Review Press; Childrens Press; Chronicle Books; Clarion Books; Crown Publishers (Crown Books for Children); Crystal River Press; Denison Co. Inc., T.S.; Dillon Press, Inc.; Dorling Kindersley, Inc.; Facts on File; Globe Fearon Educational Publisher; HarperCollins Children's Books; Humanics Limited Publishing Group; Jordan Enterprises Publishing Co., Inc.; Lerner Publications Co.; Lodestar Books; Macmillan Children's Books; Messner, Julian; Millbrook Press, The; Muir Publications, Inc, John; New Discovery Books; Orchard Books; Pando Publications; Pocahontas Press, Inc.; Prometheus Books; Pumpkin Press Publishing House; Putnam's Sons, G.P.; Scientific American Books for Young Readers; Simon & Schuster Children's Books; Sterling Publishing Co., Inc.; Tab Books; Tudor Publishers, Inc.; University Editions, Inc.; Walker and Co.; Williamson Publishing Co.; Willowisp Press

Self Help. American Bible Society; American Education Publishing; Avon Books/Books for Young Readers; Bethany House Publishers; Crystal River Press; Dawn Publications; Fiesta City Publishers; Free Spirit Publishing; Herald Press; Hunter House Publishers; Jordan Enterprises Publishing Co., Inc.; Lerner Publications Co.; Little, Brown and Company; Metamorphous Press; Orchard Books; Parenting Press, Inc.; Rosen Publishing Group, The; University Classics, Ltd. Publishers; Victory Publishing; Volcano Press; Williamson Publishing Co.

Social Issues. American Education Publishing; Bandanna Books; Barrons Educational Series; Bethany House Publishers; Carolrhoda Books, Inc.; Childrens Press; Chronicle Books; Clarion Books; Crystal River Press; Dawn Publications; Denison Co. Inc., T.S.; Dillon Press, Inc.; Distinctive Publishing Corp.; Dutton Children's Books; Free Spirit Publishing; Greenhaven Press; HarperCollins Children's Books; Herald Press; Hunter House Publishers; Jordan Enterprises Publishing Co., Inc.; Lerner Publications Co.; Little, Brown and Company; Lodestar Books; Lucent Books; Messner, Julian; Millbrook Press, The; Muir Publications, Inc, John; New Discovery Books; Orchard Books; Pando Publications; Parenting Press, Inc.; Perspectives Press; Prometheus Books; Pumpkin Press Publishing House; Putnam's Sons, G.P.; Scientific American Books for Young Readers; Simon & Schuster Children's Books; Tudor Publishers, Inc.; Volcano Press; Ward Hill Press; Waterfront Books; Weigl Educational Publishers; Willowisp Press; Women's Press; Carolrhoda Books, Inc.; Childrens Press

Special Needs. Crystal River Press; Free Spirit Publishing; Globe Fearon Educational Publisher; Humanics Limited Publishing Group; Jordan Enterprises Publishing Co., Inc.; Magination Press; Meadowbrook Press; Our Child Press; Pando Publications; Rosen Publishing Group, The; Speech Bin, Inc., The; University Classics, Ltd. Publishers; Volcano Press; Whitman & Company, Albert; Woodbine House

Sports. Aegina Press/University Editions; Archway Paperbacks/Minstrel Books; Avon Books/Books for Young Readers; Bess Press; Bradbury Press; Capstone Press Inc.; Childrens Press; China Books; Cloverdale Press; Cobblehill Books; Council for Indian Education; Crestwood House; Crown Publishers (Crown Books for Children); Crystal River Press; Dial Books for Young Readers; Enslow Publishers Inc.; Facts on File; Four Winds Press; Golden Books; Grosset & Dunlap, Inc.; Harcourt Brace & Co.; HarperCollins Children's Books; Holiday House Inc.; Ideals Children's Books; Jewish Publication Society; Jordan Enterprises Publishing Co., Inc.; Knopf Books for Young Readers; Lerner Publications Co.; Lodestar Books; Lucent Books; Millbrook Press, The; Orchard Books; Pando Publications; Pelican Publishing Co. Inc.; Pocahontas Press, Inc.; Price Stern Sloan; Pumpkin Press Publishing House; Random House Books for Young Readers; Scholastic Hardcover; Standard Publishing; Sterling Publishing Co., Inc.; Sunbelt Media, Inc./Eakin Press; Tudor Publishers, Inc.; University Editions, Inc.; Victor Books; Walker and Co.; Whitman & Company, Albert; Willowisp Press; YMAA Publication Center; Sterling Publishing Co., Inc.

Textbooks. Aegina Press/University Editions; Bandanna Books; Behrman House Inc.; Bess Press; Davis Pubilcations, Inc.; Denison Co. Inc., T.S.; Globe Fearon Educational Publisher; Jalmar Press; Jordan Enterprises Publishing Co., Inc.; Merrill Publishing; Sadlier, Inc., William H.; Speech Bin, Inc.,

The; Tudor Publishers, Inc.; University Classics, Ltd. Publishers; Winston-Derek Publishers, Inc.

Magazines: Fiction

Adventure. Atalantik; Boys' Life; Bread for God's Children; Calliope; Chickadee; Child Life; Children's Digest; Counselor; Cricket, The Magazine for Children; Crusader; Discoveries; Disney Adventures; Faith 'n Stuff; Focus on the Family Clubhouse; Goldfinch, The; Guide Magazine; Hicall; Hob-Nob; Hopscotch; Kids Today Mini-Magazine; Ladybug, the Magazine for Young Children; Magazine for Christian Youth!, The; My Friend; New Era Magazine; Odyssey; Owl Magazine; Power and Light; Primary Days; R-A-D-A-R; Seventeen Magazine; Straight; Teenage Christian Magazine; Turtle Magazine; U.S. Kids; Venture; Writer's Open Forum

Animal. Animal Trails; Atalantik; Boys' Life; Bread for God's Children; Cat Fancy; Chickadee; Child Life; Children's Digest; Children's Playmate; Clubhouse; Cochran's Corner; Counselor; Cricket, The Magazine for Children; Faith 'n Stuff; Focus on the Family Clubhouse; Discoveries; Friend Magazine, The; Goldfinch, The; Guide Magazine; Highlights for Children; Hob-Nob; Hopscotch; Humpty Dumpty's Magazine; InSights; Ladybug, the Magazine for Young Children; Magazine for Christian Youth!, The; Otterwise; Owl Magazine; Primary Days; R-A-D-A-R; Ranger Rick; Touch; Turtle Magazine; U.S. Kids; Writer's Open Forum

Contemporary. Advocate, The; American Girl; Boys' Life; Bread for God's Children; Brilliant Star; Child Life; Children's Digest; Children's Playmate; Clubhouse; Cochran's Corner; Cricket, The Magazine for Children; Crusader; Day Care and Early Education; Discoveries; Disney Adventures; Faith 'n Stuff; Focus on the Family Clubhouse; FreeWay; Friend Magazine, The; Guide Magazine; Hicall; Highlights for Children; Hob-Nob; Home Altar, The; Hopscotch; Humpty Dumpty's Magazine; Kids Today Mini-Magazine; Ladybug, the Magazine for Young Children; Listen; Magazine for Christian Youth!, The; My Friend; New Era Magazine; Noah's Ark; On the Line; Owl Magazine; Pockets; Power and Light; R-A-D-A-R; Seventeen Magazine; Shofar; Single Parent, The; Story Friends; Straight; Teen Power; Teenage Christian Magazine; Touch; Turtle Magazine; U.S. Kids; Venture; With; Wonder Time; Writer's Open Forum

Fantasy. Advocate, The; Boys' Life; Chickadee; Child Life; Children's Digest; Children's Playmate; Cochran's Corner; Cricket, The Magazine for Children; Day Care and Early Education; Disney Adventures; Faith 'n Stuff; Hicall; Highlights for Children; Hob-Nob; Hobson's Choice; Hopscotch; Humpty Dumpty's Magazine; Ladybug, the Magazine for Young Children; Magazine for Christian Youth!, The; Magic Realism; New Era Magazine; Noah's Ark; Owl Magazine; Pockets; Ranger Rick; Seventeen Magazine; With; Writer's Open Forum

Folktales. Advocate, The; Appalachian Bride; Brilliant Star; Calliope; Chickadee; Child Life; Children's Digest; Children's Playmate; Cricket, The Magazine for Children; Faces; Focus on the Family Clubhouse; Friend Magazine, The; Goldfinch, The; Highlights for Children; Hob-Nob; Hobson's Choice; Home Altar, The; Hopscotch; Magic Realism; Noah's Ark; Odyssey; Turtle Magazine; With; Writer's Open Forum

Health. Cat Fancy; Child Life; Children's Digest; Clubhouse; For Seniors Only; Hopscotch; Humpty Dumpty's Magazine; Listen; Magazine for Christian Youth!, The; Noah's Ark; Otterwise; Straight; Turtle Magazine; U.S. Kids

History. Aim Magazine; American Girl; Atalantik; Boys' Life; Bread for God's Children; Brilliant Star; Calliope; Child Life; Children's Digest; Children's Playmate; Clubhouse; Cobblestone; Cochran's Corner; Cricket, The Magazine for Children; Faces; Focus on the Family Clubhouse; Friend Magazine, The; Goldfinch, The; Guide Magazine; Hicall; Highlights for Children; Hob-Nob; Hopscotch; InSights; Kids Today Mini-Magazine; Magazine for Christian Youth!, The; My Friend; Noah's Ark; Odyssey; On the Line; Pockets; R-A-D-A-R; Touch

Humorous. Advocate, The; Atalantik; Boys' Life; Brilliant Star; Chickadee; Child Life; Children's Digest; Children's Playmate; Clubhouse; Cochran's Corner; Cricket Magazine; Crusader; Day Care and Early Education; Disney Adventures; Faith 'n Stuff; Focus on the Family Clubhouse; For Seniors Only; FreeWay; Friend Magazine, The; Guide Magazine; Hicall; Highlights for Children; Hob-Nob; Hopscotch; Humpty Dumpty's Magazine; InSights; Kids Today Mini-Magazine; Listen; Magazine for Christian Youth!, The; My Friend; New Era Magazine; Noah's Ark; On the Line; Owl Magazine; R-A-D-A-R; Ranger Rick; Shofar; Single Parent, The; Story Friends; Straight; Teen Power; Teenage Christian Magazine; Touch; Turtle Magazine; U.S. Kids; Venture; With; Writer's Open Forum

Multicultural. Aim Magazine; American Girl; Appalachian Bride; Brilliant Star; Child Life; Cricket, The Magazine for Children; Faces; Faith 'n Stuff; Friend Magazine, The; Hob-Nob; Hopscotch; Magazine for Christian Youth!, The; Power and Light; Student Leadership Journal; U.S. Kids; With; Young Salvationist

Nature/Environment. Advocate, The; Animal Trails; Bread for God's Children; Chickadee; Child Life; Counselor; Cricket, The Magazine for Children; Crusader; Focus on the Family Clubhouse; Guide Magazine; Hob-Nob; Hopscotch; Listen; Magazine for Christian Youth!, The; Noah's Ark; Otterwise; Power and Light; Skipping Stones; Straight; Turtle Magazine; U.S. Kids; Venture; With; Writer's Open Forum

Problem-Solving. Atalantik; Bread for God's Children; Brilliant Star; Children's Digest; Listen; Single Parent, The; Sleuth; Wonder Time; Writer's Open Forum

Religious. Bread for God's Children; Brilliant Star; Clubhouse; Cochran's Corner; Crusader; Faces; Focus on the Family Clubhouse; FreeWay; Friend Magazine, The; Guide Magazine; Hicall; Hob-Nob; Home Altar, The; Magazine for Christian Youth!, The; My Friend; New Era Magazine; Noah's Ark; On the Line; Pockets; Power and Light; R-A-D-A-R; Seventeen Magazine; Shofar; Story Friends; Straight; Student Leadership Journal; Teenage Christian Magazine; Touch; Venture; With; Wonder Time; Young Christian; Young Salvationist

Romance. Advocate, The; Atalantik; Cochran's Corner; Hicall; Hob-Nob; Magazine for Christian Youth!, The; New Era Magazine; Seventeen Magazine; Touch

Science Fiction. Advocate, The; Boys' Life; Bread for God's Children; Cochran's Corner; Cricket, The Magazine for Children; Highlights for Children; Hob-Nob; Hobson's Choice; Humpty Dumpty's Magazine; Kids Today Mini-Magazine; Ranger Rick; Seventeen Magazine; Writer's Open Forum

Sports. Boys' Life; Bread for God's Children; Brilliant Star; Chickadee; Child Life; Children's Digest; Children's Playmate; Clubhouse; Counselor; Cricket Magazine; Crusader; Faith 'n Stuff; For Seniors Only; FreeWay; Friend Magazine, The; Guide Magazine; Hicall; Highlights for Children; Hob-Nob; Hopscotch; Humpty Dumpty's Magazine; InSights; International Gymnast; Kids Today Mini-Magazine; Ladybug, the Magazine for Young Children; Listen; New Era Magazine; Noah's Ark; On the Line; Owl Magazine; Primary Days; R-A-D-A-R; Seventeen Magazine; Shofar; Straight; Teen Power; Teenage Christian Magazine; Turtle Magazine; U.S. Kids; Venture; With; Young Salvationist

Suspense/Mystery. Advocate, The; American Girl; Atalantik; Boys' Life; Bread for God's Children; Brilliant Star; Child Life; Children's Digest; Children's Playmate; Cricket, The Magazine for Children; Crusader; Disney Adventures; Faith 'n Stuff; Friend Magazine, The; Guide Magazine; Hob-Nob; Humpty Dumpty's Magazine; Ladybug, the Magazine for Young Children; My Friend; On the Line; Owl Magazine; R-A-D-A-R; Seventeen Magazine; Single Parent, The; Sleuth; Teenage Christian Magazine; U.S. Kids; Venture; Writer's Open Forum

Magazines: Nonfiction

Animal. Advocate, The; Animal Trails; ASPCA Animal Watch; Cat Fancy; Child Life; Children's Digest; Children's Playmate; Cochran's Corner; Counselor; Cricket, The Magazine for Children; Crusader; Day Care and Early Education; Disney Adventures; Dolphin Log; Faith 'n Stuff; FFA New Horizons; Focus on the Family Clubhouse; Friend Magazine, The; Guide Magazine; Highlights for Children; Hob-Nob; Hopscotch; Humpty Dumpty's Magazine; InSights; Ladybug, the Magazine for Young Children; National Geographic World; Nature Friend Magazine; On the Line; Otterwise; Owl Magazine; Primary Days; R-A-D-A-R; Ranger Rick; Scholastic Math Magazine; Scienceland; Superscience Blue; Teenage Christian Magazine; 3-2-1 Contact; Turtle Magazine; U.S. Kids; Venture

Arts/Crafts. Advocate, The; Bread for God's Children; Brilliant Star; Calliope; Cat Fancy; Challenge; Chickadee; Child Life; Children's Digest; Children's Playmate; Counselor; Cricket, The Magazine for Children; Crusader; Focus on the Family Clubhouse; Friend Magazine, The; Goldfinch, The; Highlights for Children; Hob-Nob; Hopscotch; Kids Today Mini-Magazine; Ladybug, the Magazine for Young Children; My Friend; Noah's Ark; Odyssey; On The Line; Primary Days; Scholastic Math Magazine; Scienceland; Teenage Christian Magazine; Turtle Magazine; U.S. Kids

Biography. Advocate, The; Brilliant Star; Calliope; Child Life; Children's Digest; Children's Playmate; Cobblestone; Counselor; Cricket, The Magazine for Children; Crusader; Disney Adventures; FFA New Horizons; Focus on the Family Clubhouse; Friend Magazine, The; Goldfinch, The; Guide Magazine; High Adventure; Hob-Nob; Hobson's Choice; Hopscotch; International Gymnast; Kids Today Mini-Magazine; Magazine for Christian Youth!, The; New Era Magazine; Noah's Ark; Odyssey; On the Line; Owl Magazine; Primary Days; Scienceland; Skipping Stones; Teenage Christian Magazine; Writer's Open Forum

Careers. Advocate, The; Career World; Careers and Colleges; Child Life; DynaMath; FFA New Horizons; For Seniors Only; Hob-Nob; Hobson's Choice; Hopscotch; Magazine for Christian Youth!, The; New Era Magazine; Scholastic Math Magazine; Scienceland; Single Parent, The; Straight; Teenage Christian Magazine; 2 Hype and Hype Hair

Concept. Magazine for Christian Youth!, The; Straight

Cooking. Calliope; Chickadee; Child Life; Children's Digest; Children's Playmate; Choices; Dyna-Math; Focus on the Family Clubhouse; Friend Magazine, The; Hopscotch; Noah's Ark; Odyssey; On the Line; Otterwise; Racing for Kids; Single Parent, The; U.S. Kids

Fashion. New Era Magazine; 2 Hype and Hype Hair

Games/Puzzles. Advocate, The; Atalantik; Brilliant Star; Calliope; Cat Fancy; Challenge; Chickadee; Child Life; Children's Digest; Children's Playmate; Cobblestone; Cricket, The Magazine for Children; Crusader; Disney Adventures; Dolphin Log; DynaMath; Faces; Focus on the Family Clubhouse; For Seniors Only; FreeWay; Friend Magazine, The; Goldfinch, The; Guide Magazine; Hob-Nob; Hopscotch; Kids Today Mini-Magazine; My Friend; New Era Magazine; Noah's Ark; Odyssey; On the Line; Scholastic Math Magazine; School Mates; Scienceland; Shofar; Skipping Stones; Teen Power; Teenage Christian Magazine; Turtle Magazine; 2 Hype and Hype Hair; U.S. Kids

Geography. Brilliant Star; Challenge; Child Life; Children's Playmate; Cricket, The Magazine for Children; Dolphin Log; Scholastic Math Magazine; Venture; Writer's Open Forum

Health. Cat Fancy; Challenge; Child Life; Children's Digest; Choices; Current Health I; Current Health II; FFA New Horizons; For Seniors Only; Hopscotch; Humpty Dumpty's Magazine; International Gymnast; Magazine for Christian Youth!, The; My Friend; On the Line; Otterwise; Racing for Kids; Scholastic Math Magazine; Scienceland; Straight; Teenage Christian Magazine; 3-2-1 Contact; Turtle Magazine; 2 Hype and Hype Hair; U.S. Kids

History. Advocate, The; Atalantik; Brilliant Star; Calliope; Child Life; Children's Digest; Children's Playmate; Cobblestone; Cochran's Corner; Counselor; Cricket, The Magazine for Children; Faces; Focus on the Family Clubhouse; Friend Magazine, The; Goldfinch, The; Guide Magazine; Highlights for Children; Hopscotch; InSights; Kids Today Mini-Magazine; Magazine for Christian Youth!, The; My Friend; National Geographic World; Noah's Ark; On the Line; Pockets; Primary Days; Racing for Kids; R-A-D-A-R; Scholastic Math Magazine; Scienceland; Single Parent, The; Skipping Stones; Student Leadership Journal; Teenage Christian Magazine; U.S. Kids; Writer's Open Forum

Hobbies. Advocate, The; Bread for God's Children; Challenge; Child Life; Cricket, The Magazine for Children; Crusader; FFA New Horizons; Focus on the Family Clubhouse; Hob-Nob; Hopscotch; Magazine for Christian Youth!, The; My Friend; On the Line; Primary Days; Racing for Kids; Scholastic Math Magazine; Teenage Christian Magazine; 2 Hype And Hype Hair; U.S. Kids; Writer's Open Forum; Young Salvationist

How-to. Atalantik; BK News; Bread for God's Children; Brilliant Star; Career World; Careers and Colleges; Cat Fancy; Challenge; Child Life; Children's Playmate; Clubhouse; Cochran's Corner; Counselor; Cricket, The Magazine for Children; Day Care and Early Education; DynaMath; FFA New Horizons; Focus on the Family Clubhouse; For Seniors Only; FreeWay; Friend Magazine, The; Goldfinch, The; Guide Magazine; Highlights for Children; Hob-Nob; Hobson's Choice; Hopscotch; Humpty Dumpty's Magazine; InSights; Listen; Magazine for Christian Youth!, The; My Friend; Mythic Circle, The; National Geographic World; Noah's Ark; On The Line; Primary Days; R-A-D-A-R; Scholastic Math Magazine; Scienceland; Seventeen Magazine; Superscience Blue; Teen Power; Teenage Christian Magazine; 3-2-1 Contact; 2 Hype and Hype Hair; U.S. Kids; Writer's Open Forum; Young Salvationist

Humorous. Advocate, The; Atalantik; Brilliant Star; Careers and Colleges; Child Life; Children's Digest; Children's Playmate; Cochran's Corner; Cricket, The Magazine for Children; Crusader; Day Care and Early Education; FFA New Horizons; Focus on the Family Clubhouse; For Seniors Only; FreeWay; Friend Magazine, The; Guide Magazine; Hob-Nob; Hopscotch; Humpty Dumpty's Magazine; InSights; Ladybug, the Magazine for Young Children; Magazine for Christian Youth!, The; National Geographic World; New Era Magazine; On the Line; Owl Magazine; Ranger Rick; Scholastic Math Magazine; Seventeen Magazine; Shofar; Single Parent, The; Skipping Stones; Straight; Teenage Christian Magazine; Touch; U.S. Kids; Venture; With; Writer's Open Forum

Interview/Profile. Advocate, The; Aim Magazine; Atalantik; BK News; Brilliant Star; Career World; Careers and Colleges; Chickadee; Child Life; Children's Digest; Cobblestone; Cochran's Corner; Cricket, The Magazine for Children; Crusader; Disney Adventures; Dolphin Log; DynaMath; Exploring; Faces; Faith 'n Stuff; FFA New Horizons; Focus on the Family Clubhouse; For Seniors Only; FreeWay; Goldfinch, The; Hicall; Highlights for Children; Hob-Nob; Hobson's Choice; Home Altar, The; Hopscotch; Humpty Dumpty's Magazine; InSights; International Gymnast; Kids Today Mini-Magazine; Listen; Magazine for Christian Youth!, The; My Friend; Mythic Circle, The; New Era Magazine; Noah's Ark; Owl Magazine; Pockets; Racing for Kids; R-A-D-A-R; Scholastic Math Magazine; Seventeen Magazine; Sharing the Victory; Shofar; Single Parent, The; Skipping Stones; Story Friends; Student Leadership Journal; Teen Power; Teenage Christian Magazine; 3-2-1 Contact; Touch; 2 Hype and Hype Hair; U.S. Kids; Young Salvationist

Math. DynaMath; Hobson's Choice; Hopscotch; Ladybug, the Magazine for /Young Children; Racing for Kids; Scholastic Math Magazine

Multicultural. Aim Magazine; Appalachian Bride; Brilliant Star; Child Life; Cricket, The Magazine for Children; Dolphin Log; FreeWay; Hopscotch; Ladybug, the Magazine for Young Children; National Geographic World; Racing for Kids; Scholastic Math Magazine; Skipping Stones; Student Leadership Journal; Teen Power; 3-2-1 Contact; Turtle Magazine; U.S. Kids; Young Salvationist

Nature/Environment. Advocate, The; Animal Trails; ASPCA Animal Watch; Brilliant Star; Challenge; Child Life; Children's Digest; Counselor; Cricket, The Magazine for Children; Current Health I; Current Health II; Disney Adventures; Dolphin Log; FFA New Horizons; Focus on the Family Clubhouse; Guide Magazine; Highlights for Children; Hob-Nob; Kids Today Mini-Magazine; Ladybug, the Magazine for Young Children; Magazine for Christian Youth!, The; My Friend; National Geographic World; Nature Friend Magazine; Noah's Ark; On the Line; Otterwise; Primary Days; Racing for Kids; Scholastic Math Magazine; Scienceland; Skipping Stones; Story Friends; Straight; Student Leadership Journal; Superscience Blue; 3-2-1 Contact; Turtle Magazine; U.S. Kids; Venture; With; Writer's Open Forum; Young Salvationist

Problem-Solving. BK News; Brilliant Star; Listen; New Era Magazine; Single Parent, The; Sleuth

Religious. Bread for God's Children; Brilliant Star; Cochran's Corner; Counselor; Crusader; Faces; Focus on the Family Clubhouse; Friend Magazine, The; Guide Magazine; High Adventure; Home Altar, The; Magazine for Christian Youth!, The; My Friend; New Era Magazine; Noah's Ark; Pockets; Primary Days; R-A-D-A-R; Shofar; Skipping Stones; Straight; Student Leadership Journal; Teen Power; Teenage Christian Magazine; Touch; Venture; With; Wonder Time; Young Christian; Young Salvationist

Science. Animal Trails; Child Life; Cricket, The Magazine for Children; Crusader; DynaMath; Focus on the Family Clubhouse; Highlights for Children; Hob-Nob; Hobson's Choice; Hopscotch; Magazine for Christian Youth!, The; My Friend; Odyssey; Racing for Kids; Scholastic Math Magazine; Science Weekly; Straight; Superscience Blue; 3-2-1 Contact; Turtle Magazine; U.S. Kids; Venture

Social Issues. Careers and Colleges; Challenge; Child Life; Choices; Counselor; Focus on the Family Clubhouse; For Seniors Only; FreeWay; Guide Magazine; Hicall; Magazine for Christian Youth!, The; Noah's Ark; Primary Days; Scholastic Math Magazine; Seventeen Magazine; Straight; Street Times; Student Leadership Journal; Teen Power; Teenage Christian Magazine; U.S. Kids; Venture; With; Young Salvationist

Sports. Brilliant Star; Challenge; Children's Digest; Cricket, The Magazine for Children; Crusader; Current Health II; Disney Adventures; DynaMath; FFA New Horizons; Focus on the Family Clubhouse; For Seniors Only; FreeWay; Friend Magazine, The; Guide Magazine; Highlights for Children; Hob-Nob; International Gymnast; Kids Today Mini-Magazine; Magazine for Christian Youth!, The; My Friend; National Geographic World; New Era Magazine; Racing for Kids; Scholastic Math Magazine; Sharing the Victory; Skipping Stones; Teenage Christian Magazine; Turtle Magazine; U.S. Kids

Travel. Atalantik; Brilliant Star; Careers And Colleges; Chickadee; Child Life; Children's Digest; Children's Playmate; Cobblestone; Cochran's Corner; Cricket, The Magazine for Children; Exploring; Faces; For Seniors Only; Goldfinch, The; Kids Today Mini-Magazine; Magazine for Christian Youth!, The; National Geographic World; New Era Magazine; Owl Magazine; R-A-D-A-R; Scholastic Math Magazine; Skipping Stones; Teenage Christian Magazine; U.S. Kids; Writer's Open Forum

General Index

More Books to Help You Get Published!

The Children's Writer's Word Book—This handy reference book offers everything you need to ensure your writing speaks to your young audience, including word lists, a thesaurus of listed words and reading levels for a variety of synonyms. You'll also find samples of writing for each reading level, and guidelines for sentence length, word usage and theme at each level. *#10316/352 pages/ $19.95, hardcover*

Writing for Children and Teenagers—Filled with practical know-how and step-by-step instruction, including how to hold a young reader's attention, where to find ideas, and vocabulary lists based on age level. This third edition provides all the tips you need to flourish in today's children's literature market. *#10101/265 pages/$12.95, paperback*

How to Write & Illustrate Children's Books—A truly comprehensive guide that demonstrates how to bring freshness and vitality to children's text and pictures. Numerous illustrators, writers, and editors contributed their expert advice. *#30082/143 pages/$22.50, hardcover*

Guide to Literary Agents & Art/Photo Reps—Interviews with top reps and agents in the field answer the most often asked questions about getting representation; then over 500 listings of literary and script agents, and art/photo reps will help you find one that's right for you. *#10363/ 240 pages/$18.95, paperback*

How to Write a Book Proposal—A step-by-step guide that helps you check the salability of your book ideas, offers inside tips and addresses to help you get additional help, and a complete sample proposal. *#10173/132 pages/$11.95, paperback*

Writer's Digest Guide to Manuscript Formats—An easy-to-follow guide to all types of manuscript formats preparation and presentation—from books and articles to poems and plays. *#10025/198 pages/$18.95, hardcover*

Artist's Market—The 2,500 listings of art buyers listed, along with helpful interviews from top professionals in the art field, make this the ultimate marketing tool for illustrators, designers, and fine artists. *#10341/672 pages/$22.95, hardcover*

Use the order form below (photocopy acceptable) and save when you order two or more books!

☐ **Yes!** I want the following books to help me get published:

Book #	Brief title	Price
_____	_____	_____
_____	_____	_____

Credit Card Orders Call TOLL-FREE 1-800-289-0963

Subtotal _____

Tax (Ohio residents only, 5½%) _____

Please add $3 for shipping and handling for one book; shipping is FREE when you order 2 or more titles.

Shipping* _____

Total _____

Check enclosed $ _____   ☐ Visa ☐ MasterCard

Acct # _____ Exp. _____

Name _____ Signature _____

Address _____

City _____ State _____ Zip _____

Stock may be limited on some titles; prices subject to change without notice.

Mail to: Writer's Digest Books, 1507 Dana Ave., Cincinnati, OH 45207

Write to this address for information on *Writer's Digest* magazine, *Story* magazine, Writer's Digest Book Club, Writer's Digest School, and Writer's Digest Criticism Service.